2021

The Supreme Court Review

"Judges as persons, or courts as institutions, are entitled to no greater immunity from criticism than other persons or institutions . . . [J]udges must be kept mindful of their limitations and of their ultimate public responsibility by a vigorous stream of criticism expressed with candor however blunt."

—Felix Frankfurter

". . . while it is proper that people should find fault when their judges fail, it is only reasonable that they should recognize the difficulties. . . . Let them be severely brought to book, when they go wrong, but by those who will take the trouble to understand them."

—Learned Hand

THE LAW SCHOOL

THE UNIVERSITY OF CHICAGO

Volume 2021

The Supreme Court Review

EDITED BY

DAVID A. STRAUSS

GEOFFREY R. STONE

JUSTIN DRIVER

AND WILLIAM BAUDE

THE UNIVERSITY OF CHICAGO PRESS

CHICAGO AND LONDON

The Supreme Court Review, Volume 2021

Published annually by The University of Chicago Press.
www.journals.uchicago.edu/SCR/

Subscriptions: Individual subscription rates are $84 print + electronic and $67 e-only. Institutional print + electronic and e-only rates are tiered according to an institution's type and research output: $117 to $206 (print + electronic), $102 to $179 (e-only). For additional information, including back-issue sales, classroom use, rates for single copies, and prices for institutional full-run access, please visit www.journals.uchicago.edu /SCR/. Free or deeply discounted access is available in most developing nations through the Chicago Emerging Nations Initiative (www .journals.uchicago.edu/ceni/).

Please direct subscription inquiries to Subscription Fulfillment, 1427 E. 60th Street, Chicago, IL 60637-2902. Telephone: (773) 753-3347 or toll free in the United States and Canada (877) 705-1878. Fax: (773) 753-0811 or toll-free (877) 705-1879. E-mail: subscriptions@press .uchicago.edu.

Standing orders: To place a standing order for this book series, please address your request to The University of Chicago Press, Chicago Distribution Center, Attn. Standing Orders/ Customer Service, 11030 S. Langley Avenue, Chicago, IL 60628. Telephone toll free in the U.S. and Canada: 1-800-621-2736; or 1-773-702-7000. Fax toll free in the U.S. and Canada: 1-800-621-8476; or 1-773-702-7212.

Single-copy orders: In the U.S., Canada, and the rest of the world, order from your local bookseller or direct from The University of Chicago Press, Chicago Distribution Center, 11030 S. Langley Avenue, Chicago, IL 60628. Telephone toll free in the U.S. and Canada: 1-800-621-2736; or 1-773-702-7000. Fax toll free in the U.S. and Canada: 1-800-621-8476; or 1-773-702-7212. In the U.K. and Europe, order from your local bookseller or direct from The University of Chicago Press, c/o John Wiley Ltd. Distribution Center, 1 Oldlands Way, Bognor Regis, West Sussex PO22 9SA, UK. Telephone 01243 779777 or Fax 01243 820250. E-mail: cs-books@wiley.co.uk.

The University of Chicago Press offers bulk discounts on individual titles to Corporate, Premium, and Gift accounts. For information, please write to Sales Department—Special Sales, The University of Chicago Press, 1427 E. 60th Street, Chicago, IL 60637 USA or telephone 1-773-702-7723.

This book was printed and bound in the United States of America.

ISSN: 0081-9557
E-ISSN: 2158-2459
ISBN: 978-0-226-82509-0 (cloth)
E-ISBN: 978-0-226-82508-3 (ebook)

TO

JUSTICE STEPHEN BREYER

Scholar, jurist, educator, public servant,
committed to reason, pragmatism,
and humanity

CONTENTS

ERADICATING BUSH-LEAGUE ARGUMENTS ROOT AND BRANCH: THE ARTICLE II INDEPENDENT-STATE-LEGISLATURE NOTION AND RELATED RUBBISH 1
Vikram David Amar and Akhil Reed Amar

MAHANOY v. B.L. & FIRST AMENDMENT "LEEWAY" 53
Mary-Rose Papandrea

SAFETY, HEALTH, AND UNION ACCESS IN CEDAR POINT NURSERY 99
Benjamin I. Sachs

SHOWDOWN AT CEDAR POINT: "SOLE AND DESPOTIC DOMINION" GAINS GROUND 125
Cynthia Estlund

FOCUSING THE CFAA IN VAN BUREN 155
Orin S. Kerr

WHAT CHRISTIANITY LOSES WHEN CONSERVATIVE CHRISTIANS WIN AT THE SUPREME COURT 185
Russell K. Robinson

EXECUTIVE DECISIONS AFTER ARTHREX 225
Jennifer Mascott and John F. Duffy

LATE-STAGE TEXTUALISM 267
Ryan D. Doerfler

THE ROBERTS COURT AND THE TRANSFORMATION OF CONSTITUTIONAL PROTECTIONS FOR RELIGION: A STATISTICAL PORTRAIT 315
Lee Epstein and Eric A. Posner

INJURY IN FACT, TRANSFORMED 349
Cass R. Sunstein

SCALIA'S SLIP 375
Owen Fiss

THE INSTITUTIONALIST TURN IN COPYRIGHT 417
Shyamkrishna Balganesh

VIKRAM DAVID AMAR AND
AKHIL REED AMAR

ERADICATING BUSH-LEAGUE ARGUMENTS ROOT AND BRANCH: THE ARTICLE II INDEPENDENT-STATE-LEGISLATURE NOTION AND RELATED RUBBISH

The biggest news of October Term 2020 was what *didn't* happen: In the run-up to, and aftermath of, yet another tight and hard-fought presidential election, the Supreme Court declined to double down on some of the worst aspects of the execrable *Bush v. Gore*[1] opinions of twenty years ago.

But a close look at the Term reveals that there was a brief moment of genuine constitutional peril, a week when it seemed quite possible that the Court might once again—as it did in 2000—besmirch itself and plunge the country into a jurisprudential abyss.

In the days preceding the election of 2020, a veritable carnival of litigants—let's call them *Bush*-Leaguers—teed up several cases based on a seemingly plausible but ultimately preposterous constitutional

Vikram David Amar is Dean and Iwan Foundation Professor of Law, University of Illinois College of Law. Akhil Reed Amar is Sterling Professor of Law and Political Science, Yale University.

Authors' note: Special thanks to Will Baude, Evan Caminker, Justin Driver, Larry Lessig, Andy Lipka, Jason Mazzone, Ayoub Ouederni, Michael Schaps, and Hayward Smith.

[1] 531 U.S. 98 (2000) (per curiam). The case is sometimes referred to as *Bush II*.

The Supreme Court Review, 2022.
 Published by The University of Chicago Press. https://doi.org/10.1086/720128

theory that had won the support of three notable justices back in 2000. Echoing the Rehnquist-Scalia-Thomas concurrence in *Bush v. Gore*, the 2020 *Bush*-Leaguers correctly noted that Article II permits each state to use its "legislature" to decide how that state's presidential electors are to be chosen. From this correct starting point, *Bush*-Leaguers quickly careened off course, claiming that state courts could not properly tweak state voting laws to bring these laws into alignment with state constitutions (as construed by these state-court jurists). Perilously, four justices at various points in the autumn of 2020 appeared to fall for this beguiling *Bush*-League idea—an idea often referred to as the "Independent State Legislature" (ISL) theory. None of the other five justices came close to explaining all the reasons—and there are several—why this theory fails.

In what follows, we show why *Bush*-League arguments were wrong twenty years ago; how they were shown to be wrong by sound scholarship in the ensuing years; and why they are even more wrong today, thanks to recent and dispositive Supreme Court case law. All sensible constitutionalists—whether on the Court or off it, whether originalists or precedentalists, whether left or right of center—should bury *Bush*.

We also aim to demonstrate that the errors and evils of *Bush v. Gore* went far beyond the ISL ideas at the heart of the Rehnquist-Scalia-Thomas concurrence. *Bush* was wrong in just about every way that it is possible for a case to be wrong. If ever there were a bad seed, *Bush* was it. The recent efforts to revive and rehabilitate *Bush*'s reputation are thus genuine cause for jurisprudential concern—even alarm. We urge today's Court to make a sharp and clean break with *Bush* as soon as possible, and to do so well before the next contested presidential election, which may be quite harrowing enough without any monkey business from the Court.

I. The Bad Seed in a Nutshell

The *Bush v. Gore* litigation in 2000 went through several rounds, but the most momentous ruling occurred on December 12, 2000. That day, a majority of the Court held that the ongoing recounting of votes in various Florida counties, as overseen by the Florida Supreme Court, violated the Equal Protection Clause because this recount was proceeding in different ways and under different standards throughout the state. Rather than remanding the matter to the Florida courts to devise recounting procedures that would satisfy the *Bush* Court's newly minted equal protection rules, a majority consisting of five Republican-appointed justices ended the vote recounting and thus guaranteed that Republican candidate George W. Bush would become the President.

Within hours, notable scholars came out swinging, condemning the *Bush* Court's decision in the strongest possible terms on a wide range of issues implicated by the case.[2]

Were these scholars right to do so? And why does any of this matter today?

As we shall show, the early and harsh critics were indeed right. (We take pride that we ourselves were among them.) And all this matters because the Constitution matters, because our constitutional culture matters, and because elections matter. The entire American constitutional project is imperiled if judges, lawyers, law professors, law students, lay opinion leaders, and the citizenry more generally grossly misunderstand first principles of American constitutional law and American democracy. And strong post-decision criticism was particularly important back in late 2000 and early 2001 because the Court had rushed into the case at breakneck speed, without the usual deliberative timetable enabling scholarly expertise to guide the Court pre-decision, via amicus briefs and the like.

True, some prominent conservative scholars tried to push back against the early and harsh critics of *Bush*.[3] But until 2020, the harsh

[2] Jeff Rosen captioned his cover story for the *New Republic* "Disgrace" and proclaimed the Court's decision "a shabby piece of work." Jeffrey Rosen, *Disgrace*, NEW REPUBLIC (Dec. 24, 2000), https://newrepublic.com/article/70674/disgrace. In the *Los Angeles Times*, Akhil concluded by saying that he would tell his students that they must accept the Court's ruling but that they should not respect it. Akhil Reed Amar, *Should We Trust Judges?*, L.A. TIMES (Dec. 17, 2000), https://www.latimes.com/archives/la-xpm-2000-dec-17-op-1126-story.html. Early scholarly articles and book chapters by distinguished constitutional scholars piled on. Jed Rubenfeld railed against the "illegality," "breathtaking indefensibility," and "wrongness" of the justices' action, proclaiming it "worse even than the notorious *Plessy*." Jed Rubenfeld, *Not as Bad as* Plessy. *Worse.*, *in* BUSH V. GORE: THE QUESTION OF LEGITIMACY 20, 20–21 (Bruce Ackerman ed., 2002). Jack Balkin and Bruce Ackerman were no less emphatic. *See, e.g.*, Jack M. Balkin, *Legitimacy and the 2000 Election*, *in id.* at 210, 210 (describing the Court's decision as "illegal[]"); Bruce Ackerman, *Off Balance*, *in id.* at 192, 195–96 (characterizing the Court's arguments as "preposterous" and its ultimate ruling as an "act of usurpation").

[3] Sad to say, several of the most notable defenders of the indefensible were and still are closely linked in the public mind to the University of Chicago Law School, the sponsor of the very volume in which we today voice our views. *See, e.g.*, Richard A. Epstein, *"In Such Manner as the Legislature Thereof May Direct": The Outcome in* Bush v. Gore *Defended*, *in* THE VOTE: BUSH, GORE & THE SUPREME COURT 13 (Cass R. Sunstein & Richard A. Epstein eds., 2001); Michael W. McConnell, *Two-and-a-Half Cheers for* Bush v. Gore, *in id.* at 98; Richard A. Posner, Bush v. Gore: *Prolegomenon to an Assessment*, *in id.* at 165; RICHARD A. POSNER, BREAKING THE DEADLOCK: THE 2000 ELECTION, THE CONSTITUTION, AND THE COURTS (2001).

critics' view had become increasingly orthodox among scholars of all stripes and, seemingly, among the justices themselves. Court insiders reported that several current and retired justices had come to view the case with profound embarrassment. Many conservative legal academics began to admit, quietly, that the case reeks. In a 2015 *Time* magazine survey of constitutional scholars, *Bush v. Gore* was repeatedly condemned as one of the worst decisions of the previous half-century. Perhaps most telling of all, no majority opinion of the Court had ever cited the case with approval.[4]

Many sophisticated commentators thus had good reason to think that *Bush v. Gore* had been quietly plowed under. Perhaps the time was not yet ripe for loud judicial denunciation of the case, à la *Dred Scott*[5] and *Plessy*.[6] But surely, many thought, *Bush* was viewed by polite society and by the justices themselves as an embarrassing judicial fart that we could all pretend not to hear or smell.

Alas, in 2020, it became clear that *Bush* has in fact not been laid to rest in our constitutional culture. There are powerful efforts afoot to revive certain aspects of this misbegotten ruling. And thus it becomes imperative to explain—once more, with feeling—just how wrong the case was, in so many ways.[7]

For starters, the *Bush* Court's overeager decision to jump into the electoral college controversy itself ran counter to text, structure, precedent, and prudence.

The Constitution's text expressly makes each congressional house the "judge" of elections to its own chamber.[8] And for analogous reasons, the Constitution's text also makes Congress (though not the vice president individually!) the ultimate arbiter of contested electoral votes for the presidency.[9]

---

[4] *See* Akhil Reed Amar, The Constitution Today: Timeless Lessons for the Issues of Our Era 10 & 437 n.2 (rev. ed. 2018); *see also* Andrea Sachs, *The Worst Supreme Court Decisions Since 1960*, Time (Oct. 6, 2015), https://time.com/4056051/worst-supreme-court-decisions.

[5] Dred Scott v. Sandford, 60 U.S. (19 How.) 393 (1857).

[6] Plessy v. Ferguson, 163 U.S. 537 (1896).

[7] We aim today to offer readers a definitive one-stop-shop evisceration of *Bush v. Gore*—and to offer that evisceration at a moment when various forces on and off the Court seem bent on reviving the case and restoring its reputation. If, as we believe, the case truly deserves to rot in judicial hell, the legal community deserves a comprehensive statement of its most egregious faults and a full response to the various *Bush* apologists over the years.

[8] U.S. Const. art. I, § 5, cl. 1 ("Each House shall be the Judge of the Elections, Returns and Qualifications of its own Members. . . .").

[9] *See* U.S. Const. art. II, § 1, cl. 3, *amended by* U.S. Const. amend. XII.

The underlying structural logic here is emphatically democratic. The Constitution creates a democratic pyramid in which earlier-mentioned and more directly democratic institutions form the popularly legitimated building blocks supporting later-mentioned and rather more elitist institutions. The Preamble comes first, making clear to all that the Constitution itself derives from a special popular mandate—from We, the People, directly, as embodied in special ad hoc conventions selected in uniquely democratic fashion.[10] In 1787–88, more folk were legally allowed to vote on how they and their posterity would be governed than had ever been allowed to vote on anything, anywhere, in the entirety of human history.[11] Next, Article I structures a democratic legislature in which the first-mentioned House consists of members chosen directly by voters—a clear break with the pre-existing Congress under the Articles of Confederation. Article II structures the ensuing tier of the democratic pyramid. That Article envisions a president who is not, strictly speaking, directly elected, but whose indirect selection will be initiated by a process that will likely involve ordinary voters, and will be ultimately certified by Congress meeting in special joint session. Finally, Article III at the narrow apex of the pyramid provides that federal judges and justices will be chosen by a rather less directly democratic process, via presidential nomination and Senate confirmation.

The obvious architecture of this grand structure is that presidents should pick justices, but justices should not pick presidents. When justices do the picking, the democratic pyramid is improperly inverted; smaller, less democratic building blocks are dangerously bearing too much weight, and the entire democratic edifice is at risk of toppling.

In all closely contested presidential elections prior to *Bush v. Gore*—1800–01, 1824–25, and 1876–77—Congress, not the Court, decided the matter, and rightly so. The idea that the Supreme Court should have thrust itself into any of these electoral college contests would have seemed bizarre to the jurists and statesmen of those eras.[12]

Having impetuously and arrogantly decided to leap onto center stage rather than wait in the wings—God forbid that Congress be allowed

---

[10] *See generally* Akhil Reed Amar, America's Constitution: A Biography ch. 1 (2005).

[11] *See id.* at 7–10 & 503–07 nn.1–12; Akhil Reed Amar, The Words That Made Us: America's Constitutional Conversation, 1760–1840, at 225–27 (2021).

[12] In 1876–77, Congress chose to involve certain individual members of the Court as adjuncts to Congress itself, not as the Supreme Court sitting as such, as happened in *Bush*.

to play the lead role prescribed by text, structure, and tradition!—the *Bush* Court at a minimum should have acted in either a stately or lawyerly fashion (ideally, both). Alas, the Court's actions flunked both the demands of statecraft and the demands of law.

As a matter of pure pragmatism and putting aside all legal niceties,[13] the best argument for Supreme Court intervention was that America in late 2000 was deeply and closely divided. The country needed a wise, unifying, and respected decision-maker—a Hercules, a Solomon, a bevy of Platonic guardians—to save the day.

In late 2000 the incoming House and Senate were themselves set to be narrowly and sharply divided. Although the (legally irrelevant) national popular vote clearly favored Gore, the (juridically decisive) national electoral vote would come down to a single raucous and fractious state. As Florida would go, so would go the nation, legally. Alas, the Florida popular vote was a statistical dead heat.[14] Someone needed to step forward to lead the country. Who better than America's most trusted branch post-Watergate and post-Vietnam—namely, the federal judiciary?

But if this was the best pragmatic and realpolitik reason for judicial intervention, the Court should have offered America a unanimous or nearly unanimous decision, in the tradition of *Brown*[15] and the *Nixon Tapes Case*.[16] If such a consensus decision seemed achievable when the *Bush* Court initially decided to jump onstage, but later became unlikely as the justices examined matters more closely, a truly wise Court would have stepped back by dismissing the writ of certiorari as improvidently granted.

The least statesmanlike resolution of all was what the *Bush* Court eventually gave the country: a final line-up that was not merely closely and sharply divided, but partisan in the ugliest imaginable way. The five justices most praised by candidate Bush in the preceding months aimed to stop the recount and crown him king, while the four justices

---

[13] *Cf.* Posner, *supra* note 3.

[14] Florida would not have been tied had it not been for the disastrous butterfly ballot used in Palm Beach county. As most honest observers understood at the time, and as later scholars have confirmed, the misleading design of this ballot caused Gore to lose thousands of votes, far more than Bush's margin of victory in the final official tally. *See, e.g.* Jonathan N. Wand et al., *The Butterfly Did It: The Aberrant Vote for Buchanan in Palm Beach County, Florida*, 95 Am. Pol. Sci. Rev. 793 (2001).

[15] Brown v. Bd. of Educ., 347 U.S. 483 (1954).

[16] United States v. Nixon, 418 U.S. 683 (1974).

most lauded by candidate Gore aimed to continue a recount in which he seemed to have the momentum.

In fact, upon close inspection, the five justices in the majority didn't really agree among themselves, although they pretended to do so for appearance's sake. Two justices sincerely (but erroneously) believed in one theory (equal protection), while three other justices embraced a different—and almost logically inconsistent—theory (Article II ISL). The only thing that truly united the narrow majority of the Court (all Republican appointees) was that the recounting must stop and the Republican candidate must win.

None of the foregoing pragmatic criticisms would be decisive if the legal arguments advanced by the majority justices actually held water. Alas, what the *Bush* Court said and did was lawless in the extreme.

The equal protection argument sincerely endorsed by two justices in the majority (O'Connor and Kennedy) and by a third justice who opposed ending the recount (Souter) was not only wrong, but also almost self-refuting. The recount was in fact designed to mitigate some of the most glaring racial and class inequalities of the initial count itself; the judicially supervised recount ordered by the Florida Supreme Court was more truly equal than Florida's initial, wildly uneven, and less judicially supervised tally. True equality argued for continuing the recount, not squelching it.

Plus, the O'Connor-Kennedy opinion (technically, a per curiam) had almost no precedential support or precedential logic backward or forward. Looking backward, we find no prior Court ruling remotely close on its facts. Looking forward, the *Bush* justices themselves openly announced that the case should not set a precedent for later cases.[17] The ruling was thus pure ad hocery—a judicial train ticket good for one day only. And few believe that if the parties were reversed, the same justices would have done for Gore what they did for Bush. Viewed in this light, the decision was the very antithesis of neutral principles.

And on the issue of remedy, the *Bush* Court also bungled badly. The justices refused to allow the Florida courts to continue the recount: Time was up, said the Supremes. In fact it wasn't, and the Florida Supreme Court should have been the one to decide, under state law, whether it was more important for Florida to get the recount done fast or done right.

---

[17] Bush v. Gore, 531 U.S. 98, 109 (2000) ("Our consideration is limited to the present circumstances. . . .").

Nor does the *Bush* equal protection argument fare any better if viewed through the lens of originalism. The Fourteenth Amendment's Equal Protection Clause was emphatically designed as a rule regulating civil rights, and was universally understood at the time of its drafting and ratification as utterly inapplicable to political rights such as voting. The clause speaks of "persons" as pointedly distinct from "citizens." Indeed, it was particularly aimed to elaborate the rights of aliens—paradigmatic nonvoters, as a rule.[18]

Of course, in most situations, this originalist point might seem a pedantic quibble, because almost all of the countless Supreme Court cases relying on the Equal Protection Clause to protect voting rights can be justified under a different clause, the Article IV provision guaranteeing each state a proper republican form of government.[19] But this Article IV clause is inapt in presidential elections, which are governed by an entirely different matrix of constitutional provisions in which strict voting equality need not be the rule. For example, under the express terms of Article II, a state legislature could (if permitted by its state constitution[20]) directly pick electors even if that legislature were controlled by a party that lost the statewide popular vote in the most recent election.

Which takes us straight to the Article II ISL argument endorsed by three other *Bush* justices—Chief Justice Rehnquist and Justices Scalia and Thomas, whom we shall call the *Bush* three. This argument was actually even more self-refuting than was the equal protection argument, whose obvious flaws it was designed to sidestep. The *Bush* three failed to understand (or even acknowledge) that a state legislature is properly defined and bounded by the state constitution that gives the legislature life. When state jurists attend to the state constitution in interpreting state election statutes, these judges are enforcing Article II, not undermining it. Even if a state constitution somehow does not apply *of its own force*, it nevertheless applies whenever a state legislature prior to a presidential Election Day has *chosen to incorporate* state constitutional principles into its state legislative schema for presidential elections, as the Florida legislature plainly had chosen to do prior to Election Day, 2000. This is a right and choice permitted to

---

[18] *See* Akhil Reed Amar, America's Unwritten Constitution: The Precedents and Principles We Live By 185–88 (2012); *see also* Minor v. Happersett, 88 U.S. (21 Wall.) 162 (1875).

[19] U.S. Const. art. IV, § 4, cl. 1 ("The United States shall guarantee to every State in this Union a Republican Form of Government. . . .").

[20] On the enormous importance of this parenthetical proviso, see *infra* note 117.

states and their legislatures by Article II itself. By disregarding this elemental and elementary point, the *Bush* three thus violated the very Article they were claiming to champion. Their argument not only fails, it implodes. It self-contradicts.

To make matters worse, it is extremely hard to believe *both* the equal protection and the Article II argument, as the three concurring justices purported to do.[21] Without their willingness to join the equal protection argument, even as they held their noses, there would have been no single opinion of the Court. Even inexpert journalists in the moment would have seen in a flash that a majority of the Court had in fact rejected each of the only two arguments put forth by Bush's lawyers for ending the recount. Only three justices truly believed in the equal protection argument: O'Connor, Kennedy, and Souter (and of course Souter thought the recounting should continue). And only three justices (Rehnquist, Scalia, and Thomas) truly believed in the Article II argument.

II. Wading Into the Weeds

A closer look at *Bush v. Gore* makes all this more clear.[22]

A. EQUAL PROTECTION

The Bush lawyers' theory of equal protection focused on claims of disuniformity in the judicially monitored recount process. But these claims needed to be considered against the backdrop of the disuniformity of *the original counting*: Different counties used different ways of generating the initial count that the *Bush* Court effectively reinstated when it ended the recount.

Given the flaws of the original count, the *Bush* Court's equal protection argument gets it exactly backward. The late November and

[21] The more one insists on the plenary power of state legislatures under Article II to call the shots in presidential elections, the more awkward it is to also insist that the state must satisfy a super-strict system of voting equality, down to uniform microstandards for evaluating chads, regardless of the counting and recounting system established by the legislature itself. Much of the recount unevenness that the *Bush* per curiam complained about was in fact the product of a decentralized/checkerboard election system that had been devised by the state legislature pursuant to Article II—the very system the *Bush* three purported to champion, even as they also purported to join the per curiam attacking that system.

[22] Some of this section borrows heavily from Akhil's 2009 Dunwody Lecture, delivered in Florida in the presence of several of the state jurists who prominently participated in the *Bush v. Gore* litigation, and first published as Akhil Reed Amar, *Bush, Gore, Florida, and the Constitution*, 61 FLA. L. REV. 945 (2009) [hereinafter *Dunwody Lecture*].

early December 2000 recount monitored by Florida judges had *fewer* equality glitches than the initial, less-monitored counts on Election Day and shortly thereafter. The recount aimed to correct some of the most glaring inequalities of the original count.

Concretely, nonwhite voters were roughly *ten times* as likely not to have their votes correctly counted as were white voters—and this in a former slave state, a former Confederate state, a former segregationist state, a state with a sorry history of open and avowed racial disenfranchisement late into the twentieth century.[23] True, the recount was imperfect (as are most things in life), but the recount's imperfections were not systematically racist, as were some of the structural inequalities in the initial count.[24] In many ways, the recount process unfolding under the Florida Supreme Court represented the last best chance to *reduce* and judicially *remedy* the inequalities, inaccuracies, and disenfranchisements that had tainted the initial counting process.

Some of the problems that seemed to surface in initial and intermediate stages of the recount might well have been cured by later corrective action from state judges, had these judges been allowed to proceed without interference from the U.S. Supreme Court, and with Congress waiting in the wings as the ultimate monitor and constitutionally mandated final judge.

Alternatively, the U.S. Supremes might have identified their specific concerns about the unfolding recount and sent the matter back to state courts with guidelines for a still-better recount process. Instead, by abruptly demanding an end to the recount process—NOW!—the *Bush* Court simply froze in place inequalities of the same sort, and of a greater extent and more racially imbalanced nature, than the inequalities the Court claimed to care about. According to the *Bush* per curiam,

> [T]he standards for accepting or rejecting contested ballots might vary not only from county to county but within a single county from one recount team to another. . . . A monitor in Miami-Dade County testified at trial that he observed that three members of the county canvassing board applied different standards in defining a legal vote. And testimony at trial also revealed that at least one county changed its evaluative standards during the

---

[23] *See* Laurence H. Tribe, *eroG .v hsuB: Through the Looking Glass*, *in* Bush v. Gore: The Question of Legitimacy, *supra* note 2, at 50.

[24] On the importance of effects and not merely intent in the voting context, see Vikram David Amar & Alan Brownstein, *The Hybrid Nature of Political Rights*, 50 Stan. L. Rev. 915 (1998).

> counting process.... This is not a process with sufficient guarantees of equal treatment.[25]

But if the Florida recount was constitutionally flawed, why wasn't the initial Florida count—which the Court's judgment in effect reinstated—even more flawed? The initial count, we must remember, featured highly uneven standards from county to county. Different counties used different ballots (including the infamous butterfly ballot), and even counties using the same ballot used different interpretive standards in counting them. This happened not just in Florida, but across the country. Were all these elections unconstitutional?

The idea that the Constitution requires absolute perfection and uniformity of standards in counting and/or recounting ballots is novel, to put it gently. For decades, if not centuries, American voters have been asked to put their "X" marks in boxes next to candidate names, and human umpires have had to judge if the "X" is close enough to the box to count. On Election Day, different umpires officiating in different precincts have always called slightly different strike zones. If these judgments are made in good faith and within a small zone of close calls, why are they unconstitutional? And if they are unconstitutional, then every election America has ever had was unconstitutional.

Regardless of what the U.S. Supremes may themselves have thought at the time, it was a mistake to believe that the Florida recount process was proceeding in some especially bad-faith manner that should have caused that process to be viewed with more suspicion than the initial counting process, which occurred without much judicial oversight. The *Bush* Court claimed that its newfangled equality principles applied only to judicially supervised state recounts, and not necessarily to other aspects of the electoral system.[26] But the Court gave no reason for this absurdly ad hoc limitation. The key facts of the case cut precisely against the per curiam: Generally speaking, cheating is *less* likely when judges and special masters—and the eyes of the world—are watching a recount unfold; and a court with a statewide mandate could help mitigate inequalities across different parts of the state. True, in a recount it might

---

[25] 531 U.S. at 106–07 (citations omitted).

[26] *Id.* at 109 ("The recount process, in its features here described, is inconsistent with the minimum procedures necessary to protect the fundamental right of each voter in the special instance of a statewide recount under the authority of a single state judicial officer. Our consideration is limited to the present circumstances, for the problem of equal protection in election processes generally presents many complexities.").

at times be foreseeable that a particular ruling might tend to favor a given candidate, but this is also true of various rulings made during or even before initial counting.

Critics of the recount, both on and off the Supreme Court, were far too quick to think they had somehow established smoking-gun evidence of foul play—"*Aha*!"—whenever they pointed to certain changes in counting protocols over time or certain variations across space. True, various Florida counties in the past had not counted dimpled chads. But the Florida Supreme Court had not blessed this past practice, and no uniform anti-dimple rule applied in the many sister states that, like Florida, affirmed the primacy of voter intent.[27]

Facts matter. If, for example, certain precincts in 2000 had particularly high rates of dimples or other mechanical undercounts, that might well be evidence of chad buildup or machine deterioration over the years. A strict anti-dimple rule that made sense in 1990 might not have been sensible a decade later, given older machines, more buildup, and a higher incidence of machine undercounts.

So too, the chad rule in precincts with short lines might not sensibly apply to precincts with much longer lines, where some voters may have felt a special need to vote fast so that others could take their turns. If the rates of dimpled chads or other undercounts were especially high in precincts where lines were longest and voters were most hurried (or were especially elderly and frail, or especially unlikely to understand English-language instructions about the proper use of punch-card styluses), it might well make sense to treat dimples in those precincts as particularly likely to reflect genuine attempted votes rather than intentional nonvotes.[28]

These sorts of issues could not have been easily addressed in each precinct on Election Day itself. But, they were just the sort of problems that a statewide court might have been able to sensibly address with an adequate factual background developed in the very process of recounting, a process in which fine-grained data about the precinct-by-precinct (and even machine-by-machine) distribution of each sort of voting problem would become available. The *Bush* Court, however, short-circuited the whole recount and remedy process, privileging the less accurate, less inclusive, and more discriminatory initial counting

[27] *See, e.g.*, Delahunt v. Johnston, 671 N.E. 2d 1241 (Mass. 1996).

[28] *See* Tribe, *supra* note 23, at 45–46.

process—and privileging that highly unequal process in the name of equality, no less!

As previously noted, the *Bush* Court per curiam failed to cite even a single case that, on its facts, came close to supporting the majority's analysis and result. To be sure, we can find lots of forceful voting-equality language in the Supreme Court's pre-*Bush* case law. But these cases were mainly about citizens simply being denied the right to vote (typically on race or class lines) or being assigned formally unequal voting power, with some (typically white) districts being overrepresented at the expense of other (typically black) districts.

The Equal Protection Clause was, first and foremost, designed to remedy the inequalities heaped upon blacks in America. The Fifteenth Amendment extended this civil-rights idea by prohibiting race discrimination with respect to the vote. Yet state governments in the former Confederacy, including the Florida government, mocked these rules for most of the twentieth century. For decades, most American blacks were simply not allowed to vote. When Congress finally acted to even things up with the Voting Rights Act of 1965, inequality persisted as a practical matter. In Florida, for example, black precincts in 2000 typically had much glitchier voting machines, which generated undercounts *many times* the rate of wealthier (white) precincts with sleek voting technology.[29] In raw numbers, this sizable inequality vastly exceeded the picayune discrepancies magnified by the *Bush* Court. Poor maintenance of voting machines, chad buildup, long voting lines in poor precincts—these were some of the real ballot inequalities in Florida 2000.

Accordingly, those who were the most serious about real equality, as envisioned by the architects of Reconstruction, persuasively argued that the government should not ignore the very large and racially non-random voting-machine skew. Rather, the government should do its best to minimize and remedy that skew, albeit imperfectly, via manual recounts. Even if such recounts were not required by equality, certainly they were not prohibited by equality.[30] In fixating on the small glitches of the recount rather than on the large and systemic defects of the machines, the *Bush* Court majority turned a blind eye to the real inequalities staring them in the face, piously attributing the problems to

---

[29] *See id.* at 50.

[30] *See* 531 U.S. at 147 (Breyer, J., dissenting).

"voter error" (as opposed to outdated and seriously flawed machines) and inviting "legislative bodies" to fix the mess for future elections.[31]

B. ARTICLE II ISL

In his concurring opinion, Chief Justice Rehnquist, joined by Justices Scalia and Thomas, declared that by straying from the text of the election law adopted by the Florida legislature, the Florida Supreme Court had violated Article II, Section 1, Clause 2 of the Federal Constitution. That clause provides that "[e]ach State shall appoint, in such Manner as the Legislature thereof may direct," presidential electors. For these three justices,[32] the key word here is *legislature*. The U.S. Constitution says that the state legislature can make the rules about how presidential electors are to be chosen. And, the argument runs, if the state judiciary deviates from those rules, the Federal Constitution itself authorizes federal judges to step in to protect the state legislature's federally guaranteed role. Under this Article II "independent-state-legislature" (ISL) reading, the Federal Constitution empowers each state legislature to discharge the legislature's Article II powers and duties independent from—and unencumbered by—the state constitution and the state judiciary interpreting that constitution.

In 2000, this ISL theory first arose in a lawsuit filed in state court as *Palm Beach County Canvassing Board v. Harris*, an earlier round of the *Bush* recount litigation.[33] In a unanimous decision handed down in late November 2000, the Florida Supreme Court openly referred to its decades-long tradition of construing the Florida election statutes in light of the Florida Constitution when it ordered the state official responsible for certifying election results to accept manually recounted ballots returned by county boards of election past a statutory deadline. In particular, the Florida justices stressed the right to vote as expressed in the Florida Constitution's Declaration of Rights:

> Because election laws are intended to facilitate the right of suffrage, such laws must be liberally construed in favor of the citizens' right to vote. . . . Courts must not lose sight of the fundamental purpose of election laws: The laws are intended to facilitate and safeguard the right of each voter to express

[31] 531 U.S. at 103–04 (per curiam).

[32] And for many subsequent scholarly apologists, such as Professors Epstein and McConnell and Judge Posner. *See supra* note 3.

[33] 772 So. 2d 1220 (Fla. 2000) (per curiam).

> his or her will in the context of our representative democracy. Technical statutory requirements must not be exalted over the substance of this right.[34]

For this reason, the Florida Supreme Court declared that provisions of the Florida Election Code for presidential elections were valid only if the provisions "impose no 'unreasonable or unnecessary' restraints on the right of suffrage" guaranteed by the state constitution.[35] On December 4, 2000, in *Bush v. Palm Beach County Canvassing Board* (which came to be known as *Bush I*) the U.S. Supreme Court unanimously vacated the Florida Supreme Court's ruling and remanded to the state court for more explanation.[36] The *Bush I* Court had granted review to address, inter alia, the following question:

> [W]hether the decision of the Florida Supreme Court, by effectively changing the State's elector appointment procedures after election day ... changed the manner in which the State's electors are to be selected, in violation of the legislature's power to designate the manner of selection under Article II, § 1, clause 2 of the United States Constitution.[37]

Media attention and the parties' briefing in that first Supreme Court foray focused extensively on the Article II questions.[38] The oral argument in the first Supreme Court hearing also zeroed in on whether the Florida Supreme Court had "made" law and thereby deprived the Florida legislature of its prerogatives, in violation of Article II.

Because the basis of the Florida Supreme Court's initial ruling was not entirely clear, the U.S. Supreme Court ended up resolving *Bush I* without ruling at all on the merits of the Article II question. As the *Bush I* Court put it, "there is considerable uncertainty as to the precise ground for the [Florida Supreme Court's] decision.... This is sufficient reason for us to decline at this time to review the federal questions asserted to be present."[39] Accordingly, the *Bush I* Court merely remanded the case for clarification by the state judiciary.

---

[34] *Id.* at 1237 (internal footnote omitted); *see also id.* at 1239 ("[T]he right to vote is the preeminent right in the Declaration of Rights of the Florida Constitution....").

[35] *Id.* at 1236.

[36] 531 U.S. 70 (2000) (per curiam) (*Bush I*).

[37] *Id.* at 73.

[38] *E.g.* Brief for Petitioner § II, *Bush I*, 531 U.S. 70 (2000) (No. 00-836); Reply Brief of Respondents Al Gore, Jr. & Fla. Democratic Party § IV, *Bush I*, 531 U.S. 70 (2000) (No. 00-836).

[39] *Bush I*, 531 U.S. at 78 (internal quotation omitted).

As part of its remand in *Bush I*, the Court foreshadowed events to come in the more (in)famous *Bush II* by quoting from an 1892 case, *McPherson v. Blacker*, on the meaning of Article II:

> Although we did not address the same question petitioner raises here, in *McPherson v. Blacker*, 146 U.S. 1, 25 (1892), we said: "[Article II, § 1, cl. 2] does not read that the people or the citizens shall appoint, but that 'each State shall'; and if the words 'in such manner as the legislature thereof may direct,' had been omitted, it would seem that the legislative power of appointment could not have been successfully questioned in the absence of any provision in the state constitution in that regard. Hence, the insertion of those words, while operating as a limitation upon the State in respect of any attempt to circumscribe the legislative power, cannot itself be held to operate as a limitation on that power.[40]

Article II and the offhand meaning given to it in *Blacker* made a return appearance in the second—and dispositive—Supreme Court go-around in the Florida matter, in the concurring opinion by the *Bush* three. In the immediate aftermath of *Bush*, several notable conservative scholars praised the *Bush* three's Article II ISL argument.[41]

Alas, many other scholars at the time and in the ensuing years allowed the ISL argument to fly under the radar screen. The ISL theory did not clearly command five votes in *Bush*;[42] and, as we have already seen, *Bush* said and did *so many* other troubling things requiring careful

---

[40] *Id.* at 76 (alteration in original).

[41] *See supra* note 3.

[42] The majority opinion did in one brief passage nod toward ISL:

> The individual citizen has no federal constitutional right to vote for electors for the President of the United States unless and until the state legislature chooses a statewide election as the means to implement its power to appoint members of the Electoral College. This is the source for the statement in *McPherson* v. *Blacker*, 146 U.S. 1, 35 (1892), that the state legislature's power to select the manner for appointing electors is plenary; it may, if it so chooses, select the electors itself, which indeed was the manner used by state legislatures in several States for many years after the Framing of our Constitution. History has now favored the voter, and in each of the several States the citizens themselves vote for Presidential electors. When the state legislature vests the right to vote for President in its people, the right to vote as the legislature has prescribed is fundamental; and one source of its fundamental nature lies in the equal weight accorded to each vote and the equal dignity owed to each voter. The State, of course, after granting the franchise in the special context of Article II, can take back the power to appoint electors. See *id.*, at 35 ("[T]here is no doubt of the right of the legislature to resume the power at any time, for it can neither be taken away nor abdicated") (quoting S. Rep. No. 395, 43d Cong., 1st Sess.).

Bush v. Gore, 531 U.S. 98, 104 (2000) (per curiam) (citation omitted).

refutation. So why bother with an argument that did not receive five square votes in *Bush* and has never received five votes in any later case?

Bother we must today, because an entire generation of young conservatives in the Federalist Society and similar circles[43] have been taught to parrot and admire the *Bush* three's ideas. As we argued long ago (and in some instances even before the 2000 election),[44] and as we shall argue again today, the *Bush* three's ideas were truly fake news—erroneous and outlandish on Day One. But these memes, unfortunately, have in recent years apparently gone viral in various right-leaning legal circles. Many young conservatives were evidently *Bush*-League activists and *Bush*-League law clerks in OT 2020. So bother we must today because one of the *Bush* three now sits as the Court's most senior justice, and an extremely influential justice at that. Bother we must because this Justice, Clarence Thomas, quite evidently continues to subscribe to the sincere but misguided ideas he embraced back in 2000. And bother we must because there are now at least two members of the current Court beyond Justice Thomas who seem to agree with the original *Bush* three.

Thus, we now stress—because it matters—that the Rehnquist/Scalia/Thomas ISL theory flew in the face of: (1) original constitutional understandings; (2) definitive actions by state legislatures themselves (the very bodies ISL claims to care about); and (3) the best reading of Supreme Court case law circa 2000.

1. *Originalism—Text, History, Structure*. ISL theory comes in two parts. First, it claims that under Article II (and also, apparently, under the companion language of Article I, governing congressional elections[45]) each state legislature enjoys a federal right to have its enactments relating to election logistics fully implemented notwithstanding any conflicts between its enactments and the state constitution that creates and bounds the legislature itself. Second, ISL says that, if any

---

[43] See, e.g., Richard L. Hasen, *Trump Is Planning a Much More Respectable Coup Next Time*, Slate (Aug. 5, 2021), https://slate.com/news-and-politics/2021/08/trump-2024-coup-federalist-society-doctrine.html; Jane Mayer, *The Big Money Behind the Big Lie*, New Yorker (Aug. 2, 2021), https://www.newyorker.com/magazine/2021/08/09/the-big-money-behind-the-big-lie.

[44] *E.g.* Vikram David Amar, *The People Made Me Do It: Can the People of the States Instruct and Coerce Their State Legislatures in the Article V Constitutional Amendment Process?*, 41 Wm. & Mary L. Rev. 1037 (2000); Vikram Amar & Alan Brownstein, Bush v. Gore *and Article II: Pressured Judgement Makes Dubious Law*, 48 Fed. Law. 27, 30–33 (2001); *Dunwody Lecture*, *supra* note 22.

[45] For one possible difference between the words of the relevant companion clauses, see *infra* note 90.

state constitutional limits do in any way constrain a given state legislature, *federal* courts must decide what those limits are, and how best to interpret state election statutes. Prominent believers in ISL are coy about whether their approach means *de novo* review by federal judges, or instead federal review with some (limited) deference to state judicial and executive interpretations. But make no mistake: either way it does not mean business as usual, in which federal courts almost invariably accept state law as pronounced by state adjudicatory entities.

Both halves of this "we-must-protect-the-state-legislatures" theory are, as an originalist matter, not just lawless—that is, not grounded in the law—but actually law-defying. They stand lawful federalism on its head. The theory invokes constitutional provisions designed to protect states against federal interference (including interference from federal courts) and instead uses these provisions to disrespect both the wishes of the state peoples who create, empower, and limit their legislatures, and the wishes of the elected legislatures themselves. The theory gives near carte blanche to *federal* judges, when the key point of Article II's election language (and the companion language of Article I) was to empower *states*.

Let's start with constitutional text: Articles I and II do create powers and duties on the part of the "Legislature" of each state.[46] But what, precisely, is a state "legislature" for these purposes? One aspect of this question is definitional: who must or can be counted as a "legislature?" Can a "legislature" include a veto-pen-wielding governor? Can it consist of an independent agency, or the people themselves engaged in direct democracy via initiatives and town meetings? Another aspect is whether the "legislature," however defined, can override state constitutional directives on how elections must be run.[47]

---

[46] U.S. Const. art. I, § 4, cl. 1 ("The Times, Places and Manner of holding Elections for Senators and Representatives, shall be prescribed in each State by the Legislature thereof. . . ."); U.S. Const. art. II, § 1, cl. 2 ("Each State shall appoint, in such Manner as the Legislature thereof may direct, a Number of Electors. . . .").

[47] These two aspects—the first of which might be seen as broadly "procedural" and the second broadly "substantive," blur at the margins. Definitionally, we might say that a "legislature" under a given state constitution is a body that includes a veto-pen-wielding governor. But of course we might also say that, definitionally, a "legislature" under that very same state constitution is a body that must allow absentee voting (even for congressional and presidential elections) or an entity that may not pick presidential electors itself or try to reserve a power to judge contested presidential elections. On this latter—and critical—point, see *infra* note 117. For a recent—and, we believe, unsuccessful—effort to posit a sharp distinction between these two aspects, see Michael T. Morley, *The Independent State Legislature Doctrine*, 90 Fordham L. Rev. 501 (2021).

Remarkably, the *Bush* three advocates of ISL offered nothing—*nothing!*—to suggest that anyone at the Founding would have understood state "legislature" to mean a free-floating body untethered to the state constitution. Or, a body whose legislative work-product would be free from state court jurisdiction and instead subject largely or wholly to federal judicial interpretation.

In fact, the public meaning of state "legislature" was clear and well accepted at the Founding: A state's "legislature" was not just an entity created to represent the people; it was an entity *created and constrained by the state constitution.*

The adoption of new, republican state constitutions up and down the American continent was a truly transcendent achievement in the late 1770s, acclaimed and revered by Americans everywhere. These new state constitutions were the very heart and soul, legally, of the American revolution.[48] These state constitutions were universally understood as creations of the American people themselves. So of course state constitutions were understood as supreme over state legislatures at the Founding! And of course state courts could—and did—enforce these state higher laws against state legislatures themselves. Notable state judicial review under state constitutions in fact predated the Philadelphia Convention, *Federalist No. 78*, and *Marbury v. Madison*.[49] Indeed, state constitutions formed the basic template for the Federal Constitution itself in 1787–88.[50]

The clear language and logic of the Article VI Supremacy Clause emphatically confirmed the general supremacy of state constitutions over mere state statutes, in the very same breath that the document similarly affirmed the supremacy of the Federal Constitution over mere federal statutes. The Clause textually enumerated five types of law, and in every instance, the *textual* order of each type of law tracked its *lexical* order, from highest law to lowest law: The U.S. Constitution came first, then federal statutes, then federal treaties, then state constitutions, then state statutes. *In that order, both textually and legally*: "[1] This Constitution, and [2] the Laws of the United States which shall be made in Pursuance thereof; and [3] all Treaties made, or which shall be made, under the Authority of the United States, shall be the

---

[48] *See* AMAR, *supra* note 11, at 152–62; GORDON S. WOOD, THE CREATION OF THE AMERICAN REPUBLIC, 1776–1787, at 46–132 (rev. ed. 1998).

[49] 5 U.S. (1 Cranch) 137 (1803).

[50] *See* AMAR, *supra* note 11, at 186–96.

supreme Law of the Land; and the Judges in every state shall be bound thereby, any thing in [4] the Constitution or [5] Laws of any State to the Contrary notwithstanding."[51]

An analogy here will drive the point home.[52] The Appointments Clause states: "Congress may by Law vest the Appointment of such inferior Officers, as they think proper, in the President alone, in the Courts of Law, or in the Heads of Departments."[53] Imagine that Congress passed a law vesting appointment power for an assistant Attorney General in the Attorney General, the head of the Justice Department. Would sensible interpreters argue that the President does not have the right to require that his Attorney General refrain from appointing person X as assistant Attorney General? No, even though the Constitution clearly distinguishes here between the "President" and "Heads of Departments." Most everyone would concede presidential power to cabin Attorney General power here and would not read the reference to "Heads of Departments" to mean "Independent Heads of Departments." IHD theory—to coin a phrase—makes no sense because there exists a backdrop understanding of unitary executive power over executive department heads. The president is his underlings' master, their superior.

So too, as a backdrop principle, state peoples and state constitutions are masters of state legislatures.[54] Thus we should not read the words of Article II, Section 1 (or the similar words of Article I, Section 4, for that matter) as excluding control by state peoples and state constitutions. Since the Revolution, every state legislature has been defined and circumscribed, both procedurally (e.g., *What counts as a quorum? Is the governor involved in legislation?*) and substantively (e.g., *What rights must the legislature respect?*) by its state constitution, which in turn emanates from the people of each state. When a state legislature violates the procedural or substantive state constitutional limitations upon it, it is no longer operating as a true state legislature for these purposes.

---

[51] U.S. Const. art. VI, cl. 2. For more on this textual and lexical ordering, and its profound implications for the status of federal treaties vis-à-vis federal statutes, see Amar, *supra* note 10, at 302–07 (citing, among other things, John Marshall's pointed reminder in *Marbury* that the Supremacy Clause listed the Constitution first, before later-mentioned and lower-level types of law).

[52] This analogy is drawn from Amar, *supra* note 44, at 1046–47.

[53] U.S. Const. art. II, § 2, cl. 2.

[54] In both the ISL and IHD contexts, the backdrop historical and structural principle was also expressly textualized in the Federal Constitution itself—in the Article VI Supremacy Clause and the Article II Vesting Clause, respectively.

The matter is really no different from what Chief Justice John Marshall said in *Marbury v. Madison* and what Alexander Hamilton said before that in the *Federalist No. 78*, and what the Constitution itself said even earlier in the Article VI Supremacy Clause and elsewhere: When *Congress* enacts an unconstitutional bill, its actions simply cease to have the force of law. The same first principles hold true when a state legislature enacts a bill violative of its state constitution.

In this regard, consider Article I, Section 4, which vests backup power to regulate various aspects of congressional elections in "the Congress." No sober person would suggest that this provision vests final substantive power in Congress to do things forbidden by other parts of the Federal Constitution itself, a Constitution that indeed creates and bounds Congress. Imagine, for example, a Congressional statute proclaiming John Smith by name as ineligible to run for Congress, in obvious violation of the spirit of the Article I, Section 9 ban on federal bills of attainder.[55] Or imagine a Congressional statute proclaiming Catholics ineligible, in plain contravention on the Article VI ban on federal religious tests,[56] to say nothing of the later First Amendment. No one would seriously suggest that federal courts lack power to interpret federal statutes regulating congressional elections with an eye toward harmonizing those statutes with constitutional rights. Nor would anyone deny that Congress has in fact deputized federal courts to perform these very functions.

All this is of course true for every provision of Article I that vests power in Congress. But the point is particularly sharp when we juxtapose "the Congress" and "the Legislature" of "each state" in Article I, Section 4. If the *federal* Congress is quite obviously not independent of the *Federal* Constitution, why should anyone think that the *state* legislature in this very same clause is somehow independent of its *state* constitution?

Indeed, at the Founding, the "legislatures" of each state to which Articles I and II refer were, as a general matter, far from free agents. Voters in many states claimed the power to formally "instruct" their state representatives and thus legally bind them on specific issues. The right to instruct had appeared explicitly in the constitutions of at least

---

[55] U.S. Const. art. I, § 9, cl. 3 ("No Bill of attainder ... shall be passed.").

[56] U.S. Const. art. VI, cl. 3 ("[N]o religious Test shall ever be Required as a Qualification To any Office or public Trust under the United States.").

five states, namely, the Pennsylvania and North Carolina Constitutions of 1776, the Vermont Constitutions of 1777 and 1786, the Massachusetts Constitution of 1780, and the New Hampshire Constitution of 1784.[57]

Founding-era state legislatures were not independent sovereign entities; they were then, and state legislatures remain today, delegatees of the sovereign power of the people. That is why the devices of instruction, recall, referendum, and initiative (to say nothing of judicial review) do not improperly invade the powers of state legislatures, but instead operate as mechanisms that further define the scope of state legislatures' legitimate authority. The Tenth Amendment preserves broad power of the people of the states to shape governments in whatever ways they want, and the Guarantee Clause of Article IV generally requires the federal government to respect and protect—not disregard and override—these state choices about how to create, divide, limit, and implement lawmaking powers.[58]

Early practice under the new Federal Constitution provides still further reason to reject the *Bush* three's ISL ideas. Four of the six state constitutions that were adopted or revised in the Constitution's earliest years of operation—George Washington's first term—regulated the manner of federal elections, and in so doing cabined the power of the state legislature. The Delaware Constitution of 1792 explicitly required that voters elect congressional representatives "at the same places" and "in the same manner" as state representatives. Three other state constitutions—Georgia's in 1789, Pennsylvania's in 1790, and Kentucky's in 1792—required "all elections" to be "by ballot" rather than *viva voce*. Though congressional and presidential elections were not specified as such, these provisions by their express terms applied to *all elections*—popular elections for statewide offices, to be sure, but also biennial elections for federal House members and any popular elections for presidential electors that might be held in the future. Early statesmen read these provisions to mean just what

---

[57] *See* Akhil Reed Amar, *The Bill of Rights as a Constitution*, 100 Yale L.J. 1131, 1154 (1991).

[58] *See generally* Deborah Jones Merritt, *The Guarantee Clause and State Autonomy: Federalism for a Third Century*, 88 Colum. L. Rev. 1 (1988). As Hamilton recognized, so long as it remains majoritarian and responsive to popular will, many a type of state government will generally comport with the Guarantee Clause. The Federalist No. 21 (Alexander Hamilton); *see* Akhil Reed Amar, *The Central Meaning of Republican Government: Popular Sovereignty, Majority Rule, and the Denominator Problem*, 65 U. Colo. L. Rev. 749 (1994).

they said.[59] These post-1789 state constitutions built squarely on strong pre-1787 precedents. Article V of the Articles of Confederation expressly provided that "delegates [to the Confederation Congress] shall be annually appointed in such manner as the *legislature* [emphasis added] of each State shall direct." But all three of the most relevant state constitutions in the Confederation era nonetheless directly and expressly regulated how state legislatures had to act in the appointment of Confederation Congressmen: state legislatures in these key states were emphatically NOT independent. Thus, the 1778 South Carolina Constitution required state lawmakers to choose Confederation Congressmen "by ballot"; the Massachusetts Constitution of 1780 specified the month and manner in which the legislature had to appoint these Congressmen (June, meeting in joint session in one room); and the New Hampshire Constitution of 1784 prescribed the timing of legislative action and the qualifications of eligible Congressional delegations, among other things. Not only did these state constitutions mandate various specific procedures and substantive constraints that state legislatures had to follow when picking Congressmen, but these constitutions also mandated that the legislatures themselves do the picking. (Note that the Articles, standing alone, allowed state legislatures—if permitted by their state constitutions!—to provide for popular election; in two states, Connecticut and Rhode Island, the legislature by law in fact opted to give a role to the voters themselves.)[60]

---

[59] *See* DEL. CONST. of 1792, art. VIII, § 2; GA. CONST. of 1789, art. IV, § 2; PA. CONST. of 1790, art. III, § 2; KY. CONST. of 1792, art. III, § 2. Although Kentucky in 1799 shifted gears and required in its constitution that federal and state elections be held by voice vote rather than ballot, see KY. CONST. of 1799, art. VI, § 16, this 1799 provision was every bit as inconsistent with ISL theory as its "ballot" predecessor in Kentucky's first constitution. It is worth mentioning that these provisions constrained governors as well as state legislatures, and that governors would have to obey these limits even when discharging the power conferred by Article I, section 2 to the "Executive Authority [to] issue Writs of Election to fill" House vacancies. Thus, there is no "Independent State Governor" (ISG) theory" that would apply here, and we are not aware of anyone who has even argued for one. For more on these early constitutions, see the important new work by Hayward H. Smith, *Revisiting the History of the Independent State Legislature Doctrine*, 53 ST. MARY'S L.J. (forthcoming 2022).

[60] S.C. CONST. of 1778, art. XXII; MA. CONST. of 1780, ch. IV; N.H. CONST. of 1784 (unnumbered clause beginning "The delegates of this state to the Congress"). A quick note on our tally: Prior to 1787, only three states—South Carolina in 1778, Massachusetts in 1780, and New Hampshire in 1784—adopted or revised state constitutions after ratifying the Articles of Confederation, whose text was not finalized until November 1777. As noted, all three state constitutions contradict ISL theory. For more on congressional selection in Connecticut and Rhode Island under the Confederation, see AMAR, *supra* note 10, at 64, 528 n.16.

All told, more than half of the eleven states that ratified the Constitution in 1787–88 thus had state constitutions that expressly regulated state legislatures in the context of federal elections in the 1780s and early 1790s. All these states acted in ways precisely contrary to modern ISL theory.[61] On the other side of the ledger, modern ISL theorists have identified no strong and specific evidence from *any* of the remaining states indicating that constitution-makers affirmatively embraced ISL ideas. In these states, the issue simply may not have arisen; or constitution-makers may have preferred, for reasons of pure policy, to leave their state legislatures untrammeled in regards to federal elections.

In addition, at least two early states that provided for vetoes for general legislative action employed such veto provisions in the process by which federal election rules were made. In Massachusetts, bills regulating federal elections were not considered by the legislative houses alone but were presented to—and subject to disapproval by—the governor. And in New York, such bills were subjected to a council of review that included not only the governor, but also members of the state judiciary.[62]

---

[61] Obviously, prior to 1787, no state constitution would have aimed to regulate Article I congressional elections and Article II presidential elections because Articles I and II did not yet exist. The U.S. Constitution did not truly commence operation until early 1789, and over the next four years, only six states revised their prior constitutions or adopted new ones: Georgia in 1789; Pennsylvania and South Carolina in 1790; and Delaware, Kentucky, and New Hampshire in 1792. As noted, Delaware quite pointedly repudiated the ISL notion; Georgia, Pennsylvania, and Kentucky also expressly did so, albeit in more general language. Adding up all the data: The three key states (South Carolina, Massachusetts, and New Hampshire) that squarely rejected ISL under the Articles, when added to three more key states (Delaware, Georgia, and Pennsylvania) that squarely rejected ISL shortly after the Constitution, form a majority of the eleven states that launched the Constitution in 1789. Kentucky, which also rejected ISL early on, joined the Constitution a bit later.

[62] *See* Hayward H. Smith, *History of the Article II Independent State Legislature Doctrine*, 29 Fla. St. U. L. Rev. 731, 759–61 (2001). As the New York episode evidences, state judges in some places had legislative roles. Also, state legislators at times had judicial roles; several states at the Founding vested judicial duties in the upper chamber of the state legislature. The superstrict distinction that ISL proponents rely upon—a sharp delineation between state legislatures and state courts—simply did not exist at the Founding. Also, efforts by some scholars, see e.g., Saikrishna Bangalore Prakash and John Yoo, *People ≠ Legislature*, 39 Harv. J. L. & Pub. Pol'y 341 (2016), to demonstrate that the Founding generation often distinguished between the "legislature" and the "people" are largely beside the point. The ISL crowd does not come remotely close to asking, much less persuasively answering, the key analytic questions. Concretely, what specific evidence suggests that the Founders actually intended to exalt state legislatures over state constitutions and override ordinary principles of state judicial review? How does any of this square with Revolutionary ideology celebrating state constitutions, or with widespread early state constitutional practice flatly contrary to ISL? How can it truly be that state legislatures cannot *if they choose* enlist state courts in

Thus, the Constitution in both Articles I and II takes state legislative bodies as it finds them, subject to pre-existing control by the people of each state—the ultimate masters of state legislatures—and the state constitutional limits that those people create.[63] And of course the Constitution also plainly recognizes the general role of state courts as the last word on the meaning of state law, including state constitutions, even when those constitutions constrain state legislatures.

To see all this one final way, let us return to the key text of Article II. If, for all the reasons we have identified, the term "legislature" cannot mean "independent legislature," why is it there? The most obvious explanation relates to efficiency and expense. The Framers knew that each of the thirteen then-existing states had an ordinary standing legislature, and Article II created a simple, inexpensive, and self-executing default that, *unless a future state constitution specified otherwise by creating a special ad hoc legislative body or process*, the state's ordinary pre-existing state legislature would be the body to adopt federal election regulations. And, to repeat, nothing in the Federal Constitution suggests that the *ordinary* state legislature would have federal carte blanche to act in *extraordinary* ways contrary to the general rules limiting the legislature in the very state constitution that created and bounded that legislature.

In 1787, state appointment practice varied widely under then-existing state constitutions. In some states, legislatures had wide appointment authority; in other states, executives played a larger role alongside others (often, council members).[64] Also, within a given state, different appointment rules sometimes applied to different appointments. In the absence of Article II's mention of "legislature," it thus might have been unclear in some states who was to play the default role in directing the manner of appointment of the Federal Constitution's newly created presidential electors. Going forward, however, Article II's text rather plainly gave each state, via any future state constitution or state constitutional amendment it might adopt, broad authority.[65] A future state

administering federal elections? And shouldn't at least some weight be given to a century of clear Supreme Court precedent (along with two centuries of actual state constitutional practice!) rejecting broad ISL claims?

[63] *See* Amar & Brownstein, *supra* note 44, at 31.

[64] *See generally* Wood, *supra* note 48, at 148–150, 407, 433–35, 452.

[65] So too, Article IV's Republican Government Clause guaranteed each state its existing governmental system while allowing future republican reforms of that system at the state constitutional level. *See supra* note 58.

constitution could thus directly regulate the elector-appointment process itself in whole or in part; create a special legislative body or legislative process to do the regulation; and/or continue to allow the ordinary legislature to direct electoral appointment, even allowing the legislature to make appointments itself[66]—all subject to whatever general rules that future state constitution might provide. That is why, textually, Article II empowers "Each State" *as such* to "appoint" electors and says merely that the state legislature "may"—not "shall" or "must"—"direct" the "Manner" of appointment. With all this in mind, the reader should now re-read the words of Article II, with our emphasis added: "Each *State shall* appoint, in such a Manner as the *Legislature* thereof *may* direct. . . ."

2. *State Legislative Practice.* A second and entirely distinct refutation of *Bush*-Leaguers is equally devastating: Even if state constitutions somehow do not apply *of their own force*, they would almost always apply because they have been *incorporated by reference* by the state legislature itself—a key argument nowhere addressed by *Bush*-Leaguers on or off the Court.

Undeniably, even if each state legislature were somehow free to ignore the state constitution that creates and bounds it, each state legislature could *choose* to abide by its state constitution and to invite state courts to enforce the provisions of that constitution as the basic backdrop of all election-law statutes. In fact, each state legislature, including Florida's, generally has so chosen, at least implicitly. This simple fact also guts the second part of the *Bush* three's ISL argument—namely, that *federal* courts must protect the *state* legislatures. State legislatures have already indicated whom they want to protect their interests: *state* adjudicatory bodies.

Notice, importantly, that Articles I and II do not say that state legislatures should be the final word on all aspects of federal elections, but only that state legislatures shall (Article I) or may (Article II) lay out the "manner" of holding federal elections. But the manner of (s)election of officials may certainly involve other branches; surely a state legislature may properly enlist state agencies[67] and state courts to put

---

[66] This is to be distinguished from the federal legislature, which of course lacks comparable appointments power under other parts of Article II.

[67] But compare Justice Gorsuch's provocative remarks (joined by Justice Alito) in a pre-election case brought by North Carolina Republicans challenging a ruling by the North Carolina State Board of Elections. The Justice relied on his own plain-meaning textualist analysis of the

the state legislature's plan into effect. And that is exactly what state legislatures have done in almost all states in almost all elections. In dialogue with state courts over the years, *and mindful of the accountability to state electorates and constituencies that state judges have (and that federal judges lack)*, state legislatures have chosen to incorporate into state statutes state constitutional norms and state judicial involvement, in both federal and state elections, to vindicate those norms. Especially in light of the historical links between state legislatures and state judicial bodies,[68] it is implausible to think that state legislatures have chosen to have federal, rather than state, judges decide what state statutes mean.[69]

One big reason state legislatures have consistently involved state courts and state constitutions in federal elections is the practical need to align state and federal voting systems. As a rule, voters use a unified ballot and participate in a unified election schema—when to vote, where to vote, how to vote—to elect candidates in both systems.

To see this point clearly, consider a thought experiment in which the Florida Supreme Court in 2000 had, in response to that fateful remand in *Bush I*, said the following quite clearly and several days before the Supreme Court impulsively jumped back into the fray in *Bush II*:[70]

> Just as Article II of the U.S. Constitution permits the Florida legislature to direct the process of selecting presidential electors, Article II of course also allows the Florida legislature, if it chooses, to cabin its own power in light of our state constitution, and to delegate the last word to resolve and manage disputed presidential elections in Florida to the Florida judiciary. We hereby hold that the Florida legislature has done just that by deputizing us, the Florida judiciary, to construe the Florida statutes and regulations regarding presidential elections against the backdrop of the Florida Constitution.

North Carolina state constitution, pooh-poohing the idea that he should seek out definitive state court rulings or otherwise "rifl[e] through state law." Based on his own two-sentence(!) glance at, and his own confident interpretation of, the state constitution, he expressed strong doubt that "the North Carolina General Assembly could delegate its Elections Clause authority to other officials." Moore v. Circosta, 141 S. Ct. 46 (2020) (mem.) (Gorsuch, J., dissenting from denial of application for injunctive relief). In earlier cases, Justice Gorsuch has been a prominent advocate for a robust nondelegation doctrine for federal lawmaking. *See, e.g.*, Gundy v. United States, 139 S. Ct. 2116 (2019) (Gorsuch, J., dissenting). In *Moore*, he evidently tried to use a variant of ISL ideology to move toward imposing a strict nondelegation vision on state governments in the context of federal elections.

[68] *See supra* note 62.

[69] *See* Robert A. Schapiro, *Conceptions and Misconceptions of State Constitutional Law in* Bush v. Gore, 29 Fla. St. U. L. Rev. 661, 680–81 (2001).

[70] For an earlier version of this idea, see *Dunwody Lecture*, *supra* note 22, at 953–56.

Indeed, the Florida legislature has empowered us, the Florida judiciary, to equitably adjust and modify the sometimes hypertechnical and confusing maze of election regulations and code provisions so as to bring the letter of election law into harmony with the spirit and grand principles of the state constitution.

As our longstanding case law makes clear, the Florida Constitution emphatically affirms the people's right to vote and right to have every lawful vote reflecting a clearly discernable voter intent counted equally. We need not decide today whether, in a presidential election, the Florida Constitution applies *of its own force*. Rather, we hold that the Florida Constitution applies simply because the Florida legislature has *chosen to make it applicable* and has deputized us to vindicate its spirit in presidential elections here in Florida.

This legislative power is not merely consistent with Article II; it derives from Article II. In general, no federal court (not even the U.S. Supreme Court!) may lawfully intervene to "protect" the Florida legislature from the Florida courts in the name of Article II, for any such federal court intervention would itself violate the very principle of Article II being asserted. To repeat: pursuant to Article II, the Florida legislature has designated the Florida judiciary as its chosen deputy in this matter.

Doubtless Article II would have been satisfied had the Florida election statute explicitly stated that "every provision of this presidential election code should be construed or judicially revised to conform to the letter and spirit of the right to vote under the Florida Constitution's Declaration of Rights, as that Declaration has been and will continue to be definitively construed by the Florida judiciary." We believe—and so hold—that the Florida statute has done just that in substance, albeit in different words.

Here is why: *The Florida Election Code rules for presidential elections are the same as the Florida Election Code rules for other elections, including state elections for state positions.* It is absolutely clear that the Florida Constitution does apply to these other elections. It is equally clear that this Court—the Florida Supreme Court—is broadly empowered to protect the fundamental state constitutional right to vote in these state elections, even if protecting that right may require this Court to go beyond and behind the strict and at times hypertechnical words of the statutes and regulations. Unless the state legislature clearly indicates otherwise—*and it has never done so*—the same interpretive principles concerning the importance of the right to vote and the authority of Florida judges to construe all rules and regulations against the backdrop of that right apply to presidential elections as well.

For example, if a voter were to use an ink pen rather than a lead pencil to fill in the oval bubble that appeared next to a candidate's name on a printed ballot, longstanding Florida case law makes it clear that this pen mark would ordinarily constitute a valid vote, even if the instructions told voters to use number two pencils when marking their ballots. Given that pen marks on a particular ballot should be counted in an election for state representative, or for any other state, local, or federal official, *surely the presidential-election section of the ballot should be handled the same way*. It would be odd indeed—absent a very clear legislative indication to the contrary—to count pen marks everywhere else on this ballot and yet refuse to count virtually identical pen marks in the presidential-election section of the very same ballot.

The takeaway here is that unless the state legislature speaks clearly to the contrary, it is most sensible to assume that the legislature wants the *entire* ballot and the *entire* election process to be governed by the same basic rules. Since the state-election parts of the ballot are undeniably controlled by the state constitution operating of its own force, the federal election parts of the ballot should be controlled by the state constitution *because state legislatures have chosen to create unified ballots, with unified electoral timetables and unified electoral logistics and unified electoral implementation.*

Even before the Constitution was ratified, leading Federalists predicted that states would do just that, and publicized this fact as a great systemic virtue of the document's envisioned model of cooperative federalism. Thus, Alexander Hamilton concluded his *Federalist No. 61* by extolling "the convenience" of enabling states to "hav[e] the elections for their own governments and for the national government" on the same date and, presumably, in the same manner.

In any event, if there be any fair doubt about whether in a given instance the legislature of state X did in fact mean to incorporate state constitutional norms, this fair doubt is to be resolved by the state supreme court, which is of course the definitive expounder of the meaning of state law.[71]

---

[71] The incorporation of state constitutional norms thus need not be explicit—or at least there is no proper warrant for the U.S. Supreme Court to demand explicitness if state courts think otherwise. There is no general federal common law of state statutory interpretation—no general requirement, for example, that state statutory interpretation must be "textualist," even if the U.S. Supreme Court were to embrace "textualism" (whatever that might mean) as its own general approach to federal statutory interpretation. Federal courts should in general not dictate to state courts how they should construe state law in a situation in which federal law, properly understood, is utterly indifferent—that is, a situation in which either interpretation of a fairly disputable substantive state law at issue fully vindicates all relevant federal-law interests. For more discussion and elaboration, see *infra* Section V.

To view the matter from another angle, let us concede, arguendo, that questions concerning the "true" meaning of state congressional and presidential election laws are, technically, federal questions under Articles I and II, respectively. Even so, the desired functional uniformity to be achieved in most situations (as exemplified by Florida in 2000) is not uniformity *across* states (to be accomplished by the U.S. Supreme Court's promulgation of one-size-fits all rules of interpretation of state election statutes), but rather uniformity *within* each state. The functional and structural idea is for each state that so desires to have a tolerably uniform election scheme harmonizing its rules for state candidates and its rules for federal candidates—that is, congressional and presidential candidates. (So too, the original Constitution aimed to

For this reason, exercise—even significant exercise—of state judicial power vindicates rather than violates the choice made by the state legislature. To be sure, whenever a legislature provides for judicial enforcement of its work, there is always a risk that courts might err in discerning the best meaning of statutes. But as long as state courts are truly acting as courts and doing what they usually do and have usually done[72]—expounding state law in good faith—there is no basis for officious federal court involvement in discerning, much less federal court de novo second-guessing of, the "real" meaning of state election law.

3. *Pre-Bush* Precedent. What about the cryptic language in *Blacker*[73] mentioned in *Bush I* and relied on by the *Bush II* opinions? Does/did *Blacker* truly support the daft notion that, at least for Article II (and perhaps Article I?) purposes, state legislatures somehow float independently of and outside the very state constitutions that created and bounded them? Actually, *Blacker*'s dictum, fairly read, says very little about the "independence" of state legislatures in these settings.

On its facts, *Blacker* did not in any way involve a conflict between what a state constitution said or a state people wanted, on the one hand, and what the elected legislature preferred, on the other. Instead, the question in *Blacker* was whether the legislature's chosen method of selecting electors by means of district-by-district (as opposed to statewide) election was permissible under Article II. The *Blacker* Court quite correctly upheld the legislature's choice in this regard. There was never

harmonize voter-eligibility law for state assembly races with voter-eligibility rules for congressional contests.) Where federal law aims to piggyback on state-law systems so as to achieve state-desired intrastate uniformity as opposed to interstate uniformity, federal courts should adjudicate formal federal-question cases by copying state courts. *See generally* Paul J. Mishkin, *The Variousness of "Federal Law": Competence and Discretion in the Choice of National and State Rules for Decision*, 105 U. Pa. L. Rev. 797 (1957). We suspect that this point would have been far more clear to all observers in 2000 had Florida's election involved razor-thin contested races for various state offices implicating the exact same chad/voter intent/etc. issues as did the razor-thin presidential contest that same day. Alas, because only the presidential contest was a statistical toss-up, many commentators and justices wrongly saw the dispute as a uniquely federal matter warranting an unduly robust role for the nine eminences on One First Street.

Finally, note that in states whose written laws, whether statutory or constitutional or both, permissibly aim to regulate federal elections somewhat differently from state elections, *see infra* note 84, state supreme court expositions of these state laws should generally be conclusive for federal courts for the simple reason that Articles I and II were designed to give states leeway here, and state courts are of course key components of states. Federal courts are not. *See infra* note 79.

[72] *See infra* Section V.

[73] McPherson v. Blacker, 146 U.S. 1 (1892).

any claim that the legislature's enactment conflicted with, or needed to be harmonized with, the state constitution. The only question was whether what the legislature chose was permissible under the *Federal* Constitution.[74] Nor did the case in any way involve an ostensible conflict between the wishes of the legislature and the views of the state judiciary. As such, the case on its facts had nothing—*nothing!*—to do with the ISL theory.

True, the *Blacker* opinion did mention and purport to rely on an 1874 report written by Senator Perry Morton of Indiana that contained the following sentences:

> This power [to appoint Electors] is conferred upon the legislatures of the States by the Constitution of the United States, and cannot be taken from them or modified by their State constitutions any more than can their power to elect Senators of the United States. Whatever provisions may be made by statute, or by state constitution, to choose electors by the people, there is no doubt of the right of the legislature to resume the power at any time, for it can neither be taken away nor abdicated.[75]

But Morton cited no historical authority for his assertion, which, as we have seen, ran counter to much of what was said and done at the Founding. What's more, the *Blacker* Court itself cast strong doubt on the ISL idea when it elsewhere stated in the opinion that "[t]he legislative power is the supreme authority *except as limited by the constitution of the State*."[76] This part of *Blacker* was never quoted, much less explained, by the majority or concurring opinions in the *Bush* litigation.

In any event, if the case for ISL is to be built on Supreme Court authority, twentieth-century decisions—decisions post-*Blacker*—strongly undercut the *Bush* three.

Consider first the 1916 case of *Ohio ex rel. Davis v. Hildebrant*.[77] Ohio's state constitution included a provision that legislative power was vested

---

[74] *See* Schapiro, *supra* note 69, at 669.

[75] *See Blacker*, 146 U.S. at 35 (quoting S. Rep. No. 43-395, at 9 (1874)). Important developments over the ensuing decades undermined Morton's overconfident and conclusory claims about the Senate. As we have explained elsewhere, the famous Oregon Plan, enacted by ordinary voters prior to the Seventeenth Amendment, did in fact use that state's direct lawmaking process to constrain state legislative selection of United States Senators, see Amar, *supra* note 44, at 1068–71; Amar, *supra* note 10, at 411, 615 n.17.

[76] 146 U.S. at 25 (emphasis added); *see also supra* text accompanying note 40 (quoting cryptic *Blacker* comment that "the legislative power of appointment could not have been successfully questioned *in the absence of any provision in the state constitution* in that regard") (emphasis added).

[77] 241 U.S. 565 (1916).

not only in the state legislature, but also "in the people[,] in whom a right was reserved by way of referendum to approve or disapprove by popular vote any law enacted by the General Assembly."[78] The Ohio General Assembly passed a redistricting act for congressional elections, and enough persons petitioned for the measure to be subject to voter approval through a referendum. In that referendum, voters rejected the redistricting act. In *Hildebrant*, the Supreme Court squarely rejected ISL as applied to Article I, which authorizes state legislatures to regulate congressional elections. The *Hildebrant* Court held that "the referendum constituted *a part of the state constitution* and laws and was contained within *the legislative power* and therefore the claim that the law which was disapproved and was no law under the constitution and laws of the state was yet valid and operative, is conclusively established to be wanting in merit."[79] In other words, a state legislature under Article I is not independent of its state constitution, but is rather bound by it. And, we would add, the same holds true for Article II. Article I's rules for state legislative regulation of congressional elections are structurally and intratextually akin to Article II's rules for state legislative regulation of presidential elections.[80]

Consider next the 1932 case of *Smiley v. Holm*.[81] The two houses of the Minnesota state legislature had passed a bill dividing the state into nine new congressional districts following a decennial census, but the bill was returned by the governor without his approval. The Minnesota legislature took the position that under Article I, section 4 of the Federal Constitution, the governor's approval was not necessary for the redistricting measure to go into effect. The U.S. Supreme Court disagreed, ruling that ordinarily "the exercise of the authority [to regulate congressional elections] must be in accordance with the method which the State has prescribed for legislative enactments."[82] Because normal laws in Minnesota were subject to gubernatorial veto under the state

[78] *Id.* at 566.

[79] *Id.* at 568 (emphasis added). The *Hildebrant* Court also made crystal clear, contra ISL ideology, that the U.S. Supreme Court should generally consider state supreme court interpretations of state election laws as dispositive: "As to the state power . . . it is obvious that the decision below [of the state supreme court] is conclusive on the subject. . . ." *Id.* at 567–68.

[80] On the use—and importance—of intratextualism in constitutional interpretation, see generally Akhil Reed Amar, *Intratextualism*, 112 HARV. L. REV. 747 (1999). For an interesting wrinkle on the kindred electoral clauses of Articles I and II see *infra* note 90.

[81] 285 U.S. 355 (1932).

[82] *Id.* at 367.

constitution, the redistricting measure returned by the governor could not be effective.

Together, *Hildebrant* and *Smiley* put the lie to ISL in its strong form. The "legislature" in Article I means "legislative process" as structured by state constitution. And what is sauce for Article I should also be sauce for Article II.

The *Bush* three concurrence championing ISL ideology simply ignored all this (just as the concurrence ignored Founding-era understandings and expectations, and state legislative practice), making no mention whatsoever of *Hildebrant* and *Smiley*.

III. *Bush*-Pruning: Post-2000 Case Law

Post-*Bush* cases have built squarely upon *Smiley* and *Hildebrant* and have authorized state constitutions to displace state legislatures altogether in certain aspects of congressional elections covered by Article I. In these cases, even conservative justices have directly rejected the *Bush* three's ISL ideas, at least for Article I (and thus, we would argue, for Article II as well). These cases make even more clear that the Federal Constitution in general takes state legislatures as it finds them, subject to state constitutional limitations—limitations that state courts are empowered to enforce.

In 2015, the Court decided a landmark case, *Arizona State Legislature v. Arizona Independent Redistricting Commission (AIRC)*.[83] The *AIRC* Court ruled that Article I allowed the people of Arizona, via their state constitution, to do congressional redistricting through an independent redistricting commission created by a popular initiative—a commission not controlled by the ordinary state legislature.

Poetically, Arizona voters had passed the initiative in question—Proposition 106—in November 2000, the very same day as the presidential election that led to *Bush*.[84] Arizona's legislature argued that

[83] 576 U.S. 787 (2015) (*AIRC*).

[84] Poetic, too, is the implicit reminder here that presidential Election Day is also state-law Election Day; the two electoral systems are tightly integrated in virtually every state—a key consideration that ISL ideologues fail to appreciate. *See supra* note 71. Quoting Hamilton's *Federalist No. 61*, the *AIRC* majority itself drew attention to the "convenience" of allowing each state to unify and harmonize the timing and manner of its state and federal elections. 576 U.S. at 819. Of course, the majority also recognized that states have the legitimate discretion to manage state and federal elections differently. 576 U.S. at 819 n.25.

Article I prevented the state from giving the power to draw congressional districts to an entity distinct from the ordinary state legislature itself.

In rejecting this ISL argument, the *AIRC* majority opinion penned by Justice Ginsburg relied extensively on *Hildebrant* and *Smiley*, and in the process strongly undercut the ISL logic of the *Bush* three. One alumnus of the *Bush* majority actually joined the Court's opinion, albeit a justice who had never squarely endorsed the *Bush* concurrence: Anthony Kennedy.

The *AIRC* majority opinion made emphatically clear that when the U.S. Constitution refers to a state "Legislature" in the context of a provision calling for state lawmaking,[85] the word "Legislature" means a state lawmaking process *as prescribed by the state constitution*. It's hard to imagine language that more plainly repudiates the core ISL idea than the wording used by the *AIRC* Court: "*Nothing in [Article I] instructs, nor has this Court ever held, that a state legislature may [regulate] the . . . manner of holding federal elections in defiance of provisions of the State's constitution.*"[86]

If "Legislature" in Article I means "legislature free to do what it wants unconstrained by state constitutions," *AIRC* could not have come out the way it did. Full stop. And, we hasten to repeat, what is sauce for Article I's rules about state legislative regulation of congressional

---

[85] The Court distinguished the issue at hand from situations in which the Constitution authorizes state legislatures to perform functions different from fashioning general regulatory policy—as when Article V gives state legislatures a role in ratifying federal constitutional amendments, and Article I (pre–Seventeenth Amendment) gave state legislatures the power to pick U.S. Senators. *Cf.* Hawke v. Smith, 253 U.S. 221 (1920); Leser v. Garnett, 258 U.S. 130 (1922). For an argument that even some of these cases and settings do not support ISL, see Amar, *supra* note 44.

[86] 576 U.S. at 817–18 (emphasis added). *AIRC* arguably went beyond *Hildebrandt* and *Smiley* insofar as the Arizona Constitution displaced rather than supplemented the elected legislature's power. But if the Arizona Constitution could permissibly have left districting in the hands of the elected legislature while prescribing the criteria the legislature had to use down to the last jot and tittle, the state constitution should also be allowed to create a new body—like the Independent Redistricting Commission—and effectively designate that new body the relevant state "legislature" for districting purposes. Similarly, state courts should be federally permitted not merely to veto unconstitutional congressional district maps drawn by state legislatures, but also to draw congressional district maps themselves to remedy state legislative lapses. *See* Vikram David Amar, *Concluding Thoughts on the Invocation of the Independent-State-Legislature (ISL) Theory in the North Carolina Emergency Relief Application at the Supreme Court: Part Six in a Series*, Justia.com (Mar. 14, 2022), viewable at: https://verdict.justia.com/2022/03/14/concluding-thoughts-on-the-invocation-of-the-independent-state-legislature-isl-theory-in-the-north-carolina-emergency-relief-application-at-the-supreme-court-part-six-in-a-series.

elections should be sauce for Article II's rules about state legislative regulation of presidential elections.

AIRC was a 5-4 ruling, decided over the dissents of the Court's conservative wing. But in 2019, *AIRC* was embraced by all the Court's conservatives in a case about partisan gerrymandering of congressional districts, *Rucho v. Common Cause*.[87]

Chief Justice Roberts, who had dissented in *AIRC*, wrote for the majority in *Rucho*. In direct opposition to ISL theory, the Chief Justice's opinion blessed state constitutional constraints enforced by state courts against state legislatures in congressional elections. This opinion directly built upon *AIRC*'s key holding by pointing approvingly to measures in Michigan and Colorado that were in all relevant respects identical to the Arizona initiative measure at issue in *AIRC*. The opinion also blessed anti-ISL developments in Florida, of all places!

The Chief Justice's remarkable language is worth savoring: "[We do] not condone excessive partisan gerrymandering. Nor does our conclusion [to limit the federal judicial role in controversies over congressional gerrymandering] condemn complaints about districting to echo into a void. The States . . . are actively addressing the issue on a number of fronts. In 2015, the Supreme Court of Florida struck down that State's congressional districting plan as a violation of the Fair Districts Amendment to the Florida Constitution. *League of Women Voters of Florida* v. *Detzner*, 172 So. 3d 363 (2015) . . . [And] in November 2018, voters in Colorado and Michigan approved constitutional amendments creating multimember commissions that will be responsible in whole or in part for creating and approving district maps for congressional and state legislative districts. See Colo. Const., Art. V, §§44, 46; Mich. Const., Art. IV, §6."[88]

Note that this passage expressly mentioned that Michigan's and Colorado's constitutional provisions applied not just to state legislative districting, but also to congressional districting under Article I. Note also that this key passage expressly endorsed both the right of

---

[87] 139 S. Ct. 2484 (2019).

[88] *Id.* at 2507. For two recent state supreme court cases invalidating the state legislature's congressional district map (as well as its state-legislative district map) as violative of the state constitution (as construed, of course, by the state supreme court itself), see *League of Women Voters v. Commonwealth*, 178 A.3d 737 (Pa. 2018); and *Harper v. Hall*, No. 413PA21, 2022 WL 496215 (N.C. Feb. 14, 2022). Relying on, inter alia, *Rucho*, *Smiley*, and *AIRC*, *Harper* explicitly rejected the ISL argument raised by the North Carolina Republicans. *See Harper*, 2022 WL 496215, at *41–42.

the Florida Constitution to constrain the Florida legislature, and the right of the Florida Supreme Court to interpret and implement that state constitution—even to the point of invalidating an enactment of the Florida state legislature. This *Rucho* passage was thus a square repudiation of ISL—both prongs. And much of this passage was, to repeat, all about federal elections in *Florida* as regulated by the *Florida Supreme Court* using the *Florida Constitution* to trump the *Florida legislature*. Take that, *Bush* three! Justices Thomas, Alito, Gorsuch, and Kavanaugh all joined this passage in full.

This brings us back to our key intratextual claim[89] that Article I and Article II are in this respect *in pari materia*. If ISL is wrong for Article I, as *AIRC* and *Rucho* make clear it is, it is also wrong for Article II.

Consider once again the relevant texts. Article I, Section 4 provides: "The Times, Places and Manner of holding Elections for Senators and Representatives, shall be prescribed in each State by the Legislature thereof. . . ." We could reorder this language (without changing its meaning) to say: "The Legislature of each State shall prescribe the manner of electing members of Congress." Article II, Section 2 says: "Each State shall appoint, in such Manner as the Legislature thereof may direct, a Number of Electors [to the Electoral College]. . . ." We could likewise reorder this language (also without changing its meaning) to say: "The Legislature of each State may direct the manner of appointing members of the electoral college." When we lay the two reformulations side-by-side, the similarity is obvious and overwhelming: "The Legislature of each State shall prescribe the manner of electing members of Congress" and "The Legislature of each State may direct the manner of appointing members of the electoral college."[90]

IV. The Bitter Fruit of the Poisonous *Bush*

Given all this, we were, we confess, surprised and dismayed when we saw the Article II ISL theory sprouting up again like a stubborn weed in the weeks leading into the 2020 presidential election.

---

[89] The *AIRC* dissenters themselves explicitly embraced the notion that the term "Legislature" at various points in the Constitution should be informed, intratextually, by the interpretation that word has been given elsewhere in the document. 576 U.S. at 829 (Roberts, C.J., dissenting) (citing Amar, *supra* note 80). For a similar thought, see *Chiafalo v. Washington*, 140 S. Ct. 2316, 2329–31 (2020) (Thomas, J., concurring).

[90] If anything, the language of Article II is less legislature-centric. The technical subject of the key sentence is the "State," not the legislature, and the legislature "may" (rather than "shall") direct the "manner" of (s)election. *See supra* text accompanying notes 65–66.

On October 26, a week before the election, Justice Kavanaugh weighed in, ominously. The case, *Democratic National Committee v. Wisconsin State Legislature*, involved a lower *federal* court's invocation of the Fourteenth Amendment's right-to-vote principles to enjoin Wisconsin from enforcing its state election laws.[91] Kavanaugh joined four other justices in chiding the district court for intervening in an election so close to the voting date. But then, in a startling footnote, he added:

> A *federal court's* alteration of state election laws such as Wisconsin's differs in some respects from a *state court's* (or state agency's) alteration of state election laws. That said, under the U. S. Constitution, the state courts do not have a blank check to rewrite state election laws for federal elections. Article II expressly provides that the rules for Presidential elections are established by the States "in such Manner as the *Legislature* thereof may direct." §1, cl. 2 (emphasis added). The text of Article II means that "the clearly expressed intent of the legislature must prevail" and that a state court may not depart from the state election code enacted by the legislature. *Bush v. Gore*, 531 U.S. 98, 120 (2000) (Rehnquist, C.J., concurring); *see Bush v. Palm Beach County Canvassing Bd.*, 531 U.S. 70, 76–78 (2000) (per curiam); *McPherson v. Blacker*, 146 U.S. 1, 25 (1892). In a Presidential election, in other words, a state court's "significant departure from the legislative scheme for appointing Presidential electors presents a federal constitutional question." *Bush v. Gore*, 531 U.S. at 113 (Rehnquist, C.J., concurring). As Chief Justice Rehnquist explained in *Bush v. Gore*, the important federal judicial role in reviewing state-court decisions about state law in a federal Presidential election "does not imply a disrespect for state *courts* but rather a respect for the constitutionally prescribed role of state *legislatures*. To attach definitive weight to the pronouncement of a state court, when the very question at issue is whether the court has actually departed from the statutory meaning, would be to abdicate our responsibility to enforce the explicit requirements of Article II." *Id.* at 115. The dissent here questions why the federal courts would have a role in that kind of case. *Post* at 45, n.6 (opinion of Kagan, J.). The answer to that question, as the unanimous Court stated in *Bush v. Palm Beach County Canvassing Bd.*, and as Chief Justice Rehnquist persuasively [!!!] explained in *Bush v. Gore*, is that the text of the Constitution requires federal courts to ensure that state courts do not rewrite state election laws.[92]

Two days later, three other justices joined the fray in *Republican Party of Pennsylvania v. Boockvar*.[93] In this case, Pennsylvania Republican

[91] 141 S. Ct. 28 (2020) (mem.).

[92] *Id.* at 34 n.1 (Kavanaugh, J., concurring in denial of application to vacate stay) (citations cleaned).

[93] 141 S. Ct. 1 (2020) (mem.).

Bush-Leaguers directly invoked the Article II ISL theory to ask the Roberts Court to step in to undo rulings by the Pennsylvania Supreme Court tweaking the date by which mail-in ballots needed to be sent in.

The state supreme court had acted to accommodate the state constitutional right to vote in the face of COVID. The state statutes facially required all mail-in ballots to be *received* by 8 PM on Election Day, but the state supreme court ruled, long before Election Day, that the state constitution allowed votes to be counted provided they were *postmarked* by Election Day and received no later than three days thereafter. Part of the logic was that a hard-to-predict-in-advance COVID spike on or just before Election Day might make it impossible or dangerous for some voters who had been planning to vote in person to do so as planned, and that a relaxed mail-in deadline would better vindicate the fundamental right to vote enshrined in the state constitution.

As applied to elections directly and undeniably governed by the state constitution—for example, state legislative elections—this tweaking was uncontrovertibly within the proper sphere of the state justices. And the state legislature had given no indication in its statutes that different deadlines and procedures should apply to federal elections. Thus the state legislature implicitly incorporated the state constitution into its unified general election laws and implicitly invited the state courts to play their traditional election role for all parts of the election, even if federal elections strictly speaking somehow fell outside the ambit of the state constitution operating of its own force.[94] And of course, *AIRC* and *Rucho*, to say nothing of *Hildebrandt* and *Smiley*, gave additional strong support to what the Pennsylvania Supreme Court had done. Under the logic of these cases, the state constitution did indeed apply of its own force even to congressional and presidential elections.

Yet Justice Alito, joined by Justices Thomas and Gorsuch (but not, notably, by Justice Kavanaugh) condemned the Pennsylvania Supreme Court and urged his colleagues to leap onstage, in a re-enactment of *Bush v. Gore*. Justice Alito's embrace of the *Bush* three's Article II ISL theory was emphatic and unrepentant:

---

[94] To repeat, the ultimate decision about what Pennsylvania's election law did and did not mean, implicitly and explicitly, is a decision reserved to the Supreme Court of Pennsylvania, not the Supreme Court of the United States. *See supra* notes 71, 79; *infra* Section V.

> The Supreme Court of Pennsylvania has issued a decree that squarely alters an important statutory provision enacted by the Pennsylvania Legislature pursuant to its authority under the Constitution of the United States to make rules governing the conduct of elections for federal office. *See* Art. I, §4, cl. 1; Art. II, §1, cl. 2; *Bush v. Palm Beach County Canvassing Bd.*, 531 U.S. 70, 76 (2000) (per curiam).... It would be highly desirable to issue a ruling on the constitutionality of the State Supreme Court's decision before the election. That question has national importance, *and there is a strong likelihood that the State Supreme Court decision violates the Federal Constitution. The provisions of the Federal Constitution conferring on state legislatures, not state courts, the authority to make rules governing federal elections would be meaningless if a state court could override the rules adopted by the legislature simply by claiming that a state constitutional provision gave the courts the authority to make whatever rules it thought appropriate for the conduct of a fair election.* See *Art. I, §4, cl. 1; Art. II, §1, cl. 2. For these reasons, the question presented by the Pennsylvania Supreme Court's decision calls out for review by this Court—as both the State Republican and Democratic Parties agreed when the former applied for a stay.*[95]

What is perhaps most astonishing is that none of the four current justices (just one shy of the number needed to blow up presidential elections yet again) who invoked the ISL notion carefully engaged the manifold and manifest problems with the theory. No history, no discussion of state legislative practice, and no awareness, even, of the incorporation-by-reference argument, which provides its own distinct, sufficient, and devastating refutation of *Bush*-League ideology. No originalist or structural explanation for why Article II would ever single out one state lawmaking institution and immunize it from the state constitutional definitions and constraints to which it would ordinarily be subject. And no close analysis of cases such as *Hildebrandt*, *Smiley*, *AIRC*, and *Rucho*. Instead, Justice Kavanaugh cited *Bush I*—the Palm Beach County case—as if it had made law, even though the Court specifically "decline[d] at th[at] time to review the federal questions asserted to be present."[96] And, unfathomably, neither Kavanaugh nor

---

[95] 141 S. Ct. at 1–2 (statement of Alito, J.) (emphasis added) (citations cleaned). Although due allowance should be made for impassioned judicial rhetoric, Justice Alito's claim that an ISL reading is necessary to avoid rendering the relevant constitutional text "meaningless," is flatly wrong. *See supra* text accompanying notes 64–66. Once it is seen that this rhetorical claim is, strictly speaking, false, the claim loses all legal and logical force. Contrary to Justice Alito's assertion, both ISL and non-ISL readings of the text make the clause *meaningful*, although the two readings attribute quite different meanings to the words. The question, then, is simply this: Which reading is more sound as a matter of text, founding history and ideology, structure, precedent, and so on?

[96] 531 U.S. 70, 78 (2000) (per curiam). Justice Alito was more coy in his citation to *Bush I*, but the implication was the same.

Alito even mentioned much less distinguished *AIRC* or the subsequent *Rucho* case embracing *AIRC*.[97]

Nor did Justice Kagan, who wrote a dissent in the Wisconsin case[98] joined by Justices Breyer and Sotomayor, set her colleagues straight with the requisite clarity and detail. All Justice Kagan said was:

> At the same time that Justice Kavanaugh defends this stance by decrying a "federal-judges-know-best vision of election administration," he calls for *more* federal court involvement in "reviewing state-court decisions about state [election] law." It is hard to know how to reconcile those two views about the federal judiciary's role in voting-rights cases. Contrary to Justice Kavanaugh's attempted explanation, neither the text of the Elections Clause nor our precedent interpreting it leads to his inconstant approach. *See Arizona State Legislature v. Arizona Independent Redistricting Comm'n*, 576 U.S. 787, 817–818 (2015); *Smiley v. Holm*, 285 U.S. 355, 372 (1932).[99]

---

[97] In early 2021, after the 2020 election craziness had subsided and President Biden was safely in office, Justice Thomas—one of the original *Bush* three, it will be recalled—expressly doubled down on the discredited ISL theory, and indeed cited the *Bush* three's concurrence with evident approval:

> Because the Federal Constitution, not state constitutions, gives state legislatures authority to regulate federal elections, petitioners presented a strong argument that the Pennsylvania Supreme Court's decision violated the Constitution by overriding "the clearly expressed intent of the legislature." *Bush v. Gore*, 531 U.S. 98, 120 (2000) (Rehnquist, C.J., concurring).

Republican Party v. Degraffenreid, 141 S. Ct. 732, 733 (2021) (mem.) (Thomas, J., dissenting from the denial of certiorari) (citations cleaned). In a separate dissent from the denial of certiorari in the same case, Justice Alito, joined by Justice Gorsuch (but not, we note again, by Justice Kavanaugh), also continued to cast his lot with ISL. In doing so, he expressly repeated his troubling *Boockvar* language, and cited not to the *Bush* three concurrence but the *Bush I* ruling—the *Palm Beach* case:

> The provisions of the Federal Constitution conferring on state legislatures, not state courts, the authority to make rules governing federal elections would be meaningless if a state court could override the rules adopted by the legislature simply by claiming that a state constitutional provision gave the courts the authority to make whatever rules it thought appropriate for the conduct of a fair election. . . . *see also Bush v. Palm Beach County Canvassing Bd.*, 531 U.S. 70, 76 (2000) (per curiam).

141 S. Ct. at 738 (Alito, J., joined by Gorsuch, J., dissenting from the denial of certiorari) (citations cleaned). On the plain error of the "meaningless" meme, see *supra* note 95.

On the certworthiness of the issue presented in *Degraffenreid*, we actually agree with these three dissenters: The Court should indeed grant review on the contentions raised there. But, we hasten to add, the Court should do so precisely to repudiate once and for all the specious ISL claims featured in these dissenting opinions.

[98] Democratic Nat'l Comm. v. Wis. State Legislature, 141 S. Ct. 28 (2020) (mem.).

[99] *Id.* at 47 n.7 (Kagan, J., joined by Breyer & Sotomayor, JJ., dissenting) (alterations in original) (cleaned up).

Bench memo to Justice Kagan: The key point is not merely that neither the constitutional text nor the Court's precedents *lead to* Justice Kavanaugh's approach. The point is that text and precedent emphatically *reject and refute* Justice Kavanaugh's approach. One would think that as multiple justices seemed to be on the verge of replaying the *Bush v. Gore* nightmare, there would have been a greater sense of urgency and a more robust explanation of just how jurisprudentially wrong-headed that would be.[100]

And what shall we say about recent commentators who are trying to bring ISL back to life? Professor Michael Morley—perhaps the most energetic scholar in this camp—has asserted that the "text of the Constitution[] [and] the history of the Elections Clause and Presidential Electors Clause ... strongly support the ... interpretation[] [under which] only a state's institutional legislature ... may regulate federal elections."[101] Alas, he has offered no persuasive textual or structural analysis, and his history comes almost entirely from decades that are either far too late or far too early—far too late to carry much originalist weight and far too early to have strong precedential weight given more recent and definitive Supreme Court case law (*Hildebrant*, *Smiley*, *AIRC*, and *Rucho*).[102]

---

[100] As this Article was going to press, Republican ISL advocates in North Carolina and Pennsylvania sought Supreme Court aid in a pair of cases involving state court decisions remedying state constitutional violations by state legislatures in congressional districting. The Court declined to get involved, but in the North Carolina case, *Moore v. Harper*, 142 S.Ct. 289 (2022), Justice Alito, joined by Justices Thomas and Gorsuch (but not Justice Kavanaugh), dissented. Yet again, these three Justices voiced at least provisional agreement with ISL, claiming that the text of Article I could have empowered "each state" but instead empowered the "legislature thereof." Of course, as we have noted, Article II does explicitly empower "each state." For a sharp critique of the *Moore* dissent on this point and others, see Amar, *supra* note 86.

[101] Michael T. Morley, *The Independent State Legislature Doctrine, Federal Elections, and State Constitutions* 15 (Oct. 30, 2020), https://ssrn.com/abstract=3530136 (posted draft on file with authors).

[102] None of Morley's material involves any clear ruling by the U.S. Supreme Court itself (if we put to one side, as we should, the opaque dicta of McPherson v. Blacker, 146 U.S. 1, 37–39 (1892)). At best, we think that Morley has interestingly but irrelevantly shown that some nonauthoritative folks have at some post-Founding times said some unpersuasive things. We should also make clear that we ourselves have not carefully double-checked all of Morley's proffered evidence post-Founding and pre-*Bush*. Given that we find various claims he has made about both the Founding and the *Bush* litigation highly problematic, we caution future scholars against relying uncritically on Morley's other assertions. And although we ourselves have not comprehensively canvassed past and current state constitutions, a recent and extraordinarily detailed piece by Hayward Smith is now bringing to light *dozens* of state constitutions over the years that have regulated congressional and/or presidential elections in

Morley's treatment of recent precedent also falls short (to put it mildly). He has said that *Bush I* "is perhaps the most important ruling stemming from the 2000 election concerning the independent state legislature doctrine."[103] In fact, as previously noted, the justices in that case chose not to reach the merits of *any* question, stating explicitly that "[we] decline . . . to review the federal questions asserted to be present" in the cert petition.[104] Morley has gone on to assert that the Court in that case "concluded" that "[c]ertain parts of the Florida Supreme Court's opinion . . . incorrectly suggested that the Florida Constitution might [permissibly] limit the legislature's authority to regulate presidential elections."[105] Wrong again. To repeat: the *Bush I* Court did not "conclude" *anything*.

Morley has also claimed the *Bush I* Court "vacated . . . and remanded so that the Florida Supreme Court could reconsider the issue exclusively under the Florida Election Code, without allowing the state constitution to influence its interpretation."[106] The Court gave no such direction on remand; it said only that "there is considerable uncertainty as to the precise grounds for the [lower court] decision" and that "[t]his is sufficient reason for us to decline at this time to review the federal questions asserted to be present."[107] So the only (implicit) direction on remand was for the state court to be more clear in the bases for its decisions.

Indeed, if a unanimous Court in *Bush I* had held what Professor Morley and various careless justices in recent months have said it held, how is it that just two weeks later, in *Bush v. Gore*, a more full-throated articulation of the same proposition—that state constitutions cannot cabin state legislatures in this arena—garnered the votes of only three justices and was explicitly rejected by four?[108]

---

ways that squarely contradict ISL ideology. *See* Smith, *supra* note 62. Morley's work has apparently overlooked tons of evidence that Smith is now uncovering.

[103] Morley, *supra* note 101, at 64.

[104] 531 U.S. 70, 78 (2000) (per curiam).

[105] Morley, *supra* note 101, at 60.

[106] *Id*. at 61.

[107] 531 U.S. at 78.

[108] The four objectors were, of course, Justices Stevens, Ginsburg, Breyer, and Souter. Note that in response to criticism by Vikram, Morley later recanted, in the final published versions of his works, some of the most untenable claims that we have cited in this section.

V. Maintaining Federalism's Garden

The axiom that state courts rather than federal courts are the ultimate interpreters of state law comes not just from both the Federal Constitution's deep structure and the watershed Supreme Court case of *Erie Railroad Co. v. Tompkins*,[109] but also from a landmark ruling over a century earlier, *Green v. Lessee of Neal*.[110] In *Green*, the Marshall Court made clear that when state courts construe state statutes, those interpretations of state legislative enactments must be respected by federal courts.[111] For decades upon decades, when federal judges have

[109] 304 U.S. 64 (1938).

[110] 31 U.S. (6 Pet.) 293 (1832).

[111] The matter is of course different if there exists a federal right that depends on whether a state-law interest exists. In these situations, in which state law is logically antecedent to a federal right, a state court cannot be allowed to manipulate the antecedent state-law issue, especially when the dependent downstream federal right is a right against the state itself. For example, if a state court could simply say, however implausibly, that no valid contract was ever made at Time T under state law, and if federal courts could never second guess that implausible claim (by carefully examining state case law as of Time T), the Article I, § 10 Contracts Clause could easily become a dead letter. So too, if a state court simply denies that a state-law property interest was created at Time T, a federal court must be able to say otherwise in order to protect the Fifth Amendment just-compensation right as incorporated against states by the Fourteenth Amendment. *See generally* Martin v. Hunter's Lessee, 14 U.S. (1 Wheat.) 304 (1816); Ward v. Love Cty., 253 U.S. 17 (1920); Hart & Wechsler's The Federal Courts and the Federal System ch. V (Richard H. Fallon, Jr. et al., eds., 7th ed. 2015). In the ISL context, however, there is no dependent federal right at stake.

Cf. Henry Paul Monaghan, *Supreme Court Review of State-Court Determinations of State Law in Constitutional Cases*, 103 Colum. L. Rev. 1919 (2003). Whereas the text, history, and structure of the Seventeenth Amendment do evidence a real federal interest in protecting state governors from their (often malapportioned and gerrymandered) state legislatures in the context of Senate vacancies—see *infra* text accompanying notes 112–113—Professor Monaghan does not identify anything truly comparable in Article II aiming to protect state legislatures from state courts in the context of presidential elections. Monaghan rightly worries about willful or bad-faith state courts that rewrite state laws retroactively in ways that threaten various federally protected interests, such as those implicated by the Contracts Clause and the Takings Clause. In these contexts, careful Supreme Court oversight of state-court rulings is warranted. But a general across-the-board rule-of-law concern about possible state judicial willfulness or bad faith cannot allow the U.S. Supreme Court to transmogrify any alleged misinterpretation of state law into a substantial federal question. Otherwise, all state-law rulings would become federal-law issues—goodbye, federalism!

Importantly, Monaghan only fleetingly mentions the main issues at the heart of ISL: whether state constitutions in presidential elections apply either of their own force or simply because state legislatures have chosen to incorporate them into unified state election laws. (Monaghan discusses the former theory in two pages—1929–30—and the latter issue not at all.)

Indeed, Monaghan's rule-of-law concern that state courts might change the rules retroactively under the guise of mere interpretation is essentially orthogonal to the ISL debate. His discussion of the propriety of the *Bush* II concurring opinion explicitly takes as its starting point the assumption that the concurring justices' ISL understanding of Article II is correct as a matter of text, history, structure and judicial precedent—an assumption the present article thoroughly debunks. And even applying Monaghan's approach on its own terms to the Florida 2000 situation, we note that long before *Bush v. Gore*, Florida state courts had made clear that the state

confronted particularly sensitive state-law questions, these judges have generally understood that they must either follow the lead of state court rulings on point (if such guidance is available) or (if not) certify state-law questions to state courts. Federal courts are not allowed to simply ignore state supreme courts and decide for themselves what state law is or ought to be.

True, state courts might at times misinterpret state constitutions. *But so might federal judges—and indeed, they are generally more likely to do so*. Also, state legislatures have vastly more control over state courts than they do over, say, Justices Gorsuch, Thomas, and Alito (who are not remotely experts on the meaning of fifty state constitutions, to put it mildly).

Does all this mean that federal courts have absolutely no meaningful part in adjudicating disputes concerning federal elections? Certainly not. What it does mean is that federal courts need to leave *state* law to *state* courts and stay focused on enforcing *federal* rights and *federal* policies. In general, there is no Article I or Article II federal right or federal policy that confers special powers or protections upon elected state legislatures vis-à-vis other institutions of state government. Relatedly, there is no substantive federal value, in either Article I or Article II, demanding emphatically literal (or narrow) adherence to the text of state legislative enactments.

In other words, there is in this domain no general federal interest in implementing any particular intra-state separation-of-powers regime or any specific textual interpretative methodology. Instead, whatever federal rights and policies that federal courts can be helpful in enforcing must come

---

constitution (as they had construed it and would continue to construe it) applied to, constrained, and supplemented state election statutes promulgated by the state legislature. What's more, on the substantive merits of the voting-law disputes in Florida in 2000—the importance of voter intent, and the need to construe voting law liberally in favor of expansive voting rights, regardless of statutory technicalities and administrative glitches—what the Florida Supreme Court was trying to do in the *Bush v. Gore* litigation was utterly consistent with what that court had been doing for decades. *See, e.g.*, Palm Beach Cnty Canvassing Bd. v. Harris, 772 So. 2d 1220, 1227–28 (Fla. 2000) (per curiam) ("Twenty-five years ago, this Court commented that the will of the people, not a hyper-technical reliance upon statutory provisions, should be our guiding principle in election cases. . . . 'By refusing to recognize an otherwise valid exercise of the right of a citizen to vote for the sake of sacred, unyielding adherence to statutory scripture, we would in effect nullify that right'"—a right guaranteed by "'[o]ur federal and state constitutions.'") (quoting Boardman v. Esteva, 323 So. 2d 259, 263 (Fla. 1975)). Monaghan does not so much as mention *Boardman*; nor does he analyze any other pre-2000 Florida voting cases. The court that in fact retroactively changed the rules and changed its stripes—the court that willfully rewrote the law while claiming merely to interpret earlier constitutional texts and prior precedents—was the U.S. Supreme Court, not the Florida Supreme Court. *See Dunwody Lecture*, *supra* note 22.

either from other parts of the Constitution, or, importantly, from Congress, which has been given a role in both congressional and presidential elections.

As to the Federal Constitution, certainly the Fourteenth, Fifteenth, Nineteenth, Twenty-Fourth and Twenty-Sixth Amendments confer rights that states must respect, under penalty of federal-court enforcement. But state respect for these rights has nothing to do with intrastate separation-of-powers. State legislatures, state courts, state agencies, and the people of states acting via direct democracy all must respect the values underlying these landmark Amendments.

True, some provisions of the Constitution, unlike Articles I and II, use specific language that reflects specific historical concerns with some state governmental institutions vis-à-vis others. For example, Section 2 of the Seventeenth Amendment, in a single sentence, pointedly differentiates between the legislatures and executive authorities of states, and confers appointment powers only on the latter.[112] The special concern over malapportionment (and the racial discrimination it often reflected) weighed on the proponents of direct election for U.S. Senators and generated an express Seventeenth Amendment preference for governors over state legislatures in filling Senate vacancies. (Governors, elected statewide, were generally immune from gerrymandering and malapportionment.[113]) But no comparable pointed linguistic contrast between a state legislature and other state organs—much less between a state legislature and the state constitution that creates it—exists

[112] U.S. Const. amend. XVII, § 2 ("When vacancies happen in the representation of any State in the Senate, the executive authority of such State shall issue writs of election to fill such vacancies: Provided, That the legislature of any State may empower the executive thereof to make temporary appointments until the people fill the vacancies by election as the legislature may direct."); *see* Vikram David Amar, *Are Statutes Constraining Gubernational Power to Make Temporary Appointments to the United States Senate Constitutional Under the Seventeenth Amendment?*, 35 Hastings Const. L.Q. 727. (2008).

[113] For elaboration on the precise text of and specific history surrounding the Seventeenth Amendment in this regard, see Amar, *supra* note 112. Consider also the Electoral College. Unlike state legislatures, presidential Electors did not pre-exist the federal Constitution. Unlike state legislatures, presidential Electors were not ordinary creatures of state constitutions, but rather acted as specially created federal functionaries of a certain sort, pointedly designed to be formally independent in key respects—federally required to meet simultaneously in many different spots on one (and only one) day and federally required to vote by secret ballot. *See* Vikram David Amar, *A Backward- and Forward-Looking Assessment of the Supreme Court's "Faithless Elector" Cases: Part One in a Two-Part Series*, Justia.com (July 14, 2020), viewable at: https://verdict.justia.com/2020/07/14/a-backward-and-forward-looking-assessment-of-the-supreme-courts-faithless-elector-cases.

in Articles I and II; nor, it is crucial to add, is there any history to support such distinctions.

In addition to these formal constitutional provisions, the structural principle of federal supremacy could, under certain circumstances, trigger federal scrutiny of state constitutional rules that treat federal-election matters worse than analogous state-election matters. Under *Testa v. Katt*[114] and related cases, state courts cannot disrespect federal claims by excluding them without explanation from state courts while allowing analogous state-law claims. So too, unexplained differential treatment of federal and state voting rules might warrant federal judicial inquiry. Oftentimes there may be innocent explanations,[115] but differential treatment could in some settings suggest problematic disrespect. Once again, the applicable principles would of course constrain all state entities and types of law alike: legislatures, courts, commissions, statutes, initiatives, and constitutions.

As for federal statutes, some may create substantive entitlements that states need to respect and federal courts need to enforce. For example, if Congress were to provide that congressional district lines must be drawn without regard to political partisanship, or with an eye toward remedying historical racial discrimination, those edicts would have to be followed by state districting entities. But again, this would be true whether the state districting entity were the elected legislature or an independent citizen commission or a state court for that matter. Relatedly, the federal statute would of course constrain not just ordinary state statutes, but also state constitutions.

Other federal statutes focus not on substance but on timing: Members of Congress and presidential electors are to be selected/appointed on the federal Election Day.[116] That does not mean that their identity must be known by 11:59 PM on Election Night, but it does mean that the antecedent facts—who voted for whom—have to be locked into place on or before Election Day. Prior to the holding of an election, a state has broad federally approved power to tinker with its election administration regime without running afoul of Congress's designation

[114] 330 U.S. 386 (1947).

[115] *See* 576 U.S. 787, 819 n.25 (2015) (*AIRC*) ("A State may choose to regulate state and national elections differently, which is its prerogative under the [Election] Clause. *E.g.*, Ind. Code § 3-3-2-2 (creating backup commission for congressional but not state legislative districts).").

[116] 3 U.S.C. § 1.

of an Election Day.[117] But after Election Day, a state cannot reject its pre-election system simply because, say, the state now knows how close the election is and wants to use its newfound leverage as a decisive swing state to induce the candidates to bid for the state's good will. Such gamesmanship would frustrate the very reason Congress requires states to lock into a system of selection ex ante. Here, too, the relevant rules constrain not just state courts but also elected state legislatures and other state governmental entities.[118]

From one angle, state courts are akin to the ballot-counting machines or in-person vote counters themselves; the courts are a relatively ministerial part of the apparatus for determining who validly voted, and for whom. Just as a machine or an individual election official seeks to recognize a valid vote from an invalid one, a judge may do the same thing, albeit at a more categorical level. Provided, of course, that judicial involvement was built into the system that was in place as of Election Day. If it wasn't, then involving the courts could potentially be seen as violating Congress's timeline for making decisions about who is elected

---

[117] Note, however, that a state constitution, as definitively construed by the state supreme court, might well constrain the choices of the state legislature long before Election Day. In some states, the state constitution might well prevent the legislature from itself choosing presidential electors. That is, the constitution, best read, might require that ordinary voters must choose the electors. *See, e.g.*, COLO. CONST. § 20 ("The general assembly shall provide that after the year eighteen hundred and seventy-six the electors of the electoral college shall be chosen by direct vote of the people.").

So, too, a state constitution might well be best read to prevent a state legislature from trying to make itself the "judge" of a contested presidential vote within the state. Such an effort might violate state constitutional separation-of-powers provisions vesting general adjudicatory power in such cases in the regular state courts and not the state legislature. *See, e.g.*, PA. CONST. art. VII, § 13 ("The trial and determination of contested elections of electors of President and Vice-President, [along with various state offices,] shall be by the courts of law. . . .").

The scenarios herein envisioned—attempted power-grabs by state legislatures in the upcoming presidential-election derby—are not outlandish hypotheticals. There are movements now afoot in various right-wing circles to empower red-tilting state legislatures in states that have bluish-purple presidential electorates—Arizona, Georgia, Wisconsin, Virginia, Pennsylvania, and Michigan, to name some of the most obvious jurisdictions. It is not hyperbole to suggest that the outcome of the next presidential election—and even, perhaps, the fate of the world—could pivot on the technical questions at the heart of this footnote and this Article more generally.

[118] And federal officials, for that matter. For an eye-popping account of shenanigans by one Senator in 2020, see *Inside Ted Cruz's Last-Ditch Battle to Keep Trump in Power*, WASH. POST (Mar. 28, 2022), https://www.washingtonpost.com/politics/2022/03/28/ted-cruz-john-eastman-jan6-committee/. We shall not today explore in any detail the many wrinkles of the Electoral Count Act. A quick word, however, is warranted on the Act's provision empowering state legislatures to play a post-election role in the event a state holds an election that "fail[s] to make a choice." 3 U.S.C. § 2. A *failed* election, within the meaning of this statute, is certainly not the same thing as merely a *close and hotly contested* election. *See Dunwody Lecture*, *supra* note 22, at 959–60.

and appointed; judges, no less than other actors, could be tempted to play games to extort candidates.

But what about the fact that judges, unlike machines, have political biases? Potential bias by judges is present in any setting, and yet we don't as a general matter say that fact forecloses courts from performing their general dispute-resolution and norm-declaration roles throughout our legal system. As long as state judges in congressional-election or presidential-election disputes are engaged in the same kinds of judicial processes and doing the same kinds of interpretive things they have done historically under state law in resolving state election contests, federal courts should defer to state court understandings of state statutory and constitutional law principles.

The bar for finding that a state court has failed this rule-of-law test is thus quite high, just as it is in other areas that remain the domain of pure state law.[119] Not only would the evidence of improper intent by state-court judges need to be compelling before such a finding were made; but also, the precise federal right or policy being infringed by such manipulation would need to be clearly and specifically identified by a second-guessing federal court. If the asserted federal value is simply a due-process concern for regularity and predictability in elections, the state-law interpretations in question would have to be truly outlandish (no less so for federal than state contests) before they would create a substantial federal question.

To recap: The test cannot be whether a state supreme court is suitably "textualist," as various Supreme Court *Bush*-Leaguers might seek to define textualism. The Supreme Court itself is not now and never has been relentlessly textualist, even as some careless justices now threaten to impose such a narrow method on states in the context of federal elections. There is nothing in the U.S. Constitution that speaks to the issue of state-court interpretive methodology over state law in general or over state law relating to federal elections in particular. (And surely there is no clear and literal federal statutory or constitutional *text* that speaks to this issue!) A given state legislature, the state people who elect that state legislature, and the spirit of that state's overarching state constitution that gave birth to and sustains that state legislature might well *prefer* a state-law jurisprudence that is more purposive, or more structural/holisitic, or more precedent-based, or more

---

[119] For situations beyond the "domain of pure state law"—situations where federal rights and interests depend on or intertwine with state law—see *supra* note 111.

representation-reinforcing, or more democracy-promoting, or more canon-driven, than relentlessly textual. And who is the U.S. Supreme Court to dictate otherwise—*especially* if the Court purports to intermeddle in the name of the state legislature, which, by hypothesis, prefers a different interpretive method![120]

So the proper question for the Supreme Court to ask is not "Was the state supreme court suitably *textualist*?" Nor is the proper question "Did the state legislature *explicitly* and *textually* incorporate by reference the state constitution in its federal-election-law schema?" Rather, the proper questions are "In the federal-election case at hand, was the state supreme court doing the kinds of things it has generally done in other cases (especially cases involving the same types of statutes and state constitutional provisions at issue) in years past?" and "Was the state court and/or the state constitution treating federal elections similarly to state elections?" If the answer to either question is *no*, closer Supreme Court scrutiny is warranted to determine if any genuine federal interest—which must, we repeat, be carefully identified and shown to be truly inherent in federal law—is at risk.

The various statements over the years by *Bush*-League justices and *Bush*-League scholars fall laughably short of this high bar. Casual references to the Article II (and Article I) word "legislature" and careless[121] claims that this word would be "meaningless" unless one embraces full-blown ISL ideology don't cut it. *Bush*-Leaguers have failed to identify any deep and valid federal interest grounded in historical understandings or structural values that would warrant aggressive federal judicial intrusion into the traditionally close partnership between state legislatures and state courts, both operating under the valid superintendence of state peoples and state constitutions. *Bush*-Leaguers actually do violence to the very state legislatures they claim to respect—state

---

[120] Suppose a state presidential-election statute says X at time T_1, and is then interpreted by the state supreme court at time T_2 to mean Y (which is rather close to X and in fact best captures the spirit of X, but does undeniably deviate from the strict letter of X). If the state legislature at time T_3 modifies other aspects of the presidential-election statute but leaves intact the X/Y provision, whose T_2 judicial gloss the state legislature quite likes at T_3, would *Bush*-Leaguers on the U.S. Supreme Court truly be faithful to the state legislature—the very state legislature the *Bush*-Leaguers claim to care so much about—if they insist the state law really means X and not Y? Even though this is emphatically not how the U.S. Supreme Court itself goes about federal statutory interpretation, as a general matter? (Statutory precedent routinely—indeed, almost always—trumps textual plain meaning for federal statutes at issue in the U.S. Supreme Court.)

[121] And demonstrably wrong, see *supra* note 95.

legislatures who live under and profess loyalty to state constitutions, who answer to state voters (as do many state judges), and who have historically closely partnered with state judges and other state officials to create integrated and unified intra-state election systems for state and federal races.

VI. Green Shoots? The Chief Justice and Justice Kavanaugh

Much of our analysis thus far has reflected deep disappointment with the work-product of several members of the current and recent Court. But there are also at least two reasons for optimism.

First, Chief Justice Roberts got things just right in the October 26 Wisconsin case, where he wrote:

> [T]his case presents different issues than the applications this Court recently denied in *Scarnati v. Boockvar*, and *Republican Party of Pennsylvania v. Boockvar*. While the Pennsylvania applications implicated the authority of *state courts* to apply their *own constitutions* to election regulations, this case involves *federal* intrusion on state lawmaking processes. Different bodies of law and different precedents govern these two situations and require, in these particular circumstances, that we allow the modification of election rules in Pennsylvania but not Wisconsin.[122]

Second, Justice Kavanaugh, who in some sense planted the Court's first kernel of *Bush*-League thinking in the 2020 election cycle in the October 26 Wisconsin case, did not, two days later, join Justices Alito, Thomas, and Gorsuch in their statement that the Pennsylvania Republicans likely had a winning Article II ISL claim on the merits.[123] Why the apparent switch-in-time?

We cannot know for sure. Perhaps we may never know, even after the current justices' papers become public in the distant future. But we can say this: In between Justice Kavanaugh's unfortunate remarks in the Wisconsin case on October 26 and his admirable silence in the Pennsylvania case two days later, various legal commentators—including both of us, along with Professor and former Acting Solicitor General Neal Katyal in the *New York Times*—weighed on this issue to remind the world of the many weaknesses of ISL reasoning.[124] Also,

---

[122] Democratic Nat'l Comm. v. Wis. State Legislature, 141 S. Ct. 28, 28 (2020) (mem.) (Roberts, C.J., concurring in denial of application to vacate stay).

[123] *See supra* text accompanying notes 91–95; *see also* note 100.

[124] Akhil Reed Amar, Vikram David Amar, and Neal Kumar Katyal, *The Supreme Court Should Not Muck Around in State Election Laws*, N.Y. Times (Oct. 28, 2020), https://www.nytimes.com

in this very same dramatic two-day window, Amy Coney Barrett formally joined the Court: Chief Justice Roberts administered the judicial oath to Justice Barrett on the morning of October 27.

We have no way to know if the frank and timely expression of our considered views as constitutional scholars in the *Times* had any effect on Justice Kavanaugh's seeming pullback from the edge. But if our timely and *Times*-ly intervention did somehow reach Justice Kavanaugh's desk at a moment when it truly mattered, when the Court was poised on the brink of disaster, then perhaps he did exactly what every good justice should do, always: pause and revisit one's instincts in light of the expert input of scholars.

In mid-December 2000, *Bush II* did not have the benefit of extensive scholarly input. Rather, most of the *Bush* justices galloped off on their own with no real time for academics to saddle up and warn the justices that they were wildly charging the wrong way—toward a cliff. And at one key perilous moment in OT 2020, it seemed as though the current justices were about to make the same horrible mistake.

The hope that what scholars say might at times matter to the Court—even when those scholars mince no words and speak candidly as true *amici curiae*—is part of the very *raison d'être* of *The Supreme Court Review*, now in its seventh decade of publication. If (and we admit it's a big if) Justice Kavanaugh in fact is rethinking his initial position as a result of scholarly input, this switch in time would be cause for optimism. To borrow an expression that famously appeared more than a half-century ago here in the pages of *The Supreme Court Review*, it might even be an occasion for "dancing in the streets."[125]

/2020/10/28/opinion/supreme-court-elections-state-law.html. This piece went online in the wee hours of the 28th.

[125] Harry Kalven, *The New York Times Case: A Note on "The Central Meaning of the First Amendment,"* 1964 Sup. Ct. Rev. 191, 221 n.125 (quoting Alexander Meiklejohn, quoting Motown, regarding a case all about the *New York Times*).

MARY-ROSE PAPANDREA

MAHANOY v. B.L. & FIRST AMENDMENT "LEEWAY"

Mahanoy Area School District v. B.L.[1] promised to resolve an issue that had been vexing the lower courts for decades: When may public schools rely on *Tinker v. Des Moines Independent Community School District*[2] to restrict their students' "off campus" expressive activities—i.e., when those students are not at school, under school supervision, or otherwise participating in school activities?[3] Fourteen long years after it expressly left open this issue in *Morse v. Frederick*,[4] the Court resolved this pressing question with a deeply unsatisfying answer: it depends. Although the Court ruled 8-1 in favor of a student who had posted

Mary-Rose Papandrea is Samuel Ashe Distinguished Professor of Constitutional Law, University of North Carolina School of Law.

[1] 141 S. Ct. 2038 (2021).

[2] 393 U.S. 503 (1969).

[3] This Article will use the term "off-campus speech" to describe expression that does not take place on school grounds, is not part of a school course or activity, and is not otherwise subject to school supervision. Like the Third Circuit, I use the phrases "on campus" and "off campus" "with caution" because "the schoolyard's physical boundaries are not necessarily coextensive with the 'school context.'" B.L. v. Mahanoy Area Sch. Dist., 964 F.3d 170, 178 (3d Cir. 2020).

[4] The Court acknowledged—and dodged—this issue in *Morse v. Frederick*, 551 U.S. 393 (2007), where it upheld the suspension of a student who held up a "BONG HiTS 4 JESUS" banner while attending the Olympic Torch Relay under school supervision. In that case, the Court simply noted that "[t]here is some uncertainty at the outer boundaries as to when courts should apply school speech precedents . . . but not on these facts." *Id.* at 401.

The Supreme Court Review, 2022.
 https://doi.org/10.1086/720294

"fuck cheer" on Snapchat after she did not make the varsity cheerleading team, *Mahanoy* is no victory for students.

Not only does the Court conclude that schools may use *Tinker*'s more relaxed constitutional standard to regulate their students' expression wherever and whenever it might occur, *Mahanoy* also embraces an *ad hoc* inquiry as its mode of analysis. The allure of the "special First Amendment leeway"[5] *Mahanoy* affords public schools is that it allows the Court to avoid articulating a clear student speech doctrine, but it leaves schools and judges free to consider any factors they wish to evaluate the constitutional rights of millions of public-school students on a case-by-case basis. The Court offers no guardrails to prevent schools from overextending their authority over student speech aside from essentially warning judges to "be careful." This dramatic expansion of school authority leaves students uncertain about what remaining speech rights they might have and creates even more instability in an already confusing and arguably incoherent area of the law.[6]

The Court may have thought its decision in *Mahanoy* was narrow; it is full of statements suggesting judicial modesty.[7] In addition, giving schools First Amendment leeway to regulate student speech may have seemed appealing because it offers flexibility as technology continues to develop.[8] Although the case specifically addressed the application of

---

[5] *Mahanoy*, 141 S. Ct. at 2045, 2046.

[6] *See* Guiles ex rel. Guiles v. Marineau, 461 F.3d 320, 321 (2d Cir. 2006) (remarking that "[t]his case requires us to sail into the unsettled waters of free speech rights in public schools, waters rife with rocky shoals and uncertain currents."); Geoffrey R. Stone, *Free Speech in the Twenty-First Century: Ten Lessons from the Twentieth Century*, 36 Pepp. L. Rev. 273, 288 (2009) (observing that the First Amendment law relating to "special circumstances" like student speech "is filled with deep ambiguities and complexities"); Kristi L. Bowman, *Public School Students' Religious Speech and Viewpoint Discrimination*, 110 W. Va. L. Rev. 187, 222 (2007) ("Constitutional law governing student speech disputes is becoming notoriously unpredictable.").

[7] *See*, *e.g.*, 141 S. Ct. at 2045 ("We are uncertain as to the length or content of any such list of appropriate exceptions or carveouts to the Third Circuit majority's rule."); *id.* at 2046 ("We leave for future cases to decide where, when, and how these features mean the speaker's off-campus location will make the crucial difference."); *see also id.* at 2049 (Alito, J., concurring) (asserting "it is not prudent for us to attempt at this time" to adopt a broadly applicable constitutional rule for off-campus speech). Justice Thomas criticizes the majority for "transparently" taking a "common-law approach to today's decision" and announcing "just one rule: Schools can regulate speech less often when that speech occurs off campus." *Id.* at 2063 (Thomas, J., dissenting).

[8] *See* Mark S. Kende, *The Supreme Court's Approach to the First Amendment in Cyberspace: Free Speech as Technology's Hand-Maiden*, 14 Const. Comment. 465, 466, 469 (1997) (Breyer's "wait and see" approach in cases involving new technology "may seem appealing because it resembles the quickly changing world without boundaries of cyberspace, and seems to facilitate that development").

Tinker to off-campus speech, it could be read as collapsing the increasingly complex set of student speech cases into one single inquiry regardless of where the student speech occurs. This approach to First Amendment questions reflects Justice Breyer's long-standing advocacy for a proportionality approach, where the Court's traditional free speech doctrines provide helpful "rules of thumb" but are not determinative.[9] Importantly, however, *Mahanoy* is not obviously a proportionality inquiry but instead an ad hoc analysis of a specific set of facts.

This Article contends that the Court's willingness to embrace an ad hoc inquiry in *Mahanoy* reflects the underlying fault lines in the Court's student speech cases and its First Amendment jurisprudence more generally. Although in many ways *Mahanoy* seems like a simple—and silly—case, it raises complicated questions not only about the proper scope of school authority but also about the rights of minors more generally, the distinction between public (or political) and private speech, protections for harassment and bullying, and the constitutionality of restrictions on lewd or profane speech. An ad hoc approach allows the Court to dodge these questions in the name of the "special circumstances" of public schools.

Part I reviews the facts of the case and the opinions of the Third Circuit and Supreme Court. Part II examines the First Amendment fault lines the Court dodges by embracing an ad hoc inquiry granting schools "First Amendment leeway" to regulate off-campus student speech. These doctrinal fault lines are based both in the Court's ordinary First Amendment jurisprudence as well as in its student speech cases specifically. Part III argues that the Court afforded schools "leeway" to regulate student speech wherever it might occur to paper over important doctrinal differences. This approach is distinct from a true proportionality inquiry that offers a potentially promising framework for evaluating student speech rights, provided that the Court does

[9] *See, e.g.*, Iancu v. Brunetti, 139 S. Ct. 2294, 2304 (2019) (Breyer, J., concurring in part and dissenting in part) (arguing the Court should regard its "speech-related categories not as outcome-determinative rules, but instead as rules of thumb"); Reed v. Town of Gilbert, 135 S. Ct. 2218, 2235 (Breyer, J., concurring) (arguing it is better to regard the rule against content discrimination as a "rule of thumb, finding it [a] helpful, but not determinative legal tool, in an appropriate case, to determine the strength of a justification"); United States v. Alvarez, 567 U.S. 709, 730 (2012) (Breyer, J., concurring) (contending that the inquiry should be whether a "statute works speech-related harm that is out of proportion to its justifications"); Pleasant Grove City v. Summum, 555 U.S. 460, 484 (2009) (Breyer, J., concurring) ("[T]he 'government speech' doctrine is a rule of thumb, not a rigid category.").

not lightly disregard bedrock First Amendment principles or afford unwarranted deference to school authorities.

I. The Case

A. The Facts

Fourteen-year-old Brandi Levy, a student at Mahanoy Area High School, a public high school in Pennsylvania, was a school cheerleader and played on a private softball team. At the end of her freshman year, she tried out for the varsity cheerleading squad and was placed on the JV team. Adding insult to injury, an incoming freshman made the varsity team. Levy took to Snapchat to voice her disappointment. On a Saturday, Levy and a friend (not a cheerleader) took a "selfie" at the Cocoa Hut, a local convenience store and student hangout. In this photo, they both had their middle fingers raised, and they posted the photo on Snapchat with the caption "fuck school, fuck softball,[10] fuck cheer, fuck everything."[11] This post was visible for 24 hours and potentially seen by about 250 of Levy's friends, some of whom went to the same school and some of whom were cheerleaders. Levy also posted a follow-up snap stating, "Love how me and [my friend] get told we need a year of jv before we make varsity but that doesn't matter to anyone else." This second post also had an upside-down smiley-face emoji.[12]

Posts on Snapchat disappear after 24 hours, but at least one student captured Levy's posts on her cellphone and circulated them to other members of the cheerleading team; in turn, a member of the team showed the snaps to her mom, who was one of the team's coaches.[13] Other students also learned about Levy's communications. Several students were reportedly "visibly upset and voiced their concerns to [Coach] Luchetta-Rump repeatedly for several days."[14] In addition, students talked about the posts during an Algebra class one of the coaches taught. After talking with the school principal, the coaches decided to punish her for using profanity in connection with an

[10] Levy was also disappointed she did not get to play her desired position on a private softball team. *Mahanoy*, 141 S. Ct. at 2043.

[11] *Id.*

[12] *Id.*

[13] B.L. *ex rel.* Levy v. Mahanoy Area Sch. Dist., 376 F. Supp. 3d 429, 433 (M.D. Pa. 2019), *aff'd*, 964 F.3d 170 (3d Cir. 2020), *aff'd*, 141 S. Ct. 2038 (2021).

[14] *Id.*

extracurricular activity, in violation of team rules banning "foul language and inappropriate gestures" and prohibiting "any negative information regarding cheerleading, cheerleaders, or coaches placed on the internet."[15] Levy apologized, but to no avail; she was suspended from the cheer team for a year.

B. THE LAWSUIT

After failing to convince the superintendent and school board to overturn the cheer suspension, Levy's parents filed a complaint in federal district court on their daughter's behalf. The district court granted their motion for summary judgment.[16] On appeal to the Third Circuit, the school district "principally defend[ed] its actions based on its power 'to enforce socially acceptable behavior' by banning 'vulgar, lewd, obscene, or plainly offensive' speech by students" pursuant to *Bethel School District No. 403 v. Fraser*.[17] The court responded that the Third Circuit had already determined that *Fraser* did not apply to off-campus speech,[18] and it rejected the district's argument that it had more leeway to punish vulgar speech when it related to an extracurricular activity.[19] The Third Circuit also rejected the district's "fall back" argument relying on *Tinker*.[20] Although a concurrence argued that the court could have simply assumed that even if *Tinker* applied, the school district had not satisfied its standard, the majority decided to confront the question to avoid the "chilling effect" of the legal uncertainty.[21] The court also noted that the application of the *Tinker* test in the context of extracurricular activities "has bedeviled our sister

[15] The school district claimed Levy violated the Respect Provision and the Negative Information Rule of the Cheerleading Rules she was required to sign as a condition of participation. These Rules state: "Please have respect for your school, coaches, teachers, other cheerleaders and teams. Remember you are representing your school when at games, fundraisers, and other events. Good sportsmanship will be enforced, this includes foul language and inappropriate gestures." The Rules also warn: "There will be no toleration of any negative information regarding cheerleading, cheerleaders, or coaches placed on the internet." *Id.* at 433.

[16] *Id.* at 434.

[17] *Mahanoy*, 964 F.3d at 181 (3d Cir. 2020) (quoting Appellant's Br. 7–8 and citing Bethel Sch. Dist. No. 403 v. Fraser, 478 U.S. 675 (1986)).

[18] *Id.* at 181 (citing Layshock *ex rel.* Layshock v. Hermitage Sch. Dist., 650 F.3d 205, 216–17, 219 (3d Cir. 2011)).

[19] *Id.* at 181–82.

[20] *Id.* at 181–83 (rejecting the school district's argument based on *Fraser* and then noting the district "falls back on *Tinker*").

[21] *Id.* at 185.

circuits" and would require the court to address "complex and unresolved constitutional questions."[22]

The court noted that the "digital revolution" had complicated *Tinker*'s famous reference to the "schoolhouse gate" as determinative of the scope of a school's authority.[23] At the same time, the court explained, "the Supreme Court, in defining the scope of schools' authority, has consistently focused not on physical boundaries but on the extent to which schools control or sponsor the forum or the speech."[24] The Third Circuit defined "off campus" speech as speech that "is outside school-owned, -operated, or -supervised channels and that is not reasonably interpreted as bearing the school's imprimatur."[25] The court then rejected the holdings of its sister circuits permitting the application of *Tinker* to off-campus speech.[26] The circuit court observed that "one unmistakable trend from the case law is that the most challenging fact patterns have produced rules untethered from the contexts in which they arose."[27] Apparently sharing these concerns about challenging fact patterns, the Third Circuit reserved judgment about the scope of school authority to regulate "off-campus speech threatening violence or harassing particular students or teachers."[28] The court noted that while it "disagree[d] with the *Tinker*-based theoretical approach . . . [its] opinion takes no position on the school's

---

[22] *Id.* at 184.

[23] *Id.* at 175.

[24] *Id.* at 179.

[25] *Id.* at 189.

[26] Some held that speech is considered student speech when there is a "reasonably foreseeable risk that [the speech] would come to the attention of school authorities" and cause a substantial disruption. *See* Wisniewski v. Bd. of Educ., 494 F.3d 34, 38 (2d Cir. 2007); *see also* D.J.M. *ex rel.* D.M. v. Hannibal Public Sch. Dist. No. 60, 647 F.3d 754, 766 (8th Cir. 2011) (embracing the "reasonably foreseeable" test). Another group of courts embraced a test asking whether the speech at issue has a sufficient "nexus" with the school's "pedagogical interests" to justify school action. *See, e.g.*, McNeil v. Sherwood Sch. Dist. 88J, 918 F.3d 700, 707–08 (9th Cir. 2019) (holding "courts considering whether a school district may constitutionally regulate off-campus speech must determine, based on the totality of the circumstances, whether the speech bears a sufficient nexus to the school" and noting that this standard is "always" met "when the school district reasonably concludes that it faces a credible, identifiable threat of school violence"); *see also* Bell v. Itawamba Cnty. Sch. Bd., 799 F.3d 379, 396 (5th Cir. 2015) (en banc) (declining to adopt any "rigid" jurisdictional standard but applying *Tinker* to threatening off-campus speech that a student "intentionally direct[ed] to the school community"); Kowalski v. Berkeley Cnty. Schs., 652 F.3d 565, 573–75 (4th Cir. 2011) (citing favorably both the "reasonably foreseeable" and "nexus" tests).

[27] B.L. v. Mahanoy Area Sch. Dist., 964 F.3d 170, 187 (3d Cir. 2020).

[28] *Id.* at 190.

bottom-line power to discipline speech in that category" that might either satisfy existing First Amendment doctrine or warrant the creation of "a narrow exception to students' broader speech rights."[29]

C. AT THE SUPREME COURT

The Court granted certiorari to resolve whether schools can rely on *Tinker* to regulate speech that does not take place on school grounds or as part of a school activity. At oral argument, Justice Breyer said, "I can't write a treatise on the First Amendment in this case."[30] He expressed concern about the expanding role of schools to serve as "caretaker," the complications added by the Internet, and the lack of a standard in *Tinker*.[31] Instead, he offered, he could write an opinion extending *Tinker* outside the schoolhouse gates when expression causes a substantial disruption, with "some kind of test, like proportionality or something else,"[32] and with the warning that this speech is "primarily the domain of the parents," that even inside the school this authority is limited, and that judges need to "be careful."[33] Justice Breyer did exactly what he outlined at oral argument in his majority opinion for an almost unanimous Court. Only Justice Thomas dissented.

The Court began by expressly rejecting the argument that *Tinker*'s "highly general statement about the nature of a school's special interests" has no applicability to "off-campus" speech in light of "the many different kinds of off-campus speech, the different potential school-related and circumstance-specific justifications, and the differing extent to which those justifications may call for First Amendment leeway."[34] The Court explained that three "features" of off-campus speech "diminish the strength of the unique educational characteristics that might call for special First Amendment leeway."[35] First, the Court said, schools rarely stand "in loco parentis" with respect to off-campus speech, which is generally "within the zone of

---

[29] *Id.*

[30] Transcript of Oral Argument at 43, Mahanoy Area Sch. Dist. v. B.L., 141 S. Ct. 2038 (2021) (No. 20-255). Justice Kavanaugh echoed these sentiments. *See id.* at 102 ("I think you can answer the question presented here [whether *Tinker* applies off-campus] without writing a treatise.").

[31] *Id.* at 73–74.

[32] *Id.* at 74.

[33] *Id.* at 43–44.

[34] *Mahanoy*, 141 S. Ct. at 2045.

[35] *Id.* at 2046.

parental, rather than school-related, responsibility."[36] Second, "courts must be more skeptical of a school's efforts to regulate off-campus speech, for doing so may mean the student cannot engage in that kind of speech at all."[37] Schools will have "a heavy burden" when they attempt to regulate "political or religious speech."[38] Third, "the school itself has an interest in protecting a student's unpopular expression" because "America's public schools are the nurseries of democracy."[39] The Court emphasized the importance of the "marketplace of ideas" to our democracy, which includes "the protection of unpopular ideas, for popular ideas have less need for protection," and added that "schools have a strong interest in ensuring that future generations understand" the importance of tolerating and even defending speech that they hate.[40] The Court offered no guidance on how lower courts should apply or evaluate these "features," instead expressly noting it would "leave for future cases to decide where, when, and how these features mean the speaker's off-campus location will make the critical difference."[41] This approach resembles the "Judge, be careful" holding Breyer promised at oral argument.[42]

In applying its announced approach to Levy's speech, the Court considered a variety of factors, including the nature of the speech; when, where, how, and to whom she spoke; and the school's interest in prohibiting her speech. Although her speech contained profanity, her expression did not constitute fighting words and was not obscene, and it contained "criticism of the rules of a community of which B.L. forms a part,"[43] which the Court implied was a matter of public concern.[44] Furthermore, she used her personal cellphone to transmit her messages to a private circle of friends, "her posts appeared outside of school hours from a location outside the school,"[45] and she did not

---

[36] *Id.*

[37] *Id.*

[38] *Id.*

[39] *Id.*

[40] *Id.*

[41] *Id.*

[42] Oral Argument Transcript, *supra* note 30, at 44.

[43] *Mahanoy*, 141 S. Ct. at 2046.

[44] The Court is not entirely clear whether it regards her speech as relating to a matter of public concern. *See infra* text accompanying notes 147–151.

[45] *Mahanoy*, 141 S. Ct at 2047.

identify the school or "target any member of the school community with vulgar or abusive language."[46] The school did not stand "in loco parentis" when she was at the Cocoa Hut. The Court also found that the school's asserted interests in teaching good manners and preventing disruption were insufficient to overcome Levy's expressive interests.[47] The school presented no evidence "of any general effort to prevent students from using vulgarity outside of the classroom."[48] Finally, the Court concluded that there was no evidence of a substantial disruption at school or any serious disruption of team morale.[49]

Notably, *Mahanoy* does not require school officials to make any sort of threshold or "jurisdictional" showing to take advantage of the *Tinker* standard, an approach common among the lower courts[50] and one that both the school district and federal government supported even though such an approach limited school authority, at least theoretically. The Court's opinion offers no explanation why it avoided taking this popular path, but at oral argument, various Justices expressed skepticism about how to apply these threshold approaches and whether they provided any meaningful limit on the school's authority.[51] In any event, the upshot is that *Mahanoy* collapses these two previously separate inquiries into one single, all-encompassing inquiry that evaluates the legitimacy of the school's interest in regulating the speech at issue.

As in *Morse*,[52] Justice Alito joined the *Mahanoy* majority opinion but also authored a separate concurrence, which Justice Gorsuch joined, because "it is important that our [majority] opinion not be misunderstood."[53] In this concurrence, Alito attempts to make sense of the

---

[46] *Id.*

[47] *Id.*

[48] *Id.*

[49] *Id.* at 2048.

[50] *See infra* note 26.

[51] *See, e.g.*, Oral Argument Transcript, *supra* note 30, at 15, 47 (Justice Alito remarking, "I have no idea what it means to target the school" and expressing a need for "clear lines"); *id.* at 19–20 (Justice Sotomayor noting that "most [students'] conversation[s] are about school"); *id.* at 39 (Chief Justice Roberts questioning the targeting inquiry when most teenagers' friends are also their classmates); *id.* at 50 (Justice Kagan remarking that it seems like "really everything that mentions a school at all is school speech").

[52] Morse v. Frederick, 551 U.S. 393, 422 (2007) (Alito, J., concurring) (asserting he joined the majority opinion based on the understanding that its holding is limited).

[53] 141 S. Ct. at 2048–49 (Alito, J., concurring).

Court's student speech cases as a whole (arguably the "treatise" approach Justice Breyer wanted to avoid). Justice Thomas filed a solo dissent criticizing the majority for simply "posit[ing] three vague considerations and reach[ing] an outcome."[54] He argued that the historical doctrine of *in loco parentis* controls, and under that doctrine, the Constitution places no limits on public schools to restrict their pupils' expression and conduct that "has a proximate tendency to harm the school, its faculty or students, or its programs."[55]

II. First Amendment Fault Lines in *Mahanoy*

Prior to *Mahanoy*, the Court decided five cases that form the modern framework of the student speech doctrine. As with the rest of the Court's First Amendment decisions involving the government operating in its "managerial" authority over certain government institutions, the Court has relaxed its ordinary First Amendment principles so that public schools can achieve their legitimate institutional objectives.[56] The problem is that, over time, the Court has created an inconsistent, unclear, and often incoherent student speech doctrine.[57] In *Mahanoy*, the Court was plainly unwilling to clean up this mess. Rather than engaging in a careful calibration of the competing interests and a close consideration of First Amendment principles to develop more precise rules to guide schools, students, and judges, the Court simply engages in an ad hoc analysis in its apparent belief that this is a narrow resolution of the issue before it. Perhaps inadvertently, however, the Court manages to create more problems than it solves with its new approach to student speech rights.

This Part argues that fault lines within the student speech doctrine and First Amendment more generally made this case more difficult

---

[54] *Id.* at 2059–63 (Thomas, J., dissenting).

[55] *Id.*

[56] *See, e.g.*, Frederick Schauer, *Towards an Institutional First Amendment*, 89 Minn. L. Rev. 1256, 1270 (2005) (arguing the First Amendment should treat different settings, institutions, and contexts differently); Robert C. Post, *Between Governance and Management: The History and Theory of the Public Forum*, 34 UCLA L. Rev. 1713, 1717, 1775 (1987) (distinguishing between "managerial" authority over government institutions, where "the state can in large measure control speech on the basis of an organization's need to achieve its institutional ends," and "governance" of the ordinary public, where "ordinary and generally applicable principles of first amendment adjudication" apply).

[57] For an examination of the evolution of the Court's student speech jurisprudence, see Mary-Rose Papandrea, *Student Speech Rights in the Digital Age*, 60 Fla. L. Rev. 1027, 1038–53 (2008).

than it might have appeared at first blush. These fault lines include (1) a lack of a clear and robust First Amendment doctrine governing harassment, threats, and "disrespectful" speech, as well as general concerns about applying existing law to new technology; (2) unresolved questions about the *Tinker* standard; and (3) a lack of a coherent understanding of the expressive rights of juveniles, especially with respect to lewd, profane, and offensive speech.

A. THREATS, HARASSMENT, DISRESPECTFUL SPEECH, AND TECHNOLOGY

In *Mahanoy*, the Court appears to panic about the possibility of resolving the issue before it given the challenges of new technology and its concerns about giving schools the authority they need to protect members of the school community from harassment, bullying, violence, and disrespectful expression that undermines the educational process. This panic leads it to reject a per se rule prohibiting the application of *Tinker* to off-campus student speech and to open the door to school regulation of their students' expression wherever it might occur.

1. *Technology concerns.* At the outset of its opinion, the Court explained that the "school's regulatory interests remain significant in some off-campus circumstances," including expression made traveling back and forth to school; expression during remote learning; severe or serious targeted harassment or bullying; threats; expression that exhibits a failure to follow rules for school lessons, assignments, the use of computers, or other online school activities; breaches of school security devices; and extracurricular activities.[58] The Court admits "[w]e are uncertain as to the length or content of any such list of appropriate exceptions," but "[p]articularly given the advent of computer-based learning, we hesitate to determine precisely which of the many school-related off-campus activities belong on such a list."[59] The Court added that the list "might vary, depending upon a student's age, the nature of the school's off-campus activity, or the impact upon the school itself."[60]

This opening portion of the Court's opinion suggests that the Court may have misunderstood and overestimated the impact of

---

[58] *Mahanoy*, 141 S. Ct. at 2045.

[59] *Id.*

[60] *Id.*

technology on a school's authority over student speech and did not appreciate the existing tools in every public school's toolbox prior to *Mahanoy*. To start, although courts and commentators continue to use the phrases "on campus" and "off campus" speech to delineate the authority of school officials, it has long been clear that the relevant boundary "is not constructed solely of the bricks and mortar surrounding the school yard."[61] Indeed, the Court's own decision in *Morse* made this clear. There, the Court explained that the case was a "school speech case" because it involved student expression at a school-approved and school-supervised event.[62] The Third Circuit's approach did not restrict school authority along strictly geographical lines. Although *Mahanoy* accurately notes how the Third Circuit used the terms "on campus" and "off campus,"[63] the Court seemed to forget the technical definition of these terms once its analysis got underway.

In addition, the dramatic increase in online instruction during the pandemic may have caused the Court to panic unnecessarily about school authority over student speech physically occurring off school grounds. As Justice Alito points out in his *Mahanoy* concurrence, the Court's list of situations potentially requiring an extension of *Tinker* off of school grounds includes "speech that takes place during or as part of what amounts to a temporal or spatial extension of the regular school program, *e.g.*, online instruction at home, assigned essays or other homework, and transportation to and from school."[64] But while these activities might be geographically off-campus, they are not considered "off campus" speech, as defined by the Third Circuit. This is because even prior to *Mahanoy*, schools would have authority under the Court's previous school speech cases to regulate speech occurring in these circumstances. In the case of expression during remote instruction, homework and assessments, and other online school activities, schools can rely on the much more permissive standard of *Hazelwood School District v. Kuhlmeier*,[65] which allows schools to regulate expression as long as they can demonstrate that the regulations

---

[61] Layshock *ex rel.* Layshock v. Hermitage Sch. Dist., 650 F.3d 205, 216 (3d Cir. 2011).

[62] Morse v. Frederick, 551 U.S. 393, 401 (2007).

[63] 141 S. Ct. at 2044.

[64] *Id.* at 2054 (Alito, J., concurring).

[65] 484 U.S. 260 (1988).

"are reasonably related to legitimate pedagogical concerns."[66] Schools can rely on *Tinker* (and *Morse* and *Fraser*) to regulate speech on school-controlled transportation (like the school bus).[67] The Court therefore wildly overstates the problem facing schools.

As a result, *Mahanoy* is out of step with the Court's more cautious approach to government speech restrictions on the Internet, even when intended to protect children. For example, in *Packingham v. North Carolina*,[68] the Court struck down a North Carolina law prohibiting registered sex offenders from using social media, explaining that it "must exercise extreme caution before suggesting that the First Amendment provides scant protection for access to vast networks in that medium" of social media.[69] *Packingham* quoted *Reno v. ACLU*,[70] where the Court rejected efforts to regulate speech on the Internet in the name of protecting children and explained that the Internet offers "vast democratic forums" and "relatively unlimited, low-cost capacity for communication of all kinds."[71] And in *Brown v. Entertainment Merchants Ass'n*,[72] the Court struck down a law restricting the sale of

---

[66] *Id.* at 273; *see, e.g.*, Collins v. Putt, 979 F.3d 128, 132–34 (2d Cir. 2020) (applying *Hazelwood* in rejecting a challenge to an instructor's decision to remove a student's offensive contribution to a virtual classroom's online message board), *cert. denied*, 141 S. Ct. 1465 (2021).

[67] The Court may have been worried about school authority over "walkers" traveling between school and home. *See* C.R. Eugene Sch. Dist. 4J, 835 F.3d 1142, 1150–52 (9th Cir. 2016) (upholding the punishment of a student who sexually harassed two disabled students on the way home from school at a park next to school grounds); *see also Mahanoy*, 141 S. Ct. at 2054 (Alito, J., concurring) (arguing schools may maintain authority over "[a]busive speech that occurs while students are walking to and from school" because this is a "temporal or spatial extension of the regular school program"). The majority also mentioned a school's interest in monitoring the proper use of school computers. *Mahanoy*, 141 S. Ct. at 2045. Schools have "acceptable use policies" or "responsible use policies" governing the use of school-issued devices and networks. Although students and their guardians usually must agree to such policies, arguments that they voluntarily waived their constitutional rights would be subject to an unconstitutional conditions challenge. In addition, strict enforcement of such agreements raises serious policy concerns. At the very least, students from low-income families, who cannot afford to purchase their own electronic devices, would be subject to school oversight in a way their wealthier peers would not. *See* Catherine J. Ross, Lessons in Censorship: How Schools and Courts Subvert Students' First Amendment Rights 234 (2015) (remarking that "[s]urely this would be a socially unacceptable outcome even if it did not violate the Constitution"); *see also* Barbara Fedders, *The Constant and Expanding Classroom: Surveillance in K-12 Public Schools*, 97 N.C. L. Rev. 1673, 1716–17 (2019) (arguing that the monitoring of school-issued devices has a disparate impact on low-income students, students of color, and LGBTQ students).

[68] 137 S. Ct. 1730 (2017)

[69] *Id.* at 1736.

[70] 521 U.S. 844 (1997).

[71] 137 S. Ct. at 1735 (quoting *Reno*, 521 U.S. at 868, 870).

[72] 564 U.S. 786 (2011).

violent video games to minors, asserting that "whatever the challenges of applying the Constitution to ever-advancing technology, 'the basic principles of freedom of speech and the press, like the First Amendment's command, do not vary' when a new and different medium for communication appears."[73]

Although *Mahanoy* leaves both students and school officials equally unsure about how to apply its ad hoc approach, this uncertainty greatly benefits school officials and simultaneously undermines student speech rights significantly.[74] It is hard to imagine a more dramatic chilling effect on the speech of minors.[75] Furthermore, school officials will almost always be able to claim qualified immunity given that it is anyone's guess how the Court would rule in any other case.[76]

2. *Threats, harassment, and disrespectful speech.* As the Third Circuit noted,[77] most of the student speech cases where the lower courts embraced the *Tinker* standard for off-campus speech have fallen into one of three categories: (1) depictions of violence or perceived threats of violence;[78] (2) criticism or hurtful comments about other students;[79]

---

[73] *Id.* at 790.

[74] *See* Jenny Diamond Cheng, *Deciding Not to Decide*: Mahanoy Area School District v. B.L. *and the Supreme Court's Ambivalence Toward Student Speech Rights*, 74 VAND. L. REV. EN BANC 511, 513 (2021) ("[T]he Court's qualified immunity doctrine effectively converts legal ambiguity into government power.").

[75] The only thing that might reduce the chilling effect is that most students would never guess their schools have such potentially broad authority to punish them for their off-campus speech. That Levy won in *Mahanoy* might also obscure the power the Court has given schools.

[76] Morse v. Frederick, 551 U.S. 393, 429–30 (2007) (Breyer, J., concurring) (arguing the case should be dismissed under qualified immunity doctrine).

[77] B.L. v. Mahanoy Area Sch. Dist., 964 F.3d 170, 187 (3d Cir. 2020) (noting that "one unmistakable trend from the case law is that the most challenging fact patterns have produced rules untethered from the contexts in which they arose").

[78] *See, e.g.*, Wynar v. Douglas Cnty. Sch. Dist., 728 F.3d 1062, 1069 (9th Cir. 2013) (holding *Tinker* standard applies when a student makes an "identifiable threat of school violence" online); Wisniewski v. Bd. of Educ., 494 F.3d 34, 38 (2d Cir. 2007) (upholding punishment of student who sent another student an image of a pistol firing a bullet at a teacher's head); Porter v. Ascension Parish Sch. Bd., 393 F.3d 608, 618 (5th Cir. 2004) (holding constitutionally protected a picture a student drew at home of the school under military-like attack).

[79] S.J.W. *ex rel.* Wilson v. Lee's Summit R-7 Sch. Dist., 696 F.3d 771, 773 (8th Cir. 2012) (upholding the punishment of students who created a blog with "a variety of offensive and racist comments as well as sexually explicit and degrading comments about particular female classmates, whom they identified by name"); Kowalski v. Berkeley Cnty. Schs., 652 F.3d 565, 567–68 (4th Cir. 2011) (holding the school could punish student who created a group webpage ridiculing a fellow student as a "slut" who had herpes).

and (3) criticism or derision of teachers, staff, and other school administrators.[80] The Court's concerns about the ability of "ordinary" First Amendment principles to handle these situations, combined with its panic and confusion about new technology, clearly impacted its opinion in *Mahanoy*. Rather than resolve the difficult question of whether and when schools should have the authority to regulate these troublesome types of expression, the Court simply embraced the *Tinker* standard.

School officials' claims that they need the flexibility of *Tinker*'s more forgiving standard to address the problems with the effective and safe operation of their schools in these contexts are sympathetic, at least in some instances.[81] As Justice Sotomayor pointed out at oral argument, the "traditional categories" of low-value speech, such as true threats, fighting words, obscenity, child pornography, defamation, etc. are very strictly drawn and hard to satisfy.[82] Some student speech depicting or threatening violence on the school will satisfy the requirements of incitement or true threats, but not all;[83] some offensive or harassing speech that arguably undermines the learning environment might constitute fighting words, defamation, or targeted severe and pervasive harassment, but much will not. Speech criticizing or making fun of adults in the school community might constitute defamation, true threats, or fighting words, but in many cases, this expression is fully protected speech. Allowing schools to operate

---

[80] *See, e.g.*, Bell v. Itawamba Cnty. Sch. Bd., 799 F.3d 379, 394 (5th Cir. 2015) (en banc) (applying *Tinker* to a rap recording that threatened and intimated two teachers); J.S. *ex rel.* Snyder v. Blue Mountain Sch. Dist., 650 F.3d 915, 926–31 (3d Cir. 2011) (assuming without deciding that the *Tinker* standard applied to an offensive fake online profile of the principal a student created, but the standard was not met). *But see* Layshock *ex rel.* Layshock v. Hermitage Sch. Dist., 650 F.3d 205, 207–08 (3d Cir. 2011) (holding a school lacked the authority to punish a lewd and offensive parody profile of a school principal on MySpace).

[81] Of course, the simple desire to "close and control" all student speech on social media is not as sympathetic. *See* Clay Calvert, Tinker's *Midlife Crisis: Tattered and Transgressed But Still Standing*, 58 Am. U. L. Rev. 1167, 1187 (2009) (noting that school officials would like to control students who "post material that openly mocks and pokes fun at classmates, teachers, and administrators in a public forum available to people all around the world").

[82] Oral Argument Transcript, *supra* note 30, at 81.

[83] For example, under ordinary First Amendment principles, advocacy of illegal conduct at some indeterminate future time is protected speech. *See, e.g.*, NAACP v. Claiborne Hardware Co., 458 U.S. 886 (1982) (holding constitutionally protected the public statement of an NAACP official that "[if] we catch any of you going in any of them racist stores, we're gonna break your damn neck"); Hess v. Indiana, 414 U.S. 105 (1973) (reversing disorderly conduct conviction of individual who shouted during an anti-war demonstration, "We'll take the fucking street later [or again].").

under the "First Amendment leeway" of *Tinker*'s standard means that schools do not have to worry about the constitutional difficulties of regulating cyberbullying or harassment under "ordinary" principles. As Justice Barrett noted at oral argument, the school has "good policy reasons" for extending *Tinker* so that it can address these situations.[84]

Calibrating the authority schools should have over harassment, threats of violence, and expressions of disrespect is not an easy task. For example, schools assert an interest in prohibiting speech that is disrespectful of teachers and school administrators. In the classroom, disrespectful speech during class directly and immediately undermines a school's teaching mission; few would question schools' authority to restrict such speech. Disrespectful speech outside of the classroom, however, poses a trickier issue because the disruption is not as direct, and the value of the speech is potentially high. Permitting schools to restrict their students' critical speech runs headlong into bedrock First Amendment doctrine protecting criticism of public figures and officials, such as *Hustler Magazine, Inc. v. Falwell*[85] and *New York Times Co. v. Sullivan*,[86] and this interest is not limited to "whistleblowing" about illegal conduct. Such speech can help inform public understanding about the operation of schools—even if just among students themselves—and also serve as an important release valve for the frustrations common among young people as they assert their independence from authority.

Adjusting the constitutional level of protection for harassment and threats of violence would likewise be tricky, even though the school interest might be more sympathetic. For example, the Court has never formally explored the relationship between the First Amendment and restrictions on hostile environment harassment, even though it has suggested multiple times that they can coexist.[87] Justice Alito's concurrence specifically notes that "[p]erhaps the most difficult category [to define with the precision required for a regulation of speech]

[84] Oral Argument Transcript, *supra* note 30, at 33.

[85] 485 U.S. 46 (2011).

[86] 376 U.S. 254 (1964).

[87] *See, e.g.*, Harris v. Forklift Systems, 510 U.S. 17 (1993) (recognizing a hostile environment sexual harassment claim under Title VII based solely on verbal conduct without any mention of the First Amendment, even though the issue had been briefed).

school's interest in regulating "*serious or severe* bullying or harassment *targeting* particular individuals" and "threats *aimed at* teachers or other students."[111] Combined with the Court's emphasis on the "marketplace of ideas" and toleration of unpopular ideas,[112] this language suggests the Court would not permit schools to restrict speech to protect students from emotional trauma and hurt feelings resulting from offensive speech, absent a showing that the speech targeted a particular individual. But it seems dangerous to read too much into these sparse tea leaves.

Relatedly, *Tinker* did not make clear whether the disruption must be caused by the student-speakers themselves or whether the disruption can be caused by a hostile reaction to the speakers. Although the Court had rejected the "heckler's veto" in 1966,[113] and portions of *Tinker* could be read to prohibit the silencing of a speaker based on a hostile audience reaction, *Tinker* does not squarely address this issue. Indeed, *Tinker*'s emphasis on the need to protect order at schools suggests that it is reasonable to interpret that decision as permitting schools to restrict any speech that causes or contributes to disruption, regardless of whether it is the speaker or audience who causes that disruption.[114] At various times during oral argument the School District asserted that *Tinker* does not tolerate a "heckler's veto," even though lower courts are not in consensus on this point. Justice Alito was quick to

[111] *Id.* (emphasis added).

[112] *Id.* at 2046.

[113] Brown v. Louisiana, 383 U.S. 131, 133 n.1 (1966) ("Participants in an orderly demonstration in a public place are not chargeable with the danger . . . that their critics might react with disorder or violence.").

[114] In addition, lower courts have disagreed whether *Tinker* bans all viewpoint discrimination, only political-viewpoint discrimination, or any content-based discrimination. *See* Frank D. LoMonte, *Shrinking* Tinker: *Students Are "Persons" Under Our Constitution—Except When They Aren't*, 59 Am. U. L. Rev. 1323, 1329 (2009) (making this point and citing cases). *Tinker* also does not explain how much deference courts should give school officials' predictions of disruption or how to evaluate whether their predictions of disruption are simply an "undifferentiated fear or apprehension of disturbance." Tinker v. Des Moines Indep. Cmty. Sch. Dist., 393 U.S. 503, 508 (1969). For example, *Tinker* suggests that school officials can restrict student speech based on a reasonable prediction of a substantial disruption (regardless of whether such disruption occurs). *See* Mary-Rose Papandrea, *The Great Unfulfilled Promise of* Tinker, 105 Va. L. Rev. Online 159, 170 (2019); *see also* Driver, *supra* note 103, at 76 (noting *Tinker* "can be understood to contain no fewer than three different, competing approaches for regulating student speech"). Lower courts have generally embraced this interpretation of *Tinker* and afforded schools broad deference in determining the "reasonableness" of their predictions.

including the content, form, and context; "no factor is dispositive."[124] The Court has noted the "difficulty of forcing state and federal judges to decide on an *ad hoc* basis which publications address issues of 'general or public interest' and which do not."[125] Despite these difficulties, the Court first made the availability of constitutional protection turn explicitly on whether the speech addresses a public matter in the government-employee speech context[126] and has since embraced the distinction in additional cases, such as in *Dun & Bradstreet v. Greenmoss Builders*[127] and *Snyder v. Phelps*.[128]

It is unclear whether *Mahanoy* purposefully used the terms "political" and "religious" speech rather than the more common distinction between matters of "public concern" and "private concern," but most likely the Court made this choice because prior student speech cases tend to use this terminology.[129] Regardless of the terminology, it is not clear what "work" the Court intends for the political/non-political distinction to do and whether it suggests a significant change in the Court's approach to student speech cases. Although decided just one year after *Pickering v. Board of Education*, which set up a balancing test to evaluate the constitutional rights of public employees,[130] *Tinker*

---

[124] *Id.*

[125] Gertz v. Robert Welch, Inc., 418 U.S. 332, 346 (1974).

[126] *See* Cynthia L. Estlund, *Speech on Matters of Public Concern: The Perils of an Emerging First Amendment Category*, 59 Geo. Wash. L. Rev. 1, 20–23 (1990) (tracing this history and noting the embrace of the public/private dichotomy "was unprecedented except for the ill-fated *Rosenbloom* foray").

[127] 472 U.S. 749 (1985) (holding that actual malice is not required in private-concern libel action brought by a private figure seeking presumed and punitive damages).

[128] 562 U.S. 443, 451 (2011) (holding viability for intentional infliction of emotional distress claim based on offensive speech "turns largely on whether that speech is of public or private concern"). Justice Breyer advocated for this distinction in his concurring opinion in Bartnicki v. Vopper, 532 U.S. 514, 539 (2001) (Breyer, J., concurring) (arguing that the relevant factor in analyzing the constitutionality of a statute prohibiting the publication of intercepted information is whether the information is a matter of substantial public concern).

[129] Justice Alito used the phrase "political or social issue" in his *Morse* concurrence. Morse v. Frederick, 551 U.S. 393, 422 (2007) (Alito, J., concurring) (arguing that the majority's opinion in *Morse* "provides no support for any restriction of speech that can plausibly be interpreted as commenting on any political or social issue"). In *Mahanoy*, Alito describes speech at the heart of the First Amendment as expression "that addresses matters of public concern, including sensitive subjects like politics, religion, and social relations." Mahanoy Area Sch. Dist. v. B.L., 141 S. Ct. 2038, 2055 (2021) (Alito, J., concurring).

[130] 391 U.S. 563, 568 (1968) (holding that constitutional rights of public employees are determined based on "a balance between the interests of the [employee], as a citizen, in commenting upon matters of public concern and the interests of the State, as an employer, in promoting the efficiency of the public services it performs through its employees").

notably did not set up a balancing test; instead, the Court held that the First Amendment rights of students could be regulated only if their expression substantially interferes with the work of the school or with the rights of others. In other words, under *Tinker*, the nature and value of the expression does not impact the inquiry.[131]

That said, the Court's subsequent decisions in *Fraser* and *Morse* suggest that the Court has narrowed *Tinker* such that its protective standard does not apply, or at least permits exceptions, when schools regulate non-political student speech. In both cases, the Court emphasized that the expression at issue was not political—in contrast to the clear political speech in *Tinker*—and suggested that therefore the Court was free to create additional exceptions to *Tinker*.[132] One possible conclusion to draw from *Fraser* and *Morse* is that the Court's approach to student speech rights is, in practice, a balancing test weighing the strength of the school's interest in regulating the expression against the value of the expression.[133] *Mahanoy* gives an additional reason to embrace that reading of the Court's caselaw in this area.

It will be interesting to watch how the lower courts apply *Mahanoy*'s new ad hoc test going forward, and specifically how they will interpret the Court's admonishment that schools regulating political and religious speech must meet a "heavy burden." The lower courts' struggle to determine the constitutional rights of public employees provides a crystal ball predicting the issues they are likely to confront, especially given that some lower courts have invoked the public-employee doctrine when analyzing student speech rights.[134] In *Pickering*, the Court adopted a balancing test to evaluate the speech claims of public

[131] Some lower courts have expressly rejected attempts to read a "public concern" requirement into *Tinker*. *See, e.g.*, Pinard v. Clatskanie Sch. Dist. 6J, 467 F.3d 755, 767 (9th Cir. 2006) ("[W]e do not read *Tinker*, its progeny or our own cases applying its standard as importing [a] public concern test into the public education context.").

[132] *Morse*, 551 U.S. at 403 (noting "not even Frederick argues that the banner conveys any sort of political or religious message"); *id.* at 403 ("[T]his is plainly not a case about political debate over the criminalization of drug use or possession."); Fraser v. Bethel Sch. Dist. No. 403, 478 U.S. 675, 680 (1986) (noting the "marked distinction between the political 'message' of the armbands in *Tinker* and the sexual content of [Fraser]'s speech").

[133] *See* Bowman, *supra* note 6, at 220 (analyzing the Court's pre-*Mahanoy* cases as suggesting that "a school's ability to restrict student speech depends on the strength of the government interest and the character of the speech itself").

[134] This is especially true in the context of extracurricular activities. *See, e.g.*, Lowery v. Euverard, 497 F.3d 584, 597 (6th Cir. 2007) (concluding that the legal principles from the public employment context are relevant in analyzing the free speech claims of football players disciplined for circulating a petition critical of their coach).

artistic expression—even on matters trivial, vulgar, or profane."[145] As one court explained, just because the Court has emphasized the importance of protecting speech on matters of public concern, this does not "imply[] that employee speech on other matters lying within the [F]irst [A]mendment's general protection should be accorded little weight in the public employee speech balancing process."[146]

Mahanoy's application of its new approach to Levy's Snapchat posts offers little guidance for future cases, particularly on how to determine whether speech is political or religious (or a matter of public concern). The Court gives mixed messages about the speech's value. On the one hand, the Court insists that "[p]utting aside the vulgar language, the listener would hear criticism of the team, the team's coaches, and the school—in a word or two, criticism of the rules of a community of which B.L. forms a part."[147] If she were an adult, the Court explained, "the First Amendment would provide strong protection" to this "kind of pure speech."[148] The Court then cites *Snyder v. Phelps*, which held that the offensive speech of the Westboro Baptist Church was a matter of public concern, and *Rankin v. McPherson*, which protected a government employee's right to make statements of public concern.[149] But by the end of the majority opinion, the Court comments that her expression "might seem a trifling and annoying instance of individual distasteful abuse of a privilege," and that "[i]t might be tempting to dismiss B.L.'s words as unworthy of robust First Amendment protections."[150] The Court nevertheless concludes that "sometimes it is necessary to protect the superfluous in order to preserve the necessary."[151]

It may be that the Court did not feel it was necessary to classify Levy's speech given that the school's interests in regulating the speech were so weak. But the two cases the Court cites as examples of speech on matters of public concern reveal how tricky this inquiry can be. *Snyder* notoriously involved hateful speech that the Court labeled

[145] *Berger*, 779 F.2d at 1000.

[146] *Id.* at 999–1000.

[147] Mahanoy Area Sch. Dist. v. B.L., 141 S. Ct. 2038, 2046 (2021).

[148] *Id.* at 2046–47.

[149] *Id.* at 2047 (citing Snyder v. Phelps, 562 U.S. 443 (2011) and Rankin v. McPherson, 483 U.S. 378 (1987)).

[150] *Id.* at 2048.

[151] *Id.*

speech on a matter of public concern even though some of the signs "were viewed as containing message related to Matthew Snyder or the Snyders specifically."[152] The Court concluded that this "would not change the fact that the overall thrust and dominant theme of Westboro's demonstration spoke to broader public issues."[153] *Rankin*, a public-employee case, split the Court 5-4 on the nature of the employee's private comment to a co-worker, upon hearing about the assassination attempt on President Reagan, that "if they go for him again, I hope they get him."[154] The majority held that this speech addressed a matter of public concern, but the dissenters argued that it did not because it was "a statement lying so near the category of completely unprotected speech"—such as fighting words or incitement—that it "cannot fairly be viewed as lying within the 'heart' of the First Amendment's protection."[155] Furthermore, under *Connick*, speech like Levy's would probably not be considered speech on a matter of public concern because it sounds much like a personal "workplace" grievance.

While it surely is worthwhile for the Court to embrace the idea that children can contribute to this marketplace of ideas—something that had been missing from the Court's school speech opinions since *Tinker*[156]—*Mahanoy* erroneously suggests the marketplace of ideas is the only animating theory of the First Amendment. Protecting the marketplace of ideas and the advancement of democratic self-governance are the dominant theories in the Court's jurisprudence.[157] But the Court has never held that speech on matters of private concern fall outside of the First Amendment entirely,[158] and it is dangerous to gives schools broad authority to regulate expression on

[152] *Snyder*, 562 U.S. at 454.

[153] *Id.*

[154] *Rankin*, 483 U.S. at 379–80.

[155] *Id.* at 394–98 (Scalia, J., dissenting).

[156] *See* Mary-Rose Papandrea, *The Missing Marketplace of Ideas Theory*, 94 Notre Dame L. Rev. 1725, 1735–41 (2019) (arguing that the Court has failed to embrace the marketplace of ideas theory in its student speech cases after *Tinker*).

[157] *See* Ashutosh Bhagwat, *The Democratic First Amendment*, 110 N.W.U. L. Rev. 1097, 1102 (2016) (noting a "broad consensus" that the fundamental animating theory of the First Amendment is the advancement of democratic self-governance).

[158] *See* Randy J. Kozel, *Business Courts and Parity: A Theory of Public Employee Rights*, 53 Wm & Mary L. Rev. 1985, 2016 (2012) (noting the Court has never held private concern speech is "subject to suppression").

Fraser reads like a grab bag of justifications for granting schools this broad authority; indeed, as the Court later admitted, "[t]he mode of analysis employed in *Fraser* is not entirely clear."[171] The Court gave lip-service to *Tinker*'s assertion that students retain their constitutional rights at school, and that the "fundamental values" of "a democratic society" must "include tolerance of divergent political and religious views."[172] But the Court also deferred to the school's "basic educational mission" to teach "the boundaries of socially appropriate behavior" and proclaimed that "[e]ven the most heated political discourse in a democratic society requires consideration for the personal sensibilities of the other participants and audiences."[173]

Fraser also rests on the principle that "the constitutional rights of students in public school are not automatically coextensive with the rights of adults in other settings."[174] The Court memorably quipped that "'the First Amendment gives a high school student the classroom right to wear Tinker's armband, but not Cohen's jacket.'"[175] In *Cohen v. California*,[176] the Court held that Paul Cohen had a constitutional right to proclaim his political opposition to mandatory conscription with his "Fuck the Draft" jacket. *Cohen* noted that this slogan was not "obscene,"[177] and that Cohen's use of a four-letter word was not "fighting words" because "[n]o individual actually or likely to be present could reasonably have regarded the words on appellant's jacket as a direct personal insult."[178] There was also no evidence that Cohen intentionally provoked a hostile reaction, or "that anyone who saw Cohen was in fact violently aroused."[179] Citing *Tinker*, the Court declared that "an 'undifferentiated fear or apprehension of

[171] Morse v. Frederick, 551 U.S. 393, 404 (2007). *Morse* said *Fraser* might have been decided based on the content of Fraser's speech, or it might have been about deferring to school officials to determine the appropriate manner of speech in a classroom or school assembly. *Id.*

[172] *Fraser*, 478 U.S. at 681.

[173] *Id.*

[174] *Id.* at 682. The Court repeats this sentence in *Morse* to support another *Tinker* exception for speech reasonably interpreted to promote illegal drug use. *Morse*, 551 U.S. at 404–05.

[175] *Fraser*, 478 U.S. at 682 (quoting Thomas v. Bd. of Educ., Granville Cent. Sch. Dist., 607 F.2d 1043, 1057 (2d Cir. 1979) (Newman, J., concurring in result)).

[176] 403 U.S. 15 (1971).

[177] *Id.* at 20 ("It cannot plausibly be maintained that this vulgar allusion to the Selective Service System would conjure up such psychic stimulation in anyone likely to be confronted with Cohen's crudely defaced jacket.").

[178] *Id.*

[179] *Id.*

exposure to patently offensive depictions of sex."[209] Likewise, he dissented in *United States v. Playboy Entertainment Group, Inc.*,[210] which concerned a federal statute regulating the problem of "signal bleed" from sexually oriented cable channels. There, Breyer argued that "our prior cases recognize that, where the protection of children is at issue, the First Amendment poses a barrier that properly is high, but not insurmountable."[211]

Perhaps this evolving doubt about the constitutional status of profanity regulations and the scope of minors' speech rights explains why *Mahanoy* stopped well short of holding that schools cannot restrict lewd or profane student speech on social media. Rather than adopting that bright-line rule, *Mahanoy* held merely that the school's asserted interest in "teaching good manners and consequently in punishing the use of vulgar language aimed at part of the school community" was "insufficient" under the facts of the case.[212] Citing both Brennan's *Fraser* concurrence and the *Morse* dicta, the Court stated that the strength of the school's interest "is weakened considerably by the fact that B.L. spoke outside the school on her own time."[213] The Court also mentioned the content of her message, noting that not only were Levy's posts made away from school, but they "encompassed a message, an expression of [her] irritation with, and criticism of, the school and cheerleading communities."[214] The Court added that the school failed to show a "general effort to prevent students from using vulgarity outside the classroom."[215] *Mahanoy* therefore leaves room for schools to restrict the manner or mode of off-campus speech in cases that are factually distinct, such as where the speech lacks a meaningful message of any kind and/or where the school has engaged in an effort to prevent students' use of vulgarity wherever they might be. In comparison, the district court had specifically rejected the idea that a school could "circumvent *Tinker* [and] *Fraser* . . . by simply defining its educational mission in a way that prohibits off-campus vulgarity," adding that under such an approach,

---

209 *Id.* at 743 (Breyer, J.) (plurality opinion).

210 529 U.S. 803 (2000).

211 *Id.* at 847 (Breyer, J., dissenting).

212 Mahanoy Area Sch. Dist. v. B.L., 141 S. Ct. 2038, 2047 (2021).

213 *Id.*

214 *Id.*

215 *Id.*

schools would be able to punish students for making a vulgar remark at a private party and serve as the "Thought Police."[216]

Some courts have been reluctant to rely on *Fraser* to uphold restrictions on speech created outside of school,[217] and for good reason. As Justice Sotomayor remarked at oral argument, among young people, "how much you curse is a badge of honor."[218] But after *Mahanoy*, it appears that schools might be able to regulate students' use of lewd, profane, indecent, or offensive expression off campus in some instances. The Court's failure to grapple explicitly with how to reconcile *Cohen*, *Brunetti*, *Fraser*, *Ginsberg*, *Pico*, *Pacifica*, and *Brown* leaves the precise contours of this power unclear. In future cases, the Court will have to grapple more directly with schools' authority to restrict profanity and other kinds of "offensive" speech when students are not on school grounds or otherwise engaged in a school activity. In addition, the Court should address the possibility that school officials would use authority to regulate "good manners" as a "pretext" for regulating critical or mocking speech.[219] As the Court asserted in *Cohen*, "[W]e cannot indulge the facile assumption that one can forbid particular words without also running a substantial risk of suppressing ideas in the process. Indeed, governments might soon seize upon the censorship of particular words as a convenient guise for banning the expression of unpopular views."[220]

III. Special Circumstances and "First Amendment Leeway"

In ordinary First Amendment cases, the Court abhors ad hoc balancing tests and has never embraced proportionality review. In *United States v. Stevens*,[221] for example, the Court rejected the

---

[216] B.L. *ex rel.* Levy v. Mahanoy Area Sch. Dist., 376 F. Supp. 3d 429, 442 (M.D. Pa. 2019), *aff'd*, 964 F.3d 170 (3d Cir. 2020), *aff'd*, 141 S. Ct. 2038 (2021).

[217] *See*, *e.g.*, Kowalski v. Berkeley Cnty. Schs., 652 F.3d 565, 573–74 (4th Cir. 2011) (declining to address whether schools also had authority to punish a student's lewd and vulgar online speech under *Fraser*); Bell v. Itawamba Cnty. Sch. Bd., 799 F.3d 379, 391–92 (5th Cir. 2015) (en banc) (applying *Tinker* in a case involving speech that allegedly threatened a teacher; the court noted that the school board did not claim it disciplined the student for the lewdness of his comments).

[218] Oral Argument Transcript, *supra* note 30, at 20.

[219] Stone, *supra* note 6, at 277 (explaining "we learned that government officials will often defend their restrictions of speech on grounds quite different from their real motivations for the suppression, which will often be to silence their critics and to suppress ideas they do not like").

[220] Cohen v. California, 403 U.S. 15, 26 (1971).

[221] 559 U.S. 460 (2010).

government's argument that additional categories of unprotected speech could be determined "on the basis of a simple cost-benefit analysis" balancing the "relative social costs and benefits" of protecting and not protecting the speech.[222] The Court reiterated its disdain for a "'simple balancing test'" in *Brown*, even though the state asserted an interest in protecting children.[223] In *Reed v. Town of Gilbert*,[224] six Justices declared that content-based laws are always subject to strict scrutiny "regardless of the government's benign motive, content-neutral justification, or lack of 'animus toward the ideas contained' in the regulated speech."[225] Many scholars have criticized the Court's strict categorical approach to First Amendment questions and have urged the Court to consider "some form of doctrinal adjustment."[226]

When Chief Justice Roberts assigned the *Mahanoy* opinion to Justice Breyer, it was clear what sort of opinion he would write (and not only because Breyer announced his intentions from the bench[227]). Breyer has long argued that categorical rules "lack the flexibility necessary to allow government to respond to very serious practical problems without sacrificing the free exchange of ideas the First Amendment is designed to protect."[228] Instead, he has argued, the Court "would do better to treat this Court's speech-related categories not as outcome-determinative rules, but instead as rules of thumb."[229] He would "appeal more often and more directly to the values the First

---

[222] *Id.* at 470.

[223] Brown v. Ent. Merchants Ass'n, 564 U.S. 786, 792 (2011) (quoting *Stevens*, 559 U.S. at 470).

[224] 576 U.S. 155 (2015).

[225] *Id.* at 166 (quoting Cincinnati v. Discovery Network, Inc., 507 U.S. 410, 429 (1993)).

[226] David S. Han, *Transparency in First Amendment Doctrine*, 65 Emory L.J. 359, 424–25 (2015) ("[T]he case law suggests that the current doctrinal approach pushes too far in the direction of categorical rules at the expense of transparency and flexibility, and that some form of doctrinal adjustment is warranted."); *see also* Richard A. Posner, *Pragmatism Versus Purposivism in First Amendment Analysis*, 54 Stan. L. Rev. 737, 740 (2002) ("[T]he balancing approach has considerable merit in First Amendment cases outside the heartland of settled law. . . .").

[227] *See* notes 30–33, *supra*.

[228] Denver Area Educ. Telecomm. Consortium, Inc. v. FCC, 518 U.S. 727, 740 (1996) (Breyer, J.) (plurality opinion); *see also Reed*, 576 U.S. at 175–76 (Breyer, J., concurring in judgment) ("The First Amendment requires greater judicial sensitivity both to the Amendment's expressive objectives and to the public's legitimate need for regulation than a simple recitation of categories, such as 'content discrimination' and 'strict scrutiny,' would permit.").

[229] Iancu v. Brunetti, 139 S. Ct. 2294, 2304 (2019) (Breyer, J., concurring in part and dissenting in part).

Amendment seeks to protect" and inquire "whether the regulation at issue 'works speech-related harm that is out of proportion to its justifications.'"[230]

It is not remarkable that Breyer wrote an opinion arguing that school officials should have unstructured First Amendment "leeway" to regulate student expression.[231] What is remarkable is that he convinced everyone but Thomas to join it. As argued above, the Justices likely felt overwhelmed with the ramifications of new technology and the lack of robust First Amendment doctrine to address the most troubling issues at school. In addition, the Court has never had a particularly coherent approach to minors and the First Amendment. Given the "good policy reasons" for giving schools broad authority over student speech rights, the Court majority may not have been so concerned with entrusting the speech rights of minors to the whims of such an uncertain approach.

But *Mahanoy* illustrates some of the dangers of moving away from a structured approach to the First Amendment. First, although Breyer has long advocated for a proportionality approach to First Amendment questions, it is not entirely clear that is what he embraced in *Mahanoy*. Instead, Breyer's opinion mostly offers an ad hoc resolution of the case before the Court with a handful of "rules of thumb" that will not provide much guidance for more difficult student speech cases. Second, this approach suggests an unwarranted abandonment of bedrock First Amendment principles, at least when the government is acting in its institutional or managerial capacity.

Affording First Amendment "leeway" to the government when it acts in its managerial capacity is attractive because rigid adherence to the Court's "ordinary" First Amendment doctrine in such contexts would lead to nonsensical outcomes. For example, a strict rule against content-based or viewpoint-based discrimination in public schools would make it impossible for schools to make curricular choices and to teach effectively.[232] Similarly, in the public employment context, the government as employer must have some ability to control the speech of its employees to make sure that the work is performed

---

[230] *Id.* at 2305 (quoting United States v. Alvarez, 567 U.S. 709, 730 (2012)).

[231] Mahanoy Area Sch. Dist. v. B.L., 141 S. Ct. 2038, 2045, 2046 (2021).

[232] *See id.* at 2050 (Alito, J., concurring) (noting "it would be impossible to see how a school could function if administrators and teachers could not regulate on-premises speech, including by imposing content-based restrictions in the classroom").

effectively, and this will necessarily mean some content-based and viewpoint-based distinctions. If the government opens a new forum to promote diverse student speech, it should not be required to let non-students speak as well.[233] And the government could not function if it had no ability to choose the content of its own messages.[234]

But offering "leeway" is not the same as a structured proportionality inquiry. Under a proportionality inquiry, a court "asks whether the regulation at issue works harm to First Amendment interests that is disproportionate in light of the relevant regulatory objectives."[235] As Justice Breyer himself has explained, this proportionality inquiry "requires examining the seriousness of the harm to speech, the importance of the countervailing objectives, the extent to which the law will achieve those objectives, and whether there are other, less restrictive ways of doing so."[236] Although Justice Breyer has long advocated for a proportionality approach to constitutional law questions, he does not expressly label his analytical approach in *Mahanoy* a proportionality inquiry, or even as a balancing test. Breyer also does not cite any of his prior opinions embracing a less rigid approach to First Amendment questions. It is not clear whether Breyer meant this opinion to be a proportionality inquiry or whether he purposefully avoided using that label, perhaps to secure the votes of the other Justices.

First Amendment "leeway" also gives schools more power to restrict speech without having to worry about "ordinary" First Amendment principles. *Mahanoy* suggests that most of these principles are negotiable, including parental rights to govern the upbringing of their children, minors' rights to speak and receive speech, the ban on a heckler's veto, concerns about content-based and viewpoint-based speech restrictions, and general distrust of the government when it claims to be regulating merely the "mode" of expression. A true proportionality inquiry would not only interrogate the school's interests

[233] *See, e.g.*, Rosenberger v. Rector & Visitors of Univ. of Va., 515 U.S. 819 (1995) (analyzing student activity fund restrictions).

[234] Walker v. Tex. Div., Sons of Confederate Veterans, Inc., 576 U.S. 200, 207–08 (2015) (explaining why "[w]hen the government speaks, it is not barred by the Free Speech Clause from determining the content of what it says").

[235] Reed v. Town of Gilbert, 576 U.S. 155, 179 (2015) (Breyer, J., concurring).

[236] *Id.*; *see also* Vicki C. Jackson, *Constitutional Law in an Age of Proportionality*, 124 YALE L.J. 3094, 3098–101 (2015) (outlining the "structured proportionality analysis" common in many other countries).

carefully and evaluate the speaker's rights vigorously, but would also consider whether there are less restrictive means to achieve the school's objectives and (under a "proportionality as such" inquiry) whether the strength of the school's interest is sufficient to justify the specific harm to a student's free speech rights.[237]

Granting schools unstructured "leeway" to regulate student speech is dangerous; in contrast, a true proportionality inquiry is much more palatable and could bring order to the disorder of the Court's jurisprudence in this area. Although the question presented to the Court was solely whether *Tinker* should apply to off-campus speech, *Mahanoy* could be read as advancing a new, universal approach for all student speech cases. To be sure, the Court nowhere indicates that this is its intention; at the outset of the majority opinion, the Court recites its prior school speech cases as the governing framework.[238] The Court also suggests that the opinion is meant to be narrow. Nevertheless, it is not hard to imagine how the Court's student speech cases could be collapsed into a single inquiry applicable in every situation, regardless of what sort of speech is at issue and where it takes place. After all, such an inquiry would permit a court to evaluate the strength of a school's interest—whether it is preventing disruption of the educational process (*Tinker*), teaching students about civil discourse (*Fraser*), protecting them from speech that advocates illegal drug use (*Morse*), or controlling speech that bears the imprimatur of the school (*Hazelwood School District v. Kuhlmeier*[239]). The showing the school would need to make in each instance could vary depending on the strength of the school's interest and the value of the student speech at issue (with political speech getting more protection).

This approach to student-speech issues could have some benefits.[240] It would eliminate the "proliferation of categories of student speech" that are "very cumbersome for school officials and lower court judges to understand and use."[241] Theoretically, a proportionality

---

[237] Jackson, *supra* note 236 (explaining how proportionality review works in other countries).

[238] *Id.* at 2044–45.

[239] 484 U.S. 260 (1988).

[240] A cynic might add that this approach would also have the benefit of "produc[ing] a result, in every case, that will make a majority of the Court happy with the law." Morrison v. Olson, 487 U.S. 654, 734 (1988).

[241] Ross, *supra* note 67, at 53.

approach could also result in more robust student speech protection.[242] For example, currently schools do not have to make any showing at all when regulating lewd, obscene, or indecent expression occurring on campus (*Fraser*), or when regulating expression reasonably interpreted as advocating for illegal drug use (*Morse*), and under *Hazelwood*, schools can restrict speech bearing the imprimatur of the school whenever they can show a legitimate pedagogical interest (essentially a "reasonable" basis, the lowest level of constitutional scrutiny). Under a proportionality approach, the constitutionality of a speech regulation would vary case by case, and in cases where the school's interest is relatively weak and the student's interest is strong, the student might prevail. Courts might expand their inquiry to ask whether schools could handle troublesome student speech in alternative ways, such as through counseling, "teachable moments," or less draconian punishments.

But it seems extremely unlikely that students would receive more speech protection under a proportionality approach unless the Court confronts head-on the many unresolved issues it has dodged with respect to school speech. Moving to a proportionality inquiry would mean that schools would no longer have to shoehorn their speech regulations to fit the requirements of *Tinker*, *Fraser*, *Morse*, and *Hazelwood*. In cases involving harassing, violent, and disrespectful speech, courts might deeply discount the value of any such expression, particularly if it regards the speech as "private" speech, and emphasizes instead the harms such speech caused or could potentially cause. The Court's failure to reconcile its school speech cases and non-school juvenile speech cases would continue to grow.

A related problem is that courts tend to be very deferential to school authorities, both when evaluating a school's interest in regulating speech and when evaluating a school's interpretation of the student speech at issue. In *West Virginia Board of Education v. Barnette*,[243] the Court rejected the suggestion that it lacked "competence" to judge what is best for public education, stating that "we act in these [schoolhouse] matters not by authority of our competency but by force of our commissions."[244] The Court concluded that schools

---

[242] A balancing can result in the expansion or contraction of constitutional rights. *See* T. Alexander Aleinikoff, *Constitutional Law in the Age of Balancing*, 96 Yale L.J. 943, 960–61 (1987).

[243] 319 U.S. 624 (1943).

[244] *Id.* at 640–41.

"have, of course, important, delicate, and highly discretionary functions, but none that they may not perform within the limits of the Bill of Rights."[245] As time went on, however, the Court's deference has grown, expanding to include even deference to a school's interpretation of the meaning of its students' speech.[246]

Furthermore, the Court needs to be careful about relying on the checks and balances of the political system to provide the guardrails on government overreaching. This approach is often both empirically and theoretically questionable. As a practical matter, the government entity embracing a speech regulation does so under the radar without much (or any) public oversight. In *Mahanoy*, for example, the school gave the cheer coaches freedom to draft their own rules and conditions for cheer team membership. To be sure, the school is subject to the oversight of the school board, which in turn is subject to democratic oversight through public meetings and elections. But in this instance, the total delegation of power to the coaches means that there was no meaningful oversight. It is a mistake to assume that the public has engaged in meaningful democratic deliberation on speech policies, especially because state boards of education or even local school boards often defer to school officials to adopt whatever policies they want.[247] As a theoretical matter, deference to the democratic process when constitutional rights are at issue is troublesome, particularly in the context of First Amendment rights. As the Court itself recognized in *Mahanoy*, "popular ideas have less need for protection" under the First Amendment.[248]

Conclusion

In the intervening years between *Tinker* and *Mahanoy*, the Court decided several public school Fourth Amendment cases that

---

[245] *Id.*

[246] Morse v. Frederick, 551 U.S. 393, 401 (2007) (holding that the interpretation of a banner as advocating the use of illegal drugs is "plainly a reasonable one"). In his *Morse* concurrence, Breyer made clear his preference to defer to school officials, arguing that "school officials need a degree of flexible authority to respond to disciplinary challenges" and "no one wishes to substitute courts for school boards, or to turn the judge's chambers into the principal's office." *id.* at 428 (Breyer, J., concurring in part).

[247] *See* Gia B. Lee, *First Amendment Enforcement in Government Institutions and Programs*, 56 UCLA L. Rev. 1691, 1716–17 (2009) (discussing the lack of meaningful democratic oversight of school speech policies).

[248] 141 S. Ct. at 2046.

demonstrated increasing deference to school officials with a corresponding lack of concern for students' constitutional rights. In *New Jersey v. T.L.O.*,[249] the Court rejected the probable cause standard for school searches and replaced it with a balancing test that considers the "reasonableness, under all the circumstances, of the search."[250] In his separate opinion, Justice Brennan attacked the majority's decision to embrace a "Rohrschach-like 'balancing test'" that "finds support neither in precedent nor policy and portends a dangerous weakening of the purpose of the Fourth Amendment to protect the privacy and security of our citizens."[251] Brennan predicted that the new "reasonableness" test "will likely spawn increased litigation and greater uncertainty among teachers and administrators."[252] Brennan concluded that the increasing use of "balancing tests" in this case and in others is "doctrinally destructive nihilism" that is a "convenient umbrella under which a majority that cannot agree on a genuine rationale can conceal its differences."[253]

Justice Brennan could have written the same dissent in *Mahanoy* had he still been on the Court. While *Mahanoy* may have reached the correct result on the facts before it, the Court's embrace of an ad hoc analysis threatens to obliterate student speech rights. The Court also papers over some significant doctrinal questions. Some of these questions concern public school students specifically, such as whether *Tinker* tolerates a heckler's veto. Other questions concern the First Amendment more generally, such as what sort of speech rights minors enjoy as speakers, whether the First Amendment should embrace a hierarchy of speech, and whether and when the government can restrict profanity. First Amendment "leeway" is not the same thing as a structural proportionality inquiry, which could offer a more promising and coherent approach to student speech rights. If the Court embraces a proportionality approach to student speech rights more generally, it should make sure it does not disregard bedrock First Amendment principles and fail to recognize the dangers of granting school officials broad authority to regulate student speech wherever it might occur.

---

[249] 469 U.S. 325, 341 (1985).

[250] *Id.* at 341.

[251] *Id.* at 357–58 (Brennan, J., concurring in part and dissenting in part).

[252] *Id.* at 365.

[253] *Id.* at 369–70.

BENJAMIN I. SACHS

SAFETY, HEALTH, AND UNION ACCESS IN CEDAR POINT NURSERY

From the late 1960s until the mid-1970s the United Farm Workers (UFW) union was embroiled in a war, and not merely a figurative one, with a corrupt coalition of agricultural employers and the International Brotherhood of Teamsters (IBT). During this era, union organizing of California farmworkers was plagued by open, violent conflict. After years of such bloody confrontations, the California legislature enacted a labor law designed to allow the UFW to engage in peaceful unionization efforts and win representation rights through secret ballot elections. Winning union elections, in turn, would position the UFW to secure its substantive goals: collective bargaining agreements that protect farmworkers from pesticide poisoning and raise their wages. The Agricultural Labor Relations Act (ALRA) of 1975 was thus California's attempt to replace open warfare with a union elections process that would enable farmworkers to peacefully bargain for safety and health and livable wages.[1] The access provision

Benjamin I. Sachs is Kestnbaum Professor of Labor and Industry, Harvard Law School.

Author's note: The author thanks Kate Andrias, Yochai Benkler, Molly Brady, Jerry Cohen, and David Strauss for helpful discussion and suggestions. He thanks Anita Alem, Mackenzie Bouverat, Rachel Casper, Jon Levitan, Fred Messner, and Nikita Rumsey for superb research assistance.

[1] *See* Cal. Lab. Code Ann. §§ 1140 et seq.

The Supreme Court Review, 2022.
 Published by The University of Chicago Press. https://doi.org/10.1086/720408

challenged in *Cedar Point Nursery v. Hassid*[2]—which gives union organizers the right to talk to farmworkers on grower property as part of the election process—is an integral piece of that labor law.[3]

California needed to enact a special labor law for farmworkers because agricultural workers are excluded from the coverage of federal labor law and have been since the beginning; the National Labor Relations Act's (NLRA) definition of employee does "not include any individual employed as an agricultural laborer."[4] The ALRA however provides farmworkers with a process for organizing and electing union representatives similar to the one contained in the NLRA.[5] The process involves union organizers speaking with farmworkers, asking them to sign cards authorizing union representation, and then petitioning for a secret ballot election in which the workers vote yes or no on unionization.[6] If the workers vote to unionize, the grower-employer then has a legal obligation to bargain collectively with the workers' union over terms and conditions of employment, including safety and health.[7]

Given the difficulties inherent in building electoral support among a highly mobile workforce,[8] the Agricultural Labor Relations Board (ALRB)—the state agency charged with administering the Act—promulgated a rule establishing that the right to unionization includes "the right of access by union organizers to the premises of an agricultural employer for the purpose of meeting and talking with employees and soliciting their support."[9] Under this access provision, a maximum of two union organizers may enter an employer's property

---

[2] 141 S. Ct. 2063 (2021).

[3] *See* Cal. Code Regs., tit. 8, § 20900(e).

[4] *See* 29 U.S.C. § 152; Ira Katznelson, When Affirmative Action Was White: An Untold History of Racial Inequality in Twentieth-Century America 54–71 (2005).

[5] For a description of that process, see, for example, Benjamin I. Sachs, *Enabling Employee Choice: A Structural Approach to the Rules of Union Organizing*, 123 Harv. L. Rev. 655, 664–67 (2010). There are important differences between the NLRA and the ALRA. *See generally* Philip Martin, *A Comparison of California's ALRA and the Federal NLRA*, 37 Cal. Agric. 6 (1983); Tracy E. Sagle, *The ALRB—Twenty Years Later*, 8 San Joaquin Agric. L. Rev. 139 (1998).

[6] *See* Cal. Lab. Code. Ann. §§ 1152, 1156, 1156.3.

[7] *See* Cal. Lab. Code Ann. §§ 1153(e), 1155.2.

[8] *See, e.g.*, Agric. Lab. Rels. Bd. v. Superior Ct., 16 Cal. 3d 392, 414–15 (1976); *see also infra* text accompanying notes 80–85.

[9] Cal. Code Regs., tit. 8, § 20900(e).

in order to speak to workers for a maximum of three hours in a day—one hour before work begins, one hour during the workers' lunch break, and one hour after work ends—during a maximum of four thirty-day periods in a year.[10] Because the right to access is tied to the union electoral process, it terminates after an election is held.[11] A stated purpose of both the statute and the regulation is "bringing certainty and a sense of fair play to presently unstable and potentially volatile conditions in the agricultural fields of California."[12]

The access provision was challenged by two large California agricultural employers ("growers") as effecting an unconstitutional taking of property under the Fifth and Fourteenth Amendments.[13] In its opinion, the Supreme Court is clear about its normative orientation to the challenge: it writes that judicial protection of property rights "is necessary to preserve freedom" and "empowers persons to shape and to plan their own destiny in a world where governments are always eager to do so for them."[14] Wary of California interfering with large agricultural employers' ability to shape their own destinies, the Court holds that the union access provision "appropriates for the enjoyment of third parties the owners' right to exclude."[15] And because the "right to exclude is one of the most treasured rights of property ownership," the state regulation granting limited access to the growers' property constitutes a per se physical taking.[16] California, if it wishes to provide union organizers access to grower property, must pay the growers for that access.

The practical implications of the *Cedar Point* holding for labor law, outside the California farmworker context, are—for better or worse—most likely limited.[17] This is true because union access rights in the

[10] *See id.* § 20900(e)(3)(A)–(B).

[11] *See id.* § 29000(e)(1)(C).

[12] *See* 1975 Cal. Stat. 4013, § 1; CAL. CODE. REGS., tit. 8, § 20900(d).

[13] *Cedar Point*, 141 S. Ct. at 2069–70. Cedar Point Nursery is a strawberry grower with approximately 500 employees; Fowler Packing a grape and citrus grower with more than 2,000 employees. *Id.*

[14] *Id.* at 2071 (internal citations omitted).

[15] *Id.* at 2072.

[16] *Id.* (internal quotation marks omitted).

[17] I say most likely because, as Professor Nikolas Bowie points out, the "right to exclude" could theoretically be read to encompass the right of an employer to fire an employee. *See* Nikolas Bowie, *Antidemocracy*, 135 HARV. L. REV. 160, 196 (2021). As Bowie puts it, "[t]o take

rest of the private sector have already been decimated by the Supreme Court through its cramped reading of the NLRA. In *Lechmere, Inc. v. NLRB*, decided in 1992, the Court held that union organizers have no right to access employees on company property except in the very rare cases where employees are "by virtue of their employment, . . . isolated from the ordinary flow of information that characterizes our society."[18] Describing the union's burden of establishing the requisite isolation as a "heavy one," the *Lechmere* rule allows access only in contexts like logging and mining camps—contexts that hardly exist today.[19]

To be sure, *Cedar Point* meaningfully limits the prospects for legislative amendments to the NLRA that would expand organizer access rights. Recognizing, as California did, the critical importance of such access rights—recognizing, as the access regulation itself states, that the effectiveness of unionization rights "depends in some measure on the ability of employees to learn the advantages [] of organization from others"[20]—numerous scholars and policy makers have argued that the NLRA ought to be amended in just this way.[21] Those attempts now face a constitutional barrier. And *Cedar Point* may also threaten, or at least raise questions about, other important NLRB doctrines, including those regarding access rights for off-duty employees and off-site employees,[22] and potentially those regarding employee use of employer email systems[23] and employee rights to discuss unionization at work.[24]

---

the vocabulary of *Cedar Point*, firing is nothing more than the 'right to exclude' a worker from the employer's private property." If this is correct then labor law's prohibition on discharging employees for union activities—a core component of any imaginable labor law regime—would amount to an uncompensated taking.

[18] 502 U.S. 527, 540 (1992).

[19] *Id.*

[20] Cal. Code Regs., tit. 8, § 20900(b).

[21] *See, e.g.*, Sharon Block & Benjamin Sachs, Clean Slate for Worker Power: Building a Just Economy and Democracy 50 (2018) ("[T]he new statute must provide union organizers with expanded access rights to workers. Critically, these rights must include the ability to meet with workers at work.").

[22] *See, e.g.*, First Healthcare Corp. v. NLRB, 344 F.3d 523 (2003).

[23] *See, e.g.*, Purple Commc'ns, 361 N.L.R.B. 1050 (2014), *rev'd* by Caesars Ent., 368 N.L.R.B. 143 (2019).

[24] *See* Republic Aviation Corp. v. NLRB, 324 U.S. 793 (1945). These doctrines all involve the rights of the property owner's employees—who enjoy a license, albeit limited to one degree or another, to enter the property in question—and so would require a different analysis than the one provided by the *Cedar Point* Court.

The focus of this essay is not, however, on what *Cedar Point* may or may not imply about future doctrinal development. Nor is it about the very important ways in which the case exemplifies this Supreme Court's privileging of business interests over workers' rights,[25] its elevation of property values over democratic ones,[26] and its denigration of unions across multiple areas of law.[27] Instead, this essay makes a different argument: that *Cedar Point* is internally inconsistent and that it is wrong on its own terms. The fact that such internal inconsistency—with its predictable political slant—is all too common for this Court neither excuses the practice nor renders a critique of it moot.

The inconsistency in *Cedar Point* can be traced to the trio of exceptions, which the Court announces, to the general rule that a regulation granting access to property "appropriates" the right to exclude and thereby constitutes a per se taking.[28] It is the third in this trio of exceptions that is relevant here.[29]

According to the Court, the government can require property owners to cede a right of access as a condition of receiving "certain benefits," or in order to avoid a "risk posed to the public," without effecting a taking.[30] The Court explains that the benefits conveyed or the risks avoided by such access conditions must constitute a "legitimate police power purpose."[31] And, borrowing from the *Nollan* and *Dolan* cases, the Court holds that the access condition must bear an "essential nexus" to that police-power purpose and there must be a "rough proportionality" between the police-power purpose and the

---

[25] *See generally* Mark Tushnet, In the Balance: Law and Politics on the Roberts Court 204, 213 (2013); Jedidiah Purdy, *Beyond the Bosses' Constitution: The First Amendment and Class Entrenchment*, 118 Colum. L. Rev. 2161 (2018).

[26] Bowie, *supra* note 17, at 195–96.

[27] *See, e.g.*, Janus v. AFSCME, 138 S. Ct. 2448 (2018); Epic Sys. v. Lewis, 138 S. Ct. 1612 (2018).

[28] Cedar Point Nursery v. Hassid, 141 S. Ct. 2063, 2078–80 (2021).

[29] The first exception is that the holding "does nothing to efface the distinction between trespass and takings," and thus that "[i]solated physical invasions, not undertaken pursuant to a granted right of access, are properly assessed as individual torts rather than appropriations of a property right." *Id.* at 2078. The second exception is, as the Court explains, that "many government-authorized physical invasions will not amount to takings because they are consistent with longstanding background restrictions on property rights," and thus "the government does not take a property interest when it merely asserts a pre-existing limitation upon the landowner's title." *Id.* at 2079 (internal citations omitted). Much can be said about these other two exceptions as well. *See, e.g.*, *id.* at 2088–89 (Breyer, J., dissenting); Bowie, *supra* note 17, at 195–96.

[30] *Cedar Point*, 141 S. Ct. at 2079–80.

[31] *Id.* at 2079.

extent of the access condition imposed on the property owner.[32] The Court gives, as an illustrating example of such an access condition that does not constitute a taking, government safety and health inspections. In particular, the Court points to a regime of EPA pesticide inspections.[33] As the Court puts it, "unlike standard health and safety inspections, the [California union] access regulation is not germane to any benefit provided to agricultural employers or any risk posed to the public."[34]

Cedar Point is internally inconsistent because the union access provision that the Court holds to be a taking fits comfortably within the Court's third exception to its takings rule. There are two ways to see why this is so. One, the ALRA and its access provision are a response to the kind of violence that can overtake union organizing in the absence of an institutionalized process for workers to form and join unions.[35] In fact, the ALRA and its access regulation were a direct response to widespread violence that engulfed California farms in the years leading up to the Act's passage. Such violence—the quintessential threat to public safety whose quelling is the quintessential police power purpose—was the product of a war that the growers and their partners in the Teamsters union waged against the UFW.[36] California

---

[32] *Id.* (citing Nollan v. Cal. Coastal Comm'n, 483 U.S. 825 (1987), and Dolan v. City of Tigard, 512 U.S. 374 (1994)).

[33] 141 S. Ct. at 2079–80. According to the Court, "[w]hen the government conditions the grant of a benefit such as a permit, license, or registration on allowing access for reasonable health and safety inspections, both the nexus and rough proportionality requirements" are easily satisfied. *Id.* at 2079.

[34] *Id.* at 2080. The ways in which the Court's analysis here mirrors the analysis in *Lochner* are uncanny. *See infra* text accompanying notes 125–128.

[35] *See, e.g.*, Donald R. Gitto, *Strike Violence: The NLRB's Reluctance to Wield its Broad Remedial Power*, 50 Fordham L. Rev. 1371, 1371 (1982) ("In the early days of the American labor movement, numerous bloody confrontations between labor and management marred the workers' struggle for higher wages, shorter hours and safer working conditions. The passage of the National Labor Relations Act . . . in 1935 manifested the federal government's concern for labor peace and the concomitant reduction of industrial strife."); Mariano-Florentino Cuéllar et al., *Twentieth-Century America as a Developing Country: Conflict, Institutions, and the Evolution of Public Law*, 57 Harv. J. on Legis. 25, 43–44 (2020) ("The sharp decline in the level of industrial violence is one of the greatest achievements of the National Labor Relations Board." (quoting Philip Taft & Philip Ross, *American Labor Violence: Its Causes, Character, and Outcome*, *in* Violence in America: Historical and Comparative Perspectives, 281, 384 (Hugh Davis Graham & Ted Robert Gurr eds., 1969)).

[36] Organizers involved in the conflict, as well as scholars of the period, routinely use "war" to describe the nature of farmworker organizing at the time. *See, e.g.*, Susan Ferriss & Ricardo Sandoval, The Fight in the Fields: Cesar Chavez and the Farmworkers Movement 182 (1997) (quoting UFW member Clementina Carmona Olloqui); Ronald B.

legislators and regulators understood that one way to end the violence in the fields was by establishing a routinized system of union elections and collective bargaining, supported by a series of protections for union organizing activity, including a limited right of organizer access to grower property. Understood this way, the access provision is entirely germane to a benefit provided to agricultural employers and to a risk posed to the public: the benefit was public safety in the truest sense of the term; the risk was its opposite. Moreover, allowing a tightly limited number of union organizers limited access to farm property in order to end deadly clashes should also satisfy the essential nexus and rough proportionality requirements.

Two, the ALRA and its access provisions are a regulatory approach to protecting public and workplace health and, in particular, protecting workers and consumers from the risk posed by pesticides—the very risk *Cedar Point* uses to exemplify a context where granting access rights does not effect a taking. Indeed, in the years leading up to enactment of the ALRA, one of the UFW's primary missions was protecting farmworkers and consumers from pesticide poisoning, and the union campaigned explicitly on the platform of using collective bargaining as a means to achieve this end. By facilitating unionization, the ALRA and its access provisions facilitated collective bargaining agreements that contained a robust system of safety and health measures, including an entire raft of pesticide protection measures. Collective bargaining, in other words, serves as a functional substitute for a safety and health inspections regime: it addresses the same risk and requires the same limited grant of access rights. According to the Court's own reasoning, the access provision in the ALRA – like a safety and health inspections regime—qualifies for the third exception to the Court's takings rule.

I. From "Blood in the Fields"[37] to Union Elections

As the UFW grew in strength across the mid and late 1960s—including through its organizing of a national grape boycott, "the most ambitious and successful boycott in American history"[38]—its

Taylor, A Study in the Acquisition & Use of Power: Chavez and the Farm Workers 293 (1975).

[37] Ferriss & Sandoval, *supra* note 36, at 159.

[38] *Id.* at 139.

efforts were met with wrathful opposition by growers. California agribusiness turned to the courts to shut down the UFW's activity, and successfully secured a slew of (generally unconstitutional) injunctions against the union's strikes and pickets.[39] They also relied on oftentimes brutal local law enforcement action to suppress the union's activism.[40] But the growers had a third strategy for halting farmworker progress: they enlisted the cooperation of a rival union, the IBT, to block the UFW.[41] Indeed, across multiple stages of the UFW's struggle to win collective bargaining protections for field workers in California, a similar dynamic played out: the UFW pushed hard for meaningful changes in the way work was organized in the agricultural industry, and the growers responded by signing representation agreements with the Teamsters—even though the Teamsters had no legitimate claim to represent farmworkers.[42]

For example, when the grape boycott ended in 1970, the UFW began organizing efforts in the lettuce fields of Salinas county.[43] In response, the growers' trade association—the Growers-Shippers Vegetable Association (GSVA)—sent a delegation to meet with the Teamsters to "explore the possibility of securing a Teamster contract over the field workers."[44] Within a day of the meeting, all grower-members of the GSVA had signed recognition agreements with the Teamsters "even though the union did not claim to represent any agricultural

[39] *See, e.g.*, Jennifer Gordon, *Law, Lawyers and Labor: The United Farmworkers' Legal Strategy in the 1960s and 1970s and the Role of Law in Union Organizing Today*, U. Pa. J. Lab. & Emp. L. 1, 17, 20 n.64 (2005); Englund v. Chavez, 8 Cal. 3d 572 (1972). In a suit to stop the grape boycott, growers claimed $25 million in lost sales. *See* Ferriss & Sandoval, *supra* note 36, at 155.

[40] *See, e.g.*, Miriam Pawel, The Union of Their Dreams: Power, Hope, and Struggle in Cesar Chavez's Farm Worker Movement 121–22 (2009); Taylor, *supra* note 36, at 43 (1975); Ferriss & Sandoval, *supra* note 36, at 42–44, 102. Law enforcement, in support of the growers, often invented their own injunctions. In one example, the Kern County sheriff banned the UFW from using the word *Huelga*—Spanish for strike and a rallying cry for UFW picketers—on the ground that "it was not American." Taylor, *supra* 36, at 142. Picketers who violated the ban were threatened with arrest. Taylor, *supra* 36, at 142–44. The sheriff's order, like many of the injunctions secured by the growers, eventually was declared unconstitutional. Taylor, *supra* 36, at 144.

[41] Frank Bardacke, Trampling Out the Vintage: Cesar Chavez and the Two Souls of the United Farmworkers 245 (2011).

[42] For detailed histories of this dynamic, see Bardacke *supra* note 41; Ferris & Sandoval, *supra* note 36; Linda C. Majka & Theo J. Majka, Farmworkers, Agribusiness, and the State (1982).

[43] *See, e.g.*, Majka & Majka, *supra* note 42, at 201.

[44] *Id.*

employees at th[e] time."[45] It was only after the Teamsters and the growers had signed the agreements that the Teamsters sought worker support. At that point, the growers granted to Teamster organizers the very thing they now challenge in *Cedar Point*: access to farm property. As Ronald Taylor describes, at the growers' invitation a "Teamster task force [went] through the fields . . . forcing [workers] to sign cards."[46]

When the growers announced that they had signed contracts with the Teamsters, the UFW and its supporters responded aggressively. In early August, the UFW sponsored a march on the town of Salinas to protest the grower-Teamster pact, and over 3,000 UFW members took part.[47] The UFW then instituted boycotts against a set of growers who had recognized the Teamsters, demanding that "these companies rescind their Teamster contracts and recognize the UFW."[48] In addition, the union called for strikes against the Teamsters and the lettuce growers,[49] and between 7,000 and 10,000 workers walked off the job and joined picket lines across the county.[50]

The Teamster-grower alliance thus set the stage for an intense struggle with the UFW and its supporters. The contours of that struggle were shaped, in large measure, by the fact that there was simply no legal process for determining which union was the workers' legitimate representative. Had agricultural workers been covered by federal labor law, an election mechanism would have been available to the UFW to test the Teamster's representative capacity.[51] Federal law

---

[45] Taylor, *supra* note 36, at 254.

[46] *Id.* at 255; *see also* Bardacke, *supra* note 41, at 244 (one major grower "welcomed Teamsters into their fields" as part of a plan to stage a sham election). The growers' motivation for turning to the Teamsters as a "shield against Chavez" was clear. "The grape boycott scared the heck out of the farmers. . . . [So, the growers] felt that the Teamsters were the best organization to represent the farmworkers . . . and they thought if they could sign a contract with [them] it would forestall Cesar trying to come in and take over the industry." Ferriss & Sandoval, *supra* note 36, at 161.

[47] Majka & Majka, *supra* note 42, at 201; *see also Table of Contents 8—No Title*, L.A. Times 2 (Aug. 3, 1970) ("Cesar Chavez told a crowd of 3,000 his United Farm Workers Organizing Committee has authorized a strike and boycott in Salinas Valley. Chavez, attending a rally which climaxes a symbolic march from Delano to protest attempts of the Teamsters' Union to unionize farm workers in Salinas Valley, said the Teamsters have signed only 1% of the workers in the area.").

[48] Majka & Majka, *supra* note 42, at 202.

[49] Taylor, *supra* note 36, at 255.

[50] Majka & Majka, *supra* note 42, at 203.

[51] *See* 29 U.S.C. § 159.

also would have invalidated the Teamster agreements on the ground that they were signed by a union lacking majority support of the workers covered by those agreements.[52] Without access to the federal mechanism, and with no state law yet on the books to provide similar administrative processes, the fight between the unions quickly descended into violent confrontation.

In essence, the growers requested and paid for Teamster members to keep UFW organizers off grower property and to attack UFW strikers and picketers. Two scholars of the farmworkers' movement describe the 1970 clashes as follows:

> [M]en armed with chains and shotguns were imported by the Teamsters to attack pickets and intimidate UFW supporters. . . . Shots were fired at UFW headquarters; the UFW-Watsonville office was bombed; three pickets were shot; and bomb threats were nearly a daily occurrence.[53]

Another observer captures the events this way:

> From Santa Maria north 200 miles to Salinas the coastal valleys were scenes of chaos as roving bands of pickets tried to prevent farmers from importing strike breaking crews; lawmen and teamster "guards" appeared in the fields, and along the back roads, carrying guns. . . . UFW [general] counsel Jerry Cohen was jumped by a 300-pound, 6-foot-2 inch "guard" who held him in a bear grip while another guard beat him unconscious. Cohen was hospitalized for four days with a brain concussion and cuts and bruises.[54]

The 1970 battle in the lettuce fields ended with a weak détente between the Teamsters and the UFW which did not hold.[55] The contracts that the UFW won as a result of the national grape boycott were set to expire in 1973, and the Teamsters approached the growers and offered to, again, act as a shield against the UFW.[56] The growers

---

[52] *See id.* § 158(a)(2); *see also* Int'l Ladies' Garment Workers' Union v. NLRB, 366 U.S. 731, 737 (1961) (noting that the employer granted recognition to a union "selected by a minority of its employees, thereby impressing that agent upon the nonconsenting majority," and holding that "[t]here could be no clearer abridgment of § 7 of the Act, assuring employees the right 'to bargain collectively through representatives of their own choosing'").

[53] Majka & Majka, *supra* note 42, at 204.

[54] Taylor, *supra* note 36, at 259–60.

[55] *See* Majka & Majka, *supra* note 42, at 206–07.

[56] The invitation was made by Teamsters president Frank Fitzsimmons at a December 1972 convention of the American Farm Bureau Federation, an organization of growers. *See* Bardacke, *supra* note 41, at 425; *see also* Gordon, *supra* note 39, at 28–29. As the convention's keynote speaker, the Teamster president "attacked the UFW as a 'revolutionary movement that is perpetrating a fraud on the American public,' and called on the Farm Bureau to join

subsequently refused to renew the UFW contracts and instead agreed to "throw in their lot with the Teamsters."[57] In fact, after the UFW grape contracts expired in 1973, 90% of the grape growers signed collective bargaining agreements with the Teamsters union,[58] despite the fact that the Teamsters had not won a single election nor proved by any other mechanism that they represented the workers for whom they ostensibly bargained.

The UFW responded to the Teamsters-growers 1973 collusion by sending its members back to the picket lines.[59] The Teamsters and the growers then initiated the next round of violence. Three hundred Teamster "freelance enforcers" were brought in from cities like Los Angeles and were paid to break the strike and crush the picket lines.[60] On June 8, for example, "members of the two unions met head-on in a pitched battle in the middle of Highway 195, east of Mecca"; it took "40 Riverside County deputies and California Highway patrolman to break up the fight."[61] On June 19, a "bomb exploded under the hood of a car belonging to [] a UFW[] member,"[62] and on the 21st, "two Teamsters organizers were arrested by Riverside deputies on assault charges and for kidnap and attempted murder. . . . [T]he Teamsters had abducted a worker; mistaking him for a member of the UFW[], they had stabbed him six times with an icepick and beat him."[63] On June 23rd, the Teamsters launched a "rock attack on a car caravan in which [UFW President Cesar] Chavez was riding, and a nighttime arson that destroyed the trailer home of a UFW picket captain."[64] Then:

> [t]he violence peaked the next morning, Saturday, June 24th. After a ritualistic exchange of insults, one of the [Teamsters] threw a firecracker, and some 200 Teamster guards charged about twice as many UFW pickets. For

---

the Teamsters in 'an alliance . . . and accommodation, which will work for the benefit of your organization and mine.'" BARDACKE, *supra* note 41, at 425.

[57] *Id.* at 427.

[58] *See* Gordon, *supra* note 39, at 29.

[59] *See, e.g.*, FERRISS & SANDOVAL, *supra* note 36, at 182 ("This new Teamster double cross unleashed six months of turbulence that rolled from Coachella up to the San Joaquin Valley, following the path of the grape harvest. On April 16th, more than one thousand workers struck in Coachella to protest the Teamsters' invasion.").

[60] BARDACKE, *supra* note 41, at 431.

[61] TALYOR, *supra* note 36, at 301.

[62] *Id.*

[63] *Id.*

[64] BARDACKE, *supra* note 41, at 436.

> more than a half-hour, according to a Riverside County sheriff's deputy, there was a "mad melee of fights and beatings all over the fields." . . . Another startled deputy reported that as soon as the fighting started, "weapons, including iron pipes, clubs, tire irons, machetes, and belts seemed to come out of nowhere." When the deputies finally established order, six Teamsters and five Chavistas were arrested, and five people (all UFW members) were taken to the hospital. . . .[65]

UFW member Clementina Carmona Olloqui, reflecting on 1973, stated bluntly, "[i]t was like being in a war."[66]

As was true in 1970, in 1973 the UFW lacked a legal mechanism for testing the Teamsters' representative status or for challenging the Teamster-grower contracts. In 1973, however, in the midst of the expanding violence, UFW President Cesar Chavez and his general counsel, Jerry Cohen, concluded that such a legal mechanism—a labor law for farmworkers—was the right path forward for farmworker organizing in California. With Jerry Brown's election as governor of California in 1974, the political prospects for such legislation became plausible, and Cohen drafted an initial version of a bill.[67] After months

[65] *Id.*

[66] Ferriss & Sandoval, *supra* note 36, at 182. The violence was widely publicized and became a major news story in California, and beyond. *See, e.g.*, *Order Bans Violence by Teamsters*, Hartford Courant, Apr. 14, 1974, at 11A ("Violence, including two deaths, marked the struggle"); *Watergate Figure Accused of Helping Anti-Chavez Campaign: Meany Charges Charles Colson With Participating in Teamsters Drive to Blame UFWA for Farm Violence*, L.A. Times, Apr. 17, 1974, at C1 ("Meany said the farm workers 'were victims of brutality, not the perpetrators. Hundreds of farm workers were beaten, many hospitalized, two killed.'"); Earl Caldwell, *Picket Shot, Many More Arrested in Grape Strike: Violence-Caused Arrests Opposition to Chavez Meany-Fitzsimmons Talks Farm Union Blamed*, N.Y. Times, Aug. 3, 1973, at 29 ("Arrests and violence swept across the San Joaquin Valley today as the United Farm Workers Union pressed its strike against California table grape growers. . . . But the cause of most concern was an outbreak of shooting that began late yesterday [in] Tulare County. . . . [A] farm union picket had been shot. . . . [D]uring the attack several bullets had also pierced the car of a free-lance photographer from San Francisco. . . . In all, the sheriff's department said that about a dozen shots had been fired."); Frank Del Olmo, *30 Teamsters Arrested After Battle at Ranch: Violence Spreads to Bakersfield; 4 Chavez Pickets Hospitalized*, L.A. Times, June 29, 1973, at A3. ("Thirty members of the Teamsters Union were arrested near Bakersfield Thursday after they allegedly attacked rival United Farm Workers Union pickets. . . . At least four UFW[] members were taken to Kern County's General Hospital in Bakersfield with injuries, among them a 60-year old man with a possible skull fracture. A sheriff's department spokesman said all the Teamsters were booked on suspicion of conspiracy to a commit a felony in addition to individual charges which range from disturbing the peace to assault with a deadly weapon."); *UFW-Teamsters Disputes Ripening Along With Grapes*, Atlanta Const., July 2, 1973, at 7B. ("For the past two months UFW pickets and Teamsters hired to guard the fields have cursed, spat, thrown rocks and bottles and worn a rut between the fields and the county jail. Violence hit a peak June 23 when 350 pickets and Teamsters swarmed at each other with iron pipes, clubs, bells, tire irons and machetes in what officers called a 'mad melee.' About 30 minor injuries and 11 arrests were reported.").

[67] *See* Gordon, *supra* note 39, at 30–31.

of negotiations between Cohen and Brown's office, Cohen secured Brown's agreement to adopt most of the UFW's favored provisions,[68] and following a special legislative session that Brown called at Chavez's request, the bill was passed into law as the California Agricultural Labor Relations Act.[69]

The Act set up an election mechanism as the exclusive process through which unions could establish their representative status and earn the right to bargain collectively with growers.[70] To reinforce the point that elections were to be the exclusive path for union recognition, section 1153 of the Act made it illegal for an agricultural employer to "recognize, bargain with, or sign a collective-bargaining agreement with any labor organization not certified pursuant to the provisions" of the Act.[71] And section 1154 made it illegal for a union to require "any employer to recognize or bargain with a particular labor organization as the representative of his agricultural employees if another labor organization has been certified as the representative of such employees."[72]

In conjunction, these provisions of the ALRA rendered illegal the Teamsters-growers collusion: having not been elected by the farmworkers, continued collective bargaining by and with the Teamsters would violate the Act. The statute likewise gave the UFW a mechanism to establish their own status as the exclusive representative of farmworkers, and to extinguish the Teamster contracts once the UFW was elected.[73] In fact, according to Gordon, "a staggering 45,915 farm workers voted in 382 elections during the first five months after the

[68] *Id.* at 31.

[69] *See* David Winder, *California Farm Bill Seeks Peace in the Fields*, Christian Sci. Monitor, June 5, 1975, at 11; *see also id.* at 32. Gordon provides an excellent synopsis of the bill's broader political constituency, and opponents, among groups as varied as growers, the Teamsters, supermarkets, county administrators, and sheriffs. *See id.* at 31–32.

[70] Thus, section 1156 of the Act states that "Representatives designated or selected by a secret ballot for the purposes of collective bargaining by the majority of the agricultural employees in the bargaining unit shall be the exclusive representatives of all the agricultural employees in such unit for the purpose of collective bargaining with respect to rates of pay, wages, hours of employment, or other conditions of employment." Cal. Lab. Code Ann. § 1156. Elections, moreover, could be requested only by unions that already enjoyed significant support from the workforce—cards signed by 50% of the relevant bargaining unit were required. *Id.* § 1156.3.

[71] *Id.* § 1153.

[72] *Id.* § 1154.

[73] *See id.* § 1156.7(a) (West 1975); *id.* § 1155.3(a)–(b) (West 1975); *see also* Gordon, *supra* note 39, at 33.

ALRA's passage,"[74] and those elections overwhelmingly favored the UFW.[75] Elections, moreover, did come to replace the kind of warfare that defined agricultural labor relations prior to the Act's passage.[76]

The Act's purpose of ending violence and restoring public safety was reflected in its preamble, the first sentence of which states that "[i]n enacting this legislation the people of the state of California seek to ensure peace in the agricultural fields."[77] Similarly, when Governor Brown signed the Act into law, he characterized it as "a beginning toward ending ten years of turmoil in the fields."[78] Contemporaneous media coverage and commentary also understood the ALRA as a means of bringing peace to California agriculture. Thus, the *Wall Street Journal* reported that "[t]he law should curtail the violence that has marked the farm-labor dispute in California," while the *Hartford Courant* wrote that "[a] new state law to provide farm workers with state-supervised secret ballot union elections brings hope for peace in the strife-torn vineyards and fields of California."[79]

The access provision at issue in *Cedar Point* was part and parcel of this system of union elections that the UFW had sought, and that California had adopted, as a means to bring an end to violence in the fields. As reflected in contemporaneous court decisions and in the hearings on the provision, farmworkers often worked for multiple growers and lived in multiple locations during a single harvest season, and thus it could be difficult—if not impossible—for the union to determine who was eligible to vote in a particular election unless the union could talk with the workers *on farm property where they worked.* The California Supreme Court, in a case upholding the access provisions' constitutionality, explained this dynamic as follows:

---

[74] Gordon, *supra* note 39, at 39.

[75] Linda C. Majka, *Labor Militancy Among Farm Workers and the Strategy of Protest: 1900–1979*, 28 Soc. Probs. 533, 544 (1981).

[76] *See, e.g.*, *Farm Workers Maintain Lead Over Teamsters in Coast Vote*, N.Y. Times, Jan. 3, 1976, at 19 ("Supporters of the law note that, despite controversy over its implementation, violence has been kept at a minimum during the election process, which began in early September.").

[77] *See* 1975 Cal. Stat. 4013, §1.

[78] Jerry Gilliam, *Brown Signs Farm Labor Compromise: Governor Calls Law Start Toward Ending Violence in the Fields*, L.A. Times, June 6, 1975, at B3.

[79] William Wong, *Fruitful Harvest: California Notes Farm-Labor Election Bill, Presaging a New Unionizing Drive in Fall*, Wall St. J., May 30, 1975, at 30; *Law in California Seeks Labor Peace*, Hartford Courant, June 9, 1975, at 8A, *see also* Winder, *supra* note 69.

> Many farmworkers are migrants; they arrive in town in time for the local harvest, live in motels, labor camps, or with friends or relatives, then move on when the crop is in. Obviously home visits, mailings, or telephone calls are impossible in such circumstances. According to the record, even those farm workers who are relatively sedentary often live in widely spread settlements, thus making personal contact at home impractical. . . .[80]

In light of these realties, a member of the first ALRB commented during the access provision hearings that unions "can't even know who to organize; who you are going to have to try to talk to if you don't have some access to the workers there."[81] While a UFW organizer testified, "[t]here is absolutely no way for us to know who the workers on the ranch are unless we go on the ranch and make contact with them."[82] Put simply, the system of union elections enacted by the ALRA depended on unions knowing who the electorate *was*, which depended on unions being granted access to grower property.

Moreover, the ALRA not only required elections but rapid elections: the statute mandates that secret balloting be conducted within seven days after a request for an election is filed.[83] The short time frame again reflects the highly transitory nature of the agricultural labor force: if elections dragged on for longer periods of time, the workforce could turn over and require the union to continually update its organizational efforts, potentially rendering the election process futile.[84] The access provisions aimed to mitigate this problem and thus to enable viable elections. As the California Supreme Court concluded, given the statutory requirement of "swift elections," the union has only a few days to communicate its views to the workers and thus "most of the channels of communication which have been used in organizing industrial laborers . . . are simply too slow to be effective."[85]

---

[80] Agric. Lab. Rels. Bd. v. Superior Ct., 16 Cal. 3d 392, 414–15 (1976).

[81] *Hearings Before the California Agricultural Labor Relations Board*, E-10 (Cal. 1975) (statement of Board Member Leroy Chatfield).

[82] *Public Hearings on the Access Provision: Hearings Before the California Agricultural Labor Relations Board*, C-66 (Cal. 1975) (statement of Lea Ybarra, UFW organizer).

[83] *Superior Court*, 16 Cal. 3d at 316 (1976); CAL. LAB. CODE ANN. § 1156.3(a).

[84] *See* Gordon, *supra* note 39, at 33–34. The swift election period also limited growers' ability to mount anti-union campaigns. *See id.*

[85] *Superior Court*, 16 Cal. 3d at 416. The same principle was reflected in the access regulation itself, which states that: "Generally, unions seeking to organize agricultural employees do not have available alternative channels of effective communication. Alternative channels of effective communications which have been found adequate in industrial settings do not exist or are insufficient in the context of agricultural labor." CAL. CODE. REGS., tit. 8, § 20900(c).

In brief, California decided to address the problem of violence in the agricultural industry by enacting a system of union elections. The success of that elections system depended, in the view of the administrative agency tasked with developing it, on limited access rights. Access rights were thus instrumental to securing public safety.

Contrary to the Court's assertion, then, the ALRA and its access provision were in fact germane to a "benefit provided to agricultural employers [and] a risk posed to the public"—namely, the benefit of public safety and the risk of public violence.[86] And it is difficult to imagine any police-power purpose more traditional, more "legitimate" in the words of the Court, than the purpose of ending public violence and ensuring public safety. This implies that the access provision, rather than being classified as a per se taking, ought to have been analyzed under the third exception to the Court's per se taking rule.

The provision would have qualified for that exception upon a finding that the limited access granted to union organizers had an "essential nexus" and bore a "rough proportionality" to the legitimate goal of curbing the violence that had plagued California agriculture for years. Although the nexus and proportionality tests are notoriously indeterminate,[87] seeing the nexus and proportionality here should, for the reasons described above, be relatively easy for a neutral decisionmaker. The nexus test requires a determination that there is a connection between the legitimate state interest at issue and the access condition chosen to effectuate it.[88] By enacting a system of union elections, California provided an alternative method—a non-violent method—for resolving labor disputes. To ensure the functionality of

[86] Cedar Point Nursery v. Hassid, 141 S. Ct. 2063, 2080 (2021).

[87] *See, e.g.*, Robyn L. Salder, Dolan v. City of Tigard: *Takings Clause Doctrine Remains Vague Under the Rough Proportionality Standard*, 31 WILLAMETTE L. REV. 147, 150–51 (1995) (predicting that the court's *Nollan* and *Dolan* standards will "fai[l] to provide the guidance necessary to enable the judiciary and local governments to reach consistent results with land use regulations" because they are overly vague); Christopher J. St. Jeanos, Dolan v. Tigard *and the Rough Proportionality Test*, 63 FORDHAM L. REV. 1883, 1889–93 (1995) (arguing that state courts attempting to apply *Dolan*'s "rough proportionality" test apply dramatically different degrees of scrutiny over factual determinations supporting land use regulations).

[88] Nollan v. California Coastal Comm'n, 483 U.S. 825, 837 (1987) (holding that land use regulations must "further the end advanced as the justification for the prohibition"); *id.* at 838 (noting that the California Coastal Commission argued that the state's interest in public access to beaches would be advanced by requiring the Nollans to provide access to their beach); Golf Course Ass'n, LLC v. New Castle Cnty., 2016 WL 1425367, at *15 (Del. Super. Ct. 2016) ("The government may constitutionally demand the conveyance of property as a condition to obtaining a land use permit so long as (1) there is a nexus between the required conveyance and the public interest.").

the union elections system, California requires limited access rights to union organizers. Hence the connection between access and the goal of ensuring public safety. The rough proportionality test requires a determination that there is a "reasonable relationship"[89] between the extent of the access condition and the "social costs"[90] occasioned by the owner's exercise of their property rights—here, the unencumbered right to exclude. Given the very significant social costs involved in the public violence that prevailed in the absence of a viable labor law, the limited access rights required by the regulation—two organizers on farm property for an hour at a time—are, to say the least, proportional to those costs.[91]

II. Collective Bargaining for Pesticide Safety

Elections and access rights served the goal of ending violent conflict, but they also facilitated collective bargaining between the UFW and the growers. Elections and access thus served the *substantive* goals that the union demanded at the bargaining table. Primary among such UFW demands was safety and health, and pesticide safety in particular. The union had been aware, since the late 1960s, that rampant and largely unregulated pesticide usage in California agriculture was resulting in severe health consequences for both farmworkers and consumers. By 1969, when he testified before the United States Senate Labor Committee, Chavez was willing to state that "[t]he issue of the health and safety of farm workers in California . . . is the single most important issue facing the United Farm Workers,"[92] and that "the issue of pesticide poisoning is more important today than even wages."[93] Having tried and failed to convince the state to ensure pesticide safety through government inspections and enforcement, the UFW attempted—and often succeeded—in writing pesticide

---

[89] Dolan v. City of Tigard, 512 U.S. 374, 391 (1994) (noting that there is general agreement among state courts "that the dedication should have some reasonable relationship to the needs created by the [development]" (citing Call v. West Jordan, 606 P.2d 217, 220 (Utah 1979)).

[90] Koontz v. St. Johns River Water Mgmt. Dist., 570 U.S. 595, 604–06 (2013).

[91] Also relevant here is the fact that, when it suited their goal of *blocking* the UFW, growers invited Teamster organizers onto their property in their efforts to get farmworkers to sign authorization cards. *See supra* text accompanying notes 45–46.

[92] *Migrant and Seasonal Farmworker Powerlessness: Hearing Before the Subcomm. on Migratory Lab. of the S. Comm. on Lab. & Pub. Welfare*, 91st Cong. 3397 (1969) [hereinafter *Hearings*] (statement of Cesar Chavez, Founder/President, United Farm Workers).

[93] *Id.* at 3390.

rules into collective bargaining agreements. The collective bargaining agreements signed between the UFW and growers were thus a functional substitute for a state-run pesticide inspection regime.

As an organization built of and for farmworkers, the UFW had first-hand experience with the health consequences of pesticide exposure.[94] Union organizers began reporting on such consequences in the mid-1960s, and Chavez's testimony to the Senate committee is replete with such accounts.[95] In one example of many, Chavez testified:

> On a large California ranch in the fall of 1965 a group of Mexican-American workers and their families were picking berries. A three-year-old girl and her four-year-old brother were playing around an unattended spray rig next to where their mother was working. The four-year-old apparently took the cap off a gallon can of 40% tetraethyl phyrophosphate (TEPP, a phosphate ester cholinesterase inhibitor) pesticide left on the rig. The three-year-old put her finger in it and sucked it. She vomited immediately[,] became unconscious, and was dead on arrival at the hospital where she was promptly taken.[96]

The experiences being reported to UFW organizers were soon confirmed by studies conducted by local health agencies. For example, in January 1969 the California Department of Health examined 774 farmworkers and found that 548 (or 71%) had one or more symptoms of pesticide poisoning.[97] Those symptoms included: eye irritation, nausea or vomiting, unusual fatigue, unusual perspiration, headaches, dizziness, skin irritation, difficulty in breathing, pain in the fingernails (some workers lost their fingernails), nervousness and/or insomnia, itching in their ears, nosebleeds, burning and sore throats, swollen hands and feet, loss of hair, diarrhea.[98] Based on the conclusions contained in this study, the state director of public health estimated that about 100,000 farmworkers were suffering nonfatal pesticide poisoning each year.[99] A similar study, this one focused on farmworker children, run by a doctor at the Salud Clinic in Tulare County at the same time, found that about

---

[94] For example, one organizer brought to the general counsel's office "several women who were covered in rashes, nauseated and sweating, talking about a white powder on the vines in which they worked." Gordon, *supra* note 39, at 25.

[95] *See Hearings*, *supra* note 92, at 3397–400 (statement of Cesar Chavez).

[96] *Id.* at 3398.

[97] *See* Robert Gordon, *Poisons in the Fields: The United Farm Workers, Pesticides, and Environmental Politics*, 68 PAC. HIST. REV. 51, 58 (1999).

[98] *See Hearings*, *supra* note 92, at 3397–98 (statement of Cesar Chavez).

[99] Gordon, *supra* note 97.

half of those children tested had elevated levels of DDT—a toxic pesticide—in their blood.[100]

Faced with the reality of pesticide poisoning, the UFW attempted to secure state cooperation in improving safety and health protections in California agriculture. But to no avail. In the late 1960s, California had a modest system of pesticide regulation, one that involved registration of pesticides and evaluation of their adverse effects by the state combined with permitting of individual pesticide use by county agricultural commissions.[101] When the UFW sought simple disclosure of permitting and use records—in its effort to learn about the type and quantity of chemicals being sprayed on fields where UFW members worked—the local agricultural commissioner denied the request on the ground that such information was "confidential."[102] The firm responsible for spraying the pesticides at issue then quickly secured an injunction against the requested disclosure.[103] The union general counsel described the year-long contest over mere access to these permitting records as "[p]erhaps the most painful proof of the inadequacy of current governmental regulations."[104]

Rather than relying on state regulation, the UFW instead turned to the collective bargaining process as the means by which it would fight for pesticide safety—for both farmworkers and consumers. Both Chavez and his general counsel made clear in their congressional testimony that this was to be the union's approach. After detailing numerous instances of pesticide exposure among UFW members, Chavez told the Senate labor committee that "[t]he United Farm Workers . . . is attempting to solve this pervasive problem by the collective bargaining process."[105] Cohen, in testimony focused on the

---

[100] *See* Ronald B. Taylor, *Nerve Gas in the Orchards*, NATION (June 22, 1970); *Hearings*, *supra* note 92, at 3397.

[101] *See* TIMOTHY MALLOY ET AL., GOVERNANCE ON THE GROUND: EVALUATING THE ROLE OF COUNTY AGRICULTURAL COMMISSIONERS IN REDUCING TOXIC PESTICIDE EXPOSURES 6 (2019).

[102] TAYLOR, *supra* note 36, at 240.

[103] *Id.*; Gordon, *supra* note 39, at 25.

[104] *Hearings*, *supra* note 92, at 3012 (1969) (statement of Jerry Cohen, General Counsel, United Farm Workers).

[105] *Id.* at 3400 (statement of Cesar Chavez); *see also* Taylor, *supra* note 100, at 732 ("What can be done to protect workers? Chavez has decided that this issue is one of the main problems the UFWOC faces. In recently completed contract negotiations with Perelli-Minetti vineyards, of Delano, the UFWOC and the company worked out a model health and safety clause that deals primarily with pesticide protections. A special committee, made up of company and union members, governs the safe use of pesticides in the vineyards.").

pesticide DDT, stated that because state officials were not "serving the interests of the consuming public" it was "clear to the Union that to ban DDT we must take the route of collective bargaining."[106] The union's strategy was also captured succinctly in its organizing and boycott literature, as the below poster from 1969 illustrates: "Only a Union Contract Can Protect Farmworkers & Consumers From Dangers of Poisonous Pesticides."[107]

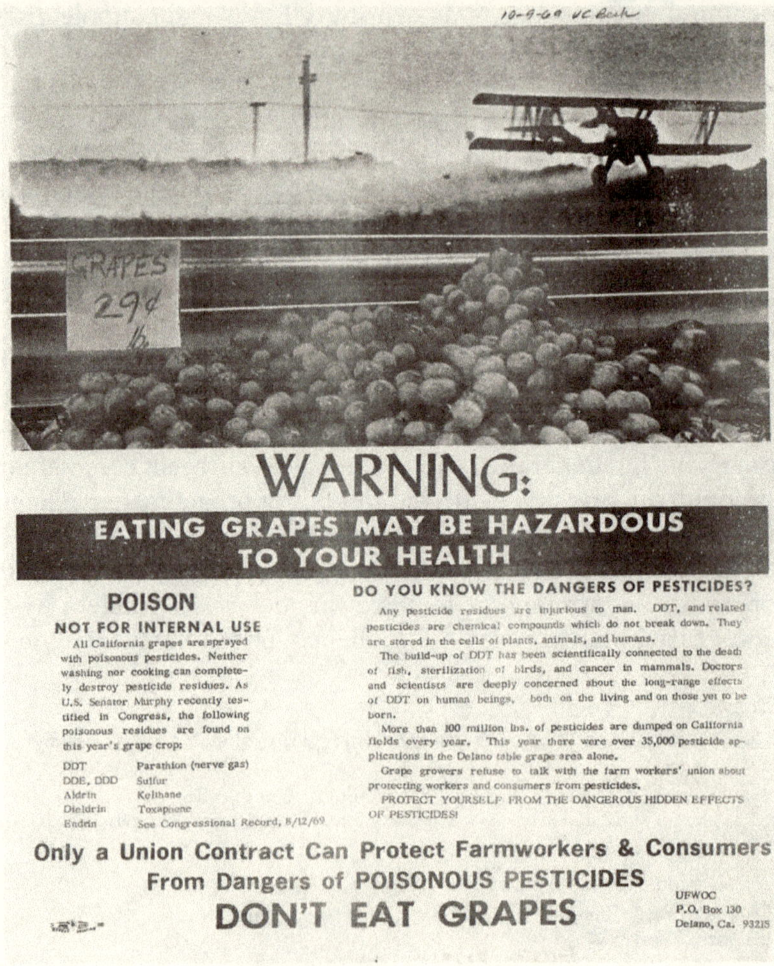

[106] *Hearings*, *supra* note 92, at 3011–12 (statement of Jerry Cohen).

[107] *Poster*, United Farmworker Org. Comm. (1969), https://dp.la/primary-source-sets/the-united-farm-workers-and-the-delano-grape-strike/sources/1320.

And, indeed, the UFW—when it was able to successfully secure bargaining rights and conclude collective bargaining agreements with growers—negotiated robust protections against pesticide exposure. For example, section XVIII of the 1970 collective bargaining agreement between the UFW and grower Wonder Palms Ranch laid out an extensive set of Health and Safety rules. These provisions included: an outright ban on the use of a series of pesticides (DDT, Aldrin, Dieldrin, Endrin, Parathion, and TPPP); the creation of a workers' Health and Safety Committee (which was to be granted access to all records concerning pesticide use, and which was to participate in the formulation of rules governing the use of pesticides including the length of time during which workers would be prohibited from entering fields after they had been sprayed); mandated recordkeeping regarding types of pesticide applied, and the locations, amount and method of application; baseline testing, at the grower's expense, of blood levels relevant to pesticide exposure; the provision of protective clothing and gear; and the right of all workers to refuse to work when there was risk of exposure to pesticides.[108] Other collective bargaining agreements bargained at the time contained the same pesticide protections.[109]

The collective bargaining agreements thus went far beyond what state pesticide regulation promised as a matter of substantive protections. Just as critically, the agreements offered an enforcement mechanism that public law lacked. Under the collective bargaining agreements' dispute resolution clause, the parties committed to submit disputes arising under the contract—including disputes regarding the pesticide rules—to binding arbitration if those disputes could not otherwise be resolved by the parties within seven days.[110] As the UFW

[108] *See* Collective Bargaining Agreement Between United Farm Workers Organizing Committee, AFL-CIO and Wonder Palms Ranch 9–11 (Oct. 31, 1970) [hereinafter *CBA*] (on file with author).

[109] *See, e.g.*, *Hearings*, *supra* note 92, at 3400–401 (statement of Cesar Chavez) (describing similar provisions from the 1969 collective bargaining agreement between the UFW and the Perelli-Minetti Company).

[110] *See CBA*, *supra* note 108, at 11. As one small measure of the collective bargaining agreement's effectiveness, Chavez noted during his Senate testimony that the contracts allowed the UFW to obtain the same information that the county agricultural commissioner had prevented the union from obtaining. *See Hearings*, *supra* note 92, at 3393 (testimony of Cesar Chavez).

general counsel put it, "you could enforce the regulations with the grievance procedure when the state wasn't bothering to enforce."[111]

Indeed, the UFW's strategy of securing and enforcing safety and health protections through collective bargaining—for both workers and the public—is not unique to agricultural unionization but is common across union contexts. This can be seen, first, in the direct impact that unions have on safety and health outcomes. For example, researchers recently examined the impact of unionization on infection and mortality rates from COVID-19 in nursing homes. The authors found that the presence of a union representing the nursing home's health care workers was associated with a 42% relative decrease in COVID infection rates and a 30% relative decrease in the COVID mortality rate as compared to facilities without unionized health care workers.[112]

Unionization also increases the efficacy of government safety and health inspection regimes, as David Weil's seminal study on enforcement of the federal Occupational Safety and Health Act (OSHA) showed.[113] As Weil explains, OSHA "is premised upon the active enforcement of detailed safety and health standards in the nation's workplaces[, and e]nforcement, in turn, is achieved by workplace inspections."[114] What Weil finds is that unions "dramatically increase enforcement" of OSHA.[115] This is true for several reasons. One, the presence of a union substantially increases the probability that OSHA

[111] Interview of Jerry Cohen by LeRoy Chatfield (May 19, 2009) at 18:47 to 19:01 (on file with author). In 1972 and then again in 1974, some of the pesticide rules that the UFW bargained in its collective agreements were adopted as state regulations, including the timing of field re-entry following pesticide application and the provision of protective clothing. *See*, e.g., Cal. Code. Regs., tit. 3, §§ 12980–12988. The UFW's strategy of fighting for pesticide safety through collective bargaining agreements remained the same, however. As one scholar put it, "[u]nfortunately, the new provisions failed to address the fundamental problem of enforcement," and thus "[w]hile stronger regulation helped in the short run," the union continued to believe that "the only way to bring about permanent change was by empowering farm workers." Robert W. Gordon IV, Politics and Pesticides 105, 110 (1993) (masters thesis on file with author).

[112] Adam Dean, Atheendar Venkataramani & Simeon Kimmel, *Mortality Rates from COVID-19 Are Lower in Unionized Nursing Homes*, 39 Health Affs. 1993, 1998, 1997 (2020).

[113] *See* David Weil, *Enforcing OSHA: The Role of Labor Unions*, 30 Indus. Rels. 20 (1991).

[114] *Id.* at 21. Because the OSHA inspection force cannot inspect every workplace in the country, however, the Act grants employees the right to participate in the complaint and inspection process, including the right to initiate inspections and to participate in those inspections: with "workers as 'partners' in this regulatory process, the chances for OSHA success are significantly improved." *Id.*

[115] *Id.* at 34.

will conduct a workplace inspection.[116] Two, OSHA inspectors spend more time conducting inspections at unionized workplaces than they do at nonunion workplaces, in part because union workers exercise their right to participate in inspections significantly more frequently than do nonunion workers.[117] Unions also increase the number of violations cited following an OSHA inspection and increase the penalty received per violation.[118] Weil's findings were confirmed recently by Aaron Sojourner and Jooyoung Yang, who conclude on the basis of a regression discontinuity analysis that union certification "increases OSHA activity—inspection rates, violations cited, and penalties assigned."[119]

Understood in this way, then, unionization and collective bargaining function as substitutes for—and complements to—government health and safety inspection regimes. Yet, the *Cedar Point* Court holds that "government health and safety inspection regimes will generally not constitute takings."[120] And again, the Court cites a federal pesticide inspection regime as an example of one that would not constitute a taking.[121] That regime involves the mandatory grant of property access to "officers or employees of the Environmental Protection Agency" for the purpose of conducting pesticide inspections.[122] What distinguishes, for takings analysis, the mandatory grant of access rights to EPA officers (for the purpose of ensuring pesticide safety) from the mandatory grant of access rights to union organizers (for the purpose of bargaining rules to ensure pesticide safety)? According to the *Cedar Point* Court, the answer is that "unlike standard health and safety inspections, the access regulation is not germane to any benefit provided to agricultural employers or any risk posed to the public," and thus "[t]he access regulation amounts to a simple appropriation of private property."[123]

---

[116] *Id.* at 26–27.

[117] *Id.* at 28–29.

[118] *Id.* at 26–33.

[119] Aaron Sojourner & Jooyoung Yang, *Effects of Unionization on Workplace-Safety Enforcement: Regression Discontinuity Evidence* 4 (Inst. Lab. Econ. Discussion Paper, 2015).

[120] Cedar Point Nursery v. Hassid, 141 S. Ct. 2063, 2079 (2021).

[121] *See* 7 U.S.C. § 136g(a)(1)(A).

[122] *Id.*

[123] 141 S. Ct. at 2080. Although the particular inspection regime cited by the Court involves entry onto private property by government agents, there is no reason why—and the Court certainly does not explain why—the non-governmental status of union organizers

There are, however, very clear ways in which the union access provision in *Cedar Point* is germane to precisely the same benefits and risks to which an inspection regime is directed. In fact, in the context of the struggle for pesticide safety in California agriculture, the UFW's view that collective bargaining was likely to be *more effective* than a state-run inspection regime is supported both by the union's contemporary experience with the state regime and by recent empirics regarding unionization's general health and safety effects. As such, and put simply, collective bargaining and an inspection regime are alternative ways to advance the goals of pesticide safety. They both address the same risk and they both similarly require a limited grant of access rights. According to the Court's own reasoning, then, the access provision should not constitute a taking but instead be immune from takings challenges under the third exception to the per se takings rule.[124]

Of course, *Cedar Point* is not the first case in which the Supreme Court has ascribed constitutional infirmity to a state labor law on the ground that the law did not advance safety and health through a particular, Court favored, means. This is also what the Court did in *Lochner v. New York*.[125] That case involved a challenge to a state statute limiting the number of hours an employee could work in a bakery. For the *Lochner* Court, the questions were whether the statute advanced an end within the police power of the state and whether the statute bore a "direct relation"—one might say "essential nexus"—to that legitimate end.[126] On the first question, the *Lochner* Court held that the police power of the state did indeed extend to protecting "public health," including "the health of the individual engaged in the occupation of a baker."[127] But the *Lochner* Court did not believe that New York's chosen method of advancing this legitimate health goal was closely related enough to that goal. Indeed, the *Lochner* Court contrasted the

---

changes the legitimate purpose, the essential nexus, or the rough proportionality components of the takings analysis. And, of course, the takings cases on which the Court relies to craft the third exception to its rule—e.g., *Nollan* and *Dolan*—are cases involving the grant of access to the public, not to government agents. *See* Nollan v. Cal. Coastal Comm'n, 483 U.S. 825, 827 (1987); Dolan v. City of Tigard, 512 U.S. 374, 377–78 (1994).

[124] The same nexus and rough proportionality analysis would apply to the state's interest in safety and health as applies to the state's interest in public safety. *See supra* text accompanying notes 87–91.

[125] 198 U.S. 45 (1905).

[126] *Id.* at 57.

[127] *Id.* at 61, 57.

maximum hours law before it from what it deemed the only proper approach to securing the health of bakery workers and the public that consumed baked goods: "[All the State] could properly do has been done by it with regard to the conduct of bakeries, as provided for in other sections of the act, [which] provide for the inspection of the premises where the bakery is carried on."[128] In *Lochner*, inspections rather than maximum hours laws were the means to advance safety and health and avoid a Due Process challenge; in *Cedar Point*, inspections rather than collective bargaining are the means to advance safety and health and avoid Takings Clause challenges.

III. Conclusion

In *Cedar Point* the Court establishes the rule that a regulation granting even limited access rights to private property interferes with the property owner's right to exclude and therefore constitutes a per se physical taking. But the Court also enumerates exceptions to that rule. According to one of those exceptions, the government can, without effecting a taking, require property owners to cede access rights—can require property owners to compromise their right to exclude—in order to avoid a risk posed to the public. As this essay has shown, the union access right at issue in *Cedar Point* was instrumental in avoiding two kinds of public risks. First, the open violence that plagued union organizing in the absence of a viable process for agricultural union elections. And, second, the profound threat to the health of farmworkers and consumers posed by the unregulated use of agricultural pesticides. The Court's own reasoning dictated that, as a means to avoid those risks, the limited union access rights that the Court held to violate its per se takings rule qualified for the exception to that rule.

[128] *Id.* at 61.

CYNTHIA ESTLUND

SHOWDOWN AT CEDAR POINT: "SOLE AND DESPOTIC DOMINION" GAINS GROUND

Blackstone famously declared: "There is nothing which so generally strikes the imagination, and engages the affections of mankind, as the right of property; or that sole and despotic dominion which one man claims and exercises over the external things of the world, in total exclusion of the right of any other individual in the universe."[1] That seems to be so, if not for all "mankind," then at least for the current majority of the Supreme Court.

In the modern era, the deregulatory impact of property rights and takings law has been blunted by the dominant role of ad hoc balancing. Advocates, scholars, and judges seeking to sharpen the takings challenge to regulation have thus focused their efforts on creating and expanding "per se rules" that circumvent the default regime of balancing. So perhaps it should be no surprise that the first major takings case decided by the lopsidedly conservative Supreme Court that took the bench in 2020 produced a resounding victory for private property

Cynthia Estlund is Catherine A. Rein Professor of Law, New York University School of Law.

Author's note: I would like to thank Niko Bowie, Tom Merrill, and Katrina Wyman for their extraordinarily thoughtful feedback on earlier drafts, and Jacob Metz-Lerman for excellent research assistance.

[1] 2 W. Blackstone, Commentaries *2.

The Supreme Court Review, 2022.
 Published by The University of Chicago Press. https://doi.org/10.1086/720149

rights in the form of a much-expanded per se rule for government-authorized physical invasions.

It was indeed no great surprise that the Court in *Cedar Point Nursery v. Hassid*[2] struck down the broad right of access for union organizers that California law had prescribed for agricultural workplaces. More surprising was how they won. What might have been an incremental ratcheting up of scrutiny for physical intrusions on private property—say, one that confined union organizers' access rights to the very narrow boundaries the Court had previously established under federal labor law—became instead a bellwether case. The Court's 6-3 decision was eye-opening in its breadth, its divergence from precedent, its implications for longstanding regulatory practices, and its provocative rhetoric, including its paean to "sole and despotic dominion." The immediate impact of *Cedar Point* may be limited to government-authorized physical invasions, which are relatively unusual. Yet the decision may signal a new willingness on the part of the newly fortified conservative majority of the Court to constitutionalize restrictions on the regulatory state through takings law.

I. A Very Short History of Regulatory Takings Before *Cedar Point*

For at least a century after its promulgation, the Fifth Amendment's Takings Clause was thought to have no bearing on government regulation of property.[3] In inaugurating the concept of regulatory takings in *Pennsylvania Coal Co. v. Mahon*, Justice Holmes underscored the elusiveness of the enterprise: "The general rule, at least, is that, while property may be regulated to a certain extent, if regulation goes too far, it will be recognized as a taking."[4] *Mahon* offered rather little guidance about how to decide how far was too far, except that "the extent of the diminution" in value was critical.[5] That accorded with the purpose of the Takings Clause, as it was later described, "to bar Government from forcing some people alone to bear public burdens which, in all fairness and justice, should be borne by the public as a

---

[2] 141 S. Ct. 2063 (2021).

[3] As the Court has acknowledged. Murr v. Wisconsin, 137 S. Ct. 1933, 1942 (2017). *See generally* William M. Treanor, *The Original Understanding of the Takings Clause and the Political Process*, 95 Colum. L. Rev. 782 (1995).

[4] 260 U.S. 393, 415 (1922).

[5] *Id.* at 413 (1922).

whole."[6] But the next half-century of regulatory takings cases produced little by way of doctrine.

In *Penn Central Transportation Co. v. New York City*[7]—the landmark case about landmarks—the Court attempted to corral its dozens of takings cases since *Mahon*. Finding a succession of "essentially *ad hoc*, factual inquiries," it prescribed more of the same.[8] But it "identified several factors that have particular significance" in those inquiries:

> The economic impact of the regulation on the claimant and, particularly, the extent to which the regulation has interfered with distinct investment-backed expectations are, of course, relevant considerations. So, too, is the character of the governmental action. *A "taking" may more readily be found when the interference with property can be characterized as a physical invasion by government* than when interference arises from some public program adjusting the benefits and burdens of economic life to promote the common good.[9]

Applying what came to be called the "*Penn Central* balancing test," the Court held that New York City committed no taking when it barred the erection of a skyscraper atop Grand Central Station, which had been designated a historical landmark. *Penn Central* did not involve a physical invasion, but it plainly signaled that its balancing test—with economic impact as its linchpin—should apply to government action that could be "characterized as a physical invasion";[10] that fact simply weighed in the balance, like a metaphorical thumb on the scale in favor of the owner.

Justice Rehnquist dissented. On two issues in particular, he took more categorical positions that harkened back to old common-law principles of property.[11] First, on what presumptively counts as a taking: "Property is taken in the constitutional sense when inroads are made upon an owner's use of it to an extent that, as between private parties,

---

[6] Armstrong v. United States, 364 U.S. 40, 49 (1960) (internal quotation marks omitted).

[7] 438 U.S. 104, 123 (1978).

[8] *Id.* at 124.

[9] *Id.* (emphasis added) (citations omitted).

[10] *Id.*

[11] And that harkened as well to analytical moves made by Justice Holmes in *Mahon* that had not crystalized into doctrine—see Pennsylvania Coal Co. v. Mahon, 260 U.S. 393, 413 (1922) (identifying the right to remove a column of coal beneath a third person's home as "an estate in land," and suggesting that it could be taken without compensation only to abate a "public nuisance")—and that were repudiated after *Penn Central* in Keystone Bituminous Coal Co. v. DeBenedictis, 480 U.S. 470 (1987).

a servitude has been acquired."[12] (That, for Justice Rehnquist, included the restrictions on Penn Central's use of its "air rights," which amounted to a negative easement.)[13] Second, on what kinds of government actions are nonetheless exempt from takings scrutiny: mainly those that prevent noxious, nuisance-like harms to the public.[14] (That, in his view, did not include disfigurement of historic landmarks.) Rehnquist's dissent laid out a takings agenda for the anti-regulatory wing of the Court.

A. PHYSICAL INVASIONS BEFORE *CEDAR POINT*

Just one year later Justice Rehnquist garnered a majority for an opinion that carried echoes of his *Penn Central* dissent into the realm of physical invasions. In *Kaiser Aetna v. United States*, the Court found a taking in the federal government's assertion of the navigational servitude—a public right of access—to a pond that had been dredged and made navigable by the owner's substantial investments.[15] But was that because the government had taken an easement—a kind of servitude—or because the *Penn Central* factors favored the owner? Justice Rehnquist's majority opinion pointed both ways. It began in the key of balancing, repeating *Penn Central*'s prescription of "essentially *ad hoc*, factual inquiries" into the economic impact of the regulation, its interference with reasonable investment-backed expectations, and the character of the governmental action.[16] And it emphasized Kaiser-Aetna's expectancies and expenditures in the wake of the government's "consent" to the dredging.[17] But Justice Rehnquist concluded in more categorical-sounding terms:

> In this case, we hold that the "right to exclude," so universally held to be a fundamental element of the property right, falls within this category of interests that the Government cannot take without compensation. . . . [T]he imposition of the navigational servitude in this context will result

[12] *Penn Central*, 438 U.S. at 146 (internal citations omitted).

[13] *Id.* at 143 (Rehnquist, J., dissenting).

[14] *Id.* at 145. Rehnquist also allowed for regulations that secure an "average reciprocity of advantage," like zoning laws that apply to all owners within broadly defined areas. *Id.* at 147. That concession to twentieth-century regulatory practice had already been blessed in *Mahon*, 260 U.S. at 160.

[15] 444 U.S. 164 (1979).

[16] *Id.* at 175.

[17] *Id.* at 178–80.

> in an actual physical invasion of the privately owned marina. And even if the Government physically invades only an easement in property, it must nonetheless pay just compensation.[18]

The opinion thus managed both to honor *Penn Central*'s balancing test and to undermine it in the context of physical invasions.

That ambiguity in *Kaiser-Aetna* was dispelled just one year later in *Pruneyard Shopping Mall v. Robins*.[19] Rehnquist, again writing for the majority, *rejected* a takings challenge to California's recognition of a state constitutional right of peaceful expression in the interior corridors of a large shopping mall: "It is true that one of the essential sticks in the bundle of property rights is the right to exclude others [citing *Kaiser Aetna*.] And here there has literally been a 'taking' of that right."[20] But that did not end the inquiry. The constitutional takings question, said the Court, turned on "such factors as the character of the governmental action, its economic impact, and its interference with reasonable investment-backed expectations."[21] There was no showing here that the physical presence of peaceful protesters would "unreasonably impair the value or use of their property as a shopping center"; unlike in *Kaiser-Aetna*, the owners had thus "failed to demonstrate that the 'right to exclude others' is so essential to the use or economic value of their property that the state-authorized limitation of it amounted to a 'taking.'"[22] After *Pruneyard* it was clear (again) that government-authorized physical invasions were subject to *Penn Central* balancing and turned on a showing of significant economic impact. The physically invasive dimension put a "thumb on the scale," as seen in *Kaiser-Aetna*'s finding a taking based on much less economic impact than the owner suffered in *Penn Central*; but *Pruneyard* showed it was not dispositive.

That is where the law of physical takings stood when the Court carved out an exception to *Penn Central* balancing in *Loretto v. Teleprompter*.[23] There the Court held that compelling landlords to permit installation of a cable and cable box on their buildings, by imposing a

---

[18] *Id.* at 179–80 (citations omitted).

[19] 447 U.S. 74 (1980).

[20] *Id.* at 82.

[21] *Id.* at 83 (citing *Kaiser Aetna*, 444 U.S. at 175).

[22] *Id.* at 83–84.

[23] 458 U.S. 419 (1982).

"permanent physical occupation," had effected a per se taking without regard to its magnitude or its economic impact.[24] As to the tiny space that was occupied, the owner had lost not only the right to exclude but the right to possess, use, or effectively convey the property; a permanent occupation "does not simply take a single 'strand' from the 'bundle' of property rights: it chops through the bundle, taking a slice of every strand."[25]

Justice Marshall, writing for the majority, went to great lengths to confine the new rule to *permanent occupations*, and to emphasize that other physical invasions were still subject to balancing. For example, the Court relied on a very old decision contrasting the installation of telephone poles along a street—a permanent occupation—to the "temporary and shifting" presence of "[t]he ordinary traveler, whether on foot or in a vehicle, [who] passes to and fro along the streets."[26] Similarly, the Court distinguished *Kaiser Aetna* as a case that had required balancing, for "the easement of passage, not being a permanent occupation of land, was not considered a taking *per se* . . ."[27] Both *Kaiser-Aetna* and *Pruneyard*, as well as past cases of "intermittent flooding," were "subject to a more complex balancing process to determine whether they are a taking," because "they [did] not absolutely dispossess the owner of his rights to use, and exclude others from, his property."[28]

The *Loretto* dissenters attacked the new per se rule as an "anachronistic," "formalistic," and unjustified departure from *Penn Central*.[29] The rule did create an anomaly in the law of regulatory takings by ignoring impact on the use or value of property. (Indeed, cable access probably increased the rental value of the affected property.) The new per se rule applied even where there were no substantial burdens on the owner at all, much less ones that, "in all fairness and justice, should be borne by the public as a whole."[30] In its original form, however, the *Loretto* anomaly did not seem very important. The category of

---

[24] *Id.* at 437.

[25] *Id.* at 435.

[26] *Id.* at 428–29 (quoting St. Louis v. W. Union Telegraph Co., 148 U.S. 92, 98 (1893)).

[27] *Id.* at 434.

[28] *Id.* at 435 n.12.

[29] *Id.* at 442 (Blackmun, J., dissenting).

[30] Armstrong v. United States, 364 U.S. 40, 49 (1960).

permanent physical occupations seemed very narrow and its boundaries clear enough to avoid sliding down a slippery slope.[31]

Alas, the slippery slope proved irresistible to those like Justice Scalia who aimed to expand takings liability and to shrink the role of ad hoc balancing. In *Nollan v. California Coastal Commission*,[32] a majority held that the state's imposition of a public easement along the dry-sand portion of a privately-owned stretch of Pacific beach would be a per se taking. ("Would be," that is, if done unconditionally; the main issue in *Nollan* was whether public beach access was nonetheless a valid condition on the grant of a building permit; it wasn't.) After citing *Loretto*'s per se rule for permanent occupations, Justice Scalia for the majority simply asserts: "We think a 'permanent physical occupation' has occurred, for purposes of that rule, where individuals are given a permanent and continuous right to pass to and fro, so that the real property may continuously be traversed, even though no particular individual is permitted to station himself permanently upon the premises."[33] In the footnote to that audacious misreading of *Loretto*, the majority distinguished both *Pruneyard* (where "the owner had already opened his property to the general public, and in addition permanent access was not required") and *Kaiser Aetna* (which "was affected by traditional doctrines regarding navigational servitudes"); neither case "involved, as this one does, a classic right-of-way easement."[34]

After *Nollan*, the category of "permanent physical occupations" included "permanent access" (as in the case of the "ordinary traveler . . . [who] passes to and fro along the streets"). *Nollan* transformed *Loretto*'s small anomaly into a beachhead in the movement to fortify traditional private property rights vis-à-vis the regulatory state. *Penn Central* balancing was not fit for that purpose; per se rules were the weapons of choice. That was later underscored in *Lucas v. South Carolina Coastal Council*,[35] which announced a new per se rule for government actions that "eliminate all economically beneficial . . . use" of the property in question.[36]

---

[31] Though the dissenters argued otherwise. *Loretto*, 458 U.S. at 448–51 (Blackmun, J., dissenting).

[32] 483 U.S. 825 (1987).

[33] *Id.* at 832.

[34] *Id.* at 832 n.1.

[35] 505 U.S. 1003 (1992).

[36] *Id.* at 1015.

B. DOCTRINAL BATTLEGROUNDS IN REGULATORY TAKINGS AND THE IMPORTANCE OF PER SE RULES

As of *Cedar Point*, the overall landscape of regulatory takings had acquired a certain symmetry. Nearly all regulatory impingements on land—both government-authorized physical invasions and restrictions on land use—were subject to *Penn Central*'s balancing test, albeit with a thumb on the scale in physical invasion cases. After *Loretto* and *Lucas*, the default domain of balancing was flanked on each side by a per se rule—one for permanent physical occupations and one for regulations eliminating all economically viable use. Two issues became critical within each branch: How broad were the per se categories? And within those categories, what were the exceptions to per se treatment? Beginning with the latter:

1. *Inherent Limitations on Title.* Both per se rules had "exceptions" where the government action corresponded to a built-in limitation on the owner's property rights. Per *Lucas*: "Where the State seeks to sustain regulation that deprives land of all economically beneficial use, we think it may resist compensation only if the *logically antecedent inquiry into the nature of the owner's estate* shows that the proscribed use interests were not part of his title to begin with."[37] It was a "logically antecedent inquiry" because it replicated what should be the threshold question in any takings case, whether headed for balancing or per se treatment: What rights did the owner have apart from the challenged government action, and did that action take anything away from that baseline bundle of rights? This "safe harbor" for preexisting limitations on title applied to all takings cases, but it mattered most in cases governed by per se rules. Within the balancing test, the government could press the importance of its goals and the reasonableness of its actions; but those were irrelevant in a per se case unless they could be squeezed into the rubric of preexisting limitations on title.

In the case of use restrictions, the quintessential pre-existing limitation, per *Lucas*, lay in nuisance law: No one has the right to use their land so as to commit a private or public nuisance.[38] (Ironically, what counts as a nuisance typically turns on a balancing test.[39]) *Lucas* pointed

[37] *Id.* at 1027 (emphasis added).

[38] *Lucas*, 505 U.S. at 1029.

[39] The Court underscored the point by referring to the balancing test prescribed by the RESTATEMENT (SECOND) OF TORTS §§ 826–831 (Am. L. Inst. 1979), for most private nuisance

to a corresponding safe harbor within the physical invasion branch: The common law doctrine of public or private necessity could sanction an otherwise trespassory physical invasion. And although permanent occupations were presumptively per se takings, "we assuredly *would* permit the government to assert a permanent easement that was a pre-existing limitation upon the landowner's title."[40] In that case the owner simply did not have the right to exclude that was allegedly taken.

Lucas intimated, however, that not all pre-existing law was created equal for these purposes: limitations on title with old common-law roots were more likely to be deemed "inherent" in the owner's baseline property rights than statutory restrictions that strayed from the common law.[41] The point was later underscored in *Palazzolo v. Rhode Island*,[42] which held that statutory restrictions do not necessarily limit the owner's baseline property rights for takings purposes upon their enactment or with the passing of time or title. Under *Lucas* and *Palazzolo*, the restrictions that "inhere in the title itself" are the "common, shared understandings of permissible limitations derived from a State's legal tradition."[43] That included old common-law doctrines like nuisance, but not the restrictions on coastal development or destruction of wetlands challenged in *Lucas* and *Palazzolo*.[44]

In denying the legislature's plenary power to modify property rights prospectively—that is, for those who acquire land after legislative action—the *Palazzolo* majority said: "The State may not put so potent a Hobbesian stick into the Lockean bundle."[45] The Lockean bundle? Locke is a progenitor of the notion that property rights are not mere creations of positive law but are pre-political and grounded in (God-given) natural law.[46] Perhaps this was merely a rhetorical flourish by the *Palazzolo* majority, for it seemed at odds with the reigning positivist dogma that property rights are defined by state law.

---

actions. *Lucas*, 505 U.S. at 1030–31. But the Court also instructed the state court, in applying the "nuisance exception," to stick closely to existing state court precedents applying nuisance law. *Lucas*, 505 U.S. at 1031.

[40] *Lucas*, 505 U.S. at 1028–29.

[41] *Id.* at 1029–30.

[42] 533 U.S. 606 (2001).

[43] *Id.* at 630 (citing *Lucas*, 505 U.S. at 1029–30).

[44] *Lucas*, 505 U.S. at 1007–08; *Palazzolo*, 533 U.S. at 614.

[45] *Palazzolo*, 533 U.S. at 627.

[46] Jeremy Waldron, The Right to Private Property 139 (1990).

Yet one couldn't help but notice that, in identifying limitations that inhere in the owner's title, the Court seemed to be pointing back through the mists of time—to a prelapsarian and pre-New Deal past. Statutes regulating "noxious" threats to human health and safety and conventional "Euclidian" zoning laws—both blessed by the 1920s—appeared to be safe. But regulatory schemes protecting the natural environment, like coastal beaches or wetlands (*Lucas* and *Palazzolo*), or affording public access to nature (*Nollan* and *Dolan)* were outside that safe harbor and exposed to takings liability. The old common law wasn't much concerned with those interests when they ran up against property rights. Nuisance law, in particular, dealt poorly with harms that were diffuse or latent, or that arose incrementally from seemingly innocuous activities—that is, with much of what modern environmental regulation has come to address. If nuisance had somehow remained the only legal framework available for dealing with those harms, it might have evolved; aggregate forms of litigation and structural injunctions might have helped to address some of nuisance law's blind spots. But the profusion of environmental legislation of the last half-century effectively preempted that evolutionary process and left nuisance law behind in its pre-modern state. It is thus ironic if not perverse that this stunted version of nuisance law has become a benchmark for what regulations are safe from takings liability.

The anachronistic shape of the "pre-existing limitation" safe-harbor from takings liability is most important within the per se categories. Under the balancing test, the benefits and burdens of regulation can be weighed in a more holistic and less hidebound way. The larger the per se categories, however, the greater the latitude for litigants, advocates, and judges to pursue an aggressive deregulatory agenda, and to foreclose consideration of regulatory gains, in the name of conventional property rights. And so the battle was on, after *Loretto* and *Lucas* respectively, to expand the reach of the per se rules.

2. *Expanding Per Se Categories.* In the case of land use restrictions, the battle was centered around shrinking the "denominator"—the whole, "all" of which must be taken to fall under *Lucas*'s per se rule.[47] *Lucas* itself involved a ban on new development that covered two

[47] The "denominator problem"—not yet so-named—arose in *Mahon* itself, and was one target of Justice Brandeis's dissent. The problem received its classic exposition in Frank I. Michelman, *Property, Utility, and Fairness: Comments on the Ethical Foundations of "Just Compensation" Law*, 80 HARV. L. REV. 1165, 1190–93 (1967).

whole undeveloped lots along a vulnerable strip of South Carolina's coastline; that counted, for the Court, as eliminating all economically beneficial use.[48] *Lucas* cast a pall over regulations protecting beaches, wetlands, or wildlife habitat, which often banned development over large tracts of land. But *Lucas*'s per se category threatened to metastasize if owners were allowed to tailor the "denominator" to fit the regulation. Imagine if the owner of a partly restricted 100-acre tract could divide that tract (in fact or conceptually) into separate lots such that some were now subject to a complete ban on development.[49] Or if the owner of undeveloped land could characterize a temporary moratorium on development as a total taking of a leasehold of corresponding duration.[50] *Lucas* set off a decades-long legal battle over how to determine the "denominator." But the Court has resisted entreaties to tinker with the denominator, and has stuck with the "entire parcel," as measured "by the metes and bounds that describe its geographic dimensions and the term of years that describes the temporal aspect of the owner's interest."[51] Skirmishes remain and reversals are possible, but we will leave those aside.

Our focus here is on the parallel battle to expand the per se category for permanent physical occupations. As we've seen, despite Justice Marshall's strenuous efforts to confine it in *Loretto*, the category was enlarged in *Nollan* to include "permanent access" in the form of a "classic right-of-way easement." Thereafter, the Court returned to the "physical invasions" branch of takings law only in passing before *Cedar Point*. But the anti-regulatory wing of the Court, with Justices Rehnquist and Scalia in the vanguard, still found opportunities to hint at future expansions of the per se category. In introducing *Lucas*'s new per se rule for some use restrictions, Scalia described *Loretto*'s per se rule as covering "regulations that compel the property owner to suffer a physical 'invasion' of his property. In general (at least with regard to permanent invasions), no matter how minute the intrusion, and no matter how weighty the public purpose behind it, we

[48] Surely it didn't render the land either useless or valueless; tents or trailers, e.g., were permitted. But the Court adopted a questionable lower court finding to this effect. *Lucas*, 505 U.S. at 1009.

[49] Such a claim was belatedly made in *Palazzolo*, but the Court refused to consider it. Palazzolo v. Rhode Island, 533 U.S. 606, 631 (2001).

[50] Tahoe-Sierra Pres. Council, Inc. v. Tahoe Reg'l Plan. Agency, 535 U.S. 302, 313 (2002).

[51] *Id.* at 331–32; *see also* Murr v. Wisconsin, 137 S. Ct. 1933, 1944 (2017).

have required compensation."[52] Then in *Dolan v. City of Tigard*, in which the owner was required to dedicate a fifteen-foot-wide strip of land for passage by pedestrians and bicycles as a condition for a building permit, Rehnquist wrote for the majority: "Without question, had the city simply required petitioner to dedicate a strip of land . . . for public use, rather than conditioning the grant of her permit to redevelop her property on such a dedication, a taking would have occurred."[53] He could have stopped there, as *Nollan* was right on point. But he added a favorite line from *Kaiser Aetna*: "Such public access would deprive petitioner of the right to exclude others, 'one of the most essential sticks in the bundle of rights that are commonly characterized as property.'"[54]

The stage was now set and the plot was in motion, even if neither of the lead script writers, Justices Rehnquist and Scalia, would live to see the denouement in *Cedar Point*.

II. *Cedar Point* and the Resurrection of Blackstonian Property Rights

Cedar Point took up a challenge to a forty-year-old California regulation that entitled union organizers to meet with workers at their work site for up to three non-working hours per day—before and after employee shifts and during lunch breaks—for up to four thirty-day periods each year. The regulation was adopted under California's Agricultural Labor Relations Act of 1975 (ALRA), a crowning achievement of Cesar Chavez and the United Farm Workers.[55] The access regulation, which contained safeguards against disruption of employers' operations, applied whether or not workers lived on site; they did not in the cases at issue.

From the outset the claim was litigated for the Supreme Court on the theory that the regulation amounted to a per se physical taking.[56] The growers, represented by the conservative Pacific Legal Foundation, made no effort to show any economic impact or interference

---

[52] *Lucas*, 505 U.S. at 1015.

[53] 512 U.S. 374, 384 (1994).

[54] *Id.* (quoting Kaiser Aetna v. United States, 444 U.S. 164, 176 (1979)).

[55] *See* Benjamin I. Sachs, *Safety, Health, and Union Access in* Cedar Point Nursery, 2021 S. Ct. Rev. 99.

[56] Brief Amicus Curiae of Property Law Professors in Support of Respondents at 3–5, Cedar Point Nursery v. Hassid, 141 S. Ct. 2063 (2021) (No. 20–107).

with use of the property, as required under *Penn Central*. As for their per se theory, even with the Court's conservative majority fortified in 2020, the case seemed a big stretch beyond *Nollan*. Access was far from "permanent"; timewise, it covered at most four percent of any given year. And it did not resemble any conventional type of easement, much less a "classic right-of-way easement."

The petitioners' claim hit its target when it reached the Court, with the six conservative Justices agreeing that the California regulation effected a per se taking. Chief Justice Roberts, writing for the majority, jettisoned the term "permanent physical occupation"—already stretched to the breaking point in *Nollan*—along with *Loretto*'s painstaking efforts to cabin the category's reach. Rather, the ALRA regulation was held to have physically "appropriated" property.[57] What exactly did the ALRA regulation appropriate? It "appropriate[d] a right to invade the growers' property";[58] or "appropriate[d] for the enjoyment of third parties the owners' right to exclude";[59] or "appropriate[d] an easement."[60] The majority used that exquisitely capacious formulation seven times in one or another of those variations. After *Cedar Point*, it is now clear that nearly all recurring physical invasions imposed or authorized by the government—at least as to property closed to the public—are per se takings, however minimal the impact on the use and value of the property.[61]

In leaving behind the limiting term "permanent physical occupation" in favor of "appropriation," Chief Justice Roberts made use of his own handiwork several years earlier in *Horne v. Department of Agriculture*.[62] *Horne* was a rare takings case involving personal property; it challenged the government's seizure of part of the owners' raisin crop. The Court described that as a "physical appropriation," and relied heavily on the per se takings rule for real property that was announced in *Loretto* and expanded in *Nollan*.[63] But the limiting term "permanent physical occupation" simply disappeared in *Horne*, which described *Loretto* as having "reaffirmed the rule that a physical *appropriation* of

[57] *Cedar Point*, 141 S. Ct. at 2072.

[58] *Id.*

[59] *Id.*

[60] *Id.* at 2073 (quoting *Kaiser Aetna*).

[61] *Id.* at 2072–74.

[62] 576 U.S. 350 (2015).

[63] *Id.* at 357–64.

property gave rise to a *per se* taking."[64] "Appropriation" was thus ready for service in *Cedar Point* as the linguistic bridge from *Loretto*'s narrow per se rule to the newly engorged version.

What was plainly new in *Cedar Point* was the breadth of the per se category. In support of that innovation, the majority recast several old precedents as illustrating the per se rule, even though they had explicitly relied on significant interference with the owner's use of land.[65] In *Portsmouth Harbor*,[66] the government had trained guns, and occasionally discharged them, directly over the owner's summer resort. The Court observed: "There is no doubt that a serious loss has been inflicted upon the claimant, as the public has been frightened off the premises by the imminence of the guns."[67] In *United States v. Causby*, planes had flown over the owner's chicken farm, "grazing the treetops and terrorizing the poultry."[68] "As many as six to ten . . . chickens were killed in one day by flying into the walls from fright."[69] *Causby* emphasized: "Flights over private land are not a taking, unless they are so low and so frequent as to be a direct and immediate interference with the enjoyment and use of the land."[70] And in *Kaiser Aetna*, as noted above, the Court emphasized the economic impact of the navigational servitude, which granted to the public a right of access that the owner had planned to sell. Yet the Court in *Cedar Point* cited all three cases, along with *Loretto* and *Nollan*, for the proposition that "government-authorized invasions of property—whether by plane, boat, cable, or beachcomber—are physical takings requiring just compensation," without regard to their economic impact.[71]

As for *Pruneyard*, the one post-*Penn Central* holding that seemed to defy the Court's new rule, the Court observed: "Limitations on how a business generally open to the public may treat individuals on the premises are readily distinguishable from regulations granting a right

[64] *Id.* at 360.

[65] *Cedar Point*, 141 S. Ct. at 2073–74.

[66] Portsmouth Harbor Land & Hotel Co. v. United States, 260 U.S. 327, 330 (1922).

[67] *Id.* at 329.

[68] *Cedar Point*, 141 S. Ct. at 2073 (citing United States v. Causby, 328 U.S. 256, 259 (1946)).

[69] *Causby*, 328 U.S. at 259.

[70] *Id.* at 266.

[71] *Cedar Point*, 141 S. Ct. at 2073–74.

to invade property closed to the public."[72] Distinguishable, yes, but hardly ringingly reaffirmed. It remains to be seen, for example, how much latitude owners will have going forward to define the scope of their invitation to the public and to label as an "appropriation" of their residual right to exclude a law that limits their ability to pick and choose among members of the public.[73] We'll return to this point.

Beyond disingenuously recasting its own takings precedents, the Court blew past other hurdles within state law. For one, the kind of access called for in the ALRA regulation did not fit the definition of an easement under California law "because the access right may not be transferred, does not burden any particular parcel of property, and may not be recorded."[74] Before *Cedar Point*, Professor Thomas Merrill had argued that the Court's regulatory-takings jurisprudence—including its recent elevation of the concept of "appropriation"—could be understood as guarding against circumvention of the law of eminent domain.[75] On that view, takings liability was reserved for cases in which the government had effectively acquired or condemned a distinct interest in property recognized under state law and conventionally bought and sold among private parties. That could be said of the easements at issue in *Loretto* and *Nollan*, but not of the episodic access in *Cedar Point*.[76] Yet the Court brushed aside this objection: "The Board cannot absolve itself of takings liability by appropriating the growers' right to exclude in a form that is a slight mismatch from state easement law."[77]

The *Cedar Point* majority also fudged the basic state law question of whether the growers had any right to exclude the organizers under California law to begin with. In other words, what was the growers'

---

[72] *Id.* at 2077.

[73] I'm indebted to Niko Bowie for underscoring this point to me. He asks: Suppose a vineyard had a winery "open to the public," but sought to exclude union organizers claiming a right of access to its workers under state law? If that would give them a takings claim after *Cedar Point*—and it might—then a whole raft of laws barring discriminatory exclusion from places "open to the public" might now be subject to takings challenges. For more on this point, see Nikolas Bowie, *Antidemocracy*, 135 Harv. L. Rev. 160 (2021). I return to the point briefly in Part III.C. below.

[74] *Cedar Point*, 141 S. Ct. at 2075.

[75] *See* Thomas Merrill, *The Compensation Constraint and the Scope of the Takings Clause*, 96 Notre Dame L. Rev. 1421 (2021); Thomas Merrill, *The Eagle Theory*, 9 Brigham-Kanner Prop. Rgts. J. 17 (2020).

[76] Thanks to Professor Merrill for drawing my attention to this feature of *Cedar Point*.

[77] *Cedar Point*, 141 S. Ct. at 2075–76.

baseline bundle of rights from which the government action allegedly subtracted? At one level the question was answered by the challenged regulation itself: Since 1976—well before the Cedar Point growers began operating[78]—California law had limited agricultural employers' right to exclude labor organizers from meeting with farm workers where they work. Arguably, then, nothing was "taken" in 2015 with the organizers' entry because their right of access was built into the bundle of rights these owners had acquired. But *Palazzolo* instructs us to ask how the ALRA regulation measures up against older or more basic "common, shared understandings" and "legal tradition[s]."[79]

The Court in *Cedar Point* dutifully nods to positivist dogma about the property rights baseline in declaring: "no one disputes that, without the access regulation, the growers would have had the right under California law to exclude union organizers from their property," citing a 1993 California decision affirming a private medical center's right to eject anti-abortion protesters.[80] But the point was indeed disputed. As one *amicus curiae* brief explained, California law on employers' right to exclude *union* speakers from their property is quite nuanced.[81] The California Supreme Court in 1981, after surveying criminal trespass law going back to the 1950s, declared that "the general trespass statutes do not prohibit [otherwise] lawful union activity at the jobsite."[82] That court later summarized the civil law of trespass, in light of state constitutional and statutory rights of access: "Since at least 1964, . . . California law has protected the right to engage in labor speech—including picketing, distributing handbills, and other speech activities—on private land in front of a business that is the subject of a labor dispute."[83] That was the context within which the ALRA regulation was enacted in 1975.

---

[78] *Our Story*, Cedar Point Nursery (last visited Mar. 12, 2022), https://cedarpointnursery.com/our-story.

[79] Palazzolo v. Rhode Island, 533 U.S. 606, 631 (2001).

[80] *Cedar Point*, 141 S. Ct. at 2076 (citing Allred v. Harris, 18 Cal. Rptr. 2d 530, 533 (Cal. Ct. App. 1993)).

[81] *See* Brief of Amici Curiae United Food and Commercial Workers Western States Council and Teamsters Joint Council 7 in Support of Respondents Hassid, et al., *Cedar Point*, 141 S. Ct. 2063 (No. 20-107).

[82] *In re* Catalano, 29 Cal. 3d 1, 10–13 (1981); *see also In re* Zerbe, 60 Cal. 2d 666, 669 (1964).

[83] Ralphs Grocery Co. v. United Food & Com. Workers Union Loc. 8, 290 P.3d 1116, 1123–25 (2012) (citations omitted).

It turns out that, on a close reading of California law, owners usually *do* have the right to exclude union speakers from property that is closed to the public, unlike common areas of large shopping malls and outdoor entrances to retail businesses.[84] Except, that is, for farms covered by the ALRA regulation itself. On a positivist reading of *Palazzolo*, one might conclude that ALRA access was consistent with the growers' baseline property rights under state law, given its congruence with other even-older union access rights under California law. But the Court in *Cedar Point* ignored that possibility, along with the nuanced state law on this point, in favor of a generic assertion of the right to exclude others.

The point is underscored by the Court's account of the access rights that *do* count among the "pre-existing limitation[s] upon [a] land owner's title" and that can therefore still foreclose a takings claim after *Cedar Point*.[85] The Court mentions only narrow privileges of access with a very old common-law pedigree: the privilege of necessity and the government's power to effect an arrest or a reasonable search on private property.[86] (The dissent asks: "Do only those exceptions that existed in, say, 1789 count?"[87]) The majority ignores broader and more relevant privileges against trespass that treatise writers have identified in the caselaw for nearly a century. The first *Restatement of Torts* in 1934 stated: "A duty or authority imposed or created by legislative enactment carries with it the privilege to enter land in the possession of another for the purpose of performing or exercising such duty or authority in so far as the entry is reasonably necessary to such performance or exercise...."[88] Is that not what ALRA does?[89] As

[84] *Id.* at 1120–21.

[85] *Cedar Point*, 141 S. Ct. at 2079 (citing *Lucas*, 505 U.S. 1003, 1028–29 (1992)).

[86] *Id. Lucas* had previously noted that a preexisting permanent easement would also count as a "pre-existing limitation upon the land," 505 U.S. at 1028; but it's unclear whether easements whose *legal* foundations were of modern vintage would count for those purposes.

[87] *Cedar Point*, 141 S. Ct. at 2089 (Breyer, J., dissenting).

[88] Am. L. Inst., Restatement of Torts § 211 (1934). Comment d specifies that private persons may be authorized to enter private lands by legislative action. *See also* 63 Corpus Juris § 121 (1933) (noting that "one acting under authority from the government may justify acts which would otherwise be a trespass," and citing examples including regulatory inspections and official surveys).

[89] One might argue that, just because an individual has a privilege against trespass liability when acting under the authority of state legislation, that does not mean the government can give itself a free pass from *takings* liability by fiat. But the Court strongly implies otherwise—that is, the government does have a free pass—as to the privileges it does recognize. *Cedar Point* extends not just liability but per se liability for the first time to exactly the sort of

Professor James Casner put it in his 1954 treatise, *American Law of Property*: "[P]rivileges to intrude upon private land exist as a balance between the rights of the occupant to freedom from intrusion and the needs of society to impose reasonable burdens upon such land for the general welfare."[90] But apparently that is the kind of new-fangled thinking that the *Cedar Point* Court aims to discredit.

So we find the Court distorting its own takings precedents as well as both state law and general common-law limitations on private property rights, skewing them at every turn toward the breadth and essentiality of owners' right to exclude others. Scattered phrases to that effect had appeared in the caselaw, though almost always anchored to holdings and analyses that were consistent with balancing. *Cedar Point* cements them for the first time into a categorical condemnation of "physical takings" and a powerful presumption about the baseline rights of owners to exclude others that casts actual state law in a subservient role. What's going on here?

Thus far we've ignored one glaring clue: In underscoring the fundamentality of the right to exclude, the Court in *Cedar Point* cites Blackstone's famous proclamation that "the very idea of property entails 'that sole and despotic dominion which one man claims and exercises over the external things of the world, in total exclusion of the right of any other individual in the universe.'"[91] In harkening to "sole and despotic dominion," *Cedar Point* sides with those contemporary property theorists for whom an owner's right to exclude others is the defining essence of property.[92] Indeed, the Court outflanks those scholars in making the right to exclude nearly inviolable by the state.[93] As for those property scholars for whom interdependency and

---

government-authorized entries that the treatise writers deemed privileged. The point is underscored by *Cedar Point*'s analysis of government inspections. *See infra* text accompanying notes 119–139.

[90] 6A American Law of Property § 28.10 (A. James Casner ed., 1954).

[91] *Cedar Point*, 141 S. Ct. at 2072.

[92] J. E. Penner, The Idea of Property in Law 69–71 (1997); Thomas W. Merrill, *Property and the Right to Exclude*, 77 Neb. L. Rev. 730, 740–55 (1998); Shyamkrishna Balganesh, *Demystifying the Right to Exclude: Of Property, Inviolability, and Automatic Injunctions*, 31 Harv. J.L. & Pub. Pol'y 593, 661 (2008).

[93] It is one thing to say that a right to exclude others is an essential attribute of property; it is quite another to say that the state's denial of one slice of that right to exclude is necessarily a taking of property even if the owner retains the right to exclude nearly anybody at nearly all times.

relational justice take precedence over exclusion,[94] they are apparently beneath the Court's notice.

Property scholars have previously highlighted the hyperbolic quality of Blackstone's dictum relative to his own description of the common law.[95] Carol Rose in particular has brilliantly contrasted the "sole and despotic dominion" passage with the more nuanced and complex account of common-law property rights that follow it in Blackstone's treatise.[96] Indeed, Blackstone offers some support to more heterodox and social conceptions of property—for example, in his account of duties to admit and serve the public on the part of property owners engaged in "common callings" like inn-keeping.[97] Rose characterizes "Blackstone's opening definition of property as exclusive dominion . . . *as metaphor, as trope*," not just for later property thinkers but for Blackstone himself.[98] Yet Blackstone remains linked in the modern legal mind with the "sole and despotic dominion" conception of property. So it's with apologies to Blackstone that I refer here to "Blackstonian property rights."

The Court's invocation of Blackstone's "sole and despotic dominion" trope suggests that more is afoot than a lazy imprecision about past precedents on the right to exclude others. *Cedar Point* implies that limitations on the right to exclude that diverge from a Blackstonian (or pre-New Deal) conception of property rights don't count as part of the "common, shared understandings" that determine property rights in the context of a takings claim. Even longstanding, authoritative interpretations of state trespass law itself appear not to inhere in an owner's baseline property rights, and to afford a safe harbor from takings liability, if they deny the "fundamental" right to exclude.[99] Thus read, *Cedar Point* amplifies the anti-positivist overtones of both *Lucas*

[94] For examples of the latter, see Gregory S. Alexander, Property and Human Flourishing (2018); Gregory S. Alexander & Eduardo M. Peñalver, An Introduction to Property Theory (2012); Hanoch Dagan, A Liberal Theory of Property (2021); Hanoch Dagan & Avihay Dorfman, *The Human Right to Private Property*, 18 Theoretical Inqs. L. 391 (2017); and Joseph William Singer, *Democratic Property: Things We Should Not Have to Bargain For*, in Research Handbook on Private Law Theory (Hanoch Dagan & Benjamin C. Zipursky eds., 2020).

[95] *See* Carol Rose, *Canons of Property Talk, or, Blackstone's Anxiety*, 108 Yale L.J. 601 (1998); David Schorr, *How Blackstone Became a Blackstonian*, 10 Theoretical Inqs. L. 103 (2009).

[96] Rose, *supra* note 95, at 603–06.

[97] *Id.* at 603–04; *see* Joseph William Singer, *No Right To Exclude: Public Accommodations and Private Property*, 90 Nw. U. L. Rev. 1283, 1308–10 (1996).

[98] Rose, *supra* note 95, at 603 (emphasis added).

[99] Cedar Point v. Hassid, 141 S. Ct. 2063, 2072, 2077 (2021).

and *Palazzolo* and undercuts prevailing positivist dogma about the source of property rights. Like the takings claim that the Rehnquist Court *rejected* in *Pruneyard*, it would suggest "that the common law of trespass is not subject to revision by the State"; as Justice Marshall said in his *Pruneyard* concurrence, such a view "would freeze the common law as it has been constructed by the courts, perhaps at its 19th-century state of development," and "would represent a return to the era of *Lochner v. New York*."[100] One can only imagine Justice Marshall's response to *Cedar Point* and its metastasized version of the per se rule that he first elaborated and tried to cabin in *Loretto*.

III. Some Consequences of *Cedar Point*

Cedar Point has direct implications for what we might call "stranger access rights," especially in the workplace, and for government inspections across the regulatory landscape. More expansive readings of the decision would imperil larger swaths of the law of work and beyond.

Before turning to substance, it's worth making two preliminary points about takings litigation that may amplify the consequences of *Cedar Point* (and of takings jurisprudence generally). First, the Court in 2019 eliminated what it called a "preclusion trap" created by its prior decisions, and cleared a straight path into federal court for many claims that had previously been tied up in state litigation.[101] That will bring more takings cases before the Court and give it ample opportunities to further expand takings liability if it is so inclined.

The second point is about remedies. It might seem that claims under *Cedar Point* will be easily defused by providing for trivial amounts of compensation, given the lack of any demonstrable interference with the use or value of the affected properties. But demands for "just compensation" will often trigger the right to a hearing—or even, as in California, a jury trial—on how much compensation is due.[102] Takings

---

[100] Pruneyard Shopping Mall v. Robins, 447 U.S. 74, 93 (1980) (Marshall, J., concurring).

[101] For many years before the Court's decision in *Knick v. Township of Scott*, 139 S. Ct. 2162 (2019), as the Court in that case explained, most claims were not ripe until fully litigated in state court, but were then barred from federal court review by preclusion. As Tom Merrill pointed out to me, *Cedar Point* itself might have been blocked as not "ripe" before *Knick*: Because the organizers had apparently violated the terms of the ALRA regulation, *see Cedar Point*, 141 S. Ct. at 2069–70, the growers probably had a remedy under state law, possibly in trespass.

[102] Cal. Const. art. I, § 19(a). That might be avoidable if the nature and impact of the physical taking is uniform for all affected owners, as it was in *Loretto* (where one dollar was

claims come with what Professor Thomas Merrill calls a "due process tax" that can make takings (and eminent domain) far more costly to the government than the value of what was taken.[103] With that in mind, let us consider the kinds of regulations that are likely to trigger *Cedar Point*'s per se rule, and to be held up by demands for a hearing and just compensation.

A. *CEDAR POINT* AND STRANGER ACCESS RIGHTS

Cedar Point took direct aim at the relatively robust rights of access for union organizers under California's ALRA. But what about other access rights for union organizing, such as those under federal labor law (from which agricultural workers are excluded)?[104] The Court in *NLRB v. Babcock & Wilcox Co.* held that organizers have a right under the National Labor Relations Act (NLRA) to enter employer property only in rare cases in which "the location of a plant and the living quarters of the employees place the employees beyond the reach of reasonable union efforts to communicate with them"[105]—that is, mainly in workplaces that are vestiges of a pre-industrial economy, like logging camps and remote rural resorts, where workers live on the employer's property. (Recall that this was not true in *Cedar Point* itself, though it is for many agricultural workers.[106]) The Court alluded to takings law,[107] but rested its decision on the statute, in which it found a "distinction ... of substance" between employees' right to communicate among themselves and the rights of union organizers to communicate with them at work.[108] Reaffirming *Babcock* more recently, the Court in *Lechmere, Inc. v. NLRB* stressed the statute's text: "By its plain terms, ... the NLRA confers rights only on *employees*, not on unions or their nonemployee organizers."[109] As I've written elsewhere, *Babcock*

found to be "just compensation" for any who challenged the mandatory cable installation). *See* Loretto v. Teleprompter Manhattan CATV Corp., 446 N.E.2d 428 (N.Y. 1983). But that shortcut probably won't work for the more varied category of entries by human beings, like union organizers or government inspectors.

[103] Thomas W. Merrill, *Economics of Public Use*, 72 CORNELL L. REV. 61, 90 (1986).

[104] For a more extensive discussion of this issue, *see* Sachs, *supra* note 55.

[105] 351 U.S. 105, 113 (1956).

[106] *See* Sachs, *supra* note 55.

[107] 351 U.S. at 112 ("Organization rights are granted to workers by the same authority, the National Government, that preserves property rights. Accommodation between the two must be obtained with as little destruction of one as is consistent with the maintenance of the other.").

[108] *Id.* at 113.

[109] 502 U.S. 527, 532 (1992).

and *Lechmere* misconstrue both the text and the purpose of the NLRA.[110] But that is where things stand.

Can even those inordinately narrow access rights survive after *Cedar Point*?[111] (If so, then similarly narrowed access rights under a revised ALRA regulation—that is, for farm workers living on employer property—would also survive.) The majority is rather cagey on this point, declining to consider "[w]hatever specific takings issues may be presented by the highly contingent access right we recognized under the NLRA."[112] Justice Kavanaugh, in concurrence, was more forthcoming: "As I read it, *Babcock* recognized that employers have a basic Fifth Amendment right to exclude from their private property, subject to a 'necessity' exception similar to that noted by the Court today."[113] If a future majority were (unexpectedly) to follow this suggestion, and recognize a *necessity* for unions to educate and recruit otherwise-isolated workers at their workplace, that would save the notoriously stingy union access rights allowed by *Babcock* and *Lechmere*. Even then, however, any future move in Congress to expand statutory access rights for union organizers beyond *Babcock* would be blocked by *Cedar Point*.[114] To be sure, this might be quite academic, given the political logjam that has long blocked private sector labor law reform in Congress.[115]

Turning from labor legislation to state common-law provisions for "stranger access," consider *State v. Shack*, in which the New Jersey Supreme Court held that an agricultural employer had no right under

---

[110] As I've argued at length elsewhere: Cynthia Estlund, *Labor, Property, and Sovereignty after* Lechmere, 46 Stan. L. Rev. 305 (1994). For one thing, the NLRA sought to empower workers to organize across workplaces, and specified that the term "employee . . . shall not be limited to the employees of a particular employer." 29 U.S.C. § 152(3). Union organizers are both "employees" of their union under the NLRA and the agents of thousands of other employees—that is, union members who are seeking to expand the union and its bargaining power.

[111] *Loretto* had expressly distinguished organizer access rights under the NLRA on the then-obvious ground that they did not entail a permanent occupation of property. Loretto v. Teleprompter Manhattan CATV Corp., 458 U.S. 419, 434 n.11 (1982).

[112] Cedar Point v. Hassid, 141 S. Ct. 2063, 2077 (2021).

[113] *Id.* at 2080.

[114] That could still leave room for legislation granting union access to employer property that is open to the public, like the shopping center parking lot in *Lechmere*, as suggested by the Court's treatment of *Pruneyard*. But that depends on how the Court ends up construing the scope of owners' invitation to the public. *See supra* text accompanying notes 72–73.

[115] Cynthia Estlund, *The Ossification of American Labor Law*, 102 Colum. L. Rev. 1527, 1591 (2002).

the state's trespass law to exclude individuals offering legal and medical aid to migrant farm workers who lived on the employer's land.[116] No positive legislation or constitutional doctrine was at hand, but none was required, to support the claimed right of entry, for New Jersey law simply did not recognize it as a trespass. State law has thus limited the right to exclude since 1969. But under *Cedar Point*, that might not count, any more than California's union access rights, as among the "longstanding background restrictions on property rights" that offer a safe harbor from takings liability. Indeed, if a majority finally takes up conservative entreaties to recognize "judicial takings,"[117] *State v. Shack* itself could be challenged as a taking. After all, as the Court declared in *Palazzolo*, "[f]uture generations must also have a right to challenge unreasonable limitations on the use and value of land."[118]

B. ACCESS FOR GOVERNMENT INSPECTORS

Cedar Point also imperils innumerable state and federal regulatory regimes that require property owners to submit to government inspections pursuant to laws protecting workers, consumers, or the general public.[119] Let's first note how out of place takings law is here, given its purpose of preventing "[g]overnment from forcing some people alone to bear public burdens which, in all fairness and justice, should be borne by the public as a whole."[120] That incongruence between the reach and the purpose of takings law underscores again the anomalous nature of the per se rule for physical takings, which rules out consideration of why and how much a law burdens private property owners, not to mention the "fairness and justice" of doing so.

The majority suggested that "government health and safety inspection regimes will generally not constitute takings."[121] But why not? Don't those laws "appropriate a right to invade" private property and thus fall within *Cedar Point*'s newly expanded per se rule? Well, yes. *Cedar Point* assumes that government inspection regimes will now

[116] 277 A.2d 369 (1971).

[117] A majority demurred, without rejecting the concept of judicial takings, in *Stop the Beach Renourishment v. Florida Dep't of Environmental Protection*, 560 U.S. 702 (2010). Needless to say, the composition of the Court has shifted since then.

[118] Palazzolo v. Rhode Island, 533 U.S. 606, 627 (2001).

[119] Cedar Point v. Hassid, 141 S. Ct. 2063, 2087–89 (2021) (Breyer, J., dissenting).

[120] Armstrong v. United States, 364 U.S. 40, 49 (1960).

[121] *Cedar Point*, 141 S. Ct. at 2079.

constitute per se takings if imposed outright. The Court found no "inherent limitation" on property owners' right to exclude legally authorized government inspectors, only one for "government searches [or arrests] that are consistent with the Fourth Amendment."[122] (As noted above, the Court ignored a longstanding privilege to enter another's land to perform or exercise a "duty or authority . . . created by legislative enactment"—one that had often been applied to government inspections.[123]) Instead, the majority in *Cedar Point* suggests that regulatory inspections might be permissible conditions on "the grant of a benefit such as a permit, license, or registration."[124] Let's see how secure a defense this doctrine affords to government inspection regimes.

The Court quotes *Nollan* for the basic logic of exactions: "a permit condition that serves the same legitimate police-power purpose as a refusal to issue the permit should not be found to be a taking if the refusal to issue the permit would not constitute a taking."[125] The test for "exactions" can only be described as exacting: the condition must bear an "essential nexus" to the purpose behind the permit requirement, and its burdens must be "roughly proportional" to the impact of what is permitted. According to the *Cedar Point* majority, "when the government conditions the grant of a benefit such as a permit, license, or registration on allowing access for reasonable health and safety inspections, both the nexus and rough proportionality requirements of the constitutional conditions framework should not be difficult to satisfy."[126] That's good to know. But those two tests require a predicate—that is, a government "benefit such as a permit, license, or registration"—whose denial would not itself constitute a taking, and to which relevant conditions can be attached. And therein lies a problem for many inspection regimes.

Consider first a prototypical "government health and safety inspection regime": Under the Federal Meat Inspection Act (FMIA),[127] nearly all meat producers are required to register with the U.S. Department of Agriculture (USDA), and "meat food products prepared

[122] *Id.*

[123] *See* Am. L. Inst., *supra* note 88.

[124] *Cedar Point*, 141 S. Ct. at 2079.

[125] *Id.*

[126] *Id.*

[127] Federal Meat Inspection Act, 21 U.S.C. §§ 601–683.

for commerce" are subject to USDA inspection "at all times, by day or night, whether the establishment be operated or not, to every part of said establishment."[128] Before *Cedar Point*, the whole regulatory scheme would have been subject to "rational basis" review; and a takings challenge to inspections, if not dismissed out of hand, would have plainly failed under *Penn Central* balancing.[129] After *Cedar Point*, however, the FMIA inspection regime would be a per se taking—an "appropriation" of meat producers' right to exclude—unless it could be justified as a valid condition on a benefit or permit that the government could lawfully deny. The government might easily satisfy both nexus and proportionality requirements. But that only avoids takings liability if the government could lawfully deny registration, and prohibit production of meat for commerce, without committing a taking.

Maybe the FMIA regime passes muster, given the public health threat posed by tainted meat. In many cases, however, there is no such predicate for the *Nollan* and *Dolan* tests; not all laws that authorize inspections require regulated firms to secure a "permit, license, or registration" to operate. For example, most employers across the country are subject to federal labor standards that are administered by the Department of Labor (the Occupational Safety and Health Act (OSHA), the Fair Labor Standards Act (FLSA)) and that provide for inspections and audits.[130] Those employers are not required to have a permit or the like from the Department of Labor to operate; they are simply required to comply with applicable labor standards, and are subject to inspections to that end. But those legally authorized inspections now fall under *Cedar Point*'s per se rule, and are justifiable only on the *Nollan-Dolan* theory as permissible conditions on a permit, license, or the like.

In theory, legislatures could add permit requirements for any businesses subject to regulatory inspections. But that won't happen. Imagine the politics of a proposal to require all businesses subject to OSHA or FLSA to secure a permit from the DOL to operate at all. And if it did happen, the Court would have to decide whether the government had the power to deny ordinary businesses—those with no particular impact on public health and safety—the right to operate

[128] *Id.* § 606.

[129] Subject to procedural due process constraints on the manner of inspection.

[130] 29 U.S.C. § 657(a); 29 U.S.C.A. § 211(a).

at all; for that would be the necessary predicate for upholding a condition, like inspections, that would otherwise be a per se taking.

The Court has made some rather confusing pronouncements on this point, several of them in a single decision. In *Horne*,[131] the Court held that, even if "the government may prohibit the sale of raisins without effecting a per se taking,"[132] it couldn't condition the right to sell raisins on the owner's handing over a sizable portion of the raisin crop (as part of a price support program).[133] That appropriation was a per se taking, period.[134] Per *Horne*, "basic and familiar uses of property" like "[s]elling produce in interstate commerce,"[135] cannot be "h[e]ld hostage, to be ransomed by the waiver of constitutional protection."[136] That is, the right to sell raisins, "although certainly subject to reasonable government regulation, is . . . not a special governmental benefit" that can be subject to conditions that would be per se takings if imposed outright. Similarly, said the Court in *Horne*, "the right to build on one's own property—even though its exercise can be subjected to legitimate permitting requirements—cannot remotely be described as a 'governmental benefit'" of the sort that can be "held hostage."[137] Recall that *Nollan* had seemed to imply that the government *could* have denied a building permit in that case (on the ground that a larger house would block the public's view of the ocean), and therefore *could* have imposed permit conditions that advanced the same regulatory aims, including conditions that would be per se takings if imposed unilaterally.[138] But the Court in *Nollan* only assumed without deciding those points,[139] which might now return to the Court in a challenge to regulatory inspections.

---

[131] Horne v. Dep't of Agriculture, 576 U.S. 350 (2013).

[132] As the grower had conceded. *Id.* at 362.

[133] *Id.* at 354, 366.

[134] Without any opportunity to satisfy the *Nollan-Dolan* test for exactions. *Id.* at 364–66.

[135] *Id.* at 366.

[136] *Id.* The Court in *Horne* distinguished *Ruckelshaus v. Monsanto, Co.*, 467 U.S. 986 (1984), in which the Court upheld a requirement that pesticide producers turn over certain trade secrets—information about chemical components—as a condition for any license to sell such pesticides.

[137] *Horne*, 576 U.S. at 366 (quoting Nollan v. Cal. Coastal Comm'n, 483 U.S. 825, 833 n.2 (1987)).

[138] *Nollan*, 483 U.S. at 836.

[139] *Id.* at 835.

In short, it isn't clear what "government benefits" can be subject to "exactions," or conditions that would otherwise be per se takings. That uncertainty might presage future limits on the government's power to require permits for "basic and familiar uses of property," and thus its power to require inspections as conditions on such permits. In the meantime, the exactions framework offers no viable defense of inspections that aren't attached to discretionary permitting processes (such as those under existing labor laws or any politically imaginable revision of those laws). The treatment of regulatory inspections as presumptive per se physical takings gives the Court's conservative majority a new deregulatory lever, and a backdoor route to undercutting what it regards as regulatory overreach.

C. SHARPENING *CEDAR POINT*

Cedar Point marks the first time since the *Lochner* era that the Court has overturned *any* labor and employment statute or regulation on takings grounds. But it is not the first time that labor laws have come into conflict with property rights. In *Republic Aviation Corp. v. NLRB*, for example, the Court upheld workers' rights under the NLRA to wear union insignia, distribute literature, and solicit union support at the workplace during non-work hours.[140] When the Court later extended *Republic Aviation* in *Eastex v. NLRB*[141] to include other types and topics of communication, Justice Rehnquist pointed out in dissent that both decisions sanctioned common-law trespasses by overriding conditions that employer-owners had imposed on workers' entry onto their property: "A licensee who goes beyond the rights and privileges granted by the license becomes a trespasser."[142] In protecting worker activities that the employer-owners vigorously opposed, the NLRA impinged on the owners' right to exclude others.

Such conflicts between labor rights and traditional trespass law appear at every turn. The very decision upholding the constitutionality of the NLRA in 1937, *NLRB v. Jones & Laughlin Steel*, sanctioned a common-law trespass by enforcing an NLRB order to reinstate employees whom the employer had fired for union activity.[143] Similarly,

[140] 324 U.S. 793 (1945).

[141] 437 U.S. 556 (1978).

[142] *Id.* at 580 (Rehnquist, J., dissenting).

[143] 301 U.S. 1 (1937).

Title VII of the Civil Rights Act of 1964 abrogated employer property rights that many states then recognized—that is, the right to exclude or expel workers from their property because of their race.[144] The cases contain no hint that Title VII might constitute a taking. (On the contrary, the analogous takings objection to the public accommodations provisions of the 1964 Act was dismissed unanimously and summarily in *Heart of Atlanta Motel v. United States*.[145]) Innumerable other federal and state statutes similarly protect activity that employers oppose, such as whistleblowing, and require reinstatement of workers who are wrongfully fired. We could go on, but the point is plain: Laws protecting workers' rights often constrict employer property rights, including the right to exclude—and have done so without triggering a takings claim that was thought worthy of mention.

The law of work is not the only body of law that bars the ejection of individuals voluntarily admitted onto private property for the owner's gain, or that bars discrimination among would-be admittees. Laws against discrimination in public accommodations or housing rentals, or against retaliatory eviction of tenants could all be depicted, in *Cedar Point*'s terms, as an "appropriation" of the right to exclude and a per se taking. Thus far the Court has declined to follow that path. In *Yee v. City of Escondido*, for example, the Court refused to apply *Loretto*'s per se rule to a California statute sharply limiting the eviction of mobile home residents from their rented "pads."[146]

The government's power to grant rights to workers, tenants, or customers, and to thus limit property owners' right to exclude or eject them, has long been taken for granted notwithstanding any conflict with conventional trespass law. But that was then. Now, *Cedar Point*, with its broad per se condemnation of "physical invasions," its paean to "sole and despotic dominion," and its backward-looking Lockean (or *Lochner*ian) conception of property rights, potentially reopens long-dormant constitutional assaults on the law of work, landlord-tenant relations, and civil rights.[147]

---

[144] 42 U.S.C. § 2000e-2.

[145] 379 U.S. 241 (1965). The Court's entire analysis was this: "Neither do we find any merit in the claim that the Act is a taking of property without just compensation. The cases are to the contrary," citing several generic no-taking decisions that did not involve physical invasions. *Id.* at 261.

[146] 503 U.S. 519 (1992).

[147] For an exploration of these potential implications of *Cedar Point*, see Bowie, *supra* note 73.

IV. Conclusion

Some modern property scholars, building on the Legal Realist critiques of the early- to mid-twentieth century, aim to dethrone owners' right to exclude others, and to contest its essentiality to property. In place of a "Blackstonian" owner- and exclusion-centered conception of property, those scholars would elevate the interests of others—workers, neighbors, the community, and all who depend on a healthy environment—within the law that governs control over valuable resources.[148] On these progressive theories of property, decisions like *State v. Shack* take center stage, along with the rousing declaration: "Property rights serve human values. They are recognized to that end, and are limited by it. Title to real property cannot include dominion over the destiny of persons the owner permits to come upon the premises."[149]

To be sure, *State v. Shack* is unusual in locating those limits within the law of property itself. Property law often requires owners to accommodate others, but mostly others with their own recognized property interests, like tenants, co-owners, or neighboring landowners. Most of the laws that require owners to accommodate non-owners—civil rights, environmental, and labor laws, for example—are normally seen as constraining property rights from without.[150] But the other-oriented property theorists hope to re-envision and transform the law of property itself, through both internal common-law evolution and legislation, into a more just and inclusive instrument of resource governance.

Cedar Point sharply repudiates those conceptions of property in favor of "sole and despotic dominion" and owner sovereignty. And it does so not within the decentralized process of common-law adjudication or the give-and-take of state or federal politics but through the federal constitutional law of property that is takings law. With its expanded per se rule for physical invasions and its anachronistic and ossified conception of the "inherent limitations" on property rights, the Court is not just weighing into debates within positive law over

[148] Hanoch Dagan, for example, argues that human autonomy and relational justice are central to both the justification and the delimitation of property rights. *See* Dagan, *supra* note 94.

[149] *State v. Shack*, 277 A.2d 369, 372 (1971).

[150] I pursue this point in Cynthia Estlund, *Is Labor Law Internal or External to Private Law? The View from* Cedar Point, 24 Theoretical Inqs. L. (forthcoming 2023).

what property rights should be; it is trumping them. Of course, constitutional rights often function as trump cards. The newly fortified conservative majority has shown itself willing not just to play the takings trump card but to pull one out of its sleeve in support of owner sovereignty against competing public interests and values.

ORIN S. KERR

FOCUSING THE CFAA IN VAN BUREN

Imagine you are focusing a lens. At first, everything is blurry. As you adjust the lens, however, the picture starts to become clearer. Shapes and colors emerge. Ideally you can reach complete focus and make everything sharp. But maybe you can only go part way. The partially-adjusted image is more revealing than when you started. But the picture is not yet sharp.

Van Buren v. United States[1] is the Supreme Court's first decision interpreting the federal computer-crime statute known as the Computer Fraud and Abuse Act (CFAA).[2] Enacted in the 1980s, the CFAA sat unexamined by the Supreme Court during an astonishing societal transformation. Computers and the Internet went from the domain of a few computer geeks to a routine part of daily life for most Americans. During that time, the CFAA's text became a source of extraordinary uncertainty. The statute might be narrow and apply rarely, the thinking went, or it might be incredibly broad and criminalize a great deal of routine computer use. Before *Van Buren*, no one knew.

Orin S. Kerr is William G. Simon Professor, University of California, Berkeley Law School.

[1] 141 S. Ct. 1648 (2021).

[2] The statute is codified at 18 U.S.C. § 1030.

The Supreme Court Review, 2022.

https://doi.org/10.1086/720376

Van Buren is best understood as a partial focusing of the CFAA. On the surface, the Court's ruling is simple: An employee with access to a computer does not violate the CFAA if he violates a workplace policy banning access for personal reasons.[3] But at a more conceptual level, *Van Buren* limits the CFAA's possible meanings much like a person sharpens an image by focusing a lens. The opinion's dialectic structure features a series of contrasting perspectives, starting from the narrowest question and ending with the broadest, that endorses the petitioner's claims with limited explanation.[4] The outcome resembles a vision though a lens that has been adjusted only part way. The Court's opinion brings new ground into focus, letting us see a range of landmarks that were blurry before. But it leaves important details hazy, leaving their resolution to future cases that can bring the CFAA into sharper focus.

After *Van Buren*, the critical question of CFAA liability is the test for authorization. The Court frames authorization as a "gates-up-or-down inquiry,"[5] but it does not directly answer the key questions: What counts as a gate, and how do you know when it is down? Closely read, however, the opinion leaves a lot of clues to answer those questions. *Van Buren*'s focusing of the CFAA provides significant support for an authentication-based understanding of CFAA liability. Under that approach, the CFAA is violated only when a user bypasses an authentication gate on access designed to limit access to certain users.[6] We will have to wait to see if lower courts take the hint and adopt that reading. But *Van Buren*'s framework gives lower courts ample grounds to conclude that the CFAA adopts an authentication test.

This Essay proceeds in three parts. Part I introduces the CFAA and explains *Van Buren*'s facts and legal context. Part II explores the reasoning of the Supreme Court's decision, showing how it focuses many sections of the statute in part without providing clear answers to what the statute covers. Part III shows how *Van Buren* helps support an authentication-based understanding of CFAA liability.

---

[3] *See Van Buren*, 141 S. Ct. at 1652.

[4] *See* Part II, *infra*.

[5] *Van Buren*, 141 S. Ct. at 1658.

[6] *See id.* at 1659 n.9 (describing the authentication standard).

I. Understanding the CFAA, and *Van Buren*'s Path to the Supreme Court

A. The CFAA

The CFAA is a computer-trespass statute.[7] It is designed to protect computers from unauthorized access roughly in the way that physical trespass statutes protect physical land and buildings from unauthorized access.[8] The basic prohibition is simple to state. You start with a "computer."[9] To satisfy the Commerce Clause, only some computers are regulated: those computers are designated "protected" computers covered by the statute.[10] For the most part, the CFAA articulates two basic acts that a person cannot do with that protected computer.[11] First, a person cannot "access" that computer "without authorization."[12] Second, if a person accesses the computer with authorization, they cannot exceed authorized access, defined as "us[ing] such access to obtain or alter information in the computer" that you are "not entitled so to obtain or alter."[13]

A person who transgresses this statutory building block—by either engaging in access without authorization or exceeding authorized access—is most of the way to violating the CFAA. The statute then lists seven distinct offenses, most of which add particular elements to the building block.[14] The most readily violated is section 1030(a)(2), which requires intentional unauthorized access that results in obtaining any information. And although section 1030(a)(2) starts off as a misdemeanor, felony liability is easily triggered: the misdemeanor becomes a felony if the act was done to make money, or if it

---

[7] Facebook, Inc. v. Power Ventures, Inc., 844 F.3d 1058, 1065 (9th Cir. 2016) ("The CFAA prohibits acts of computer trespass by those who are not authorized users or who exceed authorized use.").

[8] *See generally* Orin Kerr, *Norms of Computer Trespass*, 116 Colum. L. Rev. 1143, 1153–59 (2016).

[9] *See* 18 U.S.C. § 1030(e)(1) (defining "computer").

[10] *See id.* (defining "protected computer").

[11] I say "for the most part" because most of the crimes listed in 18 U.S.C. § 1030(a) include these two prohibitions. Not all of the § 1030(a) offenses share the structure, however. For example, 18 U.S.C. § 1030(a)(5)(A) does not address unauthorized access at all, and § 1030(a)(5)(B)-(C) prohibits access without authorization but not exceeding authorized access.

[12] Neither "access" nor "without authorization" is a defined term, although the terms are used throughout the statute. *See, e.g.*, 18 U.S.C. § 1030(a)(2).

[13] *Id.* § 1030(e)(6) (defining "exceeds authorized access").

[14] *See id.* § 1030 (a)(1)-(7).

was in furtherance of any tort or crime at the state or federal level, or if the information obtained is worth more than $5,000.[15]

B. THE STATUTORY UNCERTAINTIES BEFORE *VAN BUREN*

When the CFAA was enacted in the 1980s, computers were new and few Americans used them. The meaning of the CFAA's terms didn't matter very much. Today that is no longer true. Most Americans now spend much of their day using computer networks. According to one survey, American adults typically spend about four hours a day using computers.[16] And those computers are never far away: 85% of American adults now own smartphones, which are sophisticated computers that connect to the Internet using either the cellular telephone network or wireless networks.[17] Computers and computer networks are now fully integrated into modern life.

Juxtaposing the CFAA's raw text with the modern reality of near-universal computer use reveals a statute largely out of focus in the absence of caselaw. *Some* sorts of computer use are illegal. But which sorts? The stakes are high. Under some possible interpretations of the statute, most Americans violate the CFAA on a regular basis. Alternatively, the statute could be a very narrow law. Consider a few of the statutory uncertainties:

(1) What is "access"? An unauthorized access starts with an access. But what does it mean to "access" a computer? The statute does not define the term. Does any use of a computer access it? Does "access" require some kind of special use, such as logging on with a username and password or otherwise seeing data not available to the public?

(2) When is access "without authorization"? Assuming a computer is accessed, what makes the access "without authorization"? The statute does not define this term, either. Does authorization imply a technological standard focused on whether the computer has been

---

[15] *Id.* § 1030(c)(2)(B) (detailing the different ways that a misdemeanor violation can become a felony).

[16] Quentin Fottrell, *People Spend Most of Their Waking Hours Staring At Screens*, MARKET WATCH, https://www.marketwatch.com/story/people-are-spending-most-of-their-waking-hours-staring-at-screens-2018-08-01 ("In the first quarter of the year [2018], U.S. adults spent three hours and 48 minutes a day on computers, tablets and smartphones.").

[17] *See Mobile Fact Sheet*, PEW RSCH. CTR. (Apr. 7, 2021) https://www.pewresearch.org/internet/fact-sheet/mobile/.

programmed to limit access by computer code such as with a password gate? Or a communicated policy standard, such as when a computer owner adopts an express policy about when the computer can be accessed? Or is that a matter of norms, with some kinds of access being so out of bounds that they are implicitly without authorization?

(3) When does a user "exceed[] authorized access"? In addition to prohibiting access without authorization, the CFAA also covers a person who "exceeds authorized access."[18] Unlike "access" and "authorization," the phrase "exceeds authorized access" is a defined term: "to access a computer with authorization and to use such access to obtain or alter information in the computer that the accesser is not entitled so to obtain or alter[.]"[19] But on its face, the definition seems circular. A person exceeds authorized access if they have access with authorization (whatever that means) and then do what they are not authorized to do. But what does this add to the ban on access without authorization? Does it track the same concept but apply at a different stage, or is it a different concept entirely?

(4) When is unauthorized access "intentional"? The main provisions of the CFAA only prohibit intentional unauthorized access.[20] Does this mean only that the act must be intentional, even if the user does not realize it is unauthorized? Or does it mean that the person must have an awareness about the legal lack of authorization, or even of the scope of what the CFAA itself prohibits?[21]

(5) What is a "protected computer"? The CFAA regulates "protected computers." The word "computer" is defined, as is "protected," but the definitions are complex and little caselaw explores their limits.[22] For example, although the definition of "protected computer" appears to go as far as the Commerce Clause will allow,[23] it remains unclear how far that extends. Do all computers aggregate under a

---

[18] *See, e.g.*, 18 U.S.C. § 1030(a)(2).

[19] *Id.* § 1030(e)(6).

[20] *See, e.g.*, *id.* § 1030(a)(2) ("Whoever ... intentionally accesses a computer without authorization or exceeds authorized access...."); *id.* § 1030(a)(5)(B) ("Whoever ... intentionally accesses a protected computer without authorization....").

[21] *See* Kerr, *supra* note 8, at 1180–82 (exploring this question).

[22] *See* Orin Kerr, *Vagueness Challenges to the Computer Fraud and Abuse Act*, 94 MINN. L. REV. 1561, 1569–71 (2010).

[23] *See id.*

Gonzales v. Raich rationale, such that every computer can be regulated as a protected computer?[24] Or does the Commerce Clause apply to computers more narrowly by type or use, such that some kinds of computers are outside the Commerce Clause power?[25] And how does the concept of a "computer" apply to modern cloud computing, which replaces individual computer machines with large distributed networks of servers?

(6) When does access "obtain[] information . . . from" a protected computer? The broadest provision of the CFAA punishes unauthorized access that "thereby obtains . . . information from a protected computer."[26] Does "obtain[ing]" information merely mean seeing information, or does it require saving it or storing it in some way? And does obtaining information "from" a computer include extracting information through that computer as an intermediary, or does it only mean obtaining information that was originally sourced from that specific computer?

All of these questions were open before *Van Buren*. The Supreme Court had never interpreted any part of the law. And lower court opinions on most of the issues remained surprisingly sparse, in part because the CFAA has led to relatively few criminal prosecutions.[27] The result was a statute largely out of focus, with the scope of the CFAA a recurring uncertainty.[28]

C. CIRCUIT COURTS SPLIT ON THE INSIDER PROBLEM

Van Buren addressed the one circuit split that emerged in CFAA cases. The dispute concerns what is sometimes called the "insider"

---

[24] *See id.* at 1570 (citing Gonzales v. Raich, 545 U.S. 1, 17 (2005)).

[25] That was the apparent concern driving the recent expansion of the definition of "protected computer" to include computers used in elections. *See* Act of Oct. 20, 2020, Pub. L. 116–179, § 2, 134 Stat. 855, which added 18 U.S.C. § 1030(e)(2)(C). If aggregation of all computers is permitted for Commerce Clause purposes, that amendment was unnecessary.

[26] 18 U.S.C. § 1030(a)(2)(C).

[27] *See generally* Jonathan Mayer, *Cybercrime Litigation*, 164 U. Pa. L. Rev. 1453 (2016) (reviewing the types and quantities of litigation under the CFAA).

[28] *Cf.* Orin Kerr, *Criminal Law in Virtual Worlds*, 2008 U. Chi. Legal F. 415, 423 (noting that the unsettled scope of the CFAA made it "the usual wildcard in any discussion of computer crime law" because the law could be narrow or could "threaten[] to swallow the internet" depending on how it is interpreted).

problem.[29] When computer owners want to protect sensitive data, they have a choice of how to do that. First, they might protect data by putting up electronic walls, such as password gates, and limiting who can access the information. This is the "outsider" approach. It protects information by keeping it out of outsider's hands, regulating access by blocking it through computer code. The CFAA clearly punishes "outsider" computer misuse. An outside hacker violates the CFAA by exploiting security flaws or guessing passwords to gain access.

But there's an alternative way to try to protect sensitive information: the "insider" approach. Computer owners might want to protect sensitive information by granting technological access to it while placing explicit or implicit restrictions on how it is used. The insider approach enables technological access to sensitive information, making users technological insiders to it, but it then tries to protect the privacy of that information by placing conditions on when it can be obtained, used, or disclosed. The key question is, does the CFAA punish insiders who have technological access to information but violate expressed policies limiting its access, use, or disclosure?

Before *Van Buren*, several circuits divided on how the CFAA applies to the insider problem. The issue arose most often in the employment setting. An employer would give employees access to their network but instruct them to use the computer only for work-related reasons. The employee would instead access the computer for a personal or other corrupt reason. Circuit courts divided on whether violating the articulated limit on work-related computer use violated the CFAA. In 2010, the Eleventh Circuit ruled that this violated the CFAA.[30] Later, the Second Circuit and Ninth Circuit disagreed.[31]

D. THE FACTS AND THE CIRCUIT RULING IN *VAN BUREN*

Van Buren was an ideal case to settle the circuit split over the insider problem. Nathan Van Buren was a police sergeant in Georgia.[32] As

---

[29] In the computer context, an "outsider" is someone who has no legitimate access rights on a computer, while an "insider" is someone who has legitimate access rights. *See* S. REP. No. 104–357, at 9–11 (1996) (referring to "insiders, who are authorized to access a computer" and contrasting them with "outsiders, who gain access to a computer without authorization").

[30] *See* United States v. Rodriguez, 628 F.3d 1258 (11th Cir. 2010).

[31] *See* United States v. Valle, 807 F.3d 508 (2d Cir. 2015); United States v. Nosal, 676 F.3d 854 (9th Cir. 2012) (en banc).

[32] Van Buren v. United States, 141 S. Ct. 1648, 1653 (2021).

part of his job, his employer gave him an account to access a state law-enforcement database that included license plate information.[33] Van Buren was trained "not to use the law enforcement database for 'an improper purpose,' defined as 'any personal use.'"[34]

A local man named Andrew Albo offered Van Buren about $5,000 to access the database to check if a woman he had met at a local strip club was an undercover police officer.[35] Van Buren agreed. From his patrol car, Van Buren accessed the database and entered the license plate number Albo had provided.[36] Albo's request was part of a sting, however. Albo was working for the FBI, and the license plate number had been created by the FBI to see if Van Buren would look it up.

Van Buren was arrested and charged with both honest-services wire fraud and violating the CFAA. In Georgia, within the Eleventh Circuit, the CFAA case was airtight. Binding precedent with almost identical facts established that Van Buren had exceeded authorized access to the database.[37] Van Buren had been instructed not to access the database for any improper purpose, including any personal reason. But he accessed it for a personal and improper purpose of earning a $5,000 bribe. The Supreme Court granted review.

E. The Briefing Challenges

Briefing *Van Buren* raised two related challenges for the parties. First, each party needed both a narrow and a broad perspective on the text. The parties agreed that liability hinged on whether Van Buren "exceed[ed] authorized access."[38] Given the textualist method of interpretation favored by many of the current Justices, both sides needed to parse that defined phrase in their favor. But because the CFAA had never been interpreted by the Supreme Court before, understanding that one definition required a view of the other parts of the statute. Each party needed to offer a sensible interpretation of the statute as a whole, situating "exceeds authorized access" amidst the other open-textured terms of the statute.

---

[33] *See id.*

[34] *Id.* (quoting App. 17).

[35] *See id.*

[36] *See id.*

[37] United States v. Rodriguez, 628 F.3d 1258 (11th Cir. 2010).

[38] 18 U.S.C. § 1030(e)(6).

The uncertain scope of the question presented raised a second challenge. Van Buren had asked the Court to decide "[w]hether a person who is authorized to access information on a computer for certain purposes violates Section 1030(a)(2) of the Computer Fraud and Abuse Act if he accesses the same information for an improper purpose."[39] The government's version of the question focused more on the facts: In effect, were the facts sufficient to show that Van Buren had exceeded authorized access?[40] This framing left the scope of the case uncertain. Perhaps *Van Buren* was a narrow case about the facts, or about whether violating a purpose-based expressed limit on access rendered use unlawful. Alternatively, perhaps the case raised the broader conceptual question of whether violating an expressed limit on access rendered use unlawful, with the facts of *Van Buren* happening to involve a limit based on purpose.

II. The Reasoning of *Van Buren*

Van Buren's holding is simple to state. In an opinion by Justice Amy Coney Barrett, the Court ruled that that the ban on exceeding authorized access "covers those who obtain information from particular areas in the computer—such as files, folders, or databases—to which their computer access does not extend. It does not cover those who, like Van Buren, have improper motives for obtaining information that is otherwise available to them."[41] As the conclusion rephrases the point, "an individual 'exceeds authorized access' when he accesses a computer with authorization but then obtains information located in particular areas of the computer—such as files, folders, or databases—that are off limits to him."[42] Because Van Buren was authorized to use the database for official reasons, he did not exceed authorized access when he accessed the computer for an improper purpose.

---

[39] *See* Petition for Writ of Certiorari at i, Van Buren v. United States, 141 S. Ct. 1648 (2021) (No. 19-783).

[40] "Whether the evidence was sufficient to establish that petitioner, a police sergeant, exceeded his authorized access to a protected computer to obtain information for financial gain, in violation of 18 U.S.C. 1030(a)(2)(C) and (c)(2)(B)(i), when in exchange for a cash payment, he searched a confidential law-enforcement database for information about whether a particular person was an undercover police officer." Brief in Opposition at i, *Van Buren*, 141 S. Ct. 1648 (No. 19-783).

[41] *Van Buren*, 141 S. Ct. at 1652.

[42] *Id.* at 1662.

Although straightforward on the surface, the opinion's foundation is opaque. Computers do not naturally consist of "areas." And the important question, unanswered by the Court's holding, is what makes an area "off limits" to a user. The gap between *Van Buren*'s holding and the many questions about the CFAA's meaning that preceded *Van Buren* naturally prompts the question of what light the decision sheds on those questions. Answering that requires a close reading of the opinion. This will not be a thrilling project, as *Van Buren*'s reasoning is dense.[43] And it will win no awards for theory. But it's the only way to understand how *Van Buren* will reshape CFAA debates going forward.

The challenge of understanding *Van Buren* owes to its dialectic structure. The opinion explains the parties' positions in a series of cycles. It begins with the narrowest question, offering an extended analysis of the word "so" in the definition of "exceeds authorized access." It then broadens its attention, addressing the broader structure of the statute and implications of each side's argument. At each stage, the Court finds the defendant's arguments more persuasive. But the opinion shies away from identifying exactly what test results from that judgment or what the implications might be for future cases. The reader often is left to interpret the statute primarily by inference, with the Court's statement of Van Buren's position left as an indirect guide to what the statute means.

This dynamic explains why I analogize *Van Buren* to partially focusing a lens. Reviewing the positions of the parties on various parts of the statute, and indicating general agreement with the defendant, offers many clues about what the CFAA means. But indicating general agreement without resting the opinion on its own bottom leaves important questions blurry. The resulting opinion is broad but shallow. It offers tools that will frame future debates over the CFAA without directly resolving how the statute applies. The Court's opinion makes the overall picture clearer without leaving anything sharp, much like a lens that brings a picture into partial focus.

This section tracks the analysis of *Van Buren*, starting with the narrowest statutory question and then looking more broadly. At each stage, it explains the Court's reasoning and considers what lessons might be drawn about the CFAA.

---

[43] Having recently taught *Van Buren*, I can report that my students shared this reaction.

A. THE ANALYSIS OF "SO," LEADING TO A STRUCTURAL VIEW OF ACCESS

The Court's analysis begins with the word "so." Recall the definition: To exceed authorized access, the statute says, means "to access a computer with authorization and to use such access to obtain or alter information in the computer that the accesser is not entitled *so* to obtain or alter[.]"[44] By my eyes, that definition is entirely circular. A person exceeds authorized access, the definition says, when they have access but exceed it. The word "so" seems to add nothing to an already circular definition. But the parties gamely argued that the word "so" cinched their case. The Court dwelled on their arguments at surprising length, ultimately agreeing with Van Buren.

Van Buren argued that the word "so" was a reference to the prior authorization.[45] Van Buren was entitled to access the database for an official reason. As a result, he said, his violation of the computer use policy obtained information in the computer that he was still entitled to obtain.[46] In the government's view, by contrast, the word "so" imposed a specific limit on "the particular manner or circumstances in which he obtained it."[47] Van Buren had exceeded authorized access, the government argued, because his conduct in violation of the computer use policy was outside the initial authorization to access the database.[48]

The Court contrasted the two views with a hypothetical:

> On [Van Buren's] reading, if a person has access to information stored in a computer—e.g., in "Folder Y," from which the person could permissibly pull information—then he does not violate the CFAA by obtaining such information, regardless of whether he pulled the information for a prohibited purpose. But if the information is instead located in prohibited "Folder X," to which the person lacks access, he violates the CFAA by obtaining such information.
>
> . . .
>
> As the Government sees it, an employee might lawfully pull information from Folder Y in the morning for a permissible purpose—say, to prepare for a business meeting—but unlawfully pull the same information from Folder Y in the afternoon for a prohibited purpose—say, to help draft a resume to submit to a competitor employer.[49]

---

[44] 18 U.S.C. § 1030(e)(6) (emphasis added).

[45] *Van Buren*, 141 S. Ct. at 1654.

[46] *See id.*

[47] *Id.*

[48] *See id.* at 1654–55.

[49] *Id.*

The Court agreed with Van Buren's interpretation. According to the Court, the word "so" "refers to a stated, identifiable proposition from the preceding text," which here was "to access a computer with authorization."[50] As a result, "[t]he phrase 'is not entitled so to obtain' is best read to refer to information that a person is not entitled to obtain by using a computer that he is authorized to access."[51]

What does this passage tell us about the CFAA? The lesson so far is modest, and it mostly concerns the stages of the CFAA. According to *Van Buren*, the CFAA distinguishes between an initial stage of access to a computer and a subsequent stage of access to particular information on the computer. The prohibition on access without authorization governs the first stage, and the prohibition on exceeding authorized access governs the second stage. Further, authorization at the initial stage can govern authorization at the subsequent stage. This doesn't tell us much, at least not yet, in part because we don't yet know the big question: When does a person "lack[] access" to information, making it "off limits," so that she is "not entitled to obtain" it? At this point in the opinion, the picture remains blurry.

B. THE SURPLUSAGE ARGUMENT, LEADING TO A VIEW OF CFAA AS AN ON/OFF SWITCH

The next section addressed whether Van Buren's interpretation of "so" was unpersuasive because it rendered that word surplusage.[52] This particular skirmish considered how much "so" added to the definition of exceeds authorized access. Again, the ground seems puzzling. Readers may wonder just how much weight the word "so" can be expected to carry. But the Court again laid out the two sides and agreed with Van Buren, adding an additional layer of understanding about the CFAA.

According to the government, Van Buren's interpretation of "so" was wrong because "exceeds authorized access" would have the same meaning without it.[53] The word "so," the government claimed, was Congress's way of "incorporat[ing] all of the circumstances that might qualify a person's right to obtain information"[54] into the

[50] *Id.* at 1655.

[51] *Id.*

[52] *See id.* at 1656.

[53] *See id.*

[54] *Id.*

prohibition. Because the use policy was such a circumstance, violating the policy exceeded authorized access. Van Buren disagreed, arguing that "so" served a different purpose: it prevented a person from using their right to access a physical copy of data to obtain the same data from a computer. Without "so," Van Buren argued, an employee could use his authority to get a file in physical form (such as by asking for it) to claim a right to access the same file in digital form (such as by hacking into a computer to get it).[55]

The Court sided with Van Buren. "The statute is concerned with what a person does on a computer,"[56] the Court concluded. It is "the right to access the information by using a computer"[57] that counts. As a result, a "hacker" who engaged in "hacking into an electronic personnel file"[58] was not authorized just because he "could have walked down the hall to pick up a physical copy."[59] The Court's answer adjusts the lens slightly once more. We learn that the CFAA is only about access rights on a computer, and that those access rights do not rest on mere "circumstances that might qualify" authorization. The right of access under the CFAA, whatever it is, acts as an on/off switch. Either a person has authorization to access that information on a computer or she does not.

C. THE COMMON MEANING OF "EXCEEDS AUTHORIZED ACCESS," RESULTING IN GUIDANCE ON INTERPRETING THE CFAA GENERALLY AND THE MEANING OF "ACCESS"

Having mined the meaning of "so," the Court next considered the government's argument that "any ordinary speaker of the English language would think that Van Buren exceeded his authorized access."[60] The Court rejected this common parlance argument on two grounds. The first was obvious enough. Exceeding authorized access was a defined term, so the statutory definition, not common parlance, controlled.[61] But the Court's second ground for rejecting this argument

---

[55] *See id.*

[56] *Id.*

[57] *Id.*

[58] *Id.*

[59] *Id.*

[60] *Id.* at 1657.

[61] *See id.*

is more important for understanding the CFAA, as it offered general guidance on methods of interpreting the CFAA and supplied a functional definition of "access."

The Court's second ground started as more a note of uncertainty than a counterargument. According to the Court, it was hardly obvious that an ordinary speaker of English would think that Van Buren had exceeded authorized access. This was true because an "appropriately informed"[62] speaker of English would understand the CFAA as a technical statute that used terms that had "technical meanings."[63] Because "access" was a specialized term in a statute about computers, the meaning of "access" within the specialized world of computer geeks mattered:

> When interpreting statutes, courts take note of terms that carry "technical meaning[s]." A. Scalia & B. Garner, Reading Law: The Interpretation of Legal Texts 73 (2012). "Access" is one such term, long carrying a "well established" meaning in the "computational sense"—a meaning that matters when interpreting a statute about computers. American Heritage Dictionary 10 (3d ed. 1992). In the computing context, "access" references the act of entering a computer "system itself " or a particular "part of a computer system," such as files, folders, or databases.[64]

The Court here dropped a footnote citing a string of dictionaries, ranging from general dictionaries from the late 1980s to period computer dictionaries—specifically *A Dictionary of Computing* (from 2008), the *Microsoft Computer Dictionary* (from 1999), and the *Computer Dictionary and Handbook* (from 1980)[65]—to explain the meaning of access in the computer context. From that perspective, it was at least plausible to interpret "exceeding authorized access" in common parlance as "the act of entering a part of the system to which a computer user lacks access privileges."[66]

Although this passage begins very tentatively—it begins with what is uncertain, rather than what is correct—it ends up adding real meaning to the CFAA. It introduces a general interpretive method for understanding the statute that you might call "techie textualism." When interpreting the CFAA, the meaning of terms that have a

[62] *See id.* (quoting Caleb Nelson, *What Is Textualism?* 91 Va. L. Rev. 347, 354 (2005)).

[63] *Id.*

[64] *Id.*

[65] *Id.* n.6.

[66] *Id.* at 1658.

"specialized meaning . . . in the computer context"[67] is presumptively what Congress had in mind. This is a useful tool given the CFAA's open-textured words. Seeking a specialized meaning in the computer context from the time the statute was enacted can significantly narrow the scope of interpretive debates.

Equally importantly, that general method yields a specific definition of access. Access, we are told, is "the act of entering a computer system itself or a particular part of a computer system, such as files, folders, or databases."[68] What it means to "enter" a computer can be open to interpretation. But recall how the Court's holding was phrased in the introduction. Exceeding authorized access, the Court stated, "covers those who obtain information from particular areas in the computer—such as files, folders, or databases—to which their computer access does not extend."[69] The similar phrasing suggests entering a computer means obtaining information from the computer. The passage therefore suggests a resolution of a longtime scholarly debate over the meaning of access in the CFAA:[70] Access is entering that part of the computer by obtaining information from inside it.

D. THE "WIDER LOOK AT THE STATUTE'S STRUCTURE," INTRODUCING THE GATES-UP-OR-DOWN METAPHOR AND EXPLAINING THE RELATIONSHIP BETWEEN ACCESS WITHOUT AUTHORIZATION AND EXCEEDS AUTHORIZED ACCESS

The opinion turned next to a "wider look at the statute's structure."[71] In this section, the Court treats the degree of fit with other parts of the statute as a guide to help interpret exceeding authorized access. Van Buren's interpretation of exceeding authorized access is more plausible, the Court reasons, because it makes more sense of the rest of the statute.[72] This "wider look" allows the majority to shed

---

[67] *Id.* at n.7.

[68] *Id.* at 1657.

[69] *Id.* at 1652.

[70] *Compare* Orin S. Kerr, *Cybercrime's Scope: Interpreting "Access" and "Authorization" in Computer Misuse Statutes*, 78 N.Y.U. L. Rev. 1596, 1646–48 (2003) (arguing that access should be construed broadly to include "any successful interaction with a computer") *with* Patricia L. Bellia, *Defending Cyberproperty*, 79 N.Y.U. L. Rev. 2164, 2254 (2004) (arguing for a narrow interpretation of "access" that only applies to acts that bypass code-based restrictions).

[71] *Van Buren*, 141 S. Ct. at 1658 (quoting Romag Fasteners, Inc. v. Fossil Group, Inc., 140 S. Ct. 1492 (2020)).

[72] *Van Buren*, 141 S. Ct. at 1658–59.

light on several CFAA concepts not directly at issue in the case. In particular, the Court adopts a clear view of the relationship between access without authorization and exceeding authorized access.

This section was rooted, yet again, in the parties' dueling arguments. According to Van Buren, the two prohibitions provided "complementary protections"[73] against the same conduct at different stages. The ban on access without authorization targeted "outside hackers" who accessed the computer system with no authorization at all,[74] while the ban on exceeding authorized access targeted those who accessed the computer with permission but then accessed "certain areas within the system" without authorization.[75] As the Court put it, Van Buren's approach framed the CFAA around a "gates-up-or-down-inquiry,"[76] in contrast to "one that depends on the circumstances."[77] The government, by contrast, agreed with the "gates-up-or-down inquiry" for the ban on access without authorization but advocated a circumstances-dependent understanding of exceeds authorized access that would follow "purposes-based limits contained in contracts and workplace policies."[78]

The Court again adopted Van Buren's view. Understanding the two prohibitions as the same test at different stages "makes sense of the statutory structure" by treating the clauses "consistently,"[79] the Court reasoned. The CFAA is "aimed at preventing the typical consequences of hacking,"[80] and was therefore "focus[ed] on technological harms—such as the corruption of files—of the type unauthorized users cause to computer systems and data."[81] The statutory structure make the statute "ill fitted . . . to remediating 'misuse' of sensitive information that employees may permissibly access using their computers."[82] Van Buren's conduct was "illustrative," the Court

---

[73] *Id.* at 1658.

[74] *Id.*

[75] *Id.* at 1658–59.

[76] *Id.*

[77] *Id.* at 1659.

[78] *Id.*

[79] *Id.* at 1658.

[80] *Id.* at 1660 (quoting Royal Truck & Trailer Sales & Serv., Inc. v. Kraft, 974 F.3d 756, 760 (6th Cir. 2020)).

[81] *Id.* at 1660.

[82] *Id.*

added; although Van Buren violated the workplace rule, he did not "harm the database system itself."[83]

Two contrasting footnotes help bookend this conclusion. On one hand, footnote 9 hinted that the CFAA's gates-up-or-down inquiry might adopt an authentication test.[84] The ban on password trafficking in 18 U.S.C. § 1030(a)(6) "contemplates a specific type of authorization,"[85] the Court suggested: "authentication, which turns on whether a user's credentials allow him to proceed past a computer's access gate, rather than on other, scope-based restrictions."[86] The Court added a *cf.* to one of the dictionaries earlier used to define access, noting that the dictionary's definition of authorization as a "process by which users, having completed an … authentication stage, gain or are denied access to particular resources based on their entitlement."[87]

On the other hand, footnote 8 disavowed a broad reading of the Court's holding. "For present purposes," the opinion cautions, "we need not address whether this inquiry turns only on technological (or 'code-based') limitations on access, or instead also looks to limits contained in contracts or policies."[88] The footnote added a *cf.* to an amicus brief I had filed that advocated a code-based approach to CFAA liability that would require bypassing a technological restriction on access.[89] In practice, my approach would mirror the authentication standard hinted at in footnote 9.[90] Footnote 8 makes clear that the Court was leaving that question for another day.

---

[83] *Id.*

[84] *Id.* at 1659 n.9.

[85] *Id.*

[86] *Id.*

[87] *Id.* (quoting A Dictionary of Computing 30 (6th ed. 2008)).

[88] *Van Buren*, 141 S. Ct. at 1659 n.8.

[89] *Id.* (citing Brief for Professor Orin S. Kerr as Amicus Curiae in Support of Petitioners at 7, *Van Buren*, 141 S. Ct. 1648 (No. 19–783) (urging adoption of code-based approach)).

[90] I have argued for authentication as the best way to enact a code-based restriction. *See* Kerr, *supra* note 8 (arguing for an authentication test as a way to implement a code-based approach to interpreting the CFAA). Although they are similar, an authentication standard does not always require a code-based restriction. For example, limits on physical access can impose an authentication requirement. If a computer is in a person's physical office, to which only that person has permitted access, the key required to gain access to the room is an authentication standard just like an electronic password. A person who breaks into the room and accesses a computer that is not password-protected engages in an unauthorized access under an authentication standard because the physical key system serves as the authentication mechanism.

A lot is happening in this section of *Van Buren*. First, we know now that CFAA liability hinges on bypassing gates. Either the gates are up, permitting access, or the gates are down, denying access. We don't yet know exactly what counts as a down gate. But the gates metaphor now frames the authorization test. Second, and equally importantly, under *Van Buren* a single test governs the authorization question in the two prongs of CFAA liability. Access without authorization and exceeding authorized access use the same test at different stages; one regulates initial access to the computer while the other regulates subsequent access to parts within it. This is a major step toward understanding the statute. As Section III will explain, we have preexisting tools for interpreting criminal law elements about lack of authorization. Equating the more novel exceeding-authorized-access language with the more familiar access-without-authorization test can allow courts to root the CFAA in the latter, more familiar, element.

E. THE SCOPE OF CRIMINALITY, AND THE IMPACT OF DRAFTING PRACTICES BY PRIVATE PARTIES ON LIABILITY

Van Buren's final analysis section turns to the consequences of adopting the government's interpretation. Adopting the government's view would mean that the statute criminalized "a breathtaking amount of commonplace computer activity."[91] That was not necessarily legally problematic, according to the Court—Van Buren prevailed without the Court applying interpretive canons such as the rule of lenity or constitutional avoidance—but to the Court it "underscore[d] the implausibility"[92] of the government's interpretation.

Two points are worth noting. First, the Court discussed but did not rely on the government's suggestion that language other than "exceeding authorized access" might considerably limit CFAA liability. Perhaps the mens rea requiring intentional unauthorized access would limit liability, the government had argued.[93] Or perhaps the requirement of section 1030(a)(2) that information be obtained "from" a computer only applied if that computer was the ultimate source of the information.[94] Although the government suggested these possible

---

[91] *See Van Buren*, 141 S. Ct. at 1661.

[92] *Id.*

[93] *Id.* at 1661–62.

[94] *See id.*

limits, the Court rejected reliance on them in part because the government "stops far short of endorsing such limitations."[95]

Second, and more importantly, the Court added a "final observation"[96] about the government's position that seems to limit the role of use policies in the CFAA. The observation addressed a concession the government had made in its Brief in Opposition that the CFAA does not punish downstream information misuse.[97] Under that view, the Court reasoned, interpreting CFAA liability to hinge on the written terms of an access policy would make CFAA liability arbitrary. There was no real difference between a written ban on using information from a computer for a prohibited purpose (which, in the government's view, was a legally irrelevant use restriction) and a written ban on accessing a computer for that prohibited purpose (which, in the government's view, was a legally binding access restriction).[98] An interpretation of the statute that hinged on such a detail was problematic: "An interpretation that stakes so much on a fine distinction controlled by the drafting practices of private parties is hard to sell as the most plausible."[99]

This passage offers a final insight about the point left unresolved in footnote 8. Recall that this footnote left unanswered whether the gates-up-or-down inquiry "also looks to limits contained in contracts or policies."[100] The Court's final warning about the drafting practices of private parties suggests at least a partial answer to that question. To the extent limits contained in contracts or policies have any future relevance to CFAA liability, that relevance cannot turn on "fine distinction[s]"[101] of their drafting.

III. *Van Buren* and the Authentication-Based CFAA

Van Buren rejected the government's broad purpose-based theory of CFAA liability. For those of us worried about overly broad interpretation of criminal laws, this is cause for relief. Although the

---

[95] *Id.* at 1661.

[96] *Id.* at 1662.

[97] *See id.*

[98] *See id.*

[99] *Id.*

[100] *See id.* at 1659 n.8.

[101] *Id.*

Court insisted that its holding was required by the word "so" and not by the policy implications of ruling for the government, those policy implications were remarkable. Adopting the government's view would have turned the CFAA into the statute that swallowed the Internet. If Van Buren's violation of his workplace policy made his computer use unlawful, it would be hard to see how the Court could avoid concluding that essentially all computer use in violation of imposed rules would not meet the same fate. *Van Buren* is therefore a story of frightening outcomes avoided.

But if that's what the ruling avoids, what exactly does the ruling embrace? As mentioned earlier, I see *Van Buren* as a partial focusing of the CFAA. The opinion gives some meaning to nearly every major term and concept in the statute. But while we can see much more than before, a great deal remains unfocused. That limit may simply reflect how *Van Buren* was litigated. The petition for certiorari focused on the role of purpose-based limits, and answering that did not require resolving every CFAA debate.[102] Or perhaps that limit reflects the challenge of group decisionmaking on a multi-member court; the opinion may have been narrowed to secure a majority.[103] Whatever the reason, the majority opinion provides tools more than answers.

Despite this limitation, I think *Van Buren* does provide substantial help toward resolving the most important question of CFAA liability: the meaning of "authorization" itself. *Van Buren* teaches that both exceeding authorized access and access without authorization depend on a "gates-up-or-down inquiry." Several aspects of the opinion point to an authentication-based understanding of access without authorization, in which CFAA liability "turns on whether a user's credentials allow him to proceed past a computer's access gate."[104] Under this view, a "gate" is "down" when a user must enter some credentials such as a password to gain access. Entering the correct password lifts the gate "up." Access without authorization or exceeding authorized access occurs when a user bypasses a gate that requires credentials by using someone else's password or by exploiting a security flaw.

---

[102] *See* Section 1.E., *supra*.

[103] The vote in *Van Buren* was 6–3, and the opinion took a long time to come down: Oral argument was held on November 30, 2020, and the decision was published on June 3, 2021. We can only speculate, but caveats such as the addition of footnote 8—which expressly disavows taking a position on at least some of the possible implications of the rest of the opinion—may have been needed to secure a majority.

[104] *See Van Buren*, 141 S. Ct. at 1659 n.9.

Although *Van Buren* does not establish that theory, its approach to focusing the CFAA makes that result particularly plausible. This section explains why, pointing to the likely arguments that will be made in CFAA litigation after *Van Buren*. It starts by applying "techie textualism" to authorization; turns next to the Court's framing of the CFAA as an anti-hacking statute; next focuses on the role of "fine print" in CFAA liability; and concludes with a closer look at the dissent. None of these aspects of *Van Buren* alone establishes with certainty that the CFAA adopts an authentication standard. But they all point in that direction.

A. TECHIE TEXTUALISM AND THE MEANING OF AUTHORIZATION

The first reason to construe access without authorization as an authentication test is the Court's endorsement of techie textualism. *Van Buren* teaches that CFAA language should be interpreted as used "[i]n the computer context."[105] We need to ask how the community of computer users would have interpreted the technical word "authorization" at the time of the CFAA's enactment. As the Court explained in interpreting "access," period computer dictionaries help reveal how technical terms like access and authorization were understood. Those dictionaries largely support an authentication test for authorization

Van Buren itself starts us on this path. Footnote 9 recognizes that one such dictionary, *A Dictionary of Computing*, equates authorization and authentication. Authorization, that dictionary teaches, is a "process by which users, having completed an . . . authentication stage, gain or are denied access to particular resources based on their entitlement."[106] *Van Buren* also relied on the *Microsoft Computer Dictionary*, which explains that "[a]uthorization is typically set up by a system administrator and verified by the computer based on some form of user identification, such as a code number or password."[107]

Other period computer dictionaries share this understanding of authorization as authentication. The *Dictionary of Information Technology* defines authorization in more general terms, as "the right given

[105] *Id.* at 1658 n.7.

[106] *Id.* at 1659 n.9 (quoting A DICTIONARY OF COMPUTING, *supra* note 87).

[107] MICROSOFT COMPUTER DICTIONARY 43 (5th ed. 2002), https://burmastarrecords.files.wordpress.com/2009/12/microsoft_computer_dictionary__fifth_edition1.pdf; *see Van Buren*, 141 S. Ct. at 1657 n.6.

to a user to communicate with or make use of a computer system," but then it defines "authorization code" more specifically as "a code used to protect against unauthorized access" that "normally consists of a user id (identification) and password."[108] A National Institute of Standards and Technology report similarly defines authorization as "[t]he process of initially establishing access privileges of an individual and subsequently verifying the acceptability of a request for access."[109]

Not all period dictionaries expressly equate authorization with authentication. Other computer dictionaries do not define authorization at all,[110] and the general-purpose dictionaries I have reviewed do not include definitions of authorization specifically from the computer context. Still, *Van Buren*'s techie textualism generally supports the authentication-based understanding of authorization.

B. The CFAA as an Anti-Hacking Statute

Van Buren's discussions of the CFAA's goals, and its focus on technological harms, provide a second basis for an authentication-based understanding of authorization. The opinion frames access without authorization as about hacking and bypassing password gates. Although *Van Buren* does not establish that the former only means the latter, its focusing of the CFAA drops several clues that support the connection.

Van Buren's discussion of exceeding authorized access repeatedly frames the CFAA as an anti-hacking statute. For example, the Court endorses Van Buren's claim that access without authorization "target[s] so-called outside hackers—those who access a computer without any permission at all," while exceeding authorized access "target[s] so-called inside hackers—those who access a computer with permission, but then exceed the parameters of authorized access by entering an area of the computer to which that authorization does not extend."[111]

---

[108] Dennis Longley & Michael Shain, The Dictionary of Information Technology 22 (2d ed. 1985) (providing definitions of authorization and authorization code).

[109] Arthur E. Oldehoeft, Foundations of a Security Policy for Use of the National Research and Educational Network 43 (1992), https://nvlpubs.nist.gov/nistpubs/Legacy/IR/nistir4734.pdf.

[110] *See, e.g.*, Kent Porter, The New American Computer Dictionary 18 (1985) (defining an authorized library and authorized program, but not including a definition of authorization generally).

[111] *Van Buren*, 141 S. Ct. at 1658 (internal quotation marks omitted).

The prohibition on exceeding authorized access exists, the Court also says, so that the CFAA "does not excuse hacking into an electronic personnel file if the hacker could have walked down the hall to pick up a physical copy."[112] The Court's view that unauthorized access targets hackers is consistent with the view that the statute embraces an authentication standard. In public discussions of computer security, a "hacker" is ordinarily understood to be a person who breaks into a computer by bypassing a technological access gate.[113]

Van Buren's discussion of the CFAA's broader structure provides greater support for this reading. Notably, the Court refers to a person who has authorized access to a file as a user who "has access"[114] to it. In contrast, a user who lacks authorized access is described as a person who "lacks access."[115] An understanding of authorization governed by one who has or lacks access suggests a technological standard, as only a technological barrier gives access to authorized users while taking it away for unauthorized users. The opinion also states that the CFAA's terms "focus on technological harms—such as the corruption of files—of the type unauthorized users cause to computer systems and data."[116] In contrast, the statute is "ill fitted . . . to remediating 'misuse' of sensitive information that employees may permissibly access using their computers."[117] An authentication-based understanding of the CFAA nicely matches this focus, in that computer owners typically prevent the corruption of files by imposing technological barriers to their access

The Court's discussion of the password-trafficking section of the CFAA provides additional support.[118] The password-trafficking provision, section 1030(a)(6), criminalizes trafficking "in any password or similar information through which a computer may be accessed without authorization."[119] The Court said that section 1030(a)(6) "aligns" with its reading of the CFAA in that it "contemplates a 'specific type

[112] *Id.* at 1656.

[113] *See, e.g.*, *What is a Hacker?*, Cisco (last accessed on Apr. 9, 2022), https://www.cisco.com/c/en/us/products/security/what-is-a-hacker.html ("A hacker is a person who breaks into a computer system.").

[114] *Van Buren*, 141 S. Ct. at 1654.

[115] *Id.*

[116] *Id.* at 1660.

[117] *Id.*

[118] *Id.* at 1659 n.9.

[119] 18 U.S.C. §1030(a)(6).

of authorization—that is, authentication,' which turns on whether a user's credentials allow him to proceed past a computer's access gate, rather than on other, scope-based restrictions."[120] A statute that "contemplates" an authentication-based understanding of authorization likely adopts that understanding.

C. THE LIMITS OF FINE DISTINCTIONS IN WRITTEN POLICIES

Van Buren's discussion of the limits of written policies provides a third basis for adopting an authentication standard. In its "final observation,"[121] the Court expressed skepticism that the CFAA could be read to hinge liability on the details of computer-owner policies. "An interpretation that stakes so much on a fine distinction controlled by the drafting practices of private parties," the Court wrote, "is hard to sell as the most plausible."[122] This passage provides further support for a technological authentication standard, I think, because any interpretation of the CFAA that depends on statements of policy raises a similar problem.

To see why, return to *Van Buren*'s hypothetical involving a user who has access to Folder Y but lacks access to Folder X. If access is governed by an authentication gate, then lacking access to Folder X typically will mean that accessing X requires a password that our user does not have. In that case, authorization is simple: The password gate governs authorized access, and the lines will be clear. But imagine access is controlled by words instead of technology. For example, say our user is an employee who has technological access to the workplace computer that hosts both folders. At this workplace, however, only employees authorized to work on the X account are supposed to access Folder X. Our hypothetical employee has not been authorized to work on the X account. The boss therefore imposes a policy about which folder the employee can access: "You are authorized to access Folder Y, but you are not authorized to access Folder X." Can the employer's stated policy control authorization, such that the employee accessing Folder X commits an unauthorized access under the CFAA?

---

[120] *Van Buren*, 141 S. Ct. at 1659 n.9 (quoting Patricia L. Bellia, *A Code-Based Approach to Unauthorized Access Under the Computer Fraud and Abuse Act*, 84 GEO. WASH. L. REV. 1442, 1470 (2016)).

[121] *Id.* at 1662.

[122] *Id.*

Although footnote 8 of *Van Buren* does not foreclose the view that a policy might close a gate, the Court's "final observation" about arbitrary lines drawn by written policies suggests that a policy should not have this effect. The problem is that pairing *Van Buren*'s holding that purpose-based policies cannot control authorization with a rule that other non-purpose-based policies can do so would create the same arbitrariness that *Van Buren* found problematic. Any effort to rely on policy to control authorization has implicit limits, and those implicit limits will be hard to distinguish from the purpose-based limits rejected in *Van Buren*.

Consider different policies that could be imposed on our employee user in the Folder X hypothetical. An employer might try to limit the employee's access by phrasing the policy in several ways:

1) Employees are authorized to access Folder X only for authorized purposes.
2) Employees are authorized to access Folder X only if they have a purpose to conduct authorized work on the X account.
3) Employees are authorized to access Folder X only to conduct authorized work on the X account.
4) Employees are authorized to access Folder X only if they have been authorized to work on the X account.
5) You are not authorized to access Folder X unless you are specifically authorized to work on the X account.
6) You are not authorized to access Folder X.

If policies can control authorization, which of these policies does so? Policy 1 is functionally identical to that in *Van Buren*, which we know cannot control authorization. Policy 6 is the most direct and complete ban. If any policy controls authorization, that's the one. But if some policies can control authorization, there must be a distinction somewhere between Policy 1 and Policy 6—that is, a line between those policies that control CFAA authorization and those that do not. But where is it?

As I see it, the possible lines are all "fine distinction[s] controlled by the drafting practices of private parties," which under *Van Buren* are "hard to sell as the most plausible."[123] When computer owners make

[123] *Id.* at 1662.

access technologically available, but they then try to limit access by policy, they will always have in mind some kinds of accesses they want to allow and others they want to stop. After all, if they wanted to prohibit *all* kinds of access, they could just impose a password gate. Permitting technological access while imposing a policy is useful precisely because it allows some kind of access in some circumstances. *Van Buren* considered expressions based on purpose, in which the policy hinges on goals of the access. But computer owners can articulate the line between permissible and impermissible access in various ways, and differences between purpose-based written policies and other written policies will be thin.

The core problem is that switching from control by technology to control by policy inherently changes the key question from identity to an external condition. When a password gate is used, imposing a technological test, authorization is about identity. The technology grants access to the account holder (for any reason) and denies it to others (for any reason). In contrast, control by policy always implies that access is permitted if some external condition is met. The external condition may be something formal, whether stated explicitly or left implicit, such as an employee receiving permission to work on the X account. Or the external condition may be something informal, such as an employee having a forbidden subjective intent. But giving legal effect to some conditions and not others requires a judge-made jurisprudence of policy-writing. As *Van Buren* teaches, it seems unlikely that Congress intended to draft a criminal statute that hinges on such subtleties.[124]

D. ANALOGIES TO JOYRIDING STATUTES FROM THE DISSENT

A final argument comes from the unlikely source of Justice Thomas's dissent, which inadvertently provides an additional argument in favor of an authentication standard: Authentication emerges as the most plausible reading of the CFAA's authorization standard even using the interpretive tools favored by the dissent.

Justice Thomas's dissent reasoned that Van Buren exceeded authorized access because consent in the law is traditionally bounded by its scope. Thomas invoked the example of joyriding: "A valet, for example, may take possession of a person's car to park it, but he

[124] *See id.*

cannot take it for a joyride." [125] The valet has limited permission, and exceeding that permission would violate criminal laws on joyriding, Justice Thomas contended. Taking the car for a joyride would be exerting "unauthorized control" over the property, amounting to criminal conversion under joyriding statutes. To Justice Thomas, this traditional principle answered *Van Buren*. Because Van Buren had permission to access the database only for law-enforcement purposes, he exceeded authorized access by accessing the database for personal reasons, just like the valet engaged in criminal joyriding.

The analogy to joyriding statutes appears only in the dissent, and so it may not illuminate how to interpret the CFAA going forward. But I think the interpretive method favored by the dissent, when properly applied, ends up supporting the authentication standard for unauthorized access. The joyriding comparison is a sound one in theory, as it involves a prohibition on unauthorized use of property much like the CFAA prohibits unauthorized access to a computer. The problem is that Justice Thomas misunderstood the law governing his persuasive analogy. A closer look at the law of joyriding shows that it points in a very different direction from what Justice Thomas claims. It supports an authentication standard, not reliance on expressed policies.

Contrary to Justice Thomas's claim, statutes on joyriding have generally been interpreted narrowly, using the common-law distinction between fraud in the factum and fraud in the inducement. As a prominent treatise has summarized: "One who obtains the owner's consent to drive his car by fraudulently misrepresenting the use to be made of it, is not guilty of operating a car without the consent of the owner although the owner would not have consented to the use actually made."[126] The basic idea is that misrepresentation negates consent only if the misrepresentation is to the thing consented to (fraud in the factum). Consent based on misrepresentation as to what someone will do with property is still consent (fraud in the inducement). As a result, "an offense which requires the absence of consent is not committed if there was consent to exactly what was done, even if such consent was induced by fraud."[127]

---

[125] *Id.* at 1662 (Thomas, J., dissenting).

[126] Rollin M. Perkins, Perkins on Criminal Law 859 (1957).

[127] *Id.*

Some caselaw shows how this works. In the early case of *State v. Boggs*,[128] the owner of a car permitted the defendant to borrow his car for fifteen or twenty minutes. The defendant instead drove the car around town, picked up some friends, and drove from Ottumwa to Muscatine, about 100 miles away. The defendant was charged under a joyriding statute that punished any persons who "without the consent of the owner take, or cause to be taken, any automobile or motor vehicle, and operate or drive or cause the same to be operated or driven."[129] The Supreme Court of Iowa held that the joyriding statute was not violated. The owner had consented to Boggs driving the car, and Boggs driving the car beyond the scope of the owner's permission was irrelevant: "The statute was not designed to punish one who obtains consent of the owner to take and operate his motor vehicle by misrepresentation or for a fraudulent purpose, but one who takes possession thereof without permission or consent of the owner."[130]

Other cases reflect the same principle. In *State v. Mularkey*,[131] the defendants rented a car for a short trip and agreed to return the car the next morning. Instead, they went on a long trip and abandoned the car. Held: "the mere unauthorized or extended use of such a vehicle by one who has lawfully obtained the consent of the owner to its taking"[132] was not a joyriding crime, as the crime of joyriding targets "the obtaining of the possession in the first instance without the consent of the owner"[133] rather than exceeding of consent. The same approach is found in other cases, such as *People v. Alaboda*[134] and *People v. Cook*.[135] Some of the caselaw is complex and hinges on rather technical distinctions,[136] but it appears broadly consistent with *Boggs* and *Mularkey*.

---

[128] 64 N.W. 759 (Iowa 1917) (per curiam).

[129] *Id.* at 760 (quoting § 4823 of the 1913 Supplement to the Code).

[130] *Id.*

[131] 218 N.W. 809 (Wis. 1928).

[132] *Id.* at 810.

[133] *Id.*

[134] 198 A.D. 41, 45 (N.Y. App. Div. 1921) ("Assuming that the defendant did agree to have the car back the next morning by 7 o'clock, he merely failed to keep his agreement—he breached the contract—and was liable for any damages resulting; but he did not commit a crime.").

[135] 28 Cal. App. 2d 716, 719 (1964) ("[T]he fact that consent is obtained through misrepresentation will not supply the essential element of non-consent.").

[136] For example, where the permitted use of the car creates a bailment, and the owner withdraws the bailment before the non-permitted use occurs, the bailment ends and further use is unauthorized. *See, e.g.*, Jones v. State, 498 A.2d 622, 625–26 (Md. 1985) (holding a joyriding statute violated where an auto mechanic had the car with initial consent, was told to

Justice Thomas cites only one case in support of his very different view of joyriding liability. The decision, *In re Clayton*,[137] is puzzlingly inapt. In *Clayton*, a lawyer misused funds in a client's trust account. The funds had been received from a settlement, and the lawyer had previously agreed with his client that he would pay the funds to an insurance company to settle a lien against his client.[138] The lawyer instead used the funds to pay his own operating expenses.[139] *Clayton* concluded without elaboration that the lawyer had violated ethics rules in part because he had committed "conversion of the insurance company's funds."[140]

It's hard to see how *Clayton* supports Justice Thomas's account of the traditional standard of liability in joyriding cases. Beyond not involving joyriding, the case does not even relate to exceeding the scope of permission to use another's property. The lawyer in *Clayton* had a fiduciary responsibility to send client funds to the insurance company, and instead he simply took the money for himself. That was outright theft. The lawyer had a means of access that allowed him to commit the theft, but that seems irrelevant: The common-law requirement of "breaking bulk" before having criminal theft liability was overcome centuries ago.[141] Especially in light of caselaw like *Boggs* and *Mularkey*, Justice Thomas's view of the scope of joyriding liability seems incorrect. Looking to the law of joyriding statutes was sensible, but I believe Justice Thomas misunderstood the legal implications of the analogy.

All of this matters because the traditional distinction between fraud in the factum and fraud in the inducement, which is used to interpret the absence-of-authorization element in joyriding statutes, supports an authentication standard under the CFAA.[142] Access to a computer

---

return it, but then did not; being told to return the car entered the bailment relationship and terminated consent). This appears to explain cases where a chauffeur is told to only drive the car in a particular way or for a particular time but then exceeds those limits. *See, e.g.*, People v. Luster, 411 N.E.2d 47 (Ill. App. 1937) (explaining that because the employer is "the absolute owner and possessor of the automobile," the chauffeur only has temporary custody of the car but not possession, and "using the automobile and driving it contrary to the directions of the owner" is a trespass or even conversion).

[137] *In re* Clayton, 778 N.E.2d 404 (Ind. 2002).

[138] *Id.* at 405.

[139] *Id.*

[140] *Id.*

[141] *See* George P. Fletcher, *The Metamorphosis of Larceny*, 89 HARV. L. REV. 469, 481–86 (1976) (discussing the rise and fall of the common-law "breaking bulk" requirement).

[142] I made a similar argument in *Cybercrime's Scope*, *supra* note 70, at 1652–55.

file in violation of a policy is like fraud in the inducement. The computer operator grants technological access to the user but imposes a verbal ban on what can be done with that access, much like the car owner hands over the car to another person but imposes limits on how it can be driven.[143] The user then accesses the computer based on an implied or explicit promise to comply with those limits, much like the driver takes the car with an implied or explicit promise to follow the owner's directive. If the computer user violates the limits, the promise is broken. But the consent remains, and the access is still legally authorized, because the computer operator allowed the access to occur. The computer user who is given technological access but violates an expressed policy is like the defendant in *Boggs* or *Mularky*. Morally, he is a promise breaker. But legally, he is acting with authorization.

In contrast, access that bypasses an authentication gate is fraud in the factum that constitutes access without authorization or in excess of authorized access.[144] An authentication gate, such as a password requirement, limits who can access an account. Only the authorized user can enter the password and use the service. Because authentication verifies identity, bypassing an authentication gate tricks the computer as to whether an authenticated user has been let in. For example, a hacker who exploits a security flaw to gain access does not go through the authentication gate at all. An outsider who guesses a password to another's account, or who learns of the password and uses the account without permission, goes through the authentication gate but under false pretenses. Either way, the computer is tricked. Because authentication rests on identity, the goal of admitting only pre-authorized users is thwarted through fraud in the factum.[145]

* * *

On its face, *Van Buren* is largely a dispute about the word "so." Under the surface, however, the opinion begins to bring the CFAA into focus. The picture is still fuzzy, but we can now see the entirety of the statute in ways that will frame future disputes. A close read of the opinion suggests that it supports an authentication standard. The attention now turns back to lower courts to see if they "so" read it.

---

[143] *See id.*

[144] *See id.*

[145] This can raise subtle distinctions as to how to define the factum, of course. *See id.* at 1655 n.251.

RUSSELL K. ROBINSON

WHAT CHRISTIANITY LOSES WHEN CONSERVATIVE CHRISTIANS WIN AT THE SUPREME COURT

In *Fulton v. City of Philadelphia*,[1] the Supreme Court extended a recent trend of invalidating the application of antidiscrimination rules that protected LGBTQ people, stating that such applications violated the First Amendment's Free Exercise Clause. In 2018, the Court ruled for an evangelical baker who said that the application of a state antidiscrimination law to his refusal to bake a cake to celebrate the union of a gay couple violated his free exercise right.[2] In these two recent cases, the Court expressed rhetorical support for LGBTQ people's interest in equal treatment.[3] The holding in each case, however, privileged the asserted free exercise right over the competing equality interest. At

Russell K. Robinson is Walter Perry Johnson Professor of Law & Faculty Director, Center on Race, Sexuality & Culture, University of California, Berkeley School of Law.

Authors's note: I received very helpful comments and encouragement from participants at the Berkeley Law faculty workshop. I am also grateful to Erwin Chemerinsky, Seth Davis, Justin Driver, David Pozen, Chris Scott, David Simson, Steve Sugarman, and Leti Volpp for insightful comments. Isabella Coelho, Eliana Machefsky, and Aysha Spencer provided excellent research assistance. Edna Lewis of the Berkeley Law library provided additional help.

[1] 141 S. Ct. 1868 (2021).

[2] Masterpiece Cakeshop, Ltd. v. Colo. C.R. Comm'n, 138 S. Ct. 1719 (2018); *see also* Russell K. Robinson, *Justice Kennedy's White Nationalism*, 53 U.C. Davis L. Rev. 1027, 1065–71 (2019) (discussing *Masterpiece Cakeshop*).

[3] *See, e.g.*, *Masterpiece Cakeshop*, 138 S. Ct. at 1727.

The Supreme Court Review, 2022.
 https://doi.org/10.1086/719566

the same time, the opinions stopped short of overruling *Employment Division v. Smith*[4] and announcing a broad right of religious people and organizations to disobey generally applicable laws. That question was squarely before the Court in *Fulton*, and three Justices appeared prepared to jettison *Smith*. But Chief Justice Roberts, Justice Kavanaugh, and Justice Barrett hesitated to go that far, which preserved *Smith*—at least for the moment. This Essay identifies and analyzes what is at stake for the Supreme Court and for Christianity if the Court continues to craft a constitutional right to discriminate from the claims of a subset of conservative Christians.[5]

This Essay identifies two important reasons for the Court not to create a broad right of religious people to opt out of general laws. First, the Court's recent trilogy of religion cases—*Fulton*, *Masterpiece Cakeshop*, and *Trump v. Hawaii*[6]—as well as the lower profile pandemic worship cases[7]—call into question the Court's own neutrality on questions of religion. These decisions have impaired the Justices' ability to claim that they stand outside of politics and religion and possess the "objectivity" required to adjudicate religious liberty claims. Moreover, the enhanced politicization of the Court by the religious right, the Republican Party, and especially former President Donald Trump has boxed the Court in. The Court's legitimacy in the eyes of the public is at a precarious low, primarily because of recent political developments. This Essay seeks to show how the Court's free exercise decisions have also contributed to this vulnerability and undercut

---

[4] 494 U.S. 872 (1990).

[5] The Justices appear to be closely divided on the question of overturning *Employment Division v. Smith*, 494 U.S. 872 (1990), a landmark case limiting free exercise challenges to generally applicable laws. Recently, Justice Barrett wrote a concurring opinion, which was joined by Justice Kavanaugh and in part by Justice Breyer, explaining her decision not to join Justices Thomas, Alito, and Gorsuch in a case involving Maine's vaccine mandate. The opinion suggested that Justices Barrett and Kavanaugh's decision not to disturb *Smith* rested not only on the merits of the legal issue but also practical considerations regarding the use of the Court's emergency docket. *See* Does 1–3 v. Mills, 142 S. Ct. 17, 18 (2021) (mem.). Maine's mandate contains a medical exception but not a religious exemption. The Court denied an application for injunctive relief, which allowed Maine to proceed with its mandate. *Id.* Justice Gorsuch, joined by Justices Thomas and Alito, dissented and argued that the Maine law's provision of a medical exception required it also to include a religious exemption. *Id.* at 19 (Gorsuch, J., dissenting).

[6] 138 S. Ct. 2392 (2018).

[7] *See, e.g.*, Tandon v. Newsom, 141 S. Ct. 1294 (2021) (per curiam); Roman Catholic Diocese v. Cuomo, 141 S. Ct. 63 (2020) (per curiam); South Bay United Pentecostal Church v. Newsom, 140 S. Ct. 1613 (2020) (mem.).

certain Justices' vociferous claims that their personal backgrounds and politics are legally irrelevant.

Second, this Essay argues that the Court's validation of free exercise claims brought by conservative Christians has contributed to the conflation of "Christian" and "evangelical" in the broader culture.[8] This trend conceals the diversity and contestation among Christians as to the core of their faith and how it commands Christians to treat stigmatized groups. Thus, Supreme Court decisions in favor of conservative Christians may simultaneously be a win for them but a loss for Christians who hold a profoundly different understanding of their faith. Christianity is a complex, diverse, and constantly evolving religion. Views of Christians on sexuality and gender identity are also complex.[9] My goal is to make visible this breadth of perspectives, because one would never know the diversity of the Christian faith from reading Supreme Court opinions. This Essay's title reflects my personal understanding of Christianity and my desire to complicate the dominant understanding of the faith as aligned with conservative and anti-LGBTQ politics. I want to acknowledge that conservative Christians may see my understanding of the faith—and even the title of this essay—as a harmful distortion of true Christianity. The larger point is to reveal this intra-faith contestation and call for judges and scholars to be more attentive to it.

I. Heightened Scrutiny of Judicial Claims of Neutrality

Supreme Court Justices have long described the Court as rendering legal judgments that are distinct from politics. Legal scholars have debated these claims, and this section does not recount that long history.[10] Rather, this brief survey of recent statements by Supreme Court Justices sets the stage for my specific claim about perceptions of judicial neutrality and a recent shift in free exercise doctrine.

---

[8] *See, e.g.*, Laura Desfor Edles, *Contemporary Progressive Christianity and Its Symbolic Ramifications*, 7 Cultural Socio. 3, 4 (2013) ("[T]he rise of the 'Christian right' has resulted in the virtual equation of Christianity with political conservatism in the public sphere.").

[9] For example, some LGBTQ Christians identify as "Side A" (Christians who believe that Scripture affirms LGBTQ sexual relationships) or "Side B" (Christians who believe it is not sinful to have same-sex attraction, but Scripture requires such people not to act on that attraction). *Side A / Side B Theology Primer*, Coming out Christians, http://www.comingout4christians.net/side-a-side-b-primer.html [https://perma.cc/7388-RTEB].

[10] *See, e.g.*, Herbert Wechsler, *Toward Neutral Principles of Constitutional Law*, 73 Harv. L. Rev. 1 (1959). On various conceptions of the Court's legitimacy, see Richard H. Fallon, Jr., *Legitimacy and the Constitution*, 118 Harv. L. Rev. 1787 (2005).

Chief Justice Roberts famously asserted during his confirmation hearing, "Judges are like umpires. Umpires don't make the rules, they apply them. The role of an umpire and a judge is critical. They make sure everybody plays by the rules, but it is a limited role. Nobody ever went to a ballgame to see the umpire."[11] He also asserted: "Mr. Chairman, I come before the Committee with no agenda. I have no platform. Judges are not politicians. . . ."[12] In November 2018, President Trump denounced an Oakland, California-based district court judge who rejected his asylum policy as an "Obama judge."[13] Chief Justice Roberts, in a surprising break from judicial protocol, responded publicly, "We do not have Obama judges or Trump judges, Bush judges or Clinton judges. . . . What we have is an extraordinary group of dedicated judges doing their level best to do equal right to those appearing before them. . . . Th[e] independent judiciary is something we should all be thankful for."[14]

Trump fired back at Roberts:

> Sorry Chief Justice John Roberts, but you do indeed have "Obama judges," and they have a much different point of view than the people who are charged with the safety of our country. It would be great if the 9th Circuit was indeed an "independent judiciary". . . .[15]

He then instructed the Chief:

> Please study the numbers, they are shocking. . . . *Judicial Activism*, by people who know nothing about security and the safety of our citizens, is putting our country in great danger. Not good! . . . Judges must not Legislate Security. . . . We want the Constitution as written![16]

---

[11] *Confirmation Hearing on the Nomination of John G. Roberts, Jr. to be Chief Justice of the United States: Hearing Before the S. Comm. on the Judiciary*, 109th Cong. 55 (2005).

[12] *Id.* at 56.

[13] Robert Barnes, *Rebuking Trump's Criticism of 'Obama Judge,' Chief Justice Roberts Defends Judiciary as 'Independent,'* Wash. Post (Nov. 21, 2018), https://www.washingtonpost.com/politics/rebuking-trumps-criticism-of-obama-judge-chief-justice-roberts-defends-judiciary-as-independent/2018/11/21/6383c7b2-edb7-11e8-96d4-0d23f2aaad09_story.html [https://perma.cc/H2CJ-5EU9].

[14] *Id.*

[15] *In His Own Words: The President's Attacks on the Courts*, Brennan Ctr. for Just. (June 5, 2017) (emphasis added), https://www.brennancenter.org/our-work/research-reports/his-own-words-presidents-attacks-courts [https://perma.cc/65FU-ETVD] (quoting several tweets from Donald Trump).

[16] *Id.*

Chief Justice Roberts did not reply, but in March 2020, Roberts rebuked Senator Chuck Schumer for attacking Justices Kavanaugh and Gorsuch for their views on reproductive rights. "Justices know that criticism comes with the territory," Roberts stated, "but threatening statements of this sort from the highest levels of government are not only inappropriate, they are dangerous. . . . All Members of the Court will continue to do their job, without fear or favor, from whatever quarter."[17] The week before, Trump had called for Justices Ruth Bader Ginsburg and Sonia Sotomayor to be recused from any cases involving him or his administration.[18] Chief Justice Roberts was criticized for remaining silent in the face of these attacks by Trump, while intervening to defend two of his conservative brethren.[19]

Although they differ in many respects in terms of their identities and jurisprudence, conservative and liberal Justices appear united in their defense of the Court as neutral and objective. This discussion recounts just a few recent examples. In 2018, Justice Clarence Thomas declared: "In our great country, the judiciary is not a puppet for those in power, nor is it the engine for pioneering social change. . . . Rather, it is a safeguard against tyranny, and an assurance of neutral arbiters for those seeking the protection of the law."[20] Justice Breyer, who has spoken and written prolifically on this topic, has stated, "It is a judge's sworn duty to be impartial, and all of us take that oath seriously."[21] Justice Amy Coney Barrett—whose nomination was hustled through the process by Senate Majority Leader Mitch McConnell on the eve

---

[17] James Walker, *Chief Justice Roberts' Reprimand of Schumer Could 'Damage Public Faith,'* NEWSWEEK (Mar. 5, 2020), https://www.msn.com/en-us/news/politics/chief-justice-roberts-reprimand-of-schumer-could-damage-public-faith/ar-BB10Mld1 [https://perma.cc/3U2J-BLQ7].

[18] *See id.*

[19] *See id.* (noting that critics believed Chief Justice Roberts's failure to "repudiate" Trump's attacks on Justices Ginsburg and Sotomayor could bring "the [C]ourt's impartiality into question").

[20] Kate Brumback, *Supreme Court Justice Thomas Stresses Need For Judicial Neutrality*, CBS ATLANTA (Oct. 22, 2018), https://atlanta.cbslocal.com/2018/10/22/supreme-court-justice-thomas-stresses-need-for-judicial-neutrality/ [https://perma.cc/8RAC-M6YK].

[21] *See* STEPHEN BREYER, THE AUTHORITY OF THE COURT AND THE PERIL OF POLITICS (2021); Joan Biskupic, *Justice Breyer's Rosy View of an Apolitical Supreme Court*, WASH. POST (Sept. 17, 2021), https://www.washingtonpost.com/outlook/justice-breyers-rosy-view-of-an-apolitical-supreme-court/2021/09/16/948482b8-012b-11ec-ba7e-2cf966e88e93_story.html [https://perma.cc/G9CY-GSFG]; *see also* Ian Millhiser, *Justice Breyer's New Warning for Democrats Couldn't Have Come at a Worse Time*, VOX (May 29, 2021), https://www.vox.com/22454648/justice-stephen-breyer-supreme-court-retirement-book-harvard-court-packing-voting-democracy [https://perma.cc/B3YT-KKRE].

of the election—stated: "This Court is not comprised of a bunch of partisan hacks. . . . Judicial philosophies are not the same as political parties."[22] Justice Barrett made this assertion of neutrality, however, at an event honoring Senator McConnell.[23]

In marked contrast to Chief Justice Roberts's performance of neutrality during his confirmation hearing, Justice Kavanaugh gave an astonishingly emotional—indeed, some said unhinged[24]—defense of his character in the face of a credible charge of sexual assault by Dr. Christine Blasey Ford. Kavanaugh claimed that Democrats were engaged in a conspiracy against him on behalf of the Clintons.[25] Kavanaugh painted himself as a victim of "a calculated and orchestrated political hit, fueled with apparent pent-up anger about President Trump and the 2016 election. Fear that has been unfairly stoked about my judicial record. Revenge on behalf of the Clintons. And millions of dollars in money from outside left-wing opposition groups."[26] This highly unusual performance rallied support from Republican Senators and secured Kavanaugh's confirmation (by a razor-thin margin).[27] Rather than assure Americans that, if confirmed, he would set aside the messy political battle sparked by his nomination, Kavanaugh warned that "[t]he consequences will extend long past my nomination. The consequences will be with us for decades."[28]

Another breach of protocol came from the liberal end of the Court. In 2016, Justice Ginsburg made several comments to the press

---

[22] Adam Serwer, *The Lie About the Supreme Court Everyone Pretends to Believe*, ATLANTIC (Sept. 28, 2021), https://www.theatlantic.com/ideas/archive/2021/09/lie-about-supreme-court-everyone-pretends-believe/620198/ [https://perma.cc/DF6X-AZUV].

[23] *Id.*

[24] *See, e.g.*, Jeannie Suk Gersen, *Brett Kavanaugh's Damaging, Revealing Partisan Bitterness*, NEW YORKER (Sept. 28, 2018), https://www.newyorker.com/news/daily-comment/brett-kavanaughs-damaging-revealing-partisan-bitterness-supreme-court-confirmation [https://perma.cc/3T9N-YKXL] ("Kavanaugh often appeared to be having a petulant and distracted teen-age meltdown, interrupting the Democratic senators and rarely attempting to answer their questions directly.").

[25] *See* Louis Jacobson, *In Context: Brett Kavanaugh and 'What Goes Around Comes Around,'* POLITIFACT (Oct. 4, 2018), https://www.politifact.com/article/2018/oct/04/context-brett-kavanaugh-and-what-goes-around-comes/ [https://perma.cc/T9BE-8JW7].

[26] *Id.*

[27] *See PN2259 - Nomination of Brett M. Kavanaugh for Supreme Court of the United States*, CONGRESS.GOV (Oct. 6, 2018), https://www.congress.gov/nomination/115th-congress/2259 [https://perma.cc/DA6N-59XU].

[28] Jacobson, *supra* note 25.

indicating her contempt for Trump.[29] This was striking, and worried both conservatives and liberals. That same year, Ginsburg assailed San Francisco 49ers quarterback Colin Kaepernick, who is African American, for his political protest of kneeling during the national anthem, which she called "dumb" and "disrespectful."[30] Justice Ginsburg later apologized for these remarks.[31] However, Katie Couric, who had interviewed Ginsburg in 2016, recently disclosed the full extent of Ginsburg's critique of African-Americans who protest racial injustice. Ginsburg went on to say that Kaepernick's protest showed "contempt for a government that has made it possible for their parents and grandparents to live a decent life . . . [w]hich they probably could not have lived in the places they came from."[32] In Ginsburg's telling, a people whose ancestors were kidnapped, enslaved, treated as property, bred as if they were animals, and often brutally murdered were akin to immigrants fleeing a war-torn country in pursuit of freedom in America. Couric withheld these remarks to "protect" Ginsburg from public critique; Couric deemed them "unworthy of a crusader for equality."[33] Ginsburg's full remarks alarmingly echo the racism of her adversary Trump, who told four women of color in Congress to "go back" to their countries of origin (three of the four were born in the U.S.).[34] Justice Ginsburg's decision to intervene in public debates concerning Trump and Kaepernick further damaged perceptions of the Court's objectivity.

Public opinion polls suggest that confidence in the Court is at a historic low. A poll by a policy center at the University of Pennsylvania

---

[29] *See* Joan Biskupic, *Justice Ruth Bader Ginsburg Calls Trump a 'Faker,' He Says She Should Resign*, CNN (July 13, 2016), https://www.cnn.com/2016/07/12/politics/justice-ruth-bader-ginsburg-donald-trump-faker/index.html [https://perma.cc/27XY-PXXJ].

[30] Adam Liptak, *Ruth Bader Ginsburg Regrets Speaking out on Colin Kaepernick*, N.Y. Times (Oct. 14, 2016), https://www.nytimes.com/2016/10/15/us/ruth-bader-ginsburg-colin-kaepernick-national-anthem.html [https://perma.cc/B9HN-UQY8].

[31] *See id.*

[32] Christi Carras, *Katie Couric Scrapped RBG's Remarks on National Anthem Protests to 'Protect' Her*, L.A. Times (Oct. 14, 2021), https://www.latimes.com/entertainment-arts/books/story/2021-10-14/katie-couric-ruth-bader-ginsburg-rbg-colin-kaepernick [https://perma.cc/U9E3-V6GP].

[33] *Id.*

[34] *See* Ashley Parker, Rachael Bade & John Wagner, *Trump Says They 'Hate Our Country.' The Democrats He Attacked Say the Country 'Belongs to Everyone.,'* Wash. Post (July 15, 2019), https://www.washingtonpost.com/politics/trump-calls-on-minority-congresswomen-to-apologize-after-he-said-they-should-go-back-to-their-countries/2019/07/15/897f1dd0-a6ef-11e9-a3a6-ab670962db05_story.html [https://perma.cc/96ET-JSAC].

stated, "If the Supreme Court started making a lot of rulings that most Americans disagreed with, it might be better to do away with the court altogether."[35] Thirty-four percent of respondents agreed with that statement, compared with just 20 percent two years ago.[36] President Biden created a commission to study court reform[37] in response to a debate among Democrats about "packing the Court."[38] In addition, the Court has faced intense scrutiny for its repeated use of its "shadow docket" to make important decisions without the benefit of oral argument and writing full opinions.[39] And recently, the Court declined to invalidate an unprecedented statutory scheme out of Texas that allows private citizens to sue other citizens for terminating a pregnancy in violation of the law.[40] This recent ruling has ratcheted up public and scholarly scrutiny, possibly making the Court seem even less legitimate than it did after it effectively decided the election in

---

[35] Annenberg Pub. Pol'y Ctr., *One in Three Americans Say They Might Consider Abolishing or Limiting Supreme Court*, ANNENBERG SCH. FOR COMMS. (Oct. 5, 2021), https://www.asc.upenn.edu/news-events/news/one-three-americans-say-they-might-consider-abolishing-or-limiting-supreme-court [https://perma.cc/2QBP-AW6L].

[36] *Id.*; *see also* Linda Greenhouse, *The Supreme Court's Pain, and Our Anger*, N.Y. TIMES (Oct. 7, 2021), https://www.nytimes.com/2021/10/07/opinion/supreme-court-polls-abortion-bush-gore.html [https://perma.cc/AG48-KUNK].

[37] *See* Exec. Order No. 14,023, 86 Fed. Reg. 19,569 (Apr. 9, 2021).

[38] *See, e.g.*, Kalvis Golde, *Debate over Court Packing Continues*, SCOTUSBLOG (Feb. 8, 2021), https://www.scotusblog.com/2021/02/debate-over-court-packing-continues/ [https://perma.cc/KK8Q-SQAP]; Adam Liptak, *The Precedent, and Perils, of Court Packing*, N.Y. TIMES (Oct. 12, 2020), https://www.nytimes.com/2020/10/12/us/supreme-court-packing.html [https://perma.cc/J94N-9JXS]; Walter Shapiro, *The Case Against Court-Packing*, BRENNAN CTR. FOR JUST. (June 24, 2019), https://www.brennancenter.org/our-work/analysis-opinion/case-against-court-packing [https://perma.cc/LBA2-8W5T].

[39] *See, e.g.*, William Baude, *The Supreme Court's Shadow Docket*, 9 N.Y.U. J.L. & LIBERTY 1 (2015); Lawrence Hurley, Andrew Chung & Jonathan Allen, *The 'Shadow Docket': How the U.S. Supreme Court Quietly Dispatches Key Rulings*, REUTERS (Mar. 23, 2021), https://www.reuters.com/article/legal-us-usa-court-shadow-video/the-shadow-docket-how-the-u-s-supreme-court-quietly-dispatches-key-rulings-idUSKBN2BF16Q [https://perma.cc/3872-K55K] ("The speed and secretiveness [of the shadow docket] has drawn criticism from legal experts both on the right and left, who call it an improper use of the court's tremendous power."); Louis Jacobson, *The Supreme Court's 'Shadow Docket': What You Need to Know*, POLITIFACT (Oct. 18, 2021), https://www.politifact.com/article/2021/oct/18/supreme-courts-shadow-docket-what-you-need-know/ [https://perma.cc/JJ6X-UZQF] ("[A]s the number and importance of [shadow docket] decisions has increased, so have the concerns raised by scholars, senators, and even some of the justices themselves . . . [who] say the decisions are rushed, that they don't allow for full arguments, and that the rulings are less transparent than typical cases.").

[40] *See* Whole Woman's Health v. Jackson, 141 S. Ct. 2494 (2021); Editorial, *The Supreme Court Has to Save More than Abortion Access in Texas. It Has to Save Itself*, L.A. TIMES (Oct. 29, 2021), https://www.latimes.com/opinion/story/2021-10-29/editorial-the-supreme-court-has-to-save-more-than-abortion-access-in-texas-it-has-to-save-itself [https://perma.cc/QK8P-PQTE].

Bush v. Gore two decades ago.[41] A Gallup poll released in September 2021 found that a majority (53 percent) disapproves of the Court—the highest number in the history of the poll.[42] As Emily Bazelon wrote recently,

> The justices share an incentive to promote a vaunted status for the institution to which they devote their careers. But it's harder for any of them to argue credibly that the court is above politics when a majority of justices who were all appointed by presidents of one party change the law in ways that fulfill the most cherished hopes of that party's base.[43]

The liberal Justices expressed this anxiety pointedly during the oral argument for a Mississippi case in which the Court appears poised to overrule *Roe v. Wade*.[44] "Will this institution survive the stench that this creates in the public perception that the Constitution and its reading are just political acts?" Justice Sotomayor asked.[45] "I don't see how it is possible."[46] Public scrutiny of the Court's relationship to politics has fixated on abortion, but the next section shows how the Court's recent free exercise cases also raise questions about the Court's ability to identify anti-religious bias in a neutral, apolitical manner.

II. Fulton's Selective Depiction of "Bias"

Although the Court's decision in *Fulton* may seem narrow and fact-bound, this Part links *Fulton* to a broader significant shift in the Court's free exercise and equality jurisprudence. There is a long line of cases in which antidiscrimination laws were said to conflict with rights of religious expression, speech, or association under the First Amendment. The Court's choice since the mid-twentieth century had

---

41 *See* Greenhouse, *supra* note 36.

42 *See* Jeffrey M. Jones, *Approval of U.S. Supreme Court Down to 40%, a New Low*, Gallup (Sept. 23, 2021), https://news.gallup.com/poll/354908/approval-supreme-court-down-new-low.aspx [https://perma.cc/YDB4-FVLH].

43 Emily Bazelon, *It's Amy Coney Barrett's Supreme Court Now*, N.Y. Times (Oct. 29, 2021), https://www.nytimes.com/2021/10/29/opinion/amy-coney-barrett-supreme-court-abortion.html [https://perma.cc/C7JX-T2H9].

44 410 U.S. 113 (1973); Adam Liptak, J. David Goodman & Sabrina Tavernise, *Supreme Court, Breaking Silence, Won't Block Texas Abortion Law*, N.Y. Times (Sept. 1, 2021), https://www.nytimes.com/2021/09/01/us/supreme-court-texas-abortion.html [https://perma.cc/M7T9-8QJC] (predicting *Roe*'s demise).

45 *See* David Leonhardt & Ian Prasad Philbrick, *Abortion at the Court*, N.Y. Times (Dec. 2, 2021), https://www.nytimes.com/2021/12/02/briefing/supreme-court-abortion-case-mississippi.html [https://perma.cc/C3HR-MC3V].

46 *Id.*

typically been to affirm generally applicable antidiscrimination laws over claims of freedom to discriminate grounded in the First Amendment.[47] In some cases, the Court brushed aside the First Amendment interest as flimsy, even relegating the defense to a footnote.[48] In the 1990s, two trends emerged in cases involving LGBTQ rights. In a widely celebrated line of cases beginning with *Romer v. Evans*,[49] and culminating in *Obergefell v. Hodges*,[50] the Court expanded constitutional protections for sexual minorities under the Equal Protection and Due Process Clauses. During the same era, however, states that sought to protect LGBTQ citizens from discrimination were usually losing when private groups invoked the First Amendment as a defense.[51] At present, the Court has not extended this privileging of First Amendment interests to race and sex cases, but it also has failed to provide a rationale that would justify limiting its analysis to the LGBTQ context.

In *Fulton*, the Court continued to prioritize free exercise claims over equality interests. Indeed, the opinion barely acknowledges the equality interests of LGBTQ people. Chief Justice Roberts, writing for six Justices, explained that the dispute centered on whether the City of Philadelphia ("City") could require Catholic Social Services ("CSS"), a foster care agency, to certify same-sex couples as eligible to adopt.[52] CSS asserted that facilitating adoptions by same-sex couples would violate its faith and thus the Free Exercise Clause provided it an exemption from the City's antidiscrimination rules.[53] "No same-sex couple has sought certification from CSS,"[54] Chief Justice Roberts wrote early in the Court's opinion. "If one did, CSS would direct the couple to one of the more than 20 other agencies in the City, all of which currently certify same-sex couples."[55] The majority opinion

[47] *See, e.g.*, Roberts v. U.S. Jaycees, 468 U.S. 609 (1984).

[48] *See* Newman v. Piggie Park Enters., Inc., 390 U.S. 400, 402 n.5 (1968).

[49] 517 U.S. 620 (1996).

[50] 576 U.S. 644 (2015).

[51] *See* Hurley v. Irish-Am. Gay, Lesbian, & Bisexual Grp. of Bos., 515 U.S. 557 (1995); Boy Scouts v. Dale, 530 U.S. 640 (2000). *But see* Christian Legal Soc'y Chapter of the Univ. of Cal., Hastings Coll. of the Law v. Martinez, 561 U.S. 661 (2010).

[52] Fulton v. City of Phila., 141 S. Ct. 1868, 1874 (2021).

[53] *See id.* at 1875.

[54] *Id.*

[55] *Id.*

recounted the longstanding role of the Catholic Church in facilitating adoptions, including CSS's fifty years of service in Philadelphia.[56]

"But things changed in 2018."[57] The Chief Justice's factual summary depicts shifting cultural winds lashing a deeply rooted religious organization. After a local newspaper identified Catholic charities as refusing to certify same-sex couples, Philadelphia's City Council called for an investigation.[58] During a meeting with CSS leadership, Cynthia Figueroa, the Commissioner of the Department of Human Services, said that "things have changed since 100 years ago," and "it would be great if we followed the teachings of Pope Francis, the voice of the Catholic Church."[59] The City soon declared CSS in violation of antidiscrimination requirements, froze its existing contract with CSS, and stated that it would not renew the contract.[60] CSS brought suit. The district court and the Third Circuit ruled in favor of the City.[61] The courts deemed the antidiscrimination requirements neutral, generally applicable rules, which do not violate the Free Exercise Clause under *Employment Division v. Smith*.[62] The Supreme Court disagreed, declaring, "This case falls outside *Smith*."[63] Because the contract included language suggesting the City had discretion to grant exemptions from its nondiscrimination rule, the Court ruled, it could not deny such an exemption to CSS.[64] Relying on its recent decision in *Masterpiece Cakeshop*, the Court stated: "Government fails to act neutrally when it proceeds in a manner intolerant of religious beliefs or restricts practices because of their religious nature."[65] Chief Justice Roberts argued that one section of the contract permitted the City to make exceptions in its "sole discretion."[66] Although the City pointed to another provision barring discrimination without exception, the

[56] *Id.* at 1875–76.

[57] *Id.* at 1875.

[58] *See id.*

[59] *Id.*; *see also infra* notes 199–201 and accompanying text (discussing the Pope's refusal to judge gay people).

[60] *See Fulton*, 141 S. Ct. at 1875–76.

[61] *See id.* at 1876.

[62] 494 U.S. 872 (1990); *see also Fulton*, 141 S. Ct. at 1876–77.

[63] *Fulton*, 141 S. Ct. at 1877.

[64] *Id.* at 1878.

[65] *Id.* at 1877.

[66] *Id.* at 1878.

Chief replied that "state law makes clear that 'one part of a contract cannot be so interpreted as to annul another part.'"[67] The Court thus determined that the clause with an exception governed rather than the separate ban that lacked any exception. The inclusion of a clause permitting any exemption, the Court determined, entitled CSS to receive a pass.[68]

The City's final effort was to locate a generally applicable ban on discrimination in Philadelphia's Fair Practices Ordinance, which applies to "public accommodations."[69] Delving into the weeds of several dictionary definitions and Pennsylvania statutes, Chief Justice Roberts regarded adoption agencies as quite unlike paradigmatic public accommodations, such as "hotels, restaurants, drug stores, swimming pools, barbershops, and public conveyances."[70] In so doing, the Court departed from its usual practice of "defer[ing] to lower court constructions of state statutes."[71] Given the lack of a generally applicable rule, the Court applied strict scrutiny. *Fulton* thus narrowed the definition of "generally applicable," a trend that incrementally expands the swath of laws that are subject to strict scrutiny.[72]

Further, in this case, the Court's analysis appeared "'strict' in theory and fatal in fact."[73] The City considered three compelling interests: "maximizing the number of foster parents, protecting the City from liability, and ensuring equal treatment of prospective foster parents and foster children."[74] The Court waved away the first two asserted interests as overly general and speculative.[75] The Court

---

[67] *Id.* at 1879 (citing Shehadi v. Ne. Nat'l Bank of Pa., 378 A.2d 304 (1977)).

[68] *Id.* at 1879; *see also* Tandon v. Newsom, 141 S. Ct. 1294, 1296 (2021) (per curiam) ("[G]overnment regulations are not neutral and generally applicable, and therefore trigger strict scrutiny under the Free Exercise Clause, whenever they treat *any* comparable secular activity more favorably than religious exercise."). Scholars have described this new rule as guaranteeing religious actors "most favored nation" status. *See, e.g.*, David Simson, *Most Favored Racial Hierarchy: The Ever-Evolving Ways of the Supreme Court's Superordination of Whiteness*, MICH. L. REV. (forthcoming 2022).

[69] *Fulton*, 141 S. Ct. at 1879–80.

[70] *See id.* at 1880.

[71] *Id.* at 1881.

[72] *See, e.g.*, Ira C. Lupu & Robert W. Tuttle, *The Radical Uncertainty of Free Exercise Principles: A Comment on* Fulton v. Philadelphia, 5 AM. CONST. SOC'Y SUP. CT. REV. 221, 222 (2021); James M. Oleske, Jr., *Free Exercise (Dis)honesty*, 2019 WIS. L. REV. 689, 731–39.

[73] *See, e.g.*, Gerald Gunther, *The Supreme Court 1971 Term – Foreword: In Search of Evolving Doctrine on a Changing Court: A Model for a Newer Equal Protection*, 86 HARV. L. REV. 1, 8 (1972).

[74] *Fulton*, 141 S. Ct. at 1881.

[75] *Id.* at 1881–82.

lingered on the third state interest: "We do not doubt that this interest is a weighty one, for '[o]ur society has come to the recognition that gay persons and gay couples cannot be treated as social outcasts or as inferior in dignity and worth.'"[76] Seemingly limiting its opinion to "the facts of this case," the Court determined that the City's willingness to make exceptions "undermines the City's contention that its non-discrimination policies can brook no departures."[77]

The Court closed its opinion by offering more praise for CSS's lengthy history of service. CSS, it stated, has "long been a point of light in the City's foster-care system."[78] It also again implied that CSS had harmed no one: "CSS seeks only an accommodation that will allow it to continue serving the children of Philadelphia in a manner consistent with its religious beliefs; it does not seek to impose those beliefs on anyone else."[79] Justice Alito's concurring opinion made that claim in a more pointed fashion: "[N]ot only is there no evidence that CSS's policy has ever interfered in the slightest with the efforts of a same-sex couple to care for a foster child, there is no reason to fear that it would ever have that effect."[80]

Unlike prior cases vindicating the right to marry,[81] the opinion conspicuously omitted any discussion of the insult to the dignity and equality of same-sex couples who confront policies that deem them unworthy of becoming parents. Consider, for instance, the following hypothetical involving race. A company posts a sign saying "Blacks need not apply," and the Court holds that there was no discrimination because the applicant was hired at another company. This mode of analysis completely sidesteps the sting of discrimination, reducing the issue down to whether the person ultimately had access to a job, good or service.[82]

---

[76] *Id.* at 1882 (quoting Masterpiece Cakeshop, Ltd. v. Colo. C.R. Comm'n, 138 S. Ct. 1719, 1727 (2018)).

[77] *Id.*

[78] *Id.* (quoting Brief for Respondents at 1, *Fulton*, 141 S. Ct. 1868 (No. 19-123)).

[79] *Id.*

[80] *Id.* at 1886 (Alito, J., concurring in the judgment) ("As far as the record reflects, no same-sex couple has ever approached CSS. . . .").

[81] *See* Obergefell v. Hodges, 576 U.S. 644 (2015); United States v. Windsor, 570 U.S. 744 (2013).

[82] *See* Heart of Atlanta Motel, Inc. v. United States, 379 U.S. 241, 250 (1964) (noting "the deprivation of personal dignity that surely accompanies denials of equal access to public establishments"); Kyle C. Velte, *Recovering the Race Analogy in LGBTQ Exemption Cases*, 42 Cardozo L. Rev. 67, 109–10, 131-32, 135-36 (2020).

Although the Court never considered the discriminatory social message sent by CSS's refusal to certify same-sex couples, it rests on the following reasoning: CSS requires all couples who apply to it to be legally married. It refuses to certify any unmarried couples. Because CSS understands same-sex marriage as contrary to its faith, "it considers all same-sex couples to be unmarried."[83] Moreover, Catholic church doctrine holds that "homosexual tendencies" are "objectively disordered."[84] In short, Catholics who adhere to this teaching believe same-sex relationships can never be healthy. CSS's rationale inflicts several harms. First, it denies the commitment of married same-sex couples. Couples who have pledged to love and support each other for life and have done so in the eyes of the law are treated as if they were an unmarried couple. This reconfiguration seeks to negate the strength of the couple's bond, as they understand it. Second, Catholic doctrine regards same-sex relationships as inherently disordered or pathological, a central stereotype of homophobia, and extols male-female marriage as a healthy ideal.[85] Third, because many LGBTQ Americans were raised in non-affirming Catholic, Protestant, or Jewish families, adoption-related rejections may magnify psychological and emotional injuries inflicted by other religious figures. Fourth, some LGBTQ people rejected by agencies like CSS might be reminded of the long history of judges denying LGBTQ parents' custody of their biological children because of the parent's sexual orientation and/or gender identity. Such denials often rested on the stereotype that sexual and gender minorities are pedophiles who recruit children into homosexuality.[86] A brief filed by the Williams Institute of UCLA School of Law eloquently articulated various harms inflicted by discrimination against same-sex parents who wish to adopt, as well as children in foster care, who are disproportionately LGBTQ-identified and may benefit from having LGBTQ parents.[87]

---

[83] *Fulton v. City of Phila.*, 922 F.3d 140, 148 (3d Cir. 2019), *rev'd*, 141 S. Ct. 1868 (2021).

[84] *Stances of Faiths on LGBTQ Issues: Roman Catholic Church*, Hum. Rts. Campaign, https://www.hrc.org/resources/stances-of-faiths-on-lgbt-issues-roman-catholic-church [https://perma.cc/5HU8-KRDE].

[85] *See* Russell K. Robinson & David M. Frost, *The Afterlife of Homophobia*, 60 Ariz. L. Rev. 213, 217-18 (2018).

[86] Clifford Rosky, *Like Father, Like Son: Homosexuality, Parenthood, and the Gender of Homophobia*, 20 Yale J. Law & Feminism 257 (2009).

[87] Brief of Scholars Who Study the LGB Population as Amici Curiae in Support of Respondents at 10, *Fulton*, 141 S. Ct. 1868 (No. 19-123), 2020 WL 5020359 [hereinafter Brief of Scholars].

Although the Court's decision in *Obergefell* cited a brief by the Williams Institute and showed special concern for children raised by same-sex parents,[88] the *Fulton* Court's opinion failed even to acknowledge the existence of these harms.

Justice Alito, concurring in the judgment, wrote a lengthy opinion calling for the Court to overrule *Smith* and expand religious liberty.[89] Justice Alito wrote extensively of the vital and historic role of Catholic charities in facilitating adoptions.[90] Justice Alito and Chief Justice Roberts both argued that any same-sex couple deemed ineligible by CSS would simply turn to one of the more than 20 other agencies that accepted same-sex couples. In short, no harm, no foul.[91] By contrast, Justice Alito argued that "[b]y ousting CSS, the City eliminated one of its major sources of foster homes."[92] Justice Alito assumed that same-sex couples who are turned away by CSS because of their sexual orientation will find their way to another agency. But he claimed that couples who would have preferred to apply to CSS will fail to apply through the various other agencies that serve people of the Catholic faith. Justice Alito never explains this discrepancy. His differential assumptions as to whether the market can correct for the removal of one agency suggest an inconsistency, as well as Justice Alito's tendency to regard people of faith as uniquely disadvantaged.

Justice Alito went on to argue that the Court's expanded willingness to identify laws that "target" religious people and organizations is not subject to a uniform legal test or standard. He delineated the various layers of doctrinal uncertainty as follows:

> A threshold question is whether "targeting" calls for an objective or subjective inquiry. Must "targeting" be assessed based solely on the terms of the relevant rule or rules? Or can evidence of the rulemakers' motivation be taken into account? If subjective motivations may be considered, does it matter whether the challenged state action is an adjudication, the promulgation of a rule, or the enactment of legislation? Should courts consider the

[88] 576 U.S. 644, 668 (2015); *see also* Pavan v. Smith, 137 S. Ct. 2075, 2078–79 (2017) (invalidating Arkansas law that harmed same-sex couples who parent and their children).

[89] *Fulton*, 141 S. Ct. at 1883 (Alito, J., concurring in the judgment).

[90] *See id.* at 1884–85.

[91] Justice Alito did not reference the Williams Institute brief contesting this claim and exploring social science on how LGBTQ people respond to discrimination. Brief of Scholars, *supra* note 87.

[92] *Fulton*, 141 S. Ct. at 1886 (Alito, J., concurring in the judgment).

> motivations of only the officials who took the challenged action, or may they also take into account comments by superiors and others in a position of influence? And what degree of hostility to religion or a religious group is required to prove "targeting"?[93]

The Court's methodology for identifying anti-religious bias has vacillated considerably. The *Masterpiece* majority opinion relied heavily on what one might call "stray remarks"[94] made by executive officials enforcing the antidiscrimination law.[95] The Court latched onto ambiguous remarks made by one commissioner, but the Court did not explain the evidentiary relationship between those remarks and the decision-making of the six other commissioners who made the decision.[96] By contrast, in *Trump v. Hawaii*, the Court cited the plenary power doctrine as justification for its decision to ignore a heap of anti-Muslim remarks made by Trump before and after he was elected president.[97] The Court also seemed to think that the participation of several officials subordinate to the President cleansed the ultimate decision from discriminatory taint.[98] In *Fulton*, the opinions addressed allegations of biased remarks only in passing[99] and focused primarily on the terms of the contract and the state antidiscrimination law. The Court has made little effort to synthesize these decisions and the diverse evidentiary approaches to the question of anti-religious bias. I

---

[93] *Id.* at 1919; *see also id.* (describing disagreements among the Justices in the *Smith* majority as to evidentiary standards).

[94] *See, e.g.*, Russell K. Robinson, *Perceptual Segregation*, 108 Colum. L. Rev. 1093, 1165–66 (2008) (noting how courts tend to dismiss such racist remarks in employment discrimination cases as disconnected from the ultimate adverse employment decision).

[95] *See* Masterpiece Cakeshop, Ltd. v. Colo. C.R. Comm'n, 138 S. Ct. 1719, 1729, 1730 (2018).

[96] *See id.* at 1729.

[97] Trump v. Hawaii, 138 S. Ct. 2392, 2417, 2418–19 (2018); *see* Nelson Tebbe, *The Principle and Politics of Equal Value*, 121 Colum. L. Rev. 2397, 2465 (2021) (arguing that there was "overwhelming evidence of discriminatory intent").

[98] *See Hawaii*, 138 S. Ct. at 2421 ("The Proclamation, moreover, reflects the results of a worldwide review process undertaken by multiple Cabinet officials and their agencies.").

[99] Justice Alito cited three questionable remarks, although he did not rely on them to find a free exercise violation: (1) Philadelphia Mayor Jim Kenney said that CSS's actions were "not Christian"; (2) Commissioner Figueroa stated that CSS's policy was "out of date and out of touch with Pope Francis's teachings," which Justice Alito characterized as "disparagement"; (3) Mayor Kenney "once called on the Pope 'to kick some ass here.'" *Fulton*, 141 S. Ct. at 1919–20 (Alito, J., concurring in the judgment). The Third Circuit was not persuaded. It found: "There is nothing in the record before us suggesting that [Mayor Kenney] played a direct role, or even a significant role, in the process." Fulton v. City of Phila., 922 F.3d 140, 157 (3d Cir. 2019), *rev'd*, 141 S. Ct. 1868 (2021).

agree with Justice Alito's disappointment with "the extremely impressionistic inquiry" in recent cases.[100]

Moreover, this targeting inquiry means that the Court assumes the sincerity and good faith of religious people who seek to discriminate, at times even going so far as to rebuke government officials who question their motives.[101] By contrast, in cases like *Fulton* and *Masterpiece Cakeshop*, the Court skeptically examines the actions of government defendants (even though it declined to question the "sincerity" of President Trump in *Trump v. Hawaii*).[102] State and local government defendants are not assumed sincerely to enforce the law to protect the equality interests of LGBTQ people.[103] Rather, in this new constitutional landscape, such governments are presumed to harbor animus against Christianity, and minor details such as a flippant remark or a contractual exception that has never been used may suffice to establish a free exercise violation.[104]

The Third Circuit recognized the logical extension of the Court's heightened receptivity to free exercise claims:

> That CSS's conduct springs from sincerely held and strongly felt religious beliefs does not imply that the City's desire to regulate that conduct springs from antipathy to those beliefs. If all comment on religiously motivated conduct by those enforcing neutral, generally applicable laws against discrimination is construed as ill will against the religious belief itself, then *Smith* is a dead letter, and the nation's civil rights laws might be as well. As the Intervenors rightly state, the "fact that CSS's non-compliance with the City's non-discrimination requirements is based on its religious beliefs does

[100] *Fulton*, 141 S. Ct. at 1920. For scholarly critiques of the doctrinal landscape, see Oleske, *supra* note 72, and Lupu & Tuttle, *supra* note 72. One may agree with Justice Alito's finding of doctrinal disarray in recent free exercise cases without following his decision to overrule *Smith*. From my perspective, the Court's recent analysis of "targeting" lacks analytical form and rigor. But no Justice has proposed a replacement for *Smith* that would avoid the ad hoc decision-making typical under *Sherbert v. Verner*, 374 U.S. 398 (1963). The ambivalence expressed by Justice Barrett's concurring opinion thus is well founded. *Fulton*, 141 S. Ct. at 1882–83 (Barrett, J., concurring).

[101] *See Masterpiece Cakeshop*, 138 S. Ct. at 1723, 1729.

[102] *Hawaii*, 138 S. Ct. at 2418.

[103] This is evident from comparing the analysis of Chief Justice Roberts and Justice Alito with that of the Third Circuit. The latter court found that CSS "has failed to make a persuasive showing that the City targeted it for its religious beliefs, or is motivated by ill will against its religion, rather than sincere opposition to discrimination on the basis of sexual orientation." *Fulton*, 922 F.3d at 147.

[104] *See id.* at 158 ("[T]here is no instance in the record of Human Services knowingly permitting any other foster agency to discriminate against members of a protected class.").

> not mean that the City's enforcement of its requirements constitutes anti-religious hostility."[105]

This statement and Justice Alito's analysis reveal the tattered nature of recent free exercise jurisprudence.[106] Ultimately, however, Justice Alito evaded the big question at the heart of the case: If the Court overrules *Smith*, what standard should govern? Justice Alito stated that he leans toward the old *Sherbert* standard but admitted that it may need to be "rephrased or supplemented with specific rules."[107] These renovations, he declared, could be devised later because CSS wins under any legal test: "Philadelphia's ouster of CSS from foster care work simply does not further any interest that can properly be protected in this case. As noted, CSS's policy has not hindered any same-sex couples from becoming foster parents, and there is no threat that it will do so in the future."[108] Once again, a Justice returned to the assertion that no same-sex couple had been harmed. In this version of the claim, Justice Alito extended it to declare no possible future threat. The parties and the amici in fact vigorously disputed the harms of policies such as CSS's,[109] but Justice Alito summarily announced that any threat claimed by LGBTQ people and their allies was insignificant. He acknowledged that CSS's policy "expresses the idea that same-sex couples should not be foster parents because only a man and a woman should marry" and that "[m]any people today find this idea not only objectionable but hurtful."[110] He continued: "Nevertheless, protecting

---

[105] *Id.* at 159 (quoting Brief of Intervenors-Appellees Support Ctr. for Child Advocs. & Phila. Fam. Pride at 22, *Fulton*, 922 F.3d 140 (No. 18-2574), *rev'd*, 141 S. Ct. 1868 (2021)).

[106] *See, e.g.*, Oleske, *supra* note 72, at 744 (referring to the doctrine as a "confusing morass of irreconcilable decisions").

[107] *Fulton*, 141 S. Ct. at 1924. Justice Alito's equivocation suggests that he might continue the practice of inconsistent outcomes that prevailed before *Smith*. *See* Lupu & Tuttle, *supra* note 72, at 245 n.107 ("This is a neat invitation to weasel out of the test when it produces results with which a Justice is unhappy, as so often happened under the *Sherbert-Yoder* regime.").

[108] *Fulton*, 141 S. Ct. at 1924.

[109] *See, e.g.*, Brief for Petitioners at 7, *Fulton*, 141 S. Ct. 1868 (No. 19-123), 2020 WL 2836494 (claiming that having an "array of agencies" that specialize in serving different diverse groups "helps better serve Philadelphia's diverse population"). CSS explained that Philadelphia's foster parent recruitment website lists available agencies and encourages families to "research different agencies to 'find the best fit for [them]' so families can 'feel confident and comfortable with the agency.'" *Id.* Other parties argued that the practical effect of giving CSS a right to discriminate would be a limitation on the ability of same-sex couples to adopt, especially in rural areas dominated by religious providers. *See, e.g.*, Brief of Scholars, *supra* note 87, at 18–19.

[110] *Fulton*, 141 S. Ct. at 1924 (Alito, J., concurring in the judgment).

against this form of harm is not an interest that can justify the abridgment of First Amendment rights."[111] In short, religious groups are vindicating constitutional rights, while same-sex couples are merely complaining about hurt feelings. Justice Alito thus downgraded LGBTQ people's constitutional interest in equal treatment (as evidenced by precedent including *Romer v. Evans*,[112] *Lawrence v. Texas*,[113] and *Obergefell*[114]) to a "wisp"[115] that faded in the face of his sweeping interpretation of free exercise rights. Moreover, this diminution of state and local antidiscrimination laws could have a substantial effect on social equality because such laws typically apply not only to sexual orientation, but also to race, gender, disability, and religion.[116]

If the opinions in *Fulton* were somewhat muted in depicting traditional religious groups as under siege because of a newly "woke" consensus, Justice Alito's 2020 speech before the Federalist Society made his factual assumptions plain. He depicted a world in which obscene words have become mainstream, while traditional morality has been stigmatized as discrimination:

> In 1972, the comedian George Carlin began to perform a routine called, "The Seven Words You Can't Say on TV." Today, you can see shows on your TV screen in which the dialogue appears at time[s] to consist almost entirely of those words. Carlin's list seems like a quaint relic. But it would be easy to put together a new list called, "Things You Can't Say If You're a Student or Professor at a College or University or an Employee of Many Big Corporations." And there wouldn't be just seven items on that list. 70 times seven would be closer to the mark. I won't go down the list, but I'll mention one that I've discussed in a published opinion. You can't say that marriage is a union between one man and one woman. Until very recently, that's what the vast majority of Americans thought. Now it's considered bigotry. That this would happen after our decision in *Obergefell* should not have come as a surprise. Yes, the opinion of the court included words

[111] *Id.*

[112] 517 U.S. 620 (1996).

[113] 539 U.S. 558 (2003).

[114] 576 U.S. 644 (2015).

[115] *Fulton*, 141 S. Ct. at 1926 (Alito, J., concurring in the judgment). Justice Alito called the *Fulton* majority opinion "a wisp of a decision that leaves religious liberty in a confused and vulnerable state." *Id.* One could say the same of LGBTQ rights after *Fulton* and *Masterpiece Cakeshop*.

[116] *See* Velte, *supra* note 82, at 132. *But cf. Fulton*, 141 S. Ct. at 1925 (Alito, J., concurring in the judgment) (arguing that racial discrimination and sexual orientation discrimination are fundamentally different, and one can invoke religion to refuse serving gays and lesbians without being a "bigot").

> meant to calm the fears of those who cling to traditional views on marriage, but I could see, and so did the other justices in dissent, where the decision would lead. I wrote the following: I assume that those who cling to old beliefs will be able to whisper their thoughts in the recesses of their homes, but if they repeat those views in public, they will risk being labeled as bigots and treated as such by governments, employers, and schools.[117]

Justice Alito's speech helps to explain the lopsidedness of the *Fulton* opinions. If LGBTQ people have been embraced by the mainstream and are wielding this new clout to turn Christians into cultural minorities, the Justices' lengthy passages singing the praises of a Catholic ministry are intended to correct a social consensus that treats religious people as bigots.[118] The absence of any sustained attention to injuries experienced by same-sex couples also follows because in these Justices' minds, LGBTQ people are not "discrete and insular minorities."[119] Quite the contrary, LGBTQ people are avatars of the new progressivism.

One of the most striking aspects of *Fulton* is the silence of the liberals.[120] There are no dissents or concurrences by liberal Justices disputing or complicating Roberts's and Alito's claims and assumptions and articulating the interests of the LGBTQ community. Instead the liberal Justices joined the majority opinion and failed to supplement it by underscoring what is at stake for same-sex couples who wish to parent. *Fulton* and *Masterpiece Cakeshop* combine to establish a shift to the right in which the centrist position is to provide a narrow victory for Judeo-Christian claimants. The liberal Justices seem satisfied merely with staving off the overturning of *Smith*. None has written an opinion to underscore how ever-expanding religious exemptions could broadly undermine LGBTQ people's pursuit of

[117] *Supreme Court Justice Samuel Alito Speech Transcript to Federalist Society*, Rev (Nov. 12, 2020), https://www.rev.com/blog/transcripts/supreme-court-justice-samuel-alito-speech-transcript-to-federalist-society [https://perma.cc/3AEC-WG7G]. Justice Alito's use of "seven times seventy" is a reference to *Matthew* 18:21–22. This speech extended points that Justice Alito made in his *Obergefell* dissent. *See* 576 U.S. 644, 741 (2015) (Alito, J., dissenting).

[118] *See* Tebbe, *supra* note 97, at 2464 (arguing that the Court is "seeking to protect mainstream denominations against perceived status degradation"). Justice Alito also proclaimed: "[F]or many today, religious liberty is not a cherished freedom. It's often just an excuse for bigotry, and it can't be tolerated, even when there is no evidence that anybody has been harmed." *Supreme Court Justice Samuel Alito Speech Transcript to Federalist Society*, *supra* note 117.

[119] United States v. Carolene Prods. Co., 304 U.S. 144, 152 n.4 (1938).

[120] For an exploration of liberal "appeasement" in Establishment Clause cases, see Micah Schwartzman & Nelson Tebbe, *Establishment Clause Appeasement*, 2019 Sup. Ct. Rev. 271.

equality and belonging in society (and have ripple effects on people of color and women). This shift, in which Justice Kennedy (however inconsistent and problematic) has retired, and the most vocal Justices treat members of a majority religion as the most vulnerable, belies Alito's belief that LGBTQ rights are ascendant and secure.[121]

III. The Pandemic Worship Cases and Bias

The pandemic worship cases, although they did not involve a competing equality interest, further demonstrate the Court's shift toward perceiving religious people as presumptive losers in the political process. The pivotal decision in this line of cases, *Roman Catholic Diocese of Brooklyn New York v. Cuomo*,[122] shares *Fulton*'s dubious methodology. The Court appears to detect a "whiff" of bias against Judeo-Christianity, rushes through the strict scrutiny framework, cites little actual evidence of bias, and fails to consider counterarguments.

On November 25, 2020, the Court, in a *per curiam* opinion, enjoined the governor of New York from enforcing capacity limits on places of worship.[123] The opinion arose from two cases, one brought by the Roman Catholic Diocese of Brooklyn and the other by Agudath Israel of America, a Jewish organization.[124] The applicants argued that "the regulations treat houses of worship much more harshly than comparable secular facilities."[125] In addition, Agudath Israel argued that remarks

[121] Further complicating our understanding of the status of LGBTQ rights at the Court is a post-Kennedy majority opinion that announced that gay and transgender employees are protected by Title VII's ban on sex discrimination. Bostock v. Clayton Cnty., 140 S. Ct. 1737, 1753–54 (2020). Justice Alito might regard *Bostock* as further evidence of LGBTQ people's cultural and legal prowess. On its face, Justice Gorsuch's majority opinion relies on straightforward canons of statutory interpretation to reach its result. *See id.* at 1737. However, Cary Franklin has powerfully exposed several "shadow decision points" in the majority and dissenting opinions that tilt their analysis toward one party or another. *See* Cary Franklin, *Living Textualism*, 2020 Sup. Ct. Rev. 119, 126–27 (2021). Although Justice Gorsuch's implicit empathy for gay and transgender people may give some such people hope, he cloaked it in allegiance to textualism. *See id.* at 130–31. Moreover, he declined to opine on possible religious exemptions to the ban on sex discrimination. *See Bostock*, 140 S. Ct. at 1753–54. In *Fulton*—where the question of religious exemptions was squarely before the Court—Justice Gorsuch sided with the Catholic charity and did not write separately to express concern for the interests of same-sex couples. *See Fulton*, 141 S. Ct. at 1926 (Gorsuch, J., concurring in the judgment).

[122] 141 S. Ct. 63 (2021).

[123] *Id.* at 65.

[124] *Id.* at 66.

[125] *Id.*

made by Governor Cuomo suggested that he gerrymandered the construction of COVID-related risk zones to target the Orthodox Jewish community.[126] The Court's opinion provided "only a brief summary of the reasons why immediate relief is essential."[127] The Court suggested that "statements made in connection with the challenged rules can be viewed as targeting the 'ultra-Orthodox [Jewish] community.'"[128] But it said that even if it did not rest on such statements, the rules ran afoul of the Constitution because they "single out houses of worship for especially harsh treatment."[129] That is because a church or synagogue in a "red zone" could admit no more than ten persons, while "businesses categorized as 'essential' may admit as many people as they wish."[130] The list of "essential" businesses spanned acupuncture facilities, campgrounds, and garages.[131] In an "orange zone," "even non-essential businesses may decide for themselves how many persons to admit," while houses of worship were limited to twenty-five people. The Court cited testimony about "a large store in Brooklyn that could 'literally have hundreds of people shopping there on any given day.'"[132] A nearby church, however, would be allowed to admit no more than ten or twenty-five people.[133] This lack of facial neutrality, the Court concluded, triggered strict scrutiny.[134] "Stemming the spread of COVID-19 is unquestionably a compelling interest," but the lack of a record of an outbreak of infections at the applicants' houses of worship indicated a lack of narrow tailoring.[135] The restrictions were tighter than in prior cases and in other jurisdictions.[136] Thus, the Court concluded, New York's restrictions were "far more severe than has

---

[126] *Id.*

[127] *Id.*

[128] *Id.* (quoting Agudath Israel v. Cuomo, 980 F.3d 222, 229 (2d Cir. 2020) (Park, J., dissenting)).

[129] *Id.*

[130] *Id.*

[131] *Id.*

[132] *Id.*

[133] *Id.* at 67.

[134] *Id.* at 66 n.1, 67.

[135] *Id.* at 67.

[136] *Id.*

been shown to be required to prevent the spread of the virus at the applicants' services."[137]

The Court then considered whether virtual attendance at services sufficed to prevent "irreparable injury."[138] The Court quickly brushed aside this practice because "such remote viewing is not the same as personal attendance."[139] For Jews and Catholics, "there are important religious traditions," such as receiving communion for Catholics,[140] "that require personal attendance."[141] The Court acknowledged its lack of expertise in public health, but then pivoted to suggest that this was an especially momentous case: "by effectively barring many from attending religious services, [the restrictions] strike at the very heart of the First Amendment's guarantee of religious liberty."[142]

This opinion is notable in that it extends the practice of *Masterpiece Cakeshop* of seizing on offhand remarks by government officials as evidence of bias against Judeo-Christianity. Below is the district court's description of Governor Cuomo's contested remarks:

> At the press conference to announce the Initiative, Governor Cuomo said "the new rules are most impactful on houses of worship" and that the Initiative "is about mass gatherings" and "one of the prime places of mass gatherings are houses of worship." He also referenced his "love for the Orthodox [Jewish] community" and noted that the "Torah speaks about how certain religious obligations can be excused if you are going to save a life."[143]

The district court found that these comments indicated that "Governor Cuomo is clearly aware and concerned that EO 202.68 burdens religious practice, and particularly the religious practice of Orthodox Jews, but awareness that the burden of a law falls unequally does

[137] *Id.*

[138] *Id.* at 67–68.

[139] *Id.* at 68.

[140] Receiving communion typically involves eating and drinking in close proximity of other people, and sometimes even drinking from the same cup as other attendees. These rituals create a distinct risk of COVID-19 transmission, yet the Court did not address it.

[141] *Id.*

[142] *Id.*

[143] Roman Catholic Diocese v. Cuomo, 495 F. Supp. 3d 118, 122 (E.D.N.Y. 2020) (citations omitted) (quoting Memorandum of Law in Support of Plaintiff's Application for a Temp. Restraining Order & Preliminary Injunction at 14, *Roman Catholic Diocese*, 495 F. Supp. 3d 118 (No. 20-cv-48-44), 2020 WL 7586256), *rev'd and remanded sub nom.* Agudath Israel v. Cuomo, 980 F.3d 222 (2d Cir. 2020)).

not establish that the law was designed to target religious groups."[144] This is consistent with the legal standard in race and gender equal protection cases. Mere knowledge that a law will disproportionately harm a particular group does not suffice to show discriminatory purpose; rather, the Court has required malice, which is a desire to harm that group.[145] The Second Circuit thus treated religion as Supreme Court precedent requires it to treat race and gender-based equality claims. The Supreme Court, however, rejected the Second Circuit's interpretation without explanation. It curtly and opaquely noted that "statements made in connection with the challenged rules can be viewed as targeting the 'ultra-Orthodox [Jewish] community.'"[146] But Governor Cuomo clearly expressed "love for the Orthodox community" and said that he was adopting the restrictions because it was necessary to protect that community and those nearby from an outbreak of infections.[147] The Court never explained its decision to discredit Governor Cuomo's professed affection for the Orthodox community and desire to protect it from danger.

Whether it applied the malice standard of *McCleskey v. Kemp*[148] or the animus standard of *Romer v. Evans*[149] or some new standard (the Court did not bother to specify), the Court's conclusion implies that it found that Cuomo harbored hostility toward the Jewish community. This thinly-veiled accusation of anti-Semitism warranted a more complete and transparent explanation by the Court.[150] Moreover, because the state's restrictions similarly burdened Catholics in red and orange zones, the Court needed some theory to explain why Cuomo—a

[144] *Id.* at 129.

[145] Pers. Adm'r of Mass. v. Feeney, 442 U.S. 256, 276 (1979); McCleskey v. Kemp, 481 U.S. 279, 292 (1987); Ian Haney-López, *Intentional Blindness*, 87 N.Y.U. L. Rev. 1779, 1833–37 (2012); Russell K. Robinson, *Unequal Protection*, 68 Stan. L. Rev. 151, 175 (2016); *see also* Tebbe, *supra* note 97, at 2458–60, 2463 (arguing that the emerging "equal value" principle in free exercise cases has logical extensions to racial equality, but the Court is unlikely to apply the rule to race).

[146] *Roman Catholic Diocese*, 141 S. Ct. at 66.

[147] *Roman Catholic Diocese*, 495 F. Supp. 3d at 122.

[148] 481 U.S. at 298.

[149] 517 U.S. 620, 632 (1996).

[150] One could read the Court's statement that it was providing "only a brief summary of the reasons why immediate relief is essential" as an admission that it was releasing an incomplete opinion. *Roman Catholic Diocese*, 141 S. Ct. at 66.

Catholic—harbored animus against Catholicism.[151] Again, the Court was silent on this point.[152] Cuomo's remarks clearly fall short of the sort of "smoking gun" evidence that the Court requires in race and sex cases, which provides further support for the emergence of Judeo-Christianity as a class that enjoys heightened protections, as compared to race and sex claims.

All the Justices in *Roman Catholic Diocese* appeared to agree that treating houses of worship worse than secular businesses was presumptively unconstitutional.[153] They divided over the proper comparator for a secular business. And this is where one can see a bias in favor of Judeo-Christian religions (or—from the Court majority's perspective—the desire to protect Judeo-Christian religions) as doing substantial analytical work. To the Court and Justice Gorsuch, the proper comparators included big-box stores, bike shops, liquor stores, and cannabis dispensaries.[154] To Justice Sotomayor, in dissent, "comparable secular gatherings, includ[ed] lectures, concerts, movie showings, spectator sports, and theatrical performances."[155] An earlier influential concurring opinion by Chief Justice Roberts treated movie theaters and lectures as apt comparators and dismissed the relevance of "dissimilar activities, such as operating grocery stores, banks, and laundromats, in which people neither congregate in large groups nor remain in close proximity for extended periods."[156] The *Roman Diocese*

---

[151] *See* Jesse McKinley, *Cuomo's Virus Crackdown Angers Catholics, Who Say They're Singled Out*, N.Y. Times (Oct. 19, 2020), https://www.nytimes.com/2020/10/19/nyregion/covid-catholic-church-cuomo.html [https://perma.cc/CP5J-YKUN] (referring to Cuomo as a "conflicted Catholic" who disagrees with the church on same-sex marriage and abortion and who has cited his faith and Scripture in managing the pandemic). To be sure, one could speculate that there was a connection between the restrictions and Cuomo's testy relationship with the Catholic Church. But the Court has generally avoided wading into such matters of personal faith, and for good reason.

[152] The Court's language appears to hedge on whether it ultimately relied on Cuomo's remarks for its finding of a free exercise violation.

[153] *See, e.g.*, *Roman Catholic Diocese*, 141 S. Ct. at 79 (Sotomayor, J., dissenting).

[154] *See, e.g.*, *Roman Catholic Diocese*, 141 S. Ct. at 66 (majority opinion) (referring to acupuncture facilities, camp grounds, manufacturing plants, garages, and transportation facilities); *id.* at 69 (Gorsuch, J., concurring) (referring to restaurants, hardware stores, bike shops, acupuncturists, airports, bus stations, laundromats, banks, casinos, marijuana dispensaries, and liquor stores); *id.* at 73 (Kavanaugh, J., concurring) (referring to pet stores, grocery stores, and big-box stores).

[155] *Id.* at 79 (Sotomayor, J., dissenting); *see also* Tandon v. Newsom, 141 S. Ct. 1294, 1298 (2021) (Kagan, J., dissenting) ("[T]he law does not require that the State equally treat apples and watermelons.").

[156] South Bay United Pentecostal Church v. Newsom, 140 S. Ct. 1613, 1613 (2020) (Roberts, C.J., concurring in denial of application for injunctive relief) (mem.). Justice Gorsuch wrote a

Court threw out many potential comparators, but failed to justify its focus on big-box stores and liquor stores instead of movie theaters and lectures. The district court found that "although the [Executive Order] establishes rules specific to religious gatherings, it does so because they are gatherings, not because they are religious."[157] Citing CDC guidelines, the district court underscored other distinguishing features of religious gatherings: "congregants arrive and leave at the same time, physically greet one another, sit or stand close together, share or pass objects, and sing or chant in a way that allows for airborne transmission of the virus."[158]

None of the Supreme Court opinions sufficiently attended to the question of the relationships among people in a particular regulated space.[159] When a customer goes to a liquor store, bike shop, or laundromat, they are not going there to gather with other people. Of course, they would assume that at least one person will be present to help them complete a commercial transaction (unless an automated transaction is available, such as at most laundromats), but they are not going to that public place because they desire to be in the presence of other humans. During the pandemic, many people intentionally shopped at times when they expected few people to be present and used other strategies to minimize human interaction and the risk of virus transmission.[160] Churches and other places are different in that

---

caustic concurring opinion in *Roman Catholic Diocese*, which treated Chief Justice Roberts's concurring opinion in *South Bay United Pentecostal Church* as "expired." *Roman Catholic Diocese*, 141 S. Ct. at 70 (Gorsuch, J., concurring). The media depicted Justice Barrett's replacement of Justice Ginsburg as flipping the closely divided Court and changing the shape of the law. *See, e.g.*, Adam Liptak, *Splitting Five to Four, Supreme Court Backs Religious Challenge to Cuomo's Virus Shutdown Order*, N.Y. Times (Apr. 5, 2021), https://www.nytimes.com/2020/11/26/us/supreme-court-coronavirus-religion-new-york.html [https://perma.cc/T9BC-3UAT].

[157] Roman Catholic Diocese v. Cuomo, 495 F. Supp. 3d 118, 130 (E.D.N.Y. 2020), *rev'd and remanded sub nom.* Agudath Israel v. Cuomo, 980 F.3d 222 (2d Cir. 2020).

[158] *Id.* at 126 (citing CDC, Considerations for Communities of Faith (2020)). The Second Circuit similarly concluded: "Unlike shopping at large stores, an in-person religious service or ceremony necessarily involves a community of adherents arriving and leaving at the same time and interacting and praying together over an extended period of time." Agudath Israel v. Cuomo, 980 F.3d 222, 227 (2d Cir. 2020).

[159] Justice Sotomayor deftly demonstrated that the examples used by the majority and Justice Gorsuch did not involve "large groups of people gathering, speaking, and singing in close proximity indoors for extended periods of time." *Roman Catholic Diocese*, 141 S. Ct. at 79 (Sotomayor, J., dissenting). But she did not comment on the differences in the relationships among the people interfacing in houses of worship as compared to commercial establishments.

[160] *See, e.g.*, Lisa Bonos, *It's Not Just You. We're All Socially Awkward Now.*, Wash. Post (Aug. 16, 2021), https://www.washingtonpost.com/lifestyle/2021/04/24/awkward-social-pandemic-return/ [https://perma.cc/2ZW7-B9SU]; Maura Judkis, *Going Outside Is Our Only Escape. But Now That's*

people come together because they comprise a community of faith.[161] In the words of some Christians, they are a "church family." Furthermore, being in the physical presence of other believers is often experienced as distinct from watching a service on a screen. These bonds among people of a particular faith community also make it more likely that they will linger in close contact, hug, talk, sing, and catch up after months of isolation at home.

By contrast, to the extent that strangers in a bike shop or liquor store would strike up a conversation pre-pandemic, the life-altering stakes (especially before vaccines were widely available) meant that many strictly adhered to social distancing, minimized conversation, and shopped at "off" hours. One can recognize this difference without impugning the intentions of religious people to follow COVID restrictions.[162] The Court thought it important that a big-box store might have "hundreds of people shopping there on any given day,"[163] but it failed to ask whether such shoppers would interact like members of a church. Ultimately, a proper resolution of the pandemic worship cases should have considered the sociological question of how religious people interact in houses of worship and whether such interactions are comparable to those of strangers who happen to overlap in commercial establishments. The majority opinion is conspicuously bereft of analysis on this central question. Justice Gorsuch provided the most acerbic condemnation of New York's motive: "The only explanation for treating religious places differently seems to be a judgment that what happens there just isn't as 'essential' as what happens in secular spaces."[164] It would have been more difficult for Justice Gorsuch to

Scary, Too., WASH. POST (Apr. 7, 2020), https://www.washingtonpost.com/lifestyle/style/going-outside-is-our-only-escape-but-now-thats-scary-too/2020/04/07/c3ab9be0-7431-11ea-87da-77a8136c1a6d_story.html [https://perma.cc/AS25-VPNQ]; Marisa Dellato, *Coronavirus Etiquette: Your Guide to Work, Friends, Food Shopping and More*, N.Y. POST (Apr. 15, 2020), https://nypost.com/2020/04/15/coronavirus-etiquette-your-guide-to-work-friends-food-shopping-and-more/ [https://perma.cc/M236-XDF2].

[161] The Second Circuit referred to this as a "community of adherents." *Agudath Israel*, 980 F.3d at 227.

[162] *See, e.g.*, Does 1–3 v. Mills, 142 S. Ct. 17, 20 (2021) (Gorsuch, J., concurring) (mem.) ("A State may not assume 'the best' of individuals engaged in their secular lives while assuming 'the worst' about the habits of religious persons."); Tandon v. Newsom, 141 S. Ct. 1294, 1297 (2021) (per curiam).

[163] *Roman Catholic Diocese*, 141 S. Ct. at 67.

[164] *Id.* at 69 (Gorsuch, J., concurring). Justice Gorsuch's opinion alights on liquor, cannabis, and gambling as secular activities that were ostensibly "favored" over worship. *See id.* (referring to "marijuana dispensaries" and "liquor stores"). What kind of topsy turvy world are we in, he suggests, where "sinful" activity is deemed "essential" while worship is effectively

reach that conclusion if he had paid closer attention to "what happens in secular spaces."[165] Ultimately, the *Roman Catholic Diocese* decision provides further evidence that the current Court is inclined to rush to the conclusion that the state has violated the rights of Christians.

A leading constitutional law scholar, Cass Sunstein, has offered a more expansive, hopeful interpretation of the current state of the law. Sunstein has argued that *Roman Catholic Diocese* "can reasonably be seen as a kind of anti-*Korematsu*—as a strong signal of judicial solicitude for constitutional rights and of judicial willingness to protect against discrimination, even under emergency circumstances in which life is on the line."[166] Sunstein's interpretation is consistent with language in Justice Kavanaugh's concurrence.[167] Sunstein's interpretation, however, is in serious tension with the Court's validation of Islamophobia in *Trump v. Hawaii*, which Sunstein cites only in passing.[168] The Court's willingness to defer during wartime-like conditions seems to turn on which particular religion is seeking its protection. Although the Court tends to describe "free exercise" as if all religious people share the same rights under the Constitution, the truth is far more complex. One can synthesize the Court's recent cases to suggest a hierarchy of faiths, with conservative Christians seeking and receiving the most sustained protection from the Court.[169] As suggested by *Roman Catholic Diocese* (which involved Catholic and Jewish parties), the Court also is receptive to claims brought by Jewish litigants.[170] At the bottom of the hierarchy of faiths are Muslims, who are subject to pervasive stereotypes associating Islam with terrorism and who, even when "formally White," may be stigmatized as people of color because of their faith.[171] The

---

banned? Yet these commercial establishments generally attract strangers seeking a particular product with little incentive to associate with each other for extended periods of time.

[165] *Id.*

[166] Cass Sunstein, *Our Anti*-Korematsu, 1 Am. J.L. & Equal. 221, 222, 231 (2021).

[167] *See Roman Catholic Diocese*, 141 S. Ct. at 73–74 (Kavanaugh, J., concurring).

[168] *See* Sunstein, *supra* note 166, at 229 n.57.

[169] *See, e.g.*, Tebbe, *supra* note 97, at 2463 (arguing that the Roberts Court is "revolutionizing constitutional law in the service of a particularized blend of religiosity and libertarianism"); Robinson, *supra* note 2, at 143 (arguing that Justice Kennedy's jurisprudence "perpetuated a hierarchy in which people who identify with Christianity enjoy greater judicial protection than those who practice a minority religion").

[170] *Cf.* Caroline Mala Corbin, *Justice Scalia, The Establishment Clause, and Christian Privilege*, 15 First Amendment L. Rev. 185, 203, 206 (2016) (arguing that Jews do not receive the full protection extended to Christians).

[171] *See* Leti Volpp, *The Citizen and the Terrorist*, 49 UCLA L. Rev. 1575, 1576 (2002) (arguing that September 11, 2001 "facilitated the consolidation of a new identity category"); Khaled A.

Supreme Court's oral argument in *Trump v. Hawaii* supports this interpretation. The government downplayed the need for meaningful judicial review of its discretion to exclude foreign nationals.[172] However, when Justice Kagan, who is Jewish, posed a hypothetical in which an anti-Semitic president issued a proclamation that "no one shall enter from Israel," the government quickly pivoted and conceded that some form of judicial review was necessary.[173] When the case was perceived as only about Muslims, the government apparently saw no need for a judicial check on its discretion.[174]

The Court has also struggled with consistency in a line of cases involving death row inmates asserting access to a spiritual advisor during their execution. In a 2019 case involving a Muslim inmate seeking access to his imam, Justice Kagan's dissent called out the privileging of Christianity. "Under [the state's] policy, a Christian prisoner may have a minister of his own faith accompany him into the execution chamber to say his last rites. But if an inmate practices a different religion—whether Islam, Judaism, or any other—he may not die with a minister of his own faith by his side. That treatment goes against the Establishment Clause's core principle of denominational neutrality."[175] Moreover, Khaled Beydoun has argued that even when Muslims and Jews formally have the right of free exercise, the risk of stigma, including the threat of hate crimes, may pressure them to pass as Christian and preserve their perceived Whiteness.[176] The Court's grand declarations on free exercise tend to gloss these important legal and practical distinctions.

IV. What Christianity Loses When Conservative Christians Win at the Supreme Court

This Part argues that the recent line of free exercise cases not only poses a threat to the perception of the Court's legitimacy; it also

---

Beydoun, *Faith in Whiteness: Free Exercise of Religion as Racial Expression*, 105 Iowa L. Rev. 1475, 1520–21 (2020).

[172] Transcript of Oral Argument at 14, Trump v. Hawaii, 138 S. Ct. 2392 (2018) (No. 17-965); *Hawaii*, 138 S. Ct. at 2417, 2420 (describing the government's position).

[173] *See* Transcript of Oral Argument, *supra* note 172, at 14–18.

[174] I thank my colleague Leti Volpp for making this point.

[175] Dunn v. Ray, 139 S. Ct. 661, 662 (2019); *see also* Ian Milhiser, *The Supreme Court Finally Figures out That Religious Liberty Cases Are Hard*, Vox (Nov. 10, 2021), https://www.vox.com/22772213/supreme-court-religion-death-penalty-ramirez-collier-constitution-liberty [https://perma.cc/NGG9-QK6T].

[176] Beydoun, *supra* note 171, at 1520–21.

threatens to perpetuate the public perception that Christianity requires discrimination against LGBTQ people. Christianity is a complex, diverse, and evolving religion. Attempting to summarize different branches of the faith in a short piece is a daunting task. Although I will generally describe "right" and "left" wings, in truth there is a complex continuum, and some labels are subject to debate.[177] I fear that I will offend some readers, but that is not my intent.

The parties that seek government validation of a religiously conferred right to discriminate at the Court are typically affiliated with the right wing of the faith. This Part argues that the symbiotic relationship between conservative Christians (including some Protestants and Catholics) and the current conservative Supreme Court majority distorts the public understanding of Christianity. Moderate and liberal Christians are less likely to bring claims before the Court because they believe in inclusion of stigmatized groups. Such religious organizations have filed amicus briefs that provide a fuller understanding of how Christians of various stripes understand the relationship between discrimination and their faith. This Part highlights some examples from amicus briefs in *Fulton*.

There is much debate about what counts as "progressive Christianity." I will present my own understanding of this growing movement and contrast it with conservative Christianity. But first let me say that I do not claim to be neutral or objective. I was raised by devout Baptist parents in Dayton, Ohio. For most of my schooling, I attended Dayton Christian School, a fundamentalist, predominantly White school that has appeared before the Supreme Court to defend its understanding of religious liberty.[178] Not long after graduating from Harvard Law School, and while I was clerking for Justice Breyer, I began to come out as a gay man. During that period, I felt estranged from the church and assumed that I would have to choose between my

---

[177] *Cf.* Edles, *supra* note 8, at 5. This short piece does not allow me to engage complex questions such as the coalition between evangelicals and conservative Catholics, see Douglas NeJaime & Reva B. Siegel, *Conscience Wars: Complicity-Based Conscience Claims in Religion and Politics*, 124 Yale L.J. 2516, 2544–52 (2015), and progressives who seek to retain and remake the "evangelical" label.

[178] *See* Ohio C.R. Comm'n v. Dayton Christian Schs., Inc., 477 U.S. 619 (1986). I capitalize "White" (as well as "Black") to resist the idea that Whiteness is the absence of race and to signify the importance of reckoning with White privilege, as deftly explained by Eve Ewing. Eve L. Ewing, *I'm a Black Scholar Who Studies Race. Here's Why I Capitalize 'White,'* Medium (July 1, 2020), https://zora.medium.com/im-a-black-scholar-who-studies-race-here-s-why-i-capitalize-white-f94883aa2dd3 [https://perma.cc/35JV-VD3B].

sexuality and my faith. Over time, however, I gradually learned to embrace both and to see those dimensions of my being as beautifully knit together.[179] I attend progressive, LGBTQ-affirming churches in my hometown of Oakland, California and in cities such as New York and Chicago when I travel. These churches have helped me reimagine my faith and my understanding of God.

Christianity can be understood as divided into two major sects. While there are commonalities between the sects, including a belief in God's love and Jesus's willingness to die for humanity's sins, conservatives tend to emphasize a fear of damnation as a motivation for accepting Christ.[180] Conservatives often preach a strict code of behavior, frequently focusing on sexuality and separating from the "secular" world.[181] In my personal experience, evangelical messages about God's love were eclipsed by a tendency to carve human experience into black and white categories of forbidden or permissible activity and a refusal to admit the complexity of human experience.

Progressive Christianity understands God's love as the center of the faith.[182] Christ's sacrificial love—His willingness to suffer through crucifixion and death—embodies a perfect expression of love. Christians are called to emulate His love as much as possible. This means not just loving our neighbor but loving the "other." Jesus had a heart for those at the margins, seeking out a leper, a tax collector, and a woman who committed adultery, and offering them acceptance and

---

[179] *See generally* MATTHEW VINES, GOD AND THE GAY CHRISTIAN: THE BIBLICAL CASE IN SUPPORT OF SAME-SEX RELATIONSHIPS 162 (2015) (arguing that "the church is sinning against [gay Christians] by rejecting their intimate relationships").

[180] Some have sardonically referred to this motivation as "fire insurance."

[181] *See, e.g.*, RACHEL HELD EVANS, INSPIRED: SLAYING GIANTS, WALKING ON WATER, AND LOVING THE BIBLE AGAIN 99–101 (2018); Carey Nieuwhof, *5 Ways Judgmental Christians are Killing Your Church*, CAREY NIEUWHOF (Jan. 9, 2017), https://careynieuwhof.com/5-ways-judgmental-christians-are-killing-your-church/ [https://perma.cc/V3J9-8PQE].

[182] *John* 4:7–12 is a foundational verse in this regard:

> Beloved, let us love one another, for love is from God, and whoever loves has been born of God and knows God. Anyone who does not love does not know God, because God is love. In this the love of God was made manifest among us, that God sent his only Son into the world, so that we might live through him. In this is love, not that we have loved God but that he loved us and sent his Son to be the propitiation for our sins. Beloved, if God so loved us, we also ought to love one another. No one has ever seen God; if we love one another, God abides in us and his love is perfected in us.

redemption.[183] This love-centered faith also aspires to take seriously Christ's command "judge not, lest you be judged."[184] By some accounts, LGBTQ inclusion is the dividing line between the right and left wings of Christianity.[185] The wings also differ in their approach to race. African-Americans and other people of color are calling on progressive churches to become anti-racist,[186] and many White leaders know that they have to do better. Some progressive Christians have been influenced by the *misión integral* movement in Latin America, which seeks to integrate evangelicalism and "socio-political involvement on behalf of the poor and the oppressed."[187] Meanwhile, on the Christian right, evangelical leaders who have been linked with anti-racism or Critical Race Theory have been ousted from their positions, and prominent Black leaders have voluntarily left the fold.[188]

Another point of divergence arises from how Christians believe they are to interact with non-believers and people of other faiths. While some fundamentalists believe in a "tribal God" and urge believers to separate from the world, progressive Christians are generally more open to working with people of other faiths and even blurring the line between the church and the world.[189] Rather than extricate themselves from the world, progressive Christians work to effectuate social

---

[183] *Mark* 1:40–41; *Zacchaeus* 19:1–10 (concluding with "For the Son of Man came to seek and to save the lost"); *John* 8:2–11.

[184] *Matthew* 7:1; *see also John* 8:7 ("He that is without sin among you, let him first cast a stone at her.").

[185] *See, e.g.*, Edles, *supra* note 8, at 7-8.

[186] *See, e.g.*, Lenny Duncan, Dear Church: A Love Letter from a Black Preacher to the Whitest Denomination in the U.S. (2019). Progressive Christians are likely to draw inspiration from Dr. Martin Luther King, Jr. and the Black civil rights movement. *See* Edles, *supra* note 8, at 7.

[187] *See* Michael Clawson, *Misión Integral and Progressive Evangelicalism: The Latin American Influence on the North American Emerging Church*, 3 Religions 790, 791 (2012).

[188] *See, e.g.*, Peter Wehner, *The Evangelical Church Is Breaking Apart*, Atlantic (Oct. 24, 2021), https://www.theatlantic.com/ideas/archive/2021/10/evangelical-trump-christians-politics/620469/ [https://perma.cc/2YZB-8UHG]; Kate Shellnutt, *Two Prominent Pastors Break with SBC After Critical Race Theory Statement*, Christianity Today (Dec. 18, 2020), https://www.christianitytoday.com/news/2020/december/charlie-dates-ralph-west-southern-baptist-sbc-crt.html [https://perma.cc/5JFA-GP77].

[189] Singer-songwriter Pat Barrett's "Everything is Sacred" includes the lyric: "The ordinary shines and glows/Filled with Your intentions/You don't see the lines we draw/Between secular and sacred." *Lyrics: Everything Is Sacred*, Musix Match (Nov. 4, 2021), https://www.musixmatch.com/lyrics/Pat-Barrett/Everything-Is-Sacred [https://perma.cc/RW3S-6XE8]. Rachel Held Evans describes the Bible as "sacred yet indelibly smudged with human fingerprints." Held Evans, *supra* note 181, at 13.

justice.[190] Some progressive churches and organizations "invite all people to participate in our community and worship life without insisting that they become like us in order to be acceptable," including "agnostics" and "questioning skeptics."[191] A related theme among progressive Christians is accepting and affirming doubt. The late Rachel Held Evans was a pivotal figure in this regard as she bravely aired her struggles to make meaning of Scripture.[192] Progressive Christians often emphasize the inclusion of stigmatized people in general, including LGBTQ people, people of color, immigrants, poor people, and people in prison.[193] This work sometimes entails recasting the very image of Jesus and God. It is not surprising in progressive churches to hear a speaker refer to God as "she" or "they" or to criticize the practice of depicting Jesus with Anglo-Saxon features.[194] As writer Anne Lamott said, "[Y]ou can safely assume you've created God in your own image when it turns out that God hates all the same people you do."[195]

I examine below two examples of progressive Christianity to illustrate a version of the faith that is invisible in Supreme Court opinions.

Lauren Daigle is a contemporary Christian singer who broke into the mainstream in 2018. That fall she performed a religious song, *Still Rolling Stones*, on *Ellen: The Ellen DeGeneres Show*. She was roundly condemned by many fundamentalist Christians for appearing on a show hosted by an out lesbian. Rejecting the notion that her faith called her to judge Ellen and disassociate from her, Daigle asserted:

> I think the second we start drawing lines around which people are able to be approached and which aren't, we've already completely missed the heart of God. I don't have all the answers in life, and I'm definitely not

---

[190] Clawson, *supra* note 187, at 796. Conservative Christians might agree with this goal, but their vision of social justice is distinct—typically focused on eliminating abortion and condemning LGBTQ sexuality.

[191] Edles, *supra* note 8, at 5.

[192] Held Evans, *supra* note 181, at 68–69 ("There's nothing quite like going through the motions of Christian life—attending church, leading Bible study, singing hymns, bringing your famous lemon bars to potluck—while internally questioning the very beliefs that hold the entire culture together."); Edles, *supra* note 8, at 5 (quoting statement of Progressive Christians Uniting, which stated "[We] [f]ind more grace in the search for understanding than we do in dogmatic certainty—more value in questioning than in absolutes").

[193] *See, e.g.*, Held Evans, *supra* note 181, at 39 (noting "Scripture's call to honor the poor, welcome the stranger, and liberate the oppressed"); Duncan, *supra* note 186.

[194] *See e.g.*, Jeremiah Bartram, *Why I Believe in a Non-Binary Jesus*, Broadview (Oct. 16, 2019), https://broadview.org/non-binary-jesus/ [https://perma.cc/MGF2-ENFK].

[195] Anne Lamott, Bird by Bird: Some Instructions on Writing and Life 22 (1995).

> gonna act like I do, but the one thing that I know for sure is I can't choose who I'm supposed to be kind to and who I'm supposed to show love to and who I'm not, because that's the mission right?[196]

In a subsequent interview, Daigle was asked whether homosexuality is a sin. She was uncertain, stating "I don't know. I actually had a conversation with someone last night about it. I can't say one way or the other. I'm not God."[197] According to *The Atlantic*, "Many on Twitter quickly declared that [Daigle] could no longer be considered a Christian."[198] Daigle's comments resonate with an influential anecdote concerning Pope Francis. When the Pope was asked for his views on gay people in 2013, he replied: "Who am I to judge?"[199] In *Fulton*, Commissioner Figueroa alluded to these words when she sought to persuade CSS to follow the Pope.[200] Pope Francis later expounded on that conversation by stating: "If a person is gay and seeks out the Lord and is willing, who am I to judge that person? . . . I was paraphrasing by heart the Catechism of the Catholic Church where it says that these people should be treated with delicacy and not be marginalized."[201]

An essay by Peter Wehner, *The Forgotten Radicalism of Jesus Christ*, turns fundamentalists' judgment of Ellen on its head.[202] Wehner reminds readers that Jesus often crossed social boundaries and disregarded conventions and taboos. He healed lepers and other ill people who were regarded as unclean, he befriended Samaritans (such as the woman at the well) even though the Jews regarded Samaritans as racially inferior, and he invited Matthew to be a disciple, even though

---

[196] Jonathan Merritt, *Lauren Daigle and the Lost Art of Discernment*, Atlantic (Dec. 8, 2018), https://www.theatlantic.com/ideas/archive/2018/12/let-lauren-daigle-be-unsure-about-lgbt-relationships/577651/ [https://perma.cc/LNN2-7WAE].

[197] *Id.*

[198] *Id.*

[199] *Pope Francis Explains 'Who Am I to Judge' in His New Book*, Catholic News Agency (Jan. 12, 2016), https://www.catholicnewsagency.com/news/33231/pope-francis-explains-who-am-i-to-judge-in-his-new-book [https://perma.cc/7AEE-GTVP].

[200] *See supra* note 59 and accompanying text.

[201] *Pope Francis Explains 'Who Am I to Judge' in His New Book*, *supra* note 199; *see also* Michael O'Loughlin, *The Pope Sent Me a Letter. It Gives Me Hope as a Gay Catholic.*, N.Y. Times (Nov. 15, 2021), https://www.nytimes.com/2021/11/15/opinion/pope-francis-lgbt-community.html [https://perma.cc/7JUM-QZHL].

[202] *See* Peter Wehner, *The Forgotten Radicalism of Jesus Christ*, N.Y. Times (Dec. 24, 2020), https://www.nytimes.com/2020/12/24/opinion/jesus-christ-christmas-incarnation.html [https://perma.cc/TXW5-LXRS].

he was a reviled tax collector, someone regarded as a traitor to his people. Wehner suggests that modern-day Christians ask themselves: *Who lives in the margins today? Who do I overlook as I go about my daily life?* Wehner cites the HIV/AIDS crisis as a major failure of Christianity. AIDS victims, which included many gay men and people addicted to drugs, were the modern-day lepers, he suggests. Yet most Christians were more interested in judging or ignoring this suffering rather than ministering to their needs.[203]

I highlight progressive Christianity because it is seldom visible in mainstream media and popular culture. Christianity is more commonly linked with conservatism and evangelicalism. My argument here is loosely inspired by Richard Thompson Ford's work on race and culture.[204] Ford argues that courts should not treat certain aspects of culture as part of Black identity and thus subject to antidiscrimination laws.[205] His concern is that courts are ill equipped to define what is and is not authentically Black, and judicial opinions on this topic may ultimately undermine Title VII and influence how Black people come to see themselves.[206]

Similarly, how the courts portray Christianity may positively or negatively impact public perceptions of the faith. To be clear, by invoking Ford's work in the context of religion, I am not arguing that courts should decline to resolve free exercise claims. Instead, I argue that the Supreme Court's treatment of claims by conservative Christians may elevate and validate a particular contested version of Christianity. Justices should resolve these cases while being more mindful of how they are depicting Christianity, how their own religious backgrounds may subconsciously nudge them toward certain understandings of the faith versus others, and how their opinions may exacerbate tensions among Christians about the core of the faith.

---

[203] *See id.*

[204] *See* RICHARD THOMPSON FORD, RACIAL CULTURE: A CRITIQUE (2005).

[205] *See, e.g.*, Richard Thompson Ford, *Race as Culture? Why Not?*, 47 UCLA L. REV. 1803, 1810 (2000).

[206] *See* FORD, *supra* note 204, at 74–77. I find Ford's arguments concerning race warrant serious consideration. Yet ultimately, they do not lead me categorically to preclude courts from considering racial culture, such as Black women's assertions of a right to wear natural hairstyles at work. *See, e.g.*, Leti Volpp, *Righting Wrongs*, 47 UCLA L. REV. 1815 (2000) (characterizing as overstated Ford's claim that protecting outsider identity-related traits creates a slippery slope, arguing instead that judges are already defining race and gender, and that failing to protect traits would leave much discrimination without a remedy).

Although a majority of Americans continues to identify as Christian, this majority appears to be eroding. Moreover, some research identifies a trend in which certain Trump voters are newly identifying as "evangelical" even though they do not attend church.[207] For some of these voters, one author has argued, Trump may have replaced Jesus as the center of Christianity.[208] A Georgetown University survey suggests that younger Americans regard Christians as having "good values and principles," but also that a majority of respondents perceive Christians as "judgmental" and "hypocritical."[209] In short, the trajectory of Christianity may turn on whether the exclusionary or inclusive wing of the faith prevails in the broader imagination.

This section will review some of the briefs filed by moderate and liberal religious organizations in *Fulton* to complicate the version of Christianity that appears in the Court's opinions in *Fulton* and *Masterpiece Cakeshop*. To be clear, these briefs filed by more inclusive organizations are a subset of all the briefs filed by religious groups. I do not summarize the many briefs filed by conservative groups, as their views are generally consistent with those expressed in the majority opinions.

A brief filed by the President of the House of Deputies of the Episcopal Church, the Central Conference of American Rabbis, Methodist Federation for Social Action, and Muslims for Progressive Values, as well as several other groups, situates CSS's claim for a religious exemption in the context of the broader views of Christians. "Any suggestion that 'religion' or 'people of faith' as a whole reject LGBT equality is false and insulting to millions of Americans of faith," the brief argues.[210] The authors back up this claim with a survey that found

---

[207] Gregory A. Smith, *More White Americans Adopted than Shed Evangelical Label During Trump Presidency, Especially His Supporters*, Pew Rsch. Ctr. (Sept. 15, 2021), https://www.pewresearch.org/fact-tank/2021/09/15/more-white-americans-adopted-than-shed-evangelical-label-during-trump-presidency-especially-his-supporters/ [https://perma.cc/8NPJ-P75G]; Ryan Burge, *Why 'Evangelical' Is Becoming Another Word for 'Republican,'* N.Y. Times (Oct. 26, 2021), https://www.nytimes.com/2021/10/26/opinion/evangelical-republican.html [https://perma.cc/N4E7-6C2Y]; Wehner, *supra* note 188.

[208] *See* Wehner, *supra* note 188.

[209] Geo. Univ. Berkley Ctr. for Religion, Peace, & World Affs., PRRI/Berkley Center Poll: Millennial Values Survey 2012, https://doi.roper.center/?doi=10.25940/ROPER-31096440 [https://perma.cc/K8T7-QRGH].

[210] Brief for President of the House of Deputies of the Episcopal Church et al. as Amici Curiae in Support of Respondent at 8, Fulton v. City of Phila., 141 S. Ct. 1868 (2021) (No. 19-123), 2020 WL 5076843.

that a majority of Black Protestants (63%), Orthodox Christians (61%), Hispanic Catholics (58%), White Catholics (56%), and White mainline Protestants (54%) opposed religiously based service denials. Indeed, 44% of White evangelicals opposed such service denials. There is also general opposition to religiously based service denials among people of other faiths, including Jews (65%), Buddhists (63%), Hindus (57%), and Muslims (53%).[211]

I do not present these survey results to suggest that the Court should interpret the law to reflect the views of the majority of Christians or religious people more generally. Rather, I recount them to demonstrate how the Court's depiction of Christianity and religion may mislead readers into thinking that most religious people believe that their faith should entitle them to refuse service to stigmatized groups. Or, in the words of the Episcopal Church brief, "Petitioners [CSS] and certain amici supporting them cannot be heard to speak for all religious people."[212] The brief summarizes how various Christian churches and other faith organizations have evolved to embrace LGBTQ people and their families as members of the faith who deserve equal dignity.[213]

Other briefs demonstrated how some religious people understand their faith to require treating LGBTQ people equally. For instance, a brief for Lutheran Child and Family Services of Illinois asserted: "[I]t would be a mistake to view this case as pitting non-discrimination rules against a monolithic category of religious organizations. Many religious organizations, like amicus, believe that non-discrimination is both an imperative of their faith and a pillar of child welfare."[214] This brief also connects the discrimination against LGBTQ prospective parents to bias that harms sexual minority youth in foster care. "LGBTQ youth make up a disproportionately large percentage of children in foster care. That is no accident. Many children are forced from their homes because of their sexual orientation or gender identity."[215] The Lutheran brief goes on to argue that permitting religious exemptions in the context of adoptions threatens to reduce

[211] *Id.* at 16.

[212] *Id.* at 21.

[213] *Id.* at 12–15.

[214] Brief for Lutheran Child and Fam. Servs. of Ill. as Amicus Curiae in Support of Respondents at 2, *Fulton*, 141 S. Ct. 1868 (No. 19-123), 2020 WL 5044626.

[215] *Id.*

the availability of LGBTQ adoptive parents, which may be particularly detrimental to LGBTQ youth in the system.[216] Moreover, "'[t]he adoption of policies that reject LGBTQ* family placements . . . conveys a[n] injurious message' to LGBTQ youth that there is something wrong with them."[217]

According to the Lutheran brief, "Christian traditions recognize 'God's love and presence in the diverse and multicultural world He created,' and '[t]he dignity and value of each individual.' . . . For amicus, those values are reflected in non-discrimination policies, which ensure provision of needed services to all people, including the most vulnerable."[218]

Several briefs also highlighted the harms of discrimination beyond sexual orientation.[219] For example, some briefs argued that there is no coherent rationale for permitting religious groups to refuse service based on sexual orientation, but not race and gender. If religious organizations can refuse to facilitate adoptions for same-sex couples, then they would also have the right to turn away interracial couples. Further, a constitutional right to discriminate would mean that people of various religious backgrounds, including Protestants and Catholics, could be denied service because of their faith. A brief filed by a Baptist organization argued "nondiscrimination provisions do as much to protect religious communities as they do people of different races, genders, and sexual orientation."[220]

V. Conclusion

The preceding discussion has sought briefly to sketch the breadth of Christianity and make visible disagreement among Christians as to how their faith requires them to treat stigmatized groups. The Court tends to reduce or "essentialize" Christianity by aligning it with the most conservative and exclusionary wing. For example, in

---

[216] *Id.* at 2, 6.

[217] *Id.* at 13.

[218] *Id.* at 13; *see also* Brief of Baptist Joint Comm. for Religious Liberty et al. as Amici Curiae in Support of Respondents at 1, 4, 5, *Fulton*, 141 S. Ct. 1868 (No. 19-123), 2020 WL 5044728 ("Amici further believe that, in our pluralistic society, the free exercise of religion is not burdened—to the contrary, it is advanced—when government contractors voluntarily performing public functions are asked to adhere to governmental nondiscrimination policies.").

[219] *See, e.g.*, Brief of Baptist Joint Comm. for Religious Liberty et al., *supra* note 218, at 5, 16–17 (discussing South Carolina case involving discrimination against Catholic parents).

[220] *Id.* at 29.

Fulton, there was actually a debate among Catholics as to whether their faith permits or requires discrimination based on sexual orientation. On one side was Philadelphia Mayor Jim Kenney and Cynthia Figueroa, the Commissioner of the Department of Human Services, who are both Catholics and public officials who defended the city's antidiscrimination requirement.[221] On the other side was CSS, which argued that complying with that requirement would undermine its faith. Commissioner Figueroa invoked the Pope and the church's history of discrimination as reasons for CSS to abide by the antidiscrimination law. Whichever side is right about its view of the faith, this dispute should have been understood as a debate *among Catholics*, rather than a secular state trying to punish a Catholic charity for its faith.

More generally, the debate in *Fulton* about whether or not to overrule *Smith* pitted conservative Catholics, such as Justice Alito, against a precedent written by another conservative Catholic, the late Justice Scalia. In *Roman Catholic Diocese*, Catholic Justices such as Justice Kavanaugh disagreed with Chief Justice Roberts and Justice Sotomayor, Catholic Justices who dissented (along with Justice Breyer and Justice Kagan, who are Jewish). In marking these religious identities, I do not mean to suggest that a Justice's faith determines how she votes in any particular case. Rather, I highlight these religious identities to underscore the disagreements among Catholics that play out at the Court and in the broader society. There is no monolithic Catholic or Protestant perspective on LGBTQ rights.

This Essay ultimately calls for the Justices to take greater care in describing Christianity (and other faiths) and to consider including in their opinions the voices of more liberal Christians who file amicus briefs. Roughly one-quarter of Americans identify as evangelicals; 20 percent of Americans are Catholic; nearly 15 percent are mainline Protestants; and 7 percent are Black Protestants.[222] Although centrist and liberal religious organizations have filed scores of briefs, the Court's opinions tend to erase them. This omission not only oversimplifies the cases, but it reinforces the pervasive public conflation of Christians and evangelicals. Moreover, if the Court were to attend to the broad range of

---

[221] *See supra* note 87.

[222] *Religious Landscape Study*, PEW RSCH. CTR. (Sept. 9, 2020), https://www.pewforum.org/religious-landscape-study/ [https://perma.cc/3FD4-R9KL]. Many studies on religion treat Black Protestants as a distinct group.

religious views reflected in the briefs, this practice might counteract the risk that a particular Justice understands and represents Christianity or religion more generally exclusively through the lens of his or her own subjective religious experience as a Catholic, Protestant, or Jew.

JENNIFER MASCOTT AND
JOHN F. DUFFY

EXECUTIVE DECISIONS AFTER ARTHREX

Decisionmaking in the modern Executive Branch frequently rests on a convenient formalism. Ultimate power is typically vested in high-level "principal" officers who, under the Appointments Clause, must be appointed by the President with the advice and consent of the Senate.[1] The vast bulk of day-to-day decisions within the branch,

Jennifer Mascott is Assistant Professor of Law and Co-Executive Director, The C. Boyden Gray Center for the Study of the Administrative State, Antonin Scalia Law School, George Mason University. John F. Duffy is Samuel H. McCoy II Professor of Law and Paul G. Mahoney Research Professor of Law, University of Virginia School of Law.

[1] *See* U.S. CONST. art. II, § 2, cl. 2. The Appointments Clause does not use the phrase "principal officer." It instead prescribes a default method for appointing "Officers of the United States" (appointment by the President "by and with the Advice and Consent of the Senate") and then permits Congress "by Law" to vest the appointment of "inferior Officers" in three other locations: "the President alone," "the Courts of Law," or "the Heads of Departments." *Id.* Courts and commentators now generally use the term "principal officer" to refer to the category of non-inferior officers—those who must be appointed by the President with the advice and consent of the Senate. That terminology can be misleading. The text of the Constitution uses the term "principal officer" only once—in the "Opinions Clause," which is in the clause immediately preceding the Appointments Clause. *See id.* cl. 1. That Clause empowers the President to require written opinions from "the principal officer in each of the executive Departments." The use of the singular there suggests that each department has only one "principal" officer, and that usage is consistent with both older and more modern meanings of the adjective "principal." *Compare, e.g., Principal*, 2 NOAH WEBSTER, AN AMERICAN DICTIONARY OF THE ENGLISH LANGUAGE (S. Converse 1828) (defined to mean "[c]hief" and "the highest in rank"), *with Principal*, MERRIAM-WEBSTER.COM, https://www.merriam-webster.com/dictionary/principal (last visited Feb. 14, 2022) (defined as "chief" or "most important"). It would be far better if courts and commentators had followed the Supreme Court's lead in *United States v. Germaine*, 99 U.S. 508, 509–10 (1878), which drew the distinction between "inferior" officers and the "primary class" of officers who need appointment by the President with the consent of

The Supreme Court Review, 2022.
 https://doi.org/10.1086/720295

however, are made by thousands of lower-level officials who are either "inferior" officers appointed under the Appointments Clause[2] or mere employees lacking any official appointment under modern doctrine.[3] Those lower-level officials often wield power under contemporary norms that is as strong in practice as it is weak in theory.

United States v. Arthrex[4] marks out a constitutional limit to this modern allocation of power. Whatever de facto power lower-level officials possess as a matter of practice, the Court held in *Arthrex* that Congress cannot vest final decisional authority in subordinate civil servants not appointed by the President with the advice and consent of the Senate. In particular, the Court held that the administrative patent judges (APJs) on the Patent Trial and Appeal Board (PTAB), who are inferior officers appointed by the Secretary of Commerce, could not constitutionally hold the degree of unsupervised power that statutory law appeared to vest in them—the power to issue final executive branch decisions revoking issued patents through a discretionary administrative review process known as "inter partes review."[5]

As a remedy, the Court held that one statutory provision—section 6(c) of the Patent Act, which would otherwise prevent the Director of the U.S. Patent and Trademark Office (Patent Office) from reviewing PTAB decisions because it mandates that only the PTAB itself can rehear its own decisions—is "unenforceable as applied to the Director."[6] With that statutory provision held unenforceable, the

---

the Senate. Despite the *Germaine* terminology's superior fidelity to constitutional text, this article will, for the convenience of readers, follow the modern practice of referring to the primary class of officers as "principal officers." *See also* Gary Lawson & Steven G. Calabresi, *Why Robert Mueller's Appointment as Special Counsel Was Unlawful*, 95 Notre Dame L. Rev. 87, 135–37 (2019).

[2] U.S. Const. art. II, § 2, cl. 2 ("[H]e shall nominate, and by and with the Advice and Consent of the Senate, shall appoint Ambassadors, other public Ministers and Consuls, Judges of the supreme Court, and all other Officers of the United States, whose appointments are not herein otherwise provided for, and which shall be established by Law: but the Congress may by Law vest the appointment of such inferior Officers, as they think proper, in the President alone, in the Courts of Law, or in the Heads of Departments.").

[3] *Cf.* Jennifer L. Mascott, *Who Are Officers of the United States?*, 70 Stan. L. Rev. 443 (2018) (contending that the evidence of the Constitution's original public meaning suggests that the class of Article II officers is broader than modern doctrine presupposes and includes any official who performs a statutory duty).

[4] 141 S. Ct. 1970 (2021).

[5] 35 U.S.C. § 311.

[6] 141 S. Ct. at 1987 (plurality opinion of Roberts, C.J.); *see also id.* at 1997 (opinion of Breyer, J., concurring in part and dissenting in part) (agreeing with the remedy set forth in the plurality opinion). Section 6(c) also requires the PTAB to sit in panels of three members,

Director (who is the only officer in the Patent Office appointed by the President with the advice and consent of the Senate) could review PTAB decisions and "issue decisions himself on behalf of the Board" because the Patent Act's general provisions vest the Director with the "powers and duties" of the whole agency, including the PTAB.[7] As a result of the Court's holding, *Arthrex* and several other cases pending in the courts were remanded to the agency for further proceedings, including review of the PTAB decisions by the Director.[8]

Part of *Arthrex*'s significance is immediately clear: The Court has now, for the first time in its modern separation of powers jurisprudence, relied on a combination of the Appointments Clause and Article II's Executive Vesting Clause to invalidate statutory law not because of the tenure protections afforded to officers, but because of the distribution of decisional power between principal officers and the mass of lower-level officials. By establishing that executive power must include the authority to control outcomes in particular matters, *Arthrex* charts a course distinct from cases such as *Myers v. United States*,[9] *Bowsher v. Synar*,[10] *Free Enterprise Fund v. Public Co. Accounting Oversight Board*,[11] *Seila Law LLC v. Consumer Financial Protection Bureau*,[12] and *Collins v. Yellen*,[13] all of which focused on the statutory processes for removing officers as the key constitutional issue. Even the Court's most recent opinion on the Appointments Clause's distinction between principal and inferior officers, *Edmond v. United*

---

and thus the Director, even though a member of the Board, would need the concurrence of at least one other member of the PTAB (all of whom are inferior officers) to review a decision.

[7] 141 S. Ct. at 1987 (plurality opinion of Roberts, C.J.) (relying on the Director's general powers in 35 U.S.C. § 3(a)(1)).

[8] *Id.* at 1988 (plurality opinion of Roberts, C.J.). The Supreme Court remanded the cases pending before it to the Federal Circuit, which in turn remanded the cases to the agency if the party complaining of the Appointments Clause violation wanted the remedy afforded by the Court's decision. Not every party viewed the remedy—review by the Director—as worth the bother to pursue. *See, e.g.*, *Snyders Heart Valve LLC v. St. Jude Med., LLC*, 2021 U.S. App. LEXIS 29905 (Oct. 5, 2021) (noting that the party seeking judicial review waived its Appointments Clause challenge after the Supreme Court remanded its case to the Federal Circuit for reconsideration in light of *Arthrex*).

[9] 272 U.S. 52 (1926).

[10] 478 U.S. 714, 734 (1986) ("By placing the responsibility for execution of the Balanced Budget and Emergency Deficit Control Act in the hands of an officer who is subject to removal only by itself, Congress in effect has retained control over the execution of the Act and has intruded into the executive function.").

[11] 561 U.S. 477 (2010).

[12] 140 S. Ct. 2183 (2020).

[13] 141 S. Ct. 1761 (2021).

States, relied heavily on an unrestricted power to remove officers as a "powerful tool for control" and a key indicator that officers are sufficiently subordinate to constitute "inferior" officers under the Appointments Clause.[14] In both its holding and its remedy, *Arthrex* seems to mark a significant shift, with a principal officer's direct supervision of final adjudicative decisions sometimes constitutionally required. Instead of ready removability satisfying the constitutional requirement for supervision, *Arthrex* requires principal officer supervision on the front end of actions, with the discretion to review and reissue certain decisions before they become final for the Executive Branch.

The *Arthrex* Court relied crucially on "the traditional rule" in executive adjudications—a rule touted as being followed in "the patent system in particular"—"that a principal officer, if not the President himself, makes the final decision on how to exercise executive power."[15] Yet rather than leading back toward a traditional approach to executive power, *Arthrex* could lead to an inversion of tradition in two respects.

First, within the patent system in particular, as well as more generally, the tradition of adversarial adjudication between private parties is not merely that some principal officer has a formal power to review inferior officer decisions. The tradition is instead one of locating the primary responsibility for significant adjudicative power in principal officers. That is clearly the tradition in the judicial branch of the federal government responsible for wielding adjudicative power in private rights disputes. Presidentially appointed, Senate-confirmed federal judges do not merely supervise, in cursory and formalistic manner, the work of hundreds of inferior adjudicators who do the bulk of the work. Article III judges instead do the bulk of the work themselves, assisted with a small staff of clerks and some inferior officers such as magistrates and clerks of court. As shown in Part II below, that tradition is evident in the history of the patent system too, with presidentially appointed, Senate-confirmed officers presiding over adversarial adjudications until very recent times. And it is the tradition even for multi-member administrative agencies created in the late nineteenth and early twentieth centuries in which principal officers wield not only de jure but also de facto responsibilities over complex adjudications.

---

[14] 520 U.S. 651, 664 (1997).

[15] *Arthrex*, 141 S. Ct. at 1984.

Yet coupled with twentieth-century administrative law governing executive decisionmaking, *Arthrex* has the potential to be not a return to that tradition but an inversion of it. *Arthrex*'s holding means that the complex decisions of hundreds of inferior officers, such as administrative patent judges, must be subject to the review of a principal officer. In the Patent Office, a single person—the Director—will formally be in control of that process, supervising the rulings of "more than 200" administrative patent judges.[16] But supervising administrative patent judges is not the Director's only duty. The Director heads a multi-billion dollar agency employing over 12,000 people, including 8,000 patent examiners whom the Director is charged with supervising as they issue hundreds of thousands of patents per year.[17]

In short, the Director had a full-time job before *Arthrex* imposed the responsibility of having to supervise the adversarial adjudicative decisions of more than 200 APJs.[18] A key question, then, is whether a presidential appointee such as the Director may delegate such review (either by rule or by practice) to subordinates, including to inferior officers or even staff-level employees. The Supreme Court's mid-twentieth century decision in *United States v. Morgan* maintains that even where parties have legal rights to have their adjudication heard by a high-level executive branch official, the official should never be "subjected to [an] examination" to determine the extent to which the official actually studied the record in the case or relied on subordinates who were delegated the task.[19]

If the *Morgan* principle is applied vigorously, then principal officers like the Director of the PTO could merely in practice hand over the decision whether to review inferior officer adjudications to

---

[16] *Id.* at 1977.

[17] *See Performance and Accountability Report 2021* at 2, U.S. PATENT & TRADEMARK OFF., https://www.uspto.gov/sites/default/files/documents/USPTOFY21PAR.pdf (noting the agency's more than 12,000 employees); *id.* at 19 (noting the agency's employment of 8,073 examiners); *id.* at 148, 166 (showing the agency's budgetary resources and program costs in excess of, respectively, $4.4 billion and $3.6 billion); *U.S. Patent Statistics Chart*, U.S. PATENT & TRADEMARK OFF., https://www.uspto.gov/web/offices/ac/ido/oeip/taf/us_stat.htm (showing the issuance of 388,900 total patent grants in 2020).

[18] It is true that the staff of Article III judges grew in the twentieth century with the addition of law clerks, and judges also supervise a number of inferior officers such as magistrate judges, bankruptcy judges and court clerks. Still, the sheer scale of the number of subordinate inferior officers that the Director must now supervise, coupled with the Director's many other duties, makes the Director's supervision of each adjudication orders of magnitude less than the supervision that judges exercise.

[19] 313 U.S. 409, 422 (1941).

subordinates who either are inferior officers or lack any constitutionally valid appointment. Informal delegations of this kind are not hypothetical; it is precisely what is occurring in practice at the Patent Office in the wake of *Arthrex*. With well over a thousand complex decisions issued by the PTAB every year, the Director cannot possibly directly evaluate whether each decision merits affirmance or reversal. Thus, the Director must rely on subordinate staff to survey the decisions being issued by the PTAB and flag those that staff consider to be of import before determining the cases in which the Director will issue a new decision.[20]

A second inversion of tradition arises from the combination of *Arthrex* with *Morrison v. Olson*, which the Court has never expressly overruled and thus in theory remains good law.[21] *Arthrex*'s textual invocation of a "traditional rule" requiring principal officers to have power to review the decisions of inferior officers is expressly confined to the "context of adjudication," and in multiple places throughout the majority opinion, the Court carefully limits its statements to the context of executive branch adjudicative power.[22] This is a curious limitation—the Court identifies no reason for it. Nor does the Court acknowledge that adjudication principally is just a form of decisionmaking, rather than a separate category of power.[23] Yet the Court in its precedent has recognized that adjudication can be a method of exercising both "executive" as well as "judicial" authority.[24] (Indeed, adjudication also could provide a potential vehicle for legislative-related determinations,[25] as it constitutes just a mode of reaching determinations by the

---

[20] *See Arthrex*, 141 S. Ct. at 1987–88 (Roberts, C.J.) (plurality opinion) (noting that "the Director need not review every decision of the PTAB" but just "have the discretion to review" them and issue new decisions himself). *See also* Mascott, *supra* note 3, at 558–63 (discussing constitutional supervisory mechanisms in the context of modern administrative practice where top executive officials have authority over large numbers of subordinates).

[21] *See, e.g.*, Collins v. Yellen, 141 S. Ct. 1761, 1780 (2021) (listing *Morrison* as among the Court's "hallmark removal cases" without further comment on its validity).

[22] *Arthrex*, 141 S. Ct. at 1986 ("[W]e do not address supervision outside the context of adjudication."); *see also id.* at 1984 (describing a traditional rule applied in "adjudication"); *id.* at 1987 Roberts, C.J.) (plurality opinion) (cabining its holding to inter partes review and not other types of PTAB adjudications such as the examination process).

[23] *See* William Baude, *Adjudication Outside Article III*, 133 Harv. L. Rev. 1511, 1520 (2020).

[24] *See, e.g.*, City of Arlington v. FCC, 569 U.S. 290, 304–05 n.4 (2013); *cf.* Ortiz v. United States, 138 S. Ct. 2165, 2192 (2018) (Alito, J., joined by Gorsuch, J., dissenting) (describing executive agencies as having "conduct[ed] adjudications—often taking 'judicial' forms—since the beginning of the Republic" (internal quotation omitted)).

[25] Baude, *supra* note 23, at 1520 (discussing the possibility of an adversarial hearing in Congress to determine where to locate a post office).

application of legal rules to facts.[26]) If *Arthrex* were read as holding that *all* forms of executive adjudication must be subject to final review by a principal officer,[27] then the holding would encompass even small-scale licensing adjudications[28] and would have significant repercussions throughout the administrative state. Alternatively, the Court could have meant its holding to be limited to final executive branch determinations similar to those at issue in *Arthrex*—revocations of patent rights in adversarial proceedings between private parties. The Court may have viewed such adjudications as significant enough, and sufficiently analogous to exercises of judicial power,[29] that principal officer supervision is required.

In any event, the Court's distinction of patent revocations as more adjudicative—or perhaps, more precisely, as more judicial in appearance than classically executive acts like prosecution—could stand tradition on its head if the Court meant to distinguish *Morrison*.[30] In

---

[26] *See* Freytag v. Comm'r of Internal Revenue, 501 U.S. 868, 909–10 (1991) (Scalia, J., concurring in part and concurring in the judgment) (describing adjudicative bodies as those that "determine facts, apply a rule of law to those facts, and thus arrive at a decision").

[27] *See Arthrex*, 141 S. Ct. at 1987 (Roberts, C.J.) (plurality opinion) (emphasizing that the case concerned only supervision of APJs in inter partes review proceedings and that the Court does "not address the Director's supervision over other types of adjudications conducted by the PTAB, such as the examination process for which the Director has claimed unilateral authority to issue a patent").

[28] *See* 5 U.S.C. § 551(6)–(7) (defining adjudication as the process for formulating orders, which include final dispositions in matters including licensing).

[29] *See Arthrex*, 141 S. Ct. at 1982 (referencing an APJ's service on an appellate panel as a "judicial assignment" and observing that executive officer activities can take judicial forms); *id.* at 1985 (describing the Court's holding as regarding "the unreviewable authority wielded by APJs during inter partes review," the patent office process for revoking patent rights that Congress expanded in the 2011 America Invents Act). Just three terms before *Arthrex*, the Court in *Oil States Energy Services, LLC v. Greene's Energy Group, LLC*, 138 S. Ct. 1365 (2018), held that patent inter partes reviews were not exercises of judicial power that were required to be in Article III. The Court was divided in that case, and in fact, the authors of the majority opinions and dissents in the two cases are precisely reversed—with the Chief Justice dissenting in *Oil States* and writing the majority opinion in *Arthrex*, and Justice Thomas writing the majority opinion in *Oil States* and dissenting in *Arthrex*. The Chief Justice's view of the underlying proceeding as inherently judicial may have influenced the reasoning of the *Arthrex* opinion.

[30] We recognize that some scholarship has raised questions about the historical origins of the view of prosecution as a core executive function. *Compare, e.g.*, Lawrence Lessig & Cass R. Sunstein, *The President and the Administration*, 94 COLUM. L. REV. 1, 16–22 (1984), *with* Saikrishna Prakash, *The Chief Prosecutor*, 73 GEO. WASH. L. REV. 521, 538–39 (2005). This article does not engage that discussion, taking the Court's precedents as they stand. The Court itself has repeatedly described prosecution as a "core executive" function, and thus, its conclusions regarding the character of executive supervision should be taken as based on that conception. *See* Seila Law LLC v. Consumer Fin. Prot. Bureau, 140 S. Ct. 2183, 2200 (2020) (describing the power to "initiate criminal investigations and prosecutions" at issue in

Morrison, the Court upheld Congress's power to vest an inferior officer with the ability to make final *prosecutorial* decisions that were outside the control of the principal officers in the Department of Justice. The result, at least as the law stands now, is an inversion of the Supreme Court's traditional doctrine. Control by principal executive officers—officers accountable to the President—is *not required* for some inferior officers making core executive decisions such as the discretionary decision of whom to investigate and prosecute but *is required* for some inferior officers making adjudicative decisions.[31] This apparent consequence stemming from *Arthrex* is even more surprising given the Court's indication in 2010 that adjudication might be less susceptible than other executive acts to constitutional Vesting Clause constraints like supervision through removal.[32]

It's hard to see such a result as anything other than an inversion of the basic constitutional framework, which has placed prosecutorial decisions in a branch subject to control of the politically accountable President and judicial decisions in a branch uniquely insulated from politics. Indeed, the Court in *Humphrey's Executor v. United States* even paid lip service to that traditional allocation of power, for the Court there permitted officers to have some insulation from political control on the grounds that they were performing "quasi" judicial functions, not executive functions.[33]

These two potential inversions of tradition may, however, be merely temporary. *Morrison*, for example, seems ripe for overruling. That precedent now has so little practical weight that the Court in *Arthrex* did not even bother to cite it. Similarly, the *Arthrex* opinion suggests the Court is now recognizing not merely a *power* in principal

---

Morrison v. Olson as "core executive power"); Free Enter. Fund v. Pub. Co. Acct. Oversight Bd., 561 U.S. 477, 494–95 (2010) (describing the Court's position that the inspector general, "wield[ing] the full power of a prosecutor," was "undoubtedly an executive officer" as opposed to "quasi-legislative or quasi-judicial" (internal quotation omitted)); *cf.* INS v. Chadha, 462 U.S. 919, 1002 (1983) (White, J., dissenting) ("A legislative check on an inherently executive function, for example that of initiating prosecutions, poses an entirely different question.").

[31] *But see* Jennifer L. Mascott, *Constitutionally Conforming Agency Adjudication*, 2 Loy. U. Chi. J. Regul. Compliance 22, 24–25 (2017) (discussing first principles in relation to executive branch adjudication as an exercise of traditional executive power).

[32] *Free Enterprise Fund*, 561 U.S. at 484, 507 & n.10 (2010) (explicitly carving out administrative law judges from the scope of its holding that executive officers could not be subject to two levels of tenure protections in the context of the Public Company Accounting Oversight Board).

[33] *See* 295 U.S. 602, 628 (1935) (asserting that the Federal Trade Commission "cannot in any proper sense be characterized as an arm or an eye of the executive").

officers to review the decisions of inferior officers, but a *responsibility* to do so by exercising discretion to reverse or issue a new determination when necessary.[34] And while twentieth-century administrative law appeared to have a flat prohibition against inquiries into the actual processes by which high-level officers made decisions, more recent administrative law—most notably the Court's recent decision in the *Census Case*[35]—appears to erode that doctrine. In agencies that issue hundreds or even thousands of decisions per year and that have few presidential appointees (such as the Patent Office), the agency head will be tempted to delegate the *Arthrex* review to subordinates, including other inferior officers and staff. Indeed, that is precisely what is happening at the Patent Office. Parties will surely litigate (and indeed are already in the process of litigating) whether such delegations satisfy *Arthrex*'s ideal of having "a transparent decision for which a politically accountable officer must take responsibility."[36]

I. The Path to *Arthrex*, the Court's Decision, and Immediate Implications

Understanding *Arthrex* requires an appreciation of the background leading up to the litigation, a precise understanding of what the Court decided, and knowledge of the agency proceedings following the Supreme Court's remand in the case.

A. The Origins of the Constitutional Problem: Statutory Changes from 1975

The origins of the constitutional tensions presented in *Arthrex* extend over several decades during which Congress made a series of statutory changes to the Patent Office along two significant dimensions. First, starting in 1975 Congress reduced in significant measure the number of presidentially appointed, Senate-confirmed officers in the Patent Office. At the beginning of that year, a high watermark of sorts, the Office had 19 Senate-confirmed officers, but Congress cut

[34] *See, e.g.*, United States v. Arthrex, 141 S. Ct. 1970, 1980 (2021) (indicating that one necessary aspect of inferior officer status is being subject to the direction and supervision of a higher-level officer); *id.* at 1988 (Roberts, C.J.) (plurality opinion) (requiring the Director to have the discretion to review APJ decisions even though he need not review all of them).

[35] Dep't of Com. v. New York, 139 S. Ct. 2551 (2019).

[36] *Arthrex*, 141 S. Ct. at 1982.

the number to only four and then, after 1999, to just one. Second, legislation over time vastly increased the administrative powers of the agency. Although increased administrative power alone was not the genesis of the Appointments Clause problem at issue in this case, the combination of it along with the dearth of presidentially appointed, Senate-confirmed officers led to the issue of supervision over final decisionmaking being presented in a particularly dramatic form. The greater the amount of patent authority held by increasingly fewer non-inferior officers, the greater the challenge for final executive branch decisional authority to be vested in an officer directly accountable to the President.

The numerically largest decline in presidentially appointed, Senate-confirmed officers in the Patent Office happened on the day after New Year's in 1975, when Congress reduced the number from 19 to 4, with only the Commissioner of Patents (at the time, the title of the agency's head), a deputy, and two assistant commissioners left as non-inferior officers.[37] The appointments of all "examiners-in-chief" (the predecessors of APJs) were switched to appointment by the Secretary of Commerce within "the classified civil service," with the new appointment structure also conferring standard civil-service tenure protections.[38] That change left the agency's main adjudicative board—then known as the Board of Appeals—with a majority of its members appointed in a manner constitutionally permissible only for inferior officers and insulated in part from removal by any principal officer.

Still, the agency's four remaining presidentially appointed officers were members of the appellate Board, and those four officers could supervise and control the final decisions of the Board. Therefore, if one conceives of *Arthrex* as having been about only determining the kinds of tasks that inferior officers may perform, there was no

---

[37] *See* 35 U.S.C. § 3 (1970 ed.) (authorizing the appointment of nineteen officers by the President with the advice and consent of the Senate); Act of Jan. 2, 1975, Pub. L. No. 93–601, § 1, 88 Stat. 1956 (amending 35 U.S.C. § 3 to leave only four officers appointed by the President with the advice and consent of the Senate). That same day, another new statute renamed the agency the Patent and Trademark Office. *See* Act of Jan. 2, 1975, Pub. L. No. 93–601, § 3, 88 Stat. 1949. For simplicity, we will use the name "Patent Office" to identify the agency even after this name change—a practice followed in some recent Supreme Court opinions. *See, e.g.*, Cuozzo Speed Techs., LLC v. Lee, 579 U.S. 261 (2016).

[38] *See* Act of Jan. 2, 1975, §§ 1–2, 88 Stat. 1956, 1956 (amending 35 U.S.C. § 3 to give the Secretary the power to appoint and also amending 35 U.S.C. § 7 to require that examiners-in-chief be appointed in the civil service).

problem in 1975. If constitutionalizing the structure of the Patent Office also requires that the Director at the head of the Office have the capacity to direct the outcome of final decisions, then there still likely was no problem because the Director had partial supervisory power through his ability to order rehearings of the Board to occur before any three of the Board's four presidentially appointed members.[39] Similar directive authority to form boards for initial appellate inter partes review was considered inadequate to constitute constitutional supervision in *Arthrex* itself.[40] But in contrast to the composition of the PTAB at the time of the *Arthrex* litigation, the 1975 Board members were themselves directly subject to presidential supervision through presidential appointment and Senate consent and the presumed presidential removal and directive authority that typically accompanies principal officer appointments. The Patent Office of the era thus could be properly viewed as having a single head for most of its operations but a multi-headed panel of four principal officers to supervise the agency's adjudicative operations.

The Board maintained four presidential appointees until 1999 when legislation made three significant changes. First, the agency head—now called the Director of the Patent and Trademark Office—became the sole presidential appointee in the agency. Second, the agency's other three top officers, who had been presidential appointees, were now appointed by the Secretary of Commerce and given new titles—the Deputy Director, the Commissioner for Trademarks, and the Commissioner for Patents.[41] Third, all of the "examiners-in-chief" were given the title "administrative patent judge," and the power

[39] *See* 35 U.S.C. § 7 (1970 ed.) (requiring the Board to sit in panels of "at least three members" and vesting it with the "sole power to grant rehearings"). The rules of panels of at least three members selected by the agency head and rehearings ordered only by the Board remained constant from the enactment of the Patent Act of 1952 through to the time of the *Arthrex* litigation. *See* Patent Act of 1952, Pub. L. No. 593, § 7, 66 Stat. 792, 793. The Commissioner's power to designate a new panel for a rehearing of an appeal was controversial, but a majority of the en banc Federal Circuit upheld the power, holding that the Patent Act did not place "any limitations on the Commissioner's ability to designate Board panels, including Board panels for 'rehearing' purposes" and that such an interpretation was "consistent with the broad supervisory authority that Congress has granted the Commissioner" over the agency operations. *In re* Alappat, 33 F.3d 1526, 1534–35 (Fed. Cir. 1994) (en banc).

[40] *See* 141 S. Ct. at 1977, 1981–82 (indicating that the Director's authority to constitute inter partes review board and to select or reselect the membership of Board panels is inadequate without accompanying authority to review the substance of the final decision itself).

[41] Patent and Trademark Efficiency Act, Pub. L. No. 106–13, App. I, § 4713, 113 Stat. 1501A–575 (1999) (amending 35 U.S.C. § 3). The unusual citation form arises because the

to appoint them was transferred from the Secretary of Commerce to the agency's Director, giving them no constitutionally valid appointment as officers of any kind.[42] The changes left the Board with one presidential appointee, a few inferior officers appointed by the Secretary, and a majority of APJs who lacked any constitutionally valid appointment.

After these 1999 statutory changes, the Board had a very clear constitutional problem. Not only was the outcome of Board proceedings not controlled by principal officers, but most Board panels included no constitutionally appointed officers at all. Surprisingly, that situation continued for more than half a decade until legal scholarship pointed out that the "method of appointment [of APJs] is almost certainly unconstitutional."[43]

After news reports publicized the constitutional defect,[44] Congress acted swiftly in 2008 to shift the power to appoint patent judges to the Secretary of Commerce.[45] The same day that the statute was enacted, the Secretary reappointed all of the APJs initially appointed by the Director—supposedly with retroactive effect back to their earlier appointment dates.[46] From that point forward, the Board then

---

relevant provisions were contained in a pending bill that was incorporated by reference into an appropriations act that instructed the Archivist of the United States to publish the incorporated-by-reference bills (nine in total) as "appendices" to the U.S. Statutes at Large. *Id.* § 1000 (a)–(b), 113 Stat. 1501A–535 to 36. It is unclear whether the appendices were presented to the President as the Constitution's Presentment Clauses might seem to require, *see* U.S. CONST. art. I, § 7, cl. 2–3.

[42] Patent and Trademark Efficiency Act § 4717, 113 Stat. at 1501A–580 to 81 (amending 35 U.S.C. § 6). The statute also removed the Deputy Director from the Board, but the Deputy was added back to the Board in 2002. *See* 21st Century Department of Justice Appropriations Authorization Act, Pub. L. No. 107–273, § 13203(a), 116 Stat. 1902 (2002).

[43] John F. Duffy, *Are Administrative Patent Judges Unconstitutional*?, 2007 PATENTLY-O PATENT L.J. 21, 25 (2007). An updated version of the original paper was published as John F. Duffy, *Are Administrative Patent Judges Unconstitutional?*, 77 GEO. WASH. L. REV. 904 (2009).

[44] *See, e.g.*, Adam Liptak, *In One Flaw, Questions on Validity of 46 Judges*, N.Y. TIMES (May 6, 2008), http://www.nytimes.com/2008/05/06/washington/06bar.html.

[45] Act of Aug. 12, 2008, Pub. L. No. 110–313, § 1(a), 122 Stat. 3014 (amending 35 U.S.C. § 6(a)).

[46] *See* Brief for the Respondent in Opposition on Petition for a Writ of Certiorari at 15, DBC v. Patent & Trademark Office, 55 U.S. 816 (2009) (No. 08-1284), 2009 WL 1703247, at *15 (representation of fact by the Solicitor General). The 2008 statute purported to give the Secretary power to "deem" all judges as having new secretarial appointments retroactively effective to the dates of the Director's earlier appointments. *See* § 1(a)(1)(C), 122 Stat. at 3014 (adding 35 U.S.C. § 6(c)). No reported court decision has ruled on whether those retroactive appointments were constitutional. *See* Stryker Spine v. Biedermann Motech GmbH, 684 F. Supp. 2d 68, 88 (D.D.C. 2010) (refusing to reach the party's constitutional challenge to the Secretary's "retroactive

comprised one presidentially appointed, Senate-confirmed officer alongside dozens of Secretary-appointed inferior officers.[47]

Over this multi-decade period while Congress was decreasing the number of the Board's principal officers, Congress was simultaneously granting the Board more substantive power. In 1980, for example, Congress authorized "ex parte reexamination" of issued patents—giving the agency a new power to review and potentially revoke issued patents.[48] In 1999, 15 years after extending the Board's power to cover invention priority determinations in interference proceedings,[49] Congress authorized "inter partes reexamination" proceedings, which authorized "[a]ny person" to be able to seek a reexamination of any issued patent in adversarial proceedings in the Patent Office.[50]

Still, despite those jurisdictional expansions and the dearth of principal officers, the Board might have passed constitutional scrutiny as of 2008 because the Director held significant controls influencing Board adjudication. Examination of initial applications were still (as they are now) statutorily committed to the authority of the Director, and while the Board had (and still has) the power to reverse examiners' rejections of applications, such reversals resulted only in remands to the examiners.[51] The Patent Act continued to vest control over the agency's examination functions with the Director, so the power of the Board to reverse examiners could be interpreted as a process by which inferior officers oversaw lower-level bureaucratic examiner actions subject to the ultimate supervision of the presidentially appointed Director. Indeed, when the Board eventually acquired a role in judging interferences, the statute seemed quite explicitly to recognize the Director's overarching power over the examination process. The statute provided that the Director "*may* issue a patent to the applicant

---

appointment" authority because the Board panel reheard, and reaffirmed, its prior decision after the Secretary's appointments of the judges).

[47] As of May of 2008, the Board had 74 APJs. *See* Liptak, *supra* note 44.

[48] Act of Dec. 12, 1980, Pub. L. No. 96–517, § 301, 94 Stat. 3015, 3015.

[49] Patent Law Amendments Act of 1984, Pub. L. No. 98–622, §§ 201–02, 98 Stat. 3383, 3386–87.

[50] Patent and Trademark Efficiency Act § 4604, 113 Stat. 1501A–561 (adding 35 U.S.C. §§ 311–18 to the Patent Act).

[51] *See* 37 C.F.R. § 41.54 (2010) (dictating that the proceeding would "be returned to the examiner" after the Board's decision).

who is adjudged the prior inventor" by the Board.[52] All of the new proceedings enacted between 1980 and 1999 were placed within the agency's patent examination functions, which remained committed to the Director's power.[53] And the Director retained substantial levers of power to control outcomes in individual cases by controlling the proceedings both below and above the Board. For example, in ex parte reexamination proceedings, a previously issued patent can be revoked only with the concurrence of the Director. Similarly, in now-repealed inter partes reexamination procedures, the Director was the appellee in all appeals from Board judgments and could decline to defend the Board's decision on judicial review, which should result in remand to the agency.[54]

In the 2011 America Invents Act, however, Congress authorized a jurisdictional expansion of a substantially different kind. Congress replaced inter partes "reexamination" with two new inter partes "review" processes placed entirely outside the scope of the Director's examination authority. Rather than providing for examination followed by appeal to the Board, the new post-issuance review processes started and stopped at the administrative level with "trials" conducted solely at the Board. The shift was captured succinctly in the Board's new moniker—the Patent *Trial* and Appeal Board.[55] Furthermore, in the judicial review proceedings after the administrative trials, the Director's power was reduced to just a "right to intervene" rather than the right to be the appellee in the court proceedings.[56] This newly granted Board independence from Director influence, coupled with the absence of presidential appointees to form majorities on the Board's three-member panels, led to the constitutional challenge in the *Arthrex* litigation.

[52] 35 U.S.C. § 135(a) (2000) (emphasis added).

[53] *Id.* § 131.

[54] *See, e.g.*, Flo Healthcare Solutions, LLC v. Kappos, 697 F.3d 1367 (Fed. Cir. 2012) (naming Director Kappos as an "Appellee" in the proceeding seeking judicial review of the Board's inter partes reexamination decision); *see also* SKF USA, Inc. v. United States, 254 F.3d 1022, 1029–30 (Fed. Cir. 2001) (sustaining an agency's ability to seek and, excepting a statutory command dictating a particular result or other "unusual circumstances," to obtain a remand where the agency believes the "original decision is incorrect on the merits").

[55] Robert P. Merges & John F. Duffy, Patent Law and Policy 921 (8th ed. 2021) (noting that the 2011 America Invents Act conferred "new power to run more formalized 'trials' concerning the validity of issued patents"); *see also* Leahy-Smith America Invents Act, § 7, 125 Stat. 313 (amending 35 U.S.C. § 6 to rename the Board).

[56] Leahy-Smith America Invents Act, § 7(b)(2) (amending 35 U.S.C. § 143).

B. THE *ARTHREX* LITIGATION

The litigation that would lead to the Supreme Court's decision began in 2015 with Arthrex being issued Patent No. 9,179,907, which covers a purportedly novel surgical device capable of more easily reattaching soft tissues (such as tendons) to bones.[57] Within months, Arthrex sued Smith & Nephew for infringement in federal district court,[58] and as many infringement defendants now do, Smith & Nephew responded by filing, in 2016, a petition for inter partes review at the Patent Office.[59] Smith & Nephew argued that Arthrex's patent, which claimed "priority" to several earlier filed patent applications dating back to 2000, was not entitled to receive those earlier priority dates. Without those earlier priority dates, many of Arthrex's patent claims would not be novel due to technology that existed by 2014, the time when Arthrex filed the application that ultimately issued as its patent. The Board granted Smith & Nephew's request to commence or "institute" the inter partes review in 2017 and, one year later, issued a final decision holding invalid all of the challenged claims.

Arthrex sought judicial review of the Board's decision in the Federal Circuit and, for the first time in the proceedings, challenged the constitutional composition of the Board.[60] Because inter partes reviews are structured as adversarial proceedings between two private parties, not as administrative reexamination proceedings conducted by the Director, neither the Patent Office nor any other governmental party was a respondent or defendant to the judicial review proceedings. Thus, the United States entered the case as an intervenor to defend the constitutionality of the statute. The Trump Administration initially intervened to defend the constitutional validity of the administrative structure, and the Biden Administration continued in that course.

---

[57] U.S. Patent No. 9,179,907 (filed May 8, 2014).

[58] Smith & Nephew, Inc. v. Arthrex, Inc., IPR2017-00275, at 3 (P.T.A.B. May 2, 2018) (noting that Arthrex sued for infringement in the Eastern District of Texas). Arthrex actually succeeded in winning a jury verdict that Smith & Nephew had infringed the patent, and the parties then settled the infringement litigation with a stipulation that Smith & Nephew's challenge to the validity of the patent at the Board could go forward. *See id.* at 3–4.

[59] *See* Petition for Inter Partes Review, *Arthrex, Inc.*, IPR2017-00275 (Nov. 15, 2016).

[60] *See* Arthrex, Inc. v. Smith & Nephew, Inc., 941 F.3d 1320, 1326 (Fed. Cir. 2019). In allowing the constitutional issue to be raised despite Arthrex's failure to raise the issue at the agency, the Federal Circuit noted that the agency itself "could not have corrected the problem." *Id.* at 1327.

The Federal Circuit's decision had two holdings. First, the court ruled that the APJs could not constitutionally be mere inferior officers because they had too much power subject to inadequate control by a principal officer. In terms of power, the court specifically recognized that the judges wielded "significantly more authority" than their predecessors, the examiners-in-chief, who had been appointed by the President with the consent of the Senate up to 1975.[61] In terms of control, the court relied primarily on two factors: (i) that no presidential appointee had the power "to review a final written decision by the [judges]," and (ii) both the Secretary of Commerce and the Director of the agency lacked "unfettered removal authority" over the judges due to civil service protections that apply to their positions.[62]

The court's second holding was that any constitutional defect could be cured by severing the tenure protections that statutory law granted to the judges. That remedy was consistent both with the government's preferred remedy and with the remedy that the D.C. Circuit had applied in a similar case involving an Appointments Clause challenge to copyright royalty judges, who also had independent adjudicative authority and significant statutory tenure protections.[63]

C. THE SUPREME COURT'S DECISION

The outcome at the Federal Circuit "satisfied no one."[64] Both private parties and the United States sought en banc rehearing, which was denied by an 8-4 vote, and then filed petitions for certiorari.[65] The Supreme Court granted all three petitions, consolidated the cases, and limited briefing to questions presenting the Appointments Clause and remedial issues.[66] In its subsequent decision, the Court agreed with the Federal Circuit's ruling that the statutory scheme violated the Appointments Clause but disagreed on the appropriate remedy.

In its ruling on the constitutional issue, the Court subtly changed the relevant question and, in so doing, paved the way for an important

---

[61] *Id.* at 1335.

[62] *Id.* at 1329, 1332.

[63] *Id.* at 1337.

[64] United States v. Arthrex, 141 S. Ct. 1970, 1978 (2021).

[65] *Id.*

[66] Order List at 1, 592 U.S. (Oct. 13, 2020). The Court denied certiorari on the third question presented by the government, which focused on whether Arthrex had waived the constitutional issue by failing to present it at the administrative level.

doctrinal shift in Appointments Clause jurisprudence. Though the question presented in the case (as drafted by the United States and approved by the Court in granting certiorari) focused on whether the APJs "are principal officers who must be appointed by the President with the Senate's advice and consent,"[67] the majority opinion for the Court reframed the issue as "whether the nature of [the judges'] responsibilities is consistent with their method of appointment."[68] The focus on the mismatch between responsibilities and the appointment method allowed the Court to sidestep the question of how precisely to draw a sharp distinction between principal and inferior officers (a distinction that the Court previously related to a variety of factors such as the officers' tenure, the scope of their power, their statutory protections of independence and their positions in the hierarchy of the Executive Branch).

Relying on what it described as "the traditional rule" for "adjudication" that "a principal officer, if not the President himself, makes the final decision" within the Executive Branch, the Court held that the APJs' "unreviewable authority" in adjudicating the validity of issued patents in adversarial proceedings was "incompatible with their appointment ... to an inferior office."[69] That result, the Court's analysis suggests, was grounded not only in the Appointments Clause but also in two more general propositions. First, "[t]he President is 'responsible for the actions of the Executive Branch' and 'cannot delegate [that] ultimate responsibility or the active obligation to supervise that goes with it.'"[70] Second, powers that are delegated within the Executive Branch acquire "legitimacy and accountability to the public through 'a clear and effective chain of command' down from the President, on whom all the people vote."[71] Both of those propositions have previously been viewed as flowing from the Vesting Clause of Article II, but prior to *Arthrex*, the Court had primarily viewed the requirement for a "clear and effective chain of command" as satisfied principally by the ability to remove officers rather than the ability to review and correct their decisions.

---

[67] Reply and Response Brief for the United States at I, *Arthrex*, 141 S. Ct. 1970 (Nos. 19-1434, 19-1452, 19-1458).

[68] *Arthrex*, 141 S. Ct. at 1980.

[69] *Id.* at 1984.

[70] *Id.* at 1978–79.

[71] *Id.* at 1979.

The Court's doctrinal shift presaged the remedy afforded by the Court. In a plurality opinion, Chief Justice Roberts ruled that the appropriate remedy was not to hold the judges' appointments invalid (which would seem to be required if they were principal officers) nor to hold unlawful their tenure protections (as the Federal Circuit had done). Instead, the plurality concluded that the appropriate remedy for the mismatch between the judges' responsibilities and appointment process was to diminish their responsibilities by prohibiting "enforcement of statutory restrictions on the Director that insulate the decisions of APJs from his direction and supervision."[72] With that one portion of the statute held unenforceable against the Director, the general statutory powers of the Director to provide direction and supervision of the agency would extend to the review of the judges' decisions.[73] With the concurrence of Justice Breyer and two other Justices on this one point only, the Chief Justice's plurality opinion on the appropriate remedy controlled the judgment in the case.

D. THE AFTERMATH: *ARTHREX*'S EFFECT AT THE PATENT OFFICE

After the Supreme Court's decision, the *Arthrex* case itself and several other cases being held in abeyance at the Court or at the Federal Circuit were remanded back to the Patent Office. The agency quickly established a streamlined process in which parties to adversarial post-issuance processes (inter partes review and post-grant review) could seek review by the Director.[74] The Director began issuing decisions on August 2 and within six months had issued more than one hundred decisions. Three points are worth noting about the process.

First, most parties seeking review by the Director have been disappointed thus far. Arthrex itself received no relief from the process; its petition for Director review was denied on October 15, 2021, in a

---

[72] *Id.* at 1986–87 (Roberts, C.J.) (plurality opinion).

[73] *See id.* at 1987 (discussing 35 U.S.C. § 6(c) and 35 U.S.C. § 3(a)(2)(A), which vests the Director with the responsibility "for providing policy direction and management supervision for the Office").

[74] *See USPTO Implementation of an Interim Director Review Process Following* Arthrex, U.S. Patent & Trademark Off., https://www.uspto.gov/ patents/patent-trial-and-appeal-board /procedures/uspto-implementation-interim-director-review# (last modified June 29, 2021). The process authorized parties to seek review by filing a petition limited to 15 pages within 30 days of a Board decision. *See Arthrex* Q&As, U.S. Patent & Trademark Off., https:// www.uspto.gov/patents/patent-trial-and-appeal-board/procedures/arthrex-qas (last modified Dec. 3, 2021). The agency's announced policy did not authorize any responsive filings by parties opposed to review.

brief order that merely recited the fact of the Director's denial of review.[75] Arthrex's experience is typical. As of February 8, 2022, our survey of the Director's orders on petitions seeking review under *Arthrex* shows only 2 grants of review out of 142 orders—a success rate in seeking relief of less than 1.5%.[76] The PTO's interim policy also authorizes the Director sua sponte to review a decision, a provision that seems required by *Arthrex*'s mandate that the Director maintain discretion to issue a new decision in any case. As of February 2022, the Director has not reached out affirmatively to offer such review.

Second, the sheer number of petitions decided in an approximately six-month period strongly suggests that the Director must delegate some or all of the review responsibilities to others—most likely individuals working on the Director's staff or attorneys in the agency. Such staff or attorneys have no valid appointment for Appointments Clause purposes and are therefore mere employees. Therefore, akin to a judge overseeing the work of law clerks, the Director must maintain close responsibility for the work of such subordinates' decisions, to remain faithful to the *Arthrex* conclusion that a principal officer must have responsibility and accountability for all final executive branch determinations.

The third and final issue is whether, and to what extent, the *Arthrex* power can be formally delegated to other officials within the Patent Office. This issue has important theoretical implications and broad practical importance, and it is not speculative or hypothetical. All of the decisions granting and denying Director review have been issued by an inferior officer (the Commissioner for Patents) who has been delegated the functions and duties of the Director and has been exercising them since January 20, 2021. Those decisions are already

[75] *See* Order Denying Request for Director Review, Smith & Nephew v. Arthrex, IPR2017-00275 (P.T.A.B. Oct. 15, 2021).

[76] The agency database of documents filed in Board proceedings, available at https://developer.uspto.gov/ptab-web/#/search/documents, was queried for all documents concerning "Director Review." The search yielded over 300 documents. Review of those results located all orders reaching grant or denial decisions. A request to the Patent Office for data yielded confirmation of only two grants of Director review during that time period, though the agency counted 160 total decisions (not counting 8 petitions that were dismissed or withdrawn). *See* E-Mail from Thomas Krause, Acting Gen. Couns., U.S. Patent & Trademark Off., to John F. Duffy (Feb. 9, 2022) (on file with authors). The slightly higher count of total decisions in the Patent Office data appears to be due to the agency's practice of consolidating in a single order multiple decisions denying Director review in related inter partes review proceedings. The number in the text refers to the number of orders.

being challenged on several grounds, including alleged violations of the Appointments Clause.[77] As discussed below in Part II.B.3 of this article, one central issue in those challenges is whether the *Arthrex* power can be delegated to an inferior officer.

II. Is *Arthrex* a Return to Tradition for the Patent Office?

The Patent Office is one of the oldest and, prior to the twentieth century, largest administrative components of the federal government. The history of its adjudicative appointees is thus relevant as a general matter to the longstanding viability of the limited *Arthrex* holding, not just within the context of the patent system. In evaluating the ramifications of *Arthrex*, a key question is whether the traditional approach to allocating decisional power among appointees in the patent system, and across executive adjudication writ large, is consistent with the *Arthrex* majority's reasoning. The majority opinion contended that a "traditional rule" barring inferior officers from making final decisions historically applied "to the patent system in particular."[78] Was the Court correct, and even if it was, does the *Arthrex* decision nudge the law back toward that tradition?

Consistent with the narrative set forth in *Arthrex*, the history shows that in almost all circumstances, final decisional power in patent administration was vested in noninferior officers (presidential appointees confirmed by the Senate). But more importantly, the true tradition in the patent system is even stronger. The tradition is not merely against vesting any final decisionmaking authority in inferior officers, but against vesting the power to render very consequential decisionmaking authority in anyone other than principal officers.

Arthrex makes, at best, a half-step in returning to that tradition. At worst, if not applied and interpreted to require a strict form of executive supervision in which principal officers are held fully responsible for final executive branch patent determinations, then the opinion could produce an inversion of the tradition.

[77] *See, e.g.*, Arthrex Inc.'s Amended Notice of Appeal, Smith & Nephew, Inc. v. Arthrex, Inc., IPR2017-00275 (Nov. 1, 2021) (noting Arthrex's intention to raise new challenges under the Appointment Clause).

[78] *Arthrex*, 141 S. Ct. at 1984.

A. APPOINTMENTS AND THE ALLOCATION OF POWER IN THE PATENT OFFICE, 1790–1839

The first half-century of the U.S. patent system shows patent adjudications being lodged mainly in principal officers. There are, however, exceptions, which the majority opinion dismisses on the grounds that the persons making the decisions in those instances held "ad hoc positions [that] may not have even constituted offices" and exercised only "limited power under special and temporary conditions."[79] The majority's reasoning may seem like a bit of constitutional gerrymander. After all, if inferior officers cannot be vested with final decisional authority on patent validity issues (*Arthrex*'s holding), then it seems illogical to say that such power can be vested in a host of non-officers holding only "ad hoc" positions.

Yet a close examination of the history shows that the amount of power exercised by these other agents was miniscule in the extreme. The key point—a point easy to miss from a modern perspective—is that for much of the U.S. patent system's first century, the mere issuance of a patent did not have anything like the legal significance that the event has under modern statutory law, which grants a strong presumption of validity to issued patents.[80] Rather, the initial issuance of a patent in early history was more like a ministerial act of paperwork, establishing a presumptive grant of a patent that was not truly final until adjudicated through judicial challenge. Thus, if real and significant power is the focus of the analysis, the history shows such authority as lodged in principal officers in perhaps even all instances.

1. *The First Patent Act: Power Lodged in Principal Officers.* The nation's first patent statute, the Patent Act of 1790, lodged the power to grant patents in a board of three principal officers—the Secretary of State, the Secretary of War, and the Attorney General.[81] The power was significant because it was discretionary—the officers were authorized to issue a patent "if they shall deem the invention or discovery sufficiently useful and important."[82] Within that statutory grant of discretion, the Board developed some general principles to guide its assessments of patentability in future cases, according to Thomas

[79] *Id.* at 1985 (internal citations omitted).

[80] 35 U.S.C. § 282.

[81] Patent Act of 1790, ch. 7, 1 Stat. 109–110.

[82] *Id.* at 110.

Jefferson who served as Secretary of State while the first patent act was in force.[83] Yet the key point is that the three officers exercising the power were all principal officers.

2. *The 1793 Patent Act: Patent Registration and Minimal Power for "Arbitrators."* The 1790 Patent Act was quickly seen as impractical because the three principal officers charged with examining patents had very limited time to perform their many duties. As Jefferson described the problem, the "investigations" into patentability "occup[ied] more time of the members of the board than they could spare from higher duties."[84]

The successor to the 1790 statute—the Patent Act of 1793—addressed this issue by instituting a more pro forma registration system vested in the Secretary of State, leaving the ultimate determination of fully vested patent rights to a subsequent process of judicial review. Underscoring the point, William Thornton—appointed by the Secretary of State in 1802 to serve as the first "superintendent" of the Patent Office[85]—publicly stated in an 1811 pamphlet that then-existing law generally conferred "no discretionary power to refuse a patent."[86] So long as paperwork requirements were completed, a patent issued.[87]

This general rule was subject to only one exception that itself had minor legal import. Section 9 of the 1793 Act provided that in cases of "interfering applications"—where more than one applicant was seeking to patent the same invention—the matter should be "submitted to the arbitration of three persons" who as "arbitrators" would render a "decision . . . [that] shall be final, as far as respects the granting of the patent."[88]

---

[83] *See* Letter from Thomas Jefferson to Isaac MacPherson at 7 (Aug. 13, 1813) [hereinafter Jefferson Letter to Isaac MacPherson], https://www.loc.gov/resource/mtj1.046_1057_1065/ (mentioning some "general rules" governing the Board's determination "to grant or refuse patents" such as that "a change of material should not give title to a patent").

[84] *Id.*

[85] William I. Wyman, *The First Chief of the Patent Office*, 1 J. Pat. Off. Soc'y 152, 152 (1918).

[86] William Thornton, Patents (1811), *reprinted in* 6 J. Pat. Off. Soc'y 97, 98 (1923).

[87] *See* Jefferson Letter to Isaac MacPherson, *supra* note 83, at 8 (describing the 1793 statute as requiring patents to be issued as a matter "of course" to all applicants). The Senate report on the 1836 Patent Act also described the 1793 Patent Act as receiving "a practical construction" under which the grant of a patent was "but a ministerial duty." S. Rep. No. 24-338, at 2 (1836).

[88] Act of Feb. 21, 1793, § 9, 1 Stat. 318, 322–23.

At first glance, that authority might appear to lodge significant final decisional power in inferior officers, but it did not do so. As an initial matter, the process for appointing the arbiters was not constitutionally appropriate for "inferior officers," suggesting they were not viewed as officers. (In cases of two conflicting applicant claims, one arbiter would be "chosen by each of the applicants," with only the third appointed by the Secretary.) Confirming that instinct, subsequent court precedent interpreted the 1793 arbiter panel actions to have no conclusive power, therefore indicating that their decisions may not even have constituted an exercise of sovereign authority.

The key precedent is *Stearns v. Barrett*, authored by Justice Story riding circuit.[89] Stearns and Barrett filed interfering applications for the same patent rights and thus were subject to the procedures in the statute's arbitration scheme. When the conflicting claims came to light in the Patent Office, Stearns offered to submit the matter to arbitration. Barrett, however, refused to name his choice for an arbitrator, which caused the patent to issue to Stearns under the 1793 provision providing that "if either of the applicants shall refuse or fail to ch[oo]se an arbitrator, the patent shall issue to the opposite party."[90] Nonetheless, Barrett subsequently obtained his own patent on the same subject.[91] Stearns then sued Barrett under a provision allowing a party to seek a judicial order to "repeal" the issuance of the patent that had been obtained "surreptitiously, or upon false suggestion."[92]

On appeal in circuit court, Justice Story rejected the argument that Barrett had obtained his patent surreptitiously or falsely even though he refused to join in the arbitration and then applied for, and obtained, his own patent on the same invention that had already been patented by Stearns under the arbitration provisions of the 1793 Act. Story reasoned that even if the arbitration had gone forward, the arbitrators' decision "would not have been conclusive" on the issue of who was first inventor—a matter that could, for example, be raised and litigated between the same parties in any subsequent infringement litigation.[93] Because the arbitration itself was not conclusive, "a

[89] 22 F. Cas. 1175 (C.C.D. Mass. 1816).

[90] § 9, 1 Stat. at 323.

[91] 22 F. Cas. at 1176.

[92] § 10, 1 Stat. at 323.

[93] 22 F. Cas. at 1182.

fortiori, a refusal to join in an arbitration under the statute cannot be so."[94] This decision by Justice Story essentially rendered the arbitration process voluntary because if one party declined to submit to arbitration, that party could simply file another application and obtain the second of two patents issued by the government on the same invention. In that case, it would be left to courts to decide which was valid.[95] That result was theoretically consistent both with a patent system based on registration in which, as Jefferson had said, the whole matter of patent validity was "turn[ed] over to the judiciary,"[96] and with the concept of an arbitration process that is based on "mutual consent"[97] that thus lacks any sovereign effect.

3. *The 1836 Act: The Limited Power of Boards of Three Disinterested Persons.* The 1836 Patent Act fundamentally changed this registration system, replacing it with administrative examination of patent applications. The Patent Office had power to examine and deny patent applications on the ground that the applicant was not entitled to a patent,[98] subject to the supervision of the newly created office of the "Commissioner of Patents" who was appointed by the President with Senate advice and consent.[99]

The Commissioner's examination duties were subject, in every case where an applicant was dissatisfied with the Commissioner's decision, to an "appeal" to a board of "three disinterested persons" who were to be "appointed for that purpose by the Secretary of State."[100] Such boards could "reverse the decision of the Commissioner" whose subsequent

---

[94] *Id.*

[95] The case law appears never to have addressed the less common situation of three or more parties seeking the same patent rights. In such situations, the statute provided that if the parties failed to agree on the naming of the three arbitrators, then the Secretary of State could appoint all three. The reasoning of the *Stearns* case—that the arbitration process should not be viewed as "conclusive"—would still seem applicable in such circumstances.

[96] Jefferson Letter to Isaac MacPherson, *supra* note 83, at 8.

[97] 1 John Bouvier, A Law Dictionary Adapted to the Constitution and Laws of the United States 87 (T. & T.W. Johnson eds., Law Booksellers 1839); *see also id.* (noting that although arbitrations could be either "voluntary or compulsory," compulsory arbitrations are "perhaps confined to Pennsylvania").

[98] Act of July 4, 1836, § 7, 5 Stat. 117, 119–20.

[99] *Id.* § 7 (imposing examination duties on the Commissioner); § 1, 5 Stat. 117–18 (creating the position of Commissioner and specifying the appointment process); § 2, 5 Stat. 118 (referring to the Commissioner as a "principal officer"). Though the Commissioner was a principal officer, he was still subject to the "direction of the Secretary of State" as the Patent Office was a component of the Department of State. *Id.* § 1, 5 Stat. 117–18.

[100] *Id.* § 7, 5 Stat. 117, 120.

proceedings were to "be governed" by the Board's decision.[101] The Board's power to reverse the Commissioner extended to both cases in which only one applicant sought a patent on an invention and cases of interfering applications involving two or more inventors.[102]

The power of such boards of examiners to reverse a Commissioner decision, and to control the Commissioner's subsequent actions, may appear at first like a very significant power that should be exercised only by officers of the United States—and indeed, by principal officers. After all, each such board was being given power to reverse a determination of a Senate-confirmed, principal officer (the Commissioner). Yet as with the arbitrators of the 1793 Act, the examiners had only temporary positions and likely were considered private actors rather than officers. The language of the 1836 Act seemed to reflect that point. In section 2 of the 1836 Act, Congress did authorize the appointment of "an inferior officer . . . to be called the Chief Clerk of the Patent Office."[103] By contrast, in vesting the Secretary of State with the power to appoint boards of examiners, the statute describes the examiners as "disinterested persons" rather than "officers."[104]

Moreover, the actual power of the board of examiners was much less than what a modern lawyer might assume. During the registration era that preceded the 1836 Act, federal circuit court authority held that a patent itself was merely "prima facie evidence, and no more, of the right of the patentee to the subject patented."[105] The caveat "and no more" is significant. The leading commentator of the era, writing just after the enactment of the 1836 Patent Act, maintained that the prima facie weight that courts afforded patents as evidence of entitlement was "slight," was "not a matter of great practical importance," and was based only on the view that, because patent applicants had to file affidavits with the Patent Office attesting to the fact of invention, such affidavits could be "presum[ed] . . . to be true until the contrary is

---

[101] *Id.*

[102] *Id.* § 8, 5 Stat. 117, 121 (authorizing parties disappointed by a Commission decision in an interference to appeal in the same manner as in other Commission decisions concerning patent applications).

[103] *Id.* § 2, 5 Stat. 117, 118.

[104] *Id.* § 7, 5 Stat. 117, 120.

[105] Pennock v. Dialogue, 19 F. Cas. 171, 172 (C.C.E.D. Pa. 1825) (opinion by Justice Washington riding circuit). *See also* Stearns v. Barrett, 22 F. Cas. 1175, 1182 (C.C.D. Mass. 1816) (also treating the patent as prima facie evidence of the patentee's entitlement).

shown."[106] Subsequently, the Supreme Court opined in 1854 that during the registration era, patents were not "even prima facie evidence" and that "the plaintiff [in an infringement case] was bound to prove [the facts of novelty and utility] in order to make out his case."[107] That same 1854 precedent taught that after the advent of the 1836 Act's examination system, "a patent may be and generally is received as *prima facie* evidence of the truth of the facts asserted in it," and that it "may have weight with a jury"[108]—a fairly modest weight akin to a plaintiff's offering of a legally admissible expert opinion.

The real power granted to the Commissioner of Patents under the 1836 Act was the power to *deny* patent rights. While patent grants were still reviewed essentially de novo in the court, the denial of a patent would prevent an alleged inventor from ever getting to court. Board reversal of the Commissioner's decision to deny a patent was, at the time, considered relatively inconsequential because the grant of the patent carried so little weight. By contrast, the examiner boards themselves had no authority to deny patents that the Commissioner thought should issue. Thus, denials of patents—the real power granted in the 1836 Act—had to have the concurrence of the Commissioner.

The leading patent treatise writer of the time laid bare the pro forma task conducted by board members, each of whom was limited by statute to receiving no more than $10 (approximately $250 in current dollars) for each adjudication.[109] Phillips emphasized that "a common laborer . . . could hardly, at this rate of compensation, afford the time for an investigation of such a case."[110] Phillips opined that the small compensation demonstrated that the statute intended "only a very hasty and superficial trial" in which a board should not "reject the claim except in a very plain case."[111] Granting a patent—i.e., overturning the Commissioner's decision to deny a patent—meant only that the

[106] Willard Phillips, The Law of Patents for Inventions 406 (1837).

[107] Corning v. Burden, 56 U.S. 252, 271 (1854).

[108] *Id.*

[109] Act of July 4, 1836, § 7, 5 Stat. 117, 120. The inflation adjustment is based on the formula and data provided by the Federal Reserve Bank of Minnesota. *See Consumer Price Index, 1800-*, Fed. Rsrv. Bank Minneapolis, https://www.minneapolisfed.org/about-us/monetary-policy/inflation-calculator/consumer-price-index-1800-. Other inflation adjustments provide similar figures.

[110] Phillips, *supra* note 106, at 319. The 1836 Act fixed the salary of the Chief Clerk of the Patent Office at $1,700 per year. § 2, 5 Stat. 117, 118.

[111] *Id.*

Board would allow the matter of patent validity to be eventually tested in court, and that course could work "no material injury."[112] By contrast, the decision to deny a patent—which Phillips noted was a matter of "great" consequence that could "irreparabl[y]" harm the applicant's asserted rights[113]—could occur, excepting the situation of interfering applications, only where the Commissioner was in agreement with the reviewing board.

Interference proceedings where two competing applications were simultaneously under consideration presented a slightly different case, but ultimately of similarly little legal consequence. A board could reverse a Commissioner's decision granting priority to one applicant and decide that a competing applicant, or none of the applicants, should obtain a patent. This might sound of greater legal significance, but such determinations were subject to immediate judicial review and occurred prior to the grant of any patent, as part of the technical evaluation process of which party had a patentable invention. In section 16 of the 1836 Act, any party dissatisfied with a board decision in an interference could file a bill in equity to have a court "adjudge" whether the applicant was entitled to receive a patent "according to the principles and provisions of this act."[114] As the Supreme Court would hold 176 years later in interpreting a statute descended from the provision, such language indicates that the court must "make its own findings *de novo*" if the party challenging the agency's decision presents any new evidence in court.[115] Under the reasoning of that Supreme Court precedent, the boards of examiners held a quite modest influence on a question that did not constitute a final determination of a legal right.

4. *The Act of 1839: Commencing More Than a Century of Senate-Confirmed Agency Adjudicators.* The Act of March 3, 1839, amended the Patent Act to abolish the ad hoc boards of examiners, replacing their review with the opportunity to appeal to "the chief justice of the district court of the United States for the District of Columbia,"[116] who was an Article III federal judge appointed by the President with

---

[112] *Id.*

[113] *Id.*

[114] § 16, 5 Stat. at 124.

[115] Kappos v. Hyatt, 566 U.S. 431, 438 (2012).

[116] Act of March 3, 1839, § 11, 5 Stat. 353, 354.

the advice and consent of the Senate.[117] Although the judge's duties were nonjudicial in nature,[118] the 1839 statute's relocation of the appellate duties from ad hoc boards to a federal judge nonetheless began a period lasting more than a century in which the ultimate decisional power on patent grants and denials was firmly in control of presidentially appointed, Senate-confirmed officers. The 1839 statute also expanded to all parties dissatisfied with the denial of patent rights the de novo review procedure originally authorized in 1836 for applicants in interferences.[119] Like under the 1793 and 1836 Acts, patent grants continued to be of relatively little consequence in comparison to their modern significance because the issued patent constituted little more than "prima facie" evidence of patent validity.[120]

---

[117] The Judiciary Act of 1801 originally created the position as the "chief judge" of the circuit court of the District of Columbia. *See* Act of Feb. 27, 1801, § 3, 2 Stat. 103, 105. No appointment method was specified in the statute, so the default Appointments Clause method (by the President with the advice and consent of the Senate) applied. The chief judge was an Article III judge given tenure "during good behavior" and given powers identical to those of the judges of the other U.S. circuit courts. *Id.* The chief judge was authorized "to hold a district court" for the District of Columbia in 1802. Act of Apr. 29, 1802, § 24, 2 Stat. 156, 166. Even though the statute creating the position used the term "chief judge," subsequent statutes used the term "chief justice" in describing the head judge of the "circuit court for the district of Columbia." *See, e.g.*, Act of Mar. 3, 1811, 2 Stat. 660 (raising the salary of the "chief justice" and "assistant judges" of the court). The duties were exercised by Judge William Cranch who was the chief judge of the circuit court of the District of Columbia. *See* 1 Laws of the United States Relating to Patents and the Patent Office 87–150 (1848) (setting forth the patent decisions of Judge Cranch in appeals from the Commissioner of Patents).

[118] The duty was imposed on the judge, not a court, because the duty was plainly an extrajudicial duty in assisting the Patent Office in processing patent applications. The chief "justice" would "revise [the Commissioner's] decisions in a summary way" and thereafter "return all the papers to the Commissioner, with a certificate of his proceedings and decision, which shall be entered of record in the Patent Office." § 11, 5 Stat. at 355. As the Supreme Court would later rule, deciding administrative appeals from the Commissioner of Patents was "not the exercise of ordinary jurisdiction at law or in equity" but was instead "one step in the statutory proceeding [conducted] in aid of the patent-office." Butterworth v. United States *ex rel.* Hoe, 112 U.S. 50, 60 (1884). Further demonstrating that the duties were not considered judicial, Congress granted the chief justice of the District of Columbia an extra $100 "in consideration of the duties imposed" by the 1839 statute. § 13, 5 Stat. at 355.

[119] § 10, 5 Stat. at 354 (granting parties in "all cases where patents are refused for any reason whatever" the right to file a bill in equity ("served upon the Commissioner" in non-interference cases) and thereby obtain a judicial decision as to the party's entitlement to rights).

[120] Corning v. Burden, 56 U.S. 252, 271 (1854) (holding that because patent applications were then being "issued after an inquisition or examination" conducted "by skilful and sworn public officers," patent grants could be "received as *prima facie* of the truth of the facts asserted in it"—and could perhaps be given a bit more weight too: "[I]n cases where the evidence is nicely balanced, [the patent] may have weight with a jury in making up their decision as to the plaintiff's right"; *see also* Caleb Nelson, *Vested Rights, "Franchises," and the Separation of Powers*, 169 U. Pa. L. Rev. 1429, 1515 (2020) (discussing briefly the legal role of the 1839 review process).

The end result is that at the time of the 1839 statute, there were three bulwarks against the diffusion of too much power in lower-level administrative officials. First, the ultimate power for deciding the grant and denial of patent applications was located in presidentially appointed, Senate-confirmed officers. Second, decisions to deny patents were subject to de novo review in courts. Third, grants of patent rights were also subject to something close to de novo review. By the time of *Arthrex*, all three of these limitations had vanished.

5. *Principal Officer Decisionmaking and Aggrandizement of Administrative Power: 1839–1975.* For a century and a third following the 1839 enactment, Patent Office decisions on granting and denying patent applications were firmly controlled by presidentially appointed, Senate-confirmed officers. Decisions over patent applications in "ex parte" cases (where no interfering application or patent conflicted with the rights sought in the application) were formally vested with the Commissioner of Patents. In interferences, power was vested either in a board of presidentially appointed, Senate-confirmed officers[121] or in the Commissioner (either directly or via his control over examiners).[122] While as a practical matter the Commissioner was assisted by an ever-increasing cadre of patent examiners, statutory law required the Commissioner "to superintend or perform all the duties respecting the granting and issuing of patents."[123]

During this time, the legal consequences of the Patent Office's adjudications were on the rise. In the second half of the nineteenth and the first half of the twentieth centuries, the courts began to develop increasingly strong presumptions in favor of the validity of the Patent Office's decisions,[124] and that doctrine was eventually codified in the 1952 Patent Act's statutory presumption of validity.[125]

---

[121] *See, e.g.*, Act of Mar. 2, 1927, § 3, 44 Stat. 1335, 1335–36 (vesting power concerning interferences in a board of appeals, the members of which were at the time all appointed by the President with the advice and consent of the Senate).

[122] *See, e.g.*, Act of July 6, 1870, § 205, 16 Stat. 198, 205 (authorizing any party dissatisfied with a decision on an application or in interference to "appeal to the commissioner in person"); Patent Act of 1952, § 135, 66 Stat. 792, 801 (authorizing interferences to be heard by three "examiners of interferences").

[123] Act of July 8, 1870, § 7, 16 Stat. 198, 199; *see also* Patent Act of 1952, Pub. L. No. 593, § 6, 66 Stat. 792, 793 (containing similar language).

[124] *See* Radio Corp. of Am. v. Radio Eng'g Lab'y, Inc., 293 U.S. 1, 7–8 (1934) (collecting late nineteenth- and early twentieth-century cases in support of granting a presumption of validity to issued patents).

[125] *See* 35 U.S.C. § 282(a).

As the lower courts and eventually the Supreme Court held, the statutory presumption of validity requires parties challenging issued patents to prove invalidity by clear and convincing evidence.[126] That rule, and other associated rules of administrative deference, made the administrative adjudications of the Patent Office all the more consequential.

B. *ARTHREX* AT THE PATENT OFFICE: LIMITS AND RESPONSIBILITIES OF THE SUPERVISORY POWER

The history of the patent system demonstrates that, prior to the past half-century, the decisional power vested in executive branch officers was either (i) very modest or (ii) vested in presidentially appointed, Senate-confirmed officers. Early on, it was both of those, but by the time of *Arthrex*, it was neither. Large powers—including the power to revoke issued patents in adversarial proceedings between private parties—were vested by statutory law in inferior officers. The holding in *Arthrex* moves the system towards a new structure where large powers are vested in a single office, the office of the Director, that is generally (though not always) filled with Senate-confirmed presidential appointees. An important question for the future is whether that new status quo represents a return to tradition. An answer requires assessing the scope of the Director's new power.

1. *The Maximum of the Director's Supervisory Power.* Under the reasoning of the Court's *Arthrex* decision, the Director's power to supervise and revise Board decisions is almost certainly not subject to any upper legal limits as to the frequency or scope of its use. The Director could in theory review all Board decisions and change every one of them. While such a result seems dramatic, it has historical precedent. The 1870 Patent Act explicitly gave all parties "dissatisfied" with any final agency decision the *right* to appeal "in person"[127] to the Patent Office's head (then called the "Commissioner of Patents").[128]

---

[126] *See* Microsoft Corp. v. i4i Ltd. P'ship, 564 U.S. 91 (2011).

[127] § 47, 16 Stat. at 205 (authorizing parties dissatisfied with any decision of the "examiners-in-chief" to "appeal to the commissioner in person"). The statute routed all decisions on patent applications, applications for reissue of patents and patent interferences through a board of examiners-in-chief, *id.* § 46, 16 Stat. at 204–05, so the right to appeal to the commissioner covered all cases in the Office.

[128] § 2, 16 Stat. at 198.

Yet while a broad use of the Director's supervisory powers is legally permissible under *Arthrex* and has historical precedent, it seems practically unlikely for two reasons. First, the Director's time is limited. The original Patent Act of 1790 vested the power to grant patents in cabinet-level officials, but it was short-lived precisely because high-level officials cannot do—and have little inclination to do—a vast bulk of routine work. While later patent statutes such as the 1870 Act vested the head of the Patent Office with a broad and mandatory supervisory role over the work of the Office, that work has expanded greatly in the last 150 years to the point where no single individual could be expected to pass "in person" on every contested matter within the Office.[129]

A second pragmatic consideration is delay. When the PTAB was created and given power to review the validity of issued patents, Congress included statutory time limits on each step in the process. Most importantly, the agency is supposed to reach a "final determination" in inter partes review and other post-issuance proceedings "not later than 1 year" after the "institution" of proceedings, and that period can be extended by only six months "for good cause shown."[130] The statute then plainly calls for expediting reviews of issued patents in proceedings before the Board, and the Director's supervisory review significantly retards that process.

An example of the inevitable delays caused by directorial review can already be seen in the Director's first grant of rehearing, which occurred on November 1, 2021.[131] The Board proceeding there was instituted on July 16, 2020, and the Board's decision was rendered on July 15, 2021, one day before the expiration of the normal statutory deadline of one year.[132] The Director reversed the Board decision on

[129] The number of patent applications per year has grown more than thirtyfold from 1870 to 2020, *see U.S. Patent Activity Calendar Years 1790 to the Present*, U.S. Patent & Trademark Off. https://www.uspto.gov/web/offices/ac/ido/oeip/taf/h_counts.htm (reporting 19,171 applications in 1870 and 597,175 applications in 2020). The agency has also been tasked to perform a set of new-issuance procedures for determining patent validity after patent issuance—a task that was the province of the courts in the nineteenth century.

[130] 35 U.S.C. §§ 316(a)(11), 326(a)(11). The decision to initiate or "institute" full proceedings is also statutorily required to happen quickly; it must occur "within 3 months" after the close of briefing on a petition to institute proceedings. *Id.* §§ 314(b), 324(c).

[131] *See* Order Granting Request for Director Review, Ascend Performance v. Samsung, IPR2020-00349 (P.T.A.B. Nov. 1, 2021) (granting review by Andrew Hirshfeld, Commissioner for Patents, performing the functions and duties of the Director of the USPTO).

[132] *See* Termination Decision Document at 2, *Ascend Performance*, IPR2020-00349 (P.T.A.B. July 15, 2021) (recounting the procedural history of the administrative proceedings).

one point of law and remanded the case back to the Board. It has now remained pending there past January 16, 2022, the outer limit of the maximum eighteen-month period for the agency to reach a "final determination" under the statutory scheme.

The Director's supervisory review of the Board has thus pushed the agency proceedings past the statutory time limits for final determinations. That does not necessarily mean that supervisory review by the Director required by *Arthrex* has violated the statutory time limits—the statutory deadline for reaching a "final determination" could be construed to cover only the *Board's* decisional process. Yet even if the Director's supervisory review and any further proceedings thereafter are not counted within the statutory time periods, the exercise of the Director's supervisory review power will slow the process substantially. Congress might want to consider taking account of such time delays in crafting a new mandatory deadline for the issuance of Director review determinations. Congress might also find it beneficial to enact statutory provisions regulating the Director's new Court-mandated decisional review process so that future Directors are not left with discretion to fashion their own review procedures free from any externally imposed review criteria or procedural requirements.

In the hands of a willful Director, *Arthrex*'s supervisory review power left unregulated by Congress could in theory stall the agency's post-issuance proceedings indefinitely. That prospect is unlikely given that the Director already has the far greater, and unreviewable, power to deny institution of all post-issuance proceedings in their entirety. Indeed, the Director may very well exercise the *Arthrex* supervisory power sparingly to avoid the pragmatic problem of excessive delay of final determinations of patent validity.

2. *The Minimum of the Director's Supervisory Power.* More interesting than the maximum extent of the Director's power is the question of the minimum amount that the power must be exercised in terms of the scope and frequency of review. A good thought experiment to evaluate the issue is to consider a hypothetical rule stating that all Board decisions are, thirty days after they are issued, automatically adopted as decisions of the Director unless and until the Director repeals the rule. Parties could seek repeal of the rule or an exception from it, but the Director could reject such petitions as a matter of general policy without passing on the particulars of the case. Specifically, the Director could reject such petitions merely by saying (in every case) that "the Director continues to have confidence in the

decisions of the Board and, as of yet, has found no sufficient reason for deviating from a general policy of adopting the Board's decisions as the Director's decisions."

Under the Supreme Court's *Arthrex* decision, it's not clear that such a rule would be unlawful. The *Arthrex* Court itself made clear that the Director must have the power to overturn decisions of the Board, but it nowhere said explicitly that the Director had to exercise that power with any degree of frequency. To the contrary, the controlling plurality opinion said the Director "need not review every decision of the PTAB."[133] Left unanswered then is whether the Director must exercise the power in *any* case. A very basic principle of administrative law allows agencies nearly unfettered freedom to choose to do by rulemaking what they could otherwise do by adjudication.[134] The Director can clearly decline review in individual cases by adjudication—the controlling plurality in *Arthrex* said so—and so basic principles of administrative law would suggest the Director has the ability to do so by rule too.

Even aside from principles of administrative law, such a rule is not necessarily inconsistent with the precise holding of *Arthrex*. In *Arthrex*, section 6(c) of the Patent Act presented an apparent statutory barrier preventing the Director from exercising review in any case. The Court's declaration that section 6(c) could not constitutionally be enforced against the Director removes that apparent barrier. The controlling plurality opinion emphasized that "[w]hat matters is that the Director have the *discretion* to review decisions rendered by APJs."[135] A Director does not lose that discretion merely because she chooses, by rule, not to exercise it and instead leaves the matter with certain delegees of power.

The hypothetical rule posited here is unlikely to be promulgated because it might be viewed as circumventing *Arthrex*'s apparent requirement that some form of executive supervision over APJs is "necessary."[136] Rather, Directors now and in the future are likely to continue the practice currently developing, which is to grant review

[133] United States v. Arthrex, 141 S. Ct. 1970, 1988 (2021) (Roberts, C.J.) (plurality opinion).

[134] *See, e.g.*, Heckler v. Campbell, 461 U.S. 458, 467 (1983); M. Elizabeth Magill, *Agency Choice of Policymaking Form*, 71 U. CHI. L. REV. 1383, 1408 (2004) (emphasizing "the breadth of an agency's discretion to choose between rulemaking and adjudication" under administrative law precedents).

[135] 141 S. Ct. at 1988 (Roberts, C.J.) (plurality opinion) (emphasis added).

[136] *Id.* at 1982–83 (describing supervision and control as a "necessity").

in a small number of cases, point out an error in one part of the Board decision being reviewed, and then remand the case to the Board for further proceedings. But the hypothetical rule posited here raises a highly significant question that is already being litigated, the question whether the Constitution poses any constraints on the Director's ability to delegate the *Arthrex* review power.

Indeed, the Director has by rule delegated to the Board the entirety of the power to make final decisions concerning whether to institute post-issuance review proceedings, even though that power was vested by statute in the Director. Institution decisions can be very consequential, and courts have generally held them unreviewable.[137] Delegation of the supervisory power mandated by *Arthrex* would seem analogous to the already delegated statutory power over institution decisions.

3. *The Director's Power to Delegate: Constitutional Considerations.* Questions regarding the Director's ability to delegate the supervisory power recognized in *Arthrex* may have constitutional overtones. The Court's case law since at least *Freytag v. Commissioner of Internal Revenue*[138] has established that the Constitution imposes some constraints on the degree to which *statutory* law can confer authority on lower-level officials who lack a valid appointment under the Appointments Clause. Importantly, while the Clause can operate to protect the prerogatives of the Executive Branch, it also was designed generally to limit the "diffusion" of the appointment power within government as a protection against "despotism."[139] Such a policy seems to be a general limit on the structure of government—a limit not only on what Congress can do by law but also what the executive can do by rule, order, or practice.

Arthrex seems to confirm that approach to the Appointments Clause, for the Court speaks in terms of imposing a "responsibility" for principal officers to provide "necessary supervision" of inferior officers.[140] Indeed, the Court begins its legal analysis by making an explicit reference to the President's "responsibility" for all Executive Branch actions which, the Court states, carries an "active obligation

---

[137] *See* Thryv, Inc. v. Click-To-Call Techs., 140 S. Ct. 1367 (2020) (relying on 35 U.S.C. § 314(d) to hold that decisions whether to institute inter partes review, and closely related decisions, are precluded from being judicially reviewed).

[138] Freytag v. Comm'r of Internal Revenue, 501 U.S. 868 (1991).

[139] *Id.* at 883.

[140] *Arthrex*, 141 S. Ct. at 1982.

to supervise" that "cannot [be] delegate[d]."[141] From that introduction, the Court's legal analysis includes multiple passages that describe the supervisory responsibility of principal officers in mandatory terms.

The constitutional questions related to the extent to which the *Arthrex* power can be delegated might be presented by a delegation framework in two distinct ways. First, as previously mentioned, the officer who has been exercising the *Arthrex* power for more than six months is an inferior officer, Commissioner for Patents Drew Hirshfeld, who is currently exercising the functions and duties of the Director while that office is vacant. Commissioner Hirshfeld has not been appointed as an "Acting Director" under the relevant provisions of the Vacancies Reform Act.[142] Thus, the government is currently defending his exercise of the *Arthrex* review power on the theory that the Director's review power recognized in *Arthrex* is delegable, including to "a subordinate selected by the principal."[143] If the *Arthrex* power is fully delegable, then Commissioner Hirshfeld could continue to exercise that power without having an appointment as an acting officer under the Vacancies Reform Act. Indeed, he could continue to exercise the power even after a new Director is appointed if the new Director chose to keep the delegation of that responsibility in place.

But delegation of the power might indeed be unlawful under the holding and reasoning of *Arthrex*. Section 6(c) of the statute authorizes the Board alone, which must sit in panels of three, to rehear Board decisions, and the Supreme Court held that statute unenforceable *only with respect to the Director*.[144] Thus, the statute may continue to bar anyone else in the Patent Office from exercising any power of review over the Board's decisions. If so, then the Director's *Arthrex* review power may not be delegable, perhaps leaving the Secretary of Commerce as the only actor capable of exercising the review power in the absence of a confirmed director.[145]

---

141 *Id.* at 1978–79.

142 *See* Corrected Brief for the Intervenor at 17, Virnetx, Inc. v. Mangrove Partners Master Fund, Ltd., Nos. 2020-2271, 2020-2272 (P.T.A.B. Feb. 4, 2022) (brief filed by the Patent Office conceding this point). The Federal Vacancies Reform Act of 1998, 5 U.S.C. §§ 3345–3349d generally regulates the appointment of acting officers.

143 *See* Corrected Brief for the Intervenor, *supra* note 142, at 23.

144 *See Arthrex*, 141 S. Ct. at 1987 (Roberts, C.J.) (plurality opinion).

145 The Vacancies Reform Act provides that, where there is a vacancy in an office without any acting officer and there are functions and duties required by statute or regulation "to be

Another posture in which the constitutional delegation questions might arise is where a litigant argues that the Director is not actually supervising the Board's decisions but is in fact delegating the matter to underlying staff who may have no appointment whatsoever. The stakes for such a challenge are high. If the courts reject such a challenge, then the end result of *Arthrex* is likely to be a cadre of office staff reviewing and supervising the decisions of inferior officers on the Board. In other words, mere employees will be supervising the work of actual officers (albeit inferior officers). That may seem like an inversion of tradition, but it need not be seen as unconstitutional. If the Director were still formally accountable and responsible for any review, or nonreview, determination, such formal accountability might well be all the Constitution requires.[146]

On the other hand, if the courts sustain such a challenge, then the Director would almost certainly not be able to keep up with such supervisory responsibilities and the Board's work would grind to a halt. Some formidable doctrinal hurdles stand in the way of such a challenge prevailing. Most prominently, the Supreme Court's 1941 *Morgan* precedent appears to prevent courts from looking behind the formalities of administrative processes to determine how executive branch action is actually functioning.[147] Yet the Court's ruling in the *Census Case* suggests that judicial inquiry into the internal processes of executive branch agencies is not absolutely forbidden.[148] And the Court's earlier decision in the *Morgan* litigation, which famously stated that "[t]he one who decides must hear,"[149] could suggest that agency heads have some constitutional minimum in terms of the care with which they review decisions of their delegees.

performed by [that] officer (and only that officer)," those functions and duties cannot be delegated. *See* 5 U.S.C. § 3348(a)(2)(A) (defining the functions and duties for which appointments under the Vacancies Reform Act are the exclusive means for continuing to have those functions and duties exercised in the event of a vacancy); *see also* 5 U.S.C. § 3348(b)(2) (permitting only the head of the executive agency to exercise nondelegable functions and duties).

[146] *See supra* note 20 and accompanying text.

[147] *See* United States v. Morgan, 313 U.S. 409, 422 (1941) (analogizing an administrator making an adjudicative decision to a judge and instructing that an administrator should not be subjected to an examination about the process by which he reached his decision because "a judge cannot be subjected to such a scrutiny").

[148] Dep't of Com. v. New York, 139 S. Ct. 2551, 2573–74 (2019) (recognizing "a narrow exception to the general rule against inquiring into 'the mental processes of administrative decisionmakers'" and finding the exception applicable in the case) (quoting Citizens to Preserve Overton Park, Inc. v. Volpe, 401 U.S. 402, 420 (1971)).

[149] Morgan v. United States, 298 U.S. 468, 481 (1936).

The fundamental problem here is the very untraditional dearth of presidential appointees in the agency subject to direct supervision and ultimately potential removal by the President. Prior to 1975, Congress was consistently adding more presidentially appointed political officers to keep up with the work and to maintain the tradition of principal officer adjudication of significant matters in the Patent Office. If Congress does not expand the number of presidential appointees, then the courts must choose between two undesirable options: (i) to permit significant de jure or de facto delegations of supervisory power, or (ii) to impose an overwhelming supervisory responsibility on the sole presidential appointee in the Office. The former path will break *Arthrex*'s apparent promise of ensuring "a transparent decision for which a politically accountable officer must take responsibility."[150] The latter path could practically halt the Board's work and contradict the plurality's assurance that it was not creating an "unworkable statutory scheme."[151]

III. *Arthrex* and *Morrison*: Inverting the Traditions of Adjudication and Prosecution?

The most important thing to know about the *Arthrex* Court's treatment of its prior precedent *Morrison v. Olson*[152] is that the Court ignored the precedent entirely. Though both the United States and Smith & Nephew relied on *Morrison* in seeking to sustain the legality of the judges' appointments,[153] the majority opinion does not include even a passing "*cf.*" cite to *Morrison*.[154] The same is true for the Chief Justice's controlling plurality opinion on remedy.[155] Justice Gorsuch's opinion concurring on the Appointments Clause issue cites only the *Morrison* dissent.[156] In his dissent on the constitutional issue, Justice Breyer did cite *Morrison*, but only as subsequent appellate history to his quoting of then Judge Ruth Bader Ginsberg's

---

[150] *Arthrex*, 141 S. Ct. at 1982.

[151] *Id.* at 1987 (Roberts, C.J.) (plurality opinion).

[152] 487 U.S. 654 (1988).

[153] *See* Brief for the United States, *Arthrex*, 141 S. Ct. 1970 (Nos. 19–1434, 19–1452, and 19–1458), 2020 WL 7024946; Opening Brief for Smith & Nephew, Inc. and Arthrocare Corp., *Arthrex*, 141 S. Ct. 1970 (Nos. 19-1434, 19-1452, and 19-1458), 2020 WL 7060007.

[154] *See Arthrex*, 141 S. Ct. at 1976–86.

[155] *Id.* at 1986–88 (Roberts, C.J.) (plurality opinion).

[156] *See id.* at 1988 (Gorsuch, J., concurring in part and dissenting in part).

dissent in the D.C. Circuit.[157] Only Justice Thomas's dissent pays any attention to the *Morrison* majority opinion, but the attention is limited to a single paragraph making the general point that the Court has eschewed any "rigid test to divide principal officers . . . from inferior ones."[158] And even in that paragraph, *Morrison* is merely paired with Justice Scalia's opinion for the Court in *Edmond v. United States*.[159]

The Court's inattention to *Morrison* has been widely noticed, with a note in the *Harvard Law Review* describing it as the "*Lemon*-ization of *Morrison*," the turning of the precedent into "ghoul" that's not quite dead but not really alive either.[160] The total exclusion of *Morrison* was a step beyond the Court's treatment of the case in its recent separation of powers opinions. In decisions such as *Collins*,[161] *Seila Law*,[162] and *Free Enterprise Fund*,[163] the Court squarely acknowledged the continued validity of *Morrison* but distinguished it based on the status of the officers in those cases having control over an entire agency or being insulated from presidential control by two layers of for-cause removal.

In *Arthrex*, no such hierarchical distinctions with *Morrison* were readily apparent. Both the patent judges and the independent counsel were subject to removal by an executive department head who was freely removable by the President—the APJs by the Commerce Secretary and the independent counsel by the Attorney General. Therefore, neither officer was even arguably subject to the double for-cause problem cited by the Court in *Free Enterprise Fund*.[164] And neither the patent judges nor the independent counsel were situated at the top of an entire executive agency—making both positions distinct from the tenure-protected positions of the head of the Consumer Financial Protection Bureau and the Federal Housing Finance Agency that the Court found unconstitutional in, respectively, *Seila Law*[165] and *Collins*.[166]

---

[157] *See id.*

[158] *See id.* at 1999 (Thomas, J., dissenting).

[159] *Id.*

[160] *Separation of Powers—Appointment and Removal—Principal and Inferior Officers*—United States v. Arthrex, 135 HARV. L. REV. 391, 400 (2021) [hereinafter *Separation of Powers*].

[161] Collins v. Yellen, 141 S. Ct. 1761 (2021).

[162] Seila Law LLC v. Consumer Fin. Prot. Bureau, 140 S. Ct. 2183, 2199–2201 (2020).

[163] Free Enter. Fund v. Pub. Co. Acct. Oversight Bd., 561 U.S. 477, 494–95 (2010).

[164] *See id.* at 492.

[165] *See Seila Law LLC*, 140 S. Ct. at 2197.

[166] *See Collins*, 141 S. Ct. at 1783.

Nonetheless, the Court concluded in *Arthrex* that the current statutory structure unconstitutionally empowered APJs as "inferior officers" to reach final executive branch decisions without review, while *Morrison* had upheld a structure under which independent counsel decisions bearing the full weight of the prosecutorial authority of the federal government were subject to no direct review. And due to the Court's silence about *Morrison*, the current state of the law is that *Morrison* remains a seemingly valid precedent of the Court because it has never been overruled although its precedential effect seems increasingly limited just to its precise facts.[167]

The key result in *Morrison* then—the part that's most difficult to reconcile with *Arthrex*—is the independent counsel's ability, despite her status as an inferior officer, to be free from supervision in making final decisions about who to indict and who to let go. *Arthrex* can be reconciled with the result but only by drawing a line between prosecution and adjudication—a line without any immediately apparent justification. The Court in *Arthrex* expressly states that the Court is addressing supervision only within "the context of adjudication."[168] But it never explains why that context would be any different than the need for supervision over exercises of other categories of executive power. And, indeed, the Court also emphasizes generally that "since the founding, principal officers have directed the decisions of inferior officers on matters of law as well as policy" and "the exercise of executive power by inferior officers must at some level be subject to the direction and supervision of an officer nominated by the President and confirmed by the Senate."[169] Thus, under the technically limited scope of *Arthrex*, tenure-protected inferior officers can be appointed as unsupervised prosecutors but not as unsupervised adjudicators. Far from being traditional, that result is a complete inversion of centuries-old norms that have typically demanded prosecutors to be subject to more direct supervision than adjudicators within an executive chain of command that is ultimately subject to electoral accountability.

The apparent survival of *Morrison* remains relevant even if Congress never enacts another independent-counsel statute because the Department of Justice still has regulations permitting the Attorney

[167] *See Separation of Powers*, *supra* note 160, at 400.

[168] United States v. Arthrex, 141 S. Ct. 1970, 1986 (2021) (expressly stating that the Court was "not address[ing] supervision outside the context of adjudication").

[169] *Id.* at 1980, 1983.

General to appoint "Special Counsel[s]" who are guaranteed by regulation "not [to] be subject to the day-to-day supervision of any official of the Department."[170] If *Morrison* is a valid precedent, then such freedom from supervision is clearly constitutional. If, however, the rule in *Arthrex* were extended to prosecutorial function, then that regulation raises the very issue set forth as a hypothetical with respect to patent judges—whether there is a constitutional obligation on principal officers to supervise such that they cannot, by rule, delegate final decisions to inferior officers or other subordinates.

Morrison's value as a precedent has continuing practical implications, and yet it cannot be distinguished from *Arthrex* except along lines that would seem to make *Morrison* an easier case for finding the inferior officer unconstitutionally vested with too much unsupervised power. The situation is not stable. It would have been better—and more candid—if the *Arthrex* Court had disavowed some or all of the reasoning in *Morrison*. That approach would have respected the traditions of having prosecutors more subject to political control and adjudicators less so. In a broader sense, that approach would also be respecting the overarching tenor during the last century's worth of the Court's separation of powers precedents concerning executive control of subordinate officials. After the Court endorsed broad presidential powers to control subordinates in *Myers v. United States*,[171] *Humphrey's Executor* cast aside many of that precedent's teachings as "dicta" that could be "put[] aside."[172] *Morrison* in turn found that the Court's essential reasoning in *Humphrey*'s no longer comported with the Court's "present considered view."[173] The true tradition in this area is turbulence, but candid turbulence. *Arthrex* should have followed that tradition and "put aside" *Morrison*.

IV. Conclusion

The *Arthrex* decision has taken a positive step in trying to restore the traditional separation of powers approach to the supervision required within the Executive Branch's chain of command. But the step is at best a half-step, and it leaves the current law in a

[170] 28 C.F.R. § 600.7(b).

[171] 272 U.S. 52 (1926).

[172] 295 U.S. 602, 627 (1935).

[173] 487 U.S. 654, 689 (1988).

position that is decidedly untraditional. In ignoring *Morrison* entirely, the Court's precedents now require strong executive supervision of executive adjudications but not of prosecutions. In requiring executive supervision but leaving the content of that supervision unspecified, the Court has opened the door to de facto or de jure delegations of the supervisory power to agency employees having no constitutionally valid appointment.

On both points, the law seems unstable. As for *Morrison*, it seems prime for overruling. If principal officers in the Executive Branch have a constitutional power and responsibility to supervise executive adjudicators, a fortiori they should have same power and responsibility over other executive officers, especially prosecutors. Furthermore, *Arthrex* reiterates the constitutional importance of a "'clear and effective chain of command' down from the President" and relies on that imperative in requiring that final decisionmaking authority in adjudications be vested only in principal officers in that chain of command. Such reasoning further undermines the constitutional basis for the vast adjudicative powers vested in multi-member commissions currently headed by presidentially appointed, Senate-confirmed appointees who are not entirely accountable to the President due to statutory tenure protections.

The delegation issue seems far more difficult, but equally consequential. If the Court permits massive delegations of supervisory responsibility, then the *Arthrex* decision will do almost nothing to detract from the power of inferior officers in adjudications, except to shift a bit more power deeper in a bureaucratic staff having no necessary appointment or transparency. Yet if the Court tries to impose some obligation of supervision by a principal officer, it is likely to find that path difficult due to the dearth of principal officers available to do the work. The Patent and Trademark Office, with only a single principal officer position that has been vacant for a year, is a prime example. Tradition in that area may be unattainable without Congress restoring more principal officer positions in the Executive Branch who can then funnel the final decisionmaking authority up to the officer ultimately vested with the sole executive authority, the President.

RYAN D. DOERFLER

LATE-STAGE TEXTUALISM

Are "canons of construction" embarrassing?[1] For a long time, the answer was "yes." Exposed as "contradictory" by Karl Llewellyn, a generation of legal thinkers understood interpretive canons to be so malleable in their application as to operate mostly as pretext.[2] Rather than bring predictability to statutory decisions, the availability of more than one interpretive canon in nearly any appellate case meant that a canon's invocation worked mostly to obscure the choice (conscious or not) by judges between legally permissible outcomes.[3] Interpretive canons were thus tools of legal mystification, providing the appearance of law to what were, ultimately, acts of discretion.

Ryan D. Doerfler is Professor of Law, The University of Chicago Law School.

AUTHOR'S NOTE: Thanks to William Baude, Maggie Blackhawk, Brian Leiter, John Manning, Richard Re, and participants in the Colloquium on Constitutional Theory at New York University Law School, the Legislation Colloquium at Georgetown University Law Center, and the Public Law Colloquium at Northwestern Pritzker School of Law for helpful comments and suggestions, and to Alex Hall for exceptional research assistance.

[1] JOHN F. MANNING & MATTHEW C. STEPHENSON, LEGISLATION AND REGULATION: CASES AND MATERIALS 324 (4th ed. 2021) (describing "canons of construction" as "interpretive principles, or presumptions that judges use to discern—or, at times, construct—statutory meaning").

[2] Karl N. Llewellyn, *Remarks on the Theory of Appellate Decision and the Rules or Canons About How Statutes Are to Be Construed*, 3 VAND. L. REV. 395, 399 (1950).

[3] Importantly, Llewellyn did *not* defend global indeterminacy in either statutory or common law cases. Instead, he defended the much more modest (and much more plausible) thesis that legal indeterminacy was pervasive at the appellate stage. *See* Brian Leiter, *Legal Realism and Legal Positivism Reconsidered*, 111 ETHICS 278, 298–99 (2001).

The Supreme Court Review, 2022.
 Published by The University of Chicago Press. https://doi.org/10.1086/719651

This sort of skepticism about interpretive canons persisted at least until the "textualist revolution" of the late 1980s and early 1990s.[4] Partly a successful political project by elite conservative lawyers and elected officials, the elevation of a text-centric approach to statutory interpretation within the federal judiciary created a receptive environment for legal doctrines concerned mostly with sentence- and word-level inference. At the same time, legal theorists within the textualist movement helped to reconceive interpretive canons in ways that would insulate them from earlier critiques. In particular, these "modern" textualists incorporated insights from philosophers of language and linguists concerning language's practical character and, correspondingly, the sensitivity of language to interpretive context.[5] Viewed through this linguistic pragmatist lens,[6] interpretive canons were not to be thought of as "mechanical[]" rules of the sort Llewellyn understandably ridiculed,[7] but rather as broad generalizations about how people use words, admitting of myriad exceptions.[8]

Coming to the present Term, the Supreme Court is now populated even more fully by textualists following multiple appointments by Republicans during the Donald Trump presidency. With all these appointments well-versed in the teachings of modern textualism (and some contributing to those teachings through their own scholarly writing[9]), one would thus expect the use of interpretive canons in this Court to be

[4] Jonathan T. Molot, *The Rise and Fall of Textualism*, 106 COLUM. L. REV. 1, 5 (2006).

[5] John F. Manning, *The Absurdity Doctrine*, 116 HARV. L. REV. 2387, 2392–93 (2003) ("Even the strictest modern textualists properly emphasize that language is a social construct. They ask how a reasonable person, conversant with the relevant social and linguistic conventions, would read the text in context.").

[6] Here and throughout the phrase "linguistic pragmatism" is used loosely to refer both to the broader idea that linguistic meaning depends upon social practice and, more narrowly, that linguistic utterances sometimes communicate content beyond what is said, strictly speaking. For skepticism that "pragmatics" in the narrow sense has significant relevance to statutory interpretation, see Andrei Marmor, *Can the Law Imply More Than It Says? On Some Pragmatic Aspects of Strategic Speech*, *in* PHILOSOPHICAL FOUNDATIONS OF LANGUAGE IN THE LAW (Andrei Marmor & Scott Soames eds., 2011).

[7] Facebook, Inc. v. Duguid, 141 S. Ct. 1163, 1175 (2021) (Alito, J., concurring in the judgment).

[8] *See, e.g.*, RadLAX Gateway Hotel, LLC v. Amalgamated Bank, 566 U.S. 639, 646–47 (2012) (Scalia, J.) (recognizing that canons are not "absolute rule[s]," but "merely . . . strong indication[s] of statutory meaning that can be overcome by textual indications that point in the other direction"); Ali v. Fed. Bureau of Prisons, 552 U.S. 214, 228 (2008) (Thomas, J.) (observing that "interpretive canons must yield 'when the whole context dictates a different conclusion'" (quoting Norfolk & W. Ry. Co. v. Am. Train Dispatchers Ass'n, 499 U.S. 117, 129 (1991)).

[9] *See, e.g.*, Amy Coney Barrett, *Substantive Canons and Faithful Agency*, 90 B.U. L. REV. 109 (2010); Brett M. Kavanaugh, *Fixing Statutory Interpretation*, 129 HARV. L. REV. 2118 (2016) (reviewing ROBERT A. KATZMANN, JUDGING STATUTES (2014)).

flexible and linguistically pragmatic. And yet, with great embarrassment, the opposite appears to be true. In numerous cases this Term, the Court's statutory analysis received derisive commentary from scholars and journalists, having displayed the very sort of "wooden[ness]" that textualism had been caricatured with by its opponents for so many years.[10] Such wooden interpretation was especially visible in the cases involving interpretive canons, in which the Court pretended to the sort of precision and determinacy that Llewellyn so effectively mocked.

So, what happened? As with the rise of textualism, the story has to do both with legal theory and politics.

In terms of theory, modern textualism always contained within it an argumentative tension. According to one line of reasoning, what distinguished modern textualism from its "plain meaning" predecessors was, as mentioned, its incorporation of linguistic pragmatism.[11] In recognizing that the meaning of words depended greatly upon the practical setting, modern textualists effectively abandoned the ideal (and caricature) of a "mechanical" jurisprudence by opening themselves to circumstances in which the meaning of a legal text would be reasonably contestable given the numerous considerations that go into what language means *as used*.[12] This sort of humility about statutory determinacy paired naturally with earlier observations by Legal Realists, including Llewellyn, concerning the limits of legal determinacy in the context of appellate adjudication. It was thus by incorporating (to varying degrees) Realist insights as well that textualism became thoroughly modern. This line of reasoning sat in tension, however, with continuing assurances by textualist judges and scholars that their method brought "predictability" and so determinacy to statutory cases.[13] In this way, modern textualists did continue to promise, at least implicitly, something like a mechanical jurisprudence despite its having explicitly been disavowed.

As this Essay explains, this tension between predictability and linguistic pragmatism was mediated for decades by a further theoretical

---

[10] Antonin Scalia, *Common-Law Courts in a Civil-Law System: The Role of United States Federal Courts in Interpreting the Constitution and Laws*, *in* A MATTER OF INTERPRETATION: FEDERAL COURTS AND THE LAW 3, 23 (Amy Gutmann ed., 1997).

[11] John F. Manning, *Textualism and the Equity of the Statute*, 101 COLUM. L. REV. 1, 108 (2001) ("Modern textualists, however, are not literalists."); Molot, *supra* note 4, at 2.

[12] Mitchell N. Berman, *Judge Posner's Simple Law*, 113 MICH. L. REV. 777, 789 (2015).

[13] *See, e.g.*, ANTONIN SCALIA & BRYAN A. GARNER, READING LAW: THE INTERPRETATION OF LEGAL TEXTS xxix (2012) ("[T]extualism will provide greater certainty in the law, and hence greater predictability and greater respect for the rule of law.").

commitment among modern textualists to judicial *non-intervention*. Insisting that the role of judges within our constitutional democracy was to find law rather than make it, modern textualists consistently if unevenly expressed support for the idea that judges should stay their hand in one way or another in the absence of "clear[ly]" identifiable law.[14] Practically speaking, this meant declining to alter the legal status quo (for instance, rejecting a challenge to an agency ruling or declining to impose criminal liability) or otherwise deferring to the policy judgments of more politically accountable actors—so long as the statutory language at issue was relevantly "ambiguous."[15] Manifested in different doctrinal rules, textualist judges were thus at least sometimes able to resolve statutory cases without having to identify a single "best" reading of the language at issue, which is to say without having to act as if statutory language is more determinate than it is.[16]

Politically, conservatives were supportive of non-interventionist doctrines into the early 2000s. Sometime around 2015, however, the Republican Party reversed its position through official statements and, more consequentially, judicial appointments, celebrating intervention instead. Most visibly through its selection of judicial nominees who rejected the non-interventionist *Chevron* doctrine, conservative judges and Justices, while still avowed textualists, now argued that a judge's *failure* to intervene in many cases would be a violation of his or her constitutional duties. Functionally, this embrace of judicial intervention worked to empower a now firmly conservative federal judiciary, seizing discretion previously exercised by elected officials. As a matter of statutory interpretation, it meant that these 'late-stage' textualist judges were left to act as if statutory language admitted of only one plausible reading, with interpretive canons being used once again as contradictory rules of the sort Llewellyn derided.[17]

---

[14] *E.g.*, Frank H. Easterbrook, *Statutes' Domains*, 50 U. Chi. L. Rev. 533, 544–45 (1983); Antonin Scalia, *Judicial Deference to Administrative Interpretations of Law*, 1989 Duke L.J. 511 (quoting Chevron, U.S.A., Inc. v. Nat. Res. Def. Council, Inc., 467 U.S. 837, 842–43 (1984)).

[15] Easterbrook, *supra* note 14, at 533; Scalia, *supra* note 14, at 511.

[16] *E.g.*, Nat'l Cable & Telecomms. Ass'n v. Brand X Internet Servs., 545 U.S. 967, 980 (2005).

[17] The story here thus contrasts with Jeremy Kessler and David Pozen's in that ideological interests have resulted a *less* nuanced version of textualism. *See* Jeremy K. Kessler & David E. Pozen, *Working Themselves Impure: A Life Cycle Theory of Legal Theories*, 83 U. Chi. L. Rev. 1819, 1848–54 (2016).

This Essay proceeds as follows. In Part II, it describes the fall and rise of interpretive canons, moving from Llewellyn's influential critique through modern textualism's reconceptualization and rehabilitation of canons. In Part III, this Essay documents the embarrassing use of interpretive canons today, with special attention to this Term's decision in *Facebook v. Duguid*.[18] In Part IV, it describes the political and theoretical developments that led to the embrace and then rejection by textualists of a principle of non-intervention and how doing so first obscured and then heightened that methodology's basic tension. Finally, in Part V, this Essay shows how the rejection of non-intervention has made statutory interpretation more wooden and more inviting of ridicule even apart from interpretive canons, focusing specifically on two other cases from this past Term, *Niz-Chavez v. Garland*[19] and *Van Buren v. United States*.[20]

I. The Fall and Rise of Interpretive Canons

A. THE FALL

Originally published in 1950, Llewellyn's *Remarks on the Theory of Appellate Decision and the Rules or Canons About How Statutes Are to Be Construed* is regarded as one of the most causally significant pieces of scholarship in the history of the American legal academy. Though best known for its table of "dueling canons," Llewellyn's critique of interpretive canons was part of a broader effort to show that the norms of legal argumentation reliably under-determine legal outcomes in the context of appellate litigation.[21] Just as appeals to precedent were inadequate to decide common law appellate disputes owing to the numerous ways in which past decisions could "correct[ly]" be read, so too, Llewellyn tried to show, with statutory cases and invocations of interpretive canons.[22] Mostly because of Congress's limited foresight, Llewellyn explained, legislative bargains predictably fail to address, at least specifically, the full range of practical circumstances to which statutes will eventually be applied.[23] For that reason, it inevitably falls

[18] 141 S. Ct. 1163 (2021).

[19] 141 S. Ct. 1474 (2021).

[20] 141 S. Ct. 1648 (2021).

[21] Llewellyn, *supra* note 2, at 399.

[22] *Id.* at 395.

[23] *Id.* at 400 ("[I]ncreasingly as a statute gains in age . . . its language is called upon to deal with circumstances utterly uncontemplated at the time of its passage.").

upon judges to make the best of a difficult circumstance, "quarr[ying]" sense out of the statute "in light of the new situation," in an admittedly "creative" and, ultimately, pragmatic endeavor.[24]

In offering his remarks, Llewellyn was careful not to fault judges for engaging in such artistic behavior. With common law decisions, for example, Llewellyn insisted that it was "silly" to think of judges using the available "leeway as involving 'twisting' of precedent."[25] To characterize judicial behavior that way, after all, "presupposes that there was in the precedent under consideration some one and single meaning," a presupposition the "whole experience of our case-law" shows to be "false."[26] Similarly, given the unavoidable under-specification of legislative bargains, as well as, in Llewellyn's view, the reality that legislatures, like past courts, can be both "skillful and unskillful, clear and unclear, wise and unwise," courts must be allowed creative license in making sure that the statute at issue "make[s] sense" as applied to the present situation—within the permissible bounds of legal argumentation, of course.[27]

Though supportive of judges' use of sociologically "legitimate" arguments to reach practically sensible outcomes, Llewellyn did nonetheless criticize the interpretive canons as judges employed them.[28] As with case law, Llewellyn contended, courts in statutory cases had continued to adhere to the "foolish pretense" that the interpretive questions presented in the context of appellate litigation admit of "only one single correct answer."[29] Until judges "give up" that pretense, he continued, "there *must* be a set of mutually contradictory correct rules on How to Construe Statutes."[30] It is at this point that Llewellyn set forth his now-famous table of "thrusts" and "parries."[31] Assembled by research assistant Charles Driscoll, the table identified pairs of supposedly contradictory canons of construction, including what today

---

[24] *Id.*

[25] *Id.* at 399.

[26] *Id.*

[27] *Id.*

[28] Brian Leiter, *American Legal Realism*, *in* THE BLACKWELL GUIDE TO THE PHILOSOPHY OF LAW AND LEGAL THEORY 51 (Martin P. Golding & William A. Edmundson eds., 2005) ("Realist arguments for the rational indeterminacy of law generally focused on the existence of conflicting, but equally legitimate, canons of interpretation for precedents and statutes.").

[29] Llewellyn, *supra* note 2, at 399.

[30] *Id.* (emphasis added).

[31] *Id.* at 401–06.

we refer to as "substantive" canons like the presumption against retroactivity (paired with an authorization for judges to construe remedial statutes retroactively should doing so "promote the ends of justice"), but with much greater emphasis on what we call "linguistic" or "semantic" canons.[32] Llewellyn contrasted, for example, the *expressio unius est exclusio alterius* canon[33] with the interpretive maxim that statutory language "may fairly comprehend many different cases where some only are expressly mentioned by way of example,"[34] or, similarly, the presumption against surplusage[35] with the authorization to "reject[] as surplusage" language "inadvertently inserted or ... repugnant to the rest of the statute."[36] (Of special relevance here, Llewellyn also paired the presumption that "[q]ualifying or limiting words of clauses are to be referred to the next preceding antecedent" with the qualification that said presumption has no application "when evident sense and meaning require a different construction."[37])

At least according to the popular narrative, Llewellyn's critique—and, in particular, his "chart"—was profoundly impactful.[38] John Manning, for example, remarked that "Karl Llewellyn largely persuaded two generations of academics that the canons of construction were not to be taken seriously."[39] Similarly, Cass Sunstein said that, following Llewellyn's "demonstration[,] ... [a]lmost no one ... had a favorable word to say about the canons [for] many years."[40] Courts too expressed greater skepticism towards interpretive canons

[32] *Id.* It is worth mentioning, though, that "semantic" canons is potentially a misnomer insofar as many of those canons (e.g., *expressio unius*) correspond to *pragmatic* rather than *semantic* inference, as that distinction is traditionally understood. *See generally* SEMANTICS VERSUS PRAGMATICS (Zoltán Gendler Szabó ed., 2005).

[33] Llewellyn, *supra* note 2, at 405 ("Expression of one thing excludes another.").

[34] *Id.*

[35] *Id.* at 404 ("Every word and clause must be given effect.").

[36] *Id.*

[37] *Id.* at 405.

[38] John F. Manning, *Legal Realism & the Canons' Revival*, 5 GREEN BAG 2d 283, 283 (2002) ("With less impact, earlier realists had made similar claims. But Llewellyn made a chart.").

[39] *Id.* at 283–84.

[40] Cass R. Sunstein, *Interpreting Statutes in the Regulatory State*, 103 HARV. L. REV. 405, 452 (1989); *see also, e.g.*, Anita S. Krishnakumar, *Dueling Canons*, 65 DUKE L.J. 909, 913 (2016) (noting "Llewellyn article's tremendous influence on statutory interpretation scholars"); William N. Eskridge, Jr. & Philip P. Frickey, *Quasi-Constitutional Law: Clear Statement Rules as Constitutional Lawmaking*, 45 VAND. L. REV. 593, 593 (1992) (calling Llewellyn's essay "one of the most celebrated law review articles of all time").

during that period, though, in that instance, the causal significance of Llewellyn's arguments is far less certain as courts' hesitancy with respect to canons may have somewhat predated publication of his *Remarks*. In this respect, Llewellyn's critique may have merely captured a broader skepticism towards canons that was emerging at the time.[41]

More generally, the apparent success of Llewellyn's criticism of interpretive canons plausibly had as much to do with the perceived availability of alternate interpretive tools as with the force of his arguments. As Manning describes it, the loss of enthusiasm for interpretive canons coincided with the rise of the Legal Process school of statutory interpretation and, with it, a renewed enthusiasm for attention to legislative purpose.[42] Imagining legislators as "reasonable persons pursuing reasonable purposes reasonably,"[43] that school promised not only to imbue the law with moral content, critical with the rise of fascism abroad and its (wrongly[44]) perceived relationship with a thoroughgoing legal positivism, but also to allow judges to continue to act as faithful agents of Congress, "(at least putatively) implementing the goals that the democratically elected legislature had selected."[45] More concretely, Manning argues, decreasing reliance on canons as an interpretive tool was offset by increasing reliance on legislative history, which, despite earlier Legal Realist critiques by those like Max Radin, was more and more viewed as reliable evidence of "what Congress was really trying to get at."[46]

On Manning's assessment, then, Llewellyn succeeded in discrediting interpretive canons largely because judges and scholars had

---

[41] While Llewellyn's argument depended largely upon its fit with the experience of its audience, contemporary legal scholars have offered more systematic evidence in support of the position that the applicability of individual canons is under-determined. *See* Krishnakumar, *supra* note 40, at 955 (conducting an empirical study of the Supreme Court's use of "dueling" interpretive canons in recent statutory cases, finding evidence "suggest[ing] that the canons do not constrain the Justices on the . . . Court to vote against their policy preferences").

[42] Manning, *supra* note 38, at 286.

[43] *Id.* (quoting William N. Eskridge, Jr. & Philip P. Frickey, *An Historical and Critical Introduction to Henry M. Hart, Jr. & Albert M. Sacks, The Legal Process: Basic Problems*, *in* The Making and Application of Law: Basic Problems in the Making and Application of Law 1378 (William N. Eskridge, Jr. & Philip P. Frickey eds., 1994) (internal quotation marks omitted).

[44] *See* Herlinde Pauer-Studer, Justifying Injustice: Legal Theory in Nazi Germany 203–39 (2020) (arguing that Nazi law sought specifically to unify law and the morality of the Volk).

[45] *Id.* (citations omitted).

[46] *Id.* at 288 (discussing Max Radin, *Statutory Interpretation*, 43 Harv. L. Rev. 863 (1930)).

identified other interpretive tools that allowed them to at least purport to be effectuating Congress's aims rather than merely exercising judicial discretion. Those conditions of success were ironic, of course, insofar as the core of Llewellyn's critique was that the exercise of discretion was unavoidable when interpreting statutes in the context of appellate litigation, and that it was, in turn, the "foolish" denial of this reality that motivated the embarrassing contradictions his table was intended to highlight.[47] Be that as it may, because a more candid Legal Realism had come to be viewed as both democratically and morally concerning, the legacy of Llewellyn's critique was less the abandonment of the "pretense" that judges do not exercise substantial discretion in appellate decisionmaking, as Llewellyn urged, but rather the discrediting of one set of interpretive tools as inherently manipulable and so ultimately pretextual and the elevation of some other set of tools supposedly free of, or at least substantially less burdened by, those defects.[48]

B. THE RISE

Though "interred" for decades by Llewellyn's criticism,[49] interpretive canons enjoyed a renaissance with the emergence of modern textualism in the 1980s. Widely understood today as the dominant method of statutory interpretation among judges, the success of modern textualism is as much a political story as it is an intellectual one. Beginning in the early 1980s under the leadership of Attorney General William French Smith and later Attorney General Edwin Meese, conservative lawyers within the Department of Justice ("DOJ") began to emphasize the importance of adhering to text in both statutory and constitutional interpretation.[50] To some extent, this prioritization of

[47] Llewellyn, *supra* note 2, at 399.

[48] *Id.*

[49] David L. Shapiro, *Continuity and Change in Statutory Interpretation*, 67 N.Y.U. L. Rev. 921, 923 (1992).

[50] See, e.g., Memorandum from Arnold I. Burns, Deputy Att'y Gen. et al. to Stephen J. Markman, Acting Assistant Att'y Gen. (Oct. 29, 1986) (on file with author) ("[C]onstitutional language should be construed as it was publicly understood at the time of its drafting and ratification and government attorneys should advance constitutional arguments based only on this 'original meaning.' . . . As with constitutional adjudication, statutory adjudication starts from the proposition that the words of the statute have a meaning that constrains judgment; statutory language should be construed as it would have been publicly understood at the time of its enactment.").

statutory text was spillover from the ongoing project of popularizing and legitimizing constitutional originalism, which, as political scientist Calvin TerBeek has documented, was principally advanced by conservative political operatives as an alternative to the kind of "living constitutionalism" practiced by the Warren Court in cases like *Brown v. Board of Education*.[51] More generally, the belief among conservative lawyers within the DOJ was that a central problem of legal liberalism was its continuous straying from legal text, whether statutory or constitutional. In response to this perceived problem, DOJ lawyers deliberately presented textualism as a methodological alternative in both interpretive domains.[52] Meanwhile, within the legal academy, scholars like Frank Easterbrook and Antonin Scalia began to develop more theoretically sophisticated defenses and understandings of textualism, building partly on earlier Legal Realist arguments concerning the absence of shared intentions within multi-member legislative bodies as well as more recent work by public choice theorists, which offered both a more cynical picture of lawmaking than that associated with Legal Process as well as further resources for skepticism about (actual, historical) legislative purpose as an object of judicial inquiry.[53]

With the appointment of figures like Easterbrook and Scalia to the federal bench, along with DOJ alumni like Kenneth Starr, textualism began to settle as the preferred method of statutory interpretation among conservative judges. And as the Republican Party retained its commitment to textualism (and originalism) through subsequent presidential administrations, further appointments of both judges and Justices with those methodological commitments permitted both earlier and more recent conservative appointees to exercise significant influence over judicial practice in statutory cases. Such influence was most visible at the level of the Supreme Court, where the elevation of Scalia and Clarence

---

[51] Calvin TerBeek, *"Clocks Must Always Be Turned Back": Brown v. Board of Education and the Racial Origins of Constitutional Originalism*, 115 Am. Pol. Sci. Rev. 3 (2021).

[52] *See, e.g.*, *Intercircuit Panel: Hearing on S. 704 Before the Subcomm. on Cts., S. Comm. on the Judiciary*, 99th Cong. 3 n.3 (1985) (statement of James M. Spears, Acting Assistant Att'y Gen.) ("The Court has contributed to the trend in which the role of judges is viewed less as one of interpreting the Constitution and statutes, guided principally by their text and the legislative intent of the Framers and Congress, and more as one of resolving public policy questions as guided by the perceived values of an enlightened society. This Administration has consistently challenged, and taken steps to reverse, this trend of moving from interpretivism to judicial activism.").

[53] *See, e.g.*, Easterbrook, *supra* note 14.

Thomas in particular afforded textualism significant institutional legitimacy and, more practically, permitted textualists to extract methodological concessions from their liberal colleagues—refusing, for example, to join (portions of) opinions relying upon legislative history, leading to its decreasing use.[54]

Following the success of this political project, it is unsurprising that newly appointed textualist judges would express greater enthusiasm than their Legal Process predecessors for interpretive canons—in particular, linguistic or semantic canons—and thereby legitimize their use. With its attention to precise phrasing and grammatical nuance, interpretive canons that correspond to familiar linguistic subtleties like *expressio unius* or *ejusdem generis* fit naturally within a textualist approach to statutory interpretation. In turn, it makes sense that legal academics of all types would find new appreciation for interpretive canons given their professional interest in preserving relevance with an increasingly textualist judiciary. And find new appreciation they did, as scholars across the ideological spectrum began to suggest that perhaps interpretive canons could be useful tools after all.

Even in this highly conducive political environment, though, developments in legal theory plausibly contributed to, or at least shaped, the reintroduction of interpretive canons. Part of this apparent contribution was negative, with theoretical arguments from textualist legal academics rendering alternatives to interpretive canons less available. Drawing upon earlier Legal Realist reasoning and more contemporary work in public choice theory, textualist scholars, and in turn judges, called into question specifically the value of legislative history as an interpretive aid.[55] The apparent probative value of legislative history

---

[54] As Thomas Merrill explains it:

> A better explanation for the triumph of textualism, in my opinion, lies not so much in Justice Scalia's persuasiveness as in his persistence. The critical factor here is Justice Scalia's practice of refusing to join any part of another Justice's opinion that relies on legislative history. This means that in any case in which another Justice needs the vote of Justice Scalia to form a majority or controlling opinion, the writing Justice knows that if legislative history is employed he or she will lose majority status with respect to at least a portion of the opinion. The arrival of Justice Thomas, who has taken up a similar stance, effectively doubles Justice Scalia's voting clout in this regard.

Thomas W. Merrill, *Textualism and the Future of the* Chevron *Doctrine*, 72 WASH. U. L.Q. 351, 365 (1994).

[55] *See, e.g.*, Blanchard v. Bergeron, 489 U.S. 87, 97–100 (1989) (Scalia, J., concurring in part and concurring in the judgment); Cont'l Can Co. v. Chicago Truck Drivers, Helpers &

had been important to the case that inquiries into legislative purpose amounted to something other than covert exercises of judicial discretion.[56] By making such appeals seem less obviously credible, textualist thinkers thus helped recreate—or, maybe better, re-reveal—the vacuum of legal determinacy in statutory cases that legislative history, and more generally legislative purpose, had purported to fill.

Building on this opportunity, textualist scholars and judges emphasized simultaneously the virtues of determinacy and constraint that their preferred method supposedly offered.[57] And with interpretive canons in particular, scholars of various ideological and methodological stripes contended that the use of such canons contributed to legal determinacy by making legal interpretation more predictable. Manning, for example, promised that the use of linguistic or semantic canons could "foster" common "linguistic and syntactic rules" for legislators and their various audiences.[58] Contributing to a shared legal language, the use of canons could thus help facilitate effective "communication of legislative directions."[59] More ambitiously, Sunstein, and later William Baude and Stephen Sachs, argued that appeal to both linguistic *and substantive* canons was mostly unavoidable because judges are frequently confronted with "textual silence" and so resort to "background principles" is necessary to fill legislative "gaps" in a legally determinate fashion.[60]

For textualists specifically, resort to "gap-filling" talk was slightly awkward given that method's emphasis on fidelity to congressional

---

Warehouse Workers Union (Indep.) Pension Fund, 916 F.2d 1154, 1157–60 (7th Cir. 1990) (Easterbrook, J.).

[56] *See* Manning, *supra* note 38, at 287–89.

[57] *See, e.g.*, Scalia, *supra* note 10, at 17–18 ("The *practical* threat is that, under the guise or even the self-delusion of pursuing unexpressed legislative intents, common-law judges will in fact pursue their own objectives and desires, extending their lawmaking proclivities; from the common law to the statutory field."); Frank H. Easterbrook, *The Role of Original Intent in Statutory Construction*, 11 Harv. J.L. & Pub. Pol'y 59, 62 (1988) ("The use of original *intent* rather than an objective inquiry into the reasonable import of the language permits a series of moves. Each move greatly increases the discretion, and therefore the power, of the court."); *see also* William Baude, *Originalism as a Constraint on Judges*, 84 U. Chi. L. Rev. 2213 (2018) (discussing the legacy of "constraint" arguments by interpretive formalists in constitutional law, suggesting a decreasing reliance in that context).

[58] Manning, *supra* note 38, at 292.

[59] *Id.*

[60] Sunstein, *supra* note 40, at 422; William Baude & Stephen E. Sachs, *The Law of Interpretation*, 130 Harv. L. Rev. 1079 (2017).

aims and, more importantly, the illegitimacy of judicial lawmaking.[61] Even Manning's more modest thought that the use of canons might help generate—as opposed to merely reflect—shared interpretive norms faces difficulties in view of recent empirical work suggesting that legislative actors are largely inattentive to judicial cues concerning how to use statutory language.[62] More immediately, though, these different arguments from "predictability" all depend upon a rejection of Llewellyn's fundamental empirical claim that the interpretive canons themselves are contradictory. (Llewellyn's basic argument, after all, was that the application of contradictory canons created the *illusion* of legal determinacy, not its reality.[63]) And while Sunstein and others made some effort to show that Llewellyn's claim that the canons were contradictory and so not constraining was "greatly overstated," insisting, for example, that the principle that courts should construe narrowly statutes in derogation of the common law undoubtedly informs judges' "sense" of the relevant statutory "situation[s]," the popularity of Llewellyn's argument reflected less revelation to legal practitioners that their interpretive idols were false than resonance with lawyers' "whole experience" with statutory cases and the apparent manipulability of these supposed legal principles.[64] Against that pessimistic backdrop, it is somewhat difficult to imagine that assurances like those of Sunstein played a meaningful role in restoring interpretive canons as legitimate interpretive tools.

Beyond determinacy and constraint, however, proponents of modern textualism also highlighted that method's special attention to interpretive context. Contrasting their view with earlier "plain-meaning" textualists who placed emphasis on "literal meaning," modern textualists purported to incorporate insights from philosophers of language such as Ludwig Wittgenstein and Paul Grice, recognizing that words only gather meaning in a context of use.[65] Easterbrook,

[61] Baude and Sachs try to resolve this tension by characterizing interpretive canons as part of our "law of interpretation" and so rules of which members of Congress are presumed to be on notice. Baude & Sachs, *supra* note 60, at 1107–08.

[62] *See* Abbe R. Gluck & Lisa Schultz Bressman, *Statutory Interpretation from the Inside-an Empirical Study of Congressional Drafting, Delegation, and the Canons*: *Part I*, 65 Stan. L. Rev. 901 (2013).

[63] Llewellyn, *supra* note 2, at 399.

[64] Sunstein, *supra* note 40, at 452.

[65] *See* Manning, *supra* note 11, at 127 n.64 ("Textualist theory thus incorporates the insights of modern language theory often associated with Ludwig Wittgenstein."); Cont'l Can Co. v.

for example, observed that "words are not born with meanings" but instead "take their meaning from contexts, of which there are many."[66] (Easterbrook simultaneously disparages dictionaries as mere "museum[s] of words."[67]) So too Scalia, who declared it a "fundamental principle of statutory construction (and, indeed, of language itself) that the meaning of a word cannot be determined in isolation, but must be drawn from the context in which it is used."[68] Rather than fetishize dictionary definitions and the like, modern textualists thus interpreted, or at least aspired to interpret, specific words or phrases in view of a statute's subject matter, its internal coherence, or surrounding legislation, all with a view to understanding what a "reasonable user of words" would have taken that language to mean as used.[69] Such attention to linguistic nuance showed that modern textualists grasped that words were practical instruments used to "do things,"[70] with Easterbrook stating, for instance, that "we use [texts] purposively," which is why "meaning . . . will change with context, and over time" as do our practical ends.[71] Having adopted this sort of linguistic pragmatism (in the Wittgensteinian or Gricean sense, not the Posnerian), modern textualists positioned themselves to rebut criticisms like those of Llewellyn, who accused earlier plain-meaning textualists of "eviscerate[ing]" statutes through "wooden and literal reading."[72] Far from "wooden," modern textualism promised to be nimble, sophisticated, and, most importantly, attentive to the practical interests at stake.

This embrace of context sensitivity was reflected specifically in the way modern textualists talked about interpretive canons. Having expressly rejected the use of "rigid" interpretive methods, modern

Chicago Truck Drivers, Helpers & Warehouse Workers Union (Indep.) Pension Fund, 916 F.2d 1154, 1157 (7th Cir. 1990) (Easterbrook, J.). For an extended discussion of the importance of practical context to textual analysis, see Ryan D. Doerfler, *Who Cares How Congress Really Works?*, 66 Duke L.J. 979, 986–99 (2017).

[66] Frank H. Easterbrook, *Text, History, and Structure in Statutory Interpretation*, 17 Harv. J.L. & Pub. Pol'y 61, 61 (1994). In this passage, Easterbrook appears to run together various senses of "context sensitivity," as is typical of early modern textualist writing.

[67] *Id.* at 67.

[68] Deal v. United States, 508 U.S. 129, 132 (1993) (Scalia, J.).

[69] Easterbrook, *supra* note 57, at 65.

[70] J. L. Austin, How to Do Things with Words, The William James Lectures (J. O. Urmson ed., 1962).

[71] Easterbrook, *supra* note 66, at 61.

[72] Llewellyn, *supra* note 2, at 400.

textualists distanced themselves from the idea that the canons were rules that make statutory interpretation more mechanical.[73] To the contrary, Scalia insisted, "canons of interpretation . . . are not 'rules' of interpretation in any strict sense," but instead constitute interpretive "presumptions" that can be negated by context, often quite easily.[74] Thus, in his treatise with attorney and lexicographer Brian Garner, Scalia cataloged canons of all different types, from "semantic" to "syntactic" to "contextual," underscoring again and again the "defeasible" nature of these various interpretive maxims.[75] Clarence Thomas, the other most powerful judicial proponent of textualism at the time, likewise remarked that "canons of construction" were mere "rules of thumb"[76] that "must yield 'when the whole context dictates a different conclusion.' "[77] And so on, and so on.[78] By emphasizing so explicitly and so repeatedly the context sensitivity of interpretive canons, modern textualism thereby meaningfully defused Llewellyn's criticism that those canons as used were contradictory. That criticism, after all, rested upon the premise that interpretive canons pretended to operate like rigid, determinate rules. By explicitly rejecting that premise, modern textualists were free to say without embarrassment that *sometimes* the expression of one thing excludes another while *other times* things are expressly mentioned only by way of example, that *usually* every word and clause should be given effect, but that *in some circumstances* it is appropriate to reject statutory language as inadvertent surplusage.

* * *

To recap, while the readmission of interpretive canons into polite legal society was substantially a political story, developments within legal theory plausibly informed that readmission in two ways. First, by

---

[73] Doerfler, *supra* note 65, at 1044 n.209.

[74] SCALIA & GARNER, *supra* note 13.

[75] *Id.* at 171.

[76] Conn. Nat'l Bank v. Germain, 503 U.S. 249, 253 (1992) (Thomas, J.).

[77] Ali v. Fed. Bureau of Prisons, 552 U.S. 214, 228 (2008) (quoting Norfolk & W. Ry. Co. v. Am. Train Dispatchers Ass'n, 499 U.S. 117, 129 (1991) (Thomas, J.).

[78] *See, e.g., Conn. Nat'l Bank*, 503 U.S. at 254 ("When the words of a statute are unambiguous, then, this first canon is also the last.") (Thomas, J.); Marx v. Gen. Revenue Corp., 568 U.S. 371, 381 (2013) (quoting United States v. Vonn, 535 U.S. 55, 65 (2002) ("[The *expressio unius*] canon can be overcome by 'contrary indications that adopting a particular rule or statute was probably not meant to signal any exclusion.' ") (Thomas, J.); Barnhart v. Sigmon Coal Co., 534 U.S. 438, 461 (2002) ("This statute does not contain conflicting provisions or ambiguous language. Nor does it require a narrowing construction or application of any other canon or interpretative tool.") (Thomas, J.).

playing up the constraint canons supposedly bring to the interpretive process, proponents of interpretive canons promised that their use could help bring additional determinacy to statutory interpretation, which was especially important given recent criticisms concerning the use of legislative history, often by those same individuals. Second, building on more general insights concerning the sensitivity of language to context, proponents of interpretive canons took care to explain that such canons were mere generalizations about usage, and that evidence specific to a given case could always render them inapplicable. In so arguing, proponents of interpretive canons largely undercut Llewellyn's critique that such canons were contradictory, a critique that depended, again, on the idea that interpretive canons operate like legal rules, determinate and with clear conditions of application.

Importantly, there is an apparent tension between these two lines of argument, as discussed more fully below. The core of Llewellyn's critique was that it was a "foolish" belief in legal determinacy in statutory cases at the appellate stage that led judges to act as if interpretive canons are (inevitably contradictory) rules.[79] By insisting that interpretive canons are *not* rules but instead defeasible presumptions, modern textualists were mostly able to explain away Llewellyn's critique, but only by conceding that interpretive canons are less conducive to legal determinacy—which is just the same as saying less "wooden"—than one might have otherwise hoped. By contrast, arguments to the effect that interpretive canons are a source of constraint and, in turn, legal determinacy seem to depend on one's imagining that interpretive canons operate more *like rules*. As this Essay discusses below, other resources within modern textualism partially obscured this tension. With judges (and to some extent scholars) increasingly transitioning, however, from modern to what one might call "late-stage" textualism, that tension has very much come to the fore.

II. Canons of Interpretation Today

Fast forward now to October Term 2020. In *Facebook, Inc. v. Duguid*,[80] the Supreme Court was presented with a discrete question of statutory interpretation. Under the Telephone Consumer

[79] Again, "rules" in the sense of legal norms with clear conditions of application and that purport to dictate (as opposed to permit) a specific legal outcome.

[80] 141 S. Ct. 1163 (2021).

Protection Act of 1991 ("TCPA"),[81] it is unlawful to make any non-emergency call (including text message) to any cellular number using an "automatic telephone dialing system" without the express consent of the recipient.[82] The Act, in turn, defines "automatic telephone dialing system" as equipment having the "capacity" to "store or produce telephone numbers to be called, using a random or sequential number generator," and to "dial such numbers."[83] Here, Noah Duguid had received multiple text messages from Facebook alerting him that his account had been accessed from an unrecognized device or browser, a security measure Facebook provides to help prevent unauthorized access. The problem was that Duguid had no Facebook account and so had never consented to receiving such messages. After repeated, unsuccessful attempts to unsubscribe from this service, Duguid filed suit under the TCPA, alleging that Facebook's unsolicited text messages were in violation of the Act's "robocall" prohibition described above.[84]

In *Duguid*, the specific interpretive question was whether Facebook's unsolicited messages were in violation of the TCPA even though the Facebook computers used to send those messages neither stored nor produced the phone numbers dialed *using a random or sequential number generator*. According to Duguid, that Facebook had dialed only numbers entered into its system by Facebook users was beside the point because the limiting phrase "using a random or sequential number generator" as used in the statute modifies only the second of the two verbs in the preceding clause, "produce." In other words, as construed by Duguid, so long as Facebook had automatically text messaged numbers "stored" in its system without the recipient's consent, that was enough to violate the anti-robocalling provision.[85] (On Duguid's reading, the other way to violate the statute was to automatically message numbers "produce[d] . . . using a random or sequential number generator.") In response, Facebook argued that the phrase "using a random or sequential number generator" modified *both* verbs in the preceding clause, "store" and "produce," such

[81] 47 U.S.C. § 227.

[82] *Id.* at § 227(b)(1)(A). The statute also specifically exempted unsolicited calls for the purpose of debt collection. *But see* Barr v. Am. Ass'n of Pol. Consultants, Inc., 140 S. Ct. 2335 (2020) (declaring the exemption in violation of the First Amendment).

[83] *Id.* at § 227(a)(1).

[84] *Duguid*, 141 S. Ct. at 1167.

[85] *Id.* at 1169.

that a caller would have to use a device that could either "store . . . numbers . . . using a random or sequential number generator" or "produce . . . numbers . . . using a random or sequential number generator" to be in violation of the statute.[86]

By a unanimous vote, the Supreme Court sided with Facebook. Writing for eight Justices, Justice Sonya Sotomayor "beg[an]," as Justices do, "with the text."[87] The statute's "definition," Sotomayor noted, "uses a familiar structure: a list of verbs followed by a modifying clause."[88] "Under conventional rules of grammar," she explained, "'[w]hen there is a straightforward, parallel construction that involves all nouns or verbs in a series,' a modifier at the end of the list 'normally applies to the entire series.'"[89] This "series-qualifier" canon was straightforwardly applicable, Sotomayor continued, since "the modifier at issue immediately follows a concise, integrated clause: 'store or produce telephone numbers to be called.'"[90] Because this "clause 'hangs together as a unified whole,'" with the word 'or' . . . connect[ing] two verbs that share a common direct object, 'telephone numbers to be called,'" it would be "odd to apply the modifier ('using a random or sequential number generator') to only a portion of this cohesive preceding clause."[91] Sotomayor contrasted the series-qualifier canon with the inapplicable "rule of the last antecedent," invoked by Duguid.[92] Under that rule, "a limiting clause or phrase should ordinarily be read as modifying only the noun or phrase that it immediately follows."[93] The rule of the last antecedent, Sotomayor clarified, was "context dependent," and one the Court had declined to apply "where, like here, the modifying clause appears after an integrated list."[94] Worse still for Duguid, the "last antecedent before 'using a random or sequential number generator'" was "not 'produce,' . . . but rather

[86] *Id.*

[87] *Id.*

[88] *Id.*

[89] *Id.* (quoting Scalia & Garner, *supra* note 13, at 147).

[90] *Id.*

[91] *Id.* (quoting Cyan, Inc. v. Beaver County Employees Retirement Fund, 138 S. Ct. 1061, 1077 (2018)).

[92] *Id.* at 1170.

[93] *Id.* (quoting Barnhart v. Thomas, 540 U.S. 20, 26 (2003)) (internal quotation marks and alteration omitted).

[94] *Id.* (citing Jama v. Immigration and Customs Enforcement, 543 U.S. 335, 344, n. 4 (2005)).

'telephone numbers to be called,'" thus depriving Duguid of any "grammatical basis" for his otherwise "arbitrar[y]" reading.[95] Sotomayor similarly rejected Duguid's appeal to the "distributive" canon, according to which a "sentence contain[ing] several antecedents and several consequents," should be read "distributively . . . apply[ing] the words to the subjects which, by context, they seem most properly to relate."[96] That canon was of "highly questionable" application, Sotomayor insisted, "given there are two antecedents (store and produce) but only one consequent modifier (using a random or sequential number generator)," and besides, "the consequent 'using a random or sequential number generator' properly relates to both antecedents."[97]

As Justice Samuel Alito observed in his separate concurrence, Sotomayor's (along with seven other Justices') use of canons in *Duguid* is almost comically "mechanical[]."[98] Notions like "concise, integrated clause[s]" or some clause having "only one consequent modifier" as opposed to two (or three or four) are presented as determinative of legal outcomes—offered as "a series of if-then computations," to use Alito's phrasing.[99] More generally, the series-qualifier canon upon which Sotomayor places so much weight is characterized explicitly as a "*rule*[] of grammar," with narrow and specifically defined exceptions, Sotomayor suggests.[100] This picture of interpretive canons as rules is, needless to say, directly at odds with the teachings of modern textualism, which emphasized again and again that canons are "highly sensitive to context" and the application of which requires the sort of holistic and ultimately practical engagement with text, a type of engagement natural language competency so plainly involves.[101] Rather than conceive of them as "limit[ed]" and heavily "caveat[ed]" generalizations about linguistic usage, however, the Court here was opting, as in so many recent cases, to treat interpretive canons as "rigid" and "inflexible rules," precisely the conception of canons that Llewellyn successfully ridiculed.[102]

---

[95] *Id.* (quoting *Cyan*, 138 S. Ct. at 1077) (internal quotation marks omitted).

[96] *Id.* at 1172 (quoting SHAMBIE SINGER, SUTHERLAND STATUTES AND STATUTORY CONSTRUCTION 448 (2018)).

[97] *Id.* (citing Encino Motorcars, LLC v. Navarro, 138 S. Ct. 1134, 1141 (2018)).

[98] *Id.* at 1175 (Alito, J., concurring in the judgment).

[99] *Id.*

[100] *Id.* at 1169 (majority opinion).

[101] SCALIA & GARNER, *supra* note 13, at 150.

[102] *Duguid*, 141 S. Ct. at 1175 (Alito, J., concurring in the judgment).

So how did we get here? Five years earlier, the pair of interpretive canons that feature most prominently in *Duguid*—the series-qualifier canon and the rule of the last antecedent—took on contemporary relevance in *Lockhart v. United States*.[103] In that case, the provision at issue imposed a ten-year mandatory minimum sentence enhancement for persons convicted of possessing child pornography if they have a "prior conviction . . . under the laws of any State relating to aggravated sexual abuse, sexual abuse, or abusive sexual conduct involving a minor or ward."[104] The defendant in *Lockhart* had a prior state-court conviction for first-degree sexual abuse of an adult, raising the question whether the qualifying phrase "involving a minor or ward" modified only the adjacent "abusive sexual conduct" or also the earlier offenses in the list.[105] The Supreme Court divided six to two in favor of the government. Writing for the majority, Sotomayor assured that here the applicable canon was the rule of the last antecedent, which, she explained, "reflects the basic intuition that when a modifier appears at the end of a list, it is easier to apply that modifier only to the item directly before it."[106] In support of this intuition, Sotomayor relied substantially on ordinary language examples, observing, for instance, that if the general manager of the New York Yankees were to instruct her scouts "to find a defensive catcher, a quick-footed shortstop, or a pitcher from last year's World Champion Kansas City Royals," it would be "natural" for the scouts to limit their search for a pitcher to members of last year's Royals but to look more broadly for a catcher or shortstop.[107] In dissent, Justice Elena Kagan countered Sotomayor's rule-of-the-last-antecedent "thrust" with a "parry" of the series-qualifier canon.[108] Like Sotomayor, Kagan's argument depended significantly on ordinary language examples, offering that a real estate agent who promises "to find a client 'a house, condo, or apartment in New York'" is unlikely to send "information about condos in Maryland or California."[109]

---

[103] 577 U.S. 347 (2016).

[104] 18 U.S.C. § 2252(b)(2).

[105] *Lockhart*, 577 U.S. at 349.

[106] *Id.* at 351.

[107] *Id.* at 351–52.

[108] *Id.* at 364 (Kagan, J., dissenting).

[109] *Id.* at 362.

Returning to *Duguid*, there, too, Sotomayor supplemented her more schematic arguments for the applicability of the series-qualifier canon with yet another ordinary language example, this time asking the reader to imagine a teacher announcing that "students must not complete or check any homework to be turned in for a grade, using online homework-help websites."[110] In that instance, Sotomayor observed (correctly[111]) it would make no sense to regard the teacher as prohibiting students from completing their homework generally. And yet, as Alito objected in his concurrence, and as the back and forth between Sotomayor and Kagan in *Lockhart* makes clear, the availability of examples like this shows very little insofar as one could easily conjure an example with the same superficial grammatical structure generating the opposite linguistic intuition.[112] (For his part, Alito offers several, including, "It is illegal to hunt rhinos and giraffes with necks longer than three feet."[113]) What the availability of such competing examples suggests, of course, is that the same orderings of words and punctuations can be used to different practical effects, precisely the lesson of modern textualism and its insistence upon the importance of attending to interpretive context. And so (yet?), with arguments by example having been revealed as under-determinate—in part, by her having offered contrary examples in her earlier *Lockhart* opinion—it makes some sense that Sotomayor would rely more heavily on more abstract argumentation by the time of *Duguid*. By appealing to concepts like "concise, integrated clause[s]" and the like, her *Duguid* opinion achieves a tone of formality, of "technical[ity]," that creates, for some at least, the impression of law.[114]

Or does it really? As discussed more fully below, the reasoning in *Duguid* and other, similarly textually oriented opinions from this Term were met with widespread derision, with legal commentators coming close to (or even outright) mocking the Justices for discussing at length the placement of punctuations, the use of certain grammatical articles,

---

[110] *Duguid*, 141 S. Ct. at 1169.

[111] Absent more information, at least.

[112] Emphasis on *superficial* since in these cases specifically the interpretive task is to identify based on context the actual syntactic structure of the clause.

[113] *Id.* at 1174 (Alito, J., concurring in the judgment).

[114] *Id.* at 1175; *see also* Margaret H. Lemos, *The Politics of Statutory Interpretation*, 89 Notre Dame L. Rev. 849, 884 (2014) (arguing that appeal to technical interpretive arguments can provide "camouflage" for policy-driven outcomes).

and the like to explain judgments affecting matters as important as the right to an immigration hearing or potential criminal liability for workplace misconduct. Such frustration among legal scholars and journalists should hardly come as a surprise. As much as "we" may all be "textualists now,"[115] we are also all now, at least to some extent, Legal Realists. As such, efforts at mystification and appeal to "arcane rules" are less likely to succeed with legally sophisticated audiences, whose "whole experience" with the law has shown them that such technicalities rarely determine outcomes in cases litigated before the Supreme Court.[116] With *Duguid* in particular, Sotomayor and the other Justices could not help that legal commentators were reading their canon-centric opinion in a post-Llewellyn world.

Whatever the success of her efforts, the claim in this Part is that Sotomayor's treatment of interpretive canons in *Duguid* as legal rules is an illustration of a broader trend among the Justices not only of relying upon canons in statutory cases but of portraying those canons as "mechanical" and so outcome determinative. This portrayal is, again, directly at odds with efforts by modern textualists to defuse Llewellyn's critique of modern canons as contradictory by emphasizing that canons are *not* legal rules but are instead generalizations about ordinary linguistic practice the application of which involves careful attention to the specifics of the practical setting in which the legal text at issue was authored and intended to be read. This tendency to portray interpretive canons as rules reflects, at the same time, another line of argument within modern textualism, which promises that the use of canons brings greater predictability and so greater determinacy to judicial decision-making in statutory cases. As cases like *Duguid* bring out, these two lines of argument for modern textualists are inherently in tension insofar as emphasizing the context-sensitive nature of interpretive canons is just the same as saying that canons are insufficiently "rigid" to decide cases in a predictable, "if-then" fashion. By resolving that tension in favor of legal determinacy, the current Court has thus given new life to Llewellyn's "dueling canons" critique. It has also contributed to what this Essay calls "late-stage" textualism looking increasingly foolish, with

---

[115] Harvard Law School, *The 2015 Scalia Lecture: A Dialogue with Justice Elena Kagan on the Reading of Statutes*, YouTube (Nov. 25, 2015) https://www.youtube.com/watch?v=dpEtszFT0Tg.

[116] *Duguid*, 141 S. Ct. at 1175 (Alito, J., concurring in the judgment).

grammatical pedantry (or, really, sophistry) offered as legal justification in cases with real human stakes.[117]

III. Late-Stage Textualism and Legal Determinacy

If the embarrassing use of interpretive canons in cases like *Duguid* is attributable partly to the belief that canons add predictability and so determinacy to statutory interpretation, an immediate question is why this would be a problem only recently. Modern textualism, after all, has been extolling these purported virtues of interpretive canons for decades, and textualism has been the principal method of statutory interpretation among federal judges for almost as long. And to be sure, treatments of canons as "if-then" devices are scattered throughout the Supreme Court and Federal Reporters in decisions from the 1990s and early 2000s. Still, the use of interpretive canons does appear more frequent in recent years, and, as Alito observed in his *Duguid* concurrence, canons seem to play an especially "prominent" role in statutory interpretation cases today.[118]

So, what might explain this placing of greater weight on interpretive canons? As before, part of the story is political. Though textualism has been an influential method of statutory interpretation among Supreme Court Justices since the appointment of Scalia in 1986, the recent appointments of Neil Gorsuch, Brett Kavanaugh, and Amy Coney Barrett, all avowed textualists, has made it all but impossible to assemble a majority in a statutory case without heavy reliance on textual arguments. (Here, Kagan's appointment is also significant in that it marked the acceptance of textualism as a *bipartisan* method of interpretation among the Justices.) Under these conditions, it makes sense that a Justice like Sotomayor, though not obviously committed to textualism as a philosophical matter, would nonetheless phrase her arguments in terms of interpretive canons (and linguistic terminology more generally) rather than relying on, say, legislative history.

Beyond that narrowly political explanation, though, shifts in textualist thinking also plausibly contributed to treatment of interpretive

[117] Though different in her prescription, Abbe Gluck offers a similar diagnosis of the problem in her characterization of textualism as a failed effort at interpretive "formalism." Abbe R. Gluck, *Justice Scalia's Unfinished Business in Statutory Interpretation: Where Textualism's Formalism Gave Up*, 92 Notre Dame L. Rev. 2053, 2071 (2017) (observing that textualist judges often select arbitrarily among myriad interpretive rules because "text cannot answer every question").

[118] *Duguid*, 141 S. Ct. at 1173 (Alito, J., concurring in the judgment).

canons as legal rules. As described at various places, there is, or better was, a tension between modern textualism's insistence that interpretive canons are highly sensitive to context and its claim that the use of canons increases predictability and so determinacy in statutory cases. At the same time, modern textualism contained resources reducing the practical significance of that tension. Specifically, textualists like Easterbrook and Scalia articulated a commitment (or at least aspiration) to judicial non-intervention in the absence of "clearly" identifiable law. Though voiced sometimes concerning constitutional cases, a principle of non-intervention was more comprehensively theorized and adhered to at least somewhat more reliably by textualists in the context of statutory interpretation.[119]

A. LEGAL THEORY

Within legal theory, probably the canonical statement of a principle of non-intervention in statutory cases is Easterbrook's 1983 article, *Statutes' Domains*. In that paper, Easterbrook offered a defense of a text-centric approach to statutory interpretation grounded substantially in public choice theory. Advancing the idea that it is "difficult" if not "impossible" to aggregate the preferences of individual legislators into a "coherent collective choice," Easterbrook reasoned that features of the legislative process like agenda control and "logrolling" made it the case that judicial "predictions" of how legislatures would have resolved unanticipated cases were "bound to be little more than wild guesses."[120] Construing statutory language in any case in which Congress's written instruction was less than "clear" was, accordingly, an unavoidably "creative" endeavor.[121] The question for Easterbrook, then, was whether or when judges should exercise this sort of discretion. In some instances, Congress "plainly" delegates authority to federal courts to shape statutes, "creat[ing] and revis[ing] a form of common law"—with the Sherman Act, in Easterbrook's view, the most uncontroversial example.[122] In the absence of such

[119] For a notable exception, see John F. Manning, *Separation of Powers as Ordinary Interpretation*, 124 Harv. L. Rev. 1939 (2011).

[120] Easterbrook, *supra* note 14, at 547–48.

[121] *Id.* at 534.

[122] *Id.* at 544. *But see* Sanjukta Paul, *Recovering the Moral Economy Foundations of the Sherman Act*, 131 Yale L.J. 175 (2021) (contesting the status of the Sherman Act as a "common law" statute); Daniel A. Farber & Brett H. McDonnell, *"Is There a Text in This Class?" The Conflict Between Textualism and Antitrust*, 14 J. Contemp. Legal Issues 619, 641 (2005) (same).

unmistakable delegation, though, Easterbrook concluded that judges should refrain from construing a statute to resolve a case that its language does not specifically settle. Without a sense of what faithful construction would involve, courts should instead declare that the case falls "outside the statute's domain," leaving the legal status quo unchanged.[123]

Even as they moved away from public choice, modern textualists continued to urge non-intervention. Beginning in the mid-1990s and early 2000s, textualists placed greater emphasis on the more prosaic observation that compromise and tradeoffs are inherent to the legislative process because legislators are always pursuing multiple goals. Even a Congress earnestly committed to confronting climate change, for example, would need to balance its interest in a rapid reduction of carbon emissions with its desire to equitably distribute the burdens of transitioning from fossil fuels, its commitment to preserving biodiversity, and so on. Addressing such choices, members of Congress sometimes settle upon specific compromises, prohibiting, say, the licensing of new nuclear power plants or a federal job guarantee for displaced fossil fuel workers. Other times, though, members opt merely to identify their various goals, leaving it to some other actor, most often an agency, to work out the specifics. Against this backdrop, theorists like Manning argued that attending carefully to statutory language, and in particular to the level of generality at which Congress speaks, was critical to respecting and facilitating such legislative "bargains."[124] Adhering to the specifics of legislative language would both increase fidelity to Congress and decrease judicial discretion, these theorists argued, contrasting modern textualism with the "strong" purposivism associated with cases like *Church of the Holy Trinity v. United States*.[125]

Alongside this discussion of tradeoffs, modern textualists emphasized increasingly the importantly limited role of the federal judiciary within our constitutional system. In his canonical *A Matter of Interpretation*, published in 1997, Scalia noted the "uncomfortable relationship of common-law lawmaking to democracy," reasoning that "the *attitude* of a common-law judge," which aimed at achieving "desirable" outcomes, was inappropriate in an "age of legislation" and

[123] Easterbrook, *supra* note 14, at 544.

[124] Manning, *supra* note 11, at 18.

[125] *Id.* at 15–16.

"regulation."[126] Similarly, Easterbrook insisted in 1994 that judges were "faithful agents, not independent principals," and that earlier methods of interpretation that "liberate[d]" judges were "objectionable on grounds of democratic theory as well as on grounds of predictability."[127] As Manning observed, arguments concerning the limited authority of judges within our democracy were partly legal and partly normative, with emphasis on the *constitutional* assignment of policymaking authority to the political branches. More broadly, though, the picture that emerged, especially in more public settings, was one of judges as faithful agents, tasked, *appropriately* within a democracy, with identifying law rather than making it.[128] This picture of judging was captured most famously by Chief Justice John Roberts's analogizing of judges to "umpires."[129] (Ironic, given Roberts's comparative lack of commitment to interpretive formalism.[130]) Even in more sophisticated writings, though, the continuing suggestion was that judges were to abstain from asserting their own policy preferences, especially under the guise of "discovering" law where there was none.

As the previous comment suggests, this picture of judging as law identification was meant to be appropriately modern, incorporating to varying degrees insights from Legal Realists concerning the widespread indeterminacy of the law. Easterbrook, as noted above, conceded even in 1983 that the legal content of statutes often runs out in the context of appellate litigation.[131] Two decades later, Manning allowed similarly that "all legal texts . . . produce ambiguities," and that such ambiguities can be "'liquidated' only through practice."[132] And even Scalia, though much more modest in this regard (more on this below), confessed that in the "vast majority of cases" in which judges would deem a statute "ambiguous" Congress did not "intend[] a single result."[133] This sort of humility about legal determinacy led,

---

[126] Scalia, *supra* note 10, at 13.

[127] Easterbrook, *supra* note 66, at 63.

[128] *See generally* Manning, *supra* note 11.

[129] *Confirmation Hearing on the Nomination of John G. Roberts, Jr. to be Chief Justice of the United States Before the S. Comm. on the Judiciary*, 109th Cong. 55 (2005) (statement of John G. Roberts, Jr., Nominee to be Chief Justice of the United States).

[130] *See* Richard M. Re, *The New Holy Trinity*, 18 Green Bag 2d 407 (2015).

[131] Easterbrook, *supra* note 14, at 533.

[132] Manning, *supra* note 11, at 88 (quoting The Federalist No. 37 229 (James Madison) (Clinton Rossiter ed., 1961)).

[133] Scalia, *supra* note 14, at 517.

predictably, to a discussion of official discretion. And while textualist writers conceded that judicial discretion was, to some degree, unavoidable, the presumption within our constitutional scheme was, again, that such discretion rests with more democratically accountable actors. As discussed below, this presumption had specific doctrinal manifestations, with judges declining to intervene in one way or another in the absence of "clearly" identifiable law. Here, though, it is worth highlighting the broad sentiment among textualists that both legally and normatively, policymaking was better left to officials with a democratic constituency, whether direct or indirect.

Moving ahead to the 2010s and beyond, textualists continue to adhere, for the most part, to the idea that judges can and do find law rather than make it. At the same time, there has been a notable distancing from the Legal Realist premise that the law is frequently indeterminate, especially in the context of appellate adjudication. As discussed below, this trend has been most striking within judicial reasoning. Also within the legal academy, though, confidence in the determinacy of the law is on the rise among interpretive formalists. Most prominently, Baude and Sachs have argued, in a much-cited 2017 piece, that although the communicative content of statutory language often runs out, background legal principles determine systematically how judges ought to rule in such cases.[134] Even more strikingly, Sachs writing separately has argued that prevailing skepticism about judges "finding" common law is unwarranted, arguing that discovering unwritten legal rules was no more mysterious than identifying norms of fashion or etiquette.[135] Baude and Sachs's confidence in the determinacy of this sort of "background" law contrasts somewhat with the trend among formalist judges to insist upon the determinacy of legal texts. Regardless, both of these trends reflect a distancing from Legal Realism and so non-intervention. Even if judges should decline to intervene in the absence of clearly identifiable law, that condition becomes trivially satisfied if the law is always clear upon closer inspection.[136]

---

[134] Baude & Sachs, *supra* note 60, at 1082–83.

[135] Stephen E. Sachs, *Finding Law*, 107 CALIF. L. REV. 527 (2019).

[136] Baude and Sachs, notably, consider whether *Chevron* fits within their account as part of our law of interpretation. Baude & Sachs, *supra* note 60, at 1127. Though expressing some skepticism, the more fundamental concern is that Baude and Sachs allow for so many *other* background interpretive principles, with little basis for choosing among them, as to invite the sort of indeterminacy that their account is meant to dispel.

B. DOCTRINE

Though always more aspiration than real commitment, textualist judges also endorsed legal doctrines that were non-interventionist in both rationale and effect. Most visible among them was the *Chevron* doctrine, which, up until very recently, was regarded as one of the most important legal doctrines of the past half-century. It was articulated first in a 1984 opinion by Justice John Paul Stevens, decidedly not a member of the textualist vanguard but aligned ideologically with conservatives at the time. According to *Chevron*, a reviewing court was to uphold an agency's interpretation of a statute that it administered so long as the statute did not "clear[ly]" preclude the agency's reading.[137] Relevant in our context is the explicit justification of the doctrine in terms of legal indeterminacy. To construe an unclear statute, Stevens reasoned, was to "fill" a "gap" in the law left by Congress, and because courts, comparatively speaking, lacked both technical expertise and democratic legitimacy, it made sense to defer to an agency's construction in cases of statutory "silen[ce]" or "ambigu[ity]."[138] To select among "reasonable" constructions, Stevens explained, involved the sort of "policy choices" the "responsibilit[y]" for which our Constitution "vests" not in the judiciary but instead "in the political branches."[139]

Despite having been authored by an adherent to the Legal Process school, textualist judges and scholars quickly became *Chevron*'s strongest proponents—and continued to be into the 2010s. Sparring with liberal colleagues like Justice Stephen Breyer, Justice Scalia, for instance, vocally supported the doctrine for nearly all his judicial career. Beginning with his 1989 law review article on the subject, Scalia explained his support for *Chevron* mostly in the language of rules.[140] A categorical instruction that courts defer to an agency if the law is ambiguous, Scalia insisted, was superior to a case-by-case inquiry.[141] Other textualists grounded their defenses of *Chevron* in a commitment to democracy and, more specifically, the idea that policy determinations by judges should not substitute for those of more

[137] Chevron, U.S.A., Inc. v. Nat. Res. Def. Council, Inc., 467 U.S. 837, 842 (1984).

[138] *Id.* at 843 (quoting Morton v. Ruiz, 415 U.S. 199, 231 (1974)).

[139] *Id.* at 866 (quoting TVA v. Hill, 437 U.S. 153, 195 (1978)) (internal quotation marks omitted).

[140] Scalia, *supra* note 14.

[141] *Id.* at 516.

democratically accountable officials. Manning, for instance, reasoned that "because it is now generally accepted that the interpretation of an ambiguous text will involve policymaking," *Chevron* reflected "constitutional commitments to electoral accountability" by presuming that Congress would prefer agencies rather than courts to fill in statutory gaps.[142] Similarly, D.C. Circuit Judge Laurence Silberman explained that "*Chevron* rests on the sound premise that agencies enjoy a comparative institutional advantage as a matter of legitimacy," and that, while not constitutionally compelled, "policy making should be eschewed by the federal judiciary whenever possible."[143]

While mostly uniform in their support of the doctrine, it is important not to overstate textualists' reluctance to displace agency readings. Scalia, for example, opined that accepting *Chevron* was easier for textualist judges given their relative disposition to identify "clear" statutory meaning. Those "willing to permit the apparent meaning of a statute to be impeached by the legislative history," Scalia explained, "will more frequently find agency-liberating ambiguity, and will discern a much broader range of 'reasonable' interpretation that the agency may adopt."[144] For a "'strict constructionist' of statutes," by contrast, the "meaning of a statute" is more often "apparent from its text and from its relationship with other laws."[145] (Though using it approvingly here, Scalia would later disavow the label "strict constructionist.") Whatever the validity of Scalia's empirical premise, his comment indicates a continuing promise that textualism means greater legal determinacy.[146] As such, the core tension persisted between greater attending to context and making interpretation more predictable.

Enthusiasm for *Chevron* continued until sometime during President Barack Obama's second term. In the upper echelons of the

---

[142] John F. Manning, *Constitutional Structure and Judicial Deference to Agency Interpretations of Agency Rules*, 96 Colum. L. Rev. 612, 626 (1996).

[143] Laurence H. Silberman, Chevron-*the Intersection of Law & Policy*, 58 Geo. Wash. L. Rev. 821, 824 (1990).

[144] Scalia, *supra* note 14, at 521.

[145] *Id.*

[146] Remarks like this approached their logical limit in later years as textualist judges turned against the doctrine, with Judge Raymond Kethledge asserting, for instance, that he "personally" had "never had occasion" to defer to an agency under *Chevron* since, in every instance, the underlying statute proved "clear." Raymond Kethledge, *Ambiguities and Agency Cases: Reflections After (Almost) Ten Years on the Bench*, 70 Vand. L. Rev. En Banc 315, 323 (2017).

federal judiciary, the turn against *Chevron* began in earnest in 2015.[147] That year, in a trio of concurring opinions, Justice Thomas, previously a *Chevron* defender, argued for the first time that "the judicial power, as originally understood, requires a court to exercise its independent judgment in interpreting and expounding upon the laws," and that this "power was understood to include the power to resolve [statutory] ambiguities over time."[148] (In so arguing, Thomas relied heavily upon historical work by Philip Hamburger, published in 2008—that is, almost a decade prior.[149]) Thomas was joined shortly thereafter by Gorsuch, then still a circuit court judge, in a concurring opinion to his own majority opinion in *Gutierrez-Brizuela v. Lynch*, in a seeming audition for a Supreme Court appointment.[150] And though less vocal than either Thomas or Gorsuch, even Scalia began to express reservations, though notably not on constitutional but statutory grounds. In a concurring opinion, he remarked that *Chevron* was "[h]eedless of the original design of the [Administrative Procedure Act]," which contemplated that the reviewing court, and not the agency, would resolve statutory ambiguities "authoritatively."[151]

Around this same time, opposition to *Chevron* also became an open political project within the Republican Party.[152] In 2016, the Party included a rejection of *Chevron* in its platform, proclaiming that "courts should interpret the laws as written by Congress rather than allowing executive agencies to rewrite those laws to suit administration priorities," after years of expressing no reservations.[153] In 2016 and again in 2017, a Republican House of Representatives passed

---

[147] This turn was foreshadowed in 2013 in a dissent by Chief Justice John Roberts. *See* City of Arlington, Tex. v. F.C.C., 569 U.S. 290, 314–16 (2013) (Roberts, C.J., dissenting).

[148] Perez v. Mortg. Bankers Ass'n, 575 U.S. 92, 119 (2015) (Thomas, J., concurring).

[149] *See* Philip Hamburger, Law and Judicial Duty (2008).

[150] Gutierrez-Brizuela v. Lynch, 834 F.3d 1142, 1149 (10th Cir. 2016) (Gorsuch, J., concurring) ("But the fact is Chevron . . . permit[s] executive bureaucracies to swallow huge amounts of core judicial and legislative power and concentrate federal power in a way that seems more than a little difficult to square with the Constitution of the framers' design.").

[151] *Perez*, 575 U.S. at 109 (Scalia, J., concurring).

[152] Craig Green, *Deconstructing the Administrative State:* Chevron *Debates and the Transformation of Constitutional Politics*, 101 B.U. L. Rev. 619, 660–61 (2021)

[153] Republican Nat'l Comm., Republican Platform 2016 10 (2016), https://www.presidency.ucsb.edu/sites/default/files/books/presidential-documents-archive-guidebook/national-political-party-platforms-of-parties-receiving-electoral-votes-1840-2016/117718.pdf [https://perma.cc/2G62-L9JP].

legislative proposals explicitly negating *Chevron*'s holding that statutory silence or ambiguity indicated an intention to delegate primary interpretive authority to an administering agency.[154] And most importantly, throughout Donald Trump's presidential term, the Republican Party, seemingly under the guidance of Federalist Society co-chairman Leonard Leo, systematically added to the federal judiciary individuals who expressed opposition to *Chevron* as well as more general discomfort with the administrative state.[155] *Chevron* in particular gained public attention during the Supreme Court confirmation process for then-Judge Gorsuch, with the previously obscure administrative law doctrine the subject of extended news coverage. Following Gorsuch's confirmation, the nomination of "anti-administrativists" to the lower federal courts continued, such that, by 2018, the *New York Times* had identified opposition to *Chevron* as a "litmus test" for Republican judicial appointments.[156] This political strategy appeared to reflect an assessment that conservative ideological interests would be advanced by empowering the judiciary relative to the executive branch. And understandably so, as Republicans had gained control of the federal bench, seemingly for decades to come.[157]

Owing to the efforts of Gorsuch and Thomas, *Chevron* has been unmentionable in the Supreme Court the past few years. Indeed, the very suggestion that an agency's reading might warrant special consideration has triggered mockery from Gorsuch in particular.[158] Such total disinterest in the reasoning of political branch actors was on full display in *Duguid*. In that case, unmentioned in either opinion was the

---

[154] Green, *supra* note 152, at 666–68.

[155] *Id.* at 687–88; *see also* Jeremy Peters, *New Litmus Test for Trump's Court Picks: Taming the Bureaucracy*, N.Y. Times (Mar. 28, 2018), https://www.nytimes.com/2018/03/26/us/politics/trump-judges-courts-administrative-state.html.

[156] Peters, *supra* note 155.

[157] Gregory Elinson and Jonathan Gould argue further that although attitudes toward deference have varied in accordance with partisan control of the executive branch and the judiciary, increased congressional gridlock has led liberals to depend more strongly upon administrative deference to advance their regulatory agenda. *See* Gregory Elinson & Jonathan Gould, *The Politics of Deference*, 75 Vand. L. Rev. (forthcoming 2022), https://papers.ssrn.com/sol3/papers.cfm?abstract_id=3889828.

[158] *See, e.g.*, BNSF Ry. Co. v. Loos, 139 S. Ct. 893, 908–09 (Gorsuch, J., dissenting) ("Instead of throwing up our hands and letting an interested party—the federal government's executive branch, no less—dictate an inferior interpretation of the law that may be more the product of politics than a scrupulous reading of the statute, the Court today buckles down to its job of saying what the law is.").

extensive regulatory history surrounding the provision at issue. Under the TCPA, the Federal Communications Commission (FCC) is authorized to "prescribe regulations to implement" various provisions of the Act, including the subsection restricting the use of automatic dialers.[159] Pursuant to that statutory authority, the FCC promulgated an order in 1992 interpreting that subsection narrowly, construing it to exclude functions like speed dialing and call forwarding, reasoning that "the numbers called are not generated in a random or sequential fashion."[160] Eleven years later, though, responding to "significant changes in the technologies and methods used to contact consumers," the FCC construed the TCPA as including "predictive dialers," which "store pre-programmed numbers or receive numbers from a computer database and then dial those numbers in a manner that maximizes efficiencies for call centers."[161] As a practical matter, the FCC reasoned that "through the TCPA, Congress was attempting to alleviate a particular problem – an increasing number of automated and prerecorded calls to certain categories of numbers," and that construing automatic dialers as equipment that dialed stored numbers automatically, regardless of whether the numbers were randomly or sequentially generated, best served this purpose.[162] The FCC reiterated its position that predictive dialers were automatic dialers in 2008, again in 2012, and finally in 2015.[163] Throughout these orders, all adopted through notice and comment rulemaking and all enjoying the "force of law," the FCC emphasized again and again that changes in automatic dialing technology necessitated an expansive reading of the automatic dialer provision since a narrower reading would "render the TCPA's protections largely meaningless by ensuring that little or no modern dialing equipment would fit the statutory definition."[164]

---

[159] 47 U.S.C. § 227(b)(2).

[160] In the Matter of Rules & Reguls. Implementing the Tel. Consumer Prot. Act of 1991, 7 F.C.C. Rcd. 8752, 8776 (1992).

[161] *In re* Rules & Reguls. Implementing the Tel. Consumer Prot. Act of 1991, 18 F.C.C. Rcd. 14,014, 14,090 (2003).

[162] *Id.* at 14,092–93.

[163] *In re* Rules & Reguls. Implementing the Tel. Consumer Prot. Act of 1991, 23 F.C.C. Rcd. 559, 566–67 (2008); *In re* Rules & Reguls. Implementing the Tel. Consumer Prot. Act of 1991, 27 F.C.C. Rcd. 15,391, 15,392 n.5 (2012); *In re* Rules & Reguls. Implementing the Tel. Consumer Prot. Act of 1991, 30 F.C.C. Rcd. 7961, 7971–73 (2015).

[164] In the Matter of Rules & Reguls. Implementing the Tel. Consumer Prot. Act of 1991, 30 F.C.C. Rcd. 7961, 7976 (2015).

As a linguistic matter, the FCC's position was somewhat opaque. On the one hand, the FCC seemed to rely upon a "broad interpretation" of the term "capacity," explaining that a device had the "capacity . . . to store or produce telephone numbers to be called, using a random or sequential number generator," and "to dial such numbers," so long as that device could be easily modified, through the downloading of software, for example, so as to be able to perform the specified functions.[165] The D.C. Circuit rejected that reading as overbroad in a 2018 decision, reasoning that the FCC's interpretation would encompass most smartphones insofar as one could easily add software to such a phone allowing it to function as an automatic dialer.[166] In its orders, the FCC tried to limit the scope of its interpretation by emphasizing that "the basic functions of an autodialer are to 'dial numbers without human intervention' and to 'dial thousands of numbers in a short period of time.'"[167] "How the human intervention element applies to a particular piece of equipment," the FCC continued, "is specific to each individual piece of equipment, based on how the equipment functions and depends on human intervention, and is therefore a case-by-case determination."[168] In *Duguid*, the respondent offered exactly this argument in response to Justice Sotomayor's objection that his interpretation would encompass "virtually all modern cell phones."[169] Dismissing that argument in a footnote, Sotomayor "decline[d] to interpret the TCPA as requiring such a difficult line-drawing exercise around how much automation is too much."[170]

In addition to its broad reading of "capacity," the FCC also seemed to take up Duguid's position that a device need not have the "capacity . . . to *store*" telephone numbers "using a random or sequential number generator," explaining, for example, that "[i]n the past, telemarketers may have used dialing equipment to *create and dial* 10-digit telephone numbers arbitrarily," but that the industry had "progressed

[165] *See id.* at 7973.

[166] ACA Int'l v. Fed. Commc'ns Comm'n, 885 F.3d 687, 695–701 (D.C. Cir. 2018).

[167] In the Matter of Rules & Reguls. Implementing the Tel. Consumer Prot. Act of 1991, 30 F.C.C. Rcd. 7961, 7975 (2015).

[168] *Id.*

[169] Facebook v. Duguid, 141 S. Ct. 1163, 1171 (2021).

[170] *Id.* at 1171 n.6.

to the point where" it had become "far more cost effective" instead to "us[e] lists of numbers."[171] As the D.C. Circuit observed in its decision invalidating the relevant portion of the 2015 order, the FCC was not entirely clear on this issue, however, and in the court's view, while "[i]t might be permissible for the Commission to adopt either interpretation," it was "unreasonable" for it to include language in the order suggesting both.[172] (Unlike the Supreme Court, the D.C. Circuit still treats *Chevron* as law, allowing it to say such things.)

Following the invalidation of its 2015 order, the FCC twice solicited comments from interested parties on the scope of the auto dialer provision, but, by the time of *Duguid*, had yet to issue a new order.[173] Noting the FCC's ongoing consideration of the matter, as well as its lack of involvement in the litigation below, the Solicitor General declined to take a position in *Duguid* at issue at the certiorari stage.[174] During the merits briefing, though, the United States sided with Facebook, explaining that after the D.C. Circuit's 2018 decision vacating the FCC's 2015 order, the FCC had no position on the issue, and that in the view of the Solicitor General's office, the better reading of the TCPA was the narrower one recommended by the petitioner.[175] In addition to standard interpretive arguments, the Solicitor General observed as a matter of "policy" that Duguid's reading "could potentially sweep in every modern smartphone," and that if, as the FCC had claimed, "[t]echnological changes" were such that devices falling outside the Act's definition were "caus[ing] the same annoyance to consumers as the devices that the TCPA restricts," Congress could "amend the TCPA to take account of those changes."[176]

---

[171] *In re* Rules & Reguls. Implementing the Tel. Consumer Prot. Act of 1991, 18 F.C.C. Rcd. 14,014, 14,092 (2003).

[172] *ACA Int'l*, 885 F.3d at 702–03.

[173] *See* Consumer & Governmental Affs. Bureau Seeks Comment on Interpretation of the Tel. Consumer Prot. Act in Light of the D.C. Circuit's *Aca Int'l* Decision, 33 F.C.C. Rcd. 4864, 4865–66 (2018); Consumer & Governmental Affs. Bureau Seeks Further Comment on Interpretation of the Tel. Consumer Prot. Act in Light of the Ninth Circuit's *Marks v. Crunch San Diego, LLC* Decision, 33 F.C.C. Rcd. 9429, 9429 (2018).

[174] *Brief for the United States*, Facebook v. Duguid, 141 S. Ct. 1163 (2021), 2019 WL 6211316, at *11.

[175] *Brief for the United States as Respondent Supporting Petitioner*, *Duguid*, 141 S. Ct. 1163, 2020 WL 5439453, at *12–15.

[176] *Id.* at *33.

One can only speculate what led the United States to abandon the earlier, more consumer-protective position adopted by the FCC from 2003 to 2018.[177] Regardless, this complex and seemingly contentious policy debate within the executive branch makes no appearance in *Duguid* (beyond, perhaps, an unattributed, "icing-on-the-cake" endorsement of the Solicitor General's position that the earlier FCC reading was overbroad). Such a discussion would have been interesting, of course, and would have re-raised many of the questions dealt with in the cases developing *Chevron* about which executive branch positions are warranting of deference (or "respect" or some other weighting[178]) and under what conditions. Because the D.C. Circuit had invalidated the FCC's 2015 order, there was no agency interpretation enjoying the force of law to which the Court could have deferred.[179] At the same time, the Court could have at least considered whether to assign significance to the position of the Solicitor General, whether because the policy views of the executive branch more generally are better informed and more democratically legitimate than those of federal judges, or because the Solicitor General's position was the best predictor of how the FCC would rule in the future.[180] Relatedly, the Court could have solicited additional briefing from the FCC, to the extent that its position was viewed as importantly distinct from that of the Department of Justice. Such attempts to rely upon the executive branch would have seemed sensible, of course, had the Court been more candid about the complex policy choices at issue, balancing concerns with consumer protection and privacy with potentially overly expansive liability (and this is to say nothing of the political complexities, given, in particular, the tremendous influence of the technology sector). Rather than acknowledge this complex reality, though, the Court opted to ignore (by name, at least) the policy reasoning of the various political branch actors involved, pretending instead that grammatical rules and structural reasoning left only one tenable interpretive position.

---

[177] As this change in policy reflects, it is important in contexts like these to distinguish between *political* decisions and *partisan* ones.

[178] Skidmore v. Swift & Co., 323 U.S. 134, 140 (1944).

[179] *See* United States v. Mead Corp., 533 U.S. 218, 229–33 (2001).

[180] *See* Ryan D. Doerfler, Mead *As (Mostly) Moot: Predictive Interpretation in Administrative Law*, 36 Cardozo L. Rev. 499 (2014).

With the rule of lenity, the story is similar though slightly more complicated. Glossed alternatively as the principle that "penal statutes must be construed strictly"[181] or that courts should "interpret ambiguous penal statutes in favor of the defendant,"[182] some textualists have commented upon the rule critically, warning against any interpretive principle that would invite judges to deviate from a statute's "most natural" reading. As then-Professor Barrett explained, however, in a 2010 law review article on the relationship between textualism and "substantive" canons, textualists nonetheless embrace the rule of lenity so long as it is taken to apply only if a statute is truly "ambiguous."[183] In this respect, the critical commentary just mentioned is best understood as warning against a misinterpretation of the interpretive principle or, as Barrett puts it more candidly, an effort to conform the rule of lenity to a more thoroughgoing commitment to faithful agency.

The justifications offered for adherence to the rule of lenity are many. Sometimes textualists explain adherence to the rule mostly in terms of historical pedigree, observing, for instance, that the rule is "perhaps not much less old than [statutory] construction itself."[184] More commonly, textualist appeal to the idea of "fair notice," offered alternatingly as a constitutional or a purely normative justification, with Justice Gorsuch remarking, for example, that "much like the vagueness doctrine, [the rule of lenity] is founded on 'the tenderness of the law for the rights of individuals' to fair notice of the law."[185] And, as relevant here, textualists consistently describe the rule of lenity as "democracy-promoting,"[186] drawing upon Chief Justice John Marshall's explanation in *United States v. Wiltberger* that "the power of punishment is vested in the legislative, and not in the judicial, department."[187] Implicit in Marshall's reasoning, of course, is that to construe a statute as imposing criminal liability outside its unambiguous "core" would be, in effect, for a court to *create* criminal law.

---

[181] 1 William Blackstone, Commentaries *88.

[182] Barrett, *supra* note 9, at 109.

[183] *Id.* at 166.

[184] United States v. Wiltberger, 18 U.S. 76, 95 (1820).

[185] United States v. Davis, 139 S. Ct. 2319, 2333 (2019) (quoting *Wiltberger*, 18 U.S. at 95).

[186] Abramski v. United States, 573 U.S. 169, 204 (Scalia, J., dissenting) (citing *Wiltberger*, 18 U.S. at 95).

[187] *Wiltberger*, 18 U.S. at 95.

(Hence, the occasional description of the rule of lenity as a prohibition against federal criminal common law.[188])

Setting aside offered justifications, the rule of lenity also *operates* as a principle of non-intervention. Unlike administrative law settings in which agency adjudication can sometimes establish civil liability as the legal status quo, criminal liability can only be established through judicial enforcement. For that reason, if a court declines to hold a defendant criminally liable on the ground that the statute invoked by the prosecution is insufficiently "clear," one can understand that decision, ala Easterbrook, as declaring the situation "outside the statute's domain."[189] The "party relying upon the statute," after all, has failed to show that Congress resolved the dispute in the way it alleged, and so the court has declined to rule in its favor, leaving the legal status quo unaffected.[190]

Though uniform in recognizing the principle, textualists have differed and continue to differ in their enthusiasm for it. Practically speaking, this difference manifests mostly in the degree of "ambiguity" believed to be required for the principle to come into play. Scalia and Garner, while emphasizing that "[n]aturally, the rule of lenity has no application when the statute is clear," recommend that courts construe criminal statutes favorably for defendants when "after all the legitimate tools of interpretation have been applied, 'a reasonable doubt persists'" as to statutory meaning.[191] This more expansive understanding contrasts with Barrett's, according to which the rule only serves to select "between *equally plausible* interpretations of ambiguous text"[192] or Kavanaugh who says the rule "applies only in cases of 'grievous' ambiguity," which is to say circumstances in which, "even after applying all of the traditional tools of statutory interpretation," the court "can make *no more than a guess* as to what Congress intended."[193]

---

[188] Screws v. United States, 325 U.S. 91, 152 (1945) (Roberts, J., dissenting) (describing "Anglo-American conceptions of liberty" according to which "crimes must be defined by the legislature").

[189] Easterbrook, *supra* note 14, at 544.

[190] *Id.*

[191] Scalia & Garner, *supra* note 13, at 299.

[192] Barrett, *supra* note 9, at 123 (emphasis added).

[193] Shular v. United States, 140 S. Ct. 779, 788 (Kavanaugh, J., concurring) (emphasis added) (quoting Ocasio v. United States, 136 S. Ct. 1423, 1434 n.8 (2016)) (further citations omitted).

Such differences between the Justices notwithstanding, it would be misleading to suggest that the rule of lenity has played a major role in the Court's reasoning at any point in recent decades. Even when affirmatively invoked, the rule has typically been presented as removing "any doubt" as to the correct reading of the statute.[194] In this respect, the rule of lenity differs meaningfully from the *Chevron* doctrine, which, regardless of its influence over case outcomes, was the prevailing analytical frame for statutory cases involving an administering agency until very recently. Be that as it may, there does appear to be a similar if more subtle shift away from using the rule of lenity even as window dressing or as a principle that must be acknowledged if only to be dismissed as having no application. Illustrated more fully in cases from this Term discussed in the next Part, textualist Justices today (as well as Justices adhering to a textualist methodology strategically) appear increasingly to make a point of saying that the rule of lenity has no application even in opinions that construe the criminal statute at issue in favor of the defendant or to outright ignore the rule in opinions that side against the defendant. As with *Chevron*, then, this de-emphasizing of the rule of lenity, though, again, more subtle and more uneven, is further indication of a textualist Court's decreasing interest in even the appearance of a commitment to non-intervention.

Sticking for now to the narrow discussion of canons, one can see how a refusal to take advantage of lenity can lead to the sorting of "dueling canons" opinions Llewellyn parodied more than 70 years ago. Returning to *Lockhart*, in her majority opinion, Sotomayor ironically cited Llewellyn's *Remarks* as evidence that the apparent availability of the series-qualifier canon invoked by Kagan in her dissent was inadequate to prove the statute ambiguous since "[t]here are two opposing canons on almost every point."[195] And in her dissent, Kagan made a point of emphasizing that resorting to the rule of lenity was unnecessary since "the ordinary way all of us use language" was the real reason "why Lockhart should win."[196] Commenting on the

---

[194] *E.g.*, Yates v. United States, 574 U.S. 528, 547 (2015) ("Finally, if our recourse to traditional tools of statutory construction leaves any doubt about the meaning of [the statute] we would invoke the rule that 'ambiguity concerning the ambit of criminal statutes should be resolved in favor of lenity.'" (quoting Cleveland v. United States, 531 U.S. 12, 25 (2000))).

[195] *Lockhart*, 577 U.S. at 361 (quoting Llewellyn, *supra* note 2, at 401).

[196] *Id.* at 377 (Kagan, J., dissenting).

decision, Easterbrook lamented that this pair of opinions suggested an "absence of method" in statutory cases.[197] While "attracted to the dissent's approach," Easterbrook confessed that he did not "think that either the majority or the dissent in . . . Lockhart . . . can be called wrong" since, as in "most" cases reaching the Court, the language at issue in *Lockhart* was "incomplete."[198] Given this irresolvable "ambiguity," Easterbrook continued, the only principled way to resolve a case like *Lockhart* would be by appeal to lenity or some similar rule.[199] Even there, though, Easterbrook worried that disagreements about how ambiguous a statute must be to trigger the rule might render it insufficiently rule-like—a problem that might be resolved, he suggested intriguingly, through the implementation of a voting rule.[200]

IV. Beyond Canons

While the discussion above focused on interpretive canons, a more "wooden" or "mechanical" textualism has spread much further than that. In multiple cases, textualist reasoning has been the subject of mockery or outright derision in popular coverage, even in circumstances in which the outcomes reached were ones commentators otherwise praised. As illustrated below, the reason, as with the cases involving canons above, is that textualist judges today have no option but to exaggerate the determinacy of linguistic meaning.

Two additional cases from this past Term capture textualism's current position. Both cases devote extended, dictionary-supported analysis to Congress's selection of a one- or two-letter word. And much worse, both offer what purports to be careful, detailed linguistic analysis but what is, upon closer inspection, mildly elaborate obfuscation.

Start with *Niz-Chavez v. Garland*.[201] In that case, the Supreme Court considered what discretion the federal government enjoys in

[197] Frank H. Easterbrook, *The Absence of Method in Statutory Interpretation*, 84 U. Chi. L. Rev. 81, 83, 84–87 (2017).

[198] *Id.* at 87–90.

[199] *Id.* at 90.

[200] *Id.*

[201] 141 S. Ct. 1474 (2021).

issuing "a notice to appear" in a removal proceeding.[202] Under the Immigration and Nationality Act (INA), a non-citizen eligible for removal may receive discretionary relief if, among other things, she has been continuously present in the United States for at least ten years.[203] The Illegal Immigration Reform and Immigrant Responsibility Act of 1996 (IIRIRA), however, provides that a non-citizen's continuous presence "shall be deemed to end . . . when the [non-citizen] is served a notice to appear" in a removal proceeding.[204] The IIRIRA, in turn, defines "notice to appear" as "written notice . . . specifying" various things, including the nature of the proceedings against the recipient, the legal authority under which those proceedings would be conducted, and, as relevant here, their time and location.[205] In *Niz-Chavez*, the government ordered the removal of Agusto Niz-Chavez, sending him a document containing his removal charges.[206] Two months later, the government sent a second document providing Niz-Chavez with the time and place of his hearing.[207] An immigration judge eventually denied Niz-Chavez's plea for relief under the INA.[208] The Board of Immigration Appeals ("Board") affirmed, concluding in part that Niz-Chavez was ineligible for discretionary relief because the two documents sent to him by the government collectively constituted "notice to appear" under the IIRIRA and so "stop[ped]" his continuous presence prior to his accruing the needed ten years.[209]

Dividing six to three, the Supreme Court held that the Board erred in its interpretation of the IIRIRA.[210] Writing for the majority, Justice Gorsuch explained that the IIRIRA's requirement that the government serve "*a* notice to appear" was incompatible with the Board's conclusion that a *series* of documents containing the necessary

---

[202] *Id.* at 1478.

[203] 8 U.S.C. § 1229b(b)(1).

[204] *Id.* at § 1229b(d)(1).

[205] *Id.* at § 1229(a)(1)

[206] 141 S. Ct. at 1479.

[207] *Id.*

[208] Niz-Chavez v. Barr, 789 F. App'x 523, 525–26 (6th Cir. 2019), *cert. granted*, 141 S. Ct. 84 (2020), and *rev'd sub nom.* Niz-Chavez v. Garland, 141 S. Ct. 1474 (2021).

[209] *Id.*

[210] *Niz-Chavez*, 141 S. Ct. at 1486.

information was enough to end a non-citizen's continuous presence.[211] To the contrary, Gorsuch continued, Congress's use of the indefinite article indicated its intention to require the government to issue a "single document" with all the relevant information before continuous presence would cease.[212] Pushing back against this inference, the government and the dissenters, led by Justice Kavanaugh, observed that the IIRIRA defined "notice to appear" as, simply, "written notice," giving no indication such notice "must be provided in a single document."[213] Gorsuch countered that the dissenters' observation was irrelevant because the definition in question defined "notice to appear," not "*a* notice to appear," and so even if one were to substitute the supposedly helpful definition for the operative phrase, the problem posed by Congress's use of the indefinite article would persist.[214] The dissenters argued further that even *if* Congress's use of the indefinite article was deliberate (something they seemed to impliedly question), that did not preclude the issuing of "a" written notice in "installments."[215] Here Kavanaugh pointed to a handful of seemingly helpful examples, including "a job application" that may be submitted "by sending a resume first and then references as they are available."[216] Gorsuch responded with examples of his own, observing, for instance, that "someone who agrees to buy 'a car' would hardly expect to receive the chassis today, wheels next week, and an engine to follow."[217] More generally, Gorsuch observed, "[n]ormally, indefinite articles (like "a" or "an") precede *countable* nouns," suggesting that here Congress intended to refer to a "countable object ('a notice,' 'three notices')," as opposed to a "noncountable abstraction ('sufficient notice,' 'proper notice')" as the government and the dissenters were suggesting.[218]

Liberal commentators were enthusiastic about the Court's pro-immigrant outcome. At the same time, Gorsuch's text-bound opinion elicited mockery. *Slate* reporter Mark Joseph Stern, for example, belittled Gorsuch's reasoning as "persnickety libertarianism" and a

---

[211] *Id.* at 1480.

[212] *Id.*

[213] *Id.* at 1490 (Kavanaugh, J., dissenting).

[214] *Id.* at 1480 (majority opinion).

[215] *Id.* at 1491 (Kavanaugh, J., dissenting).

[216] *Id.* at 1492.

[217] *Id.* at 1481.

[218] *Id.*

"grammatical geek-out."[219] Similarly, law professor Michael Dorf called Gorsuch's argument "ridiculous," complaining that the Justice's "petty sticklerism," despite "fortuitously benefit[ing] an undocumented immigrant," was "still petty sticklerism.[220]

One sympathizes with this sort of derision. Though presented as careful linguistic analysis, Gorsuch's opinion mostly alternates between question-begging and misdirection. Gorsuch's appeal to countable nouns, for instance, is simply a non-sequitur insofar as an example like "a job application" submitted in installments *is* an example of countable nouns that *can be delivered in installments*. (In referencing "written notice" as a "noncountable abstraction," Gorsuch appears to be harkening back to the dissenters' argument based on the definition of "notice to appear," but that argument is wholly separate from the observation that singular objects sometimes are delivered in parts.) Ultimately, the best Gorsuch can muster to explain away such examples is to offer examples of his own, explaining why his are more similar.[221] Most forcefully, Gorsuch observes that one would expect "an indictment in a criminal case or a complaint in a civil case" to arrive in a single document.[222] In response, the dissenters observe that, unlike an indictment or a complaint, a notice to appear contains "charging information *and* logistical calendaring information," making it "easy to understand why a notice to appear might require two installments while an indictment requires only one."[223]

Implicit in the previous exchange, of course, is that whether Congress intended (or maybe better *precluded*) the use of multiple documents in providing "a notice to appear" turns less on the grammatical article that Congress selected than what practicalities Congress did or did not have in mind. Concerning such "policy arguments," Gorsuch candidly observes that, in this case, "[a]s usual, there are

---

[219] Mark Joseph Stern, *Neil Gorsuch's Persnickety Libertarianism Gave Immigrants a Win at the Supreme Court*, SLATE (Apr. 29, 2021, 2:54 PM) https://slate.com/news-and-politics/2021/04/gorsuch-libertarian-textualist-immigrant-rights.html.

[220] Michael C. Dorf, *Petty Sticklerism That Fortuitously Benefits an Undocumented Immigrant is Still Petty Sticklerism*, DORF ON LAW (Apr. 30, 2021), http://www.dorfonlaw.org/2021/04/petty-sticklerism-that-fortuitously.html

[221] *Niz-Chavez*, 141 S. Ct. at 1481.

[222] *Id.* at 1482 (citing Transcript of Oral Argument at 39, Pereira v. Sessions, 138 S. Ct. 2105 (2018) (No. 17–459)) (alteration omitted).

[223] *Id.* at 1492 (Kavanaugh, J., dissenting).

(at least) two sides," which is why the Court was resting its decision on Congress's "plain statutory command," and not "raw consequentialist calculation."[224] Notably, the dissenters in this regard sounded remarkably like Gorsuch, conceding that "one may reasonably debate" which of the two readings of the IIRIRA was better as a matter of policy, but that here, the Court's job was to "follow the law passed by Congress and signed by the President," the meaning of which was "clear" in their view.[225] For all nine Justices, then, the IIRIRA admits of only one plausible reading. Such an implausible claim is forced most obviously for Gorsuch, who, wishing to decide against the government but thus far unable to assemble five votes to declare *Chevron* no longer the law, must insist that the available "textual and structural clues" permit the Court to "resolve the interpretive question," thus making irrelevant any "conflicting reading the government might advance."[226] For Kavanaugh and the other dissenters, though, deferring to the Board's interpretation of the ambiguous statute would seem like an attractive, less embarrassing route to the same outcome. And yet, similarly skeptical of agency deference, the dissenters too are compelled to say that, despite the contestable underlying policy issue, Congress's instruction can only be read one way.

Consider next *Van Buren v. United States*.[227] The question there was whether the Computer Fraud and Abuse Act of 1986 (CFAA) criminalizes the use of computer access for an improper purpose.[228] Nathan Van Buren, a police officer, had run a license-plate search in a law enforcement database in exchange for money as the target of a sting operation by the Federal Bureau of Investigation. While Van Buren had been authorized to access the database for law enforcement purposes, his use of the database for personal gain plainly (and knowingly) violated departmental policy. The question in *Van Buren* was whether this conduct also violated the CFAA, which imposes criminal liability on someone who "intentionally accesses a computer without authorization or exceeds authorized access."[229] The Act in turn

---

[224] *Id.* at 1486 (majority opinion).

[225] *Id.* at 1498 (Kavanaugh, J., dissenting).

[226] *Id.* at 1480.

[227] 141 S. Ct. 1648 (2021).

[228] *Id.* at 1652.

[229] *Id.*

defines "exceeds authorized access" as "to access a computer with authorization and use such access to obtain or alter information in the computer that the accesser is not entitled so to obtain or alter."[230] According to Van Buren, the operative provision of the CFAA did not apply to his conduct because that provision concerns only information one is not permitted to access for any reason. The government, by contrast, argued that the provision applies to anyone who accesses information for an unauthorized purpose, regardless of whether that person could access the same information legitimately for some other reason.[231]

Six Justices sided with Van Buren. Writing for the Court, Justice Barrett set aside the "host of policy arguments" raised by Van Buren and the government, "start[ing]," instead, "with the text of the statute."[232] Drawing on the *Random House Dictionary of the English Language* and *Black's Law Dictionary*, Barrett observed that Van Buren was uncontestably "entitled" to obtain the license-plate information at issue given his position as a police officer.[233] But was he "entitled *so* to obtain" that information, as the CFAA required? Appealing again to *Black's Law Dictionary* and this time the *Oxford English Dictionary*, Barrett reasoned that "so," as used in the Act, "serves as a term of reference that recalls 'the same manner as has been stated' or 'the way or manner described.' "[234] And since the "only manner of obtaining information already stated" in the relevant provision is "via a computer [one] is authorized to access," it follows that one only obtains information, for CFAA purposes, one is not "entitled so to obtain" if one obtains that information using a computer one is *not* "authorized to access."[235] Against this interpretation, Barrett noted that the government read "entitled *so* to obtain" to refer to "information one was not allowed to obtain *in the particular manner or circumstances in which he obtained it*."[236] That "manner or circumstance," Barrett continued,

[230] 18 U.S.C. § 1030(e)(6).

[231] *Van Buren*, 141 S. Ct. at 1653.

[232] *Id.* at 1654.

[233] *Id.* (citing Random House Dictionary of the English Language 649 (2d ed. 1987); Black's Law Dictionary 477 (5th ed. 1979)).

[234] *Id.* (citing Black's Law Dictionary 1246; 15 Oxford English Dictionary 887 (2d ed. 1989)).

[235] *Id.* at 1654–55 (citations omitted).

[236] *Id.* at 1654 (emphasis in original).

supposedly included "any 'specifically and explicitly' communicated limits on one's right to access information."[237] Despite "surface appeal," Barrett reasoned, the government's reading "prove[d] to be a sleight of hand" since it had interpreted "so" to refer to a "manner or circumstance" but had "ignore[d] the definition's further instruction that such manner or circumstance already will 'have been stated,' 'asserted,' or 'described.'"[238] After all, on the government's interpretation, the "manner or circumstance" captured by "so" is "not identified earlier in the [CFAA]" but instead could "appear[] *anywhere*—in the United States Code, a state statute, a private agreement, or anywhere else."[239]

Like Gorsuch's opinion in *Niz Chavez*, Barrett's extended discussion of "so" in *Van Buren* also invited mockery. While here again liberal commentators were generally praising of the Court's noncarceral outcome, veteran Supreme Court reporter Marcia Coyle chided Barrett and her textualist colleague Justice Thomas (more on Thomas's dissent below) for being unable to agree on the meaning of such a simple term.[240] Similarly, law professors Leah Litman, Melissa Murray, and Kate Shaw jointly characterized Barrett's opinion as "fetishistically textualist," with Murray comparing Barrett's analysis to then-President William Jefferson Clinton's infamous disputation of the meaning of "is."[241] And law professor Nicholas Bagley summarized his assessment as follows: "The outcome is good; the analysis is daft. How many dictionaries can you cite, to so little effect?"[242]

Such disparaging commentary was understandable. As Justice Thomas observed in his dissent, Barrett's extended discussion of "so" itself proved a sleight of hand.[243] Given his status as a police officer, there was, of course, a sense in which Van Buren was "authorize[d]" to "access[]" the law enforcement database at issue. There was also,

---

[237] *Id.* at 1654–55.

[238] *Id.* at 1655 (internal quotation marks and alteration omitted).

[239] *Id.*

[240] Marcia Coyle, *So, Yeah, 'Textualists' Barrett and Thomas Won't Agree on Everything*, Nat'l L.J. (June 3, 2021), https://www.law.com/nationallawjournal/2021/06/03/so-yeah-textualists-barrett-and-thomas-wont-agree-on-everything/.

[241] *Fetishistically Textualist*, Strict Scrutiny (June 4, 2021), https://strictscrutinypodcast.com/podcast/fetishistically-textualist/.

[242] Nicholas Bagley (@nicholas_bagley), Twitter (June 3, 2021, 6:12 PM), https://twitter.com/nicholas_bagley/status/1400591220729069569.

[243] *Van Buren*, 141 S. Ct. at 1662–63 (Thomas, J., dissenting).

though, a sense in which he was not since one could also hear Van Buren's "authoriz[ation]" as having been limited to "accessing" that database *for legitimate purposes*.[244] The government noted this possible interpretation in its briefing, only for Barrett to brush it aside as lacking "any textual basis."[245] Despite this assertion, the government's alternate reading showed, however, that the case turned less on the meaning of "so" than on the nature of Van Buren's "authoriz[ation]," which was something that appeal to dictionaries was not going to settle. To the contrary, whether Congress intended a broad or narrow reading of "authoriz[ation]" depended on whether it meant to create narrow or broad criminal liability for computer misconduct, which is to say it depended on what Congress was trying to *do* with the statute.

And here we return to the "host of policy arguments," the significance of which Barrett tried to downplay at the outset.[246] On Van Buren's side was the entirely reasonable concern that the government's interpretation would subject employees prohibited from using their workplace computer for personal use to criminal liability for checking their email or reading the news. For the government, there was the nontrivial worry that a national security official might evade liability despite misusing their access to monitor a former spouse. Barrett understandably preferred not to rest her conclusion on such arguments the under-determinacy of which (in terms of Congress's intention) almost jumps off the page. At the same time, Barrett was conspicuously unwilling to place weight on the rule of lenity, seemingly an easy basis upon which to reach the resolution that she preferred but the inapplicability of which Barrett chose to highlight.[247] (In dissent, Thomas ignored the rule of lenity, reasoning instead that any ambiguity in the case could be resolved by the presumption that Congress uses the "ordinary meaning" of a term.[248]) The reason, according to Barrett, was that Van Buren's interpretive arguments left no ambiguity to be resolved.[249] As a result, Barrett was stuck with dictionaries and an extended (and irrelevant) discussion of "so."

[244] *Id.* at 1663.

[245] *Id.* at 1655.

[246] *Id.* at 1654.

[247] *Id.* at 1661 ("Because the text, context, and structure support Van Buren's reading, neither of these canons [the rule of lenity or constitutional avoidance] is in play.").

[248] *Id.* at 1688 (Thomas, J., dissenting) (citation omitted).

[249] *Id.* at 1661.

V. Conclusion

In its modern form, textualism promised to be less wooden than its earlier manifestations through careful attention to interpretive context. By recognizing the inherently flexible, *practical* nature of words, modern textualists would thus be able to avoid the embarrassing "contradictions" that saddled their predecessors. To avoid that sort of embarrassment, though, required that textualists be more modest about the determinacy of statutory language. To make their method of interpretation less wooden, after all, was to make it more nuanced and, accordingly, to make it more vulnerable to reasonable disagreement about its application in individual cases. To back away from the "foolish pretense" of statutory determinacy was awkward, though, in a legal environment disfavoring the open exercise of judicial discretion, and all the more so for proponents of an interpretive methodology grounded so explicitly in a commitment to democratic self-rule and opposition to juristocracy.[250]

To the extent that it did, modern textualism was able to incorporate a more Realist understanding of legal determinacy because it also contained a (concededly modest) commitment to judicial nonintervention. That commitment is, however, now mostly gone. Seemingly motivated by a desire to accrue power to a now firmly conservative judiciary, a combination of interpretive methodological conversions and new judicial appointments has yielded a federal judiciary committed not only to textualism but also to deciding the cases before them on the basis of "independent" judicial judgment.[251] And because the legal environment *continues* to disfavor the open exercise of judicial discretion—and understandably so, given judges' comparative lack of democratic legitimacy[252]—the result has been increasingly wooden analysis, giving new and unfortunate relevance to Llewellyn's near-century old critique.

---

[250] *See* Samuel Moyn, *Resisting the Juristocracy*, Bos. Rev. (Oct. 5, 2018), https://bostonreview.net/articles/samuel-moyn-resisting-juristocracy/.

[251] Perez v. Mortg. Bankers Ass'n, 575 U.S. 92, 119 (2015) (Thomas, J., concurring in the judgment).

[252] *See* Ryan D. Doerfler & Samuel Moyn, *Democratizing the Supreme Court*, 109 Calif. L. Rev. 1703 (2021).

LEE EPSTEIN AND
ERIC A. POSNER

THE ROBERTS COURT AND THE TRANSFORMATION OF CONSTITUTIONAL PROTECTIONS FOR RELIGION: A STATISTICAL PORTRAIT

The Roberts Court has handed down a number of decisions that suggest a new approach to the Court's religion jurisprudence. The religion clauses of the First Amendment were once understood to provide modest but meaningful protection for non-mainstream religions from discrimination by governments that favored mainstream Christian organizations, practices, or values. On the other hand, the religion clauses provided little protection for mainstream religions—indeed, under the Establishment Clause, mainstream religion's influence over government policy was restricted. Under the Roberts Court, however,

Lee Epstein is Ethan A.H. Shepley Distinguished University Professor at Washington University in St. Louis; Eric A. Posner is Kirkland & Ellis Distinguished Service Professor of Law and Arthur and Esther Kane Research Chair at the University of Chicago. Posner took a position at the United States Department of Justice after this paper was completed but before it was edited; the paper does not reflect the views of the Department of Justice.

Authors' note: Epstein thanks the John Simon Guggenheim Foundation, the National Science Foundation, and Washington University for supporting her research on judicial behavior. We thank Aziz Huq and Geoff Stone for helpful comments, and Sima Biondi, Lina Dayem, Kelly Gregg, Kenny Mok, and Candice Yandem, for research assistance. The project's website (https://www.epstein.wustl.edu/religionincourt) houses a full replication archive, including the data and documentation necessary to reproduce all results.

The Supreme Court Review, 2022.
 https://doi.org/10.1086/719348

the religion clauses have increasingly been used to protect mainstream Christian values or organizations that are restricted by secular laws or liberal constitutional protections. Or so it has been argued. Some legal scholars have denounced this apparent turn to the right, while others see only small changes that incrementally move the jurisprudence in a direction more faithful to constitutional values.[1]

It is always hazardous to claim a "transformation" in the law, especially *in medias res*. Ideological or jurisprudential disagreements can be lost in the complexities of the facts. The Justices responsible for the change in the law characteristically claim to be following precedent. Tiny doctrinal innovations can lay the groundwork for a major revision in the law, while the announcement of a new direction may later be undercut by retrenchment. To help move the debate forward, we offer a quantitative assessment of the Roberts Court's religion decisions, based on the assumption that a consistent pattern of case outcomes or votes helps show that doctrinal disagreements are meaningful rather than mere rhetoric. And, as we will show, that has indeed been the case here.

The conventional historical account of the Supreme Court's religion jurisprudence recognizes two major shifts—leftward in the 1960s and 1970s, and then rightward beginning in the 1990s. For the Free Exercise Clause, we may date the leftward turn to 1963. Before then, the Court expressed little sympathy for religious dissenters who violated statutory law.[2] In that year, in *Sherbert v. Verner*, the Supreme Court held that a state could not constitutionally deny unemployment compensation to a Seventh-Day Adventist who refused to work on Saturdays because of her religious beliefs.[3] The Court applied strict scrutiny and held that the law placed an undue burden on the plaintiff. For the next few decades, the Free Exercise Clause was largely used to protect religious minorities—Christian or otherwise—who were burdened by general laws that advanced secular or mainstream Christian

---

[1] *See* Erwin Chemerinsky & Howard Gillman, *Symposium: The Unfolding Revolution In the Jurisprudence of the Religion Clauses*, Scotusblog (Aug. 6, 2020), https://perma.cc/43BS-KQAS; Richard Garnett, *Symposium: Religious Freedom and the Roberts Court's Doctrinal Clean-Up*, Scotusblog (Aug. 7, 2020), https://perma.cc/7P5E-HP4Z; Kim Colby, *Symposium: Free Exercise, RFRA and the Need for a Constitutional Safety Net*, Scotusblog (Aug. 10, 2020), https://perma.cc/ZB6P-S9FV; Mark Rienzi, *Symposium: Amid Polarization and Chaos, the Court Charts a Path Toward Peaceful Pluralism*, Scotusblog (Aug. 5, 2020), https://perma.cc/A3N2-ALP2; Leslie Griffin, *Symposium: Religions' Wins are Losses*, Scotusblog (Aug. 4, 2020), https://perma.cc/Q2V7-DX2S.

[2] *See, e.g.*, Minersville School District v. Gobitis, 310 U.S. 586 (1940).

[3] Sherbert v. Verner, 374 U.S. 398 (1963).

values (or both).[4] While "religion" prevailed in these cases, the cases reflected a liberal sensibility—the notion that the Court's job is to protect vulnerable minorities from indifferent or hostile majorities.

Meanwhile, the Court's interpretation of the Establishment Clause also drifted leftward. In a series of cases in the 1970s and 1980s, the Court struck down statutes that provided aid to religious schools even when that aid was given to comparable private secular schools as well. The turning point was the 1971 case of *Lemon v. Kurtzman*, in which the Court struck down a statute that funded the salaries of teachers who taught secular subjects in religious schools even though the statute also applied to teachers in secular private schools.[5] The Court worried that these types of subsidies would entangle the government in religious organizations. The Court also took a hard line against state-mandated or encouraged prayer in public schools.[6] And the Court developed skepticism toward public religious displays, and blocked them when they suggested government endorsement of religious values.[7]

The rightward shift begins in the 1990s but has flowered only in the last decade or so. For Free Exercise, the turning point was *Employment Division v. Smith*.[8] In that case, the Court upheld a state government's refusal to award unemployment benefits to individuals who had been fired for using peyote, even when they did so for purely religious purposes. The decision, by Justice Scalia, produced an ideologically jumbled split between the Justices, and has sometimes been regarded as liberal. By holding that facially neutral laws are valid even if they incidentally burden religions, the decision seemed to take a strong line against constitutionally compelled religious accommodation. Moreover, the decision provoked outrage on the right, and led to the enactment of the Religious Freedom Restoration Act (RFRA), which revived the *Sherbert* test.[9] In the context of the time, the decision pushed Free Exercise jurisprudence to the right. In most jurisdictions,

---

[4] Wisconsin v. Yoder, 406 U.S. 205 (1972).

[5] Lemon v. Kurtzman, 403 U.S. 602 (1971); *see also* Comm. for Public Educ. & Religious Liberty v. Nyquist, 413 U.S. 756 (1973).

[6] Engel v. Vitale, 370 U.S. 421 (1962); Wallace v. Jaffree, 472 U.S. 38 (1985); School District of Abington Township, Pennsylvania v. Schempp, 374 U.S. 203 (1963).

[7] County of Allegheny v. American Civil Liberties Union, 492 U.S. 573 (1989).

[8] 494 U.S. 872 (1990).

[9] 374 U.S. 398; Whitney K. Novak, *The Religious Freedom Restoration Act: A Primer*, Cong. Rsch. Serv. (Apr. 30, 2020), https://perma.cc/7M5F-PT94.

the majority is Christian and will be inclined to pass laws that respect Christian values, dogma, and practices, like Sunday closing laws. *Sherbert*, a characteristic Warren Court decision, used the Free Exercise Clause to protect religious minorities. But under the actual facts of the case in *Smith*, it was a minority religion that was burdened. In her concurrence in *Smith*, Justice O'Connor called the majority opinion a repudiation of the principle that the Free Exercise Clause protects the rights of religious minorities "whose religious practices are not shared by the majority and may be viewed with hostility."[10] And, indeed, opposition to *Smith*, and support for RFRA, came from the left as well as from the right for just this reason.

The next step was to push doctrine beyond formal neutrality and into the realm of accommodation. In two RFRA cases decided roughly two decades after *Smith*, *Burwell v. Hobby Lobby*[11] and *Zubick v. Burwell*,[12] the Court held that the contraception mandate in the Affordable Care Act violated the rights of a corporation owned by a religious family and some religious nonprofits. These were not constitutional cases, but they anticipated *Masterpiece Cakeshop v. Colorado Civil Rights Commission*.[13] That case involved a baker who refused, on religious grounds, to sell a wedding cake to a same-sex couple. The Court held narrowly that the baker's Free Exercise rights were violated by the state commission that enforced its anti-discrimination law, on the grounds that its ruling exhibited animus and showed inconsistency with other rulings.

The Court has also backpedaled on its Establishment Clause jurisprudence. In a series of cases beginning in the late 1990s, it allowed the government to offer subsidies to religious schools as long as the subsidies were offered on a nondiscriminatory basis to secular schools as well.[14] In a major turnabout, the Roberts Court struck down a Montana statute that made tax subsidies available to people who donated money to secular schools but not religious schools.[15] While the majority opinion was based on the Free Exercise Clause rather than the

---

[10] *Smith*, 494 U.S. at 902 (O'Connor, J., concurring).

[11] Burwell v. Hobby Lobby Stores, 573 U.S. 682 (2014).

[12] Zubik v. Burwell, 136 S. Ct. 1557, 1560 (2016).

[13] Masterpiece Cakeshop, Ltd. v. Colorado Civil Rights Commission, 138 S. Ct. 1719 (2018).

[14] Agostini v. Felton, 521 U.S. 203 (1997); Mitchell v. Helms, 530 U.S. 793 (2000); Zelman v. Simmons-Harris, 536 U.S. 639 (2002).

[15] Espinoza v. Montana Dep't of Rev., 140 S. Ct. 2246 (2020).

Establishment Clause (Justices Thomas and Gorsuch would have relied on the Establishment Clause), the effect was to reverse the earlier Establishment Clause jurisprudence that effectively forced states to deny religious schools funds that they gave to secular schools. Less dramatically, the Court has also backed away from earlier prohibitions on sectarian (as opposed to "neutral") prayer in government settings where prayer is permitted,[16] and became more tolerant of public religious displays as well.[17]

In 2020, the Court's emerging view on religion was put to the test. In the midst of the Covid-19 pandemic, religious organizations around the country challenged state lockdown orders that blocked or limited congregation in religious buildings as well as in movie theaters, lecture halls, and other secular venues. The plaintiffs argued that these lockdowns violated the Free Exercise Clause because, in virtually every case, the lockdown order put fewer restrictions on other types of secular congregation—for example, in grocery stores, and even liquor stores and casinos. The lower courts exhibited a remarkable partisan divide. Eighty-two percent of Trump-appointed judges ruled in favor of religious organizations who challenged lockdown orders, while 100% of Democrat-appointed judges ruled for the government.[18] (Other Republican-appointed judges split.) Meanwhile, other constitutional challenges—based on freedom of speech, the right to association, due process, and the right to property—enjoyed significantly less success in the federal courts.[19]

Four of the Free Exercise challenges reached the Supreme Court in 2020 and 2021. In the first two cases, the Supreme Court ruled against the religious organizations. The majority, consisting of Roberts and the four liberals, held that lockdown orders during a public health emergency did not violate the free exercise rights of religious believers. The four remaining conservatives disagreed.[20] With the death of Ruth Bader Ginsburg, and her replacement with Amy Coney Barrett,

---

[16] Town of Greece v. Galloway, 572 U.S. 565 (2014).

[17] Am. Legion v. Am. Humanist Ass'n, 139 S. Ct. 2067 (2019).

[18] Zalman Rothschild, *Free Exercise Partisanship*, 107 Cornell L. Rev. (forthcoming 2022), https://papers.ssrn.com/sol3/papers.cfm?abstract_id=3707248.

[19] Jacob Gershman, *Challenges to Covid-19 Lockdowns Have Been Mostly Losing in Court*, Wall St. J. (Feb. 13, 2021), https://perma.cc/Q3JN-W3S2.

[20] South Bay United Pentecostal Church v. Newsom, 140 S. Ct. 1613 (2020); Calvary Chapel Dayton Valley v. Sisolak, 140 S. Ct. 2603 (2020).

the majority flipped. In *Roman Catholic Diocese of Brooklyn v. Cuomo*,[21] the Court ruled that New York's lockdown order violated the Free Exercise Clause. The Court divided along ideological and partisan lines that almost exactly mirrored those of the lower courts—with the three Trump appointees voting for the church, the three Democratic appointees voting for the state, and the non-Trump Republican appointees splitting. In *South Bay United Pentecostal Church v. Newsom*,[22] the Republican justices partially struck down restrictions on church services in California. Justices Alito, Gorsuch, and Thomas would have struck them down completely, while the three liberal Justices would have upheld them.[23]

In light of these decisions, many observers expected that the Supreme Court would strike a blow for religious rights and finally overturn *Smith* in the case of *Fulton v. City of Philadelphia*.[24] A Catholic foster care agency sued the city for refusing to contract with it unless it agreed to place children with same-sex parents, arguing that the City's nondiscrimination policy violated the agency's Free Exercise rights. While it did not overturn *Smith*, the Court held in favor of the agency on narrow grounds—essentially that because the City offered an exemption to the nondiscrimination rule, the law was not generally applicable and *Smith* did not apply. The Court held that, in these circumstances, the City's refusal to extend the exemption to the agency placed an excessive burden on its religious exercise since the agency sought only to act consistently with its religious beliefs, and not to impose them on others. Justices Alito, Gorsuch, and Thomas made clear in concurrences that they believed that *Smith* should be overruled. Justice Barrett wrote a concurrence in which she said that "the textual and structural arguments against *Smith* are more compelling [than the historical record, which was mostly ambiguous],"[25] but that it was premature to overturn *Smith*. Justices Kavanaugh and Breyer joined this opinion, except that Breyer did not concur with the first paragraph from which that quotation was taken. Thus, it is clear, consistent with the earlier cases, that the Court is likely to further expand

[21] Roman Catholic Diocese of Brooklyn v. Cuomo, 141 S. Ct. 63 (2020).

[22] South Bay United Pentecostal Church v. Newsom, 141 S. Ct. 716 (2021).

[23] *See also* Tandon v. Newsom, 141 S. Ct. 1294 (2021).

[24] Fulton v. City of Philadelphia, 141 S. Ct. 1868 (2021).

[25] *Id.* at 1882.

religious rights by overturning *Smith*—with three Justices strongly in favor, and two Justices leaning in that direction.

Our goal in this article is to supplement the doctrinal scholarship with an empirical accounting. First, we paint a statistical picture of the doctrinal development. We show that from a statistical standpoint, the Roberts Court represents a sharp break from earlier Supreme Court religion jurisprudence. Second, we ask why this doctrinal change has taken place. As we show, a large part of the answer is the appointment by Republican presidents of Supreme Court Justices who favor religious rights and liberties.

While our empirical study of the Roberts Court and religion is novel, we do not write on a blank slate. The judicial behavior literature has established that judges—including Supreme Court Justices and lower-court judges—frequently decide cases in a way that reflects factors that lie outside legal doctrine. The most common type of study uses the judge's "ideology" as the independent variable of interest, and her decision or vote in a case as the dependent variable. Ideology typically means liberal or conservative, based on the party of the appointing president, the configuration of relevant ideological positions of the president and relevant senators, the judge's own party, the ideological valence of the judge's decisions in earlier cases, the judge's political giving before she ascended the bench, and so on.

But as numerous researchers have pointed out, judges' ideological or policy dispositions are more complex than merely conservative or liberal. Numerous studies have found that a judge's religious affiliation is correlated with voting outcomes, usually in predicted directions—with religious judges usually being more pro-religion than nonreligious judges, and judges of various religions taking positions that are consistent with the theological or institutional claims of their faith. Closest to our work are Blake and Wasserman-Hardy.[26] Controlling for ideology, Blake finds that Catholic Justices in cases from 1953 to 2007 form a distinctive voting bloc. For example, they vote more conservatively on abortion cases and more liberally on death penalty cases than other Justices—more consistent with Catholic theological commitments than with either of the two main ideological perspectives in

---

[26] William Blake, *God Save This Honorable Court: Religion as a Source of Judicial Policy Preferences*, 65 Pol. Rsch. Q. 814 (2012); Lewis Wasserman & James Hardy, *U.S. Supreme Court Justices' Religious and Party Affiliation, Case-Level Factors, Decisional Era and Voting in Establishment Clause Disputes Involving Public Education: 1947–2012*, 2 Brit. J. Am. Legal Stud. 111 (2013).

the United States. With respect to the religion clauses, Catholic Justices vote more conservatively in Establishment Clause cases (meaning for the government) and more liberally in Free Exercise Clause cases (meaning against the government). Blake argues that the Catholic Justices are hostile to the Establishment Clause because of their support for parochial schools, while they support the Free Exercise Clause in order to protect Catholics from the non-Catholic majority.[27]

Wasserman and Hardy examined 53 Supreme Court decisions involving disputes about public education under the Establishment Clause from 1947 to 2012. Like other researchers, Wasserman and Hardy found that conservative Justices favored religious organizations more than liberal Justices. With respect to religious affiliation, they found that, controlling for ideology, Catholic and Protestant Justices voted similarly until the Reagan era, but since 1981 the Justices have diverged, with Catholic Justices favoring religious organizations more than Protestant Justices—by a factor of twelve.[28] With another eight years of data, we are able to further develop these results into a story of transformation during the Roberts Court.

---

[27] Blake, *supra* note 26; *see also* Kevin Walsh, *Addressing Three Problems in Commentary on Catholics at the Supreme Court by Reference to Three Decades of Catholic Bishops' Amicus Briefs*, 26 Stan. L. & Pol'y Rev. 411 (2015) (finding that in the Roberts Court, Catholic Justices voted for outcomes supported by amicus briefs filed by the United States Conference of Catholic Bishops more frequently than non-Catholic Justices did).

[28] Wasserman & Hardy, *supra* note 26. For earlier studies of the U.S. Supreme Court, *see* Stuart S. Nagel, *The Relationship Between the Political and Ethnic Affiliation of Judges, and their Decision-Making*, in Glendon A. Schubert, ed., *Judicial behavior: a reader in theory and research*, (Rand McNally, 1964); S. Sidney Ulmer, *Social Background as an Indicator to the Votes of Supreme Court Justices in Criminal Cases: 1947–1956 Terms*, 17 Am. J. Pol. Sci. 622 (1973); and Sheldon Goldman, *Voting Behavior on the United States Courts of Appeals Revisited*, 69 Am. Pol. Sci. Rev. 491 (1975). Herbert Kritzer & Mark Richards, *Jurisprudential Regimes and Supreme Court Decisionmaking: The* Lemon *Regime and Establishment Clause Cases*, 37 Law & Soc'y Rev. 827 (2003) found that *Lemon v. Kurtzman* changed the likelihood that the Court subsequently found in favor of challengers under the Establishment Clause. Various other studies have looked at state courts and federal lower courts, and found similar results. *See* James Brent, *An Agent and Two Principals: U.S. Court of Appeals Responses to* Employment Division, Department of Human Resources v. Smith *and the Religious Freedom Restoration Act*, 27 Am. Pol. Q. 2 (1999); Donald R. Songer & Susan J. Tabrizi, *The Religious Right in Court: The Decision Making of Christian Evangelicals in State Supreme Courts*, 61 J. Pol. 507, 518–22 (1999); Barbara M. Yarnold, *Did Circuit Court of Appeals Judges Overcome Their Own Religion in Cases Involving Religious Liberties? 1970–1990*, 42 Rev. Religious Rsch. 79 (2000); Gregory C. Sisk, Michael Heise, & Andrew P. Morriss, *Searching for the Soul of Judicial Decision-Making: An Empirical Study of Religious Freedom Decisions*, 65 Ohio St. L. J. 3 (2004); Gregory C. Sisk, *How Traditional and Minority Religions Fare in the Courts: Empirical Evidence from Religious Liberty Cases*, 76 U. Colo. L. Rev. 1021 (2005); Gregory C. Sisk & Michael Heise, *Ideology 'All the Way Down'? An Empirical Study of Establishment Clause Decisions in the Federal Courts*, 110 Mich. L. Rev. 1201 (2012); Michael Heise & Gregory C. Sisk, *Free Exercise of Religion before the Bench: Empirical Evidence from the Federal Courts*, 88 Notre Dame L. Rev. 1371 (2012).

I. Data

Our dataset includes every Supreme Court case that produced a judicial opinion relating to the Free Exercise or Establishment Clause from the 1953 to the 2020 term, excluding cases that were decided without oral argument.[29] The number of cases is 95, or about 1.4 per term. Figure 1 shows the percentage by Chief Justice era; the number of cases is in parentheses. The religion cases make up 1.3% (95/7,155) of the docket during this period. Religious organizations won almost 60% of the cases. By comparison, during the same period criminal defendants prevailed 42% of the time, and from the 1953 term to the 2020 term, businesses won 44% of the time.[30] Other summary statistics are reported in the Appendix.

To explain case outcomes, we look at the votes of individual Justices. The dataset consists of 841 votes cast by 32 Justices, or 1.3% of votes in all orally argued cases from the 1953 to the 2020 terms. We categorize votes as "pro-religion" if they favor a religious organization or religious outcome—typically (but not always) the plaintiff in a Free Exercise Clause case and the defendant (the state) in an Establishment Clause case.

The religion cases are important. A high percentage of the religion decisions were reported on the front page of the *New York Times* on the day after the Court issued them: 54%.[31] This compares to an average, overall, of 15%. All eleven of the Warren Court's religion cases made the front page. The percentages for the other eras are lower but still much higher than the norm. As for the Roberts Court, nine of its eighteen decisions made the front page.

II. Case Outcomes Over Time

The popular notion that the Roberts Court represents a break in the development of the jurisprudence of the religion clauses is

---

[29] The initial data come from the U.S. Supreme Court Database (http://supremecourtdatabase.org).

[30] Lee Epstein, William M. Landes & Richard A. Posner, *When It Comes to Business, the Right and Left Sides of the Court Agree*, 54 Wash. U. J.L. & Pol'y 33 (2017). Data updated by the authors.

[31] This percentage excludes orally argued per curiams, for which we lack a complete set of *New York Times* data. Only one religion-related per curiam was issued between the 1953 and 2020 terms. Coverage on the front page of the *Times* is a common measure of the importance or salience of the Court's decisions. *See* Lee Epstein & Jeffrey A. Segal, *Measuring Issue Salience* 44 Am. J. Pol. Sci. 66 (2000).

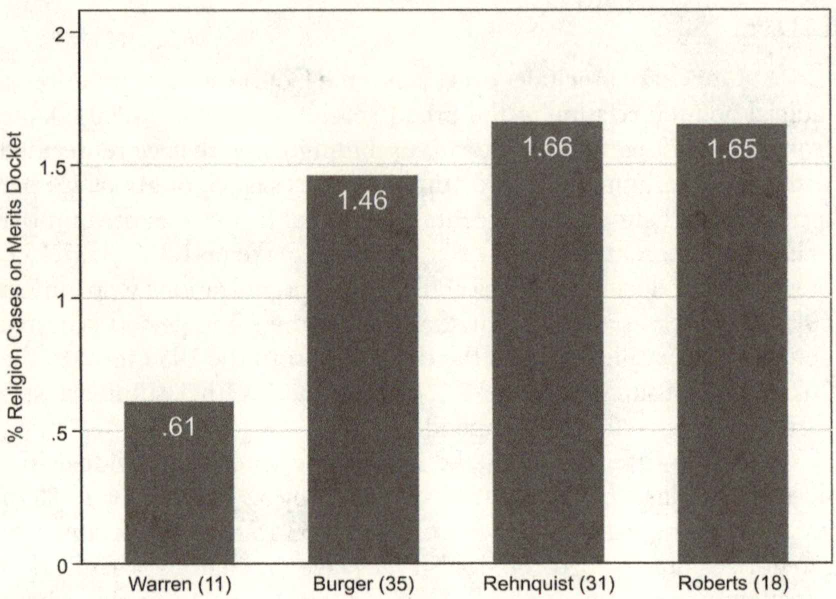

Figure 1. Religion cases as a percentage of all orally argued cases by Chief Justice era, 1953–2020 terms.

amply supported by the data. Figure 2 shows the percentage of pro-religion and anti-religion case outcomes by Chief Justice era.

Over the entire period, the Court ruled in favor of religion 59% of the time. Win rates do not differ significantly for Free Exercise Clause cases (59%) and Establishment Clause cases (57%). Across the Warren, Burger, and Rehnquist Courts the religious side prevailed about half the time, with gradually increasing success. In the Roberts Court, the win rate jumps to 83%. Relatedly, the participation of the Solicitor General in religion cases has increased over time from 9% during the Warren Court to 89% in the Roberts Court. Trump's Solicitors General supported religion in all the cases in which they participated except *Trump v. Hawaii*[32] and *Tanzin v. Tanvir*[33]—cases in which the

[32] In Trump v. Hawaii, 138 S. Ct. 2392 (2018), the Court held that President Trump's travel ban did not violate the Establishment Clause. The Court observed that the order did not ban Muslims on its face and disregarded evidence that the ban was motivated by animus or political expediency rather than national security considerations.

[33] In Tanzin v. Tanvir, 141 S. Ct. 486 (2020), the Court held that Muslim plaintiffs who had allegedly been put on the No Fly List after they refused to serve as informants against their religious community had a claim for damages under RFRA.

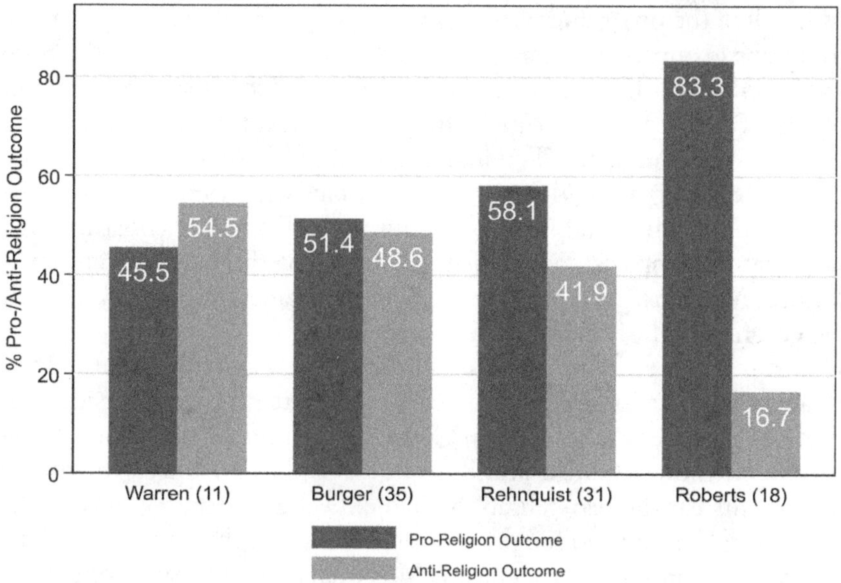

Figure 2. Outcomes in religion cases, by Chief Jusice era, 1953–2020 terms.

plaintiffs were Muslims or challenged a policy that harmed Muslims, and possibly not pro-religion but also not anti-Christian, a point which we must now address.[34]

What does "pro-religion" mean? The Warren Court religion cases were notable for protecting minority or non-mainstream religions, especially dissenting Christian denominations—the Seventh-Day Adventists in *Sherbert*, the Amish in *Wisconsin v. Yoder*.[35] Some observers argue that the Roberts Court has turned this tradition on its head by extending protections to mainstream Christian groups and values.[36] To address this argument, we try two strategies. First, we classify cases based on whether the plaintiff (not the petitioner) is affiliated with a mainstream Christian religion, or not. We find that in the Warren Court, *no* plaintiff was affiliated with a mainstream Christian religion;

[34] The Supreme Court usually rules in favor of the petitioner, presumably because the Justices search out lower court cases that they disagree with. And, indeed, the percentage of pro-religion petitioners has increased in parallel with their success in court—from 36% in the Warren Court to 78% in the Roberts Court.

[35] Sherbert v. Verner, 374 U.S. 398 (1963); Wisconsin v. Yoder, 406 U.S. 205 (1972).

[36] *E.g.*, Chemerinsky & Gillman, *supra* note 1.

thus, all of the pro-religion outcomes benefited minority or dissenting religious groups. This changes as the Court moves right. By the time we reach the Roberts Court, nine mainstream Christian plaintiffs win seven of their cases. Non-mainstream plaintiffs also did well, winning three out of four cases. The loss occurred in *Trump v. Hawaii*.[37] The Supreme Court upheld Trump's travel ban which Hawaii had challenged under the Establishment Clause as well as other constitutional and statutory provisions. Hawaii claimed that the ban discriminated against Muslims. (While Hawaii is obviously not a religious plaintiff, it acted on behalf of religious freedom.)

Second, we redefine the outcome variable as a ruling that is pro-mainstream Christian or not. The pro-mainstream Christian side won 44% of the cases in the Warren Court, 52% in the Burger Court, 57% in the Rehnquist Court, and 80% in the Roberts Court—mirroring the results for the pro-religion variable. Using this outcome variable, *Trump v. Hawaii* is no longer an anomaly but fits the pattern: the outcome is not pro-religion (it harms Muslims) but it advances, or at least is consistent with, a pro-Christian agenda. Still, while the Roberts Court favors mainstream Christian groups and values more than the earlier Courts did, the overall pattern mirrors the result for the merely pro-religion variable. One way to think about this pattern is that the Roberts Court extended the Warren Court's protections for minority religions so as to encompass majority religions as well. The Roberts Court is pro-mainstream religion, and more pro-mainstream Christian than the Warren Court, but not exclusively pro-mainstream. In a well-known speech, Justice Alito couched his criticisms of liberal Justices as a defense of religious freedom rather than as a defense of conservative religious values.[38]

III. The Justices

We turn to the most natural explanation for the transformation of religion jurisprudence: changes in the personnel of the Court. Table 1 ranks the Justices by the percentage of pro-religion votes. While the small number of cases for several Justices, including Kavanaugh and Gorsuch, prevents strong conclusions, the pattern is clear. The top

---

[37] 138 S. Ct. 2392 (2018).

[38] Samuel Alito, *Address by Justice Samuel Alito for the Federalist Society's 2020 National Lawyers Convention*, Federalist Soc'y (Nov. 12, 2020), archived at https://perma.cc/S9T3-KB5L.

five most pro-religion judges sit on the Roberts Court; they are Republican appointees; they are ideologically conservative (0 is the most conservative); and they are (as we will see) more religious than average (2 is the most devout). More broadly, Republican and conservative Justices are more pro-religion than other Justices. And the Roberts Court is obviously the most polarized as well as the most pro-religion Court, as Justices Sotomayor and Ginsburg appear at the bottom of the ranking.

Although a substantial overlap exists between pro-religion and pro-mainstream Christian,[39] certain deviations stand out. Kagan and Breyer, both liberal Justices, are relatively high on the list under the pro-religion variable (79% and 65%) but drop significantly for the pro-mainstream Christian variable (54% and 44%) as one would expect. As we will see, this is a pattern for Democratic and liberal Justices. This is because Democratic and liberal Justices often (particularly before the Roberts Court) tended to cast pro-religion votes in cases involving non-mainstream religions.[40] *Trump v. Hawaii* illustrates this pattern. The conservative Justices rejected religion in favor of national security and presidential power—but it was Muslim, not Christian religion. The liberals sided with Muslims, a frequently targeted minority religious group. The pattern then reverses for the pandemic cases. The conservative Justices side with mostly (but not entirely) mainstream Christian organizations (but also Jewish), while the liberals side with government.

To unpack these results, we start by reporting some simple correlations in Table 2.

Neither variable capturing the Office of the Solicitor General (OSG) (or party of the president in office is correlated with pro-religion votes. This may suggest these are highly personal decisions unaffected by the political environment. The remaining variables are statistically significant in these correlations.

A. POLITICAL PARTY

Overall, there is a statistically significant ($p < 0.05$) relationship between voting for religion and political party. This holds regardless of

[39] The correlation between the percentages in Table 1 is 0.80. There is also a 75% overlap in the raw votes (for religion or not) and the votes (pro-Christian mainstream or not) (552/737) (includes Barrett's vote in *Fulton v. City of Philadelphia).*

[40] The correlation between the percentages in Table 1 for the Democratic appointees is 0.70; it is 0.80 for the Republican appointees.

Table 1

Ranking Justices by Percentage of Pro-religion Votes, 1953–2020 Terms

Justice (Tenure)	% Pro-Religion (*N*)	% Pro-Mainstream Christian (*N*)	Religion	Party of Appointing President	Ideology	Devoutness
Kavanaugh (2018–)	100.0 (6)	83.3 (6)	Catholic	Republican	0.070	3.25
Thomas (1991–)	91.7 (36)	87.1 (31)	Catholic	Republican	0.160	5.00
Roberts (2005–)	88.9 (18)	86.7 (15)	Catholic	Republican	0.120	2.75
Gorsuch (2017–)	88.9 (9)	88.9 (9)	Catholic/Episcopalian	Republican	0.110	3.75
Alito (2006–)	88.2 (17)	86.7 (15)	Catholic	Republican	0.100	3.00
Scalia (1986–2016)	79.5 (39)	85.3 (34)	Catholic	Republican	0.000	4.75
Kagan (2010–)	78.6 (14)	53.8 (13)	Jewish	Democrat	0.730	3.00
Burger (1969–86)	77.1 (35)	67.7 (31)	Presbyterian	Republican	0.115	1.50
Kennedy (1988–2018)	70.3 (37)	71.9 (32)	Catholic	Republican	0.365	3.25
Rehnquist (1972–2005)	69.4 (62)	87.3 (55)	Lutheran	Republican	0.045	3.50
White (1962–93)	66.7 (57)	69.4 (49)	Episcopalian	Democrat	0.500	1.75
Stewart (1958–81)	65.6 (32)	42.3 (26)	Episcopalian	Republican	0.750	2.00
Breyer (1994–)	64.5 (31)	44.4 (27)	Jewish	Democrat	0.475	2.75
Frankfurter (1939–62)	60.0 (5)	60.0 (5)	Jewish	Democrat	0.665	1.25
O'Connor (1981–2006)	57.8 (45)	52.4 (42)	Episcopalian	Republican	0.415	3.75
Powell (1972–87)	51.4 (35)	51.6 (31)	Presbyterian	Republican	0.165	3.25
Goldberg (1962–65)	50.0 (2)	0.0 (2)	Jewish	Democrat	0.750	4.25
Blackmun (1970–94)	49.0 (51)	31.1 (45)	Methodist	Republican	0.115	3.75
Brennan (1956–90)	45.8 (59)	21.2 (52)	Catholic	Republican	1.000	4.50
Warren (1953–69)	45.5 (11)	44.4 (9)	Protestant	Republican	0.750	3.25
Marshall (1967–91)	44.9 (49)	21.4 (42)	Episcopalian	Democrat	1.000	3.25
Harlan (1955–71)	42.9 (14)	58.3 (12)	Presbyterian	Republican	0.875	2.50
Sotomayor (2009–)	41.2 (17)	13.3 (15)	Catholic	Democrat	0.780	1.75

Whittaker (1957–62)	40.0 (5)	80.0 (5)	Methodist	Republican	0.500	2.25
Clark (1949–67)	37.5 (8)	50.0 (8)	Presbyterian	Democrat	0.500	4.00
Souter (1990–2009)	36.8 (19)	18.8 (16)	Episcopalian	Republican	0.325	4.25
Black (1937–71)	35.7 (14)	41.7 (12)	Baptist	Democrat	0.875	1.50
Fortas (1965–69)	33.3 (3)	0.0 (1)	Jewish	Democrat	1.000	2.00
Stevens (1975–2010)	29.3 (58)	21.6 (51)	Protestant	Republican	0.250	1.50
Ginsburg (1993–2020)	23.3 (30)	7.7 (26)	Jewish	Democrat	0.680	2.25
Douglas (1939–75)	22.7 (22)	0.0 (19)	Presbyterian	Democrat	0.730	2.75

Sources: For the Justices' service: https://www.supremecourt.gov/about/members_text.aspx; for the Justices' religion and ideology score: Lee Epstein, et al., The Supreme Court Compendium (7th ed. 2021).

Notes:

1. Five Justices are excluded because they cast zero or one vote in religion cases: Barrett, Burton, Jackson, Minton and Reed.
2. Concerning the Justices' religion:
   - Frankfurter's religious faith was largely agnostic.
   - Gorsuch was raised Catholic but now worships at an Episcopalian church.
   - Thomas was born into a Baptist family but was raised by his grandparents as a Roman Catholic and studied for the Catholic priesthood. In his later adult years, he regularly attended a charismatic Episcopal church. In 1996 Thomas returned to the Roman Catholic Church.
3. Concerning the Justices' political party affiliation: Brennan and Powell were Democrats although appointed by Republican presidents; Frankfurter is sometimes classified as an Independent.
4. The ideology score ranges from 0 (most conservative) to 1 (liberal) and is based on an analysis of newspaper editorials prior to the Justices' confirmation (the Segal-Cover score). *See* Jeffrey A. Segal & Albert D. Cover, *Ideological Values and the Votes of U.S. Supreme Court Justices*, 83 Am. Pol. Sci. Rev. 557 (1989).
5. The "Devoutness" scores, developed by the authors, range from 1 (least devout) to 5 (most devout). For more information on the scores, see the "Devoutness" section below.

Table 2

Relationship between Pro-religion Votes and Various Explanatory Variables

Variable	Pro-Religion Votes
*Appointing President's Party	61.1% (Rs) v. 48.8% (Ds)
*Justice's Party	63.6% (Rs) v. 48.6% (Ds)
*Ideology	64.5% (conservative) v. 61.0% (moderate) v. 44.5% (liberal)
*Justice's Religion	71.1% (Catholic) v. 52.0% (Non-Catholic)
*Justice's Devoutness	62.8% (most devout) v. 57.6% (moderate devout) v. 52.2% (least devout)
*Type of Case	66.1% (free exercise) v. 51.5% (establishment)
OSG	55.2% (no participation) v. 59.2% (pro-relig) v. 61.1% (anti-relig)
Party of President in Office	56.7% (Rs) v. 58.7% (Ds)
*USSC Petitioner	61.9% (pro-religion petitioner) v. 51.4% (anti-religion petitioner)
*Case Salience	61.7% (not-salient) v. 53.8% (salient)

Notes: Total number of votes (cast by 32 Justices) = 841. * = statistically significant at $p \leq 0.05$. Case Salience is whether the decision was reported on the front page of the *New York Times* on the day after it was issued. Ideology is based on newspaper editorials (see note 4 in Table 1). For Ideology, all comparisons significant except conservative v. moderate. For Devoutness, only the comparison between the most and least devout is significant.

whether the political party is the Justice's party or the appointing president's party. However, the differences are substantively and statistically significant only for the Roberts Court Justices.[41] In the earlier Courts, the partisan divide did not map as clearly into pro- and anti-religion votes, as Figure 3 shows.

B. IDEOLOGY

We use three measures of ideology: Segal-Cover scores, which are based on newspaper editorials (see note 4 in Table 1); Martin-Quinn term-by-term scores, and Martin-Quinn career average (both derived from analyses of voting patterns).[42] (Table 2 collapses the Segal-Cover score into three categories but in the analyses, we used the raw scores.) Regardless of which we use, logit regressions (clustered on Justice and

[41] For the Burger Court, the difference is statistically significant but only when partisanship is measured as the Justice's party affiliation, not the appointing president's party.

[42] Andrew D. Martin & Kevin M. Quinn, *Dynamic Ideal Point Estimation via Markov Chain Monte Carlo for the U.S. Supreme Court, 1953–1999*, 10 Pol. Analysis 134 (2002).

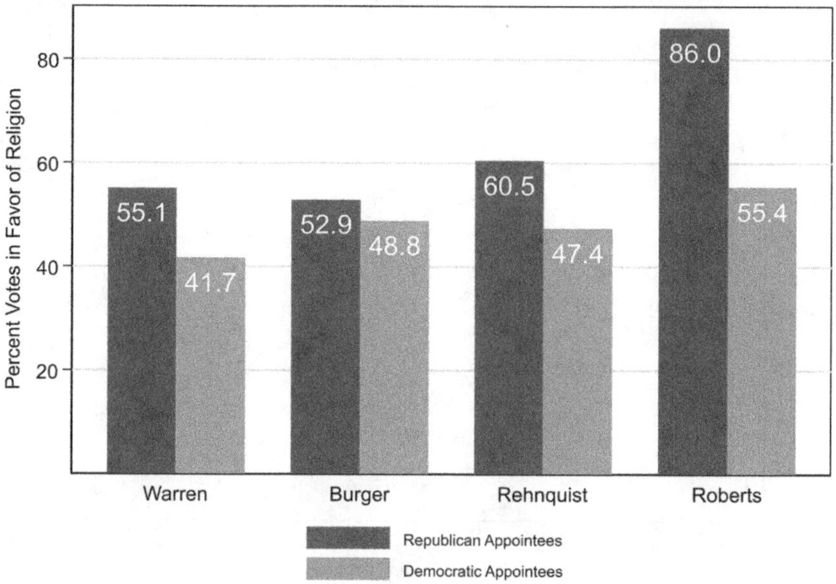

Figure 3. Votes in favor of religion by the party of the Justices' appointing presidents, 1953–2020 terms. Only the gap between the Ds and Rs on the Roberts Court is statistically significant at $p < 0.05$. N for the Warren Court = 49 R votes, 48 D votes; Burger Court = 227 R votes, 82 D votes; Rehnquist Court = 220 R votes, 57 D votes; Roberts Court = 93 R votes, 65 D votes.

controlling for whether the petitioner was pro- or anti-religion) show that ideology is a significant predictor of religion votes. Moreover, unlike partisanship the results (mostly) hold for each Court era.[43]

Figure 4 provides an example, using the Segal-Cover scores (which are easy to interpret). It shows the probability of voting in favor of religion by ideology, controlling for the petitioner (and clustered on Justice). Moving from the most conservative justices (e.g., Scalia, Kavanaugh, Alito) to the most liberal (e.g., Marshall, Brennan): the probability of voting for religion declines from about 0.71 to 0.45 when the petitioner is pro-religion. The pattern holds for the Roberts Court with one exception. The conservatives vote in favor of religion nearly all the time; Breyer, a moderate, is in the middle; and liberals Ginsburg and Sotomayor vote against religion most of the time. The exception

[43] The Warren Court is the major exception. No measure of ideology produces a significant result.

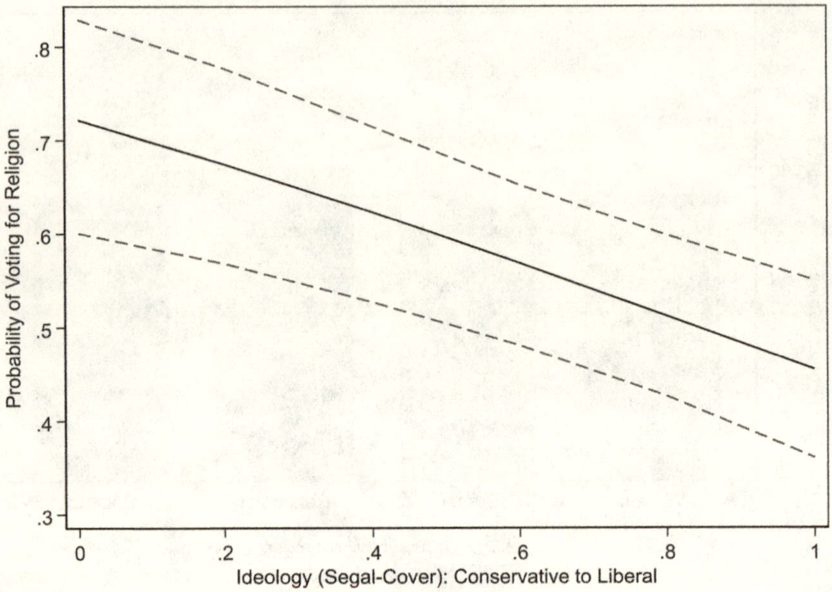

Figure 4. Probability of voting for religion by ideology, 1953–2020 terms. The dark line is the probability; the lighter lines are 95% confidence intervals. The probability is based on a logit model (clustered on Justice) that accounts for whether the petitioner in the Supreme Court is pro- or anti-religion.

is Kagan, who despite a high liberal ideology score (higher than Ginsburg's), tends to vote with the conservatives on religion, though frequently on narrower grounds (often joining a concurrence with Breyer). At the same time, Kagan differs from the conservatives by voting substantially less for the mainstream Christian position.

Overall, ideology is very important—seemingly more important than partisanship (save for the Roberts Court's Justices).

C. CATHOLIC JUSTICES

Scholars have found evidence that Catholic Justices vote differently from other Justices, and that they favor religious organizations.[44] Our results are consistent with this view. On average, Catholic Justices are significantly ($p < 0.05$) more likely to vote for religion than non-Catholic Justices are (71.1% versus 52.0%). This is largely a Roberts/

[44] Blake, *supra* note 26.

Rehnquist Court phenomenon, as Figure 5 below shows, and is easily explained. Six of the top ten most pro-religion Justices (and seven, if Gorsuch is included) are Catholic (see Table 1). All of them overlapped with one or both Courts. Only two other Catholic Justices are in our dataset. Justice Sotomayor, a liberal, ranks among the most anti-religion Justices especially on the pro-mainstream Christian variable. She is also not devout. Justice Brennan, another liberal, and the only Catholic justice during the Burger Court, accounts for the anomalous anti-religion slant of the one-person Catholic "bloc" in that Court.

Even though some of the Catholic Justices are among the most conservative in our dataset, the Catholic (or not) variable remains a significant predictor in a multivariate model that includes ideology and the petitioner in the Supreme Court (see Appendix, Table A2). All else equal,[45] for a Catholic Justice the probability of voting for religion is 0.73 [0.65, 0.81]; for a non-Catholic justice it is 0.55 [0.45, 0.66].

D. DEVOUTNESS

Not all religious judges are devout, or allow their religious commitments to influence their interpretations of the law. It seems plausible that devout Justices are more likely to vote for religious outcomes (or outcomes consistent with their particular religion) than less devout Justices. To test this hypothesis, we asked research assistants to gather biographical information about the Justices from the web, and then another group of (four) students, acting independently, to read that information and attach a numerical value from 1 (not devout) to 5 (very devout). The students (not all law students) were given only the biographical details and not told the Justice's name or that the biography was of a Supreme Court Justice. The ratings (the means of the four raters) thus reflected a collective judgment based on some rough sense of how people display their devoutness. While the ratings are obviously imperfect, they were highly correlated. There is, of course, some ambiguity whether the scores reflect true devotion or a desire to display one's religious devotion publicly.

Overall, there is generally no significant relationship between voting for religion and devoutness (regardless of how we categorize levels

[45] To make this calculation, ideology (the Segal-Cover score) is at its mean and the petitioner is pro-religion.

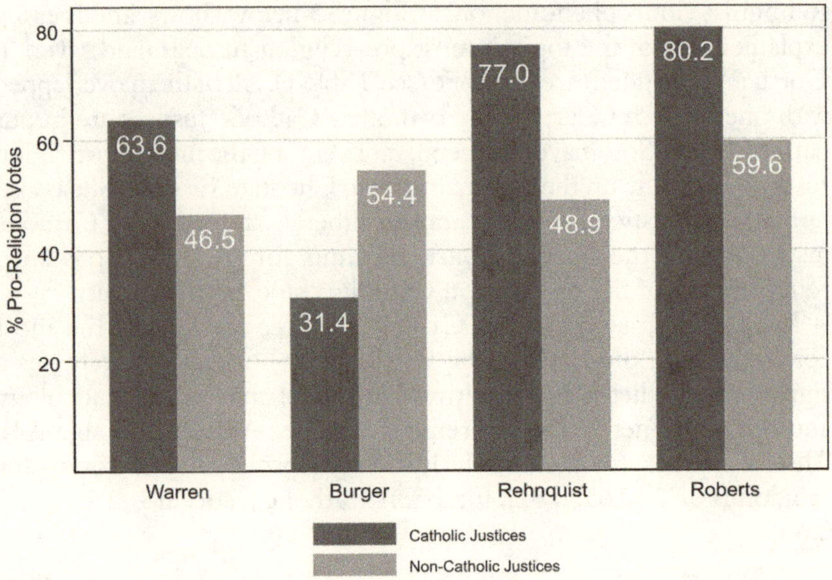

Figure 5. Voting for religion by religion (Catholic or not), 1953–2020 terms. The differences for the Rehnquist and Roberts Courts' Justices are significant in the expected direction ($p < 0.05$). The difference for the Burger Court Justice is significant but in the opposite direction. The difference for the Warren Court Justices is not significant.

of devoutness[46]). Likewise, multivariate models (controlling for petitioner and clustered on Justice) show that the devoutness variable is not statistically significant though it is positive as predicted.

Drilling down into the data helps explain this rather puzzling finding: The "devoutness" effect differs substantially by Court era, as Figure 6 shows. During the Warren years, devout and less devout (a score under 2) Justices cast a statistically equivalent percentage of votes in favor of religion. The Burger Court, once again, is anomalous. A statistically significant ($p < 0.05$) relationship exists between devoutness and votes but it is in the opposite direction: less devout Justices cast *a higher percentage* of votes in favor of religion. Only during the Rehnquist and especially Roberts Court eras, does the expected relationship emerge.

[46] Only the comparison between most and least devout is significant, as noted in Table 2.

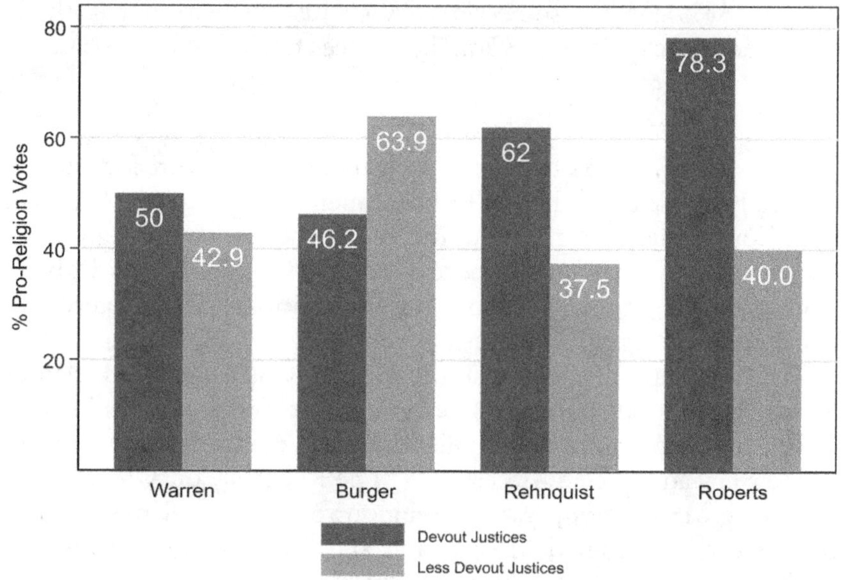

Figure 6. Voting for religion by devoutness, 1953–2020 terms. Less devout Justices are those with a score under 2 (see Table 1). The differences for the Rehnquist and Roberts Courts' Justices are significant in the expected direction ($p < 0.05$). The difference for the Burger Court justices is significant but in the opposite direction. The difference for the Warren Court Justices is not significant.

Estimating logit models (controlling for petitioner and clustered on Justice) confirms the raw data in Figure 6. For the Rehnquist Court: all else equal,[47] moving from a less devout Justice to a devout Justice, the probability of casting a pro-religion vote jumps from 0.43 to 0.67.[48] The increase is even greater for the Roberts Justices: from 0.40 (less devout) to 0.78 (most devout).[49] (Using the Justices' devoutness scores in Table 2 confirms a significant effect only for the Rehnquist and Roberts Court Justices.)

One other notable pattern is a significant relationship between votes cast by Catholic Justices and by devout Justices. Of the 186 votes cast by the least devout Justices, only 17 were by Catholic Justices (9%). And of the 164 cast by the most devout Justices, 135 were by Catholic

---

[47] This scenario sets the petitioner in the Supreme Court at pro-religion.

[48] The 95% confidence intervals are, respectively, [0.25, 0.61] and [0.53, 0.79].

[49] The 95% confidence intervals are, respectively, [0.35, 0.45] and [0.60, 0.90].

Justices (82%). While some very devout Justices were not Catholic (Goldberg, Clark, Souter), Catholic Justices tended to be devout.

E. TYPE OF CASE

On average, Justices are significantly more likely to vote for religion in Free Exercise cases than in Establishment cases. That gap exists in each Court era (see Fig. 7). But the gap in the raw data is significant only for the Warren and Roberts Courts; and only for the Roberts Court does a regression (controlling for petitioner and clustered on Justice) show a significant relationship.

The explanation is likely that the Warren Court used both clauses to protect religious minorities, leading to pro-religion votes in cases where religious minorities challenged laws and anti-religion cases where a law advanced a MS religion. The Roberts Court, focused on advancing MS religion, cast pro-religion votes in Free Exercise cases where laws constrained MS religion and pro-religion votes in Establishment clause cases where the law advanced MS religion.

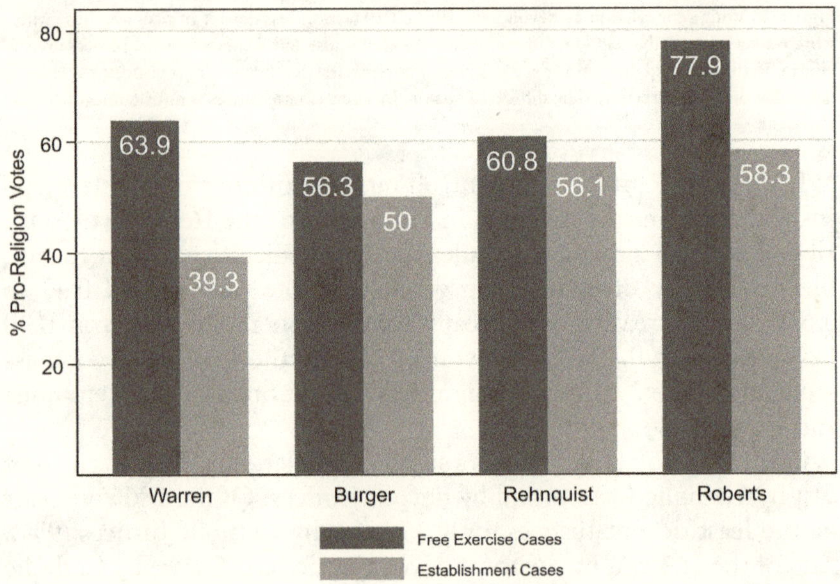

Figure 7. Relationship between pro-religion votes and type of religion case, 1953–2020 terms. For the Warren and Roberts Courts the relationship is significant ($p < 0.05$), though a regression (controlling for petitioner and clustered on Justice) shows a significant relationship only for the Roberts Court.

F. WHICH INDEPENDENT VARIABLES MATTER MOST?

Although we are hampered by a small data set, we can provide some evidence about which of the main explanatory variables appear most important in explaining the pattern of votes. We estimated several multivariate regressions that included ideology, Catholicism, devoutness, and various controls (including identity of petitioner and Court era) clustered on Justice. Overall, ideology and Catholicism matter consistently in the predicted direction, while devoutness does not. For the Roberts Court alone, all three variables are mostly statistically significant in the predicted direction, whereas in the Warren Court, none of the relationships are statistically significant (with the exception of Catholicism in one model). In the Burger and Rehnquist Courts, the relationships are more variable depending on the specification. Generally, ideology, Catholicism, and devoutness matter more (in the predicted direction) in the Roberts Court than in prior eras. The tables are in the Appendix.

IV. Discussion

Plainly, the Roberts Court has ruled in favor of religious organizations, including mainstream Christian organizations, more frequently than its predecessors. With the replacement of Ruth Bader Ginsburg with Amy Coney Barrett, this trend will not end soon and may accelerate. The quantitative results dovetail with doctrinal analysis that suggests that the Court has weakened the Establishment Clause and strengthened the Free Exercise Clause. Relaxation of the Establishment Clause has benefited mainstream Christian (including Catholic) organizations because Christianity remains the overwhelmingly dominant religion in the United States, and in many jurisdictions evangelical Christians exercise significant political power. In *Town of Greece v. Galloway*, the Court held that a town's practice of opening legislative sessions with a prayer did not violate the Establishment Clause.[50] In *American Legion v. American Humanist Ass'n*, for example, the Court held that a cross-shaped monument erected to honor soldiers who died in World War I did not violate the Establishment Clause even though it was located on public lands.[51] These cases break from older

[50] 572 U.S. 565 (2014).

[51] *See, e.g.*, Engel v. Vitale, 370 U.S. 421 (1962).

cases that disapproved of government practices with sectarian purposes or effects.

The trend with the Free Exercise Clause is more complicated and uncertain. The Court has strengthened the Free Exercise Clause which, in principle, could benefit minority religions that lack political power and so cannot block laws that interfere with their religious practices. In practice, the Court's rulings have mostly but not exclusively protected the conservative values of mainstream Christian organizations against secular laws, including public health orders to counter the Covid-19 pandemic and laws intended to prevent discrimination against sexual minorities and protect reproductive rights.[52]

One immediate question is whether our statistical results reflect selection effects rather than the changing ideologies or attitudes of the Justices. Imagine, for example, that the Roberts Court has simply encountered far more cases involving government actions and laws that are hostile to religion than earlier courts have. If so, a high rate of pro-religion outcomes is consistent with a static jurisprudence. But there are several reasons for doubting a selection-effects story, though the reason for doubt depends on the source of selection.

One possibility, for example, is that the Court grants certiorari to more extreme anti-religion cases than earlier Courts have. But it seems doubtful that earlier Courts would have ignored extreme cases. Another possibility is that courts of appeal have turned against religion, requiring correction from the Supreme Court; or that (moving backward in time) the public and legislators have become more hostile to religion in recent years. As we will see below, this set of explanations is not plausible either. A related development points in the opposite direction. Since *Employment Division v. Smith*, 21 states have enacted RFRAs, which means that state courts will have blocked anti-religion laws that might otherwise have made their way to the Supreme Court.[53]

As we turn from description to explanation, the proximate cause of the change in the Court's jurisprudence is clear. The Justices who are largely responsible for this shift are Clarence Thomas, Samuel Alito, Neil Gorsuch, John Roberts, and Brett Kavanaugh. While there are some differences among these Justices, and Kavanaugh has been

---

[52] *See* Tandon v. Newsom, 141 S. Ct. 1294 (2021); Fulton v. City of Philadelphia, 141 S. Ct. 1868 (2021); Burwell v. Hobby Lobby Stores, Inc., 573 U.S. 682 (2014).

[53] *See* Jonathan Griffin, *State Religious Freedom Restoration Acts*, NAT'L CONF. OF STATE LEGISLATURES (May 4, 2017), https://perma.cc/V2VS-K8Z8.

involved in only a handful of cases, they are clearly the most pro-religion justices on the Supreme Court going back at least to World War II. They are also all Christian, mostly Catholic, religiously devout (though this variable provides a weaker explanation than the others), and ideologically conservative. Amy Coney Barrett will likely advance this trend—though she has so far been slightly more cautious than the Alito-Gorsuch-Thomas bloc, and may turn out to be closer to Roberts than to the other conservatives.[54] By contrast, the dissenters are religiously mixed, not devout, and ideologically liberal. While correlation is not causation, it is hard to see any other explanation for the voting pattern.

But that raises an additional question, which is how all these people ended up on the Court. Republican presidents have not always appointed religiously devout, ideologically conservative jurists to the Supreme Court. In 1990, President George H.W. Bush nominated David Souter to the Court. Souter, whose ideological views were not widely known at the time, drifted left over the course of his tenure on the Court. Justice Anthony Kennedy, who had joined the Court in 1988, was more reliably conservative, including on religious issues. But he frustrated conservatives by refusing to overturn *Roe v. Wade* and by advancing constitutional protections for sexual minorities, culminating in his majority opinion recognizing the right to same-sex marriage in *Obergefell v. Hodges* in 2015.[55] Justice O'Connor was also a source of frustration for conservatives; she, too, was not an ideological standard-bearer and ended up as a swing vote on the Court. Long before O'Connor, Kennedy, and Souter left the Court, conservative Christians began devoting political resources to ensuring that Republican presidents and senators would ensure appointment of religious conservatives on the Supreme Court.[56]

But this does not seem to be the whole story. These appointments also received the enthusiastic support of the business wing of the Republican Party, as well as other non-religious mainstream Republicans. This raises the possibility that religiousness has become a screening mechanism for Republicans. The problem facing Republicans until

---

[54] South Bay United Pentecostal Church v. Newsom, 141 S. Ct. 716, 717 (2021) (Barrett, J., concurring); Fulton v. City of Philadelphia, 141 S. Ct. at 1882–83 (Barrett, J., concurring).

[55] 576 U.S. 644 (2015).

[56] Amanda Hollis-Brusky & Joshua C. Wilson, Separate But Faithful: The Christian Right's Radical Struggle to Transform Law & Legal Culture (2020).

recently was that potential nominees with ideologically impeachable credentials usually leave paper trails that can be used against them, as occurred with Robert Bork in 1987. Religiously devout people who are Republicans and familiar in conservative legal circles may have offered a way around this problem. Religious devotion is difficult to fake (at least, if it involves public acts like attending church), so a combination of religious devotion and conservative views may all but guarantee that a nominee will support conservative values on the Supreme Court and will not drift left, as so many Republican appointees did in an earlier era. Meanwhile, attacking a political nominee on religious grounds remains politically taboo, as was so clear when liberals found themselves unable to mount serious opposition to Amy Coney Barrett, even though many of her supporters made no secret of the fact that they supported her because of her conservative religious views.[57]

This hypothesis has some support in an incident that took place during the Kavanaugh nomination, described in Ruth Marcus's book *Supreme Ambition*.

> The Trump judge pickers' focus during those early discussions was not on prospective nominees' positions on the hottest-button social issues, abortion and same-sex marriage. Instead, it was on the less sexy but—to the assembled lawyers and, as significantly, to the wealthy donors who financed the Republican party—even more important matter of what Steve Bannon would later call the "deconstruction of the administrative state." Priebus laid it out: the social conservatives who had helped elect Trump might focus on abortion and same-sex marriage, but the donors cared about regulation. They were eager to undo what they viewed as the out-of-control regulatory apparatus that had been assembled since Franklin Roosevelt's New Deal.
>
> . . .
>
> And that, for all evangelical voters' focus on the Supreme Court and social issues such as abortion, was the real goal. The emphasis on social conservatism and its associated hot-button issues ended with Scalia, McGahn said at the first meeting after the election to discuss the justice's successor. It was now all about regulatory relief.[58]

---

[57] Tom Gjelten, *Amy Coney Barrett's Catholicism Is Controversial But May Not Be Confirmation Issue*, Nat'l Pub. Radio (Sept. 29, 2020), https://perma.cc/ME6G-BRMQ; Kadhim Shubber & Lauren Fedor, *Why Conservatives Have Faith in Amy Coney Barrett*, Financial Times (Sept. 26, 2020), https://www.ft.com/content/c7129d24-f48b-45c8-b11f-21aa4a6b6921 (visited on March 12, 2021).

[58] Ruth Marcus, Supreme Ambition: Brett Kavanaugh and the Conservative Takeover 63–64 (2020).

On this account, Republican presidents appoint religious lawyers (or, more to the point, conservative religious lawyers) to the Court in order to please their business constituency, not their evangelical constituency. Of course, publicly pious lawyers who publicly express hostility toward the administrative state, as Gorsuch and Kavanaugh had done, would please both constituencies.

We have so far described the transformation of the religion clauses as a political power play. But defenders of this transformation argue that it is constitutionally legitimate. Michael McConnell, for example, argued decades ago that the Supreme Court was too stingy with religious rights.[59] In an op-ed in 2020, he returned to this theme, celebrated the modern Court "as protecting pluralism—the right of individuals and institutions to be different, to teach different doctrines, to dissent from dominant cultural norms and to practice what they preach."[60] The Constitution protects religious rights, and it was wrong for earlier generations of the Court to limit those protections.

Ironically, McConnell's defense of the Court sounds more like the liberal defense of minority religious rights than the modern Court's robust protection of mainstream Christian values. But McConnell's defense could be recalibrated in the following way. The role of religion in American life has changed, and even mainstream believers should now be regarded as a "discrete and insular minority" even if not one that has historically faced discrimination. The most important change is greater tolerance for sexual minorities, exemplified by the decisions of the Supreme Court itself in *United States v. Windsor*[61] and *Obergefell*. These decisions outraged many religious conservatives, who believed that they would be compelled to respect practices that violated their religious commitments. And when a baker was ordered to sell wedding cakes to same-sex couples,[62] and a for-profit chain store run by devout Christians was forced to cover contraception in its group health care plan, those fears were vindicated[63]—until the

[59] Michael W. McConnell, *Accommodation of Religion*, 1985 Sup. Ct. Rev. 1.

[60] Michael W. McConnell, *On Religion, the Supreme Court Protects the Right to Be Different*, N.Y. Times (July 9, 2020), https://perma.cc/8UCS-GW4S.

[61] 570 U.S. 744 (2015).

[62] Masterpiece Cakeshop, Ltd. v. Colorado Civil Rights Commission, 138 S. Ct. 1719 (2018).

[63] Burwell v. Hobby Lobby Stores, Inc., 573 U.S. 682 (2014).

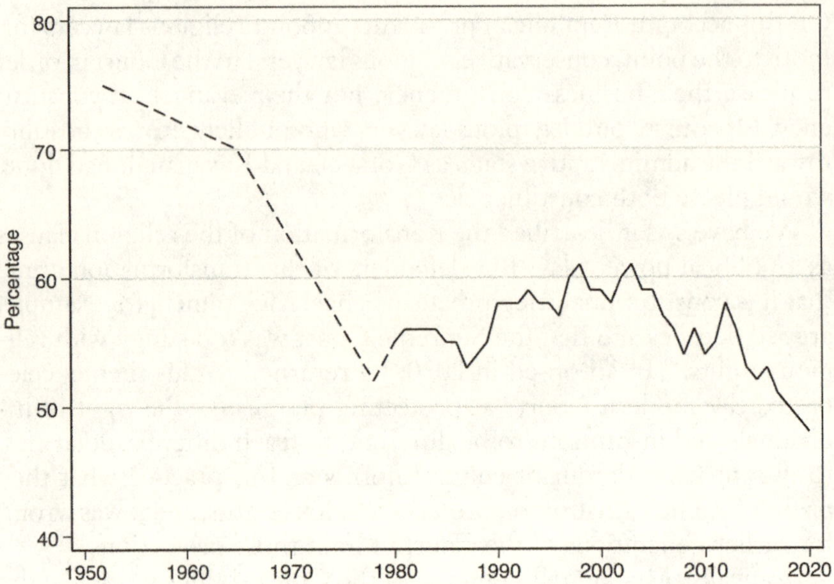

Figure 8. Percentage of Americans who responded "very important" to the question, "How important would you say religion is in your own life—very important, fairly important or not very important?" (1952–2020). The dashed parts of the line connect years without data (Gallup did not ask the question). Source: Gallup Polls, with data at https://news.gallup.com/poll/1690/religion.aspx and https://news.gallup.com/poll/245651/religion-considered-important-americans.aspx.

Supreme Court rode to the rescue. But were these cases anomalous or part of a larger secularizing trend?

There is some evidence for such a trend. Socially conservative values associated with mainstream Christianity have become less popular in the last several decades. Religious belief has declined as well, as Figure 8 shows.[64] Christianity, which was once dominated by mainstream Protestant denominations, has splintered. It has also been challenged by a variety of other religions and secular ideologies. Fewer Americans say that religion is important in their lives than in the past, though this trend has remained stable since the 1970s. Finally, the liberal Justices themselves divided in quite a few cases in the Roberts Court. Breyer and Kagan occasionally sided with the conservative majority, and even

[64] Data on religion's importance to Americans are presented at *In Depth: Religion*, GALLUP.COM, https://perma.cc/G7B5-M3LD.

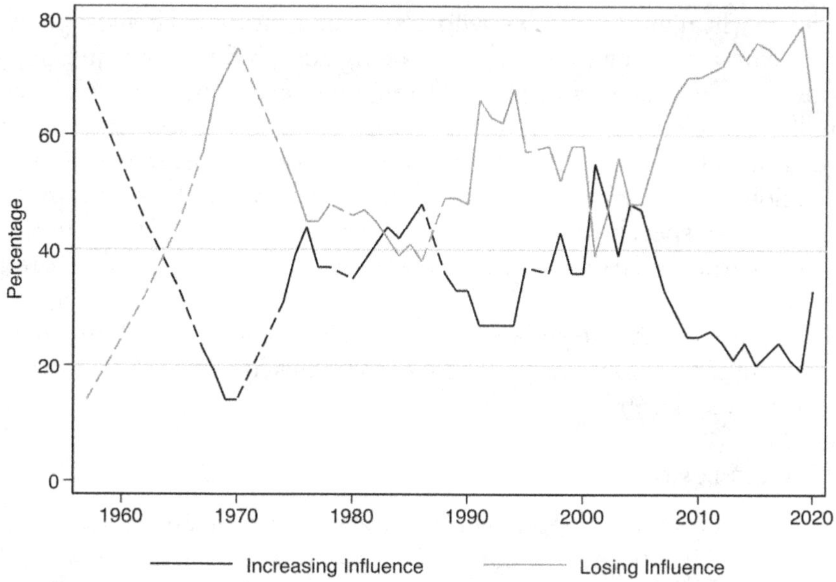

Figure 9. Responses of Americans to the question, "At the present time, do you think religion as a whole is increasing its influence on American life or losing its influence?" Americans' view of the influence of religion on life in the US. The dashed parts of each line connect years without data (Gallup did not ask the question). Source: Gallup Polls, with data at https://news.gallup.com/poll/1690/religion.aspx and https://news.gallup.com/poll/162803/americans-say-religion-losing-influence.aspx.

when they dissented, they were less scathing than Ginsburg and Sotomayor. While Breyer and Kagan tended to concur on technical grounds, one senses that they felt less hostility toward religious individuals and organizations who believed that they faced discrimination from secular authorities.[65]

A more striking statistic is the fraction of Americans who say that religion is losing its influence on American life. That number has fluctuated for decades but began a significant upswing in 2006, when 48% said that religion is losing its influence, to 76% in 2016.[66] That may

[65] *See* the disagreements between Breyer/Kagan and Ginsburg/Sotomayor in, among others, Trinity Lutheran Church of Columbia, Inc. v. Comer, 137 S. Ct. 2012 (2017); Masterpiece Cakeshop, Ltd. v. Colorado Civil Rights Commission, 138 S. Ct. 1719 (2018); Am. Legion v. Am. Humanist Ass'n, 139 S. Ct. 2067 (2019); Our Lady of Guadalupe Sch. v. Morrissey-Berru, 140 S. Ct. 2049 (2020); Little Sisters of the Poor Saints Peter & Paul Home v. Pennsylvania, 140 S. Ct. 2367 (2020).

[66] *See* Megan Brennan, *Religion Considered Important to 72% of Americans*, Gallup, https://perma.cc/6V6L-AY8X.

explain why many Christians, who were once accustomed in most places to seeing their views and practices being accepted without question, now see themselves as victims of religious discrimination. A recent poll indicates that while most Americans do not believe that their religious liberty is under threat, large majorities of evangelicals and religious Republicans do.[67] Justice Alito belongs to the latter group. As he said in a speech to the Federalist Society, "It pains me to say this, but in certain quarters, religious liberty is fast becoming a disfavored right."[68]

But the spike at the end of the period may suggest that religion may be regaining its influence—and perhaps thanks in part to the Supreme Court (see Fig. 9).

V. Conclusion

A great deal of recent work examines efforts by various Christian leaders and institutions to counter secular trends in American policy and constitutional law.[69] According to this literature, conservative Christians have taken a page from the civil rights movement and gone to the courts, hoping to expand religious rights. They have also organized and promoted legal institutions, like the Alliance Defending Freedom, which litigates on behalf of religious rights; the Blackstone Fellowship, which offers Christian-themed legal training; and law schools, like Ava Maria Law School. Christian organizations also lobby for judicial appointments that will advance their values. In just the last half century, Christian conservatism has been transformed from the mainstream ideology of the country into the agenda of a minority group, which claims to need and deserve protection under the Constitution. This group has benefited from some like-minded or sympathetic Justices, some of whom received the support of evangelical Christian organizations when they were nominated.

---

[67] *Is Religious Liberty a Shield or a Sword?*, Pub. Religion Rsch. Inst. (Feb. 10, 2021), https://perma.cc/3WVD-VTVV.

[68] *Supreme Court Justice Samuel Alito Speech Transcript to Federalist Society*, Rev (Nov. 12, 2020), https://perma.cc/JY45-QEC9.

[69] *See, e.g.*, Hollis-Brusky & Wilson, *supra* note 56.

Appendix

Table A1 provides summary statistics. The dataset is organized in two ways. For the "Court-level" analysis, an observation is a single case. For the "Justice-level" analysis, an observation is a Justice's vote.

Table A1
Summary Statistics

Outcomes		
	Court-Level	
	Conservative Christian Wins (48)	58.0%
	Liberal Wins (35)	42.0%
	Justice-Level	
	Conservative Christian Wins (360)	50.0%
	Liberal Wins (360)	50.0%
Court-Level Variables		
	Chief Justice Era	
	Warren (9)	10.8%
	Burger (31)	37.4%
	Rehnquist (28)	33.7%
	Roberts (15)	18.1%
	Type of Religion Case	
	Religious Establishment (52)	62.7%
	Free Exercise (31)	37.3%
	Petitioner in the U.S. Supreme Court	
	Liberal (31)	37.3%
	Conservative Christian (52)	62.7%
	Case Salience	
	Not Front Page NYT (37)	44.6%
	Front Page NYT (46)	55.4%
Justice-Level Variables		
	Votes by Appointing President's Party	
	Republican (518)	70.3%
	Democrat (219)	29.7%
	Votes by Justice's Party	
	Republican (435)	59.0%
	Democrat (302)	41.0%
	Votes by Catholic Justice	
	Non-Catholic (527)	71.5%
	Catholic (210)	28.5%
	Devoutness Score	
	Mean	3.08
	Median	3.25
	Ideology: Segal-Cover	
	Mean	0.43
	Most Liberal (Fortas, Marshall, Brennan)	1
	Most Conservative (Scalia)	0

Table A1 *Continued*

Ideology: Martin-Quinn Career Average	
Mean	0.06
Most Liberal (Douglas)	−4.76
Most Conservative (Thomas)	3.49
Ideology: Martin-Quinn Term by Term	
Mean	0.01
Most Liberal (Douglas)	−7.95
Most Conservative (Rehnquist)	4.52

Table A2 displays the results of various multivariate regressions, broken down by Chief Justice era (with the first column covering the entire period). The first two panels show the results when we use "pro-religion" as the dependent variable. The second two panels show the results when we use "pro-mainstream Christian" as the dependent variable. The first panel in each pair uses a dummy variable for "Justice devoutness." The second panel in each pair uses a score for "Justice devoutness."

Table A2

Multivariate Regression Using Key Variables, 1953–2020 Terms

	Pro-Religion with Justice Devoutness Dummy Variable				
	All Eras	Warren	Burger	Rehnquist	Roberts
Petitioner	0.25	0.65	−0.14	0.69	0.02
	(0.17)	(0.34)	(0.16)	(0.39)	(0.50)
Justice Ideology	−1.17*	0.20	−0.85	−0.49	−1.81
	(0.33)	(0.79)	(0.47)	(0.65)	(0.97)
Justice Catholic	0.76*	0.62	−0.26	1.09*	0.73*
	(0.24)	(0.38)	(0.31)	(0.34)	(0.33)
Justice Devout or Not	0.15	0.21	−0.52	0.64	1.30*
	(0.46)	(0.39)	(0.55)	(0.46)	(0.55)
Constant	0.36	−0.69	0.90	−0.82*	0.23
	(0.50)	(0.66)	(0.50)	(0.48)	(0.87)
Observations	841	97	309	277	158

	Pro-Religion with Justice Devoutness Score				
	All Eras	Warren	Burger	Rehnquist	Roberts
Petitioner	0.25	0.67	−0.11	0.71	0.07
	(0.17)	(0.36)	(0.18)	(0.40)	(0.49)
Justice Ideology	−1.16*	−0.02	−1.03*	−0.24	−1.90*
	(0.37)	(0.93)	(0.45)	(0.62)	(0.88)
Justice Catholic	0.77*	1.08*	0.16	0.77*	0.17
	(0.26)	(0.47)	(0.54)	(0.37)	(0.34)

Table A2 *Continued*

	Pro-Religion with Justice Devoutness Score				
	All Eras	Warren	Burger	Rehnquist	Roberts
Justice Devout Score	0.01	−0.18	−0.26	0.38	0.63
	(0.18)	(0.21)	(0.28)	(0.20)	(0.34)
Constant	0.44	0.06	1.32	−1.59*	−0.18
	(0.69)	(1.01)	(0.92)	(0.71)	(1.19)
Observations	841	97	309	277	158

	Pro-Mainstream Christian with Devoutness Dummy Variable				
	All Eras	Warren	Burger	Rehnquist	Roberts
Petitioner	0.30	−0.05	−0.15	1.05*	2.52*
	(0.18)	(0.25)	(0.16)	(0.28)	(0.21)
Justice Ideology	−2.20*	−1.93	−1.50*	−2.57*	−1.08
	(0.56)	(1.66)	(0.72)	(0.91)	(1.76)
Justice Catholic	0.70*	−0.28	−0.31	1.18*	2.20*
	(0.33)	(0.68)	(0.35)	(0.42)	(0.48)
Justice Devout or Not	0.08	−0.37	−0.42	0.39	3.45*
	(0.65)	(0.47)	(0.63)	(0.99)	(1.07)
Constant	0.50	1.34	0.89	−0.46	−5.63*
	(0.65)	(1.30)	(0.53)	(0.92)	(1.78)
Observations	737	79	273	251	134

	Pro-Mainstream Christian with Devoutness Score				
	All Eras	Warren	Burger	Rehnquist	Roberts
Petitioner	0.30	−0.03	−0.14	1.04*	2.67*
	(0.18)	(0.26)	(0.16)	(0.29)	(0.43)
Justice Ideology	−2.20*	−2.59	−1.64*	−2.48*	−2.84*
	(0.55)	(1.85)	(0.62)	(0.89)	(1.27)
Justice Catholic	0.73	0.59	−0.01	1.09*	0.57
	(0.40)	(1.04)	(0.56)	(0.54)	(0.44)
Justice Devout Score	−0.02	−0.39	−0.20	0.15	0.99*
	(0.25)	(0.23)	(0.32)	(0.36)	(0.50)
Constant	0.61	2.50	1.20	−0.65	−3.98
	(0.87)	(1.67)	(0.92)	(1.30)	(2.08)
Observations	737	79	273	251	134

Note. Each pair of tables uses separate specifications for devoutness—a dummy variable or score. Regression results are included for the effect of petitioner, ideology, religion, and devoutness on Justice vote. Cell entries of logit coefficients with robust standard errors (clustered on Justice) are included in parentheses below each. Ideology is the Justice's Segal-Cover score; Religion is 1 if the Justice is Catholic and 0 if not; Justice Devout is 1 if the Justice was scored as devout or moderately devout (a score over 2) and 0 is less devout (a score under 2). Justice Devout Score is the mean of the coders' rating of the Justice's devoutness (for our Justices, the range is from 1.25 to 5).

* $p \leq 0.05$.

CASS R. SUNSTEIN

INJURY IN FACT, TRANSFORMED

Since 1970, the law of standing has been dominated by the "injury in fact" requirement.[1] That requirement was first announced in an opinion by Justice William O. Douglas, who clearly sought both to expand the category of people entitled to challenge government action and to simplify the standing inquiry in significant ways.[2] Justice Douglas made no effort to root that requirement in the text or history of the Constitution, or indeed in any of the Court's precedents. As far as constitutional law is concerned, the injury-in-fact test was made up out of whole cloth. It appears to have come from a 1955 law review article by Kenneth Culp Davis.[3] Davis himself purported to interpret the Administrative Procedure Act (APA), not the Constitution. His interpretation of the APA was an egregious blunder.

Over the course of the last half-century, the injury-in-fact test has been transformed from a bold effort to expand the category of persons

Cass R. Sunstein is Robert Walmsley University Professor, Harvard Law School.

Author's note: I am grateful to Will Baude, Jack Goldsmith, and Adrian Vermeule for valuable suggestions, and to Eric Xu for excellent research assistance and superb comments on an earlier draft. I am also grateful to participants in a work-in-progress lunch at Harvard Law School.

[1] *See, e.g.*, Lujan v. Defenders of Wildlife, 504 U.S. 555, 560 (1992); Spokeo, Inc. v. Robins, 578 U.S. 330 (2016); Clapper v. Amnesty Int'l USA, 568 U.S. 398 (2013).

[2] *See* Ass'n of Data Processing Serv. Orgs., Inc. v. Camp, 397 U.S. 150, 154 (1970) ("Where statutes are concerned, the trend is toward enlargement of the class of people who may protest administrative action.").

[3] *See* Kenneth C. Davis, *Standing to Challenge Governmental Action*, 39 Minn. L. Rev. 353, 365 (1955).

The Supreme Court Review, 2022.
 https://doi.org/10.1086/720377

entitled to bring suit into an equally bold effort to achieve the opposite goal, by understanding judicially cognizable injuries largely by reference to the common law (and the Constitution), and by severely restricting Congress' power to create new rights and to allow people to sue to protect those rights.[4] The transformation is lawless. It is disconnected from standard sources of constitutional law.

There is an irony here, and it is in the foreground, not in the background. The administrative state arose out of grave dissatisfaction with private law principles. In diverse ways, it was founded on a recognition that various interests beyond those protected by the common law (including those of consumers, investors, workers, environmentalists, and victims of discrimination) deserve some kind of legal protection.[5] To be sure, the interests of the objects of regulation, armed with private-law rights, continued to matter, and would be a legitimate basis for a lawsuit. But in multiple domains, Congress explicitly decided that the beneficiaries of regulatory protection also ought to have access to court to protect their statutory rights.[6] And even when Congress did not make that explicit decision, the relevant provision of the APA could easily be read to authorize such access, at least in certain circumstances.[7] The irony is that the Court is now building the public law of standing directly on the private-law foundations that Congress rejected, as a matter of principle, in creating modern statutory programs and new statutory rights. As we shall see, we are witnessing a form of "*Lochner*ing."[8]

My central goal in this Article is to offer a compressed sketch of the rise and the evolution of the idea of "injury in fact" in federal standing law. It is a truly astonishing tale. The brief sketch could, of course, be

[4] *See Spokeo*, 578 U.S. at 341, explicitly rejecting the idea that "a plaintiff automatically satisfies the injury-in-fact requirement whenever a statute grants a person a statutory right and purports to authorize that person to sue to vindicate that right. . . . Article III standing requires a concrete injury even in the context of a statutory violation." For some valuable speculations about the rise of public-interest litigation, which must be counted as an important piece of the puzzle, see generally Elizabeth Magill, *Standing for the Public: A Lost History*, 95 VA. L. REV. 101 (2009).

[5] For one account, *see* CASS R. SUNSTEIN, AFTER THE RIGHTS REVOLUTION (1985).

[6] *See, e.g.*, FEC v. Akins, 524 U.S. 11 (1998); Christian Langpap & Jay P. Shimshack, *Private Citizen Suits or Public Enforcement: Substitutes or Complements?*, 59 J. ENV'T ECON. & MGMT. 235 (2010).

[7] *See, e.g.*, Norwalk CORE v. Norwalk Redev. Agency, 395 F.2d 920, 932–37 (2d Cir. 1968).

[8] Cass R. Sunstein, Lochner*'s Legacy*, 87 COLUM. L. REV. 873 (1987).

a lengthy narrative; my hope is that the main lines of the tale, and its astonishing nature, will emerge more clearly if presented in a compressed fashion.[9] I also hope that an understanding of the novelty of the injury-in-fact requirement, and its peculiar origins, might help to cast in bold relief the even newer effort to build standing principles on traditional private rights, and to expose the oddity of the associated idea that Congress lacks the authority to create rights that lack clear analogues in the common law.

II. "Legal Wrong"

Every year, people suffer innumerable injuries. You might have been hit by a car. You might have been rejected by a friend or a romantic partner. Your mother might have died of COVID-19. You might not have been hired; you might have been fired. You might have filed a request under the Freedom of Information Act, and the request might have been denied. The air you breathe might be polluted. Your favorite television show might have been canceled. You might have been subject to some kind of discrimination.

All of these are "injuries in fact," at least in human experience. But only some of those injuries are legally cognizable in the sense that law recognizes them as providing a basis for some kind of action in federal court. Whether an injury is legally cognizable would seem necessarily to depend on *law*—on whether some source of law creates a right and a cause of action.[10] Article III requires a case or controversy, and without a cause of action, there is no case or controversy.[11] People who are injured do not, by virtue of that fact, have access to federal

---

[9] For various parts of the narrative, see Magill, *supra* note 4, at 1131–99 (2009); Steven L. Winter, *The Metaphor of Standing and the Problem of Self-Governance*, 40 Stan. L. Rev. 1371 (1988); Cass R. Sunstein, *What's Standing After* Lujan? *Of Citizen Suits, "Injuries," and Article III*, 91 Mich. L. Rev. 163 (1992).

[10] *See* David P. Currie, *Misunderstanding Standing*, 1981 Sup. Ct. Rev. 41. On some of the complexities here, see William Baude, *Standing in the Shadow of Congress*, 2016 Sup. Ct. Rev. 197.

[11] For just one illustration, see Ala. Power Co. v. Ickes, 302 U.S. 464 (1938). Breaking no new ground, the Court held that competitors, facing an economic injury (in fact; no doubt about that), could not bring suit, because they did not allege a legal wrong. The Court noted that "the courts have no power to consider in isolation and annul an act of Congress on the ground that it is unconstitutional, but may consider that question 'only when the justification for some direct injury suffered or threatened, presenting a justiciable issue, is made to rest upon such an act.' The term 'direct injury' is there *used in its legal sense, as meaning a wrong which directly results in the violation of a legal right.*" *Id.* at 479 (emphasis added, and with relish). The Court added:

court; on one view, a legal right and a cause of action are both necessary and sufficient for standing.[12] As a matter of proper interpretation of the Constitution, that view is essentially right.[13] But as the law of standing has developed over the last fifty years (and counting), it is wrong.[14] The Supreme Court speaks as if the injury-in-fact test can be read off of the case or controversy requirement;[15] as a matter of language, that is a neat trick.

The law of standing of course has a long history, and I will refer to some of it here.[16] But to understand the origins of the injury-in-fact requirement,[17] we need to begin not with the Constitution, to which that test is foreign,[18] but with the enactment and interpretation of the

---

> John Doe, let us suppose, is engaged in operating a grocery store. Richard Roe, desiring to open a rival and competing establishment, seeks a loan from a manufacturing concern which, under its charter, is without authority to make the loan. The loan, if made, will be *ultra vires*. The state or a stockholder of the corporation, perhaps a creditor, in some circumstances, may, upon that ground, enjoin the loan. But may it be enjoined at the suit of John Doe, a stranger to the corporation, because the lawful use of the money will prove injurious to him and this result is foreseen and expected both by the lender and the borrower, Richard Roe? Certainly not, unless we are prepared to lay down the general rule that A, who will suffer damage from the lawful act of B, and who plainly will have no case against B, may nevertheless invoke judicial aid to restrain a third party, acting without authority, from furnishing means which will enable B to do what the law permits him to do. Such a rule would be opposed to sound reason, as we have already tried to show, and cannot be accepted.

Id. at 481. The Court cited many cases in support of the proposition that a suit by some plaintiff X would be available only in the case of a legal wrong, done to X, and not because of an economic injury. *Id.* at 481–83.

[12] *See* Currie, *supra* note 10.

[13] *See id.*; William Fletcher, *The Structure of Standing*, 98 Yale L.J. 221 (1988); TransUnion LLC v. Ramirez, 141 S. Ct. 2190, 2215 (2021) (Thomas, J., dissenting). I am bracketing the possibility that there are some outer boundaries here. *See id.* (Kagan, J., dissenting).

[14] *See, e.g.*, *TransUnion*, 141 S. Ct. 2190; Spokeo, Inc. v. Robins, 578 U.S. 330 (2016); *see also* Friends of the Earth, Inc. v. Laidlaw Env't Servs., Inc., 528 U.S. 167 (2000).

[15] *See TransUnion*, 141 S. Ct. 2190.

[16] See Winter, *supra* note 9, for a detailed discussion of the Founding period and the New Deal period; see Daniel E. Ho & Erica L. Ross, *Did Liberal Justices Invent the Standing Doctrine? An Empirical Study of the Evolution of Standing, 1921–2006*, 62 Stan. L. Rev. 591 (1910), for a fascinating treatment of the period before and after enactment of the APA.

[17] *See* Ho & Ross, *supra* note 16, at 616–20, for a clear demonstration that even in its early period, in the first decades of the twentieth century, standing doctrine did not have anything like clear content, and that it "was not a constitutional threshold." *Id.* at 619. A reading of the cases in those early decades is singularly jarring to modern readers. *See, e.g.*, Ala. Power Co. v. Ickes, 302 U.S. 464 (1938); Baltimore & Ohio R. Co. v. United States (*The Chicago Junction Case*), 264 U.S. 258, 266–69 (1924); Alexander Sprunt & Son, Inc. v. United States, 281 U.S. 249 (1930).

[18] This is not to say that the case or controversy requirement is foreign; it is anything but that. The question whether there is a case or controversy is the same as the question whether there is a cause of action, see Currie, *supra* note 10; Fletcher, *supra* note 13. Note that nothing

APA in 1946.[19] The relevant provision of the APA was an effort to codify the developing (but largely developed) body of judge-made standing law: "A person suffering legal wrong because of agency action, or adversely affected or aggrieved by agency action within the meaning of a relevant statute, is entitled to judicial review thereof."[20] This phrase, cryptic to many modern readers, was actually not cryptic at all.[21] It was designed to recognize standing in three straightforward categories of cases. All three categories had become well-established under previous law.[22] To explore them is to enter in what might seem, in the current period, to be an unfamiliar world.

I say here is meant to rule out the possibility that in very extreme cases, a congressional grant of standing might violate Article III or Article II: Imagine, for example, that Congress granted every American a kind of property right in legality, and accompanied the grant of that right with a cause of action. Lujan v. Defenders of Wildlife, 504 U.S. 555 (1992), is best understood as treating the citizens' suit, as such, as that kind of extreme case. It is of course important to pause over what makes a case extreme. For a valuable discussion, see Baude, *supra* note 10. For purposes of the present Article, the central claim is that *TransUnion* goes badly wrong insofar as it prohibits Congress from recognizing injuries, and creating causes of action, for harms foreign to the common law or the Constitution. One can accept that claim without being clear on what, exactly, makes a claim extreme. In my view, and consistent with the current near-consensus: The best view of the relevant history is that nothing in the original understanding of Article III imposes any restriction on Congress' capacity to create legal rights and causes of action. In addition, it is not straightforward to develop a nonoriginalist understanding in support of any such restrictions. But a reasonable candidate would point to broad and undifferentiated harms: If Congress said, for example, that everyone has a legal right to some state of affairs (say, clean air in Hoboken, New Jersey, or prevention against disability discrimination in Concord, Massachusetts), it might be responded that Article III is best understood to stand in the way. For broad and undifferentiated harms, the constitutionally required recourse is the political process, not the judiciary. This is a structural argument about the functions of Article III courts in the system of separation of powers. A problem with this argument is that by hypothesis, the political process has conferred the relevant right, and the relevant right will be vindicated in court if and only if the plaintiff(s) can show that the Executive (or some private actor) has violated the law. For a different view, see Baude, *supra* note 10, including the discussion of Muskrat v. United States, 219 U.S. 346 (1911), at Baude, *supra* note 10, at 206–08.

[19] Note that as standing doctrine began to emerge in the twentieth century, it was grounded in what is sometimes called "the legal interest test," by which the right to sue was closely intermingled with positive law. *See* Ho & Ross, *supra* note 16, at 616–17. My focus here is the APA, not prior years; it is, as noted, very difficult to find anything like modern standing doctrine in the first century of the American republic. *See* Raoul Berger, *Standing to Sue in Public Actions: Is It a Constitutional Requirement?*, 78 YALE L.J. 816 (1969); Louis L. Jaffe, *Standing to Secure Judicial Review: Public Actions*, 14 HARV. L. REV. 1265, 1269–82 (1961); Winter; *supra* note 9; Sunstein, *supra* note 9. A simple summary is provided by Louis Jaffe: "[T]he public action—an action brought by a private person primarily to vindicate the public interest in the enforcement of public obligations—has long been a feature of our English and American law." Jaffe, *supra*, at 302. (For those who think that the injury-in-fact requirement is part of Article III, and not a modern invention, it is worth rereading that sentence a few times.)

[20] 5 U.S.C. § 702.

[21] I draw here on Sunstein, *supra* note 9.

[22] For an excellent account, *see* Magill, *supra* note 4.

First, people could obtain standing by showing that they suffered a "legal wrong" because a common-law interest (for example, property) was at stake.[23] Suppose that an administrative agency ordered some private company to do something, or to stop doing something. An invasion of a common-law interest—such as a tort or a violation of property rights—would certainly qualify as a legal wrong. Courts presumed that anyone who could show such an invasion would be entitled to bring suit.[24]

Second, plaintiffs could show that they suffered a legal wrong within the meaning of the APA by demonstrating that their *statutory* interests were at stake.[25] Suppose, for example, that the interest of a litigant in competing on equal terms was a relevant factor under the governing statute, and that the agency was therefore required to take that interest into account. If so, the litigant would have standing to bring suit to vindicate its statutory interest (and in that sense to prevent a legal wrong).[26] Congress need not have expressly conferred standing on the plaintiff. Under the APA, the mere existence of an interest protected by statute was sufficient—hence the term "legal wrong."

As the structure of section 702 plainly shows, the third category did not involve legal wrong at all. People could also bring suit if they could show that "a relevant statute"—*a statute other than the APA*—granted them standing by *explicitly providing that those "adversely affected or aggrieved" were entitled to bring suit*. In this way, the APA recognized that in other statutes, Congress had granted people causes of action, and hence standing, even if their interests were not entitled to consideration by the relevant agency. A key example would be competitors, who might be able to sue (by the grace of Congress) not to vindicate their own interests, but to protect members of the public against unlawful harm.[27] In granting causes of action, Congress

[23] Tenn. Elec. Power Co. v. Tenn. Valley Auth., 281 U.S. 118 (1939).

[24] *See* Ala. Power Co. v. Ickes, 302 U.S. 464 (1938) (denying standing in a case in which no common-law interest was at stake); Magill, *supra* note 4, at 105. For a valuable perspective on the early days of standing doctrine, see Ho & Ross, *supra* note 16.

[25] *See* Edward Hines Yellow Pine Trs. v. United States, 263 U.S. 143, 148 (1923); Baltimore & Ohio R. Co. v. United States (*The Chicago Junction Case*), 264 U.S. 258, 266–69 (1924); Alexander Sprunt & Son, Inc. v. United States, 281 U.S. 249 (1930); S. Rep. No. 79-248, 276 (1946) ("The phrase 'legal wrong' . . . means that something more than mere adverse personal effect must be shown in order to prevail—that is, that the adverse effect must be an illegal effect.").

[26] *The Chicago Junction Case*, 264 U.S. at 266–69.

[27] FCC v. Sanders Bros. Radio Station, 390 U.S. 470 (1940).

sometimes used these very words ("adversely affected or aggrieved") in allowing competitors to sue.[28] In effect, such people could act as "private attorneys general," in the sense that they were vindicating the (legal) interests of the public. The APA thus recognized the existence of congressional authorization of actions by people lacking legal injuries and so not themselves suffering "legal wrong."

This, then, was the APA framework: standing for people whose common-law interests were at stake; standing for people whose statutory interests were at stake; standing for people expressly authorized to bring suit under statutes other than the APA. Importantly, the APA contained no innovations. It was essentially meant to codify previous law,[29] in accordance with which the principal question, for purposes of standing, was whether the law had created a legal right and conferred a cause of action. Injury in fact was neither a necessary nor a sufficient condition.[30] It had nothing to do with Article III (which required a case or controversy, and hence a cause of action). It was not part of the fabric of American public law.

III. The *Data Processing* Revolution

The defining conceptual break occurred in Justice William O. Douglas's opinion for the Court in *Ass'n of Data Processing Organizations v. Camp*,[31] which provides the basic underpinnings for the modern law of standing. In terms of its disrespect for the existing legal materials, the *Data Processing* opinion is genuinely breathtaking. The Court essentially jettisoned the entire framework of the APA, even as it purported to interpret that very statute.[32]

Data Processing itself involved a suit by an association of competitors, complaining of a decision by the Comptroller of the Currency to authorize national banks to provide data processing services,

---

[28] *See* 41 U.S.C. § 402(b)(6); *Sanders Bros.*, 309 U.S. at 476–77.

[29] *See* Kenneth E. Scott, *Standing in the Supreme Court: A Functional Analysis*, 86 Harv. L. Rev. 645, 658 (1973) ("The general understanding of [section 702 of the APA] was that it amounted to a brief description of existing law. . . .").

[30] There is one qualification to this claim. The term "adversely affected or aggrieved," as used in relevant statutes, did seem to require some kind of adverse effect—as, for example, where a competitor suffered economic harm as a result of a grant of a license of a new entrant. But the meaning of "adversely affected or aggrieved" required interpretation of the relevant statute.

[31] 397 U.S. 150 (1970).

[32] *See* Magill, *supra* note 4.

thus imposing economic injury on the association. The association could not possibly contend that it suffered "legal wrong" under the APA; its common-law interests were not at stake, and it could not contend that the agency was obliged to consider its economic interests. Nor did any statute confer standing on them as persons "adversely affected or aggrieved." In denying standing, the lower court followed the conventional framework.[33] In that court's words, "Without a legal interest or the status of an 'aggrieved' party, the complaint resolves itself into an attempt merely to show 'a common concern for obedience to law.'"[34] That was the standard way to put the matter, entirely in line with the APA. As a matter of statutory interpretation, the lower court was clearly correct. In fact, the standing issue was easy and straightforward.

In its shockingly sloppy opinion, the *Data Processing* Court abandoned the statute that it was interpreting. It concluded that a plaintiff no longer needed to show a "legal interest," a "legal injury," or a "legal wrong" to establish standing. As the Court put it:

> The first question is whether the plaintiff alleges that the challenged action has caused him injury in fact, economic or otherwise. . . . The "legal interest" test goes to the merits. The question of standing is different. It concerns, apart from the "case" or "controversy" test, the question whether the interest sought to be protected by the complainant is arguably within the zone of interests to be protected or regulated by the statute or constitutional guarantee in question. Thus, the Administrative Procedure Act grants standing to a person "aggrieved by agency action within the meaning of a relevant statute."[35]

To be sure, the "legal interest" test does go to the merits—in the sense that it depends on an interpretation of law—but under the APA, which gives pride of place to the term "legal wrong," the question of standing had never been different. Hence the *Data Processing* revolution: Instead of depending on a careful examination of the governing law to see if Congress had created a legal interest whose violation would amount to a legal wrong, the injury-in-fact inquiry was intended to be a simple and straightforward one, essentially unrelated to the underlying law. In that sense, the issue would turn (crucially) on facts, not on law. Thus it was that for the first time, the Court

---

[33] Ass'n of Data Processing Serv. Orgs. v. Camp, 406 F.2d 857 (8th Cir. 1969).

[34] *Id.* at 843 (citation omitted).

[35] *Data Processing*, 397 U.S. at 152.

invoked the idea of "injury in fact."[36] In the new *Data Processing* test, standing existed for anyone who could show (a) "injury in fact, economic or otherwise" and (b) injury "arguably . . . within the zone of interests" of the regulatory statute. (The latter part, not relevant for current purposes, can be seen as a pale echo of the "legal wrong" test.) The Court made it clear that it intended to enlarge the class of people who would be entitled to bring suit: "Where statutes are concerned, the trend is toward enlargement of the class of people who may protest administrative action. The whole drive for enlarging the category of aggrieved 'persons' is symptomatic of that trend."[37] In a crucial sentence, the Court emphasized that the interests that might give rise to standing could include "aesthetic, conservational, and recreational, as well as economic values."[38]

Maybe so. Why not?[39] But still, what a mess![40] "The whole drive for enlarging the category of aggrieved 'persons'"? What does that even mean? Whose "drive"? Why does any such "drive" matter? Why is "persons" in quotation marks? To the extent that *Congress* was embarked on a project of enlarging the category of people who could bring suit, we could perhaps speak of a "whole drive" of that sort. But the Supreme Court seems to have been speaking of developments in the lower federal courts—which had not, by the way, been enlarging the category of aggrieved "persons," or speaking in any way of "injury in fact," but which had been seeing a large number of people, above all the beneficiaries of regulation (such as those seeking to enjoy a clean environment), as suffering a "legal wrong" within the meaning

---

[36] *See* Magill, *supra* note 4, at 129 n.107 (noting that the Court had used the term "injury in fact" three times in the past, but never in the context of standing). Magill also notes the apparent source of the idea of Davis's 1955 article.

[37] *Data Processing*, 397 U.S. at 154.

[38] *Id.* It is noteworthy in this regard that only two years after *Data Processing*, Justice Douglas wrote a spirited dissenting opinion, arguing that the "critical question of standing would be simplified . . . if we fashioned a federal rule that allowed environmental issues to be litigated . . . in the name of the inanimate object about to be despoiled, defaced, or invaded by roads and bulldozers and where injury is the subject of public outrage. . . . The voice of the inanimate object . . . should not be stilled." Sierra Club v. Morton, 405 U.S. 727, 742 (1972) (Douglas, J., dissenting). Some of us would not go so far. *See* Cass R. Sunstein, *Standing for Animals (with Notes on Animal Rights)*, 47 UCLA L. Rev. 1333 (2000).

[39] The question is admittedly irreverent, but still. *See, e.g.*, Scenic Hudson Pres. Conf. v. Fed. Power Comm'n, 354 F.2d 608, 615–17 (2d Cir. 1965), *cert. denied*, 384 U.S. 941 (1966).

[40] As Magill puts it, "The Supreme Court thus completely butchered the prior law." Magill, *supra* note 4, at 131. A valuable discussion can be found in Caleb Nelson, *Standing and Remedial Rights in Administrative Law*, 106 Va. L. Rev. 703 (2019).

of the APA.[41] Those decisions had been creating a public law of standing no longer based solely on common-law foundations, but developed with fidelity and careful reference to the text of the APA; "legal wrongs" could include the (legal) harms done to the beneficiaries of regulatory statutes.[42]

One might well ask: What was the source of the injury-in-fact test? Did the Supreme Court just make it up? The answer is basically yes.[43] The concept of injury in fact did not come from Alexander Hamilton, John Jay, or James Madison. It does not appear in the debates in the Founding era.[44] It appears to have first arisen in a 1955 law review article by Kenneth Culp Davis, purporting to interpret the APA.[45] Davis relied on the APA's "adversely affected or aggrieved" language in support of his conclusion. In his view, someone is "adversely affected" if he suffers an injury "in fact." Thus, Davis titled one of the opening sections of this article with these words: "'Adversely Affected In Fact' As A Guide." (![46])

---

[41] *See, e.g.*, Norwalk CORE v. Norwalk Redev. Agency, 395 F.2d 920, 932–37 (2d Cir. 1968); Office of Commc'n of the United Church of Christ v. FCC, 359 F.2d 994, 1000–06 (D.C. Cir. 1967); *Scenic Hudson*, 354 F.2d at 615–17.

[42] *See* sources cited *id.*

[43] The idea of "proper parties" of course has a long history. *See* Winter, *supra* note 9; Frothingham v. Mellon, 262 U.S. 447 (1923).

[44] On some of the relevant history, *see* Ann Woolhandler & Caleb Nelson, *Does History Defeat Standing Doctrine?*, 102 Mich. L. Rev. 689 (2004); Sunstein, *supra* note 9. Woolhandler and Nelson make the most sustained effort to defend the idea that something like contemporary standing doctrine can find some roots in the Founding era and after, but to their credit, their own conclusions are very cautious indeed. For example:

> We do not claim that history compels acceptance of the modern Supreme Court's vision of standing, or that the constitutional nature of standing doctrine was crystal clear from the moment of the Founding on. The subsistence of qui tam actions alone might be enough to refute any such suggestion. We do, however, argue that history does not defeat standing doctrine; the notion of standing is not an innovation, and its constitutionalization does not contradict a settled historical consensus about the Constitution's meaning.

Id. at 691. In any case, the interesting evidence they muster—supporting the uncontested and clearly correct view that "eighteenth- and nineteenth-century courts were well aware of the need for proper parties," see *id.*, is generally compatible with the idea that a legal right and a cause of action are necessary and sufficient conditions for a lawsuit. *See, e.g.*, *id.* at 721: "Admittedly, these early decisions are only suggestive; they read Article III to incorporate a notion of proper parties (defined in terms of real-world interests), but they did not involve congressional attempts to confer standing."

[45] Davis, *supra* note 3.

[46] *Id.* at 354.

To support his conclusion, Davis quoted House and Senate committee reports that said that the relevant section of the APA "confers a right of review upon any person adversely affected in fact by agency action or aggrieved within the meaning of any statute."[47] But this provision was, of course, not meant to signal a *freestanding* grant of standing to anyone who had been "adversely affected in fact." As we have seen, the question was whether some independent statute granted standing to those "adversely affected and aggrieved." For that reason, the provision that Davis quoted did not support his conclusion. Davis was acutely aware that other parts of the legislative history essentially paraphrased and explained the statutory text, suggesting (for example) that a "legal wrong" must be taken to "mean something more than mere adverse effect" and "must be an illegal effect."[48] (This suggestion was very much in line with existing law.[49]) Davis brushed such statements to one side. Davis was also aware of prominent statements in the legislative history plainly stating that the section merely codified preexisting law; for example, an influential Senator quoted the Attorney General, who said plainly, "This reflects existing law."[50] But he brushed those words aside as well.[51] In his account, anyone who "is in fact adversely affected may obtain judicial review."[52]

For reasons set forth above, this was an egregious misreading of the APA; the language and history of that statute suggested no such renovation of standing law. One last time: The words "adversely affected or aggrieved" are not freestanding but are followed by "within the meaning of a relevant statute." But Davis's misreading received an authoritative endorsement in *Data Processing*.[53] By 1998, the Court

[47] *Id.* at 355 (quoting S. Rep. No. 79–248 212, 276 (1946)).

[48] *Id.* at 356.

[49] *See, e.g.*, Ala. Power Co. v. Ickes, 302 U.S. 464 (1938); Baltimore & Ohio R. Co. v. United States (*The Chicago Junction Case*), 264 U.S. 258 (1924). Lest there be any doubt, consider these words: "Loss of business, or of opportunities to get business, attributable to the activity or increase of facilities on the part of the competitor, is not enough." *The Chicago Junction Case*, 264 U.S. at 272. So much for the idea of injury in fact!

[50] Davis, *supra* note 3, at 356.

[51] *Id.*

[52] *Id.*

[53] Davis himself criticized the *Data Processing* and *Barlow v. Collins*, 397 U.S. 159 (1970) opinions, decided on the same day, as being "(1) analytically faulty, (2) contrary to much case law the Court should not have intended to overrule, (3) cumbersome, inconvenient, and artificial, and (4) at variance with the dominant intent behind the Administrative Procedure Act." Kenneth C. Davis, *The Liberalized Law of Standing*, 37 U. Chi. L. Rev. 450, 457–58

was describing the injury-in-fact requirement "as the first and foremost" of the elements of standing.[54]

IV. Of Law and Fact

What's an injury in fact, in fact? The Court seemed to think that it was a simple idea, meant to ask whether the plaintiff had been hurt ("in fact"). But as we have seen, the phrase cannot possibly be taken literally, at least if it is meant to say that all those who are injured (in fact) have a right of access to federal court. The injury must also be legally cognizable.[55] Countless injuries in fact are not enough for standing. There are infinite injuries in the world, and there is no law-free way to divine which are sufficient to justify access to federal court. As a first approximation, the question is whether Congress has elevated some injury in the world to the status of an injury in law. People might be harmed if animals about which they care are hurt or killed, but that harm is not legally cognizable unless some statute has said that it is.[56]

If the claim seems obscure, the *Havens Realty* case[57] may be helpful. One of the issues in that case was whether standing could be conferred on "testers"—people who do not intend to rent or purchase a home or apartment but who pose as renters or purchasers in order to collect information about unlawfully discriminatory racial steering.

(1970). However, his criticism was due to his desire for a "flexible and simple" injury-in-fact requirement based on Justices Brennan and White's opinion in *Data Processing* and *Barlow*. Davis, *supra*, at 450, 473.

[54] Steel Co. v. Citizens for Better Env't, 523 U.S. 83, 103 (1998).

[55] See this passage in *Lujan*:

> Nothing in this contradicts the principle that "[t]he . . . injury required by Art. III may exist solely by virtue of 'statutes creating legal rights, the invasion of which creates standing.'" *Warth*, 422 U.S., at 500 (quoting *Linda R.* S. v. *Richard D.*, 410 U.S. 614, 617, n. 3 (1973)). Both of the cases used by *Linda R.* S. as an illustration of that principle involved Congress' elevating to the status of legally cognizable injuries concrete, *de facto* injuries that were previously inadequate in law (namely, injury to an individual's personal interest in living in a racially integrated community, see *Trafficante* v. *Metropolitan Life Ins. Co.*, 409 U.S. 205, 208–212 (1972), and injury to a company's interest in marketing its product free from competition, see *Hardin* v. *Kentucky Utilities Co.*, 390 U.S. 1, 6 (1968)). As we said in *Sierra Club*, "[Statutory] broadening [of] the categories of injury that may be alleged in support of standing is a different matter from abandoning the requirement that the party seeking review must himself have suffered an injury." 405 U.S. at 738.

Lujan v. Defenders of Wildlife, 504 U.S. 555, 578 (1992).

[56] Sunstein, *supra* note 38.

[57] Havens Realty Corp. v. Coleman, 455 U.S. 363 (1982); *see* Baude *supra* note 10, at 201–02.

Without any statute, testers could not possibly have standing. It would not matter if they perceived or experienced an "injury in fact" when they were given false, discriminatorily motivated information about the housing market. Perhaps that seems like an odd claim. But in (say) 1922, a lawsuit by testers complaining of unlawful racial discrimination in housing could not have been "seen" as involving a legally cognizable injury; it would be similar to a lawsuit, today, in which people complained that the sun was shining too brightly, or not brightly enough.[58] But the plaintiffs in *Havens Realty* pointed to a statute (1) declaring it unlawful "[t]o represent to any person because of race, color, religion, sex, handicap, familial status, or national origin that any dwelling is not available for inspection, sale, or rental when such dwelling is in fact so available"[59] and (2) creating a cause of action to enforce this right.

The *Havens Realty* Court held that, in view of this statute, Congress had conferred a legal interest on testers and provided that it could be legally redressed. The injury to the "statutorily created right to truthful housing information" was sufficient for constitutional purposes.[60] It cannot be right to say that the plaintiff in *Havens Realty* suffered no injury in fact before Congress had acted, and that the civil rights statute somehow conjured up an injury ("in fact"!). Instead the relevant statute created a legally cognizable harm where none had existed before. Despite the *Havens Realty* Court's bow in the direction of injury in fact, the case shows that the real question is what harms that people perceive as such ought to be judicially cognizable. The outcome in the case had nothing to do with injury in fact. It had everything to do with the set of legal rights that Congress had conferred.

In many cases, the Court has endorsed the principle that "[t]he . . . injury required by Art. III may exist solely by virtue of 'statutes creating legal rights, the invasion of which creates standing.'"[61] For this reason, Congress may "elevat[e] to the status of legally cognizable injuries concrete, *de facto* injuries that were previously inadequate in law," such as an "injury to an individual's personal interest in living in a racially integrated community."[62] We ought to conclude,

---

[58] If that seems like a wild analogy, let me venture this prediction: Such a lawsuit will, in fact, be legally cognizable within the next century. We will see (or at least some of us will see).

[59] *Havens Realty*, 455 U.S. at 367 (citing 42 U.S.C. § 3604).

[60] *See id.* at 374.

[61] *Lujan*, 504 U.S. at 578.

[62] *Id.*

then, that despite *Data Processing*, the question of standing did not turn solely on the facts; it turned crucially on the law. And we might be inclined to think that so long as someone experiences an injury in fact, Congress can make that injury legally cognizable. Nonetheless, that proposition leaves some crucial questions unanswered. What does it even mean to say that someone experiences an injury in fact?

V. Ideological Interests and Traditional Injuries

Data Processing meant to expand the universe of people who were entitled to bring suit in federal court. But it soon became clear that the injury-in-fact test was not only a permission slip; it was also an entry requirement.[63] This is where matters start to become especially interesting.

Suppose that an environmental group challenges federal government action in California; suppose too that the group has no members in California. Does the group have standing? In *Sierra Club v. Morton*,[64] the Supreme Court ruled that the answer is "no," because the group has not been injured. Or suppose that civil-rights groups in New York object to racial discrimination that affects people in New Jersey.[65] Or suppose that people who care about animals, and who live in Nevada, are upset about violations of the Animal Welfare Act in Ohio. In a series of cases, the Court made it clear that a purely ideological interest, or an interest in law enforcement for its own sake, would not be sufficient for standing.[66] What was necessary was an injury in fact. Indeed, Congress lacks the authority to give people standing when they have not been injured.

As stated, these propositions might seem clear and simple. But they are not. Here is the missing question: What, exactly, has Congress done? Suppose that Congress has granted all Americans, wherever they live, a property right in some environmental amenity—say, a pristine area in Montana or clean air in Los Angeles—and also given all Americans, wherever they live, a cause of action to protect that right. Would they suffer an injury in fact if there is an infringement on that right? Is the idea of injury in fact a kind of Platonic form, such

[63] Sierra Club v. Morton, 405 U.S. 727 (1972); Allen v. Wright, 468 U.S. 737, 755–56 (1984).

[64] *Sierra Club*, 405 U.S. 727.

[65] *Allen*, 468 U.S. at 755–56.

[66] *See id.*

that Congress cannot simply deem certain things to fall within the category? In the same way that a dog cannot be a cat? Perhaps some legal rights do not and cannot conjure up an actual injury. Perhaps an injury in fact is not sufficient for standing. Perhaps Article III imposes limits on the kinds of interests that Congress can deem to be legally cognizable.

Does Article III impose such limits? Standing by itself (so to speak), the text of Article III contains no such limits.[67] The argument must be that something *external* to the text is properly taken to inform its interpretation, making it possible to define those limits. If so, we are not speaking of injury in fact, as such, as the issue. We are speaking of constitutional limitations on the kinds of injuries in fact that can support standing. But where would those limitations come from? The original understanding of Article III? The original understanding of Article II? Some kind of structural inference? From what?

In the decades since *Data Processing*, the Court has not answered these questions. It has insisted that people must show an injury that is both "concrete" and "particularized," and so denied standing to those whose interests can be characterized as hard to distinguish from those of members of the public as a whole.[68] In *Lujan*, the Court made it clear that Congress cannot bypass what the Court sees as the injury-in-fact requirement, which means that citizens' suits are inconsistent with Article III.[69] But *Lujan* could easily be read as a narrow ruling, authorizing Congress to elevate a host of injuries in the world to legally cognizable injuries, suitable for federal adjudication. Justice Kennedy insisted that Congress had just that authority.[70] And in the Court's own words, Congress may "elevat[e] to the status of legally cognizable injuries concrete, *de facto* injuries that were previously inadequate in law," such as an "injury to an individual's personal interest in living in a racially integrated community."[71]

In *Akins*,[72] decided in 1998, the Court read *Lujan* in exactly that way. It upheld a congressional grant of a legal right, and a cause of action, to

[67] Again: It requires a case or controversy, which imposes restrictions on what disputes, or nondisputes, federal courts can hear. Without a cause of action, there is no case or controversy.

[68] *Allen*, 468 U.S. at 737.

[69] Lujan v. Defenders of Wildlife, 504 U.S. 555 (1992).

[70] *Lujan*, 504 U.S. at 579 (Kennedy, J., concurring).

[71] *Id.*

[72] FEC v. Akins, 524 U.S. 11 (1998).

voters seeking to obtain information that bore on their decisions as voters. The Court showed no interest in the idea that Article III might limit Congress's power to create statutory rights and causes of action. Indeed, it explicitly authorized Congress to create a new right foreign to the common law. As the Court put it[73]:

> The "injury in fact" that respondents have suffered consists of their inability to obtain information—lists of [certain] donors, and campaign-related contributions and expenditures—that, on respondents' view of the law, the statute requires [be made] public. There is no reason to doubt their claim that the information would help them (and others to whom they would communicate it) to evaluate candidates for public office. . . . Respondents' injury consequently seems concrete and particular. Indeed, this Court has previously held that a plaintiff suffers an "injury in fact" when the plaintiff fails to obtain information which must be publicly disclosed pursuant to a statute.

This, then, was a clear recognition of Congress's authority to create legal rights unfamiliar to tradition and the common law.

An ambiguous signal came from *Spokeo*,[74] decided in 2016, where the Court seemed to argue in favor of respect for congressional efforts to create novel rights, but also insisted that Article III imposed some limits on congressional authority, and pointed, somewhat obscurely, to the relevance of traditional understandings of what kinds of actions are suitable for federal adjudication.[75] The Court emphasized that injuries can be "intangible" and that "Congress is well positioned to identify intangible harms that meet minimum Article III requirements," which means that "its judgment is also instructive and important."[76] The Court embraced Justice Kennedy's statement that "Congress has the power to define injuries and articulate chains of causation that will give rise to a case or controversy where none existed before."[77] But the Court rejected the idea that "a plaintiff automatically satisfies the injury-in-fact requirement whenever a statute grants a person a statutory right and purports to authorize that person to sue to vindicate that right."[78] Speaking cautiously and

[73] *Id.* at 22.

[74] Spokeo v. Robins, 578 U.S. 330 (2016).

[75] *Id.* at 340–41.

[76] *Id.* at 341.

[77] *Id.*

[78] *Id.*

without breaking new ground, the Court emphasized "the question framed by our discussion, namely, whether the particular procedural violations alleged in this case entail a degree of risk sufficient to meet the concreteness requirement."[79]

Flash forward[80] in that light to the far more radical ruling in *TransUnion v. Ramirez*.[81] In that case, the Court offered its most elaborate and firm account of what kinds of injuries in fact are sufficient to count for purposes of Article III. Emphasizing the importance of "concreteness," the Court declared that it would be necessary to ask "whether the asserted harm has a 'close relationship' to a harm traditionally recognized as providing a basis for a lawsuit in American courts—such as physical harm, monetary harm, or various intangible harms,"[82] including "reputational harm," "disclosure of private information," or "intrusion upon seclusion."[83] That is an astonishing innovation.[84]

As the Court understood it, plaintiffs would have standing if they suffered a "physical or monetary injury."[85] In addition, some intangible injuries would have "a close relationship to harms traditionally recognized as providing a basis for lawsuits in American courts."[86] Importantly, traditional harms would "include harms specified by the

---

[79] *Id.* at 342.

[80] To be sure, I am seeking the reader's indulgence here; I have briefly discussed the relevant precedents, and we are flashing forward very quickly. But for present purposes, *TransUnion* is the key case, the culmination and radicalization of a series of cases that had spoken far more cautiously and equivocally. *See, e.g.*, Lujan v. Defenders of Wildlife, 504 U.S. 555 (1992); *Spokeo*, 578 U.S. 330; Simon v. E. Ky. Welfare Rts. Org., 426 U.S. 26 (1976). Magill, *supra* note 4, offers an extended overview of relevant developments.

[81] 141 S. Ct. 2190 (2021).

[82] *Id.* at 2200.

[83] *See id.* at 2204.

[84] It is not without foundations. *See Spokeo*, 578 U.S. 330. Nonetheless, it does count as astonishing. As noted in text, *Spokeo* was far more cautious. Even in *Lujan*, which counts as astonishing in its own way, the Court made it clear that Congress could elevate various injuries to legal cognizability, even if they had no connection to traditional or common-law interests. Note the Court's crucial and uncontested acknowledgment that the plaintiffs in that case would have standing if they had a plane ticket, demonstrating that they sought to visit the endangered species at issue. *See Lujan*, 504 U.S. at 563–64. Nothing in the common law, or in tradition, recognizes as an "injury in fact" the harm done to scientists or others who are deprived of access to endangered species by virtue of the government's failure to protect such species. Recall too that in *Akins*, the Court recognized, as sufficient for standing, that injury comes from a failure to provide information that must be provided by law. FEC v. Akins, 524 U.S. 11 (1998). Nothing in the common law, or in tradition, recognizes that injury (in fact!).

[85] *TransUnion*, 141 S. Ct. at 2204.

[86] *Id.*

Constitution itself," such as abridgements of freedom of speech and free exercise.[87] Hence it would be necessary to ask whether "plaintiffs have identified a close historical or common-law analogue for their asserted injury."[88] While an "exact duplicate" would not be required,[89] Article III would not be loosened "based on contemporary, evolving beliefs about what kinds of suits should be heard in federal courts."[90]

To be sure, the Court added, judges "must afford due respect to Congress's decision to impose a statutory prohibition or obligation on a defendant, and to grant a plaintiff a cause of action to sue over the defendant's violation of that statutory prohibition or obligation."[91] But congressional judgments are not authoritative; they do not "relieve courts of their responsibility to independently decide whether a plaintiff has suffered a concrete harm under Article III."[92] To explain this conclusion, the Court emphasized that what was necessary was a "physical, monetary, or cognizable intangible harm traditionally recognized as providing a basis for a lawsuit in American courts. An uninjured plaintiff who sues in those circumstances is, by definition, not seeking to remedy any harm to herself but instead is merely seeking to ensure a defendant's 'compliance with regulatory law.'"[93]

The importance of this passage lies in the confident and even offhand use of the term "uninjured." One might think that whether a plaintiff is injured depends on what the law says. But in the Court's view, injury seems like a kind of Platonic form. Whatever Congress says, people not subjected to traditional harms *simply are not injured.* The injuries they perceive or experience are not injuries that Article III courts are authorized to "see."

---

[87] *Id.*

[88] *Id.*

[89] *Id.* at 2209.

[90] *Id.* at 2204. It is important to pause over those words, which might be seen as the equivalent to a judicial dog whistle; judicial use of "contemporary, evolving beliefs" has long been a target in certain circles. *See, e.g.*, Antonin Scalia, A Matter of Interpretation (1997). But it is one thing to suggest that constitutional rights should not be based on "contemporary, evolving beliefs." It is quite another thing to suggest that Congress lacks the authority to rely on "contemporary, evolving beliefs" to create statutory rights that are cognizable in court.

[91] *Id.* at 2205.

[92] *Id.* Justice Kavanaugh's opinion here echoes a comment written by Chief Justice Roberts after his victorious oral argument in *Lujan. See* John G. Roberts, Jr., *Article III Limits on Statutory Standing*, 42 Duke L.J. 1219, 1226 (1993): "If Congress directs the federal courts to hear a case in which the requirements of Article III are not met, that Act of Congress is unconstitutional." The statement is quite correct. But what are the requirements of Article III?

[93] *TransUnion*, 141 S. Ct. at 2206.

In a baffling and anomalous passage, the Court acknowledged that in some cases, it had recognized "informational injury," in the particular form of a "denial of information subject to public-disclosure or sunshine laws that entitle all members of the public to certain information."[94] The Court strongly indicated that Congress could grant rights to information to all members of the public and accompany those rights with a cause of action. But the Court did not explain how that conclusion squared with the proposition that what was necessary was a "harm traditionally recognized as providing a basis for a lawsuit in American courts."[95]

In *TransUnion*, the Court failed to investigate the relevant history of Article III to support its understanding of "concrete harm." Instead, it complained that a contrary view, allowing Congress to create rights and causes of action to vindicate them, "would cast aside *decades* of precedent."[96] It added that if Congress could "freely authorize *unharmed* plaintiffs to sue defendants who violate federal law," there would be an infringement on the President's authority under Article II.[97] The reason is that "the choice of how to prioritize and how aggressively to pursue legal actions against defendants who violate the law falls within the discretion of the Executive Branch, not within the purview of private plaintiffs (and their attorneys)."[98] After all, private plaintiffs "are not accountable to the people and are not charged with pursuing the public interest."[99]

---

[94] *Id.* at 2214.

[95] *Id.* at 2213.

[96] *Id.* at 2207 n.3 (italics added). I have added the italics out of mischief. Decades of precedent? *Decades*? In the scheme of things, decades are a heartbeat. If the injury-in-fact test has been around only for "decades," we really might want to question its provenance.

[97] *Id.* at 2207 (italics in original).

[98] *Id.*

[99] This is not the place for full discussion of the Article II issue, which raises puzzles of its own; for relevant remarks, *see* Sunstein, *supra* note 9, at 175–76. In brief: In *TransUnion* itself, Article II could not possibly be relevant. The case involved a suit between private parties! If Congress authorizes Private Citizen A to sue Private Citizen B in federal court, there might be an Article III issue, depending on what A is suing B for, and depending on the right conception of Article III. But it would require an adventurous understanding of Article II to think that the authority of the Executive is at stake or in danger. To be sure, the Court has thought, on occasion, that Article II is relevant to standing issues in cases in which people who are uninjured, or arguably so, are suing the Executive to force it to act, or to act in a certain way. *See* Lujan v. Defenders of Wildlife, 504 U.S. 555 (1992). To its credit, the Court has referred to Article II cautiously and without treating it as an independent barrier to standing in such cases. The reason for the caution is that for Article II purposes, it is very hard indeed to draw a distinction between cases in which people have a concrete injury (as the

Applying this analysis to the case at the hand, the Court held, first, that the standing requirements were met by those plaintiffs who argued that their credit reports contained misleading alerts that *had been sent to third-party businesses*. The relevant injury bore a sufficiently "close relationship" to the reputational harm associated with defamation.[100] To be sure, the reports were misleading, but not false, which meant that they were not defamatory. But the Court emphasized that it did not need "an exact duplicate" of the common law of defamation; the misleading statement had "a sufficiently close relationship to the harm from a false and defamatory statement."[101]

By contrast, the Court found no standing for those plaintiffs whose credit files contained misleading alerts that had *not* been sent to any potential creditors. As the Court pointed out, publication is essential to a defamation suit, and there was no historical or common-law precedent to support the idea that the existence of inaccurate information, without dissemination, counts as a concrete injury. Thus "the mere existence of inaccurate information in a database is insufficient to confer Article III standing," just as a "letter that is not sent does not harm anyone."[102]

Court understands it) and cases in which people do not. Suppose, for example, that people with plane tickets to see members of endangered species sue the Department of Interior to require it to enforce the Endangered Species Act. Under *Lujan*, there is no problem. Now suppose that people without plane tickets bring the same suit. Under *Lujan*, there is a problem. What is the difference, for Article *II* purposes? The Constitution requires the Executive to take care that the laws be faithfully executed, and that is the goal of both lawsuits. To be sure, the Executive would not be very enthusiastic about having to defend itself against a very large number of lawsuits, seeking to question and overturn its preferred enforcement priorities. But it will lose one or more of those suits if and only if it has violated the law; and it is required to comply with the law. Where is the Article II problem? The Court must be thinking that there is some Article II question if people without concrete injuries are able to force the Executive to defend its actions (or its failures to act); but why, if the ground for the attack is that the Executive has failed to comply with the law?

A possible response is that there is a difference between (1) enforcing the rights of victims, that is, those who have actually been injured and (2) enforcing the rights of the public, that is, requiring adherence to the law in cases in which there may be no victims, or in cases in which no victims are before the court. On one view, the former kind of law enforcement can be delegated to victims (as rights-holders), but the latter is an executive function. Some version of this argument may be right. But who is a victim? Who is a right holder? Who has actually been injured? In general, the answer should be settled by reference to positive law, with an acknowledgement that there might be extreme cases (as, perhaps, in *Lujan* itself, and as in a case in which Congress grants everyone a legal right to sue whenever the law is violated). I am aware that these are brisk remarks on what some people consider to be a complicated topic.

[100] *TransUnion*, 141 S. Ct. at 2208.

[101] *Id.* at 2209.

[102] *Id.* at 2209–10.

To be sure, the Court recognized that a risk of real harm, or a material risk of harm, might be enough to satisfy the requirement of concreteness: "a person exposed to a risk of future harm may pursue forward looking, injunctive relief to prevent the harm from occurring, at least so long as the risk of harm is sufficiently imminent and substantial."[103] But in a suit for damages, "a mere risk of future harm, standing alone, cannot qualify as a concrete harm—at least unless the exposure to the risk of a future harm itself causes a *separate* concrete harm."[104] The plaintiffs whose credit files contained misleading alerts were never harmed, because their files were not sent to third parties and did not result in a denial of credit. In any case, the risk of dissemination to third parties "was too speculative to support Article III standing."[105]

The Court also denied standing to those plaintiffs who objected that TransUnion had not provided them with complete credit files, as it was legally obliged to do. The files did not contain a "summary of rights" in the correct format. As the Court had it, the failure to use the correct format did not impose a concrete harm. The format of the mailings did not create "a harm with a close relationship to a harm traditionally recognized as providing a basis for a lawsuit in American courts." Insofar as the formatting violations might have created a risk of future harm, no concrete injury had been shown, because in a suit for damages, such a risk was inadequate.

Let's step back. We have come a long way from *Data Processing*. *TransUnion* clarifies that injury in fact is no longer about injury in fact at all. It is largely[106] about limiting federal courts to harms "traditionally recognized as providing a basis for a law suit." We might hope to see this as an honorably Burkean effort to ground the notion of injury in fact in traditions of legal cognizability. Unfortunately, that is a forlorn hope. The approach in *TransUnion* is a concoction. The Court has invented a tradition. *TransUnion* makes some brisk gestures in the direction of originalism,[107] but it makes no effort to ground its holding in the original understanding. That would have

[103] *Id.*

[104] *Id.* at 2211.

[105] *Id.* at 2212.

[106] Note also that the Court is willing to recognize injuries to constitutional rights and informational injuries. *See supra* notes 87, 94 and accompanying text.

[107] *See TransUnion*, 141 S. Ct. at 2204.

been exceedingly difficult to do. In the Founding-era debates, it is challenging indeed to find evidence that Article III required an "injury in fact," or anything like it.[108]

VI. *Lochnering*

Over the course of the half-century that separates *Data Processing* and *TransUnion*, what happened, exactly? It is hard not to notice that in spite of the anodyne nature of the key opinions,[109] one thing is clear: *in the most important cases in which the injury-in-fact test is causing problems for standing, the plaintiffs are typically the beneficiaries of regulatory protection.* They might be consumers, as in *TransUnion* itself;[110] they might be civil rights organizations;[111] they might be poor people;[112] they might be environmentalists.[113] In all of these cases, and many more, the people who struggle to show injury in fact do not have common-law rights at stake; they are seeking to vindicate the interests and concerns that gave rise to the relevant statutes. When common-law interests are at stake—when, for example, regulators are seeking to force companies to do or not to do something—no standing issue even arises; no question is ever asked.[114]

We could easily imagine a system of public law that is built squarely and solely on private- law foundations. In its most extreme form, such a system would insist that in order to have access to federal court, people would have to show that a common-law interest was at stake. Having such an interest would be both necessary and sufficient for standing (and as we have seen, *TransUnion* heads in this direction). We could also imagine a situation in which Congress is satisfied with that approach: common-law interests for courts; statutory interests for political processes. But we could also imagine a situation in which Congress sought to give the beneficiaries of regulatory statutes a degree of protection in federal court, perhaps because of a fear of

[108] *See* Winter, *supra* note 9; Sunstein, *supra* note 9.

[109] *See* Spokeo v. Robins, 578 U.S. 330 (2016); Summers v. Earth Island Inst., 555 U.S. 488 (2009).

[110] *See also Spokeo*, 578 U.S. 330.

[111] Allen v. Wright, 468 U.S. 737 (1984).

[112] Simon v. E. Ky. Welfare Rts. Org., 426 U.S. 26 (1976).

[113] *Summers*, 555 U.S. 488.

[114] *See, e.g.*, Entergy Corp. v. Riverkeeper, Inc., 556 U.S. 208 (2009).

interest-group capture, or perhaps because of a belief that judicial involvement could serve as an ex ante deterrent and an ex post corrective to unlawful behavior on the part of regulatory agencies. And in fact, *Data Processing* was preceded by, and seemed to ratify and extend, a set of lower court decisions that had understood the APA to authorize beneficiary suits under the "legal wrong" test, with the risk of unlawfully insufficient regulatory protection in the foreground.[115]

In these circumstances, the series of decisions that culminated in *TransUnion* had an unmistakable valence,[116] with a clear ideological overtone[117]: standing is first and foremost for the objects of regulation, armed with common-law interests, and at best dubiously for the beneficiaries of regulation, armed with statutory interests. We might call this the return of the repressed, or of the Constitution in Exile[118]—with the qualification that for Article III and Article II, something is being invented, not returned or recovered.[119] To put it bluntly: We are speaking of a modern-day analogue to *Lochner v. New York*, in the quite specific sense that like *Lochner*, *TransUnion* is an effort to use common-law baselines in such a way as to strike down actions by the democratic branches of government, and thus to limit the reach of regulatory enactments.[120]

VII. Open Questions

TransUnion raises a host of new questions.[121] Under the Freedom of Information Act, "any person" is entitled to bring suit to obtain

---

[115] *See supra* note 41 and accompanying text.

[116] On ideological valence over time, *see generally* Ho & Ross, *supra* note 16.

[117] There is an intriguing difference here from earlier periods. Consider the finding that "before 1940, liberals were far more likely to deny standing, while conservatives were far more likely to grant it. After 1940, that pattern reverses." *Id.* at 640.

[118] The term comes from Judge Douglas Ginsburg. Douglas Ginsburg, *Delegation Running Riot*, 1995 Regulation 83. It is possible, of course, to specify the meaning of the Constitution in 1789, 1872, and 1920; with respect to standing, the current understanding of constitutional meaning is emphatically current. But it does purport to be an exercise in recovery.

[119] In my view, and for reasons sketched briefly in note 99, Article II concerns do not belong in standing cases. *See* Sunstein, *supra* note 9; see also *Case Comment:* TransUnion LLC v. Ramirez, 135 Harv. L. Rev. 333, 339 (2021) (arguing that finding standing in cases involving private individuals bringing private claims does not implicate Article II concerns); F. Andrew Hessick, *The Separation-of-Powers Theory of Standing*, 95 N.C. L. Rev. 673, 675–76 (2017) (same).

[120] 198 U.S. 45 (1905).

[121] *See* Erwin Chemerinsky, *What's Standing After* TransUnion LLC v. Ramirez, 96 N.Y.U. L. Rev. 269 (2021).

information held by the government, subject to specified exemptions.[122] If people seek to vindicate their rights under the Freedom of Information Act, do they have standing? The Court's carve-out for "informational injury" would seem to suggest they do, but what is the foundation, or justification, for that carve-out? Or suppose that armed with a plane ticket to see members of endangered species, people bring suit against public officials who have failed to act in accordance with the Endangered Species Act. (*Lujan* plainly states that such people would have standing,[123] even though the relevant rights are foreign to the common law.) Or suppose that people are bringing suit to vindicate their statutory rights to be free from discrimination on the basis of race, sex, or disability. (The Court has had no trouble with such suits,[124] even though the relevant rights are foreign to the common law.)

The best approach would be to focus on the *TransUnion* holding, not the extended analysis. The central holding is exceedingly narrow: Congress cannot authorize people to sue to collect damages against a credit company on the sole ground that it has produced, and is holding, a credit report that contains inaccurate information about them. Viewed most sympathetically, the Court's holding is that Congress cannot conjure an injury out of nothing—any more than it could say that someone who lives in Texas is injured by air pollution in Maine, or that someone who lives in Utah is injured by automobile accidents in New Jersey. It is altogether different if, for example, people are discriminated against on the basis of race, sex, or disability; are deprived of information on which they would rely on in their capacity as voters;[125] are unable to see members of endangered species;[126] are unable to enjoy whale-watching;[127] or face some kind of risk of harm, including mortality.[128] Recall the Court's suggestion that Congress may "elevat[e] to the status of legally cognizable injuries concrete, *de*

---

[122] 5 U.S.C. § 552.

[123] *See* Lujan v. Defenders of Wildlife, 504 U.S. 555, 562 (1992).

[124] *See, e.g.*, Havens Realty Corp. v. Coleman, 455 U.S. 363, 376 (1982); Trafficante v. Metro. Life Ins. Co., 409 U.S. 205, 212 (1972).

[125] FEC v. Akins, 524 U.S. 11 (1998).

[126] *Lujan*, 504 U.S. at 555.

[127] Japan Whaling Ass'n v. Cetacean Soc'y, 478 U.S. 221 (1986).

[128] *See* Jonathan R. Nash, *Standing's Expected Value*, 111 Mich. L. Rev. 1283 (2013). This is of course a deeply vexed area.

facto injuries that were previously inadequate in law," such as an "injury to an individual's personal interest in living in a racially integrated community."[129] (To put it lightly, that personal interest did not implicate "harm traditionally recognized as providing a basis for a lawsuit in American courts."[130])

The challenge, of course, is to narrow the *TransUnion* ruling while also paying heed to the Court's explicit emphasis on "whether the asserted harm has a 'close relationship' to a harm traditionally recognized as providing a basis for a lawsuit in American courts—such as physical harm, monetary harm, or various intangible harms." The simplest way to do that is to note that many harms that Congress has singled out, as legally cognizable, should be understood to have a sufficiently close relationship. Air pollution can, of course, produce a physical harm or a monetary harm; it might also be akin to a common-law nuisance. But more broadly, *TransUnion* should not be taken as a train that runs over well-established categories of legally cognizable harm, or to insist on a conception of the judicial role that does not respect Congress's authority to go beyond common-law understandings of private rights. Congress has considerable room to categorize, as legally cognizable, a wide range of physical harms, monetary harms, and intangible harms, involving (for example) "aesthetic, conservational, and recreational"[131] interests, as well as the interests in avoiding discrimination, unfair or manipulative practices,[132] and risks to personal safety and health.

VIII. Conclusion

Our little tale is now complete. The injury-in-fact test was created in *Data Processing*; it is an outgrowth of an egregious misinterpretation of the APA. The Court's goal was to simplify the law of

[129] TransUnion LLC v. Ramirez, 141 S. Ct. 2190, 2204–05 (2021).

[130] *Id.* at 2213.

[131] *Id.* It is noteworthy in this regard that only two years after *Data Processing*, Justice Douglas wrote a spirited dissenting opinion, arguing that the "critical question of standing would be simplified . . . if we fashioned a federal rule that allowed environmental issues to be litigated . . . in the name of the inanimate object about to be despoiled, defaced, or invaded by roads and bulldozers and where injury is the subject of public outrage. . . . The voice of the inanimate object . . . should not be stilled." Sierra Club v. Morton, 405 U.S. 727, 742 (Douglas, J., dissenting).

[132] *See* Jamie Luguri and Lior Strahilevitz, *Shining A Light On Dark Patterns*, 13 J. Legal Analysis 43 (2021).

standing and to expand the category of persons entitled to bring suit. To say the least, the goal of simplification has not been achieved. And in the last half-century, the injury-in-fact test has turned into an increasingly serious obstacle to congressional efforts to create new rights and to give people causes of action to vindicate those rights. It is no longer clear whether and to what extent Congress can deem actual injuries, experienced in the world, to be a basis for legal injuries, cognizable in court.[133] With respect to standing, at least, public law has increasingly been understood by reference to private-law categories.

Though the idea that Congress lacks authority to create citizens' suits does not have solid foundations, it is not exactly preposterous.[134] By contrast, the idea that Congress lacks broad power to create legal rights, and to grant people causes of action to vindicate them, is indeed preposterous, which means that *TransUnion* was wrong on its facts. Nothing in the Constitution forbids Congress to create rights that are foreign to the common law or the Constitution. The most disturbing and lawless part of *TransUnion* consists in its focus on harms "traditionally recognized as providing a basis for a law suit"—and the Court's own recognition of "informational injuries" shows that it did not entirely mean what it said.

The best path forward is for the Court to make it clear that while traditionally recognized harms are indeed a legitimate basis for standing, Congress has the authority to create "new rights of action that do not have clear analogs in our common-law tradition."[135] In deciding who should have access to federal court, Congress cannot plausibly be limited, by constitutional compulsion, to private-law categories.[136] Article III does not enact Mr. William Prosser's *Law of Torts*.[137]

---

[133] *See* Heather Elliott, *Congress's Inability to Solve Standing Problems*, 91 B.U. L. Rev. 159, 167 (2011).

[134] Woolhandler & Nelson, *supra* note 44, at 691–92.

[135] Lujan v. Defenders of Wildlife, 504 U.S. 555, 579 (1992) (Kennedy, J., concurring).

[136] Once more, with feeling: A little *Lochner*, anyone? *See generally* Sunstein, *supra* note 8.

[137] *See* William Prosser, Law of Torts (2d ed. 1955). The reference is, of course, to the most famous words in Justice Holmes's dissenting opinion in Lochner v. New York, 198 U.S. 45, 75 (1905) (Holmes, J., dissenting): "The Constitution does not enact Mr. Herbert Spencer's Social Statics."

OWEN FISS

SCALIA'S SLIP

Antonin Scalia was appointed to the Supreme Court in September 1986 and served in that position until he died in February 2016. Over the course of his career he achieved great prominence and was admired by many. On his death a law school was named in his honor and in 2018 he was posthumously awarded the Presidential Medal of Freedom. His slip occurred not in the kind of social interactions that Freud envisaged, but rather in an opinion of his that appeared in the official reports of the Supreme Court. All the Justices are served by a number of law clerks and it is fair to assume that the final version of this particular opinion was carefully reviewed by one of his law clerks. It is also fair to assume that all, or at least some, of his colleagues carefully read the opinion before it was formally issued. One, Justice Clarence Thomas, joined it.

Justice Scalia issued this opinion in 2014 in *Schuette v. Coalition to Defend Affirmative Action, Integration and Immigration Rights and Fight for Equality by Any Means Necessary* (known by the acronym *BAMN*). This case arose when the state constitution of Michigan was amended to prohibit publicly financed universities of the state from

Owen Fiss is Sterling Professor Emeritus of Law, Yale University.

Author's note: This essay arises from my 2020 A Community of Equals seminar. I am grateful to the students in the seminar for the opportunity to present these ideas and to receive their comments. I also wish to thank one member of the seminar in particular—Hannah Carrese—for the extraordinary grace and rigor of her research assistance.

The Supreme Court Review, 2022.
 Published by The University of Chicago Press. https://doi.org/10.1086/718788

giving race-based preferences in their admissions processes.[1] In 2003, the Supreme Court had ruled in *Grutter v. Bollinger*—another case involving the University of Michigan, this time its Law School—that the practice of giving Blacks a modest plus in the admissions process did not violate the Equal Protection Clause of the Fourteenth Amendment of the federal Constitution.[2] Immediately prior to *Grutter*, and in the decade following, a number of states, most notably California but also Washington, Nebraska, Oklahoma, New Hampshire, Florida, and Arizona, specifically adopted laws preventing state officers from giving race-based preferences of any kind in admissions to their publicly financed universities. In effect, these provisions prohibited state officials acting under state law from taking action that the federal Constitution permitted. Michigan eventually joined this select group of states, and in the 2014 decision in *BAMN* the Supreme Court held that this action was not inconsistent with the 2003 decision in *Grutter* nor did it otherwise violate the federal Constitution.

Justice Elena Kagan did not participate in the decision, presumably because of her involvement with the litigation when she was Solicitor General. The remaining eight Justices were arrayed, essentially, in four different groups. Justice Sonia Sotomayor spoke for one group. She viewed the Michigan amendment as a change in the process by which the state universities might adopt and pursue affirmative action policies—it took the decision over affirmative action out of the hands of the elected trustees and placed it in the hands of the state-wide electorate. This change in the political process worked, Sotomayor complained, to the disadvantage of Blacks and for that reason constitutes a denial of equal protection. Only Justice Ruth Bader Ginsburg joined Sotomayor's opinion and it became the dissent.

Justice Anthony Kennedy announced the judgment of the Court and wrote an opinion that Chief Justice John Roberts and Justice Samuel Alito joined. Kennedy acknowledged that certain changes in the political process might constitute—if the change inflicted a racially specific injury—violations of equal protection. He reviewed and endorsed the applicable precedents, but in the end concluded that this standard was not met in the case before the Court. Although the Chief

---

[1] Schuette v. Coalition to Defend Affirmative Action, Integration and Immigration Rights and Fight for Equality by Any Means Necessary (*BAMN*), 572 U.S. 291 (2014).

[2] Grutter v. Bollinger, 539 U.S. 306 (2003).

Justice joined Kennedy's opinion, he also wrote a short opinion reprimanding Sotomayor for her lengthy disquisition on why race still matters and for her spirited and broad defense of affirmative action, or what she prefers to call "race-sensitive admissions policies."[3] With obvious displeasure, Roberts noted that this portion of her opinion consisted of eleven pages. Roberts also reminded Sotomayor that she herself denied that "the virtues of adopting race-sensitive admissions policies should inform the legal question before the Court."[4]

Justice Stephen Breyer supported the judgment allowing the Michigan amendment to stand, though on a unique theory. He characterized the amendment as an attempt by the electorate to gain control over admissions policies that would otherwise be set by faculty and administrators, not by elected trustees. For him, the Michigan amendment did not result in a change in the political process that worked to the disadvantage of Blacks, but rather a victory for the principle favoring democratic decision-making.

Justice Scalia spoke for the fourth group. It included Thomas and himself and, like Breyer and Kennedy and those who joined Kennedy's opinion, upheld the Michigan constitutional amendment banning affirmative action. With his customary flair, Scalia began his opinion in this way: "It has come to this. Called upon to explore the jurisprudential twilight between two errant lines of precedents, we confront a frighteningly bizarre question: Does the Equal Protection Clause of the Fourteenth Amendment *forbid* what its text plainly *requires*?"[5] In formulating the question before the Court in this way, and through the use of italics, Scalia underscored the words "forbid" and "requires," and skipped over the words that caught my eye—"its text plainly." In this way, Scalia conveyed the impression that the text of the Equal Protection Clause plainly forbids a state university from giving Blacks or other minority applicants a race-based preference. This, however,

---

[3] *BAMN*, 572 U.S. at 339.

[4] *Id.* at 315. Joan Biskupic reports Sotomayor had drafted the eleven-page section that galled Roberts to be a dissent in *Fisher v. University of Texas*, a 2012 affirmative action case. Her intended *Fisher* dissent, according to Biskupic, persuaded Justice Kennedy to change his vote in *Fisher*, and to write an opinion that remanded the case for further proceedings and thus avoided a judgment on the merits. Sotomayor joined Kennedy's opinion, so she saved the text meant to be a dissent in *Fisher* and used it in *BAMN*. *See* Biskupic, Breaking In: The Rise of Sonia Sotomayor and the Politics of Justice 205–11 (2014); *see also infra* note 11 and accompanying text.

[5] *BAMN*, 572 U.S. at 316.

is not at all the case, as anyone can see. The text—or better yet, the "plain text"—of the Equal Protection Clause does not ban race-based preferences. It only provides, in so many words: "nor shall any State . . . deny to any person within its jurisdiction the equal protection of the laws."

These words were added to the Constitution in 1868, almost immediately after the end of the Civil War, when the nation confronted the deplorable social and economic conditions of the newly freed slaves and was acutely aware of the dangers they faced. The sponsors of the Fourteenth Amendment feared that the states, primarily those that had belonged to the Confederacy but in truth all the states, North and South, might enact laws that would have the inevitable effect of perpetuating the status of Blacks as an underclass. The sponsors also feared that the states might turn a blind eye to vigilante justice and efforts by dispossessed slave owners to use all the means available to them, including violence, to oppress and maintain the perpetual subordination of the newly freed slaves. The overarching purpose of the Fourteenth Amendment, and the Equal Protection Clause in particular, was to prevent such action by the states. One further provision of the Fourteenth Amendment gave Congress the power to enact laws enforcing the rights that it conferred. This provision gave a firm constitutional basis for the various federal statutes protecting Blacks that were passed, first, between the end of the war in 1865 and the adoption of the Fourteenth Amendment in 1868, and then over the next decade, that is, before the two dominant political parties agreed, in order to settle the election of 1876, to repudiate or at least abandon Reconstruction.

The phrase the sponsors of the Fourteenth Amendment used—"the equal protection of the laws"—lends itself to many meanings. Given the historical origins of the constitutional provision and its overarching purpose, one can readily understand why it has been construed in our day to prohibit state practices that disadvantage Blacks and that use race as allocative criterion for that purpose. A rule that provides "Whites Only" clearly is a transgression of equal protection. On the other hand, given this very same understanding of the origins and overarching purpose of the Equal Protection Clause, it is difficult to read that provision as prohibiting race-based preferences for Blacks. Admittedly, whenever race is used as an allocative criterion, individuals will have to be classified according to their race—decide who is white, who is Black. In this instance, however, the racial classification is designed not to disadvantage Blacks, but rather to eradicate their status as the underclass.

By gaining admission to elite universities such as the University of Michigan, Blacks will receive significant advantages—a valuable credential, entrance to professional networks, and the special educational experience such a richly endowed university is uniquely positioned to provide. These advantages will enhance the upward mobility of those Blacks lucky enough to be admitted and in time will alter the status of Blacks in general, thereby working toward the demise of the hierarchy among racial groups that was first created by a slave system defined exclusively in racial terms and that has been perpetuated by the operation of a caste system that treats Blacks as pariahs.

Scalia read the Equal Protection Clause as a mandate for sameness, as a flat universal ban on the use of race to differentiate, classify, or distinguish among individuals, regardless of whether the differentiation disadvantages Blacks or actually improves their position. This view cannot be justified in terms of the plain text of the Equal Protection Clause. Nor has a majority of the Justices ever construed that constitutional provision to yield this flat, universal ban on racial differentiation or the use of racial classifications. For the Court, "the equal protection of the laws" requires not sameness, but rather that any differentiation, whether it be based on race or any other criterion, be appropriately justified. Unsurprisingly, throughout the history of the Supreme Court, many battles have been fought over whether any given differentiation, particularly one based on race, is sufficiently justified, and the standards and tests the Court has used to resolve that question have shifted.

I. Strict Scrutiny and Racial Classifications

Starting in 1954 and continuing through the 1960s, the Supreme Court played a crucial role in launching and then sustaining what has come to be known as the Second Reconstruction: The Court defined the duties of the states, protected the activists who led or participated in the civil rights movement, and thoroughly supported, sometimes even invited, the participation of Congress and the President in this renewed effort at reconstruction. In 1969, Earl Warren stepped down as Chief Justice, and that act marked the beginning of a period, lasting until 1975, in which President Richard Nixon and then his successor President Gerald Ford, were able to make five appointments to the Court and reconstitute the governing coalition of the Court. Then, as was made evident through a number of key decisions in the mid-1970s, the Court abandoned its leadership role in the Second Reconstruction, and in fact took upon itself the work of policing implementation of this reform program, both as it was originally formulated and then as it was refurbished in the 1980s and early 1990s by the political branches and the institutions of civil society.

This new phase of Supreme Court history, which began in 1975 and continues to this very day, might, because of the Court's stance toward reconstruction, properly be referred to as its "supervisory phase." In it the Court was called to determine whether a reconstructive practice, such as affirmative action, is constitutionally permissible, and in discharging this task the Court placed increasing emphasis on a test known as "strict scrutiny." This test is nothing more than a heuristic, a guide to the Justices in giving concrete content to the broad, general terms of the Equal Protection Clause and in determining whether a differentiation was appropriately justified. Admittedly, the application of strict scrutiny created a cloud over racial classifications, though it did not ban them altogether. Rather, strict scrutiny requires that whenever racial classifications are used, as in affirmative action, the justification for the state practice must have a very special character. Once triggered, strict scrutiny demands that the state practice be justified by a compelling public purpose and that the means chosen to pursue this purpose be narrowly tailored.

Although all the Justices might well agree with this general formulation of strict scrutiny, they have been divided over each of the three components of the heuristic: (1) What triggers strict scrutiny or makes the test applicable; (2) What qualifies as a compelling public purpose; and (3) What are the standards for judging whether the means chosen by the state to pursue this public purpose are narrowly tailored. Over the course of the phase of the Supreme Court's history devoted to policing the Second Reconstruction, which encompassed the whole of Justice Scalia's tenure (1986–2016), a majority of the Justices created a special place for racial classifications in the first and third components of the test. But they have not construed the Equal Protection Clause to require sameness or to flatly prohibit racial classifications. The majority have not said anything that might possibly excuse or even explain Scalia's slip.

A. TRIGGERS

Strict scrutiny was not applied in *Brown v. Board of Education.*[6] Without the aid of strict scrutiny, the Court concluded that a dual-school system—whites in one set of schools, Blacks in another—systematically disadvantaged Blacks by impairing the quality of education they received. In *Loving v. Virginia*, the 1967 case stemming from a challenge to a state law that forbade whites and Blacks to marry, strict scrutiny was in fact applied and resulted in the invalidation of the law.[7] Although the Virginia statute used a racial classification, the prohibition on miscegenation, like the maintenance of the dual-school system, was seen by the Court as an integral part of the caste system that systematically disadvantaged and subordinated Blacks.

Faithful to this use of strict scrutiny, even during the supervisory phase of the Court's history, a significant bloc of Justices limited the applicability of the test to situations where racial classifications are used systematically to disadvantage Blacks or other racial minorities. This group included, at one time or another, Justices William Brennan and Thurgood Marshall (the holdovers from the Warren Court), as well as Harry Blackmun, John Paul Stevens, David Souter, Stephen Breyer, Ruth Bader Ginsburg, Elena Kagan, and Sonia Sotomayor. It might have also included Justices Potter Stewart and Byron White, two of the centrists of the Warren Court, who continued to serve during the 1970s and 1980s.

These Justices were not able to prevail. Out of necessity, they aligned with members of the Court, such as Justices Anthony Kennedy and Sandra Day O'Connor, who had some sympathy for the Second Reconstruction but regarded the use of a racial classification, without regard to whether the measure of which it was part benefitted or burdened Blacks, a sufficient condition for triggering strict scrutiny. No need, on this reading, to show that the measure systematically disadvantages Blacks or was part of a larger undertaking that had such an effect. This blanket rule was the underpinning of *Grutter v. Bollinger*, which, in 2003, gave majority status to the opinion that Justice Powell (speaking only for himself) filed in 1978 in the *Bakke* case, in which he insisted that affirmative action be judged by strict scrutiny simply

[6] 347 U.S. 483 (1954).

[7] 388 U.S. 1 (1967).

because of the use of a racial classification.[8] Justice O'Connor wrote the majority opinion in *Grutter* and though Justice Kennedy dissented in that particular case, elsewhere he defended the blanket rule in part because of the divisiveness he feared racial classifications might cause, even when they are used to improve the status of the underclass.[9] Alternatively, Kennedy defended the blanket rule on the ground that using race to judge individual applications for scarce opportunities is morally offensive because it evinces a disrespect for the dignity that is owed to every person.

There are, of course, ample grounds for disagreeing with Kennedy's defense of the rule that turns all uses of racial classifications into a trigger for strict scrutiny. One may argue, for example, that the divisiveness and friction of which Kennedy spoke stems not from the use of racial classifications, but rather from the persistent and systematic subordination of Blacks as an underclass and the resentment and anger such a social structure inevitably engenders. Kennedy's claim that the use of racial classification is a violation of human dignity also seems contestable.[10] It ignores the constructive social purposes, such as school integration, that may call for the use of racial classifications.

We need not pause, however, to debate these issues here. What needs to be emphasized here is that the blanket rule disfavoring all racial classifications and making a law that deploys a racial classification subject to strict scrutiny is based either on a prudential or moralistic judgment, not a claim about the so-called "plain meaning" of equal protection. It is not based on a reading of the Equal Protection Clause that reduces that guarantee to a mandate for sameness or, as Scalia mistakenly asserted in *BAMN*, a flat and universal prohibition against racial differentiation, or racial distinctions, or racial classifications.

B. Narrow Tailoring

Justice Kennedy also allowed his wariness toward racial classifications to govern his application of the narrow tailoring requirement of strict scrutiny, though in this instance his concern was based on moral rather

[8] Regents of the University of California v. Bakke, 438 U.S. 265 (1978).

[9] Parents Involved in Community Schools v. Seattle School District No. 1, 551 U.S. 701, 797 (2007) (Kennedy, J., concurring in part and concurring in the judgment); *see* Reva Siegel, *From Colorblindness to Antibalkanization*, 120 Yale L.J. 1278 (2011).

[10] Owen Fiss, *The Law of Narrow Tailoring*, 23 U. Pa. J. Const. L. 879 (2021).

than prudential considerations. Here too he spoke for Justice O'Connor, and arguably for some of the liberal bloc.

The narrow tailoring requirement is predicated on the idea that even if the state is allowed to pursue a compelling public purpose it must economize its sacrifice of the values that are served by the underlying constitutional guarantee. Only those means that are necessary will be permitted. This rule can be easily understood in an example drawn from the First Amendment context, which is also governed by the strict scrutiny heuristic. Although the state might be allowed to guard against speech that is very likely to result in a riot (the avoidance of violence is the compelling public purpose), it cannot do so by banning public speeches or rallies that are fiercely, or even extravagantly, critical of the established order. Instead, it must utilize more tailored, or less restrictive strategies, such as those requiring advance notice to the authorities so they can deploy the force necessary to maintain order. In this way, the narrow tailoring requirement might be said to serve normative ends, or to have normative consequences, although it essentially calls for an instrumental judgment about the relationship between means and ends.

Kennedy did not, however, respect the instrumental character of the narrow tailoring requirement when he was called upon to determine whether a program designed to eradicate racial hierarchy—of which affirmative action is exemplary—passes constitutional muster. Rather, he transformed the narrow tailoring requirement into a platform for importing into equal protection analysis certain moralistic notions; for example, the need to view each applicant for admission to a university on a holistic basis and to avoid placing too much weight on race in the admissions process. In 2003 Kennedy dissented in *Grutter* because he thought the University of Michigan's reliance on race was too pronounced. However, in 2016, shortly after Scalia's death, Kennedy wrote the majority opinion for the Court upholding the University of Texas's affirmative action program in *Fisher v. University of Texas*. This was because there, as described by the district court, the race of an applicant was treated as "a factor of a factor of a factor."[11]

[11] Fisher v. University of Texas, 645 F. Supp. 2d 587, 608 (W.D. Tex. 2009), *aff'd*, 631 F.3d 213 (5th Cir. 2011), *vacated and remanded*, 570 U.S. 297 (2013), and *aff'd*, 758 F.3d 633 (5th Cir. 2014) and then *aff'd*, 579 U.S. 365 (2016).

Kennedy's insistence on holistic review of each applicant was predicated on the narrow tailoring requirement, but, at a more fundamental level, it is derived from a respect for human dignity.[12] For Kennedy, racial classifications are reductive. They deny the individuality that belongs to each person and thereby constitute an affront to human dignity. Kennedy's special regard for human dignity as a constitutional value has won him the admiration of many, especially when viewed as the source of his rulings protecting gay marriage, striking down a Texas law criminalizing sodomy, and declaring unconstitutional a newly adopted provision of the Colorado constitution that prohibited local authorities from enacting measures that would protect people from being disadvantaged because of their sexual orientation.[13] There is no provision in our Constitution protecting human dignity, although Kennedy may be of the view—first articulated by Brennan and anathema to Scalia—that human dignity is a value foundational to the Constitution and as such permeates every one of its provisions.[14]

Kennedy's otherwise admirable views about what respect for human dignity requires seem especially misguided when applied, under this narrow tailoring component of strict scrutiny, to limit the use of racial classifications in programs such as affirmative action that seek to end the subordination of Blacks. In such cases, these views have been advanced under the guise of making an instrumental or technical judgment, thereby relieving Kennedy of the burden of justifying them in substantive terms or harmonizing them with the Constitution taken as a whole. In the gay rights cases, his demand that state authorities respect human dignity was used to enlarge the constitutional protection for a vulnerable or especially disadvantaged group; as an appendage

[12] In his separate concurrence in *Parents Involved*, Justice Kennedy objects to a transfer program designed to promote school integration on the ground that it reduced applicants to "racial chits." 551 U.S. at 798. The program gave a priority to transfer applicants who would be a minority in the school to which they sought to transfer. *See* Owen Fiss, *supra* note 10; *see also infra* note 36 and accompanying text.

[13] *See* Obergefell v. Hodges, 576 U.S. 644 (2015); United States v. Windsor, 570 U.S. 744 (2013); Lawrence v. Texas, 539 U.S. 558 (2003); Romer v. Evans, 517 U.S. 620 (1996).

[14] For Brennan's idea of human dignity *see, e.g.*, William J. Brennan, Jr., The Constitution of the United States: Contemporary Ratification, Address at Georgetown University (Oct. 12, 1985) *in* 19 U.C. Davis L. Rev. 2, 7 (1985) (describing the U.S. Constitution as a "sublime oration on the dignity of man, a bold commitment by a people to the ideal of libertarian dignity protected through law"); for Scalia's notion *see, e.g.*, Planned Parenthood of Southeastern Pennsylvania v. Casey, 505 U.S. 833 (1992) and Justice Thomas's dissent in Obergefell v. Hodges, 576 U.S. 644 (2015), which Scalia joined.

to the narrow tailoring requirement of strict scrutiny, however, Kennedy's insistence that state authorities respect human dignity became the ground for limiting state programs arguably designed to further the overarching purpose of the Equal Protection Clause. The eradication of caste has as much a claim to dignity as does treating each applicant for admission as an individual; indeed, if the Civil War is to mean anything, it might have an even grander claim to the Constitution.

Perhaps in recognition of the difficulties with deploying the jurisprudence of human dignity in this context, Kennedy contemplated only a modest role for it in limiting the use of racial classifications—avoid them if you can; use them only if you must. This conditional rule against racial classifications fits well into the theoretical structure of the narrow tailoring requirement of strict scrutiny, for that requirement does not absolutely prohibit any particular means but only constrains the choice of means. Admittedly, such a conditional rule creates a cloud over racial classifications, but this cloud is faint, always subject to wind currents, and, much like the cloud generated by the blanket rule governing the triggers of strict scrutiny, it would be of no comfort to Scalia. He wanted a ban on racial classifications that is firm, universal, absolute, as though it were anchored in the words—the plain text—of the Constitution, not the philosophic speculations of some Justice or group of Justices.

C. COMPELLING PUBLIC PURPOSE

There has also been disagreement among the Justices over what counts as a compelling public purpose within the terms of the strict scrutiny test. Scalia and Thomas have taken the most stringent view on this issue. For them, only violence or the imminent threat of violence would be sufficient to justify the use of race as an allocative criterion or the use of a racial classification. They would, for example, allow a prison warden to separate Black and white inmates to quell a prison riot that arose from racial antagonisms.[15] In restricting the application of strict scrutiny in this way, Scalia and Thomas have been guided not by the ordinary understanding of the term "compelling," which connotes "especially worthy" or "very important." Rather, they

---

[15] City of Richmond v. J.A. Croson Co., 488 U.S. 469, 521 (1989) (Scalia, J., concurring in the judgment); Grutter v. Bollinger, 539 U.S. 306, 353 (2003) (Thomas, J., concurring in part).

were guided by a functional perspective, escalating the degree of worthiness required by the end to be served. Starting from the premise that the Equal Protection Clause prohibits all uses of racial classifications, they see strict scrutiny as a heuristic designed to determine whether an exception can be made to that universal rule or, put otherwise, whether a violation of that universal rule can be excused. Of necessity, exceptions to constitutional rules must be stringently confined. "Only a social emergency rising to the level of imminent danger to life and limb" would suffice, as Scalia once put it.[16]

Other than Thomas and Scalia, no other Justice who served during the supervisory phase of the Court's history has taken such a restrictive view of the compelling public purpose requirement. All the other Justices have a more generous understanding of what might qualify as a compelling public purpose and thus necessarily reject the premise upon which Thomas's and Scalia's restricted definition of "compelling" is premised. Some accept the so-called diversity rationale—that affirmative action seeks to secure the educational benefits that come from a diverse student body. Others embrace what has been referred to as the antisubordination rationale—affirmative action seeks to correct the structural inequalities that arose from slavery and were then perpetuated by the caste system.[17] What must be emphasized, however, is that both groups reject Scalia's and Thomas's understanding of the function of strict scrutiny. They do not see strict scrutiny as a test for determining whether an exception should be made to a universal ban or whether a violation to a universal ban should be excused—for them there is no such universal ban. Rather, they see strict scrutiny as a heuristic or rule that might guide them in their effort to give concrete meaning to "the equal protection of the laws" and the requirement that differential treatment be justified.

At an early point in the supervisory period, the Supreme Court held that race-based preferences in favor of Blacks could be required as part of a judicially imposed remedy against a state agency—for example, a state police force—that had been shown to have refused to hire Blacks

[16] *Croson*, 488 U.S. at 521.

[17] *See* Owen Fiss, *Groups and the Equal Protection Clause*, 6 PHIL. & PUBLIC AFF. 107, 155 (1976); Owen Fiss, *Affirmative Action as a Strategy of Justice*, 17 PHIL. & PUB. POL'Y 37 (1997); Symposium, *The Origins and Fate of Antisubordination Theory*, 2 ISSUES LEGAL SCHOLARSHIP 1 (2002).

because of their race.[18] Such a remedy was viewed not as compensation for the wrong that had occurred, since the beneficiaries of the affirmative action were not necessarily the victims of the wrong. Rather, the remedy was justified as a strategy for eliminating or correcting the effects of the wrong that had previously occurred. Past discrimination made the state police force all white; now it had to become racially integrated and race-based preferences were a device to achieve this result.

Race-based preferences to facilitate or increase the admission of Blacks to state universities were instituted in the late 1960s and early 1970s. They were also conceived of as a remedy eradicating the effects of past discrimination, here not necessarily confined to the wrongful action of the particular university—indeed, the concept of past discrimination possibly encompassed the wrongs done to generations of Blacks through slavery and the caste system. The remedy was not judicially imposed. It was instead adopted by the universities themselves, either because they felt complicit in the dynamics that resulted in the subjugation of Blacks or because they believed that every institution should do what it can to eliminate unjust social arrangements present in the community of which it is part. The question before the Court during the 1970s—indeed during the entire supervisory period, even today—is not one of obligation but rather whether this remedial action by the nation's universities is constitutionally permissible.

A wide array of Justices have embraced the antisubordination rationale for affirmative action. In the 1978 *Bakke* decision, when the Court first addressed the legality of such race-based preferences in university admissions, Justices Brennan, Marshall, Blackmun, and White upheld the practice on the theory that it is intended to eliminate the effects of past discrimination. More recently, Justices Ginsburg and Sotomayor advanced this view too. Indeed, much of Sotomayor's dissent in *BAMN*—the eleven pages that especially bothered Roberts—depicts the purpose of affirmative action in such terms. Justice Souter fully acknowledged the need to include subordinated minorities in the political life of the nation. Justice Stevens also came to that view in the course of his tenure on the Court. Traces of the antisubordination rationale can even be found in the opinions of O'Connor and Kennedy, when they considered—but avoided deciding—whether strict scrutiny

---

[18] *See, e.g.*, United States v. Paradise, 480 U.S. 149 (1987).

permits the use of race to draw electoral districts in order to comply with the requirements of the 1982 Amendments to the Voting Rights Act of 1965.[19] In *Grutter* itself, Justice O'Connor, who wrote the majority opinion, also made reference to the needs of democratic legitimacy when considering whether affirmative action satisfied the compelling public purpose component of strict scrutiny. She acknowledged the need of racial minorities for concrete assurances that positions of leadership in the political community were open to all.[20]

For the most part, however, *Grutter* rested on the so-called diversity rationale for affirmative action first articulated by Justice Powell in *Bakke* (and in that case supported by no other member of the Court). In *Grutter*, O'Connor affirmed the view of Powell, who was no longer on the Court, and secured a majority to support her. According to Powell, the compelling public purpose required by strict scrutiny can be found in a desire to obtain "the educational benefits that flow from an ethnically diverse student body."[21] Powell reached this decision because he wanted to avoid the antisubordination rationale: In a prelude to formulating and announcing the diversity rationale, Powell expressed unwillingness to treat a desire to remedy "the effects of 'societal discrimination'"[22] as the compelling public purpose required by strict scrutiny.

In taking this stance, Powell did not deny the pervasiveness of "societal discrimination." Nor did he deny that a desire to eradicate the effects of "societal discrimination"—the subordination of Blacks—was in fact the actual or stated purpose of the affirmative action program, or that such a purpose is especially worthy or important. In fact, eradication of the effects of "societal discrimination" seems far more worthy or compelling than the educational benefits that might be achieved by a diverse student body. This remains true even considering Powell's attempts to make the diversity rationale seem more compelling by anchoring it in the First Amendment and its protection of freedom of speech. No, Powell's unwillingness to treat the desire to end the subordination of Blacks as the compelling public purpose that

---

[19] Shaw v. Reno, 509 U.S. 630, 657 (1993); Miller v. Johnson, 515 U.S. 900, 923 (1995).

[20] *Grutter*, 539 U.S. at 308.

[21] Regents of the University of California v. Bakke, 438 U.S. 265, 306 (1978) (opinion of Powell, J.).

[22] *Id.* at 307.

strict scrutiny demands stemmed from a fear that there was no way of distinguishing the claims of Blacks from those that might be voiced by the multitude of other disadvantaged groups now present in our society. He was unable to appreciate the singularity of the Black experience in America—more than two centuries of slavery defined exclusively in racial terms and then a third governed by a caste system that treated Blacks as pariahs and perpetuated their status as the underclass. Powell said that "remedying the effects of societal discrimination is . . . an amorphous concept of injury that may be ageless in its reach into the past,"[23] as though the Constitution contained a built-in statute of limitations.

As race-based preference in university admissions persisted in civil society the diversity rationale gained social currency, so much so that O'Connor's adoption of it in 2003 might be seen as a codification of a social understanding that evolved from the position Powell took in *Bakke* twenty-five years earlier. In truth, however, the defeat or displacement of an antisubordination rationale may only be nominal. Antisubordination is omnipresent, always lurking in the background, the unstated but actual purpose served by the race-based preference given to Blacks in the admissions processes that govern the leading universities of the nation. Without antisubordination, and a belief in the pernicious nature of caste that it seeks to eradicate, it would be difficult to understand (a) the enormous importance attached to the educational benefits emerging from a diverse student body, especially in the sciences or in medical schools (the subject of *Bakke*); (b) why diversity should be achieved through the application of group criteria rather than individual assessments;[24] and (c) why the preference should be extended to Blacks or other especially disadvantaged groups, such as Latinos, but not to members of religious groups, ethnic groups (e.g. Greek-Americans), or applicants with felony convictions, or applicants who are fascists. Unmoored from antisubordination, and then extended from student admissions to faculty hiring, the diversity rationale might soon compromise or undermine the fundamental academic commitments of the university.[25]

---

[23] *Id.*

[24] *See* Colin S. Diver, *From Equality to Diversity: The Detour from* Brown *to* Grutter, 3 Univ. Ill. L. Rev. 691 (2004).

[25] *See generally* Anthony Kronman, The Assault on American Excellence (2019).

In *BAMN*, the diversity rationale either ensnared Justice Breyer or was used by him as a shield to hide behind. He voted to uphold the Michigan constitutional amendment that banned race-based preferences by publicly supported universities, and began his opinion by saying that if the race-based preferences were instituted as a remedy for "past exclusionary racial discrimination or the direct effects of that discrimination" this would present "different questions which may demand different answers."[26] In saying this, Breyer confused the actual purpose of the admissions policy and the purpose that a majority of Justices were willing to accept when they applied the compelling public purpose component of strict scrutiny.[27]

Breyer also tried in *BAMN* to rewrite O'Connor's *Grutter* opinion. He added the words "only" and "solely," stating that the Court in *Grutter* addressed the Fourteenth Amendment "only as it applies to, and forbids, programs that rest upon one justification: using 'race in the admissions process' solely in order to 'obtai[n] the educational benefits that flow from a diverse student body.'"[28] This made it appear that the desire to obtain the educational benefits that come from a diverse student body was the sole rationale the *Grutter* majority accepted, thereby ignoring the passage in O'Connor's opinion—which Breyer joined—where she explained that a program designed to increase the number of Blacks in the student body might enhance democratic legitimacy.[29] Perhaps more egregiously, he ignored O'Connor's clear declaration "we have never held that the only governmental use of race that can survive strict scrutiny is remedying past discrimination."[30]

Not only does diversity ill-serve affirmative action, by attributing to it a less compelling public purpose than it actually has, it also obscures the relation that exists between affirmative action and the Constitution. Even those who defend affirmative action in terms of diversity part company with Scalia and Thomas, for they deny that they are asking for

---

[26] *BAMN*, 572 U.S. 291, 332 (2014) (Breyer, J., concurring in the judgment).

[27] *See* Kimberly Reyes, *Affirmative Action Shouldn't Be About Diversity*, The Atlantic, Dec. 27, 2018. Reyes notes that Lee Bollinger, President of the University of Michigan when *Grutter* was argued, has made clear the diversity rationale was advanced largely for strategic reasons. Reyes reports Bollinger said: "We needed to win a major legal battle in the context of trying to win the hearts and minds of people about the issue. . . . On the legal side, *Bakke* made it clear that you couldn't use past discrimination as a rationale. I felt that was wrong and still feel that's wrong." *Id.*

[28] 572 U.S. at 333 (Breyer, J., concurring in the judgment).

[29] *Grutter*, 539 U.S. 306, 332 (2003).

[30] *Id.* at 328.

an exemption from a text-based universal ban on the use of race as an allocative criterion. Indeed, they deny the existence of such a ban. Their claim is only that if the purpose of the contested practice is diversity it is consistent with "the equal protection of the laws" and the demand, governed under certain circumstances by the strict scrutiny heuristic, that all differentiations be justified. Yet, the antisubordination rationale casts the relation between affirmative action and the Equal Protection Clause in a whole new light. More than consistency can be claimed. Under antisubordination, affirmative action can be seen as a means of furthering the overarching purpose of the Equal Protection Clause. Not only consistent with that constitutional provision, affirmative action should be allowed and maybe even preferred because it contributes to the progressive realization of that law's very purpose.

II. Disparate Impact and the Political Process Doctrine

Justice Scalia's willingness to disregard settled understandings of the Equal Protection Clause is not confined to the Court's decision to allow affirmative action. It extends to the technical legal question before the Court in *BAMN*. At issue in *BAMN* was not the constitutional permissibility of using race-based preferences in favor of Blacks for university admissions, but rather the permissibility of taking the decision to pursue such a policy out of the hands of the elected trustees of the university, thereby placing that decision in the hands of the state-wide electorate. To permit such a policy in Michigan the state constitution would have to be amended. This change brought into play what is called by lawyers the political process doctrine, which is rooted in a number of precedents, some reaching back to the 1960s. Scalia, with Thomas's concurrence, rejected them all.

Actually, there are two versions of the political process doctrine, each reflecting an understanding of the Equal Protection Clause that prohibits changes that work to the disadvantage of Blacks in the process through which laws are enacted or policies instituted. One version of the doctrine—endorsed in *BAMN* by Sotomayor, Ginsburg, and even Breyer—condemns changes in the political process that make it more difficult to pass laws or initiate policies that "inure primarily to the benefit of the minority."[31] Another version of the doctrine is put forth by Kennedy in his opinion in *BAMN* that Roberts and Alito joined.

[31] This phrase comes from *Washington v. Seattle Sch. Dist. No. 1*, 458 U.S. 457, 472 (1982) and is used by Sotomayor in *BAMN*, 572 U.S. at 351.

It condemns any change in the political process that poses "the serious risk, if not purpose, of causing specific injuries on account of race."[32]

For her version of the political process doctrine, Sotomayor primarily relied on the 1982 decision in *Washington v. Seattle School District No. 1*, in which the Court set aside a state-wide initiative that banned busing that might be adopted to further school integration. Kennedy cast a wider net. He reached back to the 1967 decision in *Reitman v. Mulkey* that invalidated an amendment to the California constitution protecting the right of landowners to sell their property to whomever they wished.[33] That amendment, according to Kennedy, inflicted "specific injuries on account of race" because it precluded the enactment of a fair housing law by state or local legislatures.[34] He also found his version of the political process doctrine endorsed by the Court in the 1969 decision in *Hunter v. Erickson*.[35] That decision struck down an amendment of the city charter of Akron, Ohio, that required that before any ordinance prohibiting racial discrimination in housing could take effect it had to be approved by a city-wide referendum.

For reasons I do not fully understand, Kennedy did not find the requisite racially specific injury in the Michigan constitutional amendment banning affirmative action. Maybe he was driven to this position because of his attachment to the principle, also invoked by Breyer, but qualified by *Reitman*, *Hunter*, and *Seattle*, favoring democratic decision-making. Alternatively, he, like Breyer but not Sotomayor, was ensnared by the fiction that the purpose of affirmative action was only to secure the educational benefits that come from a diverse student body and refused to acknowledge the injury that would be done to Blacks by the abandonment of affirmative action required by the Michigan amendment. In a concurrence in a 2007 case involving elementary and secondary school segregation, Kennedy acknowledged that, in terms of injury to Blacks, there was no difference between de facto and de jure segregation and, in support of that opinion, relied on the 1982 *Seattle* decision, which he then claimed protected busing that was aimed at disestablishing de facto segregation. In *BAMN*, however, he maintained that the busing remedy in the *Seattle* case was aimed at correcting school segregation attributable to assignments based on

[32] *BAMN*, 572 U.S. at 305 (opinion of Kennedy, J.).

[33] 387 U.S. 369 (1967).

[34] *BAMN*, 572 U.S. at 305 (opinion of Kennedy, J.).

[35] 393 U.S. 385 (1969).

race.[36] On this reading, Kennedy's position was dictated not by a preference favoring democratic decision-making but by a narrow conception of the injury caused by the Michigan amendment. Kennedy would have us believe that the only injury caused would be the loss of the educational benefits that come from a diverse student body where, in truth, the injury was more profound and more racially specific—the repudiation of a remedy aimed at the eradication of caste.

Scalia would have none of this. He rejected *Hunter*, *Seattle*, and by implication *Reitman* (or at least Kennedy's interpretation of that decision). He picked over the two versions of the political process doctrine offered by Kennedy and Sotomayor and found within each a multitude of failings. Yet his fundamental objection to the political process doctrine stemmed from his understanding of the Equal Protection Clause. It did not, according to Scalia, proscribe laws that had the inevitable effect of especially disadvantaging Blacks or other racial minorities. At the outset of his opinion in *BAMN* Scalia said the plain text of the Equal Protection Clause prohibited any use of race as an allocative criterion (which is not true). By the end of his opinion he seemed to have whittled down his idea of equal protection so that allocation on the basis of race is the only state practice the Equal Protection Clause prohibits: Absent a racial classification a state law can never be deemed a violation of equal protection. Scalia announced that he had to "part ways" with Kennedy and Sotomayor and the precedents they invoked because "each endorses a version of the proposition that a facially neutral law may deny equal protection solely because it has a disparate racial impact."[37] In this way, Scalia emptied the Equal Protection Clause of any meaning other than to prohibit racial classifications or the use of race as an allocative criterion.

To support this view, Scalia invoked the authority of *Washington v. Davis*, a 1976 decision that antedated *Seattle v. School District No. 1* but followed *Reitman v. Mulkey* and *Hunter v. Erickson*.[38] The fact that the majority opinion in *Washington v. Davis* was written by Justice White

---

[36] *See BAMN*, 572 U.S. at 306 (opinion of Kennedy, J.) ("[T]he legitimacy and constitutionality of the remedy in question (busing for desegregation) was assumed, and *Seattle* must be understood on that basis."). Kennedy adds, "As this Court held in *Parents Involved*, the school board's purported remedial action [in *Seattle*] would not be permissible today absent a showing of *de jure* segregation." *Id.* There was no such showing in 1982, when *Seattle* was decided.

[37] *BAMN*, 572 U.S. at 329–30 (Scalia, J., concurring in the judgment).

[38] Washington v. Davis, 426 U.S. 229 (1976).

should have given Scalia some pause in invoking the authority of that decision to repudiate the political process doctrine and thus overturn *Reitman v. Mulkey* and *Hunter v. Erickson*, because White also wrote the majority opinions in both those cases. In truth, *Washington v. Davis* did not purport to reduce the meaning of the Equal Protection Clause in the way that Scalia maintained. Instead it was, as I see it, primarily intended to downgrade the disparate impact rule first announced in *Griggs v. Duke Power Company* in 1971 from a constitutional to a statutory rule. It should be read as resting on a view about the proper allocation, between the judiciary and the political branches of government, of responsibilities for widespread social and economic changes.

The *Griggs* decision imposed an obligation on employers to use hiring or promotion standards that minimized the adverse disparate impact on Blacks. If the plaintiff demonstrates in a court of law that the hiring or employment standard has a disparate impact on Blacks, the employer would be required to show that the standard is job-related; and even if that showing is in fact made, the plaintiff would still have the opportunity to demonstrate that there are alternative standards or methods of selecting employees that would serve the employer's business interests and at the same time would minimize the disparate impact on Blacks. *Griggs* itself was brought under Title VII of the Civil Rights Act of 1964, which prohibited employment discrimination. Yet the rule emerging from that case—generally referred to as the *Griggs* principle—was soon understood by the profession as governing both statutory and constitutional claims.

Washington v. Davis involved the hiring practices of the Washington, D.C. police. As a result it implicated disparate impact claims under both the Constitution and Title VII (as amended in 1972 to cover public employers). The Court held that there was no merit to the statutory claim. That ruling necessarily implied that there would be no merit to the *Griggs* claim even if it had a constitutional basis, because constitutional and statutory standards were assumed to be identical. However, the Court did not confine itself to this ruling but, in violation of the traditional norms governing the exercise of the judicial power, went on to consider the larger constitutional question—not listed in the questions presented and thus not briefed by the parties—whether the *Griggs* principle, and disparate impact doctrine in general, had a constitutional basis. There was no need for the Court to consider whether *Griggs* governed equal protection claims.

The original 1971 decision of the Supreme Court in *Griggs* was, as a purely formal matter, presented as an interpretation of Title VII of the Civil Rights Act of 1964. There was, however, good reason to believe that the ruling was of constitutional proportions. The statute did no more than proscribe discrimination in allocating employment opportunities that were based on race. To bring disparate impact within the purview of the statute the Court cast it as a form of "indirect discrimination," and to reach that conclusion drew on constitutional understandings. The only precedent the Court cited was the 1969 decision in *Gaston County v. United States*, which the Chief Justice, who wrote for the Court in *Griggs*, described in these terms: "There, because of the inferior education received by Negroes in North Carolina, this Court barred the institution of a literacy test for voter registration on the ground that the test would abridge the right to vote indirectly on account of race."[39]

In 1976, however, the Court was no longer willing to assume responsibility for the dislocation that might be caused by disparate impact liability. The Court decided that responsibility for this legal rule would be placed on Congress, and to accomplish that purpose it had to deny, as it did in *Washington v. Davis*, that disparate impact doctrine—or "indirect discrimination"—had a constitutional basis. In reaching this conclusion, the Court did not make a comprehensive judgment about the meaning of equal protection, or the requirements of racial justice. Rather, the Court appeared to be guided by considerations of the separation of powers. As appears from the passage from the majority opinion quoted in the footnote below, the Court was unwilling to take on the responsibility for the implementation or even persistence of the *Griggs* principle—and was even more reluctant to preside over its extension as a device for protecting the poor.[40]

---

[39] Griggs v. Duke Power Co., 401 U.S. 424, 430 (1971).

[40] The crucial portion of Justice White's opinion is found in this passage:

> A rule that a statute designed to serve neutral ends is nevertheless invalid, absent compelling justification, if in practice it benefits or burdens one race more than another would be far reaching and would raise serious questions about, and perhaps invalidate, a whole range of tax, welfare, public service, regulatory, and licensing statutes that may be more burdensome to the poor and to the average black than to the more affluent white.
>
> Given that rule, such consequences would perhaps be likely to follow. However, in our view, extension of the rule beyond those areas where it is already applicable by reason of statute, such as in the field of public employment, should await legislative prescription.

Washington v. Davis, 426 U.S. 229, 248 (1976).

Given this understanding of *Washington v. Davis* and its endorsement of the *Griggs* principle as a statutory rule, it came as a surprise when, in 2009, Scalia declared in yet another concurrence—once again joined only by Thomas—that there is "a war between disparate impact and equal protection."[41] At this point in time there could be no doubt whatsoever that Congress fully approved and embraced disparate impact liability as it applied to employment decisions. Congress had acquiesced in the initial announcement of the doctrine in 1971 and then again in 1972 when it amended Title VII to cover public employers. In 1976 Congress was told that it was fully in charge, and in the following decades Congress took no action to repudiate or qualify its commitment to the *Griggs* principle. In fact, in 1991 Congress enacted a statute to correct an errant 1989 decision of the Supreme Court that lessened the burden of proof imposed on employers when called upon to demonstrate that a standard or test is job-related.[42] In that measure—the Civil Rights Act of 1991—Congress explicitly indicated its approval of the Court's initial announcement of the doctrine in the *Griggs* case and then went on to codify disparate impact doctrine as it had developed prior to the disapproved Supreme Court decision of 1989.

Scalia's announcement of a war between disparate impact doctrine and equal protection occurred in *Ricci v. DeStefano*, a case involving the use of a written test to govern promotions in the New Haven fire department. Although a number of Blacks had taken the test, eighteen whites, one Hispanic, and no Blacks had qualified for promotion under the test. Frank Ricci was one of the whites; John DeStefano was the Mayor of New Haven. Once the results of the test had become publicly known a controversy erupted in political circles, and eventually the governing board of the city set aside the results of the test. It also began to formulate plans for instituting an alternative test that, presumably, would serve the city's legitimate interest in selecting qualified leaders of the fire department and at the same time minimize racial disparate impact. Ricci then sued the city for violating Title VII, specifically in setting aside the test that had already been administered. In an opinion by Kennedy, a majority ruled in favor of Ricci, but only after concluding that the record before the Court did not adequately support

[41] Ricci v. DeStefano, 557 U.S. 557, 595 (2009) (Scalia, J., concurring).

[42] Wards Cove Packing Co. v. Atonio, 490 U.S. 642 (1989).

the city's claim that it was simply implementing, on its own, the *Griggs* principle. In limiting his ruling in favor of Ricci in this way, Justice Kennedy implied that if there is strong evidence in the record indicating the requirements of the *Griggs* principle are satisfied—as there surely would be if the principle was applied by a court after a full trial—then that principle could be lawfully applied and the results of a test that did not satisfy that principle could be thrown out.

Although Justice Scalia joined the judgment of the Court condemning the action of the city of New Haven, he was provoked by the implication of Kennedy's ruling. Scalia did not say that the *Griggs* principle violated equal protection, but only that there was a war between it and equal protection. This statement was not a description of a state of affairs, but more a performative utterance, much like a congressional declaration of war against another country that makes a change or hopes for a change in the practical world. Such a declaration was in and of itself alarming because it indicated a willingness of Scalia to strike down an interpretation of Title VII of the Civil Rights Act of 1964 that was first established by the Supreme Court in 1971, reaffirmed by the lower federal courts on countless occasions, and then explicitly endorsed by Congress in the Civil Rights Act of 1991.

Not only was such a declaration of war alarming, it also seemed completely without basis and unlikely ever to succeed. Scalia was certainly right in claiming, as he did, that the Equal Protection Clause, made applicable to the federal government by the Due Process Clause of the Fifth Amendment, prohibited Congress from requiring public employers to take action that is itself prohibited by the Equal Protection Clause. However, he never explained why a denial of the equal protection of the laws would result from a rule that acknowledges the right of public employers to use job-related tests but nonetheless insists that they choose, among these job-related tests, the one that minimizes adverse disparate impact on Blacks.

In his concurrence in *BAMN*, Scalia took the view that, by its very terms, the Equal Protection Clause prohibits governments from using race as an allocative criterion or from employing racial classifications, even when a measure seeks to benefit rather than burden Blacks. We have seen that this view about the text of the Equal Protection Clause is mistaken, and furthermore that Scalia's extravagant hostility to racial classifications cannot be rehabilitated even if it is understood as an interpretive gloss on that clause—strict scrutiny yields no such rule. In the present context, however, it is important to emphasize that the

Griggs principle does not require that race be used as an allocative criterion. No plus is given to Blacks. It does not require that individual job applicants be classified according to their race and then be given preference on the basis of that classification. The *Griggs* principle requires employers to be mindful of the impact of their standards and tests on racial groups and to take appropriate steps, consistent with their business interests, to minimize that impact, but it does not call for racial classifications or race-based preferences.

Admittedly, there is risk that public employers might, in order to guard against suits aimed at implementing the *Griggs* principle, informally or surreptitiously, give a preference to Black applicants. It is hard to believe that Scalia would worry about this, at least given his legal approach to the Equal Protection Clause: He repeatedly denied that the effect or consequence of a law might turn it into a violation of equal protection and, in repudiating the political process doctrine in *BAMN*, he reduced that constitutional provision to a ban on racial classifications. It is also important to bear in mind that the risk of employers surreptitiously giving race-based preference to Blacks as a means of insuring against litigation is not in any way confined to the *Griggs* principle. The risk arises from any measure that seeks to protect the employment opportunities of Blacks. It may arise from Title VII's prohibition against direct discrimination as much as it does from the prohibition against indirect discrimination based on the Court's 1971 interpretation of Title VII and the affirmation of that interpretation in the Civil Rights Act of 1991. Can it be that in his *Ricci* concurrence Scalia was declaring war on not just the Civil Rights Act of 1991 but also on the Civil Rights Act of 1964?

At the end of his opinion in *BAMN*, almost as coda, Justice Scalia invoked, as he did on many occasions, the famed remark of Justice John Marshall Harlan in his 1896 dissent in *Plessy v. Ferguson*.[43] Objecting to Jim Crow laws, Harlan wrote "Our Constitution is color-blind."[44] As a basis for repudiating the political process doctrine and the precedents upon which it rested, Scalia turned Harlan's aphorism into a transcendent constitutional mandate, a blanket prohibition against seeing or being aware of race. Disparate impact doctrine most assuredly transgresses this mandate, as does political process doctrine. Both are acutely

---

[43] 163 U.S. 537 (1896).

[44] *Id.* at 559.

aware of the disadvantages that might be imposed on Blacks. They are color conscious. It is difficult to understand, however, why color-blindness, understood as an affliction that prevents some people from seeing what is visible to most others, should be imposed on society as a whole or on the instrumentalities of government, as part of their obligation to provide for the equal protection of the laws. Some may believe that one day the prevailing, maybe overwhelming, differences in the status between whites and Blacks that exist in this country will, or at least should, disappear. However, no one could reasonably think—in 1868, in 1896, in 1954, in 1964, in 1976 or in 2003 or in 2014 or even today—that this change will occur if we simply enact or follow a rule that prevents government agencies from paying attention to, or acknowledging, the differences that exist between whites and Blacks that are, in the end, attributable to slavery and the operation of a caste system that, once slavery was legally abolished, perpetuated the status of Blacks as an underclass.

In his *Ricci* concurrence, Scalia, never able to resist the melodramatic, spoke of the "evil day" when the conflict between equal protection and disparate impact doctrine would have to be resolved.[45] The truth, however, is that if that conflict is rooted in an understanding of equal protection that constitutionalizes Harlan's aphorism and thereby outlaws racial consciousness, the conflict was resolved two years earlier, in the *Parents Involved* decision of 2007. That case involved elementary and secondary school integration, and it led Kennedy to make a sharp distinction between racial classifications and racial consciousness. He first placed Harlan's aphorism in context, "*Plessy*, of course, concerned official classification by race applicable to all persons who sought to use railway carriages."[46] Then he continued, "And, as an aspiration, Justice Harlan's axiom must command our assent. In the real world, it is regrettable to say, it cannot be a universal constitutional principle."[47] In *Parents Involved*, Kennedy supported the judgment of the Court, which set aside a transfer program designed to promote school integration. He issued a separate opinion to distance himself from the opinion Chief Justice Roberts had filed to explain that judgment. (Roberts' opinion was joined by Scalia, Thomas, and Alito.)

[45] 557 U.S. at 594.

[46] *Parents Involved*, 551 U.S. at 788 (Kennedy, J., concurring in part and concurring in the judgment).

[47] *Id.*

In repudiating the norm of colorblindness in this way, Kennedy not only spoke for himself, but, in effect, also for the Justices who dissented (Breyer, Stevens, Souter, and Ginsburg)—in other words, for a majority of the Court.

Throughout his career, Justice Kennedy was wary of racial classifications. He never claimed, as Scalia did in his *BAMN* opinion, that racial classifications were outlawed by the plain text of the Equal Protection Clause. Nor did he use strict scrutiny in such a way as to yield an absolute, universal rule against their use. Still, he viewed racial classifications, regardless of whether the measure that called for them benefitted or burdened Blacks, as a trigger for strict scrutiny. Kennedy also allowed his worry about racial classifications to govern his application of the narrow tailoring requirement. Racial classifications, for him, were an offense to human dignity and for that reason presumptively impermissible under the narrow tailoring requirement. In fact, in *Parents Involved* itself, he set aside modest transfer programs that the Seattle and Louisville school boards had devised to promote racial integration on the ground that they entailed a racial classification and were thus not narrowly tailored.

Under the Seattle/Louisville programs, students were initially assigned to schools on the basis of their residence, and then allowed to transfer if there was space available in a particular school. If there were more applicants than space permitted, choice among the applicants for transfer, after other priorities were satisfied, turned on comparison between the race of the applicant and the race of the students who predominated in the school to which the applicant sought to transfer. Justice Kennedy regarded the purpose of the transfer program (racial integration) as compelling, but he was prepared to invalidate that program because he could imagine other means for achieving integration that did not require racial classifications and that had not yet been shown to be inadequate or ineffective. They first must be tried.

In this context, Kennedy identified and approved of a number of ways that school boards might promote integration at the elementary and secondary school level without classifying individuals on the basis of their race and thus possibly running afoul of the Equal Protection Clause. Kennedy mentioned strategically locating new schools; drawing attendance zones with general recognition of the demographics of neighborhoods; and recruiting students and faculty in a targeted fashion. According to Kennedy, none of these methods of promoting integration involved racial classifications, or what he sometimes called "racial typing"[48]—deciding whether an individual is white or Black and then telling a rejected applicant that he or she is of the wrong race: "Sorry you're not Black," or "Sorry you're not white."[49] He fully acknowledged, however, that these broader, alternative strategies to promote integration, much like the political process and disparate impact doctrines, violate the norm of colorblindness. In pursuing these strategies state officials are fully aware of race in the most general way and then take concrete steps to stop or minimize a practice—school segregation—that especially disadvantages Blacks. Justice Kennedy said that it would be "unlikely any of [these strategies] would demand strict scrutiny to be found permissible" and then concluded: "Executive and legislative branches, which for generations now have considered these types of policies and procedures, should be permitted to employ them with candor and with confidence that a constitutional violation does not occur whenever a decision-maker considers the impact a given approach might have on students of different races."[50]

In reaching this conclusion, Kennedy was, as a purely formal matter, speaking only for himself. Yet the four Justices who dissented in *Parents Involved* also rejected the norm of colorblindness. They too believed that there was no constitutional ban on race consciousness and that there was no conflict between doctrines that took account of differential racial impacts and equal protection. The principal dissent, written by Justice Breyer and joined by Justices Stevens, Souter, and Ginsburg, primarily aimed its fire at Chief Justice Roberts's opinion. In that dissent Breyer also took issue with Kennedy, but only with his assessment of the contested transfer program. Breyer felt Kennedy was making too much out of the rule that allowed school officials, in passing on transfer applications, to consider the race of the applicant and the race of the students that predominated in the school the applicant wished to attend. Because this understanding of the alignments among the Justices is evident from the opinions filed in *Parents Involved*, presumably it was known to Justice Scalia when, in his *Ricci* concurrence filed only two years later, he declared war, in the name of equal protection, on disparate impact doctrine, the *Griggs* principle, the Civil

[48] *Id.* at 798.

[49] *See supra* notes 9–10 and accompanying text.

[50] *Parents Involved*, 551 U.S. at 789.

Rights Act of 1991, and maybe even on the Civil Rights Act of 1964. In *Ricci*, Scalia's opinion was supported by Justice Thomas, but this was a war that Scalia could not, and presumably knew he could not, possibly win.

Parents Involved was decided in 2007. *Ricci* was decided in 2009. Then in 2015, the Supreme Court, following the lead of the Courts of Appeals of all the circuits that had considered the issue, extended disparate impact doctrine from employment under Title VII to housing claims under Title VIII of the Civil Rights Act of 1968. The majority opinion was written by Justice Kennedy who, as he in effect did in *Ricci*, approved the *Griggs* principle. He found the legislative prescription that *Washington v. Davis* required in Title VIII and in the 1988 amendments to that Act.[51] Justice Alito filed a dissent objecting to Kennedy's interpretation of these statutes. Thomas joined that dissent but also filed his own—a broadside roughly organized around the theme "*Griggs* is bad enough."[52] Pointedly, Justice Scalia did not join Thomas's dissent. Without filing an opinion of his own or otherwise making comment of any kind, Scalia, like Roberts, joined Alito's dissent, which, as I said, focused on issues of statutory interpretation. Apparently, Scalia just gave up on the war between equal protection and disparate impact doctrine that he had once tried to launch.

III. A Jurisprudence of Resentment

The Second Reconstruction may have begun in 1954, with the Supreme Court's decision in *Brown v. Board of Education*, but it has extended well into the twenty-first century and even today remains a persistent subject of litigation. In the mid-1970s the Supreme Court changed its position toward that endeavor. It renounced its role as sponsor and catalyst and assumed the role of policeman: Evaluating and supervising the reconstructive measures that had been adopted by others to improve the status of Blacks and to eradicate the caste structure that evolved in the years following the end of the Civil War. Some of these measures have been instituted by state and local governments, others by institutions of civil society like the great universities of this

---

[51] Texas Dep't of Housing and Community Affairs v. Inclusive Communities Project, Inc., 576 U.S. 519 (2015).

[52] *See id.* at 547.

country, and still others by the political branches of the federal government, as manifest in the civil rights statutes that were initially enacted during the 1960s and that have remained on the books and that were, in some instances, refurbished in the 1980s and 1990s.

The record of the Supreme Court during this supervisory phase is mixed. Some reconstructive measures have survived review, though often with freshly minted limits. The Supreme Court has approved the *Griggs* principle as a statutorily based rule requiring employers and housing authorities to adopt policies and regulations that minimize adverse disparate impact on Blacks. The Court has allowed universities to give Blacks a modest, indeterminate plus in the admissions process. It has endorsed a number of strategies—though not all—that local school boards could use, if they chose, to promote racial integration in elementary and secondary education. These are significant but modest achievements.

Remarkably, Justice Scalia adamantly opposed each and every one of the Court's gestures in support of civil rights and the Second Reconstruction. For Justice Scalia, the limits his colleagues imposed on these reconstructive measures were never enough. Scalia wanted an absolute, universal prohibition on the use by state authorities of racial classifications, even when they used such classifications as part of a program to improve the status of the underclass. In voicing his opposition to the *Griggs* principle, Justice Scalia went even further and demanded that government officials be colorblind or give no consideration to the consequences of their actions upon various racial groups, including the racially defined underclass. He denied that the Equal Protection Clause proscribed laws that had the effect of specifically disadvantaging Blacks and perpetuating their subjugation.

In voicing these views, Scalia was invariably joined by Thomas. Aside from that alliance, Scalia appeared as a singular figure in his opposition to prominent programs of the Second Reconstruction, most notably affirmative action and disparate impact liability. He appeared, at least on issues of racial equality, as much at war with his colleagues as with the Second Reconstruction. On some occasions, however, Scalia participated in the formation of the controlling majority.[53] When a majority turned against reconstruction he was

[53] In *Whren v. United States*, 517 U.S. 856 (1996), Scalia wrote the opinion for the Court dismissing a racial profiling claim, and construed the Fourth Amendment in a way that made

part of it. In *BAMN*, for example, Scalia joined Kennedy, Roberts, and Alito, and even Breyer, in upholding the Michigan amendment banning affirmative action by state officials, though he went on to repudiate the political process doctrine in all its forms. For Scalia, there were no federal constitutional limits on the capacity of statewide electorates to negate the practical significance of *Grutter*. The full impact of this position on the Second Reconstruction depended on the number of states that might follow the example of Michigan.

Justice Scalia was also essential in the formation of the majority in *Shelby County v. Holder*, an even more decisive setback to the Second Reconstruction.[54] In that decision, handed down in 2013, only one year before *BAMN*, the Court struck down an important provision of the Voting Rights Act of 1965—long regarded as one of the most significant achievements of the civil rights era. Scalia did not file a separate opinion in *Shelby County*—the majority opinion was written by the Chief Justice. Yet Scalia was one of the five who supported that judgment and one of the five who turned Roberts's opinion into the opinion of the Court. Even more significantly, in the course of oral argument in *Shelby County*, Scalia made a statement about the Act, a short soliloquy, that revealed an odd perspective toward it and by implication the Second Reconstruction in general. It might even explain his slip in *BAMN*.

The Voting Rights Act of 1965 bans all tests and requirements for voting, either in state or federal elections, that have the purpose or effect of preventing Blacks from voting or diminish their capacity to elect candidates of their choice. It also contains a provision (Section 5) that established a procedure that prohibits a limited number of state and local jurisdictions from instituting new voting regulations without first having those regulations approved either by the Attorney General of the United States or by a three-judge federal court sitting in Washington, D.C. These federal officials were to determine whether

---

it difficult for such claims ever to succeed. He turned the probable cause requirement of the Fourth Amendment limiting the issuance of arrest warrants into a wholly sufficient basis for rendering warrantless arrests lawful. He also extended that rule to cover arrests stemming from any infraction of any traffic law, regardless of whether the infraction posed any threat to public safety, and concluded that any search incident to such an arrest would be lawful and thus not subject to the Fourth Amendment's exclusionary rule. Remarkably, this ruling did not provoke any objection from the liberals then on the Court and thus Scalia spoke for a unanimous Court. I am especially grateful to Charlie Crosby, of the 2020 A Community of Equals seminar, for enhancing my understanding of this decision.

[54] Shelby County v. Holder, 570 U.S. 529 (2013).

the proposed change threatened to interfere inappropriately with the exercise of the right to vote as guaranteed by the Act. This unusual procedure—referred to as preclearance—reflected the importance attached to the right to vote in a democratic society and the sad fact that for almost a century following the end of slavery and the adoption of the Fourteenth and Fifteenth Amendments, Blacks had been, as part of the caste system, systematically and grossly prevented from exercising that right. Preclearance was not designed to apply to all states and localities, but only to the worst offenders—those who had been guilty of pervasive, flagrant, and rampant interferences with the right to vote.

Section 4 established the criteria for identifying the state and local jurisdictions covered by the preclearance procedure. Lawyers from the Department of Justice played a key role in drafting the Voting Rights Act, and based on their experience in mounting, in the early 1960s, an extensive, almost monumental litigation program designed to protect the right to vote, they had a pretty good idea of which jurisdictions qualified as the worst offenders—Louisiana, Mississippi, Alabama, Georgia, South Carolina, North Carolina, and Virginia.[55] Then, through a process of reverse engineering, these lawyers developed a formula—the so-called coverage formula—to identify, in general terms, those jurisdictions that would be covered by the preclearance procedure, though provision was also made for the initiation of special proceedings that would enable particular jurisdictions either to come out from or to be added to the preclearance procedure.

The coverage formula is keyed to designated presidential elections and identifies two circumstances in those elections that would lead the state or political jurisdiction to be covered. The first reflects an understanding, derived from the extensive litigation program of the Department of Justice in the early 1960s, of the devices commonly used to disenfranchise Blacks. It requires the covered state or political jurisdiction to have maintained in a designated election a literacy test or similar device (for example, a good character requirement or one that requires the would-be voter to explain particular constitutional provisions) as a prerequisite to voting. The second reflects the intuitive proposition that massive disenfranchisement will diminish voting participation. This prong of the coverage formula requires

---

[55] On the importance of this litigation program, *see* Brian K. Landsberg, Free at Last to Vote: The Alabama Origins of the 1965 Voting Rights Act (2007).

that less than 50 percent of the voting age population in the state or political jurisdiction be registered to vote or have voted in the designated election.

Although the statute requires that both prongs of the coverage formula be satisfied, the consequences of being deemed a covered jurisdiction differ for each prong. The statute itself bans literacy tests or similar devices—referred to as "tests or devices"—in covered jurisdictions.[56] More controversially, however, another section of the statute, specifically Section 5, requires all covered jurisdictions to have any change in their laws or regulations affecting voting approved by the Attorney General or by a federal court sitting in Washington, D.C. before these changes are implemented or given effect. This prong is the heart of the preclearance procedure and the source of its name.

When the Voting Rights Act was first passed in 1965, Section 4 used the election of November 1964 as the benchmark for the coverage formula. When the Voting Rights Act was renewed in 1970, the benchmark was enlarged to include the November 1968 election, and when the Act was renewed in 1975 the benchmark was once again updated to include the November 1972 election. At that point, however, the process of updating the benchmark stopped. In 1982, Congress renewed the coverage formula for a twenty-five year period without changing the election benchmark. The Act was renewed again in 2006 for another twenty-five year period, and again the benchmark was not updated. As a result, when, in 2013, the Act came before the Court, the coverage formula of Section 4 had an archaic, almost obsolete character. Coverage turned on the use of literacy tests and on voting rates in the elections of 1964, 1968, and 1972, and it seemed highly unlikely that that formula would identify the worst offenders at the present time, almost fifty years later. As Judge Stephen Williams, of the D.C. Circuit Court of Appeals, succinctly put it, using the number of judgments against a jurisdiction for violations of Section 2

---

[56] The 1970 amendments to the Voting Rights Act banned the use of literacy tests and similar devices nationwide for a five-year period; the 1975 amendments made this ban permanent. Additionally, the 1975 amendments protected "language minority" groups. To do this, Congress added to the first prong of the coverage formula a new definition of test or device. In any state or political jurisdiction where more than five percent of the citizens of voting age belonged to a single language minority, Congress expanded the meaning of "test or device" to encompass the practice of providing materials related to the electoral process, including ballots, only in the English language. If a state or political jurisdiction satisfying this updated first prong also satisfied the second prong of the coverage formula, it would be covered under Section 4. *See* Act of Aug. 6, 1975, Pub. L. No. 94-73, 89 Stat. 400 (codified at 52 U.S.C. § 10101).

of the Act as the measure, "the five worst uncovered jurisdictions . . . have worse records than eight of the covered jurisdictions."[57] Section 2 prohibits regulations that have the purpose or effect of interfering on the basis of race or color in the exercise of the right to vote or choosing a representative of one's choice.

Roberts viewed the preclearance procedure of the Voting Rights Act through the prism of what he called the Equal Sovereignty principle. He did not try to anchor this principle in the Equal Protection Clause or the Fourteenth and Fifteenth Amendments, or for that matter in any particular clause or provision of the Constitution. It arose instead, much like the principle requiring separation of powers, from the very structure of the Constitution. Roberts spoke of "our historic tradition, that all states enjoy equal sovereignty" and repeatedly referred to Equal Sovereignty as a "fundamental principle."[58] Seen as a constraint on congressional power, Equal Sovereignty did not deny the federal government the power to differentiate among the states and their constituent parts. It only required that this differential treatment be clearly justified, as when the federal government directs hurricane relief only to Louisiana because it and it alone had been struck by a devastating hurricane. Similarly, Equal Sovereignty presumably would allow the worst offenders—those with records indicating pervasive and flagrant violations of the Fifteenth Amendment—to be singled out and made subject to prophylactic procedures such as Section 5 preclearance.

In 1965, the coverage formula set forth in Section 4 may have functioned properly, but, according to Roberts, not in 2013. It no longer functioned to identify the special circumstances that would justify such differential treatment. With this as his premise, Roberts ruled only on Section 4, and to make that abundantly clear added: "We issue no holding on Section 5 itself, only on the coverage formula. Congress may draft another formula based on current conditions."[59] Given the sharp partisan divisions in Congress when *Shelby County* was rendered, there was ample reason to doubt that Congress would be able, as a purely practical matter, to reactivate Section 5 by adopting a new coverage formula, say along the lines of the standard used by Judge Williams.

[57] Shelby County v. Holder, 679 F.3d 848, 897 (D.C. Cir. 2012), *rev'd*, 570 U.S. 529 (2013), *vacated and remanded*, 541 F. App'x 1 (D.C. Cir. 2013) (Williams, J., dissenting).

[58] *Shelby County*, 570 U.S. at 540, 542, 544 (2013) (citing Nw. Austin Mun. Util. Dist. No. 1 v. Holder, 557 U.S. 193, 203 (2009)).

[59] *Id.* at 557.

But that seemed a legal irrelevance for some, or perhaps all, of the majority. They refused to allow such a pragmatic assessment of the politics of the day to become a ground for forgiving or overlooking what appeared to them to be a violation of a fundamental constitutional principle. Apparently, the majority were also unwilling to treat the provision of the Act allowing covered jurisdictions to come out from the preclearance procedure—the so-called bailout provision—as an adequate corrective for the inadequacy of the coverage formula itself. Shelby County did not apply for a bailout and, under the terms of the statute, was clearly not entitled to one. In an earlier case, Roberts complained of the stringent requirements imposed by the statute for obtaining a bailout, though it is doubtful that a relaxation of those requirements would have saved the coverage formula. The *Shelby County* majority may have even regarded the need for a select number of states to apply for a bailout as an offense against Equal Sovereignty.

Justice Thomas joined Roberts's opinion, but wanted to go further. In a separate opinion he indicated that he would have invalidated Section 5. As though he was participating in a Senate hearing, Thomas concluded that, under current conditions, the abuse of voting rights that might justify preclearance could never be established. Scalia did not join Thomas's opinion, but expressed his rage in another way—in the course of the oral argument, a phase of the judicial proceedings in which Scalia typically took great interest and delight. Most of the Justices use this phase of the Court's proceedings, which tend to be relatively short, as an opportunity to clarify an issue in the record, or to resolve a doubt about a party's position. Not Justice Scalia. He seemed especially attracted to the possibility of sparring with the advocates, though given his elevated position—he had the power to decide—badgering might be a more appropriate word to describe Scalia's interaction with the lawyers who stood before him. More generally, Scalia used the oral argument as an opportunity to broadcast his views to the public—not just to occasional visitors to the exalted courtroom, but also to the many reporters who sit in that courtroom and then give an account of the proceedings through various media outlets. Justice Scalia was also aware that what he said would be transcribed and preserved. No unguarded moment here. Scalia tended to treat oral argument as just another platform for advancing his views, much like a faux concurrence, similar to his separate opinions in *BAMN* or *Ricci*, only for a wider audience and expressed in a much more informal and elusive manner.

The success of the Voting Rights Act of 1965 is legendary. Soon after it was sustained by the Supreme Court, in *South Carolina v. Katzenbach*,[60] the registration of Blacks increased by almost one million in ten southern states, and it increased by more than 850,000 just in the jurisdictions covered by the preclearance procedure.[61] The Census Bureau also reported that some 500,000 more Blacks living in southern states voted in the election of 1968 than in the election of 1964.[62] This was an enormous step forward in the progressive realization of the democratic aspiration of the nation and in redeeming the promise of the Fifteenth Amendment. Scalia appeared to be of another mind. At the very end of oral argument, Scalia confronted the Solicitor General, who had defended the Act, with an alternative understanding of the accomplishments of the Act. Scalia saw it as creating a "racial entitlement"—not a legal entitlement, not an egalitarian entitlement, not a democratic entitlement, but a racial entitlement.

Characterizing the Voting Rights Act in this way, Scalia put aside the lofty public purposes of the Act and referred to the Act as though it were nothing more than an exercise in interest group politics. According to this view, the Act gave one particular group a tangible benefit that could not easily be taken away from them, even though there might be good reason to do so. In pursuing this line of analysis, Scalia even managed to mock the larger public purposes—democracy, equality—that are served by this statute: "Even the name is wonderful: the Voting Rights Act. Who is going to vote against that in the future?"[63]

---

[60] South Carolina v. Katzenbach, 383 U.S. 301 (1966).

[61] *See* U.S. COMM'N ON CIVIL RTS., POLITICAL PARTICIPATION; A STUDY OF THE PARTICIPATION OF NEGROES IN THE ELECTORAL AND POLITICAL PROCESSES IN 10 SOUTHERN STATES SINCE PASSAGE OF THE VOTING RIGHTS ACT OF 1965 (1968). The ten southern states described in the Commission's report are Alabama, Arkansas, Florida, Georgia, Louisiana, Missisippi, North Carolina, South Carolina, Tennessee, and Virginia. Of these, Alabama, Georgia, Louisiana, Mississippi, North Carolina, South Carolina, and Virginia were the original preclearance jurisdictions, covered by virtue of the Section 4 formula applied to the 1964 election. By 1967, these seven original preclearance states accounted for 771,426 newly registered Black voters.

[62] *See* CENSUS BUREAU, CHARACTERISTICS OF PERSONS OF VOTING AGE: 1964 TO 1968 tbl.3 (1968); *see also* CENSUS BUREAU, REPORTED VOTING RATES IN PRESIDENTIAL ELECTION YEARS, BY SELECTED CHARACTERISTICS: NOVEMBER 1964 TO 2016 tbl. A-9 (2019).

[63] Here is Scalia's statement from the oral argument:

> I think [the repeated reenactment of the VRA in Congress] is attributable, very likely attributable, to a phenomenon that is called perpetuation of racial entitlement. It's been written about. Whenever a society adopts racial entitlements, it is very difficult to get out of them through the normal political processes. I don't think there is anything to be gained by any Senator to vote against continuation of this act. And I am fairly confident it will be reenacted in perpetuity unless—unless a

Scalia advanced the idea of "racial entitlement" in *Shelby County* for a very specific purpose: To discredit the legislative process and to explain why it would be wrong to rely on it to cure whatever defect the Voting Rights Act might have. As he put it, "Whenever a society adopts racial entitlements, it is very difficult to get out of them through the normal political processes." Scalia did not claim any originality for the idea. As he said, "It's been written about." In fact, he himself had written about it in 1979, in an article criticizing the then-recent *Bakke* decision on affirmative action.[64] At that time, Scalia had not yet become a judge. (President Ronald Reagan appointed him to the D.C. Circuit Court of Appeals in 1982.) He was then a professor at the University of Chicago, and presumably drew on the earlier work of social scientists, particularly under the sway of economics, who introduced the idea of "racial entitlement" and who defined their scholarly mission in a very special way: They seek only to explain human behavior and stand ready to have their explanations judged by the accuracy of the predictions those explanations generate. Social scientists of this stripe do not purport to offer a full description of a social phenomenon. Rather, they try to identify some easily measured feature of a social situation and then turn it into the basis of a certain number of predictions. They aspire to a certain reductionism and treat this easily measurable feature as if it were all that mattered.

Judges are not, to emphasize the obvious, social scientists. Although judges need to base their decisions on accurate information, there is no virtue to the reductionism prized by economics-oriented social scientists nor to basing their decisions on some easily measurable feature of a social situation. Their job is not to generate

---

> court can say it does not comport with the Constitution. You have to show, when you are treating different States differently, that there's a good reason for it. That's the—that's the concern that those of us who—who have some questions about this statute have. It's a concern that this is not the kind of a question you can leave to Congress. There are certain districts in the House that are black districts "by law" just about now. And even the Virginia Senators, they have no interest in voting against this. The state government is not their government, and they are going to lose . . . votes if they do not reenact the Voting Rights Act. Even the name of it is wonderful: The Voting Rights Act. Who is going to vote against that in the future?

Transcript of Oral Argument at 51:48–53:12, *Shelby County*, 570 U.S. 529. I am especially grateful to Andrea de Sa, of the 2020 A Community of Equals seminar, for initially bringing this exchange to my attention.

[64] Antonin Scalia, *The Disease as Cure: "In Order to Get Beyond Racism, We Must First Take Account of Race,"* 1979 WASH. UNIV. L. Q. 147.

testable predictions, but to do what is just, and to discharge that responsibility judges must fully understand all the social dynamics and public purposes that might account for the passage or implementation of a statute. For that reason, I would say that Scalia's use of the idea of "racial entitlements" is a misappropriation. For judges, reductionism is never a virtue, though a measure of realism may sometimes be appropriate.

Every time a court is called upon to judge the constitutionality of a legislative act, it must confront what Alexander Bickel once called "the counter-majoritarian difficulty"—the chance that unelected officials will set aside the work of an institution that is elected by a majority of citizens.[65] Democracy is not reducible to majoritarianism, but the countermajoritarian quality of judicial review is a reason for a court to be hesitant and restrained. The Supreme Court acknowledged this precept when, in the late 1930s, it reversed its stand on the New Deal, and became more accepting of legislation aimed at economic recovery. In that spirit, Justice Harlan Stone, soon to become the Chief Justice, announced in the *Carolene Products* case of 1938 that economic regulations are entitled to a "presumption of constitutionality."[66]

Stone was, however, careful to limit the scope of this presumption and in doing so, introduced an element of realism. In a footnote—Footnote 4—Stone indicated that there might be a reason to have a more skeptical attitude toward legislation that adversely affected what he called "a discrete and insular minority."[67] The risk was high that the interests of such a group would not be adequately or fairly represented in the legislative process. In carving out this exception to the presumption of constitutionality, Justice Stone, perhaps with an eye to the future, might have anticipated the civil rights decisions of the 1940s and *Brown v. Board of Education* itself as well as its progeny. Indeed, decisions like *Reitman*, *Hunter*, and *Seattle* that undergird the political process doctrine might well be predicated on Footnote 4 and the realism about the political process that it introduced.

Certainly Justice Sotomayor thought so, and she relied upon Footnote 4 of *Carolene Products* in her dissent in *BAMN*. Scalia saw Footnote 4 differently. In his *BAMN* opinion, he wrote, with a measure of disdain: "The dissent trots out the old saw, derived from

---

[65] *See* Alexander Bickel, The Least Dangerous Branch 16 (1962).

[66] United States v. Carolene Products Co., 304 U.S. 144, 148 (1938).

[67] *Id.* at 153.

dictum in a footnote, that legislation motivated by 'prejudice against discrete and insular minorities' merits 'more exacting judicial scrutiny.'"[68] True, the political power of Blacks has changed since 1938. By the time *BAMN* was decided, Blacks might have be able to build coalitions with other interest groups and thus could no longer be properly regarded as "insular" in the way that Stone imagined. But no account was taken by Scalia of the very real impediments that Blacks then faced and continue to face in those political processes, especially referendums, governed by a state-wide majority vote. These impediments arise from the fact that Blacks are a numerical minority and lack the wealth or economic power of those whose interests might be deemed threatened by affirmative action.

In *BAMN*, Scalia took no account of these factors limiting the political power of the Black community before he dismissed Footnote 4 as "dictum" and "old saw." He went even further in *Shelby County* when he invoked the theory of "racial entitlement" to discredit the "normal political process." Far from seeing Blacks as victims of majoritarianism, Scalia there suggested that, thanks to the Voting Rights Act, Blacks have an inappropriate measure of power in that process. Realism might be, in Scalia's eyes, a virtue, but the selective realism he displayed in *BAMN* and the year before in *Shelby County* is of another character altogether. Selective realism distorts the truth and rests on an unspoken premise that guides the selection. It also conveys a certain contempt for the public purposes and accomplishments of the Voting Rights Act.

Scalia's contempt was not confined to the provisions of the Act protecting the right to vote, specifically the provisions striking down registration requirements and tests that had long prevented Blacks from participating in the electoral process in any way. He also managed to belittle the 1982 Amendments of the Voting Rights Act that sought to protect Black communities from pernicious electoral districting practices that denied those communities the right to choose representatives of their choice. One such practice splintered those communities among a number of electoral districts (what civil rights lawyers called "cracking"); another diluted the power of these communities by switching from single to multimember districts, in which a majority of voters in the larger, and predominantly white, districts

[68] *BAMN*, 572 U.S. at 325.

would be entitled to elect all the members of a representative council. The 1982 Amendments were intended to correct a 1980 Supreme Court interpretation of the 1965 Act and, in much the same fashion as the Civil Rights Act of 1991, they did so by restoring and codifying a decision of the Court that was rendered in the early 1970s. In 1986, shortly before Scalia was appointed to the Court, the Supreme Court upheld the 1982 Amendments of the Voting Rights Act and established rules to guide their application and prevent abuses.[69]

In his *Shelby County* broadside, Scalia contemptuously dismissed—though not by name—all these legislative and judicial efforts to create a "hedge"[70] against the racial polarization and antagonisms that had for so long infected American electoral politics and that, for the most part, had worked to the disadvantage of Black communities. He expressed the view that a decision about the continuation or even correction of the Voting Rights Act "is not the kind of a question you can leave to Congress" because, so he reported, "There are certain districts in the House that are black districts 'by law' just about now."[71]

Scalia saw no justice in the Voting Rights Act. It was all a matter of interest group politics. One group's electoral power was increased, and that had the inevitable effect of diminishing the power of other groups, some of which may also be defined by ascriptive criteria. Such an understanding of the Voting Rights Act is likely to generate resentment: Not the petty resentment that might belong to a member of a group whose electoral power has not been increased and in fact has only been diminished, nor the resentment of those who claim they are being treated unfairly, but rather the resentment that might belong to a professional dedicated to justice and the Constitution. It is the resentment of betrayal. Those who proposed and enacted the Voting Rights Act may have proclaimed that they were furthering justice and making the Constitution a living truth. Yet if, as Scalia saw it, all is interest group politics—one group competing for power against others—the claims of justice and fidelity to the Constitution appear as a sham. The insistence by the sponsors of the measure that it is something more—that it is required by justice—would be pretense. Even more, it would be a betrayal of their sacred duty to the Constitution, and would be likely to

[69] Thornburg v. Gingles, 478 U.S. 30 (1986).

[70] *Id.* at 83 (White, J., concurring).

[71] Transcript of Oral Argument at 52:36–52:51, *Shelby County*, 570 U.S. 529.

generate that sense of resentment that animates and is implicitly conveyed by Scalia's *Shelby County* intervention.

The Voting Rights Act has, as I said before, long been seen as one of the most important and compelling provisions of the Second Reconstruction. It sought to bring to an end the massive disenfranchisement of Blacks and the corruption of the electoral process that arose after the collapse of the First Reconstruction in the 1870s and that soon became an integral part of the dynamics that gave rise to and perpetuated the caste system. If Scalia saw no justice in the Voting Rights Act, and passed it off as nothing more than an instrument of interest group politics, he was unlikely to see any justice in more modest reconstructive measures—for example, the *Griggs* principle—that were instituted in the late 1960s and early 1970s. We know from his 1979 article that he saw affirmative action in university admissions in similar terms—nothing more than an attempt to increase the share of scarce opportunities enjoyed by Blacks. The effort to defend affirmative action and the *Griggs* principle in more lofty terms especially offended him and generated the same sense of resentment that governed his response to the Voting Rights Act. The problem was not one measure or another but the Second Reconstruction itself.

It was this perspective on the Second Reconstruction that led, in my opinion, to Scalia's bizarre declaration of war against the *Griggs* principle and the statute which confirmed it, specifically the Civil Rights Act of 1991, and perhaps even the statute that first gave rise to it, the Civil Rights Act of 1964. To close the gaps between Blacks and whites in terms of unemployment rates and income, the *Griggs* principle required employers to use standards that minimized disparate adverse impact on Blacks. Justice Scalia, viewing this development through the prism of "racial entitlement," might have regarded this principle and the civil rights acts as nothing more than devices to increase the number of jobs and promotions allocated to an interest group. Scalia issued his declaration of war against the *Griggs* principle and disparate impact doctrine in his separate opinion in *Ricci v. DeStefano* in 2009, even after a majority had, two years earlier in *Parents Involved*, rejected the premises upon which it rested. He silently abandoned this campaign in 2015, when a majority of the Court once again affirmed the principle as a requirement of justice and extended it from employment to housing. Speaking for the majority in that case, Justice Kennedy saw disparate impact doctrine as playing an important role in removing obstacles to housing that otherwise might be available to Blacks and thus avoiding "the grim prophecy" of the Kerner Commission.[72] This Commission, appointed by President Johnson immediately following the riots in Detroit in July 1967, had warned when it issued its report in February 1968: "Our Nation is moving toward two societies, one black, one white—separate and unequal."[73] Scalia dissented without a quip.

The same sense of resentment that was generated by the Voting Rights Act and the *Griggs* principle might also account for much of Justice Scalia's hostility to affirmative action and his opinion in *BAMN* in particular. He had long refused to allow, on any terms, race-based preferences for Blacks in university admissions—as a technique to secure the educational benefits that come from a diverse student body or as a strategy of justice designed to eradicate caste. He announced his campaign against affirmative action and *Bakke* in his 1979 law review article and continued that campaign on the bench. Eventually he lost the battle in the 2003 *Grutter* decision, and as a result, in the early decades of the twenty-first century affirmative action survived and came to be seen as a prominent feature of the Second Reconstruction—its own poster child. The very first line of Scalia's *BAMN* opinion captures his sense of exasperation with the Second Reconstruction: "It has come to this." Scalia well understood that the Michigan constitutional amendment at issue in *BAMN* created a new way of limiting, as a practical matter, the effects of *Grutter*, and he thoroughly embraced this strategy. Indeed, to prevent this oppositional strategy from ever being denied by judges who might try to protect Blacks from the vicissitudes of state-wide referenda or initiatives, typically effectuated by secret ballots and controlled by predominantly white majorities, Scalia turned *BAMN* into a platform to repudiate all forms of the political process doctrine.

Scalia was relentless in his opposition to the Second Reconstruction. He opposed affirmative action, the *Griggs* principle, the political process doctrine, measures to enlarge the distribution of the franchise, the additional protection provided the right to vote by preclearance, and even those regulations designed to give Black communities the opportunity to elect representatives of their choice. It mattered not whether the particular measure was instituted by universities, the federal judiciary, state and local governments, the Executive Branch, or

[72] *Inclusive Communities*, 576 U.S. at 546.

[73] Nat'l Advisory Comm'n on Civ. Disorders, Report of the National Advisory Commission 1 (1968).

even the Congress of the United States. He saw no justice in any of it, only the power of an interest group—and he resented those who claimed otherwise.

Sometimes Scalia based his opposition on precedents, most notably on an extravagant reading of *Washington v. Davis*, though his general willingness to repudiate precedents and to dismiss the work and views of those Justices with whom he disagreed was almost breathtaking. For the most part, however, Scalia claimed the authority of the Constitution pure.[74] On one occasion, joining the *Shelby County* majority, he relied on the free-floating Equal Sovereignty principle. In most instances he based his opposition to the Second Reconstruction on the Equal Protection Clause.

To turn the Equal Protection Clause into a ground for opposing reconstruction Scalia needed to deny its overarching purpose—to protect the newly gained freedom of Blacks. Divorced from its historical moorings, the Justice read the Equal Protection Clause to forbid in total, and to only forbid, racial consciousness and racial classifications, whatever purpose these practices may serve or whatever effect they may have. The words of the Equal Protection Clause do not easily or naturally accommodate such a pristine and absolute rule, so on occasion, as we saw in *BAMN*, Scalia made them up, I have to assume, unthinkingly. Freud once promised that if we paid attention to slips and probed the underlying dynamics that produced them, we would discover a larger truth. I doubt he ever imagined that the truth revealed would consist of a jurisprudence of sorts.

---

[74] *See* Planned Parenthood of Southeastern Pennsylvania v. Casey, 505 U.S. 833, 984, 1000 (1992).

SHYAMKRISHNA BALGANESH

THE INSTITUTIONALIST TURN IN COPYRIGHT

It was a few minutes after 10 a.m. on October 9, 2002, a brisk Wednesday morning in Washington, D.C. Some of the crowd that had begun lining up outside the Court before daybreak to hear oral argument had successfully obtained seats in the visitor's gallery, where they now waited with great anticipation for the Court to call its first case.[1] In short order, Chief Justice Rehnquist announced that the Court was ready to hear arguments in the case of *Eldred v. Ashcroft*,[2] and Professor Lawrence Lessig began presenting the case for the petitioner, arguing that the Sonny Bono Copyright Term Extension Act (CTEA) was an unconstitutional exercise of Congress's lawmaking power.[3]

Shyamkrishna Balganesh is Sol Goldman Professor of Law, Columbia Law School.

Author's note: Many thanks to Justin Driver, Jane Ginsburg, Peter Menell, Tom Merrill, David Pozen, Matt Sag, Pam Samuelson, Tom Schmidt, Peter Strauss, and participants at the 2021 Intellectual Property Scholars Conference (IPSC) for helpful comments and suggestions. Thanks are also due to Gillian Wei for her excellent research assistance.

[1] *See* Linda Greenhouse, *Supreme Court Hears Copyright Challenge*, N.Y. Times (Oct. 9, 2002), https://www.nytimes.com/2002/10/09/business/media/supreme-court-hears-copyright-challenge.html.

[2] Transcript of Oral Argument at *4, Eldred v. Ashcroft, 537 U.S. 186 (2002) (No. 01-618), 2002 WL 31309203.

[3] Opening Brief of Petitioners at 47, *Eldred*, 537 U.S. 186 (No. 01-618).

The Supreme Court Review, 2022.
 https://doi.org/10.1086/719042

Lessig had meticulously prepared for the argument and believed himself to have developed an effective strategy that would appeal to the Court's most conservative Justices, who were generally wary of any attempted Congressional overreach.[4] Barely a few minutes into the argument, as Lessig was responding to a question from another Justice about the uniqueness of his constitutional challenge to a piece of copyright legislation, Chief Justice Rehnquist interrupted Lessig with a question about the absence of prior constitutional challenges to copyright legislation, which he delivered with his unmistakable tone of skepticism: "Well, doesn't that itself mean something, Mr. Lessig? The fact that they were never challenged, perhaps most people, and perhaps everybody felt there was no basis for challenging them."[5]

Lessig, who had fully anticipated the question, launched into his detailed response, observing how his case was fundamentally different and noting that it was "not the case that the earlier extensions were not questioned on constitutional grounds," but that a prominent copyright scholar (Melville Nimmer) had in fact considered the question and reached a similar conclusion.[6] Before he could finish, the Chief cut him off derisively, "Well, I'm talking about court challenges, not academic challenges,"[7] forcing Lessig to concede the novelty of his position: "That's right, there is no [prior] court challenge."[8] He was asking the Court to circumscribe Congress's legislative authority to enact copyright legislation, and for the first time ever since the enactment of the first federal copyright statute in 1790.[9]

Lessig went on to lose the case, with the Court deciding on a 7-2 vote that the CTEA embodied a rational exercise by Congress of its

---

[4] Lawrence Lessig, *How I Lost the Big One*, Legal Affairs, Mar.-Apr. 2004, at 57, 58; Lawrence Lessig, Remix: Making Art and Commerce Thrive in the Hybrid Economy 89 (2008).

[5] Transcript of Oral Argument, *supra* note 2, at *5.

[6] *Id.*

[7] *Id.* at *6.

[8] *Id.*

[9] To be sure, as early as 1879 the Supreme Court had held that the Intellectual Property Clause of the Constitution (Art. I, § 8, cl. 8) did not extend to trademark legislation since a trademark was not an invention, discovery, or writing within the meaning of that clause. *Trademark Cases*, 100 U.S. 82 (1879). In so doing, the Court was implicitly placing a limit on what Congress could do under the terms of the Intellectual Property Clause. Yet, its holding was that the legislation at issue was not patent or copyright legislation, while in *Eldred* the argument was that the statute was not constitutionally valid under the substantive limits of the Clause even if a species of copyright legislation. The difference is hardly subtle and should not be overlooked.

legislative powers.[10] *Eldred v. Ashcroft* has since become part of the copyright canon, where it is understood as having broken new ground by concluding that neither the Intellectual Property Clause nor the First Amendment imposed independent limitations on copyright legislation that did not alter the "traditional contours" of copyright.[11] Embedded within the logic of Justice Ginsburg's majority opinion in *Eldred* was, however, an observation that had direct echoes of the early exchange between Lessig and Rehnquist, when she observed that since the CTEA was a "rational enactment" the Court was therefore simply "not at liberty to second-guess congressional determinations and policy judgement[s] of this order, however debatable or arguably unwise they may be."[12] The Court did not relish an institutional tussle with Congress over copyright policy.

In the years since, *Eldred* has come to be seen by copyright scholars as something of a one-off decision: as a decision that set up a clash between a reading of the Constitution and copyright policy, which the Court refused to recognize and countenance. Yet, in its reasoning—captured vividly by Justice Ginsburg's quote—the Court foreshadowed an approach to its engagement with copyright law that would become obvious a few years later. Ignored in oversimplified accounts of *Eldred* is the reality that the decision planted the seeds for a general approach to copyright law, which I describe herein as the "institutionalist turn" in the Court's copyright jurisprudence.

The institutionalist turn refers to the reality that over the last decade and a half, the Court's copyright jurisprudence has come to focus less and less on directly resolving substantive issues within the landscape of copyright doctrine. It has instead become a principal site of debate and disagreement over issues that have a direct bearing on the role, competence, and legitimacy of the Court within the copyright system. The institutionalist turn does not imply that the Court's decisions have altogether avoided engaging substantive copyright issues; merely that its engagement of copyright doctrine has come to be intertwined with—and often overshadowed by—strong institutional considerations. These considerations can be seen to cluster around three analytically interrelated themes: (i) the Court's role as faithful

---

[10] Eldred v. Ashcroft, 537 U.S. 186, 187 (2002).

[11] *Id.* at 191.

[12] *Id.* at 208.

agent interpreting Congress's directives as contained in the complex Copyright Act of 1976, (ii) the nature of legislative-judicial interaction and deference in the domain of copyright lawmaking, and (iii) the continuity—or lack thereof—between copyright's adjudicative mechanisms and other legal areas.

U.S. copyright law has always been statutory in origin, with the Constitution expressly investing Congress with the power to make copyright laws.[13] While the Act of 1976 certainly altered the level of detail and complexity of the statute, interpreting its provisions proved relatively straightforward and uncontroversial in the Court's early jurisprudence under the Act.[14] The legislative origins of copyright presented the Court with no particular concerns in its adjudicatory role. This remained true even in the Rehnquist Court, where copyright opinions did not hesitate to directly engage questions of policy, despite the recognition that Congress remained the primary arbiter of such policy.[15] Not only was the Court comfortable wading into substantive copyright policy, but an overwhelming majority of copyright opinions were also decided unanimously during this period.[16] A few years into the Roberts Court this began to change, despite the text of the statute remaining unaltered. Applying the statute's various substantive provisions began generating serious disagreement among the Justices. While initially entangled with questions of copyright policy,[17] it soon became apparent that the disagreement originated in competing visions of the Court's institutional role within the copyright

---

[13] U.S. Const. art. I, § 8, cl. 8. For the statutory origins of copyright law, see Copyright Act of 1790, Pub. L. No. 1-15, 1 Stat. 124; Joseph Liu, *Regulatory Copyright*, 83 N.C. L. Rev. 87, 88 (2004); Jennifer Rothman, *Liberating Copyright: Thinking Beyond Free Speech*, 96 Cornell L. Rev. 463, 475 (2010).

[14] *See, e.g.*, Community for Creative Non-Violence v. Reid (*CCNV*), 490 U.S. 730 (1989); Harper & Row, Publishers, Inc. v. Nation Enters., 471 U.S. 539, 541–42 (1985).

[15] *See, e.g.*, Fogerty v. Fantasy, Inc., 510 U.S. 517, 526 (1994) ("[T]he policies served by the Copyright Act are more complex, more measured, than simply maximizing the number of meritorious suits for copyright infringement.").

[16] *See CCNV*, 490 U.S. at 732; Feist Publ'ns, Inc. v. Rural Telephone Serv. Co., 499 U.S. 340, 342 (1991); *Fogerty*, 510 U.S. at 519; Campbell v. Acuff-Rose Music, Inc., 510 U.S. 569, 599 (1994); Quality King Distributors Inc. v. L'anza Rsch. Int'l Inc., 523 U.S. 135, 138 (1998); Feltner v. Columbia Pictures Television, Inc., 523 U.S. 340, 342 (1998); MGM Studios, Inc. v. Grokster, Ltd., 545 U.S. 913, 918 (2005).

[17] *See, e.g.*, Kirtsaeng v. John Wiley & Sons, Inc. (*Kirtsaeng I*), 568 U.S. 519, 536 (2013) (weighing the policy concerns of granting the "holder of an American copyright . . . permanent control over the American distribution chain . . . in respect to copies printed abroad but not in respect to copies printed in America").

system, something that had rarely ever been directly addressed during the tenure of Chief Justice Rehnquist, with the exception of *Eldred.*

Much of this disagreement occurred around questions of statutory interpretation, where the issue of whether and how to give effect to Congress's intention on copyright questions soon became the principal frame for most questions of substantive copyright law. Some members of the Court took the position that owing to the comprehensive statutory nature of the field, the interpretive task was to be limited to the plain meaning of the statute, eschewing any direct engagement with considerations of copyright policy out of deference to Congress.[18] Other members disagreed, instead adopting the position that the Court was obligated to interpret the statute by discerning Congress's intention—actual or imputed—from a variety of sources.[19] All the same, the Justices agreed on one core idea: on substantive copyright questions, the answer "depend[ed] solely on statutory interpretation,"[20] which emerged as the principal frame for their decisions.

The Court's debates over statutory interpretation in copyright law, however, concealed a more foundational disagreement among the Justices of the Roberts Court. Copyright statutes prior to the Act of 1976 were sparse in detail and thus left it to courts to develop much (if not most) of copyright law incrementally, through the common law's accretive process. The Act of 1976 altered this, and codified (sometimes with alteration) much of the prior judge-made law.[21] It thus consciously replaced the symbiotic approach to copyright lawmaking with one that emphasized the primacy of the legislature, leaving it to courts to reinvent their place in this changed landscape.[22] Despite this change in the statute, neither the Burger nor Rehnquist Courts found it to require any real alteration in their approach to copyright questions. Not so in the Roberts Court, where debates over statutory interpretation were often proxies for disagreements over the appropriate

---

[18] *See* Star Athletica, LLC v. Varsity Brands, Inc., 137 S. Ct. 1002, 1006 (2017).

[19] *See Star Athletica*, 137 S. Ct. at 1034–35 (Breyer, J., dissenting); *Kirtsaeng I*, 568 U.S. at 557 (Ginsburg, J., dissenting).

[20] Mazer v. Stein, 347 U.S. 201, 214 (1954).

[21] *See* Peter S. Menell, *The Mixed Heritage of Federal Intellectual Property Law and Ramifications for Statutory Interpretation*, *in* Intellectual Property and the Common Law 63, 64 (Shyamkrishna Balganesh ed., 2013); Shyamkrishna Balganesh, *Copyright as Legal Process: The Transformation of American Copyright Law*, 168 U. Pa. L. Rev. 1101, 1103 (2020); Barbara Ringer, *First Thoughts on the Copyright Act of 1976*, 22 N.Y. L. Sch. L. Rev. 477, 477 (1977); Zechariah Chafee, Jr. *Reflections on the Law of Copyright: I*, 45 Colum. L. Rev. 503, 504–509 (1945).

[22] Pierre N. Leval, *An Assembly of Idiots?*, 34 Conn. L. Rev. 1049 (2001).

role of the Court (and the judiciary more generally) in copyright law. Dissenting opinions (and occasionally concurrences) routinely criticized the Court's opinions as interfering with Congress's prerogative to set federal copyright policy; and the Court's direct engagement with questions of copyright policy soon became taboo. The judicial role thus became a latent—and on occasion, obvious—point of disagreement in copyright opinions on the Roberts Court.

Lastly, the Court's turn toward questions of statutory interpretation and the appropriate judicial role in copyright cases was augmented by its embrace of a form of anti-exceptionalism about copyright's adjudicatory rules. In dealing with the procedural and remedial parts of copyright law—both statutory and non-statutory—the Court came to adopt an altogether different approach from the one seen in its engagement with substantive copyright doctrine.[23] Here, the Court's concern was instead in establishing the seamlessness between copyright adjudication and other forms of federal adjudication. At first blush, this may appear to run contrary to the institutional turn by evincing a degree of judicial immodesty. In reality, however, it served the institutional turn rather perfectly by relegating to the Court a domain of law that it was universally seen as best positioned to administer: the judicial process. Given that the institutionalist turn was at base about the competence and legitimacy of the Court within the copyright system, these exact same concerns were bolstered by the Court's engagement with the procedural and remedial elements of the copyright system since the Court was able to draw parallels and connections between copyright and other forms of federal adjudication.

The institutionalist turn described herein began to take shape toward the end of Chief Justice Rehnquist's time on the Court and fully crystallized several years into Chief Justice Roberts's tenure. While Roberts was formally seated as Chief Justice in 2005, it was not until several years later that the Roberts Court began its foray into copyright jurisprudence, triggering the new institutional dynamic.[24] Since that time, roughly a decade ago now, the Court has

---

[23] *See* Reed Elsevier Inc. v. Muchnick, 559 U.S. 154, 157 (2010); Petrella v. MGM, Inc., 572 U.S. 663, 667 (2014); Allen v. Cooper, 140 S. Ct. 994, 996 (2020); Fourth Estate Pub. Benefit Corp. v. Wall-Street.com, LLC, 139 S. Ct. 881, 884 (2019); Rimini Street Inc. v. Oracle USA, Inc., 139 S. Ct. 873, 874 (2019); Kirtsaeng v. John Wiley & Sons, Inc. (*Kirtsaeng II*), 136 S. Ct. 1979, 1981 (2016).

[24] *See Reed Elsevier*, 559 U.S. at 157.

decided twelve copyright cases.[25] By contrast, the Rehnquist Court decided a sum total of ten copyright cases in twice that amount of time.[26] What is additionally intriguing about the Roberts Court's copyright jurisprudence is its very selection of copyright cases and issues to address. Of the copyright decisions handed down by the Roberts Court half (six out of twelve) have been procedural and remedial,[27] i.e., adjectival. In twice as much time, the Rehnquist Court handed down only two such decisions.[28]

In what follows, I describe the origins and entrenchment of the Court's institutionalist turn in its copyright jurisprudence and show how its copyright decisions reflect a heightened concern with the Court's institutional role and legitimacy. While the turn may have resulted in substantive copyright law doctrine coming to be sidelined in the Court's jurisprudence, it nevertheless entrenched a strong prudentialist impulse in the judicial engagement of the copyright system, one that directs attention away from the polarizing justificatory debates that have long surrounded substantive copyright law—often described as the "copyright wars."[29] Yet in so doing, it also indirectly complicated copyright's own legitimacy crisis by injecting into it a new set of methodological disagreements involving statutory interpretation and the role of the judiciary in the copyright system.

In describing the institutionalist turn in the Court's engagement with copyright law, I am not suggesting that the phenomenon is unique to copyright law, or particularly trenchant therein. Indeed, the elements of the institutionalism seen in copyright are themselves

---

[25] *See id.*; Golan v. Holder, 565 U.S. 302 (2012); *Kirtsaeng I*, 568 U.S. 519; *Petrella*, 572 U.S. 663; Am. Broadcast Cos. v. Aereo, Inc., 573 U.S. 431 (2014); *Kirtsaeng II*, 136 S. Ct. 1979; Star Athletica, LLC v. Varsity Brands, Inc., 137 S. Ct. 1002 (2017); *Fourth Estate*, 139 S. Ct. 881; *Rimini Street*, 139 S. Ct. 873; *Allen*, 140 S. Ct. 994; Georgia v. Public.Resource.Org, Inc., 140 S. Ct. 1498 (2020); Google LLC v. Oracle Am., Inc., 141 S. Ct. 1183 (2021).

[26] *See* Community for Creative Non-Violence v. Reid, 490 U.S. 730 (1989); Stewart v. Abend, 495 U.S. 207 (1990); Feist Publ'ns, Inc. v. Rural Telephone Serv. Co., 499 U.S. 340 (1991); Fogerty v. Fantasy, Inc., 510 U.S. 517 (1994); Campbell v. Acuff-Rose Music, Inc., 510 U.S. 569 (1994); Quality King Distributors Inc., v. L'anza Rsch. Int'l Inc., 523 U.S. 135 (1998); Feltner v. Columbia Pictures Television, Inc., 523 U.S. 340 (1998); New York Times Co. v. Tasini, 533 U.S. 483 (2001); Eldred v. Ashcroft, 537 U.S. 186 (2003); MGM Studios, Inc. v. Grokster, Ltd., 545 U.S. 913 (2005).

[27] *See generally Reed Elsevier*, 559 U.S. 154; *Petrella*, 572 U.S. 663; *Allen*, 140 S. Ct. 994; *Fourth Estate*, 139 S. Ct. 881; *Rimini Street*, 139 S. Ct. 873; *Kirtsaeng II*, 136 S. Ct. 1979.

[28] *See generally Fogerty*, 510 U.S. 517; *Feltner*, 523 U.S. 340.

[29] PETER BALDWIN, THE COPYRIGHT WARS: THREE CENTURIES OF TRANS-ATLANTIC BATTLE (2014); WILLIAM PATRY, MORAL PANIC AND THE COPYRIGHT WARS (2009).

drawn from other areas of the Court's jurisprudence. My claim is instead that copyright law has proven to be an unexpectedly ideal vehicle for this shift in orientation, such that the trend is likely to continue into the future, so long as the concerns motivating it remain central to the Court. The noted First Amendment scholar Zechariah Chafee, Jr. once noted that "[c]opyright is the Cinderella of the law,"[30] in that its importance and relevance often emerge through happenstance and external factors. While he did not intend it as such, Chafee's metaphor is rather apt as a description of the Court's turn toward institutionalism in its dealings with copyright law.

I. The Stirring of Copyright Institutionalism

To understand the shift in the Court's approach to copyright cases that has come to be seen in its recent decisions, it is essential to note the salient features of its copyright jurisprudence in the immediately preceding era, i.e., during the Rehnquist Court. The Rehnquist Court heard and decided a total of ten copyright cases between 1986 and 2005. While they cumulatively addressed a wide range of substantive copyright issues, two in particular—decided unanimously a couple of years apart—exemplify the Court's pre-institutionalist approach: *Feist Publications v. Rural Telephone Service Co.*[31] and *Community for Creative Non-Violence v. Reid* ("*CCNV*").[32]

Decided in 1991, *Feist* involved a claim of copyright infringement brought by the producer of a telephone directory against a competitor that had copied the directory in its entirety.[33] In defense of its copying, the competitor argued that the directory did not satisfy the standard of "originality" mandated by the statute for works of authorship to become eligible for copyright. Writing for a unanimous Court, Justice O'Connor found the telephone directory to lack the requisite originality.[34] In support of its conclusion, the opinion made three significant (and interdependent) analytical moves.

To arrive at the conclusion that telephone directories were not original, the Court proceeded to reject an approach to originality

[30] Chafee, Jr., *supra* note 21.

[31] 499 U.S. 340 (1991).

[32] 490 U.S. 730 (1989).

[33] *Feist*, 499 U.S. at 342–44.

[34] *Id.* at 363–64.

that had come to be understood as the "sweat of the brow" doctrine, wherein a creator's mere expenditure of *some* intellectual labor was viewed as sufficient to meet the originality standard.[35] Instead, the Court read into the requirement of originality the need for a "creative component," an idea that it variously described as the "modicum of creativity" or the "creative spark."[36] In addition to showing that a work therefore originated in its author, the work itself needed to reveal some minimal degree of creativity to qualify as original. In so doing, the Court was actively embracing the common law development of the doctrine, an incremental evolution that had predated the Copyright Act of 1976.[37] Indeed, the manner in which the opinion found aspects of the creativity requirement in precedent was vividly reminiscent of common law adjudication, despite the originality requirement having a statutory basis under the 1976 Act.

While not irrelevant, the statutory basis of originality was seen by the Court as exerting surprisingly little constraint on its reasoning. Instead, Justice O'Connor looked to the House and Senate Reports accompanying the 1976 Act to highlight Congress's desire to preserve the judge-made standard of originality in the statute, which to the Court was an authorization for such judge-made evolution to continue.[38] To buttress this conclusion, it dug even further into the legislative history, to cite the views of the Copyright Office during the revision of the statute.[39]

Justice O'Connor's opinion for the Court made a further move that has never reappeared in copyright since. In explicating the Court's standard for originality, the opinion treated its standard as deriving from the Intellectual Property Clause of the U.S. Constitution, specifically the words "writings" and "authors" therein.[40] In

---

[35] *Id.* at 352–54. For a general overview of the doctrine, see Jane C. Ginsburg, *No "Sweat"? Copyright and Other Protection of Works of Information After* Feist v. Rural Telephone, 92 COLUM. L. REV. 338 (1992).

[36] *Id.* at 346, 359.

[37] *See generally* Shyamkrishna Balganesh, *Copyright as Legal Process: The Transformation of American Copyright Law*, 168 U. PA. L. REV. 1101, 1123–45 (2020) (discussing this evolution); Jessica Litman, *Copyright, Compromise, and Legislative History*, 72 CORNELL L. REV. 857, 858 (1987) (noting how "courts had embroidered the old statute with a wealth of common law interpretation").

[38] *Feist*, 499 U.S. at 355.

[39] *Id.* at 355 (citing to the views of the Register of Copyright during the copyright revision process).

[40] *Id.* at 346 ("Originality is a constitutional requirement.").

thus constitutionalizing the originality requirement, the Court was advancing the idea that "[t]he *sine qua non* of copyright is originality."[41] In other words, even Congress was powerless to amend the copyright statute to eliminate or modify the originality requirement, once so understood to emanate directly from the Constitution. Nothing short of a constitutional amendment (or reinterpretation of the Constitution) would empower Congress to alter copyright's originality requirement. The Constitution and its principal interpreter, the Court, rather than Congress, had final say over the doctrine.

What is salient in the Court's reasoning is the matter-of-fact manner in which it strung these three independently significant moves together to build the case for its conclusion. Each of the moves was additionally uncontroversial enough internally on the Court so as to not even fracture its unanimity. *Feist* therefore unproblematically embraced the idea that it was making new law in common law style, developed its legitimacy for such lawmaking from the history and background of the statute rather than from its text alone, and immunized its lawmaking from Congressional scrutiny/override by deriving it directly from the text of the Constitution.

As a decision, *Feist* was hardly an outlier in its manner of dealing with the subject. Just two years prior in 1989, the Court in *Community for Creative Non-Violence (CCNV) v. Reid* had interpreted a particularly controversial part of the 1976 Act—the "work made for hire doctrine"—using a rather unconventional approach.[42] Copyright's work made for hire doctrine deals with works that are produced by one individual at the behest of another and treats the latter as both the author and owner of the work.[43] It thus deviates from copyright's traditional presumption that the person actually producing the work is its author.[44] The statutory definition of a work made for hire identifies two separate circumstances under which a work is to be considered as made for hire, and *CCNV* dealt with one: where "a work is prepared by an employee within the scope of his or her employment."[45]

CCNV involved a sculpture produced by a sculptor based on an arrangement with the plaintiff non-profit organization. Despite their

[41] *Id.* at 348.

[42] 490 U.S. 730 (1989).

[43] *See* 17 U.S.C. § 101 (2020) (definition of a "work made for hire").

[44] *Id.* § 201(a)-(b).

[45] *Id.* § 101.

extensive interaction, the parties had failed to formalize their contractual arrangement and when a dispute arose as to the ownership of the sculpture, the question that emerged was whether the sculptor was an employee of the organization, thereby rendering the sculpture a work made for hire.[46] In another unanimous opinion, this time written by Justice Thurgood Marshall, the Court found the sculptor to be an independent contractor and denied the organization's work made for hire claim.[47] Yet, the route that it took to arrive at that conclusion was anything but straightforward.

Central to the entire case was the manner in which the Court was to give meaning to the term "employee" that Congress had employed in the definition of work made for hire. Presented with four possible ways in which to understand the term, the Court settled on what it saw as the "common law" meaning of the term, deriving from the judge-made law of agency.[48] It rejected the alternatives as incompatible with the "language and structure" of the statutory definition, for which it made extensive resort to the Act's legislative history.[49] Much like it would later do in *Feist*, the Court in *CCNV* set out in great detail the motivation behind the doctrine, as well as the manner in which it was gradually shaped through the legislative process to achieve a "historic compromise."[50]

To support the Court's recourse to the common law, Justice Marshall invoked the canon of common law conformity, noting that when Congress uses terms with a settled common law meaning, a court is obligated to infer a Congressional intent to incorporate that settled meaning into the statute, unless the statute suggests otherwise.[51] The Court saw the statute's use of employment terminology as indicative of just such an intent, and thus concluded "that the term 'employee' should be understood in light of the general common law of agency."[52] That general common law of agency, it further observed, was embodied in the *Restatement (Second) of Agency*, adopted in 1958.[53]

---

46 *CCNV*, 490 U.S. at 733–35.

47 *Id.* at 737.

48 *Id.* at 740.

49 *Id.* at 742.

50 *Id.* at 746.

51 *Id.* at 739 (relying on Court precedent for this canon of construction).

52 *Id.* at 741.

53 *Id.* at 740.

The Court's principal move in the case was hardly subtle. By invoking the idea of common law conformity as its primary—and sole—interpretive mechanism, *CCNV* had effectively converted a statutory term into a common law one, both in form and in substance. Not only was Congress seen as relying on the settled common law meaning, but it was to be understood as doing so in a dynamic and ongoing process, i.e., by outsourcing the meaning of the term to the state common law of agency, as it would evolve and develop even after the enactment of the statute. In due course, this approach became unworkable owing to its unpredictability. Yet at the time, the decision made a concerted effort to retain judicial control over the employment-prong of the work made for hire doctrine, on the basis of an imputed Congressional intention to this effect. This was unlike in *Feist*, where the legislative history was unequivocal in suggesting that Congress had chosen to incorporate judge-made law (and by implication, further judicial lawmaking) into the statute.[54]

Justice Marshall's opinion for the Court treated each of its inferences, imputations and presumptions as both uncontroversial and unproblematic. The Court's conversion of a statutory term into a common law one, its plunge into the legislative history of the provision and the compromise that it represented, and its decision to look to the *Restatement* as the authoritative embodiment of the common law—were seen as rather straightforward, and unworthy of any independent justification.

Viewed through the lens of the current Court's approach to copyright, both *Feist* and *CCNV* are remarkable decisions. Even while acknowledging the primacy of the statute, neither opinion shied away from engaging in the task of referencing copyright's goals and policies, as embodied in the statute's legislative history and overall constitutional structure. Today, such forays would be derided as tantamount to actual lawmaking. Both decisions instead viewed the statute as affirming (and requiring) the judiciary's involvement in developing copyright doctrine, a task that each opinion further treated as altogether unexceptional. Further, neither opinion saw its approach to statutory interpretation and reliance on specific canons and sources for that task as necessitating additional justification. Indeed, noteworthy

[54] *Feist*, 499 U.S. at 355 (quoting the House and Senate Reports which noted that the term originality was "purposely left undefined" since it was "intended to incorporate without change the standard of originality established by the courts" under the previous statute).

here is that Justice Scalia—who would go on to play a significant role in advocating a textualist approach to statutory interpretation that abjured recourse to legislative history[55]—was already a member of the Court when both *Feist* and *CCNV* were unanimously decided, and signed on to both opinions' extensive use of legislative history, engagement with copyright policy, and overt lawmaking.

Under the Rehnquist Court, copyright law was therefore neither a polarizing subject nor the site of deep methodological and institutional disagreement among members of the Court.[56] This would change over the course of the following decade. Three interrelated factors played a key role in this transformation.

The first was the change in the Court's composition. Justice Thomas joined the Court a few months after *Feist*, Justice Ginsburg in 1993, and Justice Breyer in 1994. The latter two were particularly important additions for copyright, with direct substantive expertise in the field. Justice Ginsburg had written the majority opinion for the Court of Appeals that the *CCNV* decision endorsed and affirmed,[57] and Justice Breyer was well-known in the academic world for his early scholarly work adopting a skeptical view of copyright in new technologies.[58] Their substantive clashes on copyright issues would profoundly shape the Court's jurisprudence.

The second was the emergence of "textualism" and its emphasis on the text of the statute as a distinctive approach to statutory interpretation,[59] a development that coincided with the personnel changes on the Court. Textualism's most overt champion was Justice

[55] For a general overview of Scalia's interpretive philosophy, see William N. Eskridge, Jr., *Should the Supreme Court Read* The Federalist *but Not Statutory Legislative History?*, 66 GEO. WASH. L. REV. 1301 (1998).

[56] *See generally* Matthew Sag, Tonja Jacobi & Maxim Sytch, *Ideology and Exceptionalism in Intellectual Property: An Empirical Study*, 97 CALIF. L. REV. 801 (2009) (showing that the Justice's votes in intellectual property cases are broadly predictable on the basis of ideology, but less so than in some other areas).

[57] Community for Creative Non-Violence v. Reid, 846 F.2d 1485 (D.C. Cir. 1988). She also authored a few other significant copyright opinions during her time on the D.C. Circuit. *See* Nat'l Cable Television Ass'n v. Copyright Royalty Tribunal, 724 F.2d 176 (D.C. Cir. 1983); Atari Games Corp. v. Oman, 888 F. 2d 878 (D.C. Cir. 1989); Atari Games Corp. v. Oman, 979 F.2d 242 (D.C. Cir. 1992); Cablevision Sys. Dev. Co. v. Motion Picture Ass'n of Am, Inc., 808 F.2d 133 (D.C. Cir. 1987).

[58] Stephen Breyer, *The Uneasy Case for Copyright: A Study of Copyright in Books, Photocopies, and Computer Programs*, 84 HARV. L. REV. 281 (1970).

[59] *See generally* William N. Eskridge, Jr., *The New Textualism*, 37 UCLA L. REV. 621 (1990).

Scalia, who began advancing the theory in his opinions shortly after his appointment to the Court in 1986. Characteristic of this approach was its connection to constitutional separation of powers, and thus a very particular vision of the judicial role in statutory domains.[60] Foreshadowing its impact, one prominent scholar of legislation thus predicted that if adopted, textualism would "represent a significant change in the way . . . the Court conceptualizes its role in interpreting statutes" since it represented a "bold rethinking of the Court's role."[61]

A third factor was specific to the copyright discourse. At the same time that textualism began to divide the Court methodologically and ideologically, substantive thinking about copyright law started becoming increasingly polarized.[62] Fueled by the emergence of the internet and digital technologies, copyright law began seeing deep divisions around the core substantive issues of scope, coverage, duration, and remedies; a division that came to be described as the "copyright war."[63] By the year 2000, this divisiveness started playing itself out in litigation that often pitted authors and content owners on one side against users, technology companies, and public interest groups on the other.

Then, in 2002 the "copyright war" landed on the front steps of the Supreme Court. While *Eldred v. Ashcroft*[64] was framed as a constitutional challenge to an amendment to the copyright statute, in reality it was the culmination of a decade-long effort to push back against copyright's gradual expansion. The petitioners in the case tried convincing the Court that the words "for Limited Times" in the Intellectual Property Clause of the Constitution, and the First Amendment, each independently functioned as limits on Congress's power to enact copyright legislation, which the statutory amendment transgressed.[65] In support of their argument, they relied heavily on the Court's then-recent Commerce Clause jurisprudence, which had

[60] *Id.* at 673.

[61] *Id.* at 624.

[62] *See* Patry, *supra* note 29, at 1–42 (2009); John Tehranian, Infringement Nation: Copyright 2.0 and You 15 (2011).

[63] *See* Patry, *supra* note 29; Tehranian, *supra* note 62; Lawrence Lessig, The Future of Ideas: The Fate of the Commons in a Connected World 16 (2002); Jonathan Zittrain, *How to End the Copyright Wars*, 457 Nature 264 (2009).

[64] 537 U.S. 186 (2003).

[65] *Id.* at 193.

identified Congress's legislative power as having inherent limits embedded within its very grant.[66] Congress's power to enact copyright law, the petitioners argued, was no different.

In a 7-2 decision, the Court rejected the petitioners' challenge. While the majority considered plausible defenses for the statutory amendment, it ultimately decided the case on institutionalist grounds. Writing for the Court, Justice Ginsburg concluded that as long as the amendment was a rational exercise of legislative power, it was not the judicial role to examine the wisdom or suitability of that exercise:[67]

> As we read the Framers' instruction, the Copyright Clause empowers Congress to determine the intellectual property regimes that, overall, in that body's judgment, will serve the ends of the Clause. . . . Beneath the facade of their inventive constitutional interpretation, petitioners forcefully urge that Congress pursued very bad policy in prescribing the CTEA's long terms. The wisdom of Congress' action, however, is not within our province to second-guess. Satisfied that the legislation before us remains inside the domain the Constitution assigns to the First Branch, we affirm the judgment of the Court of Appeals.

Each of the two dissenting opinions—one by Justice Breyer and the other by Justice Stevens—saw the majority's approach as an abdication of its judicial responsibility. Justice Stevens was particularly polemical:[68]

> By failing to protect the public interest in free access to the products of inventive and artistic genius—indeed, by virtually ignoring the central purpose of the Copyright/Patent Clause—the Court has quitclaimed to Congress its principal responsibility in this area of the law. Fairly read, the Court has stated that Congress' actions under the Copyright/Patent Clause are, for all intents and purposes, judicially unreviewable. That result cannot be squared with the basic tenets of our constitutional structure. It is not hyperbole to recall the trenchant words of Chief Justice John Marshall: "It is emphatically the province and duty of the judicial department to say what the law is." *Marbury v. Madison*, 1 Cranch 137, 177 (1803).

In *Eldred*, the majority emphasized a consideration that was altogether new to its copyright jurisprudence: inter-branch coordination or, to use the language of Legal Process theory, "institutional

---

[66] Lessig, *supra* note 4, at 60 (discussing petitioner's strategy of relying on *United States v. Lopez*, 514 U.S. 549 (1999), in *Eldred*).

[67] *Eldred*, 537 U.S. at 222.

[68] *Id.* at 242 (Stevens, J., dissenting).

settlement."[69] According to this principle, lawmaking power is to be allocated to different institutions on the basis of their institutional competence and decisions rendered in the exercise of such power are to be respected by other institutions absent strong countervailing considerations.[70] While copyright law had long been recognized as statutory in origin, that statutory basis had never—until *Eldred*—been seen as embodying an institutional settlement that needed to be respected and deferred to. As illustrated by both *Feist* and *CCNV*, the Court had been perfectly comfortable in sharing lawmaking responsibility with Congress, especially in areas where Congress had either endorsed such sharing or acquiesced in it.

To be sure, *Eldred* did not transform the Court's engagement with copyright law overnight. As previously noted, it presented the Court with a unique set of constitutional questions. All the same, the majority's engagement with Congress's authority to make copyright law, and its deferential approach to such authority had its roots in a commitment to the ideal of separation of powers. And by making it a distinct part of the calculus, *Eldred* forced the Court to confront its very idea of the judicial role in copyright adjudication.

Federal copyright statutes prior to the Act of 1976 were all characterized by their brevity and use of open-ended language.[71] Courts took this to imply an active role for them in the lawmaking process, through "a constructive, beneficial partnership" as one federal judge observed.[72] In the years immediately after the passage of the 1976 Act, this mindset did not change. This change was especially true of doctrinal areas that had been previously developed by courts but codified by Congress in the new statute. *Feist* and *CCNV* exemplified the continuation of this mindset while *Eldred* successfully sowed the seeds of change.

Even though *Eldred* was a constitutional challenge to the copyright statute rather than a case about the interpretation of the statute

---

[69] Henry M. Hart, Jr. & Albert M. Sacks, The Legal Process: Basic Problems in the Making and Application of Law 4 (1958) (describing it as "the central idea of law"). *See generally* William N. Eskridge, Jr. & Philip P. Frickey, *The Making of the Legal Process*, 107 Harv. L. Rev. 2031, 2045 (1994) (noting the centrality of the idea to Legal Process).

[70] *See* Ernest A. Young, *Institutional Settlement in a Globalizing Judicial System*, 54 Duke L.J. 1143, 1143 (2005).

[71] *See* Liu, *supra* note 13, at 94–101 (describing the nature of these early statutes and their reliance on judge-made law for elaboration and further development).

[72] Leval, *supra* note 22, at 1062.

as such, the decision's posture toward Congress implicitly rejected the idea of a lawmaking partnership. The Court's belief that it was "not at liberty to second-guess congressional determinations and policy judgements" in the area of copyright "however debatable or arguably unwise they may be" openly endorsed the idea that Congress was the principal lawmaking institution in copyright, which it was bound to respect.[73] *Eldred* thus set the stage for the Court's turn toward institutionalist considerations in its copyright jurisprudence.

II. Copyright's Institutionalist Turn at the Court

While *Eldred* laid the groundwork for the Court's turn toward institutional considerations in its copyright jurisprudence, it also brought to the surface a substantive philosophical difference between the two Justices on the Court most knowledgeable about copyright: Justices Breyer and Ginsburg. Breyer's lengthy dissent in *Eldred* saw the amendment at issue in the case—the CTEA—to be substantively problematic as a matter of copyright policy, since it endorsed a private benefit (to existing authors/owners) at the expense of the public domain.[74] The logic of deference that informed the majority, was to him, little more than an endorsement of the CTEA itself. His opinion therefore went to considerable length to showcase the problems with the amendment, often well beyond the positions taken by the petitioner. Ginsburg construed this statement as needless advocacy, at one point criticizing Breyer's dissent as not "restrained" but instead "[m]oving beyond the bounds of the parties' presentations, and with abundant policy arguments but precious little support from precedent."[75]

Eldred marked the beginning of an important fracturing in the Court's substantive position on copyright questions. In *Eldred*, Justice Breyer positioned himself rather firmly as a copyright-skeptic who believed that the copyright system was in need of retrenching, having advanced that position in his early academic work.[76] Justice

[73] *Eldred*, 537 U.S. at 208.

[74] *Eldred*, 537 U.S. at 255–63 (Breyer, J., dissenting).

[75] *Id.* at 199 n.4.

[76] Breyer, *supra* note 58, at 281. It is worth noting that this appears to be a departure from Breyer's own engagement with congressional expertise and statutes in other contexts. One study found that in 2005, he was the least "inclin[ed] to strike down Congressional laws," based on his voting patterns. Paul Gewirtz & Chad Golder, *So Who Are the Activists?*, N.Y. Times

Ginsburg's position was more neutral. She undoubtedly saw significant virtue in the functioning of the copyright system that Congress had developed and was suspicious of judicial efforts to thwart legislative policy in the domain. The year before *Eldred* was argued, she had penned her first copyright opinion for the Court in *New York Times Co. v. Tasini*, siding with freelance authors against their publishers in an opinion that excavated the history and logic behind a little-known provision of the copyright statute.[77] Notably, Breyer dissented in the case.[78] Justice Ginsburg's opinion in *Eldred*, in many ways, represented her overall approach to copyright: a strong presumption of rationality in the system that merited deference.

The Breyer-Ginsburg divide on copyright became undeniable by the end of the Rehnquist Court. In *MGM Studios, Inc. v. Grokster, Ltd.*,[79] decided a few months before the death of Chief Justice Rehnquist, the Court unanimously decided that a peer-to-peer filesharing service was liable for indirect copyright infringement under a new theory of "inducement" that it developed in the case. Yet, the Court's unanimity was deceptive, evidenced by the two separate concurring opinions—by Breyer and Ginsburg—that vehemently disagreed with *each other* over the scope of the Court's precedent on contributory infringement, an issue that the opinion for the full Court decided to address merely in passing.[80] During their time together on the Court,

---

(July 6, 2005), https://www.nytimes.com/2005/07/06/opinion/so-who-are-the-activists.html. Indeed, Breyer advanced this idea of deference in his non-judicial writing as well, wherein he described his philosophy as a Justice on the court. *See* STEPHEN J. BREYER, ACTIVE LIBERTY: INTERPRETING OUR DEMOCRATIC CONSTITUTION 49 (2006) ("Courts can defer to the legislature's own judgment insofar as that judgment concerns matters (particularly empirical matters) about which the legislature is comparatively expert."). In the same non-judicial writing, he however identified a limit to this deference, noting that "courts should not defer when they evaluate the risk that reform legislation will defeat the participatory self-government objective itself." *Id.* Perhaps the legislation at issue in *Eldred* and much of copyright law since its origin represents such a departure in his thinking. *See Eldred*, 537 U.S. at 265–66 (Breyer, J., dissenting) (noting his concern for deference to Congress, but concluding that the statute was deeply problematic in conferring a private benefit at the expense of the public).

[77] New York Times Co. v. Tasini, 533 U.S. 483 (2001).

[78] *Id.* at 506 (Stevens, J., dissenting). Justice Breyer joined Justice Stevens's dissent.

[79] 545 U.S. 913 (2005).

[80] *Id.* at 942 (Ginsburg, J., concurring); *id.* at 949 (Breyer, J., concurring). The disagreement revolved around the interpretation of *Sony Corp. of America v. Universal City Studios, Inc.*, 464 U.S. 417 (1984). The Court in *Grokster* sidestepped the issue altogether. *See Grokster*, 545 U.S. at 934 ("[We] leave further consideration of the *Sony* rule for a day when that may be required.").

it handed down a total of 15 copyright decisions.[81] In those decisions, Justice Ginsburg wrote an opinion 11 times and Justice Breyer on 9 occasions, indicative of their strong views on the subject. The two Justices wrote opinions specifically disagreeing with each other on 7 of those occasions and voted on opposing sides in 7 of the 15 cases. These numbers capture the extent of their disagreement on copyright matters.

It is of course difficult to know the precise effect of the Breyer-Ginsburg disagreement on the other Justices of the Court. Both Breyer and Ginsburg were reliable progressive votes among the Court's members and routinely voted on the same side on the Court's most politically charged cases.[82] Indeed, it is because of this overall alignment in views that the extent of their disagreement on copyright matters is little known outside of copyright circles.[83] All the same, the overt manifestation of their disagreement toward the end of the Rehnquist Court coincided with an underappreciated, yet readily discernible trend in the Court's approach to copyright cases under Chief Justice Roberts. And this was the Court's overt turn toward institutional considerations in copyright matters.

The Roberts Court's approach to copyright law had a direct connection to broader debates about the Court's institutional legitimacy.

---

[81] Quality King Distributors Inc. v. L'anza Rsch. Int'l Inc., 523 U.S. 135 (1998); Feltner v. Columbia Pictures Television, Inc., 523 U.S. 340 (1998); *Grokster*, 545 U.S. at 913; *Tasini*, 533 U.S. at 483; *Eldred*, 537 U.S. at 186; Reed Elsevier Inc. v. Muchnick, 559 U.S. 154 (2010); Golan v. Holder, 565 U.S. 302 (2012); Kirtsaeng v. John Wiley & Sons, Inc. (*Kirtsaeng I*), 568 U.S. 519 (2013); American Broadcast Cos. v. Aereo, Inc., 573 U.S. 431 (2014); Kirtsaeng v. John Wiley & Sons, Inc. (*Kirtsaeng II*), 136 S. Ct. 1979 (2016); Star Athletica LLC v. Varsity Brands, Inc., 137 S. Ct. 1002 (2017); Fourth Estate Pub. Benefit Corp. v. Wall-Street.com, LLC, 139 S. Ct. 881 (2019); Rimini Street Inc. v. Oracle USA, Inc., 139 S. Ct. 873 (2019); Allen v. Cooper, 140 S. Ct. 994 (2020); Georgia v. Public.Resource.Org, Inc. (*PRO*), 140 S. Ct. 1498 (2020). In addition to these, there were two cases where the Court affirmed the lower court's decision because of an equally divided 4-4 court. *See* Lotus Dev. Corp. v. Borland Int'l, Inc., 516 U.S. 233 (1995); Omega SA v. Costco Wholesale Corp., 562 U.S. 40 (2010).

[82] For a fascinating account of why Justices Breyer and Ginsburg might have disagreed within copyright, traced back to their differing approaches to adjudication, see Joshua B. Fischman & Tonja Jacobi, *The Second Dimension of the Supreme Court*, 57 Wm. & Mary L. Rev. 1671, 1674–75 (2016).

[83] *See, e.g.*, Jeremy Bowers, Adam Liptak & Derek Willis, *Which Supreme Court Justices Vote Together Most and Least Often*, N.Y. Times (July 3, 2014), https://www.nytimes.com/interactive/2014/06/24/upshot/24up-scotus-agreement-rates.html (noting how Justices Ginsburg and Breyer agreed with each other overall 88% during the 2014 Term).

Early into his term, Chief Justice Roberts emphasized that ensuring the legitimacy of the Court as an "impartial institution" would be a principal consideration during his leadership.[84] As he noted at the time, this was to be realized through fewer separate opinions and greater unanimity in the Court's decisions.[85] In reality, this vision never came to be realized, with the Court continuing to offer splintered decisions on a wide range of matters including copyright law.[86] In the ten copyright cases that the Rehnquist Court decided, seven were unanimous, five of them on substantive copyright doctrine.[87] Of the twelve decided by the Roberts Court, five were unanimous and they all involved procedural and remedial—as opposed to substantive—questions.[88]

Unanimity was not, however, the only means of furthering the Court's institutional legitimacy. Equally important to such institutional legitimacy was the Court's outward commitment to the ideal of separation of powers, which Roberts described as "respecting Congress" and adopting a norm of "deference [to the legislature] in matters of policy."[89] This approach to institutional legitimacy was, of course, controversial on its own, as the line between judicial deference (to other branches) and judicial abdication became a point of contention. Whether the other Justices shared his views on this topic or not, the norm of deference and its overt connection to the Court's institutional role and legitimacy infiltrated their reasoning in copyright matters.

---

[84] *See* Jeffrey Rosen, *Roberts's Rules*, The Atlantic, Jan.-Feb. 2007, https://www.theatlantic.com/magazine/archive/2007/01/robertss-rules/305559/.

[85] *Id.* (noting how "he had made it a priority of his first term to promote unanimity and collegiality on the Court").

[86] Cass R. Sunstein, *Unanimity and Disagreement on the Supreme Court*, 100 Cornell L. Rev. 769, 771 (2015) ("Under his leadership . . . the patterns that concerned the Chief Justice in 2006 have been maintained.").

[87] Community for Creative Non-Violence v. Reid (*CCNV*), 490 U.S. 730, 732 (1989); Feist Publications, Inc. v. Rural Telephone Serv. Co., 499 U.S. 340, 342 (1991); Fogerty v. Fantasy, Inc., 510 U.S. 517, 519 (1994); Campbell v. Acuff-Rose Music, Inc., 510 U.S. 569, 599 (1994); Quality King Distributors Inc. v. L'anza Rsch. Int'l Inc., 523 U.S. 135, 138 (1998); Feltner v. Columbia Pictures Television, Inc., 523 U.S. 340, 342 (1998); MGM Studios, Inc. v. Grokster, Ltd., 545 U.S. 913, 918 (2005).

[88] Reed Elsevier Inc. v. Muchnick, 559 U.S. 154, 157 (2010) (dealing with registration); Allen v. Cooper, 140 S. Ct. 994, 996 (2020) (dealing with state sovereign immunity for copyright infringement); Fourth Estate Pub. Benefit Corp. v. Wall-Street.Com, LLC, 139 S. Ct. 881, 884 (2019) (dealing with copyright registration); Rimini Street Inc. v. Oracle USA, Inc., 139 S. Ct. 873, 874 (2019) (dealing with the assessment of costs); Kirtsaeng v. John Wiley & Sons, Inc. (*Kirtsaeng II*), 136 S. Ct. 1979, 1981 (2016) (dealing with attorney's fees).

[89] Nat'l Fed. of Independent Business v. Sebelius, 567 U.S. 519, 538 (2012).

Much has been written and said about the Court's institutional legitimacy over the last decade.[90] Debates about the Court's legitimacy have, however, focused principally on the Court's high-profile public law cases, where perceptions of its partisanship and engagement with the other branches of government are most obvious. These same concerns have inflected the Court's copyright jurisprudence in unappreciated ways by intertwining arguments (and disagreements) over institutional legitimacy and separation of powers with questions of copyright doctrine. Institutionalism thus emerged as a common thread in the Court's copyright opinions, and often in subtle ways. As used here, "institutionalism" and "institutional considerations" are descriptors for the idea that the Court's legitimacy and public credibility are important normative considerations that ought to influence its substantive work.

Eldred had already oriented the Court toward institutional considerations in copyright law. The Court's copyright decisions between 2010 (the year that the Roberts Court decided its first copyright case[91]) and 2021 further internalized this institutionalism, which manifested itself in the Court's copyright opinions in three interconnected ways. The first manifestation involved its opinions advancing arguments of a *direct institutionalist* nature, wherein members of the Court raised questions and concerns about the appropriate role of the Court (and the judiciary more generally) in copyright matters. While relatively rare, this line of argument has become more common in the Court's most recent copyright disagreements. The second manifestation centered around arguments that were *indirectly institutionalist*. Here, debates surrounding the interpretation of the copyright statute came to be influenced by the nature and degree of deference that needed to be accorded to Congressional intent, either as manifested in the statute or other sources. While the disagreement between the Court's textualist and non-textualist Justices captured some of this indirect institutionalism, it also emerged independent of that debate, and among the next-textualist members of the Court as well.

The third form in which the Court's copyright institutionalism manifested itself was a likely consequence of the Breyer-Ginsburg

---

[90] *See, e.g.*, Richard H. Fallon, Jr., Law and Legitimacy in the Supreme Court (2018); Michael Zills, The Limits of Legitimacy: Dissenting Opinions, Media Coverage, and Public Responses to Supreme Court Decisions (2015); Tara Leigh Grove, *The Supreme Court's Legitimacy Dilemma*, 132 Harv. L. Rev. 2240 (2019) (reviewing Fallon, *supra*); Gillian E Metzger, *To Tax, To Spend, To Regulate*, 126 Harv. L. Rev. 83 (2012).

[91] *Reed Elsevier*, 559 U.S. 154.

disagreement on the Court over substantive copyright doctrine. At the same time that it became increasingly clear that the Court was likely to splinter on the most pressing substantive copyright questions and thus contribute to concerns about the Court's overall institutional legitimacy, the Justices began coalescing around aspects of the copyright system that (a) did not involve substantive copyright policy where Justices Breyer and Ginsburg each held strong and divergent views, and (b) showed significant continuity with other areas of federal litigation. In short order, the Roberts Court began granting certiorari in cases involving adjectival—i.e., procedural and remedial—aspects of the copyright system. Six of the twelve copyright matters decided by the Roberts Court fell into this category.[92]

While these grants surprised many in the copyright world given the number of crucial substantive copyright questions that the Court refused to hear, this part of the Court's copyright jurisprudence is best understood as driven by its institutionalism as well. To the extent that these adjectival questions implicated issues that were hardly unique to copyright law and focused on the enforcement and adjudication of copyright claims by reference to principles and doctrines that were somewhat universal, the Court's intervention therein supplemented—rather than detracted from—its overall strategy of legitimacy. Speaking to a jurisdictional or remedial question was something that was unlikely to be viewed as stepping on Congress's policy-making, especially if the Court was willing to speak in one voice. To the contrary, it was more likely to be seen as principally within the Court's domain and competence, as administrator of the federal judicial system. Not surprisingly, *all* of the Roberts Court's unanimous copyright decisions—a total of five—came from this category of copyright cases, which as a whole generated consensus among the Justices in all but one instance. This *adjectivalism* undoubtedly served both of Chief Justice Roberts's legitimacy goals—greater consensus and avoidance of policy—discussed previously.

The discussion that follows unpacks each of the three forms of institutionalism seen in the Roberts Court's copyright jurisprudence. It does so analytically rather than chronologically, to emphasize that the Court's turn to institutionalism in the domain of copyright law is to be understood less as a concerted strategy on the part of its members

---

[92] *See Reed Elsevier*, 559 U.S. 154; *Petrella*, 572 U.S. 663; *Kirtsaeng II*, 136 S. Ct. 1979; *Fourth Estate*, 139 S. Ct. 881; *Rimini Street*, 139 S. Ct. 873; *Allen*, 140 S. Ct. 994.

or leadership, but instead as a frame through which to understand the coherence and logic of its copyright jurisprudence.

A. DIRECT INSTITUTIONALISM: APPROPRIATE JUDICIAL ROLE

It is widely recognized that in enacting the Copyright Act of 1976, Congress envisioned a role for federal courts adjudicating copyright disputes that was fundamentally different from what they had been doing under prior statutes.[93] Instead of leaving it to courts to extend the statute's abstract principles into new contexts and thus play a coequal role in the development of copyright law, Congress now envisioned itself as the principal lawmaker in the field. This "shift in direction for the very philosophy" of copyright resulted in the 1976 Act attempting to comprehensively codify much of copyright law, including areas previously developed by courts incrementally.[94] In its level of detail and coverage, Congress implicitly demanded that its vision of copyright policy obtain a new level of deference from courts. It was not until *Eldred* that the Court overtly acceded to this demand and adopted a vision of the judicial role in copyright matters that showed open deference to Congress's policy choices in the area. To be sure, *Eldred* was a constitutional matter. Yet in the Roberts Court, its logic resonated well beyond.

Nearly a decade after *Eldred*, in what was only the second copyright case decided under Chief Justice Roberts, the Court confronted a nearly identical constitutional challenge to an amendment made by Congress to the copyright statute. In *Golan v. Holder*,[95] the petitioners argued that an amendment to the copyright statute, the Uruguay Round Agreements Act (URAA) enacted by Congress in order to give effect to international treaty obligations, was a violation of the Intellectual Property Clause and First Amendment.[96] In an opinion written by Justice Ginsburg, a majority of the Court rejected the challenge on the same grounds that it did in *Eldred*: the Court had "no warrant to reject the rational judgement [of] Congress."[97]

---

[93] *See* Liu, *supra* note 13, at 102; Litman, *supra* note 37, at 858–59.

[94] Ringer, *supra* note 21, at 479.

[95] 566 U.S. 302 (2012).

[96] *Id.* at 315–18.

[97] *Id.* at 327.

Yet unlike in *Eldred*, the petitioners in *Golan* presented the Court with a policy rationale that cut against the URAA, deriving from what is known as the "orphan works" problem, involving "older and more obscure works with minimal commercial value that have copyright owners who are difficult or impossible to track down."[98] The URAA sought to restore works that had fallen into the public domain back under copyright protection and the petitioners feared that this restoration would impose prohibitive administrative costs on those seeking to use such restored works when they were nevertheless orphaned.[99] Justice Breyer's dissenting opinion in *Golan* paid special attention to the orphan works problem, which he saw as undermining the rationality of the URAA. To the majority, this was simply not a judicial prerogative. While acknowledging the gravity of the problem, Justice Ginsburg was clear that the issue was simply not "a matter appropriate for judicial, as opposed to legislative, resolution."[100] Among her reasons were "the host of policy and logistical questions" underlying the problem and its solution.[101] Second-guessing Congress's policy choices in copyright law—in the name of constitutional scrutiny—was not an appropriate role for the Court.

For the most part, disagreement over institutional considerations in the Court's copyright jurisprudence presented itself only ever indirectly, i.e., through statutory interpretation. *Golan* raised the issue since it involved a constitutional question where the Court was *asked* to override Congress. While a few opinions alluded to the concern thereafter, debates over institutional considerations remained for the most part submerged under disagreement relating to statutory interpretation, which as we shall see was far more common. All the same, the form of direct institutionalism seen in *Eldred* and *Golan* reached an unexpected crescendo and divided the Court rather sharply in a case from its 2019 Term: *Georgia v. Public.Resource.Org., Inc.* (*PRO*).[102]

PRO involved a relatively obscure copyright doctrine known as the government edicts doctrine, which denies copyright protection to texts produced by government bodies and agencies in the exercise

[98] *Id.* at 355 (Breyer, J., dissenting).

[99] *Id.*

[100] *Id.* at 334.

[101] *Id.*

[102] 140 S. Ct. 1498 (2020).

of their lawmaking functions.[103] The principal creation of three nineteenth-century Supreme Court cases,[104] and with no mention in the text of the statute,[105] the doctrine today denies copyright to statutes, judicial opinions, administrative regulations, and a host of other legal texts. At issue in the case was the question whether it applied to annotations accompanying an official state statute, which had received the imprimatur of the state legislature and been merged into a single "official" code.[106] In a splintered 5-4 decision, the Court found the doctrine to apply and denied protection to the state annotations.

The majority opinion in *PRO* was the first—and to date only—copyright opinion written by Chief Justice Roberts. Relying on the Court's old precedents, which he rooted in the idea of authorship, Roberts developed what he saw as a "straightforward rule" in the case.[107] Since "authorship" found mention in the statute, he treated the precedents as entirely compatible with the statute and found it altogether unproblematic to extend the logic of the doctrine to annotations. His opinion provoked two independent dissents: one by Justice Ginsburg[108] and the other by Justice Thomas.[109] In his dissent, Justice Thomas challenged the majority's interpretation of the text and common law precedents, and then went one step further arguing that "the majority ha[d] strayed from its proper role" by

[103] *Id.* at 1504–05.

[104] Wheaton v. Peters, 33 U.S. (8 Pet.) 591 (1834); Banks v. Manchester, 128 U.S. 244 (1888); Callaghan v. Myers, 128 U.S. 617 (1888).

[105] It is of course not unique in this respect. Copyright law embodies other non-statutory doctrines as well, such as substantial similarity and indirect infringement.

[106] *PRO*, 140 S. Ct. at 1504–05.

[107] *Id.* at 1506.

[108] *Id.* at 1522 (Ginsburg, J., dissenting) (joined by Justice Breyer). It remains unclear why Justice Breyer chose to join Justice Ginsburg's dissenting opinion, in addition to his joining Justice Thomas's. One plausible explanation has less to do with the actual content of Justice Ginsburg's dissent, and instead with the strength of his disagreement with the majority in the case.

[109] *Id.* at 1513 (Thomas, J., dissenting) (joined by Justices Alito and Breyer). It is interesting to note that Justice Breyer refrained from joining one part and one footnote in Justice Thomas's dissent. In that Part, Part II-A, Justice Thomas unpacked the majority's textualist analysis to argue that its reasoning found little support in the text of the statute, except through the "magic wand of *ipse dixit.*" *Id.* at 1520–21. And that footnote—footnote 6—dealt with Justice Thomas's views on Supreme Court precedent that had come to be understood differently over time, even when not overruled, and the value of separate opinions in different cases. *Id.* at 1521 n.6. Presumably, Justice Breyer's disagreement with the implicit political and methodological underpinnings of these views triggered his refusal to join the footnote.

usurping policy decisions that were the exclusive prerogative of Congress to make.[110] He put the point even more sharply. Not only did he disagree with the majority's actual conclusion in the case, but he also saw that conclusion as problematic in that it was "the result of [the Court's] meddling" in copyright's legislative scheme, when it was instead "bound to respect" all of "the deliberative legislative choices" made by Congress.[111] To Justice Thomas, the majority's reasoning—in *both* form and substance—involved an inappropriate exercise of the "judicial role,"[112] a point that the Chief Justice's opinion sought to vehemently counter.[113]

The institutionalist rhetoric about "judicial role" that divided the Justices in *PRO* was no coincidence. A few months after the Court announced its decision in the case, a news report revealed that the *PRO* case had involved unusually intense internal wrangling among the Justices.[114] The report claimed that during private conference following oral argument, Justice Thomas's opinion had garnered enough votes to be the majority opinion, with the Chief Justice's view constituting the minority. Shortly thereafter, Chief Justice Roberts managed to persuade one other Justice over to his side, allowing him to "capture[] the majority" from Justice Thomas.[115] While this maneuvering was of course nowhere near as climactic as Chief Justice Roberts's last-minute switch of his vote in *NFIB v. Sibelius* that has since come to be hailed as an overt institutional move,[116] it nevertheless suggests that Roberts saw his opinion in *PRO* to be of some institutional significance, despite its arcane subject matter.

A closer look at Chief Justice Roberts's opinion suggests that a good part of that significance may have come from the desire to maintain the Court's nineteenth-century precedents rather than abrogate them on a

---

[110] *Id.* at 1522.

[111] *Id.*

[112] *Id.* at 1515.

[113] *Id.* at 1512 n.4.

[114] Joan Biskupic, *Behind Closed Doors During One of John Roberts' Most Surprising Years on the Supreme Court*, CNN (July 27, 2020), https://www.cnn.com/2020/07/27/politics/john-roberts-supreme-court-liberals-daca-second-amendment/index.html. For a similar account speculating on why Chief Justice Roberts shifted his position in *NFIB v. Sibelius*, see Mark Tushnet, In the Balance (2013).

[115] *Id.*

[116] For a full account, see Joan Biskupic, The Chief: The Life and Turbulent Times of Chief Justice John Roberts 221 (2019).

theory of desuetude. To treat them as outdated simply because they relied on an outmoded understanding of the "author" and legal publishing, struck him as too conjectural and potentially dangerous. Justice Thomas viewed the Court's nineteenth-century precedents with suspicion, worrying that they endorsed a view of lawmaking that had since been abandoned.[117] To the majority, this was not what the judicial role entailed. It instead mandated that the Court "apply the reasoning and results the Court voted on and committed to writing."[118] To Chief Justice Roberts, therefore, maintaining the integrity of the Court's own precedents was of institutional significance, a point that his opinion reiterated when directly presented with an argument from the petitioner that the precedents did not represent sound "copyright policy." Such an "appeal to copyright policy" to overturn precedent, and as an independent basis for the Court's decision, was to him simply "addressed to the wrong forum."[119]

PRO may have therefore been inconsequential as far as its own subject matter went. And yet it fractured the Court around the idea of the "judicial role" in copyright adjudication, an idea that went well beyond the domain of statutory interpretation. In all the back and forth between the opinions, it is easy to overlook the reality that both the majority opinion and Justice Thomas's dissent agreed on one crucial point: Congress, and "not the court[]," was to decide how best to pursue copyright policy, a proposition for which they each independently cited the exact same sentence from *Eldred*.[120] *PRO* thus confirmed that the Court as a whole had arrived at the recognition that the judicial role in copyright cases simply did not extend to its engagement with policy. That was instead the exclusive domain of Congress. What they disagreed on was the secondary question of *how* to give effect to that role. The logic of *Eldred* had successfully percolated deep into the Court's copyright adjudication.

B. INDIRECT INSTITUTIONALISM: STATUTORY INTERPRETATION

In the Roberts Court, institutional considerations entered copyright jurisprudence most frequently in the name of statutory interpretation.

---

[117] *PRO*, 140 S. Ct. at 1515–17 (Thomas, J., dissenting).

[118] *Id.* at 1512 n.4.

[119] *Id.* at 1511.

[120] *Id.* at 1511, 1522.

While the Copyright Act of 1976 was a comprehensive piece of copyright legislation, its component parts embodied rules of varying lineages. In some areas, such as originality and fair use, Congress merely codified pre-existing judge-made law with little to no change.[121] In others, such as collective works, public performance and first sale, it retained the prior doctrine but with significant alteration.[122] And in yet others, such as preemption and joint works, it constructed rules and doctrines anew.[123] Independent of all these categories were additional copyright doctrines such as government edicts and substantial similarity that Congress chose to ignore altogether in its codification, seemingly acquiescing in their continued existence through its silence. In short, the Act of 1976 was a complex statutory enactment and the culmination of over two decades of compromise. Surprisingly little of this complexity produced serious disagreement among the Justices during the Rehnquist Court.

Not so in the copyright jurisprudence of the Roberts Court. *All* of the Roberts Court's decisions that addressed a substantive issue in copyright law generated disagreement among the Justices around the interpretation of the statute. To be sure, some of this was a direct consequence of the rise of textualism on the Court, especially under the stewardship of Justice Scalia (and later Justice Thomas). Yet, textualism is at best a partial explanation. Disagreement on matters of statutory interpretation arose on the Court even among the non-textualist Justices. Indeed, neither Justice Ginsburg or Breyer has ever embraced textualism as their preferred approach to interpreting statutes. A large part of this disagreement arose from competing views of the Court's role in engaging Congress's vision of copyright as reflected in the statute and beyond. All the same, the disagreement masked a unified willingness among members of the Court to refrain from overtly engaging in the development of copyright policy.

Kirtsaeng v. John Wiley & Sons, Inc.[124] was the first substantive copyright matter decided by the Roberts Court. Decided the year after *Golan*, the case involved the first sale doctrine, which exempts the owner of a "lawfully made" copy to sell it without triggering the

---

[121] *See, e.g.*, 17 U.S.C. §§ 102(a), 107.

[122] *Id.* §§ 201(c), 106(4), 109(a).

[123] Id. §§ 301, 101.

[124] 568 U.S. 519 (2013).

distribution right or its subsidiary, the importation right.[125] Each of the three elements at issue was codified afresh by Congress in 1976: the first sale doctrine in § 109(a), the distribution right in § 106(3), and the importation right in § 602(a)(1). The controversy that triggered the case involved the interpretation of the phrase "lawfully made" in § 109(a), which one side interpreted as a geographic restriction and the other as a non-geographic one. In an opinion for the majority, Justice Breyer preferred the non-geographic interpretation. Interpreting the phrase using its language, context and "common law history," the majority concluded that Congress could not have intended a geographic reading of the term since it would have vitiated its own policy goals for copyright.[126]

In a scathing dissent, Justice Ginsburg saw the majority as doing anything but interpretating Congress's design. Describing the majority's position instead as a "stunning" and "bold departure from Congress' design," she chastised the opinion for substituting its own views on the first sale doctrine for Congress's in the name of interpretation.[127] After adopting a textual analysis of the statute, she then proceeded to undertake a detailed scrutiny of the provision's legislative history and the different treaty obligations that committed the U.S. to a geographic reading of the phrase.[128] Interestingly enough, Justice Ginsburg's dissent drew the support of Justices Kennedy and Scalia, with the latter joining the dissent except for its reliance on legislative history.[129]

What is interesting about the Breyer-Ginsburg disagreement in *Kirtsaeng* is less that they disagreed as such on the virtues of their respective substantive positions, with one (Breyer) preferring a narrowing of the copyright owner's rights and the other (Ginsburg) adopting a more expansive reading of those rights. It is instead that both opinions framed their disagreement as an *interpretive* one and enveloped it in

---

[125] 17 U.S.C. § 109(a).

[126] *Kirtsaeng I*, 568 U.S. at 530.

[127] *Id.* at 557 (Ginsburg, J., dissenting).

[128] *Id.* at 561–78.

[129] Which was in keeping with Justice Scalia's views on legislative history. *See* Antonin Scalia, A Matter of Interpretation: Federal Courts and the Law 35 (1997) (taking the position that legislative history is unconstitutional). For a critique, see Stuart Minor Benjamin & Kristen M. Renberg, *The Paradoxical Impact of Scalia's Campaign Against Legislative History*, 105 Cornell L. Rev. 1023 (2020); Margaret H. Lemos, *The Politics of Statutory Interpretation*, 89 Notre Dame L. Rev. 849 (2013).

the task of discerning Congress's presumed "intent" on the question. Both opinions therefore steadfastly adopted a "faithful agent" account of the Court's role in cases involving domain, even though their disagreement was substantive.[130] The very move to statutory interpretation for what was in effect a substantive disagreement over policy—the question of whether to adopt a domestic or international view of exhaustion (i.e., first sale)—highlights the institutionalism that had set in.

A similar interpretive division was to be seen the very next year in *American Broadcasting Cos. v. Aereo, Inc.*[131] The defendant in the case offered its subscribers broadcast television programming over the internet for a monthly fee. Its technology assigned each user an individual (dime-sized) antenna to pick up the appropriate broadcast signal based on the viewer's choice of programming and thereafter made a temporary copy of the content, which it streamed to the viewer. Each of these technological nuances (antenna, temporary copy) was designed to differentiate it from ordinary cable television operators.[132] Copyright owners whose content was transmitted to viewers through the platform commenced an action for infringement. The dispute centered on whether the defendant had engaged in a "public performance" in violation of the exclusive right to publicly perform the work that the statute grants copyright owners.[133]

In an opinion for a six-member majority of the Court, Justice Breyer found the defendant to have publicly performed the work. Much—if not all—of the Court's reasoning in interpreting the phrase "public performance" relied on the history behind Congress's inclusion of that

---

[130] *See, e.g.*, Amy Coney Barrett, *Substantive Canons and Faithful Agency*, 90 B.U. L. Rev. 109, 112 (2010) ("The view that federal courts function as the faithful agents of Congress is a conventional one . . . [and] disputes centered around how best to implement it."); Thomas W. Merrill, *Faithful Agent, Integrative, and Welfarist Interpretation*, 14 Lewis & Clark L. Rev. 1565, 1567–68 (2010) (noting the existence of "internal divisions" in this approach but recognizing that both textualists and intentionalists fall within this broad category); Richard H. Fallon, Jr., *The Statutory Interpretation Muddle*, 114 Nw. U. L. Rev. 269, 296 (2019) (observing how purposivists and intentionalists adhere to this general understanding of faithful agency).

[131] 573 U.S. 431 (2014).

[132] As the dissenting opinion in the Second Circuit put it, "the system is a Rube Goldberg-like contrivance, over-engineered in an attempt to avoid the reach of the Copyright Act and to take advantage of a perceived loophole in the law." WNET, Thirteen v. Aereo, Inc., 712 F.3d 676, 697 (2d Cir. 2013).

[133] *Aereo*, 573 U.S. at 437.

phrase in the statute.[134] In structuring the public performance right, Congress chose to overturn two pre-1976 decisions of the Court,[135] which had held that cable television operators did not engage in a public performance when they transmitted over-the-air broadcast content to their subscribers. To Justice Breyer, this history made amply clear that Congress intended to treat cable operators as themselves engaging in a public performance.[136] Since the defendant's activities were "substantially similar to those of [cable television] companies," the majority saw the public performance right reaching its service.[137] None of the individual technological differences that the defendant had built into its platform in order to differentiate itself from regular cable television—such as the assignment of an individual (rather than collective) antenna, the transmission of a privately made copy, and the absence of a constant transmission—were seen as material to its liability.

The majority's approach thus placed all of its interpretive emphasis on Congress's desire (as reflected in the legislative history) to treat cable television transmissions as public performances, from which it extrapolated to conclude that the defendant's services would have been within Congress's intention to cover. This approach prompted a dissent from Justice Scalia, which was joined by Justices Thomas and Alito.[138] As a substantive matter, the dissent contended that the defendant did not perform at all, since it did not satisfy the requirement of "volitional" conduct implicit in a public performance. The majority did not even so much as mention this requirement in its reasoning.

Justice Scalia's biggest problem with the majority's opinion was, however, its failure to offer a workable legal standard, instead using what he described as a "guilt by resemblance" approach to the issue.[139] That approach was hardly the product of an interpretive method, which he described as embodying "severe shortcomings" and resting

[134] *Id.* at 441–44.

[135] Fortnightly Corp. v. United Artists Television, Inc., 392 U.S. 390 (1968); Teleprompter Corp. v. Columbia Broadcasting System, Inc., 415 U.S. 394 (1974).

[136] *Aereo*, 573 U.S. at 441 (quoting the relevant legislative history in order to establish this proposition).

[137] *Id.* at 442.

[138] *Id.* at 451 (Scalia, J., dissenting).

[139] *Id.* at 457.

on "the shakiest of foundations."[140] While acknowledging that the defendant may have exploited loopholes in the statute, the dissent was clear that resemblance-based statutory interpretation was not the right mechanism of closing them, and certainly not one for the Court to adopt:

> [W]hat we have before us must be considered a "loophole" in the law. It is not the role of this Court to identify and plug loopholes. It is the role of good lawyers to identify and exploit them, and the role of Congress to eliminate them if it wishes. Congress can do that, I may add, in a much more targeted, better informed, and less disruptive fashion than the crude "looks-like-cable-TV" solution the Court invents today. . . . [T]he proper course is not to bend and twist the Act's terms in an effort to produce a just outcome, but to apply the law as it stands and leave to Congress the task of deciding whether the Copyright Act needs an upgrade.[141]

Noticeably absent from Justice Scalia's dissent was any reference to textualism, except for his observation that the majority's attempt to interpret the text of the statutory term "public performance" was a façade that falsely gave "the [majority] opinion the 'feel' of real textual analysis."[142] In short, what the dissenting opinion was objecting to was the majority's effort to create copyright policy ("just outcome") in the guise of interpreting statutory text.

Putting the dissent's criticisms to one side, the opinion for the Court is indeed characterized by an extreme intentionalist approach that it adopts to the interpretive question.[143] While Justice Breyer's interpretive philosophy had long relied on the use of legislative history to interpret statutes, that reliance has always been accompanied by an identifiable ambiguity in the text of the statute.[144] In his opinion for the Court in *Aereo*, Justice Breyer's approach was instead to reconstruct Congress's intention and directly ask if Congress would have wanted (i.e., intended) the defendant's technology to be

---

[140] *Id.* at 457–58.

[141] *Id.* at 462.

[142] *Id.* at 460.

[143] *See* William N. Eskridge Jr., *Dynamic Statutory Interpretation*, 135 U. Pa. L. Rev. 1479, 1479–80 (1987) (observing how the "'intentionalist' approach asks how the legislature originally intended the interpretive question to be answered, or would have intended the question to be answered had it thought about the issue when it passed the statute").

[144] *See* Stephen Breyer, *On the Uses of Legislative History in Interpreting Statutes*, 65 S. Cal. L. Rev. 845, 848 (1992) (describing how the use of legislative history assists in the interpretation of unclear statutory language and in the clarification of ambiguity).

treated as a public performance in the same way in which it addressed cable television. Note that this is materially different from asking if Congress's chosen conceptual or textual framework for instantiating its view of a public performance was sufficiently capacious to cover the defendant's operations. The latter would use the legislative history to examine the statute and then arrive at an answer on that basis. The former—as seen in the opinion—merely examined Congress's presumptive coverage of the matter in controversy, independent of the conceptual framework. The difference is thus between asking whether (i) the statutory definition of a public performance could be interpreted as covering internet re-transmissions, and if (ii) Congress would have wanted to cover internet re-transmissions, regardless of what it put into the statute.

The majority's effort to answer the latter accounts for its emphasis on the "similarity" between cable television and the defendant's online streaming. The dissent was perhaps right in observing that the majority opinion could have ended with its observation that "the many similarities between [the defendant] and cable companies, considered in light of Congress' basic purposes in amending the Copyright Act, convince us that this difference is not critical ... and that [the defendant] 'perform[s].'"[145] The discussion of the statute could have been mistaken for an afterthought since it was Congress's freestanding objective that formed the opinion's principal focus.

Aereo's overt intentionalism somewhat vividly showcased a further entrenchment of the institutionalist mindset in the Court's copyright jurisprudence. Not only was the Court to refrain from engaging questions of policy in the copyright arena or second-guess Congress's dictates in that domain, its task in adjudicating copyright cases was to search for a fit between the policy/purpose and the controversy at hand. While not altogether irrelevant, the framework of the statute was clearly of secondary importance in this task rather than an embodiment of operative principles. In this sense, the *Aereo* opinion was in reality less about statutory interpretation than it was about the legislature's intent on the question, pure and simple—and fit rather well with the Court's growing emphasis on institutionalism. Again, what should not be missed is the reality that both majority and dissenting opinions agreed that Congressional intent alone—not policy—needed

[145] *Aereo*, 573 U.S. at 444.

to be the basis of the Court's intervention. They simply disagreed on *how* that was to be gleaned. And while the majority left no doubt about its own view of the defendant's behavior, the dissent was equally clear that it shared the majority's position on the matter.[146] Yet to both, statutory interpretation was the only institutionally acceptable vehicle through which that was to be addressed.

Statutory interpretation emerged front and center again—with textualism now occupying the spotlight—in *Star Athletica LLC v. Varsity Brands, Inc.*,[147] a case involving the copyrightability of cheerleader uniform designs. The respondent in the case designed, made, and sold cheerleader uniforms and had obtained over two hundred copyright registrations for its designs, which consisted of combinations and arrangements of different lines, shapes, curves and colors.[148] When the petitioner copied several of these designs on its own uniforms and was sued for copyright infringement, it challenged the copyrightability of the respondent's designs under copyright's "useful article" doctrine. The useful article doctrine, contained in the copyright statute, provides that "the design of a useful article" is eligible for protection as a "pictorial, graphical, or sculptural work only if, and only to the extent that, such design incorporates pictorial, graphic, or sculptural features that can be identified separately from, and are capable of existing independently of, the utilitarian aspects of the article."[149]

The above-quoted definition had generated a significant amount of confusion and disagreement among lower courts, with each circuit effectively developing its own test for "separability," as the requirement's core principle came to be called. In its opinion reversing the district court's grant of summary judgment in favor of the petitioner, the Sixth Circuit had highlighted the nine different tests that courts around the country had come to employ in applying the principle.[150] The dissenting opinion ended by noting that "[i]t is apparent that either Congress or the Supreme Court (or both) must clarify copyright

---

[146] *Id.* at 462 (Scalia, J., dissenting) ("I share the Court's evident feeling that what [the defendant] is doing (or enabling to be done) to the [plaintiffs'] copyrighted programming ought not to be allowed.").

[147] 137 S. Ct. 1002 (2017).

[148] *Id.* at 1007.

[149] 17 U.S.C. § 101 (2020) (definition of a "pictorial, graphic, and sculptural work").

[150] Varsity Brands, Inc. v. Star Athletica, LLC, 799 F.3d 468, 484–85 (6th Cir. 2015).

law with respect to garment design . . . [since t]he law in this area is a mess and it has been for a long time."[151] The Court granted certiorari to review the matter.[152]

In another 6-3 opinion, the Court found for the respondent. The opinion for the majority was authored by Justice Thomas this time. Instead of engaging the myriad tests that had been developed for the principle, the extensive legislative history of the definition, or indeed the Copyright Office's own guidelines for the registrability of designs of useful articles, Justice Thomas's opinion presented the solution as a straightforward instance of statutory interpretation that abjured any engagement with copyright policy.[153] He thus announced at the outset that the opinion was "not a free-ranging search for the best copyright policy, but rather 'depends solely on statutory interpretation.' "[154] The clear meaning of the text was to dominate this analysis: "[w]e thus begin and end our inquiry with the text."[155]

The irony here is of course that it was that very same "clear meaning" of the text that had produced divergent interpretations among courts. Justice Thomas then proceeded to examine the wording of the statute and develop an overly simplistic two-stage inquiry that began by asking whether the design was capable of separate identification, and then proceeded to examine if it was capable of being "imagined apart from the useful article."[156] The test was tailor-made for the facts of the case, which allowed the majority to find the cheerleader designs capable of separation from the articles themselves since they could be transposed to a white background.

Justices Ginsburg and Breyer each wrote separate opinions in the case. Ginsburg's disagreed with the Court's reasoning, but concurred in its judgment.[157] Breyer's opinion on the other hand disagreed with the judgment even though it endorsed the Court's test, and was joined by Justice Kennedy.[158] Somewhat surprisingly though, neither opinion seriously challenged the Court's observation that the answer

[151] *Id.* at 496 (dissenting opinion).

[152] 136 S. Ct. 1823 (2016) (granting certiorari).

[153] *Star Athletica*, 137 S. Ct. at 1010.

[154] *Id.* (citations omitted).

[155] *Id.*

[156] *Id.* at 1010.

[157] *Id.* at 1018 (Ginsburg, J., concurring).

[158] *Id.* at 1030 (Breyer, J., dissenting).

to the problem was to be found in the text of the statute on its own. To be sure, neither separate opinion endorsed textualism either; Justice Breyer openly employed his intentionalist reliance on legislative history and Congressional intent to criticize the Court for failing to appreciate that "[c]ourts must respect [copyright's statutory] lines and not grant copyright protection where Congress has decided not to do so."[159]

Justice Thomas's opinion for the Court in *Star Athletica* set up his textualism as an alternative to a policy-based decision. In so doing, the latter was portrayed as an inappropriate exercise of the judicial function, while the former was firmly within it. The connection between textualism as a method of statutory interpretation and the institutional legitimacy of the judiciary is hardly new. One scholar has noted that "formalistic textualism urges the judge to zero in on statutory language, focusing on semantic context and downplaying policy concerns and practical consequences—the very concerns and consequences that tend to be of most interest to external observers."[160] Textualism was thus a direct mechanism of institutional legitimacy. Characterizing the text as plain and clear allowed the opinion to steer clear of a host of policy considerations that had plagued prior applications of the useful article doctrine, where courts had undoubtedly made new law by integrating such considerations into the framework of the statute. Not only did the Court refrain from engaging in such an exercise, but it also wiped the slate clean of all prior judge-made law in the area; thereby signaling to lower courts that the institutional role of the judiciary was to merely give effect to decisions put into the text of a statute by Congress.

In summary, the most obvious feature of the Roberts Court's substantive copyright decisions was the lengths to which the Justices' opinions went to treat their legal reasoning as an exercise in statutory interpretation and no more. Even when the Justices disagreed with each other, they routinely couched their criticism of each other's opinions as a disagreement about interpretation rather than as a substantive disagreement *tout court*. This in itself highlights the degree to which copyright adjudication had in the Roberts Court become little more than an exercise in statutory interpretation, a reality that is rarely

[159] *Id.* at 1034.

[160] Tara Leigh Grove, *Which Textualism?*, 134 Harv. L. Rev. 265, 303 (2020).

acknowledged. Congress, and not the Court, made copyright law; the Court was merely interpreting it as a faithful agent of Congress.

What is surprising is certainly not just the Court's near-unanimous retreat to its position as a faithful agent of Congress in the realm of copyright law.[161] It is also the stark contrast between this approach and the manner in which substantive copyright decisions were made in the Rehnquist Court, illustrated previously. Nothing about the statute had changed in the interim, and yet in the Roberts Court it produced an emphasis on interpretation and generated serious disagreement among members of the Court around that idea.

C. ADJECTIVALISM: HARMONIZING FEDERAL ADJUDICATION

Adjective law refers to "the remedial agencies and procedure by which rights are maintained, their invasion redressed, and the methods by which such results are accomplished in judicial tribunals."[162] Substantive law delineates rights and identifies actionable wrongdoing that interferes with those rights; adjective law on the other hand deals with the procedural and remedial rules through which those rights are vindicated and enforced. A hallmark of adjective law, generally speaking, is its trans-substantivity[163]: the rules and principles pertaining to the adjudication and enforcement of rights are rarely ever subject-area specific. This remains true of copyright law, where the general rules and procedures of federal litigation govern the manner in which infringement claims are commenced and adjudicated. Most of the remedies delineated in the copyright statute are themselves drawn from general equitable and common law principles seen in other areas of law.

This trans-substantivity of adjective law formed a key third element of the Roberts Court's institutionalism in its copyright cases. Half of the Roberts Court's copyright decisions focused on procedural and remedial questions in copyright law, which involved the interplay between copyright-specific rules and doctrines on the one hand, and broader principles that are universal to federal adjudication on the

---

[161] *See* sources cited in note 130.

[162] EDWIN E. BRYANT, THE LAW OF PLEADING UNDER THE CODES OF CIVIL PROCEDURE 1 (2d ed. 1899).

[163] *See* David Marcus, *Trans-Substantivity and the Processes of American Law*, 2013 B.Y.U. L. REV. 1190, 1190.

other.[164] And despite routinely involving the interpretation of the statute, an overwhelming majority (five out of six) of these cases were decided unanimously.[165] Their role in the Court's copyright jurisprudence is best viewed through the frame of its institutionalism.

Turning to copyright's adjectival component allowed the Court to avoid much of the substantive disagreement over copyright law and policy that had become obvious in its decisions, captured most vividly in the Breyer-Ginsburg disagreement but extending well beyond. As noted previously, while the substance of these disputes revolved around questions of copyright policy, in rhetoric and form they focused on statutory interpretation. Copyright's adjective law, by contrast, was an area that allowed the Court to develop greater consensus on copyright issues and speak in one voice. And a large part of its ability to do so emerged from the recognition that the issues therein focused less on engaging legislative copyright "policy" where the Court was growing increasingly wary of treading on Congress's domain, and more on the connection between copyright adjudication and other areas of federal litigation. This last feature diminished the significance of substantive copyright expertise (and related disagreement), which likely explains the heightened consensus that it generated among the Justices.

The Roberts Court's first foray into copyright law was an adjectival case pertaining to federal subject matter jurisdiction in copyright cases. In *Reed Elsevier, Inc. v. Muchnick*,[166] the Court examined whether § 411(a) of the copyright statute—which requires that a work be registered with the Copyright Office prior to bringing a claim for infringement[167]—was a limitation on courts' subject matter jurisdiction. Writing for a unanimous Court, Justice Thomas answered the question in the negative, drawing a distinction between

---

[164] Reed Elsevier Inc. v. Muchnick, 559 U.S. 154, 157 (2010); Petrella v. MGM, Inc., 572 U.S. 663, 667 (2014); Allen v. Cooper, 140 S. Ct. 994, 996 (2020); Fourth Estate Pub. Benefit Corp. v. Wall-Street.com, LLC, 139 S. Ct. 881, 884 (2019); Rimini Street Inc. v. Oracle USA, Inc., 139 S. Ct. 873, 874 (2019); Kirtsaeng v. John Wiley & Sons, Inc. (*Kirtsaeng II*), 136 S. Ct. 1979, 1981 (2016).

[165] Of the six, the one that was not unanimous was *Petrella*, 572 U.S. at 667.

[166] 559 U.S. 154 (2010).

[167] 17 U.S.C. § 411(a) ("[N]o civil action for infringement of the copyright in any United States work shall be instituted until preregistration or registration of the copyright claim has been made in accordance with this title.").

jurisdictional conditions and claim-processing rules.[168] For this distinction, he drew on the Court's precedent on jurisdictional limitations, which demanded that the section "clearly state[]" that a limitation is jurisdictional.[169] Applying it to § 411(a), Justice Thomas concluded that that provision was a mere claim-processing rule.

Especially noteworthy in the opinion was its abbreviated engagement with considerations specific to copyright law. Instead, it focused on assessing, extending and reconciling the Court's precedents relating to jurisdictional limits before applying them to copyright.[170] The rejection of copyright exceptionalism was thus an identifiable feature of the Court's opinion, and one that would be seen in many of the Roberts Court's adjectival copyright decisions. Indeed, this rejection allowed the Court to altogether sidestep considerations of "policy," which had been raised as a basis for treating the registration requirement as jurisdictional within copyright. Noting that it had rejected such considerations of policy in its jurisdictional precedents, the Court found the argument altogether unpersuasive.[171]

The Court adopted a similar approach to adjectival issues in two more recent copyright cases, each also decided unanimously: *Rimini Street, Inc. v. Oracle USA, Inc.*[172] and *Allen v. Cooper*.[173] *Rimini Street* examined the phrase "full costs" contained in § 505 of the Copyright Act, a provision that gives courts discretion to award a prevailing party litigation costs.[174] *Allen* involved the interaction between copyright and state sovereign immunity. In *Rimini Street*, Justice Kavanaugh openly rejected the idea of copyright exceptionalism in his analysis. His opinion for a unanimous Court instead adopted the position that the copyright statute was to be treated like the "more than 200 subject-specific federal statutes that explicitly authorize the award of costs to prevailing parties" absent a legislative directive to the contrary.[175] For those other statutes, the term "costs" meant the grounds specified in

---

[168] *Reed*, 559 U.S. at 160.

[169] *Id.* at 163 (quoting Arbaugh v. Y&H Corp., 546 U.S. 500, 502 (2006)).

[170] *Id.* at 167–69.

[171] *Id.* at 169 n.9.

[172] 139 S. Ct. 873 (2019).

[173] 140 S. Ct. 996 (2020).

[174] 17 U.S.C. § 505 (2020).

[175] *Rimini Street*, 139 S. Ct. at 877.

the general costs statute, which the Court extended in a straightforward manner to § 505 of the Copyright Act.

Allen on the other hand involved Congress's attempt to abrogate state sovereign immunity for infringement actions brought against states. In 1990 Congress passed the Copyright Remedy Clarification Act (CRCA), which introduced § 511(a) of the statute, specifying that states "shall not be immune, under the Eleventh Amendment [or] any other doctrine of sovereign immunity, from suit in Federal court."[176] In an infringement action brought by a private party against the state of North Carolina, the defendant argued that § 511(a) was unconstitutional under the Court's precedents specifying the conditions under which state sovereign immunity could be abrogated by Congress. The Court agreed. In a unanimous opinion authored by Justice Kagan, the Court found that its precedent controlled. Since Congress had failed to establish in the legislative record that the abrogation was congruent and proportional to the injury being prevented or remedied, the abrogation was found to exceed Congress's power.[177]

At first glance, *Allen* may seem hard to reconcile with the Court's opinions in *Eldred* and *Golan*. Whereas the latter two had refused to second-guess Congress, in *Allen* the Court readily declared §511(a) invalid. Yet *Allen* was qualitatively different and very much in keeping with the Court's institutionalism. Both *Eldred* and *Golan* had involved challenges to *substantive* copyright doctrine, which in turn were seen to embody crucial policy decisions made by Congress on the basis of its effort to balance competing interests. *Allen* on the other hand involved no substantive copyright policy of that kind. Indeed, the Court's precedent on permissible abrogations of state sovereign immunity based on Section 5 of the Fourteenth Amendment required the examination of whether such a policy concern was part of the legislative record that informed Congress's decision.[178] In *Allen* the Court found there to be no such record whatsoever—and thus by implication, no pressing policy concern that had motivated Congress.

---

[176] 17 U.S.C. § 511(a) (2020).

[177] *Allen*, 140 S. Ct. at 1004.

[178] *See* Fla. Prepaid Postsecondary Educ. Expense Bd. v. Coll. Sav. Bank, 527 U.S. 627, 629 (1999); City of Boerne v. Flores, 521 U.S. 507, 509 (1997).

Allen therefore involved no second-guessing of Congress's policy wisdom for copyright.[179]

Even if there was a discernible policy behind the abrogation of state sovereign immunity in copyright cases, the Court's move to general principles of federal litigation to decide the case was to ensure that its decision would not be seen as second-guessing Congress. It would instead highlight that the Court was constrained by what it had done on the same question elsewhere, since its slate was "anything but clean."[180] Justice Kagan's opinion therefore emphasized the continuity between copyright's attempted abrogation of state sovereign immunity and Congress's successful and unsuccessful efforts to do the same in other areas.[181] The rejection of copyright exceptionalism was thus an unmistakable thread through the opinion, borne out of the recognition that state sovereign immunity—much like issues of federal jurisdiction—transcended the specific subject matter at issue, and instead implicated broader considerations involving federalism. It is in this important sense that *Allen* is an adjectival opinion: it involved the Court's consideration of the structure of federal copyright adjudication. And given its role at the apex of the federal judiciary, applying and extending its own rules governing federal adjudication to copyright was seen as presenting no problems as such. Instead, to the extent that the Court would be perceived as the appropriate branch of government to safeguard the boundaries of federal litigation, its decision invalidating § 511(a) would instead be seen as buttressing its core institutional role. In this sense, *Allen*—much like *Rimini Street* and *Reed Elsevier*—represented the affirmative side of the Court's institutionalist approach. Affirmative in the sense of the Court's embrace of its role as gatekeeper of federal adjudication; rather than negative in the sense of its forbearance from addressing issues of substantive policy.

Not all the Roberts Court's adjectival copyright opinions exhibited the same approach. Yet, they strove hard to achieve consensus among the Court's members and routinely side-stepped copyright specific concerns. In *Fourth Estate Public Benefit Corp. v. Wall-Street.com*,[182]

---

[179] *Allen*, 140 S. Ct. at 1006.

[180] *Id.* at 1002.

[181] *Id.* (discussing the dissimilarity between bankruptcy law and intellectual property law for sovereign immunity).

[182] 139 S. Ct. 881 (2019).

Justice Ginsburg's opinion eschewed both pragmatic and policy considerations to instead focus on a textualist reading of the statute that hewed narrowly to its plain meaning. Even while acknowledging the significance of pragmatic considerations that might have urged an alternative interpretation, the opinion made clear that the problem under consideration (i.e., the backlog and consequent delays in the issuance of copyright registrations) was one that "courts cannot cure" by "revis[ing] . . . congressionally composed text."[183] The opinion was unanimous as a result, generating not even a separate concurrence from another Justice.

Focusing on copyright's adjectival component was of course no guarantee of unanimity, or of Justices Ginsburg and Breyer agreeing. In *Petrella v. MGM, Inc.*[184] the Court examined whether the equitable defense of laches could be invoked by a defendant in response to a claim for copyright infringement that was brought within the statute's period of limitation. Writing for a six-member majority, Justice Ginsburg found that laches could not be used to override the statutory period of limitations, placing reliance on the Court's jurisprudence around equitable remedies and the "province of laches."[185] In a dissenting opinion on behalf of three Justices, Justice Breyer disagreed. In essence, the dissent's objection was that the majority was not rejecting copyright exceptionalism enough, in failing to examine "the rules and practice of modern litigation."[186] His worry was therefore that the rejection of laches would result in inequities between copyright plaintiffs and defendants, and as a result situate copyright defendants differently from their counterparts in other areas.

Quite noticeably, the Breyer-Ginsburg disagreement in *Petrella* was structured around the form and extent of the other's rejection of copyright exceptionalism rather than on an interpretation of the statute as such, a clear departure from the domain of substantive copyright. The majority based its reasoning on the Court's prior jurisprudence relating to the law/equity distinction and the nature of federal litigation, which to the dissent was inadequate.[187] Submerged under the rhetoric about the nature of modern litigation was a straightforward

[183] *Id.* at 892.

[184] 572 U.S. 663 (2014).

[185] *Id.* at 668.

[186] *Id.* at 699 (Breyer, J., dissenting).

[187] *Id.* at 677–80.

disagreement over policy: the majority position advantaged copyright plaintiffs, i.e., copyright owners, who would now no longer face the risk of having their lawsuit summarily dismissed if they waited for too long but were within the statute of limitations. To Justice Breyer, a self-described copyright skeptic, this was problematic. Yet that disagreement remained buried underneath arguments about copyright's continuity/discontinuity with other areas.

Overwhelmingly, the Roberts Court's copyright adjectivalism has remained an important mechanism for the Court to safeguard and promote its institutional legitimacy in the field. The Court's willingness to actively intervene in this domain and develop a set of rules and principles that are hardly unique to copyright and instead emphasize the continuity between copyright and other areas of law was at once symbolic, cohesive, and outwardly principled. Symbolic in the sense of publicly reaffirming the Court's role as the guardian of the federal litigation process, cohesive since it generated consensus among the Justices about harmonizing copyright litigation with the rest of federal adjudication, and principled in that it was seemingly driven by well-worn ideas and norms that had long informed other areas of litigation or remedies.

* * *

Institutionalism in the Roberts Court's copyright opinions thus had both limiting and enabling elements to it, with the former dominating. The emphasis on appropriate judicial role and the Court's role as faithful agent in interpreting the copyright statute were meant to constrain the Court in its engagement with substantive copyright policy, which came to be seen as the exclusive prerogative of Congress to formulate and develop. At the same time, maintaining the continuity between copyright adjudication and other areas of federal litigation carved out an important domain for the Court to exert its own independent influence over, so as to not be seen as abdicating its role within the copyright system altogether.

The question that deserves asking, however, is whether the Court's turn to institutionalism ought to be understood as little more than a proxy for other deeper and arguably more substantive disagreements among the Justices. Hints of this concern were to be seen in some of the Justices' own criticisms of each other as using interpretation as a mask for a policy preference. Consider in this vein: Justice Ginsburg's observation that the majority in *Kirtsaeng* was departing from the legislature's design in the name of interpretation in order to adopt an international approach to first sale,[188] or Justice Scalia's assertion that the majority in *Aereo* was "distort[ing] the Copyright Act" in order to remedy the apparent wrongfulness of the defendant's technology.[189] Seen through a traditional Legal Realist lens, these observations suggest that the Justices are on occasion themselves less than convinced that another's reliance on institutional considerations was in reality not in furtherance of a substantive outcome.

A more nuanced way of understanding the concern, however, sees the fault line a little differently. Legal Process thinking—with its commitment to institutional settlement—"absorb[ed] and temper[ed] the insights of Legal Realism,"[190] and in so doing saw courts as the gatekeepers of reason engaged in the "reasoned elaboration" of law.[191] Interpretation of the statute was thus in equal measure about recognizing the primacy of congressional policy and channeling it in a principled manner through the use of reason. Viewed through this lens, the disagreements were less about the possibility of motivated reasoning (or "rationalization" as Legal Realists called it[192]) and more about the appropriate balance between policy deference and its reasoned elaboration. In short, they were disagreements about ways in which to give effect to institutionalism, the value of which was taken for granted.

III. Institutionalism Triumphant

The Court's turn toward institutionalism played a decisive role in its most recent copyright decision, characterized by some as "the copyright case of the century"[193]: *Google, LLC v. Oracle, Inc.*[194] A

[188] Kirtsaeng v. John Wiley & Sons, Inc. (*Kirtsaeng I*), 568 U.S. 519, 556 (2013) (Ginsburg, J., dissenting).

[189] American Broadcast Cos., Inc. v. Aereo, Inc., 573 U.S. 431, 462 (2014) (Scalia, J., dissenting).

[190] Morton J. Horwitz, The Transformation of American Law 1870–1960: The Crisis of Legal Orthodoxy 254 (1992).

[191] Henry M. Hart, Jr. & Albert M. Sacks, The Legal Process: Basic Problems in the Making and Application of Law 147 (1994).

[192] Laura Kalman, Legal Realism at Yale: 1927–1960, at 6–7 (1986).

[193] *See* Scott Graham, *Supreme Court, Finally, Takes Up 'Google v. Oracle'*, Law.com (Nov. 15, 2019), https://www.law.com/nationallawjournal/2019/11/15/supreme-court-finally-takes-up-google-v-oracle/; Devin Dwyer, *Google Wins Big in Supreme Court Clash with Oracle*, ABC News (Apr. 5, 2021), https://abcnews.go.com/Politics/google-wins-big-supreme-court-clash-oracle/story?id=76878814.

[194] 141 S. Ct. 1183 (2021).

plain reading of that much-anticipated opinion and its reasoning hides the complex institutional motivations that were at play in the decision. Yet when understood contextually and against the backdrop of the doctrinal maneuvering that produced it, *Google* highlights the extent to which the Roberts Court has internalized—and normalized—its institutionalism.

The rather complex facts of the case involved Google's copying of computer code that had been written and organized by Sun (which Oracle acquired) into pre-written packages (called "APIs") contained in its Java library.[195] The copying was however not of the packages in their entirety but instead merely portions of the packages that described their individual functions—known as the "declaring code."[196] When sued for copyright infringement, Google argued that the declaring code was uncopyrightable as a "method of operation," a category that Congress had identified as ineligible for protection in § 102(b) of the statute.[197] Google also argued that its copying constituted a form of fair use since it was copying the code to allow programmers familiar with Java to carry their knowledge-base with them to its new platform. While Google had prevailed at the district court on both arguments (each on a separate occasion), the Federal Circuit had reversed the district court each time.[198] The Court agreed to hear the case, despite the Solicitor General suggesting otherwise.[199]

In a 6-2 split, the Court sided with Google. In his opinion for the majority, Justice Breyer sidestepped the issue of copyrightability and concluded that Google's copying amounted to a fair use of the work. In a far-reaching expansion of the fair use doctrine, his opinion concluded that the use was transformative since it was done to ensure that

[195] *Id.* at 1191.

[196] *Id.* at 1192.

[197] 17 U.S.C. § 102(b) (2020) ("In no case does copyright protection for an original work of authorship extend to any idea, procedure, process, system, method of operation, concept, principle, or discovery, regardless of the form in which it is described, explained, illustrated, or embodied in such work.").

[198] Oracle Am., Inc. v. Google Inc., 872 F. Supp. 2d 974 (N.D. Cal. 2012); Oracle Am., Inc. v. Google Inc., No. C 10-03561 WHA, 2016 WL 5393938 (N.D. Cal. Sept. 27, 2016); Oracle Am., Inc. v. Google LLC, 750 F.3d 1339 (Fed. Cir. 2014); Oracle Am., Inc. v. Google LLC, 886 F.3d 1179 (Fed. Cir. 2018).

[199] Brief for the United States as Amicus Curiae, Google LLC v. Oracle Am., Inc., No. 18-956, 2019 WL 4750021 (U.S. Sept. 27, 2019); Google LLC v. Oracle Am., Inc., 140 S. Ct. 520 (2019) (mem.) (granting certiorari).

Google's code was interoperable with Oracle's Java platform,[200] that the fair use doctrine allowed courts to draw distinctions between different types of computer code,[201] and further that fair use required courts to examine the potential public benefits of the copying as part of the calculus.[202] On its own, the majority opinion broke new ground on fair use and its application to computer software, by effectively incorporating considerations normally associated with copyrightability into the fair use analysis. Yet what is even more far-reaching, even if entirely hidden, was the reason for the majority's reliance on fair use for its result.

At the time of oral argument, the Court was down to eight Justices: Justice Ginsburg had died the month before and her seat remained vacant.[203] During its argument, Google led with the issue of copyrightability and attempted to convince the Court that declaring code was fundamentally different from other types of code so as to render it ineligible for copyright protection under § 102(b).[204] This prompted a series of skeptical questions from several members of the Court, all of which focused on the undeniable reality that in expressly allowing for computer code to be protected, Congress had made no distinction between different types of code.[205] To recognize such a distinction would put all computer code "at risk of losing protection" under the statute and thus override Congress's "express intent."[206] Justice Gorsuch voiced the concern best when he noted his discomfort with overriding Congress's textual directive: "[w]e might not think otherwise that it should be [protected], but there it is."[207]

---

[200] *Google*, 141 S. Ct. at 1203–04.

[201] *Id.* at 1201–02.

[202] *Id.* at 1206–08.

[203] Transcript of Oral Argument at *3, *Google*, 141 S. Ct. 1183 (No. 18-956), 2020 WL 6203589.

[204] *Id.* at *3–5.

[205] *Id.* at *10 ("[Y]ou seem to rely quite a bit on Section 102. Why don't we rely on Section 101, which is more specific with respect to computer programs?") (Thomas, J.); *id.* at *17 ("How do you square your position with Congress's express intent to provide protection for computer codes?") (Alito, J.); *id.* at *20 ("I go back to the essence of the question that I think my colleagues are asking, is how do you differentiate between declaring codes and implementing codes?") (Sotomayor, J.); *id.* at *29–30 ("We might not think otherwise that it should be, but there it is. And, normally, … the specific instruction there in 101 would govern the more general idea-expression dichotomy in 102.") (Gorsuch, J.).

[206] *Id.* at *17.

[207] *Id.* at *29.

Playing into the textualist concern with overriding the language of the statute, Google's lawyer continued to describe the copyrightability claim as a "textualist" one.[208] The issue of copyrightability—emanating from § 102(b) of the statute—was anything but textual. While the provision identifies "methods of operation" as unprotectable, it says nothing further at all about what such methods are and how courts are meant to identify them. The legislative history accompanying the provision confirms that Congress intended to do no more than "re-state" judge-made law on the provision "unchanged."[209] Further, Congress saw this as perfectly compatible with the availability of protection for computer software. § 102(b) was instead meant to itself be the vehicle *through which* courts were to sift through the protectable and unprotectable parts of computer code. It put the point unequivocally: "Section 102(b) is intended, among other things, to make clear that the expression adopted by the programmer is the copyrightable element in a computer program, and that the actual processes and methods embodied in the program are not within the scope of the copyright law."[210]

Congress therefore fully intended there to be absolutely no textual inconsistency between the denial of protection to certain kinds/components of computer software under § 102(b) and its express recognition that computer software was eligible for protection under the statute. To the contrary, balancing the two was something that it expressly outsourced to courts in almost the exact same manner in which it did with the requirement of originality. But whereas the Court in *Feist* had embraced that outsourcing to expound on the doctrine,[211] the Court in *Google* saw the delegation as controversial since it effectively required reconciling judicial line-drawing under § 102(b) with an express textual directive in § 101. It mattered little that Congress was fine with this reconciliation. To several members of the Court, this was not acceptable.

Given the exaggerated textualist concern—which many Justices made obvious during oral argument—Justice Breyer's compromise was

---

[208] *Id.* at *17, *26, *38.

[209] H.R. Rep. 94-1476, at 57 (1974).

[210] *Id.*

[211] Feist Publ'ns, Inc. v. Rural Telephone Serv. Co., 499 U.S. 340, 355 (1991) (quoting the legislative history indicating that Congress had chosen to avoid defining originality in order to "incorporate without change" the judge-made law around it).

to avoid the question of copyrightability altogether under the pretext of doing no more than was "necessary to resolve the parties' dispute."[212] All the same, that avoidance was largely formal. While refraining from addressing the line-drawing and balancing that § 102(b) called for, the majority instead focused on fair use. The fair use doctrine has long been seen by the Court—and Congress—as a judge-made doctrine; and one where courts are at liberty to develop the law in incremental, common law style.[213] The Court's own unanimous 1994 opinion in *Campbell v. Acuff-Rose Music, Inc.* had endorsed such an approach and generated much jurisprudence among lower courts around the doctrine.[214] The majority however did not just invoke fair use. It instead invoked fair use and expanded it to incorporate the exact same concerns that it had dodged under §102(b).[215] The line-drawing that several Justices were so worried about was now no longer problematic, given that it presented no *textual* conflict whatsoever. In thus moving the conversation—in substance even if not in form—from copyrightability to fair use, Justice Breyer's opinion effectively blunted concerns about textualism and the fear of overriding Congress.

Justice Breyer's compromise was insufficient for Justice Thomas, whose dissent voiced the textualist concern. Emphasizing the centrality of copyrightability, the dissent repeatedly asserted that "Congress rejected any categorical distinction" between types of computer code. It recognized the majority's clever ploy in turning to fair use, noting despondently that the majority had invoked fair use to "remove copyright protection from declaring code" contrary to Congress's

---

[212] *Google*, 141 S. Ct. at 1197.

[213] *Id.* at 1197. The fair use doctrine was entirely a creation of courts in the nineteenth century. *See* Folsom v. Marsh, 9 F. Cas. 342 (C.C.D. Mass. 1841). It found no mention under prior copyright statutes. Congress eventually codified the doctrine in the Act of 1976. 17 U.S.C. § 107 (2020). Yet, it made clear that the codification was a mere restatement and that courts were to continue developing it further:

> The bill endorses the purpose and general scope of the judicial doctrine of fair use, but there is no disposition to freeze the doctrine in the statute, especially during a period of rapid technological change. Beyond a very broad statutory explanation of what fair use is and some of the criteria applicable to it, *the courts must be free to adapt the doctrine to particular situations on a case-by-case basis.* Section 107 is intended to restate the present judicial doctrine of fair use, not to change, narrow, or enlarge it in any way.

H.R. Rep. 94-1476, at 66 (emphasis added).

[214] 510 U.S. 569, 576 (1994).

[215] *Google*, 141 S. Ct. at 1201–02.

intention.[216] To Justice Thomas, "[t]he majority ha[d] used fair use to eviscerate Congress' considered policy judgement."[217] The majority was doing indirectly what it would not directly.

In one sense, Justice Breyer's strategy certainly succeeded in *Google* and enabled him to reintroduce considerations of copyrightability into fair use, thereby preserving the line-drawing between idea and expression demanded by the law. All the same, his very reliance on this strategy to achieve a majority represents something of a complete capitulation to the extreme institutionalist concerns about the judicial role in copyright, manifested in textualism and beyond. In strong contrast to his opinions in *Kirtsaeng* and *Aereo*, Justice Breyer's opinion in *Google* retreated altogether from any effort to interpret the statute (i.e., § 102(b)) for fear of losing the majority. Reframing the question as one of fair use was not without its costs, since fair use resists bright-line rules and emphasizes contextual rulings that are specific to a particular defendant's use.[218]

The coalition of textualist and non-textualist Justices that constituted the majority in *Google* thus rallied around fair use as the answer to the dispute. And while this certainly reinvigorated the role of fair use in copyright adjudication and of courts within that framework, it at the same time reaffirmed rather starkly the centrality of institutional concerns to the Court. Steering clear of Congress's "policy judgement[s]" was not just a hallmark of its interpretive approach, but it now influenced the Court's very framing and doctrinal choices. In *Google*, Justice Breyer conceivably failed to convince his colleagues that any line-drawing around copyrightability under § 102(b) was not an exercise in policy-making, forcing him to retreat to the defense of fair use where such line drawing was less of a "policy" choice, since fair use is very fact-specific and situational.

Google therefore highlights the Roberts Court's entrenched copyright institutionalism. Refraining from "policy" engagement has long been a highlight of such institutionalism. *Google* reveals the reach of this credo. The Court's disengagement with policy was not just about its refusal to "second-guess" Congress's judgements, it was instead

---

[216] *Id.* at 1213 (Thomas, J., dissenting).

[217] *Id.* at 1220.

[218] In his opinion for the Court in *Kirtsaeng I*, Justice Breyer considered the fair use defense insufficient, whereas the dissent thought that many of the problems identified by the majority could be solved by fair use. Kirtsaeng v. John Wiley & Sons, Inc. (*Kirtsaeng I*), 133 S. Ct. 1351, 1364 (2013); *id.* at 1389 (Ginsburg, J., dissenting).

about the Court's unwillingness to exercise its own judgement in domains where such judgement might be conflated with policy and thus undermine the Court's institutional legitimacy.[219]

IV. Institutionalism and Copyright's Legitimacy Crisis

The Roberts Court's copyright jurisprudence is characterized by two prominent features. The first is the complete absence of unanimity among the Justices of the Court on questions of substantive copyright law;[220] and the second is the Court's increased engagement with adjectival copyright questions that implicate non-copyright principles and where it is by contrast able to generate a significant amount of unanimity, albeit artificially.[221] The two are hardly unrelated: the lack of unanimity on substantive questions is in stark contrast to the almost complete unanimity on adjectival ones, making the Roberts Court's overall engagement with copyright—at least facially—appear less fractured than it actually is. It is therefore plausible to assume that the Court's willingness to address non-core copyright questions was motivated in large measure by its inability to speak univocally on substantive copyright law.

The unanswered question is whether the manner of the Court's engagement with copyright has aided or hurt its legitimacy, the principal impulse behind the institutionalist turn. An overly simplistic analysis of the question in terms of the Court's unanimity overlooks the manner in which the two features described above have reaffirmed each other to enable the Court to steer clear of the heavily polarized "copyright wars." While it is true that the Roberts Court's turn to institutionalism on substantive copyright failed to generate greater consensus among the Justices, it nevertheless succeeded in firmly entrenching the idea that the Court was but a faithful agent of Congress in the domain of copyright law and thus obligated to ensure that its decisions did not directly or indirectly interfere with questions of "policy" where Congress was supreme. Even when disagreeing over their interpretation of the statute, the Justices uniformly committed to disengaging from the creation of copyright policy in what was a

[219] *See* David E. Pozen & Adam M. Samaha, *Anti-Modalities*, 119 Mich. L. Rev. 729, 747 (2021).

[220] Of the six substantive copyright decisions decided, *none* was unanimous.

[221] Of the six adjectival copyright decisions decided by the Roberts Court, five were unanimous, a remarkable difference from the Court's substantive copyright docket.

significant break even from the approach of the Rehnquist Court.[222] While the Court's turn to adjectival issues may have produced greater agreement on the Court, it too reaffirmed the Court's commitment to steering clear of copyright-specific policy considerations, given that procedural and remedial issues rarely embraced such specificity and instead drew on general principles. Avoidance of copyright policy thus formed a common theme in the Roberts Court's copyright docket: both in the Justices' individual interpretive approaches, as well as in their collective choice of issues to address.

While the avoidance of policy may have sounded primarily in the ideal of separation of powers, it also embodied a copyright-specific rationality that is easy to overlook. Since the beginning of the twenty-first century, U.S. copyright law has suffered from a readily discernible legitimacy crisis. The copyright system has come to be seen as little more than a mechanism of rent-seeking for special interest groups, rent-seeking that is structured as controlling the public's access to—and use of—original expression.[223] While scholars disagree over the precise origins of and cause for this legitimacy crisis, the existence of such a crisis is uniformly acknowledged.[224] The emergence of new technologies—of both copying and control—has only contributed to this crisis, with formal law coming to be seen as but one tool that creators and users could deploy in service of their goals.

Unwittingly, federal courts have contributed to this legitimacy crisis. As the copyright landscape became increasingly polarized, courts across the country handed down decisions that seemingly supported the

---

[222] The Roberts Court's disavowal of "policy" in its opinions—both majority and dissents—is particularly noteworthy. *See* Golan v. Holder, 565 U.S. 302, 334–35 (2012) (identifying "the host of policy and logistical questions" rendering the "matter [in]appropriate for judicial, as opposed to legislative, resolution); *Kirtsaeng I*, 133 S. Ct. at 1373 (noting the majority's departure from Congress's "aim" and "design") (Ginsburg, J., dissenting); Star Athletica, LLC v. Varsity Brands, Inc., 137 S. Ct. 1002, 1010 (2017) ("This is not a free-ranging search for the best copyright policy."); Georgia v. Public.Resource.Org, Inc. (*PRO*), 140 S. Ct. 1498, 1511 (2020) ("That appeal to copyright policy . . . is addressed to the wrong forum."); *Google*, 141 S. Ct. at 1220 ("The majority has used fair use to eviscerate Congress' considered policy judgment.") (Thomas, J., dissenting).

[223] *See, e.g.*, Neil W. Netanel, Copyright's Paradox 140 (2008); Michele Boldrin & David K. Levine, Against Intellectual Monopoly (2010).

[224] *See* Jane C. Ginsburg, *How Copyright Got a Bad Name for Itself*, 26 Colum. J.L. & Arts 61, 61 (2002) ("I have a theory about how copyright got a bad name for itself; and I can summarize it in one word: Greed."); Jessica Litman, *Real Copyright Reform*, 96 Iowa L. Rev. 15–16 (2010) ("Copyright law's legitimacy has suffered marked erosion in the public's view."); Paul Edward Gellar, *Beyond the Copyright Crisis: Principles for Change*, 55 J. Copyright Soc'y 165, 175 (2008).

position of one interest group (including the public) over others.[225] If one group succeeded in obtaining an expansive interpretation of an enumerated exclusive right, another would try and ensure a broad reading of fair use or of the first sale defense to counteract that. And with courts only ever focusing on the individual case (and connected precedents) each time, they developed a form of tunnel vision that precluded them from seeing their contributory role in the broader saga.

A prime example of a federal court's entanglement was the Second Circuit's 2001 decision in *Universal City Studios, Inc. v. Corley*.[226] The case involved the application of § 1201 of the copyright statute, which deals with digital protection measures relied on by copyright owners to protect their works from copying.[227] The provision was introduced in 1998 through the Digital Millennium Copyright Act (DMCA), and among other things, it renders both the circumvention of such digital protection measures and the trafficking in technologies of circumvention independently actionable.[228] The defendant in the case had distributed an anti-circumvention code publicly (known as the DeCSS), but when sued under § 1201 relied on a host of arguments including the unconstitutional nature of the provision as well as the fair use doctrine as an embodiment of the First Amendment.[229]

The case generated an immense amount of interest and news coverage and came to be seen as something of a bellwether in a polarized copyright landscape.[230] Numerous academics, industry groups and public interest entities filed amicus briefs before the court. In finding against the defendant, the Second Circuit undertook an elaborate analysis of the DMCA, its underlying goals, and their connection to

---

[225] *See, e.g.*, Chamberlain Grp., Inc. v. Skylink Tech., Inc., 381 F.3d 1178 (Fed. Cir. 2004); MGM Studios, Inc. v. Grokster, Ltd., 380 F.3d 1154 (9th Cir. 2004); A&M Records, Inc. v. Napster, Inc., 239 F.3d 1004 (9th Cir. 2001); RIAA v. Diamond Multimedia Sys., Inc., 180 F.3d 1072 (9th Cir. 1999); Kelly v. Arriva Soft Corp., 280 F.3d 934 (9th Cir. 2002); Video Pipeline, Inc. v. Buena Vista Home Ent., Inc., 342 F.3d 191 (3d Cir. 2003).

[226] 273 F.3d 429 (2d Cir. 2001).

[227] 17 U.S.C. § 1201(a) (2020).

[228] *Id.* §§ 1201(a)(1)(A)-(a)(2).

[229] *Corley*, 273 F. 3d at 436.

[230] *See* Dow Jones, *Hollywood Studios Join Legal Battle to Stop DVD Copying*, N.Y. Times (Jan. 15, 2000), https://archive.nytimes.com/www.nytimes.com/library/tech/00/01/biztech/articles/15disc.html; *Movie Studios File DVD Hack Suit*, Wired (Jan. 14, 2000), https://www.wired.com/2000/01/movie-studios-file-dvd-hack-suit; John Leyden, *2600 Withdraws Supreme Court Appeal in DeCSS Case*, Register (July 4, 2002), https://www.theregister.com/2002/07/04/2600_withdraws_supreme_court_appeal.

the Constitution. Despite purporting to adopt an "evolutionary" and "narrow" approach to the broader questions so as to allow future courts to develop the law incrementally,[231] the court's actual opinion did far more, including making far-reaching observations about the connection between fair use and the Constitution and the overall scope of fair use under the DMCA: "[f]air use has never been held to be a guarantee of access to copyrighted material in order to copy it by the fair user's preferred technique or in the format of the original."[232] That observation was hardly minimalist.

Compounding the court's inability to avoid wading into the polarized copyright landscape was the reality that its holding was ineffective. Despite its issuance of an injunction, the anti-circumvention technology that was at issue in the case continued to be made available by various websites and defendants online, and in significant numbers even after the decision. The practice came to be seen as a form of political protest—against the decision in *Corley*, the DMCA, and the entire U.S. copyright system.[233]

Operating within this polarized landscape, the Court's turn toward institutionalism has thus preserved not just its overall institutional legitimacy, but also its domain-specific legitimacy, i.e., within the copyright system. Discussions of legitimacy tend to focus on either institutional (court-specific) or system-wide legitimacy, often overlooking how the Court's cautionary approach to a particular legal area with its own legitimacy crisis allows the Court to put some distance between its legitimacy concerns and those of the area under consideration. Instead of entangling questions of its own public legitimacy with public perceptions of copyright, the Roberts Court's effort is to situate itself as a faithful agent merely executing Congress's vision ("policy") for the area. To the degree that a particular outcome could be seen as problematic, the fault—in this narrative—would lie with Congress, rather than the Court.[234]

---

[231] *Corley*, 273 F.3d at 445.

[232] *Id.* at 459.

[233] *See* Kristin R. Eschenfelder & Anuj C. Desai, *Software as Protest: The Unexpected Resiliency of US-Based DeCSS Posting and Linking*, 20 Info Soc'y 101 (2002).

[234] *See, e.g.*, American Broadcast Cos., Inc. v. Aereo, Inc., 573 U.S. 431, 451 (2014) ("[T]o the extent commercial actors or other interested entities may be concerned with the relationship between the development and use of such technologies and the Copyright Act, they are of course free to seek action from Congress."); Georgia v. Public.Resource.Org, Inc., 140 S. Ct. 1498, 1510 (2020) ("[C]ritics of our ruling can take their objections across the street, [where] Congress can correct any mistakes it sees." (citations and quotation marks omitted)).

Assessing the Court's institutionalist turn in copyright against this metric presents a more complicated picture. On the one hand, the Court has undoubtedly succeeded in avoiding some of modern copyright's most vexing questions, both by refraining from hearing such cases and by deciding the few that it takes through non-policy approaches. Each of its interpretive decisions has been sufficiently narrow in scope: whether it be the Court's plain meaning textualism in *Star Athletica*,[235] or its overt technological intentionalism in *Aereo*.[236] Indeed, it is this narrowness that has fueled the criticism that the Court's copyright opinions do little more than decide the specifics of the case rather than clarify the law.[237] The Roberts Court has therefore maintained a sufficient level of distance from the polarizing copyright wars, such that the Court's own institutional legitimacy is hardly seen as impacted by its copyright jurisprudence.

At the same time, the Court's restraint has not been altogether costless. While refraining from addressing substantive questions of copyright policy in its decision-making, the Court's retreat to an institutionalist methodology has revealed an independent set of fault lines among the Justices, who now disagree over the Court's precise mechanisms of policy avoidance in copyright law. In the process, it has introduced an altogether new set of divergences into the copyright landscape, ones that had never existed before. These new methodological divergences draw on public law disagreements among the Court's members and thus assume an overt political dimension.[238]

In short then, while the Roberts Court's institutionalist turn in its copyright jurisprudence may have immunized the Court from debates about copyright's own public legitimacy, it has significantly complicated those debates. Disagreements at the Court over copyright's core doctrines are as a result no longer substantive and driven by the competing normative considerations underlying copyright; they are instead premised on divergent views of law-making and statutory interpretation in copyright.

The Court's decision in *Google* captures this very dynamic and will in the coming years test the effect of the Court's institutionalist turn

[235] Star Athletica LLC v. Varsity Brands, Inc., 137 S. Ct. 1002 (2017).

[236] *Aereo*, 134 S. Ct. at 2511.

[237] *See* Shyamkrishna Balganesh, *Foreword: Clarifying the "Clear Meaning" of Separability*, 166 U. Pa. L. Rev. 79, 82 (2017).

[238] *See* Nina A. Mendelson, *Change, Creation, and Unpredictability in Statutory Interpretation: Interpretive Canon Use in the Roberts Court's First Decade*, 117 Mich. L. Rev. 71 (2018).

on copyright's public legitimacy. In implicitly accepting the view that the copyrightability of computer software was a domain where Congress had spoken and the Court was therefore limited in its ability to interfere, the Court certainly refrained from engaging questions of "policy." All the same, its overt effort to reintroduce those considerations into fair use where Congress had empowered courts to be generative, showcased the Court's creative ability to lace its institutionalism with the malleability of copyright doctrine. *Google* will therefore be seen as either having confirmed the Court's inability to engage in any line-drawing judgments that implicate statutory copyright rules, or as revealing the subversive fecundity of fair use. Either way, the debate about copyright's legitimacy is certain to assume new vigor and the Court's institutionalism will be an integral part of it.

V. Conclusion

In the Roberts Court, copyright law has emerged as an important arena for the Court's emphasis on its institutional legitimacy. This has manifested itself in the Court's near-complete disengagement from issues of substantive copyright policy, both interpretively and in its selection of copyright cases to decide. The singular hallmark of the Roberts Court's approach to copyright law has been its inability to develop an appropriate equilibrium for its role within the copyright system.

To be sure, over the course of history, the nature and form of the Court's engagement with copyright law has indeed varied. During the nineteenth century, the Court freely developed an independent federal common law of copyright, which was seen as having an unproblematic existence alongside the statute.[239] In the first half of the twentieth century, this trend mostly continued except that the Court's opinions justified their lawmaking through the barebones (and undeveloped) nature of the copyright statute.[240] In the second half of the century, the Court's engagement with copyright became significantly more technocratic, with the advent of new technologies and the empowerment

[239] *See, e.g.*, Banks v. Manchester, 128 U.S. 244 (1888); Burrow-Giles Lithographic Co. v. Sarony, 111 U.S. 53 (1884); Wheaton v. Peters, 33 U.S. 591 (8 Pet.) (1834).

[240] *See, e.g.*, Fox Film Corp. v. Doyal, 286 U.S. 123 (1932); Herbert v. Shanley Co., 242 U.S. 591 (1917); Fox Film Corp. v. Knowles, 261 U.S. 326 (1923); Buck v. Jewell-LaSalle Realty Co., 283 U.S. 191 (1931).

of the Copyright Office as an agency with subject-matter expertise.[241] The 1976 Act only exacerbated this modality of engagement, given its detailed nature. Yet here too, the Court succeeded in carving out a legitimate space for itself within the copyright system.

What is crucial to appreciate is that the Act of 1976 did very little on its own to alter the nature of the Court's engagement with the subject. Neither the Burger nor Rehnquist Courts treated the Act's comprehensiveness or level of detail as requiring a significant alteration in their approach to interpreting, applying, and supplementing the statute.[242] To the contrary, some of the Court's most far-reaching doctrinal modifications emerged after the enactment of the 1976 Act. It was only in the Roberts Court, a full three decades later, that Congress's structural machinations in the statute have commanded heightened respect.

The irony of such deference emerging after an extended time period is further compounded by a more obvious reality: the Court's extreme institutionalism has left it unclear about its place in the legal landscape of copyright. Even if it is a faithful agent of Congress tasked with interpreting the legislature's statutory intentions, the Court has been unable to converge around the scope and contours of that agency. While it is one thing to avoid upsetting statutorily delineated copyright policy, it is quite another to refrain from deciding an issue when Congress delegated that task to courts. The *a priori* politics of the Justices' individual positions on questions of interpretation and separation of powers has precluded any sense of uniformity or cohesion in the Court's methodology of engaging copyright. In this sense, the Court's institutionalism has made the Court something of an outsider to the copyright system.

The ultimate beneficiaries of the Roberts Court's institutionalist turn in copyright remain altogether unclear. The politics of copyright law remain unchanged by the Court's disengagement; and the Court's own political legitimacy appears altogether unaffected by its institutional maneuvering in copyright law. By contrast, unequivocally clear are the real victims of the Court's institutionalist capitulation in this area: copyright law and policy.

---

[241] *See, e.g.*, Mazer v. Stein, 347 U.S. 201 (1954); Fortnightly Corp. v. United Artists Television, Inc., 392 U.S. 390 (1968); Goldstein v. California, 412 U.S. 546 (1973); Teleprompter Corp v. Columbia Broadcasting, 415 U.S. 394 (1974); Twentieth Century Music Corp v. Aiken, 422 U.S. 151 (1975).

[242] *See Aiken*, 422 U.S. 151; Sony Corp. of Am. v. Universal City Studios, Inc., 464 U.S. 417 (1984); Feist Publications, Inc. v. Rural Telephone Serv. Co., 499 U.S. 340 (1991); Stewart v. Abend, 495 U.S. 207 (1990).